COUNSELING THE
FOURTH EDITION
ADOLESCENT

Individual, Family, and School Interventions

Edited by

JON CARLSON and JUDITH LEWIS

Governors State University

LOVE PUBLISHING COMPANY®
Denver • London • Sydney

To Kirstin, Chris, Keith, Christine, Matthew,
Karen, Benjamin, and Kali

Some chapters in this book are adapted from selected issues of
Counseling and Human Development, *Family Counseling and Therapy*,
Focus on Guidance, and *Focus on Exceptional Children*, Copyright by
Love Publishing Company, Reprinted by permission.

Published by Love Publishing Company
Denver, Colorado 80222

Fourth Edition

Library of Congress Catalog Card Number 2001092821

Copyright 2002, 1998, 1993, 1988 by Love Publishing Company
Printed in the U.S.A.
ISBN 0-89108-291-3

Preface

A dolescence, a period of remarkable physical, intellectual, and emotional metamorphosis, presents some of the most challenging issues faced today by counselors and by society as a whole. Adolescents are unquestionably at a vulnerable developmental stage as they attempt to navigate the difficult transition from childhood to adulthood. Any life transition holds the potential for danger or for growth, but adolescence represents probably the most crucial transition, combining a general life adventure (bidding farewell to childhood and joining the adult world) with a series of specific changes (leaving one school for another, entering the work world, learning to think differently, meeting new expectations, working out more mature relationships with parents—even adapting to a new body).

While many young people manage this transition successfully, some experience major stress and find themselves engaging in behaviors that place their well-being at risk. All of us—whether in our roles as educators, as counselors, as parents, or as community members—feel a sense of urgency, a need to do something to help adolescents find healthy ways to deal with the demands they face. Although there are no simple answers to the complex problems of adolescence in modern society, some fresh perspectives can enhance our understanding and give direction to our efforts. The purpose of this book, like its earlier editions, is to give voice to those perspectives, to address the special needs of adolescents at risk, and to provide suggestions for action.

If any action with this population is to be fruitful, it must be based on an understanding of adolescent development and behavior patterns, which must be examined within a social and cultural context. We therefore begin this edition by addressing the cultural context of adolescence and discussing how this impacts the modality and content of counseling sessions. The next section of the book, "Individual Issues and Interventions," focuses on important concerns in the individual realm, such as risk behaviors, suicide, pregnancy, violence, and loss. Also included in this edition are discussions on resilience and bullying. The following section, "Family Issues and Interventions," describes changes in contemporary family life that may have strong effects on adolescent family members. The final section, "School Issues and Interventions," is directed at the school climate and suggests activities that can help schools to enhance, rather than deter, adolescents' development, including ways to implement new and effective wellness programs and conflict resolution strategies.

Whether focusing on the individual, the family, or the school, each author in this book blends theory and practice. Each provides an overview of a specific issue, describing in detail the nature of a particular problem common to adolescence, followed by workable suggestions and discussions of the most promising avenues for counselor and community intervention.

Table of Contents

Adolescent Counseling in Context

Working With Adolescents: The Cultural Context

Judith A. Lewis

1

ounselors who work successfully with adolescents usually find that they need to use multifaceted approaches that combine interventions at a number of levels. The counselor's focus at any one time may be on the individual, the family, the school, or the community. Regardless of the level of the specific intervention, however, the effective counselor is always aware that the system being addressed exists within a broader cultural context.

The Cultural Context of Adolescent Development

As adolescents make the transition from childhood to adulthood, they are faced with an astonishing array of challenges. In the few years that divide the onset of puberty and the attainment of full adult status, each individual must adjust both to a new body and to a new place in the world. Counselors and human development specialists have long recognized that adolescence brings with it the need to accomplish a number of important developmental tasks (Havighurst, 1972). What mental health professionals are beginning to see more clearly now is that the nature and meaning of these tasks are powerfully affected by cultural factors. As Lee (1995) reported:

> The process of human psychosocial development must be considered within the context of cultural diversity as it relates to the dynamics of race/ethnicity. Specifically, culture needs to be understood in terms of the developmental dynamics of those young people from racial/ethnic groups who trace their cultural origins to places outside of a Western European, European-American conceptual framework. (pp. 6–7)

What criteria should be used to decide whether a developmental task has been completed successfully? What are the earmarks of a well-adjusted adolescent and an effective adult? The answers that would be provided by the dominant culture do not necessarily represent universal values.

Dominant Versus Traditional Values

As noted by Koss-Chioino and Vargas (1992), "What is 'normative' is culturally determined" (p. 12). Consider, for instance, the commonly held view that the important tasks of adolescence include separating from the family of origin and gaining an independent self-identity. Placing a premium on the adolescent's attainment of individualism and independence reflects a value that is central to the dominant culture in the United States but that is not shared by all ethnic groups. Sue and Sue (1990) pointed out that most cultural groups "place greater value on families, historical lineage (reverence of ancestors), interdependence among family members, and submergence of self for the good of the family" (p. 123). Inclan and Hernandez (1992) also emphasized that the concepts of separation, individuation, and clear boundaries are not universally accepted across cultures. They cautioned that helpers who overemphasize the goal of personal autonomy may inadvertently be imposing definitions of normality that are at odds with a client's culture. This issue, while important throughout the life span, is especially crucial when the client is an adolescent.

During adolescence, young people raised in nondominant cultures often feel forced to reconcile conflicting pressures. They may try to conform to dominant values at school while adhering to the traditional norms of their culture at home. Discussing issues concerning Asian American youth, Yagi and Oh (1995) pointed out:

> As acculturation occurs, cultural conflict may become a reality for many Asian American youth. Socialized in a highly collectivistic culture where individual identity is often indistinguishable from family identity, many young people experience anxiety, confusion, and stress when exposed to the value of individuality characteristic to the predominant American culture. . . . Significantly, many of the psychosocial issues that confront school counseling professionals in working with Asian American students focus on the stress of meeting parental obligations while striving for individuality. (p. 64)

According to Koss-Chioino and Vargas (1992), conflicts around the issue of autonomy are also prevalent among Hispanic youth. Modern and traditional values in this area vary widely. As these authors stated, "When Hispanic parents do not lead children into autonomous behaviors that prepare them for separation from the family at the cessation of high school, and when they groom their female (and often male) children to remain at home until they marry, therapists who insist upon a certain degree of adolescent autonomy provoke misunderstandings and confusion in their clients" (p. 8).

Thomason (1995) observed that Native American students also face potential conflicts in the school milieu.

> In addition to the normal identity crises that all young people face, Native American children and teenagers often experience pressure to ignore their traditional

values and assimilate into American culture. A student's family may emphasize the importance of traditional values, whereas at school teachers and peers consciously and/or unconsciously reinforce adherence to the values of mainstream society. (pp. 110–111)

Clearly, the kinds of conflicts described by these authors do not affect all adolescents of color. Counselors can never assume that an individual student's ethnicity determines the unique values that he or she holds. Rather than stereotyping the members of any population, counselors need to recognize the heterogeneity within ethnic groups and to be aware that many of the generalizations that have found their way into the literature are based on inadequate research (Zapata, 1995). With this caveat in mind, culturally competent counselors explore with each client the nature and salience of the cultural factors that affect him or her. Only in this way can they avoid the kind of harm that can be caused by a counselor who is not awake to cultural norms.

Ina (1994) reported a distressing story that epitomizes the problems that can occur if a counselor is not awake to cultural norms. A Japanese American student was referred to her for counseling because he had been in a deep depression since his estrangement from his family. His former therapist, after constructing a genogram, had diagnosed his family relationships as dysfunctional, citing that (a) the men in the family seemed authoritarian and emotionally unavailable, (b) the boundaries between subsystems within the family seemed diffuse, and (c) the family's communication patterns involved the habit of sending messages to one another indirectly through a third party. The therapist had encouraged the student to air his concerns by confronting his father in public. It was the confrontation that had brought about his exclusion from the family.

Ina saw what the former therapist had missed. This family's interactions were not pathological; rather, they were based on the family's traditional values. The son's new behaviors, encouraged by his former therapist, had been so much in opposition to these values that his humiliated father would not speak to him. Under Ina's guidance, the student successfully reintegrated into the family by asking his eldest sister to act as an intermediary (the kind of communication that the previous therapist had viewed as dysfunctional). The culturally sensitive perspective that Ina brought to the situation allowed the family to avoid what could have been a permanent schism.

The Context of Oppression

Just as the conventional wisdom views developmental tasks from within a mainstream cultural perspective, it also works under another assumption that may be erroneous. This inaccurate assumption is that adolescents can address their developmental tasks within an environment that is essentially friendly. A related premise is that if a young person develops normally, he or she will be able to find a comfortable niche in society. Unfortunately, the existence of racism and other forms of oppression makes these assumptions unrealistic for a large number of young people. Discussing problems faced by African American children, Greene (1992) wrote:

> The image of childhood as a protected developmental period is clearly not the case for a majority of African American children, particularly those who are economically impoverished. These children grow up under conditions that sharply contrast with those of many white children, the life-styles they view in the media, and the formally espoused values of the dominant culture. Survival becomes an ongoing struggle. (p. 67)

Greene asserted that the optimal development of African American children and adolescents is threatened by an antagonistic environment that embodies "the dominant culture's insidious devaluation of persons of color" (p. 66).

Factors related to economic class place additional hazards in the paths of developing youth. Schools that serve children and adolescents in poor neighborhoods work with only a fraction of the resources available to their suburban counterparts. Reacting to the common terminology of the lack of a "level playing field," Kozol (1991) explained:

> Unlike a tainted sports event . . . a childhood cannot be played again. We are children only once; and, after those few years are gone, there is no second chance to make amends. In this respect, the consequences of unequal education have a terrible finality. Those who are denied cannot be "made whole" by a later act of government. Those who get the unfair edge cannot be later stripped of what they've won. Skills, once attained—no matter how unfairly—take on a compelling aura . . . the winners in this race *feel* meritorious. (p. 180)

People who have that "unfair edge" of privilege tend not to notice their advantage and to attribute success to their personal competence. The reverse is also true. People who are victims of oppression often internalize the negative views that are communicated so powerfully by the dominant culture. Lewis and Arnold (in press) noted:

> The most insidious effect of oppression is the internalization of the distortions and lies of the oppressor by the victims of oppression. . . . Internalized oppression is the acceptance, most often unconscious, of the myths, misinformation, and stereotypes the dominant culture constructs about one's own group. Victims take on the values and norms of the dominant group and cast aspersions on the experiences and traditional values of their own group. In order to take on the values of the dominant culture, one must repudiate one's self and live with contradictions in how one experiences self-in-the-world. . . . The process is often conflictual because it involves what would seem to be mutually-exclusive emotional responses of acceptance and rejection of one's oppressor.

The contradictions inherent in this experience are especially confusing for adolescents, who are in the process seeking their place in the world. Greene (1992) contended that African American children, as they learn to be bicultural in a hostile environment, "must learn to imitate the dominant culture whether they accept its values or not" (pp. 65–66). Sage (1991) stated that "close identification with the non-Indian world increases the American Indians' sense of invisibility, which decreases their sense of identity and self esteem" and that, "conversely, not identifying with the dominant culture (non-Indian world) leads to isolation, passivity, increased stress, anxiety, and depression" (p. 26). This conflict was also addressed by Herring (1991), who, in a discussion of the attempts of Native American youth to live as both Native Americans and Americans, wrote, "This dualistic life places much stress and strain on these young people" (p. 42). Members of all oppressed groups have to deal with both the harsh realities of external persecution and the destructive force of internalized oppression. Whether intervening at the individual, family, or school level, counselors working with young people need to use approaches that acknowledge these obstacles to development. At the same time, their approaches need to reflect an appreciation the positive resources in the client's life. As Greene (1992) pointed out, despite the barriers created by racism and poverty, "African American children have succeeded against the odds for generations" (p. 68), at least in part because of the supportive emotional environments created by family and community.

Interventions Focused on Individuals

Cultural factors and issues of oppression have implications for both the modality and the content of counseling in sessions with adolescents.

Counseling Modalities

As they work with young people of varied ethnic backgrounds, culturally sensitive counselors learn to adjust the modalities they use to the needs and preferences of their client populations. Thomason (1995), for example, presented suggestions for working with Native American students in the school milieu. He recommended that when working with individual clients the counselor be available for informal conversations that focus on problem solving and avoid intrusive questioning. He suggested, however, that group and family counseling are more valuable approaches than individual counseling for this population. Group work, he asserted, "relieves individual students of some of the pressure to talk and self-disclose and allows them to learn from the experiences of the other students" (p. 116). Family counseling is helpful both because of the family's strong influence and because "the family can provide the student with strength and support, which may not be readily available to the student in the school environment" (p. 113). Thomason also advocated the use of tribal network therapy.

> In this approach, as many as 40 people—who are related to the client by blood, friendship, need, or proximity—are called together to provide support for the client. The goal is to build the coping skills of the client within the context of the group,

both to resolve the current problem and improve the client's ability to handle future problems. This approach makes clear that problems exist in groups, rather than just in individuals, and the group is a powerful agent of change. (pp. 113–114)

Similarly, Jackson (1995) focused on group work as an appropriate vehicle for addressing the needs of Arab students, pointing out that as long as group members are all of the same sex, "group counseling would be an activity that reflects the Arab value of collectivism" (p. 49). Ho (1992) recommended group modalities for Asian clients as well.

Asian children are taught at an early age that there is pervasive awareness of mutual interdependence, and an Asian child who values interdependence and cooperation can gain significantly from the power and strength of collective group feedback. The group atmosphere can be less threatening than individual treatment. (p. 188)

Of course, while guidelines for working with specific adolescent groups are useful for practicing counselors, they can never replace careful assessment of the needs of one's own clients and setting.

Counseling Content

The content of effective counseling reflects the counselor's ability to notice the impact of environmental factors on the client. This competence is especially important when working with clients who are members of oppressed groups. As stated by Carlson, Sperry, and Lewis (1997), "The process of oppression is insidious because targeted people must face a lethal combination of overt bigotry, covert discrimination, and a socialization process that encourages internalization of negative self-views" (p. 130). To be effective, the counseling process has to address these issues directly.

In some cases, the client may be well aware that oppression is part of the problem but fearful that the counselor will avoid discussing it. Boyd-Franklin (1993) pointed out that African American clients who are concerned about racism often avoid bringing up the topic, believing that counselors "will try to talk them out of what they are feeling because they do not understand the need for African-American individuals and families to vent their rage about situations in which there is an undercurrent of racism" (p. 56). Yet, as noted by Franklin (1993), "If the impact of racism is ignored, it's unlikely that therapy will go anywhere" (p. 36). Sometimes, clients need time to explore oppression-related issues before they are ready to talk about planning for personal actions. The counselor must ensure that this process is not only allowed but encouraged.

Often, the impact of racism and other forms of oppression is not readily available in the client's consciousness. In such cases, the counseling process can help the client to understand the relevance of oppression to a particular situation. "Clients who recognize the role of oppression in their lives are most likely to be able to move from the morass of self-blame to the solid ground of self-management" (Carlson,

Sperry, & Lewis, 1997, p. 132). Without this understanding, they might remain mired in the self-condemnation that accompanies internalized oppression.

Interventions Focused on Families

As school-based family counseling becomes more prevalent, increasing numbers of counselors are working with adolescents and their families. As is the case with individual counseling, differences between norms of the dominant U.S. culture and those of other cultures soon become apparent. As already discussed, different cultural groups value individuation and family unity to varying degrees, but other cultural variations are just as important. In fact, the most basic concepts and definitions of *family* vary across cultures. Sue and Sue (1990) noted, "Middle-class white Americans consider the family unit to be nuclear (husband/wife and children related by blood), while most minorities define the family unit as an extended one" (p. 120). Most cultures characterize family life in terms of extended kinship systems that include supportive members who are not necessarily related by blood.

Extended Families

Extended family networks are common among Native Americans (Ho, 1987; Thomason, 1995), African Americans (Boyd-Franklin, 1989), Hispanics (Inclan & Hernandez, 1992), and Asians (Sue & Sue, 1990). Counselors working with diverse populations of young people need to ask their clients how they define their families rather than making unsupported assumptions based on a lack of cultural knowledge. Falicov (1994) related the story of a Puerto Rican child who was hospitalized with a serious illness. His godmother, an elderly great-aunt, spent hours at the hospital, praying and overseeing his treatment. The health care providers were upset about what they interpreted as her interference and wondered why the child's parents had allowed this person to usurp their role. These health professionals were unaware that some cultures define "family" in a way that encompasses kinship bonds, shared parenting, and multigenerational involvement.

Another story highlighting the importance of understanding family structure, which hits closer to home for counselors, was related by Sue and Sue (1990). A school counselor, working with an adolescent Latina in crisis, arranged a family conference. The counselor was surprised that, in light of the father's difficulty in taking time away from his place of employment, the student's mother was hesitant to arrange an appointment on her own. When the participation of both parents had finally been negotiated, the counselor was astonished once more. A brother-in-law, who was the student's godfather, accompanied the parents. As described in Sue and Sue (1990):

> The counselor reported being upset at the presence of the brother-in-law when it became obvious he planned to sit in on the session. At that point, she explained that

a third party present would only make the session more complex and the outcome counterproductive. She wanted to see only the family. The counselor reported that the session went poorly with minimal cooperation from the parents. (p. 119)

The helping professional here, too, showed a lack of awareness concerning the variability of family structures. The result of this misunderstanding was that the family's culturally appropriate behavior was pathologized by the counselor because it did not fit her own limited definition of family life. The counselor's ability to use the resources that could have been helpful to the student was clearly compromised.

Cultural Conflicts Within Families

The work of Szapocznik and his colleagues (Szapocznik & Kurtines, 1993; Szapocznik, Scopetta, Ceballos, & Santisteban, 1994), which began in the 1970s and continues to the present day, has focused on the idea that the individual is embedded in the family, which, in turn, is embedded within a complex cultural milieu. The original focus was on Hispanic adolescents, particularly Cuban immigrants, and their families. The researchers found that the conduct problems of many of the adolescents they studied were associated with family dynamics played out in a cultural context. They learned that they could not view these families strictly in terms of their cultures of origin, instead, they had to recognize that the adolescents and their families lived in a multicultural context, with young people acculturating to the mainstream values of the United States more quickly than their parents, who tended to remain loyal to traditional Hispanic values. In their words:

> The impact of a culturally diverse environment on these families resulted in the emergence of conflict-laden intergenerational acculturational differences in which parents and youths developed different cultural alliances (Hispanic and American, respectively). These intergenerationally related cultural differences were added to the usual intergenerational conflicts that occur in families with adolescents to produce a much compounded and exacerbated intergenerational *and* intercultural conflict. As a consequence, parents became unable to properly manage youngsters who made strong claims for autonomy and who no longer accepted their parents' traditional Cuban ways. (Szapocznik & Kurtines, 1993, p. 403)

It is still true today that families are exposed to a complex array of influences. Many of the older family members value the traditional culture of origin, but "this cultural melange also includes the hybrid culture in which the children are immersed both in school and with acculturating peers" (Szapocznik, Scopetta, Ceballos, & Santisteban, 1994, p. 23).

In response to this issue, Szapocznik and his colleagues designed a structured therapeutic approach called Bicultural Effectiveness Training (Szapocznik & Kurtines, 1993). One of the strategies used is to place the intergenerational/intercultural conflict in the role of the identified patient. The therapists then help family members to reframe their views of the conflict. As family members begin to recognize the cultural determinants of each person's world view, they establish a readiness to build new alliances across generations and cultures.

School Interventions

In any setting, to meet the needs of a diverse group of adolescents, counselors must pay attention to the context of the adolescents' lives. Within the school setting, a contextual approach involves building a comprehensive framework that addresses students' needs for direct services while, at the same time, ensures that their learning environment facilitates healthy development. Table 1.1 provides an illustration of how such a framework can be used to address cultural issues in the school milieu.

As the table indicates, this model distinguishes between direct and indirect services. Direct services provide opportunities for students to develop the knowledge, skills, and attitudes that can help them live effectively, while indirect services address the settings that affect their well-being. In other words, direct services target the students and indirect services target the environment. The model also distinguishes between schoolwide services and focused services. Schoolwide services are provided to meet the needs of the total school population and are therefore focused on development and prevention. Focused services, in contrast, are aimed at students who might need more active assistance. The model encompasses four distinct facets:

1. *Direct, schoolwide services:* These are educational programs that provide direct services to students and that are made available to the school population as a

Table 1.1   Addressing Cultural Issues: A Multifaceted Model

	SCHOOLWIDE SERVICES	FOCUSED SERVICES
DIRECT SERVICES	Multicultural education	Multicultural counseling
	Developmental programs in cultural context	
INDIRECT SERVICES	Address racism and other oppressions in school and community	Advocate on behalf of students who are victimized by racism and other oppressions

Note: Adapted from *Community Counseling: Empowerment Strategies for a Diverse Society,* by J. A. Lewis, M. D. Lewis, J. A. Daniels, & M. J. D'Andrea. Pacific Grove, CA, Brooks/Cole, 1998.

whole. When these services target cultural issues, they include both (a) educational efforts to deal with multicultural issues and (b) attention to cultural context in all schoolwide developmental programs.

2. *Direct, focused services:* These are outreach and counseling programs designed for students who need or desire additional assistance. When these services target cultural issues, they feature multicultural counseling with individuals, groups, and families.

3. *Indirect, schoolwide services:* These are efforts to make the school and community environments more responsive to the needs of the entire population of students. When these services target cultural issues, they address issues of oppression.

4. *Indirect, focused services:* These are programs that intervene in the environments of individuals or groups with special needs on behalf of these individuals and groups. When these services target cultural issues, they emphasize client advocacy efforts.

Direct, Schoolwide Services

Omizo and D'Andrea (1995) and D'Andrea and Daniels (1995) described a set of multicultural guidance activities that they have used with youngsters of various ages. The purpose of the activities is threefold: to help students better understand how people from different backgrounds might be similar to or different from themselves, to foster the development of social skills, and to encourage multicultural sensitivity. Based on structured games, the activities include Multicultural People Bingo, Cultural Warm Fuzzies, Rainbow Poster, Creating a Country, Multicultural Art, and others. The authors emphasized the fact that although these activities were developed and have been carried out by counselors, the counselors have worked closely with teachers in the hope that multicultural education would become infused into the curricula. Of course, a vast array of options are available for age-appropriate multicultural education. Counselors and teachers, working together, can easily design and implement the specific learning strategies that suit their own students.

Culturally relevant programming also includes activities that are not necessarily *about* multiculturalism but that bring cultural awareness into play. Consider, for instance, Zapata's (1995) suggestions for student leadership development. In the kinds of programs Zapata recommended, counselors can identify Hispanic students with potential for leadership involvement and recruit them for participation in leadership training. The program is about leadership, but the context emphasizes diversity.

Direct, Focused Services

Earlier sections of this chapter focused on the kinds of counseling strategies that hold the most promise for working with various client populations. As suggested earlier, the content of counseling should include attention to issues related to oppression. An important awareness for counselors is that although direct counseling will always be a part of their repertoire, it can only be one part. It is clear that if counselors are to be effective, they need to address environmental issues as well.

Indirect, Schoolwide Services

Hilliard (1995) wrote:

> The problem of privilege and oppression or inequity in education is sometimes cast as a problem of stereotyping, intergroup ignorance, or miscommunication. Stereotyping, ignorance, or miscommunication may, in fact, be problematic. However, these "problems" are merely manifestations or components of a total system that is much more complex and pervasive. Consequently, the educator who restricts his or her attention and activity to the elimination of stereotyping, intergroup ignorance, and miscommunication contributes to the appearance of problem solving when, in fact, little of importance may actually be accomplished. Stereotyping, intergroup ignorance, and miscommunication become euphemisms for the deeper problems of privilege, oppression, or inequity, which are much more difficult to address. (p. 149)

Hilliard's conceptualization suggests that the use of euphemisms reduces the scope of the problems discussed herein and makes them easier to address. He suggested that the frightening term *oppression,* could be renamed *race relations* or even *intergroup relations.* But, he noted, this reframing helps people turn their backs on the real issues.

> It is much easier to engage a school district in implementing a program to improve "interpersonal communications" than to focus on problems associated with privilege and oppression. Well-meaning educators and public policymakers succumb to the seduction of euphemisms since they reduce internal and external pressures, soothe sensitivities, and provide the illusion of progress toward important goals. (Hilliard, 1995, p. 150)

It takes hard work and dedication to provide effective direct services to adolescents: to improve "interpersonal communications." However, to address a hostile learning environment takes not only hard work and dedication but also tremendous personal courage. In any school system, counselors are among the first to know when students are victimized by hostile and punitive environments. That knowledge is what gives counselors their courage.

Indirect, Focused Services

As counselors examine the learning environment that affects all children in a school, they generally become aware of individuals and groups who need stronger advocacy on their behalf. As noted by Lewis and Arnold (in press), counselors know that

> poor children, children of color, and children for whom English is a second language are often neglected, labeled, and left to wither in the lowest tracks in our

schools. Just as counselors in agency settings alert the community to the oppression of its members, so can school counselors voice opposition to oppressive and punitive practices affecting children and youth. Just as agency counselors participate in alliances with community organizations seeking change, so can school counselors affiliate with groups working toward the creation of schools that are distinguished by warm and welcoming climates for learning.

Atkinson, Morten, and Sue (1993) suggested that, in a society characterized by oppression, client advocacy may be the service of choice.

> As an advocate, the counselor speaks on behalf of the client, often confronting the institutional sources of oppression that are contributing to the client's problems. . . . In this role, the counselor represents a client or group of clients who have brought a particular form of discrimination to the counselor's attention. Being an empathic counselor who suggests alternative ways of coping with a particular problem is not enough. (p. 301)

Summary

As counselors examine the cultural context of adolescent development, they become aware that the society's conventional view of developmental tasks may be culture-bound. For example, the mainstream, European culture in the United States dictates that adolescence is the time for young people to separate from their families and become independent. Yet, most cultures emphasize family interdependence and frown on autonomy. Recognizing the context within which adolescents live also increases awareness of racism and other forms of oppression that place barriers in front of their development.

This knowledge affects the work counselors do as they focus on individuals, on families, and on schools. Cultural competence makes counselors consider the diverse world views of their clients when they make choices about counseling modalities or emphases. It makes them ask their clients how they define their own families and whether all of the family members would answer that question in the same way. It makes counselors aware that, in their school-based interventions, they need to focus not just on providing direct services to the students but also on making the school as a whole a supportive environment for learning.

References

Atkinson, D. R., Morten, G., & Sue, D. W. (Eds.). (1993). *Counseling American minorities: A cross-cultural perspective* (4th ed.). Madison, WI: Brown & Benchmark.

Boyd-Franklin, N. (1989). *Black families in therapy: A multisystems approach.* New York: Guilford.

Boyd-Franklin, N. (1993, July/August). Pulling out the arrows. *Family Networker,* pp. 33–39.

Carlson, J., Sperry, L., & Lewis, J. A. (1997). *Family therapy: Ensuring treatment efficacy.* Pacific Grove, CA: Brooks/Cole.

D'Andrea, M., & Daniels, J. (1995). Helping students learn to get along: Assessing the effectiveness of a multicultural developmental guidance project. *Elementary School Guidance & Counseling, 30,* 143–154.

Falicov, C. (1994, August). *Cultural change on a global scale: Crossing cultural borders.* Paper presented at the 1994 Annual Convention, American Association of Marriage and Family Therapy, Chicago.

Franklin, A. J. (1993, July/August). The invisibility syndrome. *Family Networker,* pp. 33–39.

Greene, B. A. (1992). Racial socialization as a tool in psychotherapy with African American children. In L. A. Vargas & J. D. Koss-Chioino (Eds.), *Working with culture: Psychotherapeutic interventions with ethnic minority children and adolescents* (pp. 63–81). San Francisco: Jossey-Bass.

Havighurst, R. J. (1972). *Developmental tasks and education.* New York: McKay.

Herring, R. D. (1991). Counseling Native American youth. In C. C. Lee & B. L. Richardson (Eds.), *Multicultural issues in counseling: New approaches to diversity* (pp. 37–47). Alexandria, VA: American Counseling Association.

Hilliard, A. G. (1995). *The maroon within us.* Baltimore: Black Classic Press.

Ho, M. K. (1987). *Family therapy with ethnic minorities.* Newbury Park, CA: Sage Publications.

Ho, M. K. (1992). Differential application of treatment modalities with Asian American youth. In L. A. Vargas & J. D. Koss-Chioino (Eds.), *Working with culture: Psychotherapeutic interventions with ethnic minority children and adolescents* (pp. 182–203). San Francisco: Jossey-Bass.

Ina, S. (1994, April). *Culturally sensitive family therapy.* Paper presented at the national conference of the American Counseling Association, Minneapolis, MN.

Inclan, J., & Hernandez, M. (1992). Cross-cultural perspectives and codependence: The case of poor Hispanics. *American Journal of Orthopsychiatry, 62,* 245–255.

Jackson, M. (1995). Counseling youth of Arab ancestry. In C. C. Lee (Ed.), *Counseling for diversity: A guide for school counselors and related professionals* (pp. 41–60). Boston: Allyn & Bacon.

Koss-Chioino, J. D., & Vargas, L. A. (1992). Through the cultural looking glass: A model for understanding culturally responsive psychotherapies. In L. A. Vargas & J. D. Koss-Chioino (Eds.), *Working with culture: Psychotherapeutic interventions with ethnic minority children and adolescents* (pp. 1–22). San Francisco: Jossey-Bass.

Kozol, J. (1991). *Savage inequalities: Children in America's schools.* New York: Harper Perennial.

Lee C. C. (1995). School counseling and cultural diversity: A framework for effective practice. In C. C. Lee (Ed.), *Counseling for diversity: A guide for school counselors and related professionals* (pp. 3–17). Boston: Allyn & Bacon.

Lewis, J. A., & Arnold, M. S. (in press). From multiculturalism to social action. In C. C. Lee & G. Walz (Eds.), *Social action: A mandate for counselors.* Greensboro, NC: ERIC/CASS and American Counseling Association.

Lewis, J. A., Lewis, M. D., Daniels, J. A., & D'Andrea, M. J. (1998), *Community counseling: Empowerment strategies for a diverse society.* Pacific Grove, CA: Brooks/Cole.

Omizo, M. M., & D'Andrea, M. J. (1995). Multicultural classroom guidance. In C. C. Lee (Ed.), *Counseling for diversity: A guide for school counselors and related professionals* (pp. 143–158). Boston: Allyn & Bacon.

Sage, G. P. (1991). Counseling American Indian adults. In C. C. Lee & B. L. Richardson (Eds.), *Multicultural issues in counseling: New approaches to diversity* (pp. 23–35). Alexandria, VA: American Counseling Association.

Sue, D. W., & Sue, D. (1990). *Counseling the culturally different: Theory and practice* (2nd ed.). New York: Wiley.

Szapocznik, J., & Kurtines, W. M. (1993). Family psychology and cultural diversity: Opportunities for theory, research, and applications. *American Psychologist, 48,* 400–407.

Szapocznik, J., Scopetta, M. A., Ceballos, A., & Santisteban, D. (1994). Understanding, supporting and empowering families: From microanalysis to macrointervention. *Family Psychologist, 10*(2), 23–27.

Thomason, T. C. (1995). Counseling Native American students. In C. C. Lee (Ed.), *Counseling for diversity: A guide for school counselors and related professionals* (pp. 109–126). Boston: Allyn & Bacon.

Yagi, D. T., & Oh, M. Y. (1995). Counseling Asian American students. In C. C. Lee (Ed.), *Counseling for diversity: A guide for school counselors and related professionals* (pp. 61–84). Boston: Allyn & Bacon.

Zapata, J. T. (1995). Counseling Hispanic children and youth. In C. C. Lee (Ed.), *Counseling for diversity: A guide for school counselors and related professionals* (pp. 85–108). Boston: Allyn & Bacon.

The Ethical and Legal Context of Adolescent Counseling

Peggy Kaczmarek

Before discussing specific ethical and legal issues related to working with child and adolescent clients, a case vignette is presented to demonstrate some of the issues. Readers are encouraged to consider this vignette in reference to the information presented in the chapter and then to work through the ethical decision-making model provided to determine how they would handle the case if they were the treating professional. Readers are encouraged to compare their approach with the one I suggest and to discuss with colleagues about areas of agreement and disagreement. The vignette has not been constructed from an actual case.

Ethics Vignette

A 13-year-old girl named Sarah is seen on a walk-in basis at a nonprofit counseling agency. Sarah's parents have been divorced for 5 months and, although she lives primarily with her mother, she reports that she spends time with both parents on a regular basis. Sarah is an only child, and she is sad as a result of the continued tension between her parents. The divorce has not stopped the bitterness or her parents' inability to agree on decisions related to her.

Sarah's parents often ask questions about the other parent and how they spend time with her. They also ask her if the other parent is dating. Sarah reports that she has trouble falling asleep and sleeping at night because she thinks about her changed family. She is having trouble concentrating at school, and her grades have been going down. This is causing some tension with her mother.

Sarah has lost 5 pounds and has little appetite. She is highly pessimistic about the future. She reports that she has thought about suicide but does not have a plan and says she would not do that because it would make her parents and her boyfriend too sad. Sarah's boyfriend attends the same school. Her mother likes the boyfriend and approves of their seeing each other. Her father believes she is too young to have a boyfriend and wants his daughter to break up with him.

Sarah is seeking a counseling relationship that does not involve her parents. She wants some place to go where she can sort out her feelings about her changing family circumstances without worrying about hurting anyone's feelings. Sarah mentions specifically the importance to her of having a confidential therapy relationship. She reports that if the counselor involves her parents, she will not participate in therapy. Sarah also reports that her father does not support counseling; he believes that individuals should be able to handle their own problems, and if the counselor tries to involve him, he probably will forbid her to continue.

This chapter explores the differences associated with working with children and adolescents and with adults. The ethical codes will be reviewed for references to clients of minor age. Ethical and legal discussions focus on issues of competence, confidentiality, privileged communication, and informed consent. A sample professional disclosure statement for children and adolescents is provided. An ethical decision-making model is described and applied to the case vignette. Last, I provide recommendations for staying current in regard to ethical and legal issues related to children and adolescents.

Differences in Working With Minor Clients

Children and adolescents have been described in the literature as a specialized population (Corey, Corey, & Callanan, 1993), a multicultural subgroup based on age. Children are not miniature adults, and adolescents are neither children nor adults. Some of the clinically significant differences associated with working with minor clients are as follows.

■ The developmental stage of the child or adolescent can have significant implications related to minors' capacity to understand and consent to therapy, as well as limiting their autonomy in decision making. Depending on the age and cognitive maturity of the child or adolescent, parents or guardians may legally hold the decision-making capacity. Age is an important factor in deciding how much autonomy to provide minors, with children under the age of 11 more governed by their parents, adolescents age 15 and older more like adults related to decision making, and more gray areas associated with adolescents 11–14 (Sobocinski, 1990).

■ Frequently the child or adolescent does not independently seek services, but a parent or another significant adult decides that the child or adolescent would benefit from therapy and, therefore, a third party intrudes into the therapy relationship. This context raises the ethical issues of voluntariness and the right to refuse treatment.

■ Conflicts of interest may be prominent for professionals who work with minors, as the parents may have identified goals that conflict with those identified by the child (Sondheimer & Martucci, 1992) or the adolescent. Whenever a professional works with a minor client, the professional and the parents are engaging in a dual relationship because the best interests of the minor may diverge from those of the parents (Koocher and Keith-Spiegel, 1990).

■ Confidentiality is a frequently occurring ethical dilemma that is more complex with minors because of the greater need to consult with collateral contacts—parents, teachers, step-parents, physicians, and so on. The clinician will have to identify a stance on what kind of confidentiality the child/adolescent client will have in relation to the parent or significant adult seeking services. Younger children have less serious concerns than pre-adolescents and adolescents about confidentiality.

■ The clinician has to have an identified approach as to how parents will be consulted in regard to treatment, which should incorporate the wishes of the child/adolescent client.

■ The parents might identify the child or adolescent as the problem when the issue might be more of a lack of parenting skills or a family systems issue that the parent has difficulty accepting. The therapist may lose the chance to work with the family if the parents are confronted before a relationship is established.

■ Parents may consciously and unconsciously sabotage therapy. They may not want someone else to succeed where they have failed, or they may become jealous of the relationship that develops between the client and the therapist. On the other hand, parents can be a good source of background information and an ally in therapy. Axline (1969) stated that the therapy proceeds more quickly when the parents are involved.

■ Parents may decide when to terminate therapy irrespective of the needs of the child/adolescent or the therapist's recommendation.

■ Managed care guidelines are established along the line of adult contacts and may have to be adapted for work with children. Some managed care organizations permit the therapist to divide one unit into two 30-minute sessions without penalty, and others will not.

■ The therapist dealing with children or adolescents may have to assume more of a role of child advocate (Koocher & Keith-Speigel, 1990), just as social workers are trained to provide. This may involve school personnel or community agencies so the child or adolescent can receive needed services.

■ Child therapists may have to guard against being paternalistic or parental with minor clients. Child therapists have to create a role that is different from that of a parent or a teacher and that is more of a facilitator.

■ Counseling with minor clients means providing services that may be of shorter duration than adult sessions and may be more activity-oriented, depending on the client's developmental level (Vernon, 1999). Clearly, work with minor clients raises numerous issues that do not have standard answers.

Professional Codes of Ethics

Although ethical codes of conduct establish general guidelines for working with clients, these codes are based primarily on the premise that the professional relationship will be between counselors and adult clients. Therefore, the professional must generalize or adapt the guidelines to children and adolescents with little guidance or training about how to proceed (Koocher & Keith-Spiegel, 1990; Corey, Corey, & Callanan, 1993). Ethical and legal issues courses typically do not address issues related to minor clients in any depth. No seminal resources or ethical/legal casebooks are available to assist the clinician in adapting ethical codes in their work with children and adolescents. Current textbooks on child counseling, such as *Counseling Children* (Thompson & Rudolph, 2000) provide limited attention to ethical and legal issues and current journal literature is limited in this area (Lawrence & Robinson-Kurpius, 2000). Although the school counseling literature provides some guidance, resources for clinicians who work in nonschool settings are sparse.

Legal Considerations With Minors

Historically, children were viewed as the property of their parents, and the law has been reluctant to interfere with parental rights. Children and adolescents are legally defined as minors. *Black's Law Dictionary* (Garner, 1999) defines a minor as "a person who has not reached full legal age." Children and youth are viewed as incapable of making certain decisions legally, and the law defers to the parents or legal guardians to know what presumably is in the best interest of the child. Several classic court cases, however, have resulted in the expansion of rights for minors, such as in re Gault, which extended Miranda rights to minors (cited in Koocher & Keith-Spiegel, 1990).

In legal cases involving minors, the courts may appoint a *guardian ad litem* to protect the interests of minors. Many states allow minors to receive treatment for substance abuse, birth control, and medical treatment of venereal disease without involvement or notification of the parents (Kitchner & Robinson, 2000). The rationale is that treatment is in the best interest of the adolescent and that this may not occur if parents need to be notified.

The ability of a minor to obtain an abortion without parental involvement also differs by state. In Great Britain, the Children's Act of 1989 formally recognized that children are individuals and not the property of parents (Honig & Bentovim, 1996). This act provides for different levels of minors' autonomy based on age, developmental stage, and capacity to understand. These rights of minor children still need to be balanced with the legal responsibility of parents for their minor children.

Each state has mental health statutes that govern work with clients. Clinicians have to know the statutes in the state in which they practice. The differences in the law across states can be significant. For example, in most states parental permission is required to treat minor clients, but in New Mexico any child, with no age limit imposed, is entitled to verbal therapy with or without the permission of the parents (Chapter 32A, New Mexico Children's Code). Though accepting a minor client for services without parental permission may be legally possible, it might not be in the best interest of the client to exclude parental involvement.

References to Minors in Professional Ethical Codes

The ethical codes of four major professional counseling organizations are reviewed here to determine the guidance they provide in working with minor clients. Specific sections of the code are referenced and discussed.

American Psychological Association

The Ethical Principles of Psychologists and Code of Conduct (APA, 1992) includes adaptations based on age in the following sections:

■ *Principle D: Respect for People's Rights and Dignity* discusses the need for professionals to be sensitive to cultural differences based on age along with additional factors.

■ *2.04: Use of Assessment in General and with Special Populations* directs psychologists to be watchful for situations in which interventions or assessments may have to be adapted based on the client's age and additional factors.

■ In *4.02: Informed Consent,* minor clients are discussed more directly in that permission for interventions must be obtained from an adult if the client is not legally able to give consent. The code makes it clear, however, that the clinician is expected to present information to minors in language they can understand so their consent can also be obtained.

■ *4.03: Couple and Family Relationships* discusses the complexities of working with multiple parties so boundaries are established and all parties are clear on who the client is.

■ In *5.01: Confidentiality,* professionals are required to discuss the limitations of confidentiality with clients, and "to the extent feasible, minors, or their legal representative."

■ In *6.11: Informed Consent to Research,* researchers must provide information about the project in terms that are understandable to minors and to obtain their consent in addition to their legal representative.

American Counseling Association

The *Code of Ethics and Standards of Practice* (American Counseling Association, 1995) has both direct and indirect references to minors.

■ *Section A: The Counseling Relationship, A.1: Client Welfare* suggests that: it may be helpful to involve family members as a positive addition to therapy.

■ *A.3: Client Rights* emphasizes the need for the client to have freedom to chose to enter therapy or decline and *"Inability to give Consent:* When counseling minors or persons unable to give voluntary informed consent, counselors act in these clients' best interest."

■ *A.8: Multiple Clients* suggests that if a counselor is working with parents and children, the counselor must clarify who the client is and the boundaries that will be established with other individuals who are involved.

■ *B.3: Minor or Incompetent clients:* "When counseling clients who are minors or individuals who are unable to give voluntary, informed consent, parents or guardians may be included in the counseling process as appropriate. Counselors act in the best interest of clients or take measures to safeguard confidentiality."

■ *B.2: Groups and Families* suggests that in family counseling, the counselor works to protect the confidentiality of all members and does not reveal information from an individual member without his or her permission.

American School Counselor Association

Even though many of the professionals who work with children and adolescents are not in school settings, they may find some guidance from the American School Counselor Association's (1998) Ethical Standards for School Counselors, which speaks more directly than other professional codes to the issue of working with minor clients. It is divided into subheadings that address the responsibilities of the counselor to multiple groups: students, parents, colleagues and professional associates, school and community, self, and the profession. Even though the code addresses the various roles the counselor may perform, it highlights the importance of confidentiality in the counseling relationship and the need to provide students with a written disclosure document that identifies the limitations associated with confidentiality and the need to have the client sign the document after discussion.

In the section outlining responsibilities to parents, the code recognizes that parents have legal rights and responsibilities related to their children, and the counselor is encouraged to establish a collaborative relationship with parents when appropriate. Although the code recognizes the importance of a confidential relationship with the client, it suggests that parents have to be informed.

American Association for Marriage and Family Therapy

The American Association for Marriage and Family Therapy's (AAMFT, 1991) Code of Ethics is unique because it addresses the complexities of working with multiple clients in families. Related to confidentiality, the code stresses that "therapists respect and guard confidences of each individual client." It also states that related to release of information, when more than one member of a family receives counseling services, all legally competent members must sign a release for information to be provided.

A review of the preceding ethical codes illustrates the difficulty of balancing responsibilities to parents and children and identifying clear boundaries when working with more than one family member.

Ethical/Legal Issues Related to Work With Child and Adolescent Clients

Three major issues will be addressed from an ethical and legal standpoint: competence, confidentiality and privileged communication, and informed consent.

Competence

A basic ethical issue related to work with children and adolescents is the need to have the professional competence to work with this group and to demonstrate knowledge of the significant age-related developmental differences that will influence therapy. Children, adolescents, and adults are distinct populations. Counselors who work with children should have specialized training in: theory and techniques of counseling applied to children, play therapy techniques, child psychopathology, assessment techniques for children, and supervised practica working with child clients and administering assessments to this population (Kaczmarek & Wagner, 1994). Kaczmarek and Riva (1996) suggested the following specialized training for working with adolescent clients: knowledge of adolescent development, career counseling, theory and technique of adolescent counseling as applied to individual and group counseling, assessment with adolescents, and supervised experience working with adolescents at different developmental levels. In addition, it seems important that clinicians take a course that focuses on ethical and professional issues unique to children and adolescents.

Confidentiality

Confidentiality and privileged communication are related but are different terms. *Confidentiality* is the ethical obligation of the professional to protect information provided in counseling from disclosure (Koocher & Keith-Spiegel, 1990). *Privileged communication* is a legal right established by state statutes stating that information that clients provide to specified professionals may not be revealed in a court setting without the client's consent (Arthur & Swanson, 1993). The law establishes which professions will be granted privilege. The privilege belongs to the client, and in the case of minor clients, it is held by the parent.

Confidentiality is the foundation on which the therapeutic relationship is built, and this is equally true for children and adolescents. Most preadolescents and adolescents are familiar with the concept of confidentiality and they expect it (Gustafson & McNamara, 1987), but they often hold expectations of "absolute" confidentiality. Schulte and Cochrane (1992) described confidentiality as a "therapeutic promise" made by the therapist. Nemiroff and Annunziata (1990) defined confidentiality as a "one-way secret" to 4- to 7-year-olds. Their book explains the importance of confidentiality to parents and children.

Gustafson and McNamara (1987) discussed the use of the following criteria to decide the extent of confidentiality to grant to minor clients: age, cognitive maturity, identified problem, wishes of the client, and wishes of the parents. The age of the child is important, although age can be an unreliable indicator of maturity. Therefore, age should be combined with an informal assessment of cognitive maturity. The wishes of the child/adolescent are important, and often as children get older, they desire more privacy from parents. Parents' wishes is a factor that has to be considered, as is the quality of the relationship between the parent and the child/adolescent. Decisions regarding confidentiality and autonomy should be based on the competence of the child or adolescent to make rational choices (Sobocinski, 1990).

When Collins and Knowles (1995) surveyed 13- to 18-year-olds related to their beliefs about confidentiality, 56% said confidentiality was *essential* in the therapy relationship and 46% said it was *important.* There was no difference between the responses of 13-year-olds and 18-year-olds. It also was interesting that the respondents did not realize that parents or other adults might have a right to information about what goes on in counseling and that counselors have legal obligations. Elementary counselors were more likely to breach confidentiality than were secondary counselors (Isaacs & Stone, 1999).

Prior to beginning treatment the therapist should discuss with the parents and the child or adolescent a confidentiality agreement that includes a discussion of the pros and cons of confidentiality with minor children (Welch, 1999; Lawrence & Robinson-Kurpius, 2000). Parents need to understand the importance of confidentiality in the therapeutic relationship and be agreeable to granting it. The therapist is trying to balance two systems—the rights of parents to knowledge about their children and adolescents and the advantages of their involvement for the client versus the right of the minor client to confidentiality and autonomy, which may promote more self-disclosure, provided they are not a danger to themselves or to others. Parental access to information may become more important as various state courts have begun to enact laws that hold parents responsible for the illegal actions of minors.

The therapist has to decide how to access background information. The therapist might have a consultation session with the parents first so they can talk freely. Or, in the case of adolescents, it might be better to meet with both the parents and the adolescent jointly so the client does not feel the clinician has aligned with the parents. Younger children may require more parental involvement so parents can promote environmental changes that may have a positive impact. Adolescents may prefer less parental involvement.

The counselor should identify in advance how parental phone calls will be handled so as not to lose trust with the adolescent. Parents may choose to try to contact the therapist either to provide information about the adolescent or to ask questions. I inform parents that if they contact me between sessions, I will let the adolescent know.

Confidentiality is not an absolute for clients of any age (Huey & Remley, 1996). The limits of confidentiality must be clearly explained verbally and in writing, and all parties—parents and child or adolescent client—must sign a confidentiality agreement. The discussion must be clearly understandable to the developmental level of the child or adolescent. Positions the counselor can negotiate in establishing boundaries of confidentiality related to the parent/child/adolescent are the following (adapted from Hendrix, 1991 as cited in Lawrence & Robinson-Kurpius, 2000).

1. With parental approval, the minor client is given confidentiality and only general information is shared with parents.

2. No confidentiality is provided for the minor client.

3. The client is provided limited confidentiality; the therapist decides what information should be shared with the parents.

4. Limited confidentiality is provided, with the client and the therapist deciding in advance what information will be shared with the parents, and the therapist is open to the client's perspective not to disclose certain information.

All of the preceding declarations of confidentiality have associated problems. If the therapist promises confidentiality, he or she may not be able to honor this commitment, and legally, depending on the age of the minor, the parents may be able to access information about him or her. If no confidentiality will be provided, the therapist may discourage children, especially adolescents, from seeking therapy or disclosing in therapy, especially if they wish to discuss some issues about which they would prefer that their parents not have knowledge.

Lawrence and Robinson-Kurpius (2000) suggested that it is important to have an agreement between the child, parents, and therapist about what approach to confidentiality will be used, and to work to empower the minor client to make disclosures to parents as appropriate. Haley (1987) described the therapist as the "gatekeeper of information," with the responsibility of deciding when secrets are to be shared and when they need to be kept, a function that can serve to strengthen the therapeutic alliance between the client and the therapist. If parents are too removed from the therapeutic arrangement, however, they may terminate therapy (Taylor & Adelman, 1989).

The most critical issue is that all parties be clear about the approach to confidentiality. The therapist has to check the client's level of understanding to be sure he or she fully understands.

Work with child clients often involves the need to make more collateral contacts for information about how the child is doing in different systems. If the teacher, social worker, probation officer, or physician is going to be contacted, the child or adolescent should be asked for his or her permission. Younger children often have no objections, but mid-school and high-school students might object. The wishes of the child or adolescent client should be considered when making collateral contacts.

Informed Consent

Informed consent has both ethical and legal implications. Clients have a right to information that is presented in an understandable way so they can make an informed decision about whether they want to participate in therapy (Welch, 1999). Nagy (2000) identified the following aspects of informed consent:

1. The client must be presented with information about therapy that is understandable. In the case of child and adolescent clients, the therapist must explain the therapy process in terms that are appropriate given the client's cognitive developmental level. For example, parents can be asked to read to their children *A Child's First Book About Play Therapy* (Nemiroff and Annunziata, 1990), written for children between 4 and 7 years of age. The book can be used to provide general information to children and parents about the process of therapy and confidentiality.

2. The client must be able to provide consent to treatment. In many states, parents must provide consent for minor clients. The law tends to view chronological age as the marker for establishing consent (Powell, 1984). Under the age of 11, consent is seen as primarily belonging to the parents; for age 15 and older, consent on the basis of maturity can be argued for the minor; however, between 11 and 14 years of age, the therapist will have to make some fine discriminations (Sobocinski, 1990). Autonomy must be based on an assessment of the competence of the adolescent to make rational decisions. Several states permit minors to access counseling services without parental permission. New Mexico is one such state and there is no age limit.

3. The client must voluntarily agree to receive services. When parents consent to treatment for their children or adolescents, the minors must give their assent to treatment (Reid, 1999). Even though parents have the right to make decisions concerning their children, the cooperation of the child or adolescent is important if therapy is to be effective.

Powell (1984) discussed the necessity, at times, of being paternalistic, or overriding the autonomy of minors, when it promotes the well-being of the minor to receive treatment or if clients are determined to endanger themselves or others. By observing the clients and parents together, the therapist can determine if the minors are being coerced into entering therapy, and this will have to be addressed.

When discussing therapy with children and adolescents, the therapist should give them general information about why parents are seeking services for them and to get their agreement to enter counseling. If they are reluctant, they should feel free

PROFESSIONAL DISCLOSURE STATEMENTS FOR MINOR CLIENTS

Welcome. I am pleased to have the chance to get to know you better. I am a licensed psychologist, and I specialize in work with children and adolescents. I am not a medical doctor, nor do I provide medication. As a psychologist, I have been trained to help individuals deal with problems by talking about them and engaging in activities. I am often consulted when children or adolescents are having difficulty at school, when they are having trouble getting along with family members or with friends, or when they have strong emotions, such as anger or sadness, that may be related to negative events or changes that have occurred in the family.

In counseling, it is important that you and I work together. I will help you talk about your feelings and learn how they may affect your behavior. You will develop a better understanding of your strengths, and you may develop new skills that will help with problem solving. I have available a play and activity room, and you may choose to have our sessions there.

Confidentiality

Confidentiality, the duty to keep private what you share with me in counseling, is an important part of our working relationship. I will try my best to protect your privacy. You need to be aware, however, that in a few situations I am legally and ethically bound to break confidentiality.

1. If you tell me that you are being abused.
2. If you appear in my judgment to be in danger of hurting yourself or someone else.
3. If you request that I release information to someone else.

You, your parents, and I will negotiate a confidentiality agreement that will identify the role your parents will have in the therapeutic process, what kind of information will be provided to them, and what type of contact they will have with me. I will try to honor your request, but you need to be aware that, legally, your parents may be able to access information about your counseling sessions.

I will always try to discuss with you in advance any information that may be released. In this state, the age of consent is _____. If you meet this age limit, legally you are able to decide who will be able to obtain information about therapy and you will have to sign the release of information forms.

Responsibilities of Child and Adolescent Clients

Child and adolescent clients are responsible for:

1. Attending scheduled counseling sessions.
2. Actively participating in deciding what to work on.
3. Trying to complete agreed upon assignments.
4. Calling the therapist between sessions if in distress.

Rights of Child and Adolescent Clients and Parents [some of these have been adapted from Huey, 1986; Jacob & Hartshorne, 1991; Koocher & Keith-Spiegel, 1990; Ross, 1980; and Simmonds, 1976, as adapted and cited in Prout, DeMartino, & Prout, 1997].

Child and adolescent clients have the right to:

1. Be treated with respect and dignity.
2. Have confidentiality and its limits explained.
3. Develop a confidentiality agreement with the parents related to therapy.
4. Participate in decision making to the fullest extent possible.
5. Have the process of therapy and the techniques used clearly explained.
6. Contribute to the development of treatment goals.
7. Provide an opinion about what role parents, step-parents, legal guardians, or other significant adults are preferred to have in therapy.
8. Be able to ask questions and to receive answers that are understandable.
9. Have assessment results explained in clear language.
10. Provide the therapist with feedback about the counseling relationship.
11. Not be labeled as the identified client when the problem may be a family issue.
12. Receive treatment.
13. Refuse treatment as long as it is not legally mandated or school-mandated.
14. Decide who will receive information about therapy.

Parents have the right to:

1. Seek services for their children and adolescents.
2. Access information that pertains to their child or adolescent.
3. Control release of information for minor children.

Please sign that you have read the brochure and that you are in agreement with entering therapy.

_____   _____
Signature of client   **Date of Birth**   **Date**

_____   _____
Signature of parent   **Date**

to discuss their reservations openly. Children and adolescents need to become involved in the therapy process. To make an informed choice, written information should be provided at an appropriate level of understanding for minor clients. A brochure designed for children age 8 to 14 for example, should be concise but comprehensive. The language used should be at the client's level of understanding. Counselors should provide the client information about their credentials and training, approach to therapy, client rights and responsibilities, parental rights, and limits of confidentiality.

Finally, it is important to document in the client record that the information was discussed and understood and questions were answered (Krener & Mancina, 1994).

Ethical Decision-Making Model

An ethical decision-making model provides a systematic way to problem solve. This is especially important in cases related to children and adolescents, as the professional codes must be adapted to the context of working with minors. The following is an example of an ethical/legal decision-making model for working with children and adolescents, adapted from Tymchuk (1981) and Haas and Malouf 's (1989) work (as adapted and cited in Koocher & Keith-Spiegel, 1998).

1. *Recognize that certain ethical/legal issues are related to child and adolescent clients.* Just as clients are evaluated for suicidal and homicidal ideation during the initial session, all cases should be reviewed for current or potential ethical or legal dilemmas. Zuckerman (1997) discussed developing an ethical and legal consciousness that would keep the clinician proactive. For example, in work with children, parents could possibly divorce and attempt to involve the therapist in a custody battle. By anticipating ethical and legal issues, the clinician has time to research and reflect on the issues.

2. *Identify the specific ethical and legal issues and consult the relevant sections of the current professional code and the state mental health statutes for guidance. Once the relevant sections of the code and the statutes have been identified, adapt the information to a child or adolescent context.* All practicing therapists should have a current copy of their professional ethical code, a copy of their state mental health statutes, including a children's code if applicable, and a current copy of the rules and regulations developed by their professional licensing board. In addition, clinicians might develop a personal library of ethical and legal resources, such as books and articles, on topics related to children and adolescents, to be better able to make adaptations for this population (Koocher and Keith-Spiegel, 1998). For example, clinicians who work with adolescents should have resources that address suicide assessment in this population and a copy of suicide assessment criteria and a "no harm contract." An effective system of paperwork and forms will help to demonstrate that the clinician has thought through many of the ethical and legal issues associated with work with minor clients (Zuckerman, 1997).

3. *Reflect on personal beliefs and values that may influence your judgment.* It is impossible to perform value-free therapy (Corey, Corey, and Callanan, 1998). Ethical and legal issues may create strong emotional reactions in clinicians. One way to assess the impact of personal values on decision making is to have clinicians complete the Ethics Position Questionnaire (Forsyth, 1980). The questionnaire has 20 items, with 10 reflecting level of idealism and 10 reflecting level of realism. The final score provides clinicians with feedback about which one of four ethical ideologies they may favor when making ethical-decisions: situationalism, absolutism, subjectivism, and exceptionalism.

The influence of values is demonstrated in research reporting that various professionals can apply the same ethical code and arrive at different decisions (Haas, Malouf, & Mayerson, 1986). Personal variables such as gender, ethnicity, age, years of experience, and theoretical orientation also may impact decision making (Koocher & Keith-Speigel, 1998).

4. *Identify the rights and responsibilities of the child, adolescent, parents, or significant others involved.* It is important to analyze the case from the perspective of the child, the adolescent, the parents, or significant others, such as step-parents. When working with minor clients, verification of who is the custodial parent is essential. Zuckerman (1997) discussed the importance of documenting written consent from both parents to provide therapy to children when parents share a joint custody arrangement.

5. *Identify all possible courses of action, being overinclusive rather than underinclusive, and then rank order them.*

6. *Identify consequences associated with each identified action and its impact on all of those involved.*

7. *Formulate an action plan, and then consult at least two professional colleagues who have extensive experience in working with children and adolescents. Consult an attorney if legal issues are involved.* The clinician should struggle with the dilemma first and formulate a tentative course of action before consulting with colleagues. Clinicians should ask colleagues for their opinions and then provide them an opportunity to respond to the tentative plan the clinician has developed. The colleagues should be experienced in working with children and adolescents. The clinician also may choose to consult with state and national ethics committees or with an attorney experienced in mental health law. Clinicians are encouraged to document their consultations.

8. *Analyze all of the information and then make a decision.* Recognize that all courses of action may be problematic.

9. *Act on the decision.* Even though professionals may be aware of the appropriate course of action to take, they may choose not to follow through (Bernard & Jara, 1986).

10. *Document the decision, the decision-making process, the references consulted, and the rationale for the choice.*

Ethical Decision-Making Model Applied to Vignette

I now will apply the preceding ethical/legal decision-making model to the case vignette at the beginning of the chapter and share my "thinking aloud" processes. The legal issues will be addressed from the perspective of New Mexico law.

1. *Recognize that ethical/legal issues are related to minor clients.* The professional's ethical/legal sensitivity radar should send out an alarm in response to this scenario. Clinicians should be asking themselves if they can honor the minor's request to provide confidential services without involving the divorced parents. The clinician should be asking what lies behind the adolescent's request for absolute secrecy. The clinician also should be recognizing that the parents seem to disagree and be hostile in regard to issues surrounding the adolescent. The clinician must keep in mind, however, that this is only one perception of the family situation. If both parents were interviewed, other perspectives might emerge.

2. *Identify specific ethical and legal issues and then consult the relevant sections of the ethical code and the state legal statutes, recognizing that the clinician may have to adapt the guidelines of the code to work with minor clients.* As with many clinical scenarios, multiple ethical and legal issues are involved, beginning with best interest of the client, confidentiality, informed consent, and right to treatment. Initially legal issues include right to treatment, informed consent, and privileged communication.

For the sake of illustration, the ethical code of the American Psychological Association (1992) will be consulted for guidance:

■ Principle E: Concern for Other's Welfare applies as there is a 13-year-old who describes symptoms that would benefit from treatment. She has the maturity to recognize that she is in need of help and is requesting services.

■ 4.02: Informed Consent to Therapy requires that the person seeking services has the mental capacity to provide consent to treatment. To make this determination, the clinician has to be able to make an informal assessment of cognitive functioning.

■ 4.02(b) suggests that when the client is not able to legally consent to treatment, consent is sought from those who have that legal standing, such as parents.

■ 5.01: Confidentiality discusses that the limits of confidentiality have to be explained to the client. Because the parents are not involved in initiating therapy, it is not possible to discuss a confidentiality agreement with all parties in advance of services being provided. This could set in motion an angry reaction from parents if they later find out about therapy being provided, and they may demand to know information related to counseling.

The client is 13 years old, and there is a legal question related to whether an adolescent may seek mental health services without the consent of her parents. The clinician may have to make an argument for a mature minor, if the clinician decides to accept the client in therapy. In New Mexico, children are legally permitted to receive counseling services without parental consent. This does not mean it is in the best interests of the minor client to exclude the parents. In New Mexico, even though children can seek services, they do not achieve greater autonomy until they reach the age of 14—therefore this client would have to be informed that the parents could very well access information related to the services provided.

The parents are divorced, and it sounds like a joint custody arrangement, but the clinician does not know the final disposition of custody. The adolescent is troubled by the situation with her parents, and leaving them out of the counseling process may create additional conflict if they find out. Another consideration is the administrative policy from the organization that employs the clinician, as to whether the organization would support treating the minor client without parental permission.

3. *Reflect on personal beliefs and values that may influence judgment.* In this particular case, I need to explore my ethnic values, which may tend to emphasize the rights of the individual rather than looking at issues related to the family. I also would have to consider the culture of the client and the parents and contrast it with my own. Because I am a parent, I may have strong feelings about excluding parents from decision making related to their children, especially since, by client report, they seem to be the source of some of the adolescent's distress.

I have completed the Ethics Position Questionnaire, and my score has placed me in the situationalist category. I tend to be influenced by the individual circumstances of a given case, which could mean that individual circumstances may lead me to interpret the code differently in various contexts.

As a female, I also am concerned about relationship issues, and I am in the process of developing a relationship with the female adolescent. I firmly believe that treatment is better than no treatment for this client at this moment in time. I recognize that the parents, especially the father, may be highly upset with me if they find out that I accepted their daughter into counseling. I also may believe that if I involve the parents at this point, the entire case is likely to become more highly charged and complex and the adolescent probably will lose autonomy in terms of pursuing therapy.

4. *Identify the rights and responsibilities of the child, adolescent, parents, or significant others.* The clinician is caught between the rights of the adolescent and the rights of the parents. The adolescent has a right to receive treatment, and she is describing symptoms that would benefit from therapy. Nevertheless, she seems to want to set conditions for treatment that may not be in her best interest. She does have a right to autonomy in decision making, especially if she is acting in her own best interests and if she is sufficiently mature cognitively. If the client is accepted into therapy, she has a right to a confidential counseling relationship. But the clinician cannot guarantee confidentiality because the parents have been totally excluded at the adolescent's request. If the client were accepted and subsequently were to become suicidal, the therapist would have to contact the parents.

The parents in this scenario have the right to be involved in decisions that affect their child. It sounds as if their involvement potentially could lead to a change in the home environment that would have a positive impact on the client. Several times I have been pleasantly surprised when I met parents after I had listened to an adolescent describe them. Parents have a right to know of their daughter's distress and to be kept apprised of her progress in therapy.

5. *Identify all possible courses of action and then rank order the possibilities in terms of their level of acceptability.*

The following four proposed action plans are listed in order of their acceptability in my opinion.

■ Encourage the client to involve her parents in the decision, and allow the client some time to think it over. If she is still opposed, accept the client for therapy, as she appears to be a mature minor. The client is requesting services and is experiencing several symptoms of depression, which may become more severe if untreated. Spend time discussing with her the limits to confidentiality, given her minor status. She has a level of cognitive maturity that can be used to argue for autonomy in decision making.

   The parents are creating stress for her, and you may be able to work with her to reduce her symptoms enough so that she will be willing to try to include the parents later. The client has to recognize that the parents, by not being included from the beginning may be able to access her counseling records. Before the therapeutic relationship begins, the client has to fully understand the limits to confidentiality and when the therapist is bound to break confidentiality.

■ Inform the client that you will have to contact at least one parent before you can work with her, and suggest that it can be the parent of the adolescent's choice. Work with the client to find the best way to inform the parent, and see if you can get the parent to consent to therapy and to confidentiality for the adolescent.

■ Inform the client that if she wants to see you in therapy, you will have to schedule a meeting with her and her parents, so you can all discuss the distress that is being generated. Let her know that, because she apparently is in a joint custody arrangement, both parents have to be contacted, although you could meet with them separately. Work with the client to help make these meetings successful. Try to get the parents to work toward the client's best interest.

■ Suggest to the adolescent that you contact her school to see if it has a divorce adjustment group that may help the client deal with her current situation. Suggest that the client's church might have some resources available that the parents would see as acceptable.

6. *Identify consequences associated with each proposed action and its impact on all involved parties.*

■ The first option is to try to change the restrictions the adolescent placed on the therapy arrangement but agreeing to see her even if she did not change her mind. It is hoped that therapy would be able to reduce current symptoms and make her more amenable to including her parents in the future. If the parents are included later, they may be highly resentful about being excluded initially and might terminate therapy or try to access their daughter's records, which could have a negative impact on the therapeutic relationship.

Your practice is in a small town and someone may see the client leaving the center and ask one of the parents about this. The client could become angry with a parent and say that her therapist stated that parents should not place children in the middle between feuding parents. The client might become suicidal, in which case the therapist would have to notify the parents and also to inform them that she had been seeing the client in therapy. The client may be harboring a secret that may require taking action on the part of the client. Because the home environment may continue to be distressed, therapy might not be as effective as if the parents were involved.

■ Accept the client if she will permit you to obtain permission from one parent, whom she can choose. If the client chooses the mother, you may be able to negotiate a confidentiality agreement for the client and may promote a better relationship between the two. You may, however, alienate the client from the other parent, who may become hostile if he finds out that he has been left out of the process. He also may be able to access records if it is a joint-custody arrangement. The excluded parent might place the adolescent in an even more distressed environment. The client may find the terms unacceptable and decide not to enter therapy.

■ The client may find the terms of contacting both parents for permission unacceptable and decide not to enter therapy at this time. Or she may agree to invite the parents for a meeting with you and the parents may decide that therapy is not needed and the adolescent will have lost autonomy of decision-making. The client's symptoms could worsen without intervention. The parents may decide against therapy, but they may have more empathy for their daughter's current situation and make some changes.

■ The client might be willing for you to investigate school programs to see if group counseling is available, without using her name. The clinician must check to see if parental permission is required for participating in school counseling. The client might be able to present this concept more easily to her parents than the individual counseling option. She might be amenable to talking with someone from her church to try to persuade her parents to permit her to enter counseling. Or the church or another agency in town might have a divorce adjustment group, but parental permission likely would be sought for participation.

7. *Formulate an action plan, and then consult with at least two colleagues who have extensive experience working with children and adolescents. Consult with an attorney for legal advice.* I had decided to tentatively choose the first course of action described above, which was to lobby the adolescent to involve her parents, but if not successful, to accept her as a client. Having formulated a decision, I proceeded to consult with two psychologists in private practice and an attorney. The first child and adolescent psychologist was concerned that the adolescent did not want any parental involvement or even notification. The psychologist thought this was significant and should be explored more fully. She also was concerned that the adolescent might be keeping something from the therapist, waiting to receive some assurance of confidentiality, at which time she might reveal something that would

necessitate the parents' involvement, such as abuse or potential suicide. The psychologist also postulated that the adolescent was presenting one perspective on the family and information from other individuals might be useful, as well as providing a different perspective.

Further, if the therapist agreed to see the client, the client would have to be informed about the limits of confidentiality and the parents legally might be able to access her records. The psychologist recommended countering the adolescent's objections so the parents could be contacted.

The second child and adolescent psychologist in private practice responded that it might be possible to see the adolescent, but that agency rules and administration should be consulted for guidelines. She was aware that New Mexico law would not prohibit her from accepting the adolescent client. But she was bothered by the restrictions and the control that the adolescent was trying to exert over the therapeutic relationship. This psychologist did not want to agree to such a handicapped relationship, and she believed that her autonomy as a therapist was being compromised, possibly manipulated. For example, a referral for medications might be needed in the future, and this was an option that might not be available without parental involvement.

I also consulted an attorney who was experienced in mental health law. He reported that it made a difference that the adolescent was seeking therapy on her own. In New Mexico, the Children's Code states that children are entitled to verbal therapy and parental consent is not required. He cautioned, however, that if one parent in a joint custody situation would seek to initiate services for a minor client, the therapist would have to contact the other parent for consent as well, as joint custody implies joint decision making on important issues.

As the reader will note, three different professionals were consulted—and each had a slightly different perspective. This is why multiple consultations are important. The treating professional, however, must make the ultimate decision and accept the responsibility for the action and any consequences.

8. *Analyze all of the information and then make a decision.* Following consultations with colleagues and the administrator of the agency, I am beginning to rethink my decision to accept the client in counseling without parental involvement. Legally, I can see the client without parental permission, but I am not able to promise confidentiality in reference to the parents. I recognize the client's reluctance to involve hostile parents, but because they are contributing to the current problem, it would seem to be in the best interest of the client to involve the parents from the outset. I believe it would be highly conflictual if therapy were initiated and the parents were to find out later.

I practice in a small town, and the chance that a friend of the family might see the client at the agency is relatively high. The client might have to lie to the parents about her activities, and this would not be in the client's best interest. I would want to know the client's objections to contacting the parents, and I would try to work with her to overcome them. I could role-play with the client about how to approach her parents, and I would offer to support her through this process. I would offer to meet separately with each parent if this would be seen as a more acceptable option. But it may be more difficult to refuse her after talking with her than to make a decision in the abstract.

If the client were unwilling to involve her parents, as a secondary approach I would encourage her to join a group at school or at church so she could receive support. I also would encourage her to talk to her parents or another relative about how she was feeling.

Creating and Maintaining a Personal Ethical and Legal Stance in Clinical Practice

One way to generate ideas about how to stay current in the field is to ask yourself how you would respond if you were asked by a client, a colleague, a prospective employer, or an attorney to demonstrate that you are an ethical professional who practices within the scope of your state's laws. The following are some recommended actions which will help to ensure that you are staying current in ethical/legal issues in your state.

1. Join at least one national professional organization and seek membership in divisions that bring together professionals who have an interest in children and adolescents. Divisions provide an opportunity for closer networking with professionals who have similar interests.

2. Have a copy of the current ethical code of your professional organization in your desk and know the year of its publication. I observed an attorney embarrass a clinician who could not provide the date of publication of the current ethical code. More important than having a copy of the code, be sure to review it periodically. As an instructor, I assign students to read the code, and we discuss it in class. Ethical codes are dynamic, not static, and they are continually in a process of revision. The practicing clinician must take responsibility for staying current. Read the professional journals and newsletters that you receive from professional organizations, as they will discuss the revision process and upcoming changes in the ethical code.

3. Have a current copy of the state mental health statutes and any laws that specifically apply to minors. Have a copy of state statutes related to confidentiality, informed consent, and release of information related to the treatment of minor clients. The American Psychological Association is in the process of publishing a series entitled *Law and Mental Health Professionals* for each of the 50 states.

4. Research and identify an ethical decision-making model that you will apply to ethical dilemmas. The decision-making model provides a systematic way to analyze the situation. Cottone and Claus (2000) have compiled a literature review of several decision-making models.

5. Develop a personal library with resources addressing ethical and legal issues that occur with high frequency in your practice. Start an ethical file of journal articles and relevant materials. Include references that discuss the current ethical code and legal issues in your state. Inquire about obtaining continuing-education texts for home-study courses on relevant topics.

6. Join a state professional organization. They often sponsor workshops addressing legal changes within the state, and they have an ethics committee that also can provide consultation. Their newsletter will provide current relevant state information.

7. Have a copy of the current rules and regulations from your state licensing board. This resource will keep you informed about state laws.

8. Identify at least two professionals who are experienced in working with children and adolescents whom you can call upon for consultation when needed, and identify a professional whom you can consult on legal issues.

9. Attend at least one continuing-education workshop annually on ethical or legal issues. Several liability insurance companies provide a discount for such continuing-education activities.

10. Attend the national conference from your professional affiliation, and include at least one workshop on ethical issues.

11. Check professional organization websites for updates about ethical issues. Some suggestions are:
    www.apa.org./ethics/Code.html
    www.counseling.org/resources/codeofethics.htm
    www.schoolcounselor.org/ethics/standards.htm

References

American Association for Marriage and Family Therapy. (1991). *Code of ethics.* Washington, DC: AAMFT.

American Counseling Association. (1995). *Code of ethics and standards of practice.* Washington, DC: ACA.

American Psychological Association (APA). (1995). *Ethical principles of psychologists and code of conduct.* Washington, DC: APA.

American School Counselor Association (1998). *Ethical standards for school counselors.* Alexandria, VA: ASCA.

Arthur, G. & Swanson, C. (1993). *Confidentiality and privileged communication.* Washington, DC: American Counseling Association.

Axline, V. (1969) *Play therapy.* New York: Ballantine Books.

Bernard, J. L. & Jara, C. S. (1986). The failure of clinical psychology graduate students to apply understood ethical principles. In D. N. Bersoff (Ed.). *Ethical conflicts in psychology* (pp 67–71). Washington, DC: American Psychological Association.

Collins, N., & Knowles, A. (1995). Adolescents' attitudes towards confidentiality between the school counsellor and the adolescent client. *Australian Psychologist, 30,* 179–182.

Cottone, R. & Claus, R. (2000). Ethical decision-making models: A review of the literature. *Journal of Counseling & Development, 78,* 275–283.

Corey, G., Corey, M. S. & Callanan, P. (1993). *Issues and ethics in the helping professions.* (4th ed.) Pacific Grove, CA: Brooks/Cole.

Corey, G., Corey, M. S., & Callanan, P. (1998). *Issues and ethics in the helping Profession* (5th ed.). Pacific Grove, CA: Brooks/Cole.

Forsyth, D. (1980). A taxonomy of ethical ideologies. *Journal of Personality & Social Psychology, 39,* 175–184.

Froese, A. (1991). Minors' right to psychiatric treatment. *Canadian Journal of Psychiatry, 36,* 452–455.

Garner, B. (Ed). (1999). *Black's law dictionary* (7th ed.). St. Paul, MN: West Group.

Gustafson, K. E., & McNamara, R. J. (1987). Confidentiality with minor clients: Issues and guidelines for therapists (pp. 193–197). In Bersoff. (Ed.). *Ethical conflicts in psychology.* Washington, DC: American Psychological Association.

Haas. L., Malouf, J., & Mayerson, N. (1986). Ethical dilemmas in psychological practice: Results of a national survey. In D. N. Bersoff (Ed.), *Ethical conflicts in psychology* (pp. 90–98). Washington, DC: American Psychological Association.

Haley, J. (1987). *Problem-solving therapy.* (2nd ed.) San Francisco: Jossey-Bass.

Herlihy, B. & Corey, G. (1996) *ACA ethical standards casebook.* Alexandria, VA: American Counseling Association.

Honig, P., & Bentovim, M. (1996). Treating children with eating disorders—ethical and legal issues. *Clinical Child Psychology & Psychiatry, 1,* 287–294.

Huey, W. C., & Remley, T. P. (Eds.) (1986). *Ethical and legal issues in school counseling.* Alexandria, VA: American School Counseling Association.

Isaacs, M. L., & Stone, C. (1999). School counselors and confidentiality: Factors affecting professional choices. *Professional School Counseling, 2,* 258–266.

Kaczmarek, P. & Riva, M. (1996). Facilitating adolescent optimal development: Training considerations for counseling psychologists. *Counseling Psychologist, 24,* 400–432.

Kaczmarek, P., & Wagner, W. (1994). Future training requirements for counseling psychologists: Competence with children. *Counseling Psychologist, 22,* 426–443.

Kitchener, K. & Anderson, S. (2000). Ethical issues in counseling psychology: Old themes—new problems. In S. D. Brown and R. W. Lent (Eds.). *Handbook of counseling Psychology* (pp. 50–82). New York: John Wiley.

Koocher, G., & Keith-Spiegel, P. (1990). *Children, ethics, and the law.* Lincoln, NE: University of Nebraska.

Koocher, G., & Keith-Spiegel, P. (1998). *Ethics in psychology.* New York: Oxford Press.

Krener, P. K., & Mancian, R. A. (1994). Informed consent or informed coercion? Decision-making in pediatric psychopharmacology. *Journal of Child & Adolescent Psychopharmacology, 3,* 183–200.

Lawrence, G. & Robinson/Kurpius, S. (2000). Legal and ethical issues involved when counseling minors in nonschool settings. *Journal of Counseling & Development, 78,* 130–136.

Milne, J. (1995). Analysis of the law of confidentiality with special reference to the counselling of minors. *Australian Psychologist, 30,* 169–174.

Nagy, T. (2000). *Ethics in plain English.* Washington, DC: American Psychological Association.

Nemiroff, M. & Annunziata, J. (1990). *A child's first book about play therapy.* Washington, DC: American Psychological Association.

Powell, C. (1984). Ethical principles and issues of competence in counseling adolescents. *Counseling Psychologist, 12,* 57–68.

Prout, S. M., DeMartino, R. A., & Prout, H. T. (1999). Ethical and legal issues in psychological interventions with children and adolescents (pp. 26–48). In H. T. Prout & D. T. Brown (Eds.), Counseling and psychotherapy with children and adolescents. (3rd Ed.). New York, NY: Wiley & Sons.

Reid, W. H. (1999). *A clinician's guide to legal issues in psychotherapy.* Phoenix: Zeig, Tucker, & Co.

Schulte, J., & Cochrane, D. (1995). *Ethics in school counseling.* New York: Teachers College Press.

Sobocinski, M. (1990). Ethical principles in the counseling of gay and lesbian adolescents: Issues of autonomy, competence, and confidentiality. *Professional Psychology: Research & Practice, 21,* 240–247.

Sondheimer, A., & Martucci, C. (1992). An approach to teaching ethics in child and adolescent psychiatry. *Journal of American Academy of Child & Adolescent Psychiatry, 31,* 415–422.

Taylor, L. & Adelman, H. S. (1989), Reframing the confidentiality dilemma to work in children's best interest. In D. N. Bersoff (Ed.), *Ethical conflict in psychology* (pp. 198–201). Washington, DC: American Psychological Association.

Thompson, C., & Rudolph, L. (2000). *Counseling children* (5th ed.). Belmont, CA: Wadsworth/Thompson Learning.

Vernon, A. (1999). *Counseling children and adolescents.* (2d ed.). Denver: Love Publishing.

Welch, B. (1999). The hazards of working with children and adolescents. *Insight.* Amityville, NY: American Professional Agency.

Zuckerman, E. (1997). *The paper office.* New York: Guilford Press.

Individual Issues and Interventions

Jon Carlson and Judith A. Lewis

The seven essays that make up this section examine concerns that affect adolescents on an individual level. Each author combines knowledge of adolescent development with an awareness of the behaviors that tend to place young people in jeopardy.

In Chapter 3, M. Lewis Putman describes the problems experienced by adolescents with special emphasis on those with learning disabilities, as they seem to be more at-risk than their non-disabled peers. The dramatic physical, emotional, psychological, and social changes of adolescence pose unique challenges for individuals with learning disabilities.

Rosemary Lambie, Susan Leone, and Christopher Martin discuss how important resilience can be in working with at-risk children and youth. The authors offer many ideas as to how resilience can be increased.

In Chapter 5, Sharon Robinson-Kurpius discusses the growing problem of substance abuse among adolescents. According to research, most high school seniors have at some time smoked cigarettes or consumed alcohol and a large percentage have experimented with illegal drugs. Unfortunately, these phenomena coincide with increases in other at-risk and criminal behaviors. The author delves into the historical and psychosocial reasons for substance abuse and explores the possibilities for prevention, including education.

In Chapter 6, John Maag and Steven Forness provide an overview of child and adolescent depression. They describe the treatment studies that have been completed with depressed children and adolescents, as well as some of the common psychopharmacological interventions that are used. In addition, they discuss the prevalence of depression in populations with disabilities and the treatments that are available.

Next, Dave Capuzzi addresses another problem of great urgency: adolescent suicide. He provides an overview of possible causes for adolescent suicide, identifying common misconceptions and describing developmental, family, and environmental factors that may relate to the recent increase in adolescent suicide rates. He suggests a number of strategies for recognizing and preventing potential suicides and provides guidelines for managing crises that could not be prevented.

Barry Weinhold shows how bullying and school violence can lead to tragedy such as that experienced at Columbine High School. Dr. Weinhold describes effective long-range prevention methods that address many of the hidden elements present in a culture of violence.

In Chapter 9, Radha Horton-Parker builds on Weinhold's ideas and presents a firm foundation for pro-social behavior that is essential for curbing violence during the adolescent years. This chapter presents information that the counselor can use to assist parents in developing practices that will lead to pro-social outcomes in young children and last throughout their lives.

The need to understand the nature of adolescent development is made clear throughout the chapters in this section. Elkind's (1974) conceptualization of adolescent egocentrism and the key role and variability of cognitive, social, and moral development are discussed. Adolescents are expected to attain the capacity for formal operational thought. Yet, as Ingersoll and Orr (1998) point out:

> Many adolescents, perhaps a majority, do not progress beyond concrete operational thought. In the same fashion, there are no guarantees that older adolescents operate at advanced, or even middle, levels of cognitive social development. Those same adolescents who vary so widely in physical status likewise vary in intellectual and social skills. (p. 27)

Clearly, individual interventions with adolescents require that counselors understand how the adolescents attach meaning to their experiences. Awareness of the developmental level of the adolescent client is an important component in each counselor-client interaction.

Another theme that unites these chapters is the authors' shared recognition of the interactions among varied problematic behaviors. Ingersoll and Orr (1998) cite the research of Jessor and Jessor (1974), Donovan and Jessor (1985), and others to support the idea that the behaviors of drug abuse, delinquency, and early sexual activity are linked, especially by the individual's rejection of commonly held social values. It is interesting to note the similarities between Hayes and Cryer's (1998) profile of the adolescent who becomes pregnant and keeps her child and the profile of the adolescent drug abuser. As described by Hayes and Cryer (1998), the former

> is likely to express less acceptance of social norms, be biologically ready for pregnancy and childbirth, possess an inability to use information and an inability to project events into the future, have an unstable family environment, have no clearly defined religious orientation, have poor school performance and low educational aspirations, and have low self-esteem. (p. 59)

The similarity between this profile and that of the adolescent drug abuser cannot be overlooked by the counselor who hopes to understand and intervene. As Ingersoll and Orr (1998) point out,

> The linked nature of many risk behaviors suggest that categorical interventions limited to only one component of a series of problem behaviors and ignoring the others will be unsuccessful. For example, insisting that sexual abstinence is the only way to prevent teenage pregnancy ignores the interactions between drug use, antisocial acts, and early sexual activity. A given behavior may serve multiple personal needs. (p. 28)

Finally, the authors in this section share a vision of counseling that encompasses *prevention* as well as intervention. Each chapter provides a set of practical suggestions for services to address a particular issue. The guidelines presented have a number of common characteristics, including:

- a recognition that complex problems require multifaceted strategies for resolution and that no single method will always be appropriate.

- an awareness that interventions should fit the developmental level and special needs of the individual at risk and that careful assessment should be the basis for the approach to be used.

- a focus on the roles of family, peer group, and other systems in the development and resolution of problems.

- an appreciation of the need to use honest, straightforward, two-way communication in dealing with adolescents.

- a combination of broad, preventive measures and specific, targeted interventions to address each issue.

Adolescence is, for many, a difficult transitional stage. Because of the complexity of the issues involved, counseling clients who are at this stage in their development is demanding. The chapters in this section do not oversimplify this challenge, but they do provide some practical, positive strategies for coping with it.

References

Donovan, J. E., & Jessor, R. (1985). Structure of problem behavior in adolescence and young adulthood. *Journal of Consulting and Clinical Psychology, 53,* 890–904.

Elam, S., Rose, L., & Gallup, A. (1994). The 26th annual Gallup poll of the public's attitudes toward the public school. *Phi Delta Kappa, 76,* 41–56.

Elkind, D. (1974). *Children and adolescents: Interpretive essays on Jean Piaget* (2nd ed.). New York: Oxford University Press.

Hayes, R. L., & Cryer, N. (1998). When adolescents give Birth to children: A developmental approach to the issue of teen pregnancy. In Carlson, J. & Lewis, J., Eds. *Counseling the adolescent:*

Individuals, family and school interventions, (3rd ed.) Denver, CO: Love Publishing Co., 47–64.

Ingersoll, G. N., & Orr, D. P. (1998). Adolescents at risk. In Carlson, J. & Lewis, J., Eds. *Counseling the adolescent: Individuals, family and school interventions,* (3rd ed.) Denver, CO: Love Publishing Co., 19–32.

Jessor, S. J., & Jessor, R. (1974). *Problem behavior and psychosocial development: A longitudinal study of youth.* New York: Academic Press.

Problems of Adolescents

M. Lewis Putnam

Here are just a few of the challenges we face:

- Every 31 seconds an adolescent becomes pregnant
- Every 2 minutes an adolescent gives birth
- Every 78 seconds an adolescent attempts suicide
- Every 90 minutes an adolescent commits suicide
- One million adolescents drop out of high school (*Children and Teens Today Newsletter,* 1987; Mann, 1986).

This chapter provides a discussion of several social issues that all adolescents must deal with daily. This information is critical to special education teachers because students with learning disabilities (LD) are not immune to involvement in these and other social issues.

Depression and suicide, alcohol and other drug use, teenage sexuality and school dropout, along with many other pressing social issues, place adolescents at risk for social, emotional, and psychological problems. Adolescents often are involved with more than one of these social issues. They attend schools where they are expected to be attentive, complete assignments, learn in a classroom setting, earn credits toward high school graduation, and eventually enter the world of work or attend an institution of higher education. Many adolescents succeed despite their involvement in these social issues, but increasing numbers need social, emotional, and educational interventions aimed at increasing their coping skills or at reducing their involvement. Adolescents with LD are at even greater risk for involvement with these social issues than their nonhandicapped peers. Thus, special education teachers should understand the incidence, possible causes, identification, and appropriate interventions.

Problems of Adolescence

Adolescence is a developmental stage characterized by experimentation, confusion, risk-taking behaviors, and a sense of immortality and invulnerability. Teachers often hear student comments such as, "I got so blasted Saturday night that I don't remember anything," or "It's not cool to use a condom!"

Public School Responsibility

Public schools increasingly are expected to address social issues that previously were the responsibility of the family, religious organizations, and social agencies. Educators often feel overwhelmed and underprepared to deal with adolescents at-risk for depression and suicide, alcohol and other drug use, sexual activities, school dropout, and other complex social issues facing today's adolescents.

Adolescents At-Risk

Many professionals use the term *at-risk* to describe a certain category of students. Never precise, the meaning of this term varies considerably in research and in classroom practice. McWhirter et al. (1993) defined "at risk" as "a set of presumed cause/effect dynamics that place the [adolescent] in danger of negative future events" (p. 6) such as not graduating from high school (Slavin, Karweit, & Madden, 1989). Those authors contended that "at-risk" also might be viewed as a relative term, like a series of steps along a continuum rather than as a distinct category. The continuum in Figure 3.1 ranges from adolescents who are minimally at-risk to those who are involved more actively in risk-taking behaviors.

Minimal risk. Adolescents who come from high socioeconomic settings, attend good schools, and have loving, caring relationships with their friends and families are assumed to be at minimal risk for involvement with these social issues. These adolescents, however, cannot be considered as "no risk," because no adolescent can escape altogether the influences of events such as death, divorce, and so on. The extent to which these and other events lead the adolescent to risk-taking behaviors depends upon factors such as age, developmental level, personality, available resources (social and mental health support), coping skills, and so on.

Remote risk. An adolescent reaches the point on the continuum at which risk-taking behaviors, though still remote, seem more possible because of negative demographic markers involving family, school, and so forth. A combination of these markers moves the adolescent along the at-risk continuum. For example, an adolescent who is from an "impoverished, dysfunctional, ethnic minority family and who attends a poor school in a marginal neighborhood" (McWhirter et al., 1993, p. 8) is further along the continuum than an adolescent with fewer markers. Most adolescents in this group do survive these difficulties and function well. Therefore, although these markers are important, they are only partially predictive of at-risk status for an adolescent.

MINIMAL RISK
> favorable demographics
> positive family, school, and social interaction
> limited psychosocial and environmental stressors

REMOTE RISK
> negative demographics
> less positive family, school, and social interaction
> some stressors

HIGH RISK
> negative family, school, and social interaction
> numerous stressors
> development of personal at-risk markers
> negative attitudes and emotions
> skill deficiencies

IMMINENT RISK
> development of gateway or threshold behaviors and activities

AT-RISK CATEGORY
> at risk for more intensive maladaptive behavior
> adolescent's activity solidly places him or her in the at-risk category
> at risk for other categories

Source: Based on Orr & Brack (unpublished data)McWhirter, J. J., McWhirter, B. T., McWhirter, A. M., & McWhirter, E. H. (1993). *At-risk youth: A comprehensive response.* Pacific Grove, CA: Brooks/Cole. Reprinted with permission.

Figure 3.1 The At-Risk Continuum

High risk. The next set of circumstances that moves a adolescent along the continuum is the demographic markers combined with an adolescent's negative attitudes or emotions. Adolescents at this point often experience depression, anxiety, and exhibit aggressive and risk-taking behaviors. These markers often signal that an adolescent is not coping with various stressors (e.g., poor grades, few friends) and certain demographic markers.

Imminent risk. As the adolescent moves along the continuum, at-risk status becomes even greater. At this point the adolescent may begin to use alcohol or other drugs occasionally to reduce some of the stressors or may appear to be depressed at times. These behaviors, referred to as *threshold behaviors*, often progress to increasingly more frequent and severe risk-taking behaviors. For example, cigarette use is considered a threshold to alcohol use, which can be a threshold to marijuana use, which in turn can be a threshold to crack cocaine use.

At-risk. The final step in the continuum is reached when the adolescent participates in behaviors that define the at-risk categories. According to McWhirter et al.

(1993), these adolescents no longer are at-risk because they may have already attempted suicide, become involved in the abuse of alcohol and other drugs, become sexually active, or dropped out of school.

Teenage Depression and Suicide

Suicide is a growing problem among adolescents. The number of 15- to 24-year-olds who have committed suicide has risen 200% (Tomlinson-Keasey & Keasey, 1988) and now ranks as one of the top three causes of death for individuals under 24 years of age (Guetzloe, 1989).

How Many Adolescents Attempt Suicide

Suicide *ideation* (thoughts about suicide) and *parasuicide* (attempted suicide) both show a significant increase with age, particularly during adolescence (Rutter, 1986). As many as 7,000 adolescents commit suicide each year, and 400,000 to 1 million attempt to do so (Capuzzi & Golden, 1988; Robertson & Mathews, 1989). According to the results of a Gallup poll, 33% of 1,152 adolescents 15 to 19 years old have thought about suicide, 15% have seriously considered killing themselves, and 6% actually have made attempts (Peterson, 1991). In the United States, 20% of male suicides and 14% of female suicides involve adolescents (Hendlin, 1982; Robertson & Matthews, 1989). Females attempt suicide three times as often as males, but males complete suicide three times as often as females. This difference results from the more violent means, such as guns, that males use. The rate of completion by teenage girls, however, is increasing rapidly (Steele, 1983). These estimates are low because suicides often are reported inaccurately. Because of family embarrassment or religious beliefs or because of school and community discomfort, many suicides are reported as accidental or undetermined deaths (McWhirter et al., 1993).

Knowledge of the incidence of suicide by adolescents with LD is even less clear, as only a few studies directly compare depression and suicide by adolescents with mild disabilities and those without disabilities. The limited number of studies, however, suggests a discouraging picture. Adolescents with mild disabilities seem to have higher anxiety levels, more frequent and more serious bouts of depression, and higher rates of suicide than adolescents without disabilities (Dollinger, Horn, & Boarini, 1988; Hayes & Sloat, 1988; Maag & Behrens, 1989; Ritter, 1989).

Societal Myths Related to Suicide

Our society presents a negative view of suicide and of individuals who attempt suicide. As a result, many myths are associated with suicide. Accurate knowledge is one of the keys to understanding the causes and characteristics of adolescents who are at risk for taking their own lives. The most common myths are shown in Table 3.1.

Table 3.1   Societal Myths Related to Suicide

MYTH	FACT
People who talk about suicide do not attempt suicide.	8 out of 10 people who attempt to kill themselves do leave clues to their intent. Simply talking about suicide, however, does not mean a person will not attempt. Every verbal threat or reference to dying must be taken seriously. To discount a person's threat or reference is a direct rejection of his or her cry for help.
Suicide happens without warning.	Suicide often seems to be a sudden, unprovoked act only because we missed the warning signs. Sometimes, however, the clues are much more indirect unless we know what to look for. Statements such as "You won't have to worry about me much longer," or behavior such as withdrawing from friends or giving away many of their possessions can be signs that a person is preparing to die. The point is that expressed statements about dying must be taken seriously. We must learn the warning signs that the suicidal person provides.
Suicidal persons are fully intent on dying.	Most suicidal persons are ambivalent about dying. Many, especially teens and younger children, never believe they will die but that they will be rescued. Ninety percent of teenage suicide attempts are made in the home between early afternoon and midnight when parents are likely to find them. The fact that clues and warning signs most often precede the attempt also points to the ambivalence. It must be remembered, however, that the ambivalence does not reduce the risk involved.
People who attempt suicide are mentally ill.	The overwhelming despair a suicidal person feels can be caused by a sudden emotional upset, a long physical illness, the sudden loss of a loved one, or the feeling that he or she truly is a burden to others. A frequent theme of suicidal children is that they feel they are the cause of their parent's unhappiness. Suicide in most cases is not the act of psychotic persons, but persons who feel that the pain in their lives will not die, so they must. Only 12% of those who commit suicide are mentally ill. The attitude that suicide is the act of a deranged mind is exactly what keeps many potentially suicidal persons from being more open about their feelings. They fear that if they reveal their suicidal feelings, others will attempt to commit them to a psychiatric hospital. This reaction is, by far, the least helpful and is most often unnecessary.
Children are not capable of knowing how to kill themselves.	Television has given adolescents the knowledge necessary to kill themselves. They are aware of what acts are potentially lethal.
Children who attempt suicide have parents who are callous, insensitive, ignorant, and incapable of loving a child.	Most parents are sometimes the last to see the pain in their child because they love the child so much that they don't want to recognize that their child is in pain. Most parents, however, once approached, will do whatever is necessary to help their child.
People who attempt suicide are merely looking for attention.	People who threaten to attempt suicide are reaching out for help, not "merely" attention.

Source: Steele, W. (1983). *Preventing teenage suicide.* Novato, CA: Ann Arbor Publishers. Reprinted with permission.

When an Adolescent May Be Suicidal

For many, adolescence is filled with stressful events and adjustments. We must be able to distinguish between the typical turmoil that occurs during adolescence from turmoil that is life-threatening. Too many adolescents at risk for suicide have been viewed mistakenly and sometimes tragically as simply going through a stage (Metha & Dunham, 1988).

The exact cause of suicide remains a mystery. Professionals generally agree that suicidal behavior results from a complex interaction of numerous factors with no single cause (Hawton, 1986; Pfeffer, 1986). Thus, no one type of adolescent is more suicidal than another. It could be any student from the homecoming queen to the most reserved and quiet student in class.

The single most predictive factor for adolescent suicide is a previous attempt (Shaffer, 1974). Any problem that contributes to feelings of depression, worthlessness, helplessness, or hopelessness has the potential to trigger suicidal behavior in a vulnerable adolescent. Table 3.2 summarizes the most common warning signs that an adolescent may be thinking about committing suicide.

Certain psychological, social, and school characteristics can help distinguish between adolescents who are able to cope with their turmoil and those who are at risk for taking their own lives.

Psychological characteristics. These characteristics include suicidal threats or statements, extreme changes in behavior, and "getting the house in order" (e.g., giving away prized possessions) (Guetzloe, 1987). Frederick (1985) contended that suicidal individuals often suffer from the "three H's: haplessness, helplessness, and hopelessness" (p. 15). For example, suicidal adolescents may have had a series of misfortunes over which they had little or no control, such as their parents' divorce and a subsequent move (haplessness). The adolescent may not have the coping skills, such as seeking help or advice from a friend or professional, to deal with these events (helplessness). As a result, the adolescent may feel hopeless, and suicide may seem to be the only answer ("I don't know what else to do!").

Another key psychological characteristic, depression, is highly correlated with suicidal behavior. Estimates of the prevalence of depression among the general school-aged population have ranged from 1.8% to 13.9% (Pfeffer, Zuckerman, Plutchik, & Miznuchi, 1984), with higher rates reported among older adolescents. We must become aware of the signs of depression among adolescents so we can provide appropriate interventions or refer the adolescent to the school counselor or to a local social or mental health agency.

According to the *Diagnostic and Statistical Manual of the American Psychiatric Association, Third Edition, Revised (DSMIII-R)* (APA, 1987), a consideration of major depression requires at least five of the following nine behaviors and must include either a depressed mood or loss of interest or pleasure. These behaviors must have been evident nearly every day for at least 2 weeks and represent a change from the adolescent's previous behaviors:

1. Depressed or irritable mood

Table 3.2   Suicide Warning Signs

BEHAVIORAL CLUES
- Sudden changes in behavior
- Drinking, taking drugs
- Decline in school performance
- Inability to concentrate
- Withdrawing from others
- Studying all the time to the exclusion of outside activities and friends
- Fighting physically with family members
- Running away
- Giving away possessions

VERBAL CLUES
Direct:
   "I feel like killing myself."
   "Sometimes she makes me so mad, I feel like hanging (shooting, etc.) myself."
Indirect:
   "Everyone would be better off without me."
   "If this happens again …"
   "I just can't take anymore. …"
Any denial that problems exist when problems are obvious to others. Sudden interest in suicide, questions about it, ongoing discussion about it, etc.

SITUATIONAL CLUES
- Loss of relationships, friends, etc.
- Loss of status or sudden traumatic event (not making grades or team, or exclusion from peers)
- Divorce of parents
- Violence within the family
- Parental overemphasis on achievement
- First year of college
- Period of time immediately following a long bout of depression
- Physical problems along with changes in behavior or performance

Source: Steele, W. (1983). *Preventing teenage suicide.* Novato, CA: Ann Arbor Publishers. Reprinted with permission.

---

2. Loss of enjoyment or interest in normally pleasurable activities

3. Change in weight, appetite, or eating habits

4. Problems with sleeping

5. Psychomotor agitation or slowness

6. Loss of energy; feeling of fatigue

7. Feelings of worthlessness, inadequacy, self-reproach, self-depreciation, loss of self-esteem

8. Diminished ability to attend, think, or concentrate

9. Recurrent thoughts of death or suicide.

Social Characteristics. One of the major social characteristics of teenage suicide is the cluster suicides that follow or imitate another suicide. Teenagers who are part of a cluster may attempt suicide out of an impulsive reaction to someone else's suicide. When one adolescent commits suicide, the act somehow becomes "normalized" for others, and those who previously had experienced the "three H's' may begin to see suicide as a viable option. The incidence of cluster suicides suggests that one adolescent's suicide is a powerful event that influences others to take their own lives (Sturner, 1986).

A second social characteristic is related to the adolescent's home situation. Suicidal youths are more likely than non-suicidal youths to have lost a parent. Specifically, 50% to 72% of adolescent suicide attempters or completers have lost a parent through death, divorce, or abandonment (Tomlinson-Keasey & Keasey, 1988; Tomlinson-Keasey, Warren, & Elliott, 1986).

Violence in the home is another social characteristic. Some researchers have reported that nearly 60% of suicidal adolescents have experienced some degree of sexual or physical abuse at home (Kosky, 1983). In addition, a family history of suicide is prevalent in adolescents who attempt or complete suicide. According to one study, nearly 38% of adolescent suicide attempters had a close relative who had committed suicide (Metha & Dunham, 1988).

School Achievement Characteristics. Suicide also is related to the adolescent's school achievement. In one study of 12-to 15-year-olds hospitalized for self-destructive behavior and threats of suicide, 20% were not enrolled in school, 45% reported that they did not attend school regularly, and 50% were performing below their expected grade level (Gispert, Wheeler, Marsh, Davis, 1985). As we are all too aware, poor school achievement often initiates a spiral of self-doubt, failure, and negative thoughts, which may lead to depression or suicide attempts.

Identification

In addition to being aware of these psychological, social, and school achievement characteristics, two useful methods are available to determine an adolescent's suicide ideation. Teachers who feel uncomfortable about using these procedures should refer the adolescent to another professional, such as the school counselor.

Interviews. Interviews, which can disclose the severity and lethality of suicide ideation, probably are the most effective and informative way to determine the adolescent's suicide risk (McWhirter, 1993). These are conducted with adolescents who appear to be depressed or suicidal and with their parents, teachers, and friends. Information to be solicited during the interview includes:

(a) History of the presenting problem (depression, anxiety, etc.)

(b) The family structure and relationships (divorce, physical or sexual abuse, alcoholism, etc.)

(c) The developmental, medical, and academic history of the adolescent

(d) The status of interpersonal relationships

(e) Previous suicide attempts

(f) Verbal warning signs

(g) Behavioral warning signs

(h) Any stressor events that may trigger a suicide attempt (McWhirter et al., 1993, p. 195).

If suicide ideation is suspected, the degree of risk of the adolescent acting upon those thoughts must be determined. Because suicide ideation by itself is not a great risk, the severity of the threat or suspicion depends on the specificity and the lethality of the method of choice.

Therefore, we need to be knowledgeable about the risk factors of a suicidal threat as listed by Steele (1983):

1. *Suicidal plan.* The more specific a person is about the way he or she will die, the greater is the likelihood of an attempt.

2. *Availability of method.* The risk is higher whenever the method is readily available. (Example: a person who says he or she has thought of carbon monoxide poisoning but does not have a car is less at risk than the person who has a car available.)

3. *Location.* If a person has determined the place and it is accessible, the risk of suicide is high, especially if the location is inaccessible to others.

4. *Time.* If the time is specified, the risk is higher. Teens most often attempt suicide in their own homes between mid-afternoon and midnight.

5. *Ingestion of alcohol or drugs.* Whenever anyone is drinking or taking other drugs and talking suicide, the risk is very high because drugs reduce self-control and significantly increase impulsivity.

6. *Accessibility for rescue.* If a person plans to commit suicide at a time or place when or where no one is expected or able to get to, the risk is high.

7. *Lack of support.* If the person has no friends, parents who are not concerned, or if the suicidal person refuses to give information necessary to reach friends or those who could help, the risk is high. A recent loss coupled with talk of suicide portends high risk. A loss that may seem insignificant to us can be painful for that person, especially if followed by other losses. Loss may be in the form of a friend or a pet, for example. Not getting an "A," not winning an election, not being accepted into peer groups, or being rejected from a peer group can be significant losses.

8. *Previous attempts.* Those who have attempted suicide in the past are always at high-risk for suicide.

9. *Illness.* Chronic physical illness or long-standing emotional problems raise the risk for suicide.

Self-report Inventories. The second method that can be used to determine the level of depression in adolescents is the self-report inventory. Two useful inventories are the *Beck Depression Inventory* (BDI) (Beck et al., 1961) and the *Scale of Suicide Ideation* (SSI) (Beck, Kovacs & Weissman, 1979). The BDI indicates whether an adolescent is severely depressed and at-risk for suicide. The SSI focuses more on attitudes about living and dying, the characteristics and specificity of suicidal ideation, and background factors such as previous suicide attempts.

By using interviews and self-report inventories and by being aware of the warning signs and myths associated with depression and suicide, we are better able to identify adolescents who may be depressed or experience suicide ideation. Before accurate identification is possible however, we must be aware of two primary difficulties:

1. Adolescents tend not to actively volunteer information about their emotions, turmoil, and so forth (Garrison, Lewinsohn, Marsteller, Langhinrichsen & Lann, 1991).

2. Adolescents are reluctant to say that they are thinking of taking their own life or that they may be thinking of death (Reynolds, 1985).

Prevention, Intervention, and Postvention

Suicide *prevention* tends to focus on the factors that lead to suicidal ideation or parasuicide, while *intervention* is directed to treatment after an unsuccessful suicide attempt. *Postvention* consists of activities for surviving family members, friends, the school, and the community after a parasuicide or successful suicide.

Prevention. Most school-based suicide prevention programs deal primarily with detecting signs of depression and suicide ideation. In addition, prevention efforts attempt to help students to be successful in school, to grow emotionally, and to achieve up to their academic potential. School-based prevention efforts include modifying the student's school situation (e.g., changes in schedule), providing a tutor, or reducing the student's credit load. In addition, students with LD may need a change in their individualized education programs (IEPS), such as reduced time in either the special or general education classroom, and specific instruction in social skills or problem solving.

Intervention. Intervention efforts usually are initiated after an adolescent is determined to be depressed or has exhibited suicidal behaviors or attempted suicide. The focus here should not be on why adolescents view suicide as an option to their current situation but, rather on solving problems, in the home, school, or community, so suicide is no longer considered an option. The major stressors (e.g., grades, friends) that triggered the suicidal behavior or thoughts should be identified, and steps taken to reduce the pressures through school-based counseling or support groups. Again, a change in IEP may be necessary for students with LD, to address specific stressors.

At times an adolescent may have to be referred to services outside of the school system, such as a counseling center or a mental health agency. Regardless of whether interventions are in or outside of the school, the immediate task is to provide relief from feelings of the "three H's", to explore alternatives to suicidal behavior, and to instill feelings of being in control of their life (Frederick, 1985). With appropriate interventions, depressed and suicidal adolescents usually show considerable improvement (Peck, 1985), but warning signs can recur. More than 40% of adolescents who commit suicide are thought to have made previous attempts (Shaffer, 1974), and 3%–10% do so within 15 years (Otto, 1972). Therefore, school-based prevention and intervention efforts must be combined with long-term intervention and follow-up efforts, because an adolescent with suicidal tendencies may be at risk for several years after the initial threat or attempt (Guetzloe, 1988).

When teachers find themselves in a situation of interacting with a depressed or suicidal adolescent, the following set of guidelines proposed by McGee and Guetzloe (1988) may be helpful.

1. Never take suicide threats or gestures casually.
2. Don't be afraid to bring up the subject of suicide.
3. Question the student closely and carefully about a possible suicide plan.
4. Do not debate the morality of suicide.
5. Identify the major stresses or events that precipitated the suicidal behavior.
6. Do not convey the message that suicidal thoughts are ridiculous or that make the student suffer guilt.
7. Encourage the student to use other support systems such as parents, friends, church leaders, school personnel, or a counseling center.
8. If the suicidal behavior was precipitated by the loss of a romantic relationship, don't downplay it. The adolescent may view such a loss as the end of any hope for a loving relationship.
9. Don't leave the suicidal student alone.
10. Dispose of anything in the immediate environment that could be used as a weapon.
11. Mention school or community events that will be coming up later in the day, the next day, or the next week that might elicit their interest.
12. Be aware of the student's responses to your statements.
13. Be sure that the student has the telephone number of a crisis center, the suicide hotline, or a member of the school staff.
14. Do not promise to keep a student's suicidal behavior a secret.
15. Try to get a commitment from the student that he or she will not hurt himself or herself and that if he or she feels any kind of suicidal impulse, he or she will call a teacher, a counselor, or a hotline worker.
16. Always make a referral to a school guidance counselor or other appropriate professional.

These guidelines are not to be used in lieu of notifying parents or guardians or seeking other professional help.

Postvention. Despite prevention and intervention efforts, all adolescent suicides cannot be prevented. When a suicide does occur, the school should provide postvention activities. These efforts deal with issues such as cluster suicides and the grief and shock of family members, friends, and other students.

Adolescents will talk about the suicide whether we do or do not provide them with the opportunity. They need a chance to remember that having suicidal thoughts is not unusual and thinking about suicide does not mean they are destined to attempt suicide. If they talk about the suicide without adult leadership, however, their conclusions may be incorrect or negative. The leadership that the school can provide can help adolescents who might have suicidal ideations. Berkan (1986, pp. 29–30) suggested the following postvention activities.

■ The building principal should brief all teachers and staff on the situation.

■ The building principal should request assistance from the district's psychologists, social workers, and counselors to spend several days in the school and/or district talking to small groups of students about their feelings and reactions to the suicide.

■ All first-hour or homeroom classes should be informed about the facts of the situation and given an opportunity to have a short discussion of their feelings and be told about the small group sessions.

■ The immediate peer group of the student who has committed suicide should be identified and called in at once for special sessions with the support staff.

■ All students need to be told as to whom to ask for help if they or a friend are thinking of suicide.

■ Support groups should be scheduled for those who need them during school time.

■ Do not dismiss school; students need to follow a normal schedule as much as possible.

■ Do not encourage a general student body attendance at the funeral if it is held during school hours; excuse only those students who have a parental request to attend.

■ Do not dedicate a room, garden, etc., to the student's memory.

■ If the students or staff want to do something, in memory of the student, suggest helping to plan a suicide prevention effort in the school or community.

■ Emphasize that suicide is not a good choice to solve problems, that help is available, and that people care.

■ Emphasize that no one is to blame, not friends, parents, or teachers; the student chose to die by suicide and no one forced it on the student.

Alcohol and Other Drug Use

Alcohol and other drug use among adolescents is widespread and has remained stable at high levels since 1975. Marijuana remains the most commonly used drug, followed by stimulants, inhalants, hallucinogens, sedatives, and tranquilizers (Johnston, O'Malley, & Bachman, 1986). The average age at which alcohol consumption begins is 12 years, 5 months, and 23% of young people between ages of 12 and 18 have a serious drinking problem (Horton, 1985). Regardless of the substance used and the age at consumption, even occasional use can have disastrous results. The leading cause of death in adolescents is accidental death, related to the consumption of alcohol in at least 40% of cases (American Academy of Pediatrics, 1988).

Incidence

Although the substance of choice among adolescents is alcohol, estimates of alcohol consumption and other drug use vary greatly depending upon definitions. Results of two nationwide studies indicated that anywhere from 60% to 66% of high school seniors nationwide reported alcohol consumption during the month prior to the study, 4.2% - 5% of seniors reported that they drank every day, and 37.5% reported at least one incident of heavy drinking (five or more drinks in a row). In addition, about 2%-6% admitted to using stimulants, 9% used inhalants, and 5% had used cocaine. Furthermore, 16%-33% reported having experimented with marijuana (Newcomb & Bentler, 1989).

Limited data are available on the prevalence of alcohol and other drug use by adolescents with mild disabilities. Existing data are mixed, stemming primarily from clinical studies and geographically limited samples, as well as from studies with questionable technical adequacy. Devlin and Elliott (1992) found that 51% of a sample of students classified as behavior disordered (BD) showed patterns of high drug use. Only 14% of a matched nondisabled control group showed similar rates of usage. Only 28% of the BD students reported no drug use, compared with 74% of the control students. Others (see Dean, Fox, & Jensen, 1985; DiNitto & Krishef, 1984; Issacs, Buckley, & Martin, 1979; Krishef, 1986) have contended that the incidence of alcohol and other drug use in adolescents with disabilities may be greater that it is among the general population. Still others (Elmquist, Morgan, & Bolds, 1989; Leone, Greensburg, Trickett, & Spero, 1989) see no reason to believe that adolescents with disabilities have higher levels of substance use than nondisabled students.

These and other reported incidence rates probably underestimate the prevalence and incidence of drug use by adolescents. Most research studies do not include school dropouts, who are at even higher risk for alcohol and drug abuse.

Why Do Adolescents Use Alcohol and Other Drugs?

The reasons for alcohol and other drug use among adolescents are difficult to determine. Typical reasons for use of alcohol and other drugs often are linked to social influences (e.g., peer use of drugs), whereas reasons for abuse often are tied to internal processes (e.g., use of alcohol and other drugs as medication against depression, anger, frustration) (Long & Scherl, 1984).

Research suggests that some environmental, behavioral, psychological, and social risk factors are so consistently associated with alcohol and other drug use that they can be considered true causal factors (Newcomb & Bentler, 1989). This information can be used to determine the likelihood of alcohol and other drug use by students and then used to provide appropriate interventions. The more risk factors with which an adolescent is associated, the greater is the probability of alcohol and other drug use.

The most reliable predictor of future alcohol and other drug use is prior use (McWhirter et al., 1993). Adolescents who use alcohol and other drugs before age 15 have more problems of abuse in later life (Kellam & Simon, 1980). Risk factors for alcohol and drug abuse that have been identified by numerous researchers include (American Academy of Pediatrics, 1988; Capuzzi & LeCoq, 1983; Horan & Strauss, 1987; MacDonald & Blume, 1986; Webb, Baer, McLaughlin, McKelvey, & Caid, 1989):

Early and persistent behavior problems
Low commitment to school
Peer rejection in the elementary grades
School failure
Antisocial and deviant behavior
Tolerance for deviance
Sensation-seeking
Peer and parental approval and use of alcohol and other drugs
Poor relationship with parents
Family history of alcoholism or other drug use or abuse
Peer use of alcohol and other drugs
Depression
Low self-esteem
Poor parent-child communications.

Use Versus Abuse

Many adolescents experiment with alcohol and other drugs but perform well in school and go on to lead productive lives. Their use does not necessarily equate to abuse. With this in mind, we must keep the entire issue of alcohol and other drug use versus abuse in perspective. Because there is such a fine line between use and abuse, some informal identification procedures may be helpful. We must consider the context, frequency, type, and purpose for which alcohol or other drugs are used.

Informally, one of the best ways to determine an adolescent's use of alcohol and other drugs is through our own knowledge of the issue and the relationship we have established with students. The more we know about the students, the better the chances are that we may pick up on signs of alcohol and other drug use, as listed in Table 3.3.

In addition to these warning signs, teachers should be knowledgeable about the most common drugs adolescents use, their street names, and their effects. Also, to be

Table 3.3 Signs of Alcohol and Drug Abuse

CHANGES IN PERFORMANCE:

- Distinct downward turn in grades—not just from Cs to Fs, but from As to Bs and Cs
- Assignments not completed
- Loss of interest in school; extracurricular activities
- Poor classroom behavior such as inattentiveness, sleeping in class, hostility
- Missing school for unknown reasons
- In trouble with school, work, or the police
- Memory loss

CHANGES IN BEHAVIOR:

- Decrease in energy and endurance
- Changes in friends (secrecy about new friends with different lifestyles)
- Secrecy about activities (lies or avoids talking about activities)
- Borrows lots of money, or has too much cash
- Mood swings, excessive anger, irritability
- Preferred style of music changes (pop rock to heavy metal)
- Starts pulling away from the family, old friends, and school
- Chronic lying, stealing, or dishonesty
- Hostile or argumentative attitude; extremely negative, unmotivated, defensive
- Refusal or hostility when asked to talk about possible alcohol or other drug use
- Slurred speech

CHANGES IN APPEARANCE/PHYSICAL CHANGES:

- Weight loss or gain
- Uncoordinated
- Poor physical appearance or unusually neat; striking change in personal habits
- New interest in the drug culture (drug-related posters, clothes, magazines)
- Smells of alcohol, tobacco, marijuana
- Frequent use of eyedrops and breath mints
- Bloodshot eyes
- Persistent cough or cold symptoms (e.g., runny nose)
- Always thirsty, increased or decreased appetite, rapid speech
- AOD paraphernalia (empty alcohol containers, cigarettes, pipes, rolling papers, baggies, paper packets, roach clips, razor blades, straws, glass or plastic vials, pill bottles, tablets and capsules, colored stoppers, syringes, spoons, matches or lighters, needles, medicine droppers, toy balloons, tin foil, cleaning rags, spray cans, glue containers, household products)

Source: Elmquist, D. L. (1991). School-based alcohol and other drug prevention programs. *Intervention in school and clinic, 27,* 10–19. Reprinted with permission.

able to distinguish between the occasional user from the adolescent whose use has moved to abuse, teachers should be familiar with the patterns of progressive alcohol and drug use, shown in Table 3.4.

A more formal means of determining an adolescent's alcohol and other drug use is the *adolescent drinking index* (ADI) (Harrell & Wirtz, 1989). The ADI is a 24-item scale that measures the severity of drinking problems of adolescents. Severity is measured by determining the number of different areas (e.g., school, grades) in which the adolescent has had alcohol-related difficulties and the extent or intensity of the problem in those areas.

Prevention and Intervention

Prevention programs are the most common form of intervention for alcohol and other drug use, for students who have not yet experimented with the substances. At the same time, treatment for threshold drug use is instituted for students who are already users.

Many school-based prevention programs are provided through extracurricular clubs and activities that are open to all students and require no special training or selection process. These programs alone cannot be expected to have a significant effect on alcohol and other drug use and related problems. They should be *part* of a comprehensive school-based alcohol and other drug use program. The following are a few examples of clubs and activities that schools may offer to their students.

Students Against Driving Drunk (SADD). SADD meets regularly as a school club to promote the nonuse of alcohol and other drugs by peers and their parents, particularly when driving. A major component of this program is a contract for life, in which the adolescents and parents agree in writing to call for help or transportation if they are in a situation where they have been drinking and need to go home. SADD sponsors activities such as putting up posters in stores, restaurants, and bars; giving presentations in the community; arranging for speakers at school-wide assemblies; and giving presentations to students in middle and elementary schools to encourage early commitment to preventing alcohol and other drug use.

Just Say No Clubs. These clubs advocate the nonuse of alcohol and other drugs among its members and classmates. Members receive current and accurate information regarding alcohol and other drug use, as well as training in how to say no to peers, how to have fun without using alcohol and other drugs, and how to support each others' nonuse. Meeting during and after school, they often sponsor alcohol- and drug-free activities for the club and the entire school.

Lock-ins. The lock-in is an overnight alcohol- and drug-free activity sponsored by parents, students, or other clubs. Participating students engage in activities such as volleyball, basketball, swimming, and watching videos on a weekend evening. Students obtain parental permission and are not allowed to arrive or leave between certain hours, usually 9:00 P.M. until 7:00 A.M. the following morning. Lock-ins often have a special theme, and the school or local groups or agencies donate money, food, and prizes. The students are locked in to help prevent alcohol and other drug use.

Table 3.4 Patterns of Progressive Drug Abuse

EXPERIMENTATION

Behavior	*Frequency of Use*	*Emotional State*
Little effect	1 to 5 times	Excitement/daring
Denial of negative consequences	(total)	Mild euphoria
		Possible discomfort
		Mild guilt

SOCIAL/SITUATIONAL

Behavior	*Frequency of Use*	*Emotional State*
Decreased academic performance	2 to 4 times	Excitement
Loss of interest in hobbies	per week	Being "in" with the crowd
Loss of interest in special activities		Feels better with drug than
Begins to seek out drug-using friends		without it
Changes in clothing habits		Less guilt—"Drugs are OK,
Some uncharacteristic behavior		I can handle them."

HABITUAL

Behavior	*Frequency of Use*	*Emotional State*
Most friends use drugs	Daily use	"Need" for euphoric state
Beginning of family problems		Highs are very high, and
due to drug use		lows are very
Major loss of interest in		uncomfortable
school and other activities		More guilt and depression
Impulsiveness		
Erratic mood swings		
Uses drug alone		

OBSESSIVE/DEPENDENT

Behavior	*Frequency of Use*	*Emotional State*
Skips school regularly	Multiple times	Needs drug to feel "normal"
Weight loss or gain	per day	Severe discomfort if drug is
Messy, unclean appearance	depending	not available
Loss of ability to concentrate	on drug	Disorganized thoughts
Severe paranoid or depressed	Erratic behavior	
thoughts		May become psychotic or
Dangerous aggression, suicidal		suicidal
thoughts		
Stealing to obtain drugs		

Source: Kerr, M. M., Nelson, C. M., & Lambert, D. L. (1987). *Helping adolescents with learning and behavior problems.* Columbus, OH: Merrill. Reprinted with permission.

Sufficient supervision and administrative support are essential for success of these events.

Adventure-based programs. These programs are designed to fill the adolescent's need for adventure and risk-seeking behaviors. They provide stimulating and exciting activities as alternatives to alcohol and other drug use. Students build self-confidence and self-esteem and learn group problem solving and teamwork as they develop new skills and find new strengths. Canoeing, camping, mountain climbing, sailing, and hiking are some of the many possible activities.

Mini-courses and wellness days. Schools offer these programs to promote individual well-being and fun without alcohol and other drug use. For one day or all week students participate in presentations by community volunteers and professionals with themes such as wellness, hobbies, noncompetitive games, alcohol and other drug-use issues, and skills in resisting peer pressure and saying no.

School climate teams. Schools sponsor positive school activities that build school spirit and community pride. The goal is to prevent alcohol and other drug use by making the school a better place to be—more caring, nurturing, and personal. Activities include a special day for encouraging friendship, decorating lockers for birthdays, and special events that give students a sense of belonging and bonding within the school.

To ensure that these clubs and activities are effective (Contrucci, 1991):

■ Activities should be comfortable and safe for all participants.

■ A variety of individual, small-group, and whole-group activities should be offered to add diversity and interest to the program.

■ Activities should be flexible to meet individual school, and community needs.

■ Participation must be voluntary.

■ Realistic expectations should be set for each activity.

■ Advisors and school staff must receive basic training. (p. 47)

Many educational materials are available to teachers. These can be incorporated in daily instruction or utilized as part of the activities of these clubs and activities.

Teenage Sexual Activity

During the developmental stage of adolescence, sexuality takes on new dimensions. Feelings become more intense, relationships become more complex, and the consequences of sexual activities are altered radically. These changes affect not only the behavior of adolescents but also the behavior of their families, peers, and educators. Despite public opposition from a variety of sources, the need for adequate school-based sex education programs is pressing (Romaneck & Kuehl, 1992). Issues related to adolescents' sexual activities are broad and complex, including sex education, the use of contraceptives, date/acquaintance rape, sexually transmitted diseases (STDs), sexual orientation and sexual harassment.

Extent of Adolescent Activity

Although the age of first sexual intercourse varies by gender and ethnicity, the majority of adolescents are sexually active by age 18 (Hofferth, Kahn, & Baldwin, 1987; Orr, Wilbrant, Brack, Rauch, & Ingersoll, 1989). In a Time/CNN telephone survey of 500 teenagers, Gibbs (1993) found that 19% of 13- to 15-year-olds and 55% of 16-17-year-olds have had sexual intercourse. Further, 61% of teenage girls reported that they have had multiple sexual partners, up from 38% in 1971. In addition, 61% of the same population reported using birth control every time they had sex; 26% reported sometimes, and 13% reported never using birth control.

Why Do Adolescents Become Sexually Active?

The reasons adolescents become sexually active are varied. Economic status, educational goals and attainment, perceived life options, parental involvement, and familial role models are among the most influential factors associated with adolescent sexual activity. Additional factors include the adolescent's values of independence and achievement, level of self-esteem, and peer influence (Muccigrosso, Scavarda, Simpson-Brown, & Thalacker, 1991).

Family factors are highly associated with adolescents' decisions about being sexually active. Adolescents with working mothers and from single-parent families may be more likely to be sexually active (Fick, 1984). Beyond the effects of income and educational status females whose older sisters are role models and those from large families seem to be more sexually active. The extent of sexual activity by adolescents also is related directly to the quality of parent-child communication in the home. The more involved that parents are in the lives of their adolescent, the less likely their children are to be active sexually (Foster, 1986; Paget, 1988).

Sexual activities commence at a younger age in male and female adolescents who live in poverty, teenage males and females who are low achievers educationally, and females whose mothers and older sisters are low educational achievers (Foster, 1986). According to Gibbs (1993), "In the inner cities the scarcity of jobs and hope for the future invites kids to seek pleasure with little thought of the fallout" (p. 63).

Sex Education Programs

The consequences of an adolescent's sexual behavior are so potentially serious for themselves, their families, and society that learning and practicing responsible sexual behavior is imperative. The overall goal of sex education is to teach adolescents sexual responsibility and to promote the "positive perception of an individual's sexuality" (Kempton, 1988, p. 24). Adolescents learn sexual responsibility as they grow up in a family, by watching and copying the way responsible adults behave. Adolescents need to know that good relationships can suffer from acting upon one's sexual feelings. Unless adolescents understand the meaning of sexual responsibility, they are unprepared to engage in any sexual activity.

Sexual responsibility can be summarized as:

■ both partners discussing birth control and agreeing to use it every time to prevent an accidental pregnancy

■ both partners being honest about their sexual health and agreeing to use condoms to prevent sexually transmitted diseases (STDs)

■ knowing that sex involves commitment and mutual consent

■ understanding the positive and negative consequences that sex can have in their lives (Stang, 1989, p. 3).

Although sex education is still highly controversial, one study indicated that 85% of parents favor sex education in the schools and believe it fosters a healthy attitude toward sex (Harris, 1987). Much of the debate over teaching sex education in the public schools focuses on the morality of and our own attitudes toward human sexuality. As a result, it is a difficult issue on which to build consensus among teachers, administrators, and parents. The issue is complicated further by the flaunting of sexuality in the media, the lack of appropriate role models who practice responsible sexual behavior, and societal attitudes regarding sexuality.

In describing the needs for sex education for adolescents with disabilities, Shapiro (1981) stated:

Exceptional children experience the same physical and emotional changes that [nondisabled] children do, as well as the same anxiety which often accompanies adolescence. Thus, they must cope with all the emotional conflicts of their [non-disabled] teenage counterparts in addition to those produced by their handicaps. (pp. 25–26)

Price (1987) concurred that

[adolescents with handicaps] are influenced by the same pressures affecting the sexual decision making of every adolescent and teen, such as peer pressure, movies, and television. The differences lie in the [disabled] person's lack of appropriate information about physical and emotional changes of adolescence, sexuality, and birth control (p. 154)

Conger (1988) recommended three general approaches to sex education: (a) family-life planning, (b) increasing the accessibility of contraceptives to adolescents, (c) and enhancing the life options of adolescents.

Family-Life Planning. All students need current, relevant, accurate, and appropriate family-life education from the early school through high school years. Unfortunately, many students receive little information about sexuality from their parents. Only 30% of 13- to 15-year-olds and 27% of 16- to 17-year-olds reported that they learned the most about sex from their parents; 26% of the 13- to 15-year-olds and 37% of the 16 to 17-year-olds reported learning about sex from their friends, Gibbs (1993). This is discouraging because we all have heard the type of information about sex that students hear from their friends (for example, "If you have sexual inter-course while standing up, the girl can not become pregnant").

Although sex education in the context of family-life planning is important, it is not sufficient to resolve the problem of adolescent sexual activity. Sex education improves knowledge, but little conclusive proof exists that behavior is influenced by knowledge alone. Therefore, educational programs that work on improving rela-tionships, boosting self-esteem, and teaching decision-making skills must be com-bined with life-planning programs (McWhirter et al., 1993).

Increased accessibility to contraceptives. A second approach to sex education is the availability of contraceptive options to sexually active adolescents. Decisions about birth control are complicated. Age at onset of sexual activity, family income, belief in the risks associated with unprotected sexual activity, and the availability of confidential contraceptive services are crucial variables in adolescents' use of con-traceptives (Muccigrosso et al., 1991).

Contraceptives cannot be forced on adolescents, but they should be available. Access can be provided best through community- and school-based clinics that offer comprehensive, easily accessible, and high-quality health services. School-based clinics are particularly useful so sexuality can be dealt with in the context of overall health care by a school nurse who is aware of adolescents' special sexuality concerns and needs. The various methods of contraceptives available to adolescents are var-ied, controversial, and confusing. Therefore, adolescents should ask themselves some serious questions about their choice of contraceptives, such as:

- Would an accidental pregnancy be a big problem for me and my partner?

- How safe is this method for me?

- How easy is this method to use? Will I use it the right way every time, even if it sometimes is a hassle?

- How much will this method cost to use? Can I afford it?

- How does my partner feel about birth control? Can we work together to use this method?

- Will I feel embarrassed about using this method? Will my partner feel embar-rassed? Will I use it even if I feel embarrassed?

- How do I feel about touching my body?

- How often do I have sex? Do I want a method that is always in my body? Or can I pick a method to use only when I have sex?

- Do I have more than one sexual partner?

- Do I have religious or moral feelings about using birth control? Does this method fit with my religious beliefs?

At this point, the few clinics that provide comprehensive health services, includ-ing dispensing contraceptives, have shown promising results. In one school district the overall annual rate of first-time pregnancies was reduced from 80 per 1,000 to

29 per 1,000; repeat pregnancies were reduced to 1.4%, compared to 33% nationally (Kirby, 1984; Schorr, 1988).

Using contraceptives every time an adolescent has sexual intercourse can help protect against pregnancy and STDs, however, the most commonly-used form of contraceptive, the use of condoms, is still not 100% foolproof. Condoms can break, partners can be careless, and mistakes can happen. The only surefire method of contraception is abstinence. Adolescents should take the attitude that being abstinent does not mean they are not grown up but, rather, they are being sexually responsible.

Until the majority of adolescents elect abstinence, those who are sexually active should be urged to practice safe sex. Safe sex means more than using contraceptives. It also requires knowing your partner and your partners sexual history. A person is having sex not only with the partner but also with whomever the partner has ever had sex with (Adams & Gullotta, 1989).

Enhanced life options. A third approach to sex education attempts to improve adolescents' life options. McWhirter et al. (1993) contended that "when young people feel good about themselves and have a clear vision of a successful and self-sufficient future, they will be motivated to avoid pregnancy" (p. 147). In addition, Edeleman (1987) proposed that "the best contraceptive is a real future" (p. 58). A future requires opportunities to build academic and work-related skills, job opportunities, assistance with life-planning, and access to comprehensive-health services. Adolescents who are working toward personal and economic self-sufficiency tend to be more sexually responsible (McWhirter et al., 1993).

Sexually Transmitted Diseases. To many adolescents, STDs (formerly called venereal diseases) are not a concern. Thus, the risks for adolescents' contracting an STD are extremely high. Any sex education program offered in the public schools must include information on STDs, including the human immunodeficiency virus (HIV) that causes the acquired immune deficiency syndrome (AIDS). Short of abstinence, there is no surefire way to prevent contracting STDS.

The rates of STDs are escalating in adolescents. More than 2.5 million adolescents contract an STD annually (Office of Population Affairs, 1988). Nearly one-fourth of adolescents contract some STD each year (Gibbs, 1993). Adolescents must understand how STDs are contracted and their symptoms, as shown in Table 3.5.

The incidence of STDs in adolescents has increased because:

1. More adolescents are sexually active.

2. Adolescents tend to have more sexual partners.

3. Many adolescents who are asymptomatic do not know that they have an STD and spread the disease unknowingly (Gale, 1989).

AIDS is an STD caused by the human immunodeficiency virus (HIV). Over time, HIV damages the body's immune system, resulting in life-threatening infections and cancers. These illnesses are called *opportunistic diseases* and do not develop in healthy people.

Table 3.5 The Most Common Sexually Transmitted Diseases

STD	CAUSE	SYMPTOMS*	TRANSMISSION
HIV	virus	general illness swollen glands pneumonia skin cancer (Kaposi's sarcoma)	sexual contact (via blood, semen) blood transfusion dirty needles mother to fetus
Chlamydia	bacteria	itching or burning in genital or urinary areas	sexual contact mother to fetus
Giardia diarrhea	bacteria	diarrhea abdominal pain	sexual contact blood feces
Gonorrhea	bacteria	discharge from penis or vagina	sexual contact
Herpes Type I Type II	virus	painful sores around mouth and/or vagina burning or pain during urination	sexual contact
Syphilis	bacteria	pimple-like sores on genitals	direct sexual contact with sore mother to fetus
Vaginal infections	bacteria fungi yeasts	bad-smelling vaginal discharge pain during intercourse	sexual contact some infections spread on objects (towels, douche equipment)
Genital warts	virus	warty growths in genital area	sexual contact mother to infant

*may not experience all of these or may be asymptomatic

Source: Scott, M. (1988). *Family living and sex education* (p. 126). New York: Globe. Reprinted with permission.

Without doubt, AIDS is the most dangerous of the STDs that adolescents risk through their sexual activity. Because at this time AIDS is always fatal, adolescents who engage in high-risk behavior—principally, unprotected sexual intercourse or intravenous (IV) drug use are vulnerable to contracting HIV. The number of adolescents infected with HIV is unknown, but it is believed to be much higher than the prevalence of AIDS in adolescents and is doubling each year (Brooks-Gunn, Boyer, & Hein, 1988).

Approximately 1% of those diagnosed with AIDS are adolescents (Centers for Disease Control, 1989); however, individuals 20 to 29 years of age constitute 21% of those with AIDS (Hein, 1989). Given the 7- to 10-year latency period between HIV infection and the diagnosis of AIDS (National Academy of Sciences, 1989), 20% of the individuals diagnosed in the 20-29 year-old range were infected during adolescence (Centers for Disease Control, 1989). The source of infection varies substantially by gender: 38% of males are infected by homosexual activity and 37% by hemophilia; females are more likely (45%) to be infected through heterosexual activity (Centers for Disease Control, 1989).

Until researchers find a cure for AIDS or a vaccine for HIV, the only weapon against the epidemic is education. Many adolescents receive contradictory and confusing information, not only from peers but also from parents and teachers. Adolescents' lives and the lives of all their sexual partners depend on their having accurate information about AIDS. This is not an overstatement or a scare tactic. Adolescents no longer can afford to think about the pleasures of sex without knowing the risks of contracting the HIV virus.

A number of studies have found significant deficiencies in adolescents' AIDS-related knowledge and beliefs (Hingson, Strunin, Berlin, & Heeren, 1988; Strunin & Hingson, 1987). Many beliefs related to AIDS put adolescents at risk for exposure to the HIV virus. For example, 12% of a national sample believed that birth control pills provide some protection against HIV infection, and 23% believed that one can tell whether a person has AIDS by looking at them (Anderson et al., 1990). In addition, Tatum (1988) contended that adolescents often associate HIV/AIDS with gays and bisexuals ("the gay disease") , which frequently leads to homophobia (fear and mistrust of gays and lesbians).

Much of this misinformation is the result of hastily conceived programs, curricula, and educational materials that provide inaccurate information on HIV and AIDS. To ensure that the information shared with students is accurate, it must be obtained from reliable sources. The local public health department, Red Cross chapter, local and national AIDS agencies, and the public library can provide or recommend up-to-date, accurate information and educational materials.

Information provided to adolescents about HIV/AIDS should take into account the following information:

1. The risk of becoming infected with HIV can be virtually eliminated by not engaging in sexual activities and by not using illegal IV drugs.

2. Sexual transmission of HIV is not a threat to uninfected individuals who engage in monogamous sexual relations.

3. HIV can be transmitted through sexual contact with an infected person, by using needles that an infected person has used, and from an infected mother to her infant before or during birth.

4. Although no transmission from deep, open-mouth ("French") kissing has been documented, it theoretically could transmit HIV from an infected to an uninfected person through direct exposure of mucous membranes to infected blood or saliva.

5. Adolescents who engage in sexual intercourse with individuals who are at risk or whose infection status is unknown should use a latex condom and a water-based lubricant to reduce the likelihood of becoming infected.

6. Behavior that prevents exposure to the HIV virus also may prevent unintended pregnancies and exposure to STDs (*Morbidity and Mortality Weekly Report,* 1988).

Regardless of the amount of information provided to adolescents about HIV/AIDS, many continue to engage in sexual activities. These adolescents can take several precautions to greatly reduce their risk for contracting HIV (American College Health Association, 1990; Gale, 1989):

1. Make careful choices about sexual activity in (a) choosing whether to be sexually intimate, (b) choosing a partner, (c) choosing how to be sexually intimate, and (d) choosing when to be sexually intimate.

2. Communicate assertively with your sexual partner and negotiate for safer sexual practices.

3. Develop skills to express your feelings and concerns.

4. Remove alcohol and other drug use from the context of sexual activities.

5. Use latex condoms and water-based lubricants for sexual intercourse.

6. Do not share IV needles.

Date/Acquaintance Rape

Dating violence is "a pattern of abusive and coercive behaviors or actions whereby one dating partner seeks to control the other," and sexual abuse is "any sexual activity forced upon a person without his or her consent" (Tomaszewski, 1991, p. 5). All adolescents, males and females, should recognize that forcing anyone into unwanted sexual activity is rape. Forced sex is illegal, even if the person is a friend, a relative, or a date.

Rape is the most frequently committed violent crime in the United States today, and violence in dating couples does exist in adolescent relationships. Coles and Stokes (1985) reported that 14% of adolescent females in their study said they had been raped. When asked to identify the rapist, they indicated the following:

Identity of Rapist	Percentage
friend	30
stranger	29
boyfriend	16
relative	13
neighbor	9
gang rape	4

These abusive behaviors rarely stop without some form of intervention. Violence in an early intimate relationship is as an indicator of violence in future adolescent and adult relationships (Tomaszewski, 1991). Clearly, education about date/acquaintance rape is a necessary step toward prevention and early intervention.

The goals of educational programs are "to provide adolescents with information about the dynamics of violence, teach interpersonal relationship skills that could reduce the likelihood that one partner will be abusive or abused, and provide resources to either change the abusive behavior or help an abused teenager leave the relationship" (Tomaszewski, 1991, p.4). Education should focus on sexual responsibility and "sex as a loving act" (Gale, 1989, p. 120). Sex requires two consenting persons and requires that each person set his or her own limits and be accepting of their partner's limits. All adolescents should be advised to give a clear and firm message in setting their limits and not to let themselves get talked or bullied into a situation they do not want (Gale, 1989). When a partner says "no," it means NO.

Teachers cannot prevent their students from being in situations where they are forced to participate in sexual activity without their consent. Nevertheless, teachers can offer some suggestions for lessening this risk:

1. If you feel uncomfortable about going somewhere or being alone with someone, don't go.

2. Be cautious of someone who invades your personal space by doing things such as standing or sitting too close, staring at your breasts or crotch, or touching you more than you want; tell him or her clearly to stop it.

3. Be careful of someone who is domineering and selfish, who tries to get what he or she wants at your expense.

4. Be especially alert at parties involving alcohol and drugs; they lower resistance and self-control.

5. Don't accept a ride home or go somewhere alone with someone you just met.

6. Always have a back-up to get a ride home or a way out of a potential risky situation.

7. For girls—be aware that boys may misinterpret a girl's manner of dress or behavior, and be prepared to set your limits.

8. If you get in a situation in which you are being coerced, pressured, threatened, or forced, respond quickly and firmly, flee or try to flee, fight back and yell (Gale, 1989, pp. 122-124).

Sexual Orientation

Among the many controversial topics in school-based sex education programs, none has raised so many red flags as that of sexual orientation, "the emotional and physical attraction a person feels for the [opposite] and/or same sex" (Humm, 1992, p. 14). Orientation to the opposite sex is heterosexuality; to the same sex, homosexuality;

and to both sexes, bisexuality. Many female homosexuals prefer to be called lesbians, whereas many male homosexuals prefer to be called gay. Being gay is not a disease, a mental illness, or a choice. The American Psychiatric Association removed homosexuality from its list of mental disorders in 1973.

Estimates of the prevalence of homosexuality in the general population range from about 2% to 10%–12%. In multiple studies of gay men, the mean age of acknowledging sexual orientation has been identified retrospectively around the age of 13–14. Although these men usually did not consider themselves as gay until young adulthood, the feelings were there much earlier.

Because homosexuality is a sensitive subject for most adolescents, as well as their parents and teachers, we tend to avoid discussing it. Nevertheless, we may find ourselves in a situation in which a student asks us about sexual orientation. At one time or another, many adolescents wonder whether they are gay. For most, these are just mild concerns that cease as they grow older. For others, however, feelings about being gay can be confusing and emotional. As a result, they may "spend their time trying to look and act like other [adolescents] and being afraid to do anything that might make them different" (Gale, 1989, p. 111). Often they fight their feelings and, because of this insecurity, many adolescents tend to confuse masculinity/femininity with sexual orientation. The male who does not match the subjective definition of "masculine" or the female who does not match that of "femininity" are suspected of being gay.

For fear of arousing anyone's suspicions, adolescents often hesitant to discuss their feelings and think they are the only ones with the same feelings. Gay and lesbian adolescents are more likely than their heterosexual peers to drop out of school, become runaways, and abuse alcohol and other drugs. The suicide rate for gay and lesbian adolescents is two to six times higher than that of heterosexual adolescents (Pender, 1990).

In addition to the many emotions that gay and lesbian adolescents experience, they also must cope with parental, peer, and societal negative reactions to being gay. A significant amount of ridicule, discrimination, stigmatization, anger, and physical attacks (known as "gay-bashing) is directed at gays and lesbians simply because of their sexual orientation.

Although many sex education programs include the topic of sexual orientation, the information is limited and often presented in a negative, nonaccepting fashion. Many state mandated HIV/AIDS education programs, however, have opened up discussions about sexual orientation. School districts are beginning to take the initiative in educating adolescents about sexual orientation and are beginning to provide more of a healthy and safe environment for students who consider themselves to be gay. As examples: schools in Los Angeles operate a counseling and support program called "Project 10" for gay and lesbian youth; in San Francisco each school is required to designate a "gay-sensitive" staff member to whom students can turn if they have concerns; and schools in Fairfax, Virginia, integrate homosexuality into the family living/sex education curricula (Humm, 1992).

Sexual Harassment

One of the most persistent problems related to the issue of sexual harassment has been the "absence of a widely agreed upon definition, one that is broad enough to comprehend the variety of experiences to which the term refers, and yet specific enough to be of practical use" (Fitzgerald, 1992, p. 9). Because of the confusion over a definition, many students hesitate to discuss incidents with other students or school administrators. Students often feel helpless and without witnesses. Further, the burden of proof falls largely on the adolescent. The other side of the coin is that many teachers hesitant to interact with their students (put their arms around students in a friendly manner) for fear of being falsely accused themselves.

According to the American Association of Colleges (1978), behaviors that may be considered sexual harassment include:

- Verbal harassment or abuse
- Subtle pressure for sexual activity
- Sexist remarks about someone's clothing, body, or sexual activities
- Unnecessary touching, patting, or pinching
- Leering or ogling at someone's body or body parts
- Demanding sexual favors accompanied by implied or overt threats concerning one's grades, etc.

A coed expressed the following emotions after being sexually harassed by one of her teachers: "I still slink down one hall, cowering, frightened because of a teacher whose classroom is there. . . . Whenever I see him, my heart jumps a beat, I begin to sweat and I try to avoid eye contact as he stares at me" ("The Pain of Harassment," 1993). This student's feelings were the result of numerous sexual harassment incidents such as the teacher passing her in the hall and blowing her a kiss or patting her on the back or the buttocks in class; calling her "sweetheart," "honey," and "cutie"; and walking by her desk and discreetly slipping his hand inside the waistband of her jeans. Ultimately, the student informed the school's administration about the harassment. After a year of investigations and interviews, the teacher was suspended without pay with a warning that further incidents would not be tolerated.

In terms of education, adolescents need to become aware of behaviors that are considered inappropriate and what to do if they believe they are being sexually harassed. In addition, administrators must establish a school atmosphere that encourages students to report these behaviors.

Teaching Sex Education

Because sex education is such a sensitive topic, a student's question or behavior at times may be beyond what a teacher feels comfortable or knowledgeable about discussing. A model developed by Jack Annon (discussed in Muccigrosso et al., 1991), the PLISSIT model, is designed to determine the parameters and when a referral to a professional in or outside of the school is indicated. The model outlines four levels of intervention: permission, limited information, specific suggestions, and intensive therapy.

Permission (P). Some potential problems can be eliminated simply by giving permission to adolescents to experience their sexual development. Adolescents need to know they are normal in their sexuality, through statements such as, "All girls have periods. It's normal and part of being a girl. It means you're growing up, and that's exciting!" (Maksym, 1990, p. 109). This may be helpful in relieving anxiety over sexual thoughts, fantasies, and arousal (Kempton, 1988) for boys and girls alike.

Limited information (LI). This level of information provides more details but only enough to answer specific questions. Information presented through a sex education program must be keep simple: "Some bleeding comes from the vagina each month; it comes from the uterus inside the girl's body" (Maksym, 1990, p. 110). This type of information dispels myths and concerns about sexuality.

Specific suggestions (SS). Often questions can be answered by giving specific and concrete suggestions: For example, you might say to an adolescent, "Having a period is a private thing. You can talk about it just with your mother or your teacher or your best friend. Not to people on the bus, or people you don't know" (Maksym, 1990, p. 110).

Intensive therapy (IT). Teachers should not provide intensive therapy unless they have been trained in both the physical and the psychological aspects of human sexuality. This is the level at which teachers usually suggest that the individual student obtain professional counseling.

A lot of information about human sexuality can be provided to students through informal and unplanned interactions. When discussing these topics, teachers should not overemphasize technical detail, or misrepresenting facts, or omit essential options. The goal is to provide accurate, complete, and relevant information so adolescents can make informed, responsible decisions. Throughout these interactions, the following personal characteristics are essential for effective instruction in human sexuality (Romaneck & Kuehl, 1992), (p. 24):

1. *Credibility.* The ability to win the confidence and respect of students.

2. *Knowledge.* Awareness of the subject matter and confidence in one's ability to present the material in an open and straightforward manner.

3. *Trust.* Engendering in students the feeling that they can communicate freely and openly with the teacher.

4. *Acceptance.* The ability to accept individual differences.

5. *Approachability.* Communicating to students that they can express highly sensitive or private feelings to the teacher.

6. *Flexibility.* The capability of dealing with student input in a nonrigid fashion.

7. *Authenticity.* The ability to maintain an honest and sincere posture toward students.

Numerous commercial curricula are available for more formal sex education programs. Regardless of the program used, Thomas et al. (1985), have suggested that the following components be part of a sex education curriculum:

Unit 1
Introduction to human growth
and development
Communication and decision making

Unit 2
Growing up male
—anatomy and physiology
—sexual orientation
—pressures
—laws

Unit 3
Growing up female
—anatomy and physiology
—sexual orientation
—pressures
—laws

Unit 4
Teen pregnancy
—health and psychosocial risks

Unit 5
Personal hygiene for males
and females

Unit 6
Birth control
—benefits
—risks
—alternatives
—access and laws

Unit 7
Sexually transmitted diseases
—prevalence

—prevention
—detection
—treatment
—health risks
—laws

Unit 8
Factors influencing reproductive
health
—smoking
—alcohol and other drug use
—nutrition and medical care

Unit 9
Labor and pregnancy

Unit 10
Positive parenting and pregnancy
alternatives

Unit 11
Date rape and stranger rape
—prevalence
—prevention
—laws
Sexual harassment
—prevalence
—prevention
—laws

Unit 12
Conclusion
—course review
—development of personal
  reproductive life plan

In addition, Muccigrosso et al. (1991), have suggested some effective techniques for teaching sexuality to adolescents, as follows:

1. Draw out what the students already know or think they know.

2. Establish ground rules to make it safe to talk about sexuality, such as
   ■ no put-downs

- don't share information outside of the class
- everyone can pass (e.g. refuse to discuss a topic)
- no private stories
- show respect for one another
- all questions are good questions.

3. Agree on commonly understood vocabulary.

4. Use visual aids such as models, videos, and slides.

5. Create opportunities for role plays.

6. Incorporate group discussions and cooperative learning.

7. Be as concrete as possible; demonstrate and illustrate.

8. When possible, have coeducational groups.

9. Team-teach— male and female whenever possible.

10. Start with topics that are comfortable to you and the students.

School Dropout

Dropping out of school has a significant impact on a student's life as well as economic and social repercussions for the society at large. Unemployment rates are high among high school dropouts. In one study, 60% of dropouts in Miami and 46% in Philadelphia reported being unemployed and not enrolled in vocational or academic programs. In addition, high school dropouts who are employed tend to earn less than high school graduates (Dropouts' Perspective on Leaving School, 1988). The result is a loss of earnings, taxes, and social security, as well as a lack of qualified workers.

Most dropouts later regret their decision to leave school (Peng & Takai, 1983). This dissatisfaction only intensifies the low self-esteem typical of dropouts (Ekstrom, Goertz, Pollack, & Rock, 1986). Teachers, therefore, must provide appropriate opportunities for all students to learn, to be successful, and to graduate from high school as a means of reducing the ever-rising dropout-rates.

Numbers of Dropouts

One problem with the current research on dropouts is the lack of a standardized definition and inconsistent accounting procedures across school district and research studies (MacMillan, Balow, Widaman, Borthwick-Duffy, & Hendrick, 1990). The Office of Educational Research and Improvement (1987) defined a *dropout* as a student who leaves school before his or her program of study is complete, before graduation, without transferring to another school.

Another definition of school dropouts, by Voss, Wendling, and Elliott (1966) differentiated three types of dropouts:

1. Involuntary dropouts who have to leave school because of unavoidable circumstances such as a family emergency.
2. Students . . . who leave because they lack certain skills.
3. Capable students who voluntarily drop out for other reasons.

A conservative estimate of the dropout rate nationwide is 15%–25.9% of all high school students (Mann, 1985; State Education Performance, 1990). The incidence of students with mild disabilities who drop out of school may significantly exceed that of the nondisabled; approximately one in four students with mild disabilities drop out of school (Cohen & deBettencourt, 1991).

Studies that report dropout rates separately for different categories of handicapping conditions generally indicate that two groups have a higher propensity than others to leave school before graduation. The estimated dropout rate of students with severe emotional disturbances is approximately 50% (Kaufman, 1987), and for adolescents with learning disabilities, between 25% and 50% (deBettencourt, Zigmond, & Thornton, 1989). In a comparative study Zigmond and Thornton (1985), reported that half of the students with learning disabilities who began 9th grade left school before graduation. This rate was significantly higher than that for nondisabled adolescents in the same urban school.

Kinds of Students Who Drop Out of School

Numerous characteristics of students at risk for dropping out of school have been identified. Ekstrom and her colleagues (1986) focused on a sample of high school sophomores over a 2-year period and found that those who stayed in school ("stayers") differed from those who left ("leavers") across a wide variety of dimensions. Students in low socioeconomic and racial/ethnic minority groups were disproportionately represented among the leavers and were more likely to be older and male.

Specifically, these researchers found that the leavers tended to come from homes with fewer study aids and fewer opportunities for nonschool-related learning. Further, the leavers were less likely to have both birth parents living in the home, more likely to have employed mothers (who had less education and lower educational expectations for their children), and to have less parental monitoring of their in- and out-of-school activities.

The leavers also were less likely to be involved in extracurricular activities and had lower grades and test scores than the stayers. Too, the leavers did less homework— an average of 2.2 hours a week compared to the 3.4 hours reported by the stayers. The leavers also had more discipline problems in school than the stayers, were absent and late more often, cut more classes, got suspended from school more often, and had more trouble with the police.

Differences between leavers and stayers also were found in the social domain. Many of the leavers reported feelings of alienation from school. Few leavers reported being satisfied with their academic work and being popular with other students. They tended to choose friends who also were alienated from school and who had low educational expectations. Finally, the leavers were likely to have worked more hours during their high school years than the stayers. Their jobs were more enjoyable and important to them than school. Additional characteristics of dropouts and related school factors are summarized in Table 6.

Table 3.6   Characteristics of Drop-Out Students

Demographic Factors	*School Factors*
Ethnic group	Weak leadership from the principal
Gender	High level of disempowerment
Community type	experienced by staff
Social and Family Factors	Small amount of time teachers
Socioeconomic status	engage in instruction
Single-parent family	Low percentage of teaching time
Educational or motivational support	spent in interactive learning
at home	Tracking
Personality Factors	Misuse of standardized tests
Low self-concept	Fiscal arrangements that encourage
Externalized locus of control	early dismissal of dropouts
Low needs for self-development	
Early Transition into Adulthood	Overcrowding
Pregnancy	Underachieving student body
Marriage	High failure rates
Having a job	
Deviant Behavior in Society	Low degree of order and discipline
Institutionalized or incarceration	Low attendance rate
Delinquency	
Drug use	
In-School Factors	School reform
Low academic achievement and low grades	
Low IQ; reading problems	
Being held back; being over age	
Low educational and occupational	
aspirations	
Behavior problems; poor attendance	

Source: Wolman, C., Bruininks, R., & Thurlow, M. L. (1989). Dropouts and dropout programs: Implications for special education. *Remedial and Special Education, 10,* 6–20. Reprinted with permission.

Although the profile of adolescents who drop out of school helps to identify potential dropouts, the data do not tell us why these students decide to leave. Some say that factors identified by Ekstrom and her colleagues (e.g., truancy, poverty, low expectations) actually cause students to drop out of school (SMERC, 1986). Over the past 30 years dropouts have consistently reported (Dropouts' Perspective on Leaving School, 1988) their main reasons for leaving school before graduation as:

A dislike for school
The opinion that "school is boring" and not relevant
Low academic achievement and poor grades
A desire to work full-time and a need for money
Lack of belonging and a sense that nobody cared.

Prevention

Literally thousands of school programs have been designed to reduce the number of students who drop out of school. Successful programs share several common features: small size, inclusion by choice, flexibility, view of school as a community, and involvement of the community outside the school (Cuban, 1989).

Nationwide, school districts are adopting a variety of programs to reduce high school dropout rates. The underlying premise of many of these programs is to provide opportunities for student success (ways to get students through school and to accumulate credits toward high school graduation) and to improve their self-image. Many interventions emphasize support systems designed to help students overcome obstacles such as low motivation and large class size. The programs also tend to stress flexibility with regard to course requirements and grading systems, school climate, support from teachers and administrators, teacher-student contact strategies, instructional approaches, and vocational and school-community educational programs (Cohen & deBettencourt, 1991).

Some common dropout prevention programs are

■ Remedial and basic skills classes

■ Reading programs

■ Tutoring programs

■ Motivational development activities

■ On-the-job training

■ School-supervised work experience

■ Counseling activities

■ Parental involvement

■ Self-awareness classes

■ School-age parenting classes

■ Evening or weekend classes.

Generally, educators say the needs of students at risk for dropping out of school are complex and defy easy solutions (Rodenstein, 1990). Moreover, the reasons frequently are multiple (e.g., a young girl is pregnant, low-achieving, and poor) and vary from student to student.

Crisis Intervention Efforts

A number of professionals (Caplin, 1964; McWhirter et al., 1993) separate prevention into three levels: (a) *primary prevention*, efforts to reduce the incidence of involvement; (b) *secondary prevention*, efforts to work with adolescents who are involved already; and (c) *tertiary prevention*, efforts directed toward rehabilitation of the adolescent.

Primary Prevention

Primary prevention has been defined as "a process which promotes health by empowering people with the resources necessary to confront complex, stressful life conditions and by enabling individuals to lead personally satisfying, enriching lives, (Berkan, 1986, p. 4). This approach encompasses a variety of activities that help adolescents develop a positive self-image and better coping skills. Most primary prevention programs promote behavioral changes of adolescents to reduce their risk-taking behaviors. Shaw and Goodyear (1984) noted that primary prevention must:

— be group-oriented and individually focused.

— be a before-the-fact effort targeted to groups or individuals not yet involved in the social issue.

— rest on a solid knowledge base that suggests the program holds potential for preventing involvement (p. 625).

Primary prevention approaches are of four main types: information, affective, alternative, and social competence (Elmquist, 1991).

Information. Prevention efforts are considered generic when they are thought to be appropriate for all students, not just those presumed to be at-risk. Often, these efforts are information-based with the assumption that more balanced, factual knowledge about the consequences of at-risk behaviors, such as alcohol and drug use, sexual behaviors, and so on, will create more negative attitudes toward and reduce the likelihood of the adolescent's involvement.

Educators must provide accurate and timely information about these social issues. Hansen et al. (1988) found that information about relatively immediate consequences had greater effect than information about long-term consequences. In addition, adolescents are more likely to be suspicious of information presented in an obviously one-sided and biased manner than information presented in a balanced and neutral manner (Botvin & Willis, 1987).

The information approach includes scare tactics. We all have seen the television commercials that dramatically demonstrate the effects of drugs on the brain by cracking an egg into a sputtering skillet. However, scare tactics neither provide information nor prevent drug use (Horan & Straus, 1987; Newcomb & Bentler, 1989).

Fortunately, we are beginning to move away from the information approach. According to Goodstadt (1986), information-based efforts, especially alcohol and other drug-use education programs, have failed for four reasons: (a) changes in attitude do not automatically lead to changes in behavior; (b) alcohol and other use drug or sex education courses often are taught as though all students involved are nonusers or nonparticipants; (c) education programs do not make necessary links between the classroom and reality; and (d) most education programs have not been evaluated in terms of learning outcomes. Finally, Eiser, Eiser, and Bocker (1988) questioned teachers and found them dissatisfied with information-based interventions, preferring approaches based on teaching students how to make appropriate decisions.

Affective. Affective educational programs promote self-understanding and responsible decision making. They address value clarification, problem solving, self-awareness and self-esteem, and coping skills (Barnea, 1989; Jaker, 1985). An adolescent faces many decisions that require these skills (Should I have sex? Should I try marijuana? Should I have another beer?). This prevention/intervention approach is based on the assumption that by improving their psychological traits, clarifying values, and developing responsible patterns of assertiveness, refusal and decision making skills, and skills in resisting peer pressure, the adolescent will decide not to become involved in alcohol and drug use, sexual activities, and so on (Elmquist, 1991). For example, instead of focusing on actual alcohol and drug use, affective education programs attempt to eliminate the underlying reasons for their use (Bell & Battjes, 1987). Several professionals (e.g., Moskowitz, 1989; Tobler, 1986), however, claim that affective education is ineffective in influencing values, self-esteem, or behaviors.

Alternatives. The alternative prevention approach is based on the premise that an individual exhibits risk-taking behaviors because of a need to be involved in rewarding, exciting, and thrilling activities (Barnea, 1989). Adolescents often drink alcohol because they want to belong and have fun with friends. To be effective, alternative intervention programs have to offer healthy, legal alternative activities, such as the alcohol and other drug use activities and clubs described earlier, as a means of meeting these needs (Bell & Battjes, 1987).

Alternative programs have proven effective in decreasing alcohol and other drug use and in improving self-esteem, coping skills, relationships with family and friends, school attendance, school behavior, leadership skills, and academic performance (Contrucci, 1991). Participants enjoy a sense of belonging to a group that engages in meaningful, worthwhile activities where they have some responsibility and control. Using the dynamics of positive peer pressure, peer support, peer influences, and peer interaction, these programs bring together a group of unique and diverse students with the common interest of wanting to help others.

Social Competence. The social competence approach is based on the assumption that alcohol and other drug use, sexual activities, and so on often are a result of poor personal and social competence (Elmquist, 1991). An adolescent with appropriate social skills can resist and counter these pressures (Botvin, 1983).

A major component of this approach is active student participation through peer helper programs. Specially selected, responsible students are trained in specific skills and are given the opportunity to have a positive influence on their fellow students (see Contrucci, 1991 for selection and training procedures).

Secondary Prevention

Secondary prevention involves identifying adolescents who show beginning signs of depression or involvement in undesirable behaviors for whom prompt diagnosis and effective treatment might ward off more serious involvement. Simply, it is the action taken following recognition of the problem, such as the steps discussed earlier related to teenage depression and suicide.

Tertiary Prevention

Tertiary prevention consists of treating adolescents who are seriously involved in alcohol and drug abuse, sexual activities, and so on. This treatment is similar to the concept of rehabilitation—to help those who already are affected to lead as normal a life as possible (for more information see Adams & Gullota, 1989, Thompson & Rudolph, 1992).

Comprehensive Efforts

Schools should adopt a comprehensive prevention approach because no *one* approach reaches every adolescent. A comprehensive approach differs from what many schools and educators currently provide, such as the problem-of-the-week approach (Jessor, 1991) wherein efforts are mobilized to fight teenage pregnancy one week, drunk driving the next, alcohol and drug use the next, and so on.

A comprehensive approach is based on the assumption that many adolescents are involved not only in alcohol and other drug use but also in risky sexual activities. For example, the three behaviors that place individuals at highest risk for HIV infection typically are initiated during adolescence. These are (a) unprotected sexual intercourse, (b) intravenous drug use, and (c) the use of drugs and alcohol before or during sexual behavior (Rotheran-Borus & Koopman, 1991). Professionals have identified common components of comprehensive dropout prevention programs (Guetzloe, 1988; Rogers, 1991):

1. Initiated early and dealt with antecedents, not results of failure.

2. Gave one-on-one attention to students.

3. Supplied, fostered, and encouraged the development of basic skills and socialization skills.

4. Located in school and involved parents, students, and educators.

5. Had an obvious connection with the real world.

6. Had exciting leaders who related well to adolescents.

7. Were broad-based, communitywide efforts.

8. Involved multiple agencies.

Dryfoos (1991) provided examples of successful communitywide prevention programs that incorporated different kinds of programs and services (e.g., schools, public and private community agencies, parent groups, media, police, courts, clergy, businesses, universities, and students). For example, a number of efforts combined community education, media, and school interventions. In the alcohol and other drug abuse area, a communitywide health promotion campaign used local media and community education in conjunction with alcohol and other drug use prevention curricula in the local schools. A successful program in pregnancy prevention concentrated on community education through the media and a speaker's bureau; training of parents, clergy, and other community leaders; and development and implementation of comprehensive sex and family life education unit in the schools. In another example a school dropout program was implemented successfully by an all-out community effort that involved the schools with local businesses, local government agencies, and universities in planning, teacher training, and training and job placement of adolescents.

Summary and Conclusion

As we explore adolescents' involvement in social issues and as we consider prevention and intervention activities, we must keep in mind the enormous changes adolescents go through. The dramatic physical, emotional, psychological, and social changes of adolescence occur rapidly, at a rate unsurpassed at any later point in life. To this great change within adolescents we must add the changes in social expectations, changes in the structure and content of formal education, the effects of difficult conditions in our society, and the effects of having a mild disability. Only then can educators imagine how tough the transition into adulthood can be for many adolescents. As educators, we must ask how we can establish more supportive environments for adolescents' transition to adulthood in a society that place many obstacles in their paths. Hepworth and Shernoff (1989) contend that, "to be effective, education must motivate people to recognize personal risk and to take action to change behaviors that put them at risk" (p. 48).

References

Adams, G. R., & Gullota, T. (1989). *Adolescent life experiences*. (2d ed.) Pacific Grove, CA: Brooks/Cole.

American Academy of Pediatrics. (1988). *Substance abuse: A guide for health Professionals*. Elk Grove Village, IL: Author.

American Association of Colleges (1978). *Sexual harassment: A hidden issue*. Washington, DC: Author.

American College Health Association (1990). *HIV infection and AIDS*. Baltimore, MD: Author.

American Psychological Association. (1987). *Diagnostic and statistical manual of mental disorders* (3d ed. rev.) Washington, DC: Author.

Anderson, J. E., Kann, L., Haltzman, D., Arday, S., Truman, B., & Kolbe, L. (1990). HIV/AIDS knowledge and sexual behavior among high school students. *Family Planning Perspectives, 22*, 252–255.

Barnea, Z. (1989). A critical an comparative review of the prevention of drug and alcohol abuse in Israeli *Journal of Drug Education, 19*, 59–81.

Beck, A. T., Ward, C. H., Mendelson, M., Mock, J., & Erbaugh, J. (1961). An inventory for measuring depression. *Archives of General Psychiatry, 4,* 53–63.

Beck, A. T., Kovacs, M., & Weissman, A. (1979). Assessment of suicidal ideation: The scale of suicidal ideation. *Journal of Clinical and Consulting Psychology, 47,* 343–352.

Bell, C. S., & Battjes, R. J. (1987). Overview of drug abuse prevention research. In C. S. Bell & R. J. Battjes (Eds.), *Prevention research: Determining drug abuse among children and adolescents* (National Institute on Drug Abuse research Monograph

No. 63, DHHS Publication No. ADM-85-1334). Washington, DC: U. S. Government Printing Office.

Berkan, W. A. (1986). *Suicide prevention: A resource and planning guide*. Madison: Wisconsin Department of Public Instruction.

Botvin, G. J. (1983). *Life skills training (Teacher's Manual)*. New York: Smithfield.

Botvin, G. J., & Willis, T. A. (1987). Personal and social skills training: Cognitive-behavioral approaches to substance abuse prevention. In C. S. Bell & R. J. Battjes (Eds.), *Prevention research: Determining drug abuse among children and adolescents* (National Institute on Drug Abuse research Monograph No. 63, DHHS Publication No. ADM-85-1334). Washington, DC: U.S. Government Printing Office.

Brooks-Gunn, J., Boyer, C. B., & Hein, K. (1988). Preventing HIV infection and AIDS in children and adolescents: Behavioral research and intervention strategies. *American Psychologist*, 43, 958–964.

Caplin, G. (1964). *Principles of preventive psychiatry*. New York: Basic Books.

Capuzzi, D., & Golden, L. (1988). Adolescent suicide: An introduction to issues and interventions. In D. Capuzzi & L. Golden (eds.), *Preventing adolescent suicide* (pp. 3–28). Muncie, IN: Accelerated Development.

Capuzzi, D., & Le Coq, L. L. (1983). Social and personal determinants of adolescent use and abuse of alcohol and marijuana. *Personnel and Guidance Journal, 61,* 199–205.

Centers for Disease Control. (1989, December). AIDS cases reported through

November 1989. *HIV/AIDS surveillance*. Atlanta, GA: Author.

Children and Teens Today Newsletter (1987, February), p. 3.

Cohen, S. G., & deBettencourt, L. V. (1991). Dropout: Intervening with the reluctant learner. *Intervention in school and clinic, 26*, 263–271.

Coles, R. , & Stokes, G. (1985). *Sex and the American teenager*. NY: Rolling Stone Press.

Conger, J. J. (1988). Hostages to fortune: Youth, values, and the public interest. *American Psychologist*, 43, 291–300.

Contrucci, V. J. (1991). *Alcohol and other drug abuse programs: A resource and planning guide*. Madison: Wisconsin Department of Public Instruction.

Cuban, L. (1989). At-risk students: What teachers and principals can do. *Educational Leadership, 45*, 29–33.

Dean, J. C., Fox, A. M., & Jensen, W. (1985). Alcohol and drug use by disabled and nondisabled persons: A comparative study. *The International Journal of the Addictions, 20*, 629–641.

deBettencourt, L. U., Zigmond, N., & Thornton, H. (1989). Follow-up of rural learning disabled graduates and dropouts. *Exceptional Children, 56*, 40–49.

Devlin, S. D., & Eliott, R. N. (1992). Drug use patterns of adolescents with behavioral disorders, *17*, 264–272.

DiNitto, D. M., & Krishef, K. (1984). Drinking patterns of mentally retarded persons. *Alcohol, Health, and Research World, 8*, 40–42.

Dollinger, S. J., Horn, J. L., & Boarini, D. (1988). Disturbed sleep and worries among learning disabled adolescents. *American Journal of Orthopsychiatry, 58*, 428–434.

Dropouts' Perspective on Leaving School (1988). *CAPS Capsule*, 2–3.

Dryfoos, J. G. (1991). *Adolescents at risk: Prevalence and prevention*. New York: Oxford University Press.

Edeleman, M. W. (1987). *Families in peril: An agenda for social change*. Cambridge, MA: Harvard University Press.

Eiser, C., Eiser, J. R., & Bocker, M. (1988). Teachers, evaluation of a "life-skills" approach to drug education. *Educational Research, 30*, 202–210.

Ekstrom, R. B., Goertz, M. E., Pollack, J. M., & Rock, D. A. (1986). Who drops out of high school and why? Findings from a national study. *Teacher's College Record, 87*, 356–373.

Elmquist, D. L. (1991). School-based alcohol and other drug prevention programs: Guidelines for the special educator. *Intervention in school and clinic, 27*, 10–19.

Elmquist, D. L., Morgan, D. P., & Bolds, P. (1989). *Substance abuse among adolescents with disabilities*. Unpublished manuscript, Utah State University, Department of Special Education, Logan.

Fick, L. (1984). *Adolescent childbearing decisions: Implications for preventing*. St. Louis, MO: The Danforth Foundation.

Fitzgerald, L. F. (1992). *Sexual harassment in higher education: Concepts and issues*. Washington, DC: National Education Association.

Foster, S. (1986). *Preventing teenage pregnancy*. Washington, DC: Council of State Policy and Planning Agencies.

Frederick, C. I. (1985). An introduction and overview of youth suicide. In M. L. Peck, N. L. Farberow, & R. E. Litman (Eds.), *Youth suicide* (pp. 1–33). New York: Springer-Verlag.

Gale, J. (1989). *A parent's guide to teenage sexuality*. Henry Holt: New York.

Garrison, C. Z., Lewinsohn, P. M., Marsteller, F., Langhinrichsen, J., & Lann, I. (1991). The assessment of suicidal behavior in adolescents. *Suicide and Life-Threatening Behavior, 21*, 217–230.

Gibbs, N. (1993, May 24). How should we teach our children about sex? *Time*, 60–66.

Gispert, M., Wheeler, K., Marsh, L., & Davis M. S. (1985). Suicide adolescents: Factors in evaluation. *Adolescence, 20*, 753-761.

Goodstadt, M. S. (1986). School-based drug education in North America: What is wrong? What can be done? *Journal of School Health, 56*, 278–281.

Guetzloe, E. C. (1987). *Suicide and depression, the adolescent epidemic: Education's responsibility.* Orlando, FL: Advantage Consultants.

Guetzloe, E. C. (1988). Suicide and depression: Special education's responsibility. *Teaching Exceptional Children,* 20, 25–28.

Hansen, W. B., Graham, J. W., Wolkenstein, B. H., Lundy, B. Z., Pearson, J., Flay, B. R., & Anderson-Johnson, C. (1988). Differential impact of three alcohol prevention curricula on hypothesized mediating variables. *Journal of Drug Education,* 18, 143–153.

Harrell, A. V., & Wirtz, P. W. (1989). *Adolescent drinking-index.* Odessa, FL: Psychological Assessment Resources, Inc.

Harris, L. (1987). *Inside America.* New York: Vintage.

Hawton, K. (1986). *Suicide and attempted suicide among children and adolescents.* Beverly Hills, CA: Sage.

Hayes, M. L., & Sloat, R. S. (1988). Suicide and the gifted adolescent. *Journal for the Education of the Gifted,* 13, 229–244.

Hein, K. (1989). AIDS in adolescence: Exploring the challenge. *Journal of Adolescent Health Care,* 10, 105–355.

Hendlin, H. (1982). *Suicide in America.* New York: W. W. Horton.

Hepworth, J., & Shernoff, M. (1989). Strategies for AIDS education and prevention. In E. Macklin (ed.), *AIDS and Families,* p. 35–48. New York: Harrington Press.

Hingson, R. W., Strunin, L., Berlin, B. M., Heeren, T. (1988). Beliefs about AIDS, use of alcohol and drugs, and unprotected sex among Massachusetts adolescents. *American Journal of Public Health,* 78, 460–461.

Hofferth, S. L., Kahn, J. R., & Baldwin, W. (1987). Premarital sexual activity among U.S. teenage women over the past three decades. *Family Planning Perspectives,* 19, 46–53.

Horan, J. J., & Straus, L. K. (1987). Substance abuse. In M. Hersen & V. B. Van-Hasselt (eds.), *Behavior therapy with children and adolescents: A clinical approach* (pp. 440–464). New York: Wiley.

Horton, L. (1985). *Adolescent drug abuse.* Bloomington, IN: Phi Delta Kappa Educational Foundation.

Humm, A. J. (1992). Homosexuality: The new frontier in sexuality education. *Family Life Educator,* 10, 13–18.

Issacs, M., Buckley, G., & Martin, D. (1979). Patterns of drinking among the deaf. The *American Journal of Alcohol and Drug Abuse,* 6, 463–476.

Jaker, G. F. (1985, August). *Lessons learned: A review of the research in drug education.* Anoka: Minnesota Prevention Resource Center.

Jessor, R. (1991). Risk behavior in adolescence: A psychosocial framework for understanding and action. *Journal of Adolescent Health,* 12, 597–605.

Johnston, J., O'Malley, P. M., & Bachman, J. G. (1986). *Drug use among American high school students, college students, and other young adults.* Washington, DC: U.S. Government Printing Office.

Kellam, S. G., & Simon, M. C. (1980). Mental health in first grade and teenage drug, alcohol and cigarette use. *Journal of Drug and Alcohol Dependency,* 5, 273–304.

Kempton, W. (1988). *A teacher's guide: Sex education for persons with disabilities.* Santa Monica, CA: Stanfield.

Kirby, D. (1984). *Sexuality education: An evaluation of programs and their effect.* Santa Cruz, CA: Network.

Kosky, P. (1983). Childhood suicidal behavior. *Journal of Child Psychology and Psychiatry,* 24, 457–467.

Krishef, C. H. (1986). Do the mentally retarded drink? A study of their alcohol usage. *Journal of Alcohol and Drug Education,* 31, 64–70.

Leone, P. E., Greensburg, J. M., Trickett, E. J., & Spero, E. (1989). A study of the use of cigarettes, alcohol, and marijuana by students identified as seriously emotionally disturbed. *Counterpoint,* 9, 6–7.

Long, J. V. F., & Scherl, D. J. (1984). Developmental antecedents of compulsive drug use: A report on the literature. *Journal of Psychoactive Drugs,* 16, 169–182.

Maag, J. W., & Behrens, J. T. (1989). Epidemiologic data on seriously emotionally disturbed and learning disabled adolescents reporting extreme depressive symptomatology. *Behavioral Disorders, 15*, 21–27.

MacDonald, D. I., & Blume, S. B. (1986). Children of alcoholics. *American Journal of Disorders of Children, 140*, 750-754.

MacMillan, D. L., Balow, I. H., Widaman, K. F., Borthwick-Duffy, S., & Hendrick, I. G. (1990). Methodological problems in estimating dropout rates and the implications for studying dropouts from special education. *Exceptionality, 1*, 29–39.

Maksym, D. (1990). *Shared feelings: A parent guide to sexuality education for children, adolescents and adults who have a mental handicap.* North York, Ontario: The G. Allan Roeher Institute.

Mann, D. (1985). Action on dropouts. *Educational Leadership, 43*, 16–17.

Mann, D. (1986). Can we help dropouts: Thinking about the undoable. *Teachers College Record, 87*, 307–323.

McGee, K., & Guetzloe, E. (1988). Suicidal emotionally handicapped students: Tips for the classroom teacher. *The Pointer, 32*, 7–10.

McWhirter, J. J. (1993). Will he live? A suicide assessment interview. In L. Golden & M. Norwood (eds.), *Case studies in child counseling* (pp. 89–98). New York: MacMillan.

McWhirter, J. J., McWhirter, B. T., McWhirter, A. M., & McWhirter, E. H. (1993). *At-risk youth: A comprehensive response.* Pacific Grove, CA: Brooks/ Cole.

Metha, A., & Dunham, H. (1988). Behavioral indicators. In D. Capuzzi & L. Golden (eds.), *Preventing adolescent suicide* (pp. 49–86). Muncie, IN: Accelerated Development.

Morbidity and Mortality Weekly Report. (1988, January 29). *Guidelines for effective school health education to prevent the spread of AIDS.* Atlanta, GA: Centers for Disease Control.

Moskowitz, J. M. (1989). The primary prevention of alcohol problems: A critical review of the research literature. *Journal of Studies on Alcohol, 50*, 54–88.

Muccigrosso, L., Scavarda, M., Simpson-Brown, R., & Thalacker, B. E. (1991). *Double Jeopardy: Pregnant and parenting youth in special education.* Reston, VA: Council for Exceptional children.

National Academy of Sciences. (1989). *Confronting AIDS: Directions for public health, health care, and research.* Washington, DC: Author.

Newcomb, M. D., & Bentler, P. M. (1989). Substance use and abuse among children and teenagers. *American Psychologist, 44*, 242–248.

Office of Educational Research and Improvement. (1987). *Dealing with dropouts: The urban superintendents' call to action.* Washington, DC: U.S. Government Printing Office.

Office of Population Affairs. (1988, November). *Family life information exchange.* U.S. Department of Health and Human Services, Public Health, Resource Memo. Washington, DC:

Orr, D. P., Wilbrant, M. L., Brack, C. J., Rauch, S. P., & Ingersoll, G. M. (1989). Reported sexual behaviors and self-esteem among young adolescents. *American Journal of Diseases of Children, 143*, 86–90.

Otto, U. (1972). Suicidal acts by children and adolescents. *Acta Psychiatry Scandinavia, 233*, 7–123.

Paget, K. (1988). Adolescent pregnancy: Implications for prevention strategies in educational settings. *School Psychology Review, 17*, 570–579.

The pain of harassment, *Seattle Times,* Nov. 2, 1993, p. E-8.

Peck, M. L. (1985). Crisis intervention treatment with chronically and acutely suicidal adolescents. In M. Peck, N. Farberow & R. Litman (eds.), *Youth suicide* (pp. 1–33). New York: Springer-Verlag.

Pender, L. (1990). Growing up gay. *Cincinnati Magazine* (February). 26–29.

Peng, S. S., & Takai, R. T. (1983). *High school dropouts: Descriptive information from high school and beyond.* Washington,

DC: National Center for Educational Statistics (ERIC No. ED 236-366).

Pfeffer, C. R. (1986). *The suicidal child.* New York Guilford Press.

Pfeffer, C. R., Zuckerman, S., Plutchik, R., Mizruchi, M. S. (1984). Suicidal behavior in normal school children: A comparison with child psychiatric patients. *Journal of American Academy of Child Psychiatry, 23,* 416–423.

Price, M. (1987, December). Physically, mentally disabled teens require special contraceptive care. *Contraceptive Technology Update,* 154–156.

Reynolds, (1985). Depression in childhood and adolescence: Diagnosis, assessment, intervention strategies, and research. In T. R. Kratochwill (ed.), *Advances in school psychology* (Vol. 4, pp. 133–189). Hillsdale, NJ: Lawrence Erlbaum.

Ritter, D. R. (1989). Social competence and problem behavior of adolescent girls with learning disabilities. *Journal of Learning Disabilities, 22,* 460–461.

Robertson, D., & Mathews, B. (1989). Preventing adolescent suicide with group counseling. *Journal for Specialists in Group Work, 14,* 34–39.

Rodenstein, J. M. (1990). *Children at-risk: A resource and planning guide.* Madison: Wisconsin Department of Public Instruction.

Rogers, D. E. (1991). Adolescents at risk conference: Summation. *Journal of Adolescent Health, 12,* 644–647.

Romaneck, G. M., & Kuehl, R. (1992). Sex education for students with high-incidence special needs. *Teaching Exceptional Children, 25,* 22–24.

Rotheran-Borus, M. J., & Koopman, C. (1991). HIV and adolescents. *The Journal of Primary Prevention, 12,* 65–82.

Rutter, M. (1986). Depressive feelings, cognitions, and disorders: A research postscript. In M. Rutter, C. E. Izard, & P. B. Read (eds.), *Depression in young people* (pp. 491-519). New York, NY: Guilford Press.

Schorr, L. B. (1988). *Within our reach: Breaking the cycle of disadvantage.* New York: Doubleday.

Shaffer, D. (1974). Suicide in childhood and early adolescence. *Journal of Childhood Psychology and Psychiatry, 15,* 275–291.

Shapiro, C. (1981). *Adolescent pregnancy prevention: School-community cooperation.* Springfield, IL: Charles C. Smith.

Slavin. R. E., Karweit, N. L., & Madden, N. A. (1989). *Effective programs for students at risk.* Boston: Allyn & Bacon.

SMERC. (1986 January). *Information for professional excellence: Dropouts.* Redwood City, CA: San Mateo County Office of Education.

State Education Performance, 1982 and 1989. (1990, May 9). *Education Week.*

Steele, W. (1983). *Preventing teenage suicide.* Novato, CA: Ann Arbor Publishers.

Strunin, L., & Hingson, R. (1987). Acquired immunodeficiency syndrome and adolescents: Knowledge, beliefs, attitudes, and behavior. *Pediatrics, 79,* 825–828.

Sturner, W. Q. (1986). Adolescent suicide fatalities. *Rhode Island Medical Journal, 69,* 471–474.

Tatum, M. L. (1988). The AIDS challenge: Controversial issues in the classroom. *Family Life Educator, 7,* 15–19.

Thomas, L. L., Long, S. E., Whitten, K., Hamilton, B., Fraser, J., & Askins, R. V. (1985). High school students' long-term retention of sex education information. *Journal of School Health, 55,* 274–278.

Tobler, N. (1986). Meta-analysis of 143 adolescent drug prevention programs: Quantitative outcome results of program participants compared to a control or comparison group. *Journal of Drug Issues, 16,* 537–567.

Tomaszewski, E. P. (1991). Adolescent dating violence. *Family Life Educator, 10,* 4–8.

Tomlinson-Keasey, C., & Keasey, C. B. (1988). "Signatures" of suicide. In D. Capuzzi & L. Golden (eds.), *Preventing adolescent suicide* (pp. 213–245). Muncie, IN: Accelerated Development.

Tomlinson-Keasey, C., Warren, L. W., & Elliott, J. E. (1986). Suicide among gifted women: A perspective study. *Journal of Abnormal Psychology, 95,* 123–129.

Voss, H. L., Wendling, A., & Elliott, D. S. (1966). Some types of high-school drop-outs. *Journal of Educational Research, 59,* 363–368.

Webb, J. A., Baer, P. E., McLaughlin, R. J., McKelvey, R. S., & Caid, C. D. (1989). Risk factors and their relation to initiation of alcohol use among early adolescents. *Journal of American Academy of Child and Adolescent Psychiatry, 30,* 563–568.

Zigmond, N., & Thornton, H. (1985). Follow-up of postsecondary age learning disabled graduates and drop-outs. *Learning Disabilities Research, 1,* 50–55.

Fostering Resilience in Children and Youth

Rosemary A. Lambie, Susan D. Leone, and Christopher K. Martin

Resilience in children and youth at-risk has become a topic of interest within the field of education during the last few decades. Studying resilience in children who otherwise would be expected to fail provides us with clues for helping children who are living under similar circumstances. What is resilience? Simply put, resilience is about *beating the odds* (Haggerty, Sherrod, Garmezy, & Rutter, 1994; Wang & Haertel, 1995). Of students considered at-risk, 19% were found to be resilient (Peng, Wang, & Walberg, 1992). As caring professionals, our challenge is to increase the number of children who fall in the resilient category. Resilience is a valuable topic because it focuses on the positive factors that can accompany challenging life circumstances (Cowan, Cowan, & Schulz, 1996; Kaplan, Turner, Norman, & Stillson, 1996).

At-Risk Children and Youth

Professionals from varied fields have written and hypothesized about at-risk children and youth for some time (Haggerty et al., 1994; Rutter, 1994). An early definition from education is that at-risk students are those who are likely to fail either in school or in life (Frymier, 1992; Frymier & Gansneder, 1989). Risk is related to negative experiences faced, their severity and frequency, as well as other circumstances in the child's life. Professionals generally share the opinion that risk also relates to internal aspects such as biophysical factors innate to the individual (Masten, 1994).

In about 1991, professionals in the field seem to have discontinued the quest to define the term *at risk* and began to focus more on resiliency. Perhaps this is a result of the definitive study by Frymier (1992), funded by Phi Delta Kappa, providing answers sought about the terminology, etiology, and characteristics of the at-risk population.

Earlier, Slavin and Madden (1989) indicated that "a practical criterion for identifying students at risk is eligibility for Chapter 1, special education, or other remedial services under today's standards" (p. 4). Frymier and Gansneder (1989) found that between 25% and 35% of the students in their study were seriously at risk for failure. This was defined by 45 factors that previous research had linked to being at risk.

Cuban (1989) offered a new and different explanation for students considered at risk. He departed from the previous notion that these students are the cause of their own poor performance, or that their families neither prepared them for school nor provided proper support. His alternative view was that the school failed to meet the needs of the child by disregarding or devaluing the family and culture. Cuban contended that teachers from the middle class often reflected those values and criticized children with behavior and values that varied from the dominant culture. Cuban also indicated that diverse abilities and interests were not accommodated, nor were adaptations made to meet individual needs.

Slavin and Madden (1989) agreed with Cuban's view. They identified the following risk factors: low achievement, retention in grade, behavior problems, poor attendance, low socioeconomic status, and attending school with a large number of poor students.

Liontos (1991) said the term *at-risk* had become a cliche "used both as a description and a prediction" (p. 5). She viewed the term as one that describes personal, educational, and societal ills, in particular as they relate to families who are poor.

The concept of risk is familiar in medical fields as well. According to Jens and Gordon (1991), the concept of risk had recently entered the field of education and was misunderstood by many. The term implies possible negative outcome as well as the possibility of avoiding a negative outcome. "Resiliency" is the term used when the negative outcome is avoided or ameliorated.

In this chapter we provide counselors with information about, and means of working with, at-risk students, their families, and communities. We focus on the nonacademic factors related to social, personal, and environmental influences—not academics. We recognize that all children who face serious life challenges may be or might become at risk for failure. For the purposes of determining eligibility for specific programs and allocating funds, the government sets certain socioeconomic parameters to define children who are at-risk or have special needs. In actuality, children who are identified as at-risk can be found in any classroom and in every socioeconomic and ethnic group.

Lambie (in press) found that, over time, the literature on at-risk students has reflected greater emphasis on the positive. Practitioners including counselors, educators, other mental health professionals and their professors, and sociologists are focusing on possibilities and abilities; shared meaning, values, power, and experience, as well as the importance of developing of an internal locus of control within students and their families. Guidance and counseling professionals are in a unique position to be of help, having a history of working with clients' strengths and abilities. Counselors, however, have typically focused on identification of at-risk youth but have not focused specifically on increasing the characteristics of resiliency in its wholeness (Rak & Patterson, 1996).

This emphasis on the positive might be seen as a simplistic means of dealing with tightening budgets, shifting interests on the part of society, or a denial of overwhelming pain in the face of perceived hopelessness. Nevertheless, *if you train your eye to look in the right direction, you will see much beauty.* Many who work with children and youth considered at risk have overcome many family-life and personal challenges. Nietzsche wrote, "That which does not kill me makes me stronger."

Perhaps all of us who succeed are resilient and have something to offer in our stories of resiliency (Henderson & Milstein, 1996). Many counselors have painful stories that others would never imagine—stories like those told by the students who are working to beat the odds and being taught by a professional who has beaten the odds in spite of adversity. So where we choose to train our eyes and the example that this gives to others become important in our efforts to increase resilience. Proust said, "The real voyage of discovery consists not in seeking new landscapes but in having new eyes." The eye to the positive is a voyage of discovering how our vulnerable children can rise from the ashes like the Phoenix of mythology.

Models of Resilience

Professionals who have beaten the odds and risen from the ashes can make excellent models, especially when they speak from experience, offer compassion, and have chosen *a path with heart* (Shepard, 1995). This article is about them and for them and others who wish to learn from their experiences. It is about our communities joining to be part of the whole, serving not as islands but as part of the main. In being allowed the opportunity to give, we are vital links in the chain, and we know we are valuable. George Bernard Shaw said:

> This is the true joy in life, the being used for a purpose recognized by yourself as a mighty one; . . . being a force of Nature instead of a feverish little clod of ailments and grievances complaining that the world will not devote itself to making you happy.

Research demonstrates that resilient individuals beat the odds because they recover from or adapt to stress and problems found in life (McMillan & Reed, 1994; Rhodes & Brown, 1991). Professionals benefit from knowing what helps to build resiliency in children so those program attributes can be reinforced, thereby increasing resiliency.

Today, school personnel speak about a school population in which the dropout rate reaches 30% to 50%, and in which more and more students are impoverished, are classified for special education, come from various ethnic and cultural backgrounds, and have academic difficulties in our schools (Barr & Parrett, 1995). At the same time, our economy is becoming less tolerant of individuals without skills and the ability to learn and adapt. If the schools do not address the at-risk population effectively, the consequences for at-risk children and our society are clear. With the growing numbers of at-risk children and youth in America (Barr & Parrett, 1995), we must find ways of helping our schools and communities increase the numbers of resilient, at-risk students. Increasing resiliency among at-risk children is a *community* responsibility, rather than the school's responsibility alone (Waddock, 1995).

Many professionals from varied fields have written on resiliency in children (Garmezy & Rutter, 1983; Haggerty et al., 1994; Henderson & Milstein, 1996; Hetherington & Blechman, 1996; Joseph, 1994; Rhodes & Brown, 1991; Wang & Gordon, 1994; Weissbourd, 1996). We first describe factors related to resilient at-risk students in terms of personal, family, and school factors. Then we discuss characteristics of successful school programs for the at-risk population. The remainder of the chapter is devoted to increasing resiliency by promoting the wise use of resources from many contexts, including school, family, social supports, and the community at large. Counselors are encouraged to serve as *web weavers*, helping coordinate the evolution of a caring community (Noddings, 1995).

Factors Related to Resilient At-Risk Students

In this section we describe three factors related to resilience: personal, family, and school domains. Understanding these factors will enable counselors to influence and develop programs and interventions within schools and communities.

Personal Factors

Teachers have described resilient children as social, optimistic, energetic, cooperative, inquisitive, attentive, helpful, punctual, and on-task (Sagor, 1996). They laugh at their own mistakes (Young-Eisendrath, 1996). The resilient child has a personality, manifested in early childhood, that elicits a positive response from others. These children are affectionate, good-natured, cuddly, and easy to get along with (McMillan & Reed, 1994), and they actively seek out relationships (Wolin & Wolin, 1996). As they grow older, they play alone comfortably, and as they seek challenging experiences, they appear to be self-reliant and have little fear. They use art, play, and humor as creative outlets that help them escape painful circumstances (Wolin & Wolin, 1996).

They also request and receive help from adults when required (Werner, 1984). Positive reciprocity emerges at an early age. Resilient youth reach out to others assuming they will receive help. Thus, their positive attitude results in responsiveness from others. Resilient children view the world as affirming in spite of challenging circumstances. The positive attitude relates to respect for others, being prepared for school, volunteering, and being at ease with school (McMillan & Reed, 1994).

In addition, resilient at-risk children have an internal locus of control and are highly motivated to succeed (Henderson & Milstein, 1996). They feel personally responsible for their success, which they view as their own (McMillan & Reed, 1994; Wolin & Wolin 1996). They do not blame others or their environment (external locus of control) for their failures or other situations. They have clearly defined goals that they articulate in a mature manner, and they recognize the importance of goal setting as a method by which they can improve their circumstances. Thus, mastery of new experiences is important for all at-risk students. Counselors can help teachers see the importance of providing self-fulfilling activities for students that reinforce their development of an internal locus of control.

Resilience is seen in the potential individuals have for creative development (Young-Eisendrath, 1996). Resilient students often seek refuge from their troubled environments in extracurricular activities. These activities may keep them away from potentially detrimental activities such as drug abuse. Resilient youth welcome alternative positive experiences such as sports and academic clubs (McMillan & Reed, 1994). Working successfully in groups with peers and emerging as a leader within one's peer group can be rewarding to the at-risk child or youth. The recognition associated with extracurricular activities can motivate students to participate. Counselors who recognize this can collaborate with teachers and parents to encourage belief in the student's ability to succeed.

Choosing to volunteer is another personal factor related to resilient children and youth (Henderson & Milstein, 1996). A few possible volunteer experiences are tutoring, helping in the home, and visiting nursing homes. Having a purpose that aids others is associated with resiliency (Keith, 1997). Young-Eisendrath (1996) wrote of the desire, as well as ability, to "feel and understand the needs of other" and "the ability to compromise and to delay meeting one's own desires in order to meet the needs of others" (pp. 71-72). Equally valuable in extracurricular activities and volunteering alike is the exposure to a positive adult who leads or facilitates the activities and serves as a role model for resilient behavior.

The personal characteristics of resilient children and youth lend themselves to success in the face of adversity. They have achieved a wisdom that allows them to engage life's meaning as well as their personal limitations (Young-Eisendrath, 1996). Resilient children in dysfunctional and abusive homes have the capacity to develop insights about their circumstances and don't blame themselves for their family's troubles. They seek safety for themselves by creating physical and emotional distance from unpredictable parents and find productive activities to fill their time (Wolin & Wolin, 1996). Some at-risk children from families having a parent who has a psychological disorder are able to maintain a sense of separateness from their parents, making peace with them and assuming a resilient life (Rak & Patterson, 1996).

Though peers may struggle in school as well as daily life, the resilient child emerges from a stressful environment able to cope successfully. Resilient children are the kind of people whom other people want to be around. They survive and thrive despite the odds against them. A resilient child is our modern day *phoenix*. This child rises with much to teach us about life, and, if we listen and observe, we will more ably serve all children and youth and their families.

Family Factors

Family demographic factors are not predictive of resiliency. Children in intact families have no higher incidence of resiliency than single-parent families do. What influences resiliency is a strong parent-child relationship and support (Hetherington & Blechman, 1996). Parental commitment gives the family a sense of coherence. Out of this family experience, resilient children learn to feel that life makes sense and that they can exercise control of their lives. This sense of meaning is basic to their motivation.

Receiving family support is another important family factor that can promote resiliency in children (Liontos, 1991). Parents of resilient children have higher educational expectations for their children, which in turn influence the children's achievement orientation; and resilient children have more of the necessary tools and materials for learning at home and are more frequently taken to community educational activities than are those who are nonresilient (Henderson & Milstein, 1996). Under-education of parents relates to nonresiliency. Peng et al. (1992) found that less than 11% of children were resilient in families in which the parents had not earned a high school diploma. Of students whose parents had at least a high-school diploma, 23% were considered resilient. This statistic alone points to the need for parenting training in low-income and high dropout areas.

A hallmark of resilient children is that, at early ages, they seek out and access adults whom they can trust (Hetherington & Blechman, 1996; McMillan & Reed, 1994; Rak & Patterson, 1996). Trust is established in the early years. It forms the building blocks for later adjustment at school, translating to reciprocal relationships with teachers and other role models. It is difficult to "exaggerate the importance of anchors in their lives—children and adults outside their families who are caring and attentive over time" (Weissbourd, 1996, p. 63).

Parents, though important, are not essential to building trust. Other adults may provide this necessary ingredient. These adults often become as close as family. Many resilient adults recount stories of a special neighbor or a teacher who took an interest in them (Wolin and Wolin, 1993). This connection made the children feel confident in their ability to build other strong relationships. Counselors are, by training and responsibility, in a position to provide this important relationship.

A personal recollection from a resilient adult follows:

> I remember when it seemed as if everything in our family life was a struggle. My father was ill and had to retire in his 40s. My mother was overwhelmed with the responsibilities of her nursing job, my father's heart attacks and strokes, and raising us kids. When I was in sixth grade, my father went into the hospital, and the day he got out, my mother went in.

A friend of my mother's, Elena, stepped in and filled some empty spaces in my life. Elena continued to be an important person in my life throughout life. I can still hear some of the things she would say, and they serve as guides to me today. She was fun to be with and had lots of advice about dating.

When my grandmother died, Elena was right there with me at eighth-grade graduation while my mother was at the funeral across the country. Elena was also right beside me a few months later when my dad died. She was a teacher of mine in grade school and for life. She taught me a lot about people and how to lighten up. I don't think I would have made it without her presence in my life.

School Factors

Children who are resilient find support outside of the home. This often takes the form of support in school. Resilient children usually get along well with their peers and have at least one close confidante from their school. They have an informal network of people whom they can access in crisis, as well as for help in academic and other areas (McMillan & Reed, 1994).

Resilient children usually are involved in extracurricular activities and find them to be supportive, providing a sense of belonging and increased self-esteem (Werner, 1984). Service learning has become a major thrust in education, and taking advantage of the opportunities it presents will help build resiliency (Henderson & Milstein, 1996; Keith, 1997).

Resilient students often mention that teachers, counselors, and other school staff have provided personal interest in and support for them (Geary, 1988; Coburn & Nelson, 1989) that influenced them to succeed. Resilient students find the interpersonal relationship aspect as well as the competence of these adults to be important (Geary, 1988). The resilient student wants school professionals to demonstrate caring, respect them for who they are, be able to get along with ease, listen without being intrusive, take them seriously, be available and understanding, provide encouragement, and share humor. In terms of competence, resilient students want the teacher to foster group goals, listen beneath the surface before disciplining, be fair in grading and instruction, encourage success, and know them academically (McMillan & Reed, 1994).

Characteristics of Successful School Programs

Richard Sagor (1996) identified five attributes that schools can integrate within the curriculum to encourage resiliency: competence, belonging, usefulness, potency, and optimism. Sagor asserted that educators must incorporate these attributes in educational experiences. This is neither difficult nor time-consuming. Sagor pointed out that good teaching and resiliency-building are the same. Educators continue to do what already works—what already helps instill resiliency within students.

Ten attributes of successful programs have been identified for at-risk students (McMillan & Reed, 1993; Westfall & Pisapia, 1994). These categories, expanded upon in the following pages, relate to characteristics and problems of at-risk students.

Early Intervention

As has been learned from experiences such as Head Start (Berrueta-Clement et al., cited in Trachtman, 1991) and special education (Fewell, 1995), early educational experiences in quality preschool programs can serve to decrease school failure stemming from poverty. Early monitoring of progress and providing assistance can help at-risk students avoid the all too frequent school failure and high dropout rates associated with challenging life circumstances. Early education has been related to better intellectual performance, reduction in the dropout rate, and reduction of placement in special education (Trachtman, 1991). Early educational intervention can also unlink negative family patterns and habits from low school success rates and increase early exposure to resiliency-building factors.

School Climate

A welcoming and pleasant school atmosphere will help students enjoy coming to school and increase the likelihood of their success. Noddings (1995) wrote that personal manifestations of care are "more important in children's lives than any particular curriculum or pattern of pedagogy" (p. 676). Cooperative learning (Johnson & Johnson, 1994), a sense of belonging (Edwards, 1995), and a positive environment (Mullis & Fincher, 1996) can be encouraged through alternative and enrichment activities, total school programs, more direct contact with teachers, counselors, and administrators, and use of positive reinforcement. Lewis, Schaps, and Watson (1995) wrote of developing the child's ethical and social aspects through a caring community. They said formation of trust and mutually satisfying relationships are important features of schools. School counselors can assume responsibility by their involvement in and coordination of total school programs that enhance community and unity.

School Personnel

The teacher plays a significant role in creating a positive school climate and in motivating students (Hetherington & Blechman, 1996). To be successful, school professionals must be positive and believe that they and their students can be successful. They are advised to be flexible, approaching each student as an individual with different needs, providing activities that lead to the development of an internal locus of control and a positive self-image, and offering students visible touchstones of their success. School professionals do well to keep themselves focused on the positive and the possible rather than on deficits. Thus, we must include students in creating a classroom community through classroom meetings, problem solving, and democratic procedures (Lewis, Schaps, & Watson, 1995). Counselors are pivotal in helping school personnel emphasize the positive, through staff development, as models, and by promoting wellness and resiliency in all facets of school life.

Small Class and School Size

Class and school size affect how much individual attention a teacher, counselor, or administrator can provide, how flexible the counselor or teacher can be in meeting individual needs, and how quickly a counselor or teacher will be able to notice and address problems as they develop. Small classes make it easier to provide a positive school climate and to interact personally and in a timely manner with parents, resulting in fewer behavior problems and higher achievement (Achilles, 1996, 1997; Finn, 1998).

Beyond class size, Sergiovanni (1995) focused on size of high school, reiterating Goodlad's findings in *A Place Called School*, and the value of smaller schools. Wynne and Walberg (1995) seconded this value on smaller schools, especially intimacy in education that can be developed more easily in smaller schools. According to Weissbourd (1996), many larger high schools are "creating more personal environments—environments in which children spend the bulk of their day with the same group of teachers and students—by clustering teachers and students, for example, or by creating schools within schools or houses within schools" (p. 63).

Parent Involvement

When parents work with their children to prepare them for preschool, the children experience fewer difficulties when they do enter school. Counselors can impact growing families when they work with parents of students who have preschool siblings. Later, parents should be invited to be participants in their child's education both at home and in the school building (Slavin, Madden, Dolan, & Wasik, 1996). Empowering parents as co-planners in their child's education is an effective way to increase their participation and to encourage them to reinforce academic activities at home (Lambie, in press). Special education, with its emphasis on parental involvement, is a model that general education can borrow for at-risk families (Pell & Cohen, 1995).

Counselors can advocate for meaningful family involvement in the schools by helping teachers and administrators recognize its importance and overall positive impact on adjustment, achievement, and self-esteem of students (Christianson, 1997). Henry (1996) challenges us to communicate with parents in ways that encourage collaboration, value diverse perspectives, and utilize problem solving to benefit the child.

Self-Esteem Building and Support

Increasing self-esteem is critical with at risk-students (Joseph, 1994). The first step in increasing self esteem may be finding an area in which a student can be successful and recognizing the student for the success. This can *hook* the student on success.

Volunteer projects and service learning can provide students with opportunities to feel good about themselves and their ability to contribute to their world (Keith, 1997; Lewis, Schaps, & Watson, 1995; Yoder, Retish, & Wade, 1996). Including students in decision making also helps to develop a sense of ownership and influence in the school community, building self-esteem in the process. Groups led by counselors can focus on increasing self-esteem/self-efficacy of students (Sonnenblick, 1997).

Guidance and Mental Health Counseling

Schools should provide opportunities for individual and group counseling support for individual students as well as their families, both at school and in the home (Edwards & Foster, 1995; Rak & Patterson, 1996). Confidentiality must be maintained, and meetings have to be held discreetly so students and families remain comfortable with the process. Counselors who remain creative, flexible, and nonjudgmental can work successfully with this population. Brief, solution-focused approaches should recognize cultural diversity. Consultation services (Kaplan, Turner, Norman, & Stillson, 1996) are invaluable with at-risk families and students.

Social and Life Skills/Vocational Education

Prerequisites for school success are having and using social skills (Sugai & Lewis, 1996). Good social and life-skills training as well as vocational programs make education relevant to students and increase their feeling that education is worthwhile (McMillan & Reed, 1993). Counselors can use the group context effectively to help students who come to school with insufficiently developed social skills to develop appropriate human interaction skills.

Although some (e.g., Barr & Parrett, 1995) question that vocational and career education programs succeed with at-risk students, others (McMillan & Reed, 1993; Westfall & Pisapia, 1994) indicate that students involved in vocational education tend to complete school. They also related that vocational classes tend to provide many of the positive attributes described previously, including smaller classes and positive classroom climate. Counselors are in a unique position to point out these advantages to the family and students who are at-risk for school failure. They can also be instrumental in countering the stigma that vocational education has in some communities. Comprehensive career guidance programs, coordinated by the counselor, should include community and family involvement and emphasize social and life-skills.

Extracurricular Activities

Many positive benefits are associated with extracurricular activities, including a sense of belonging and community, as well as greater opportunity to pursue interests and learn new things, both of which can increase self-esteem (Geary, 1988;

McMillan & Reed, 1994; Werner, 1984). After-school activities provide students with a safe, supervised atmosphere. Evidence cited in a review of at-risk students, by McMillan & Reed (1993), also suggests that extracurricular activities decrease the likelihood that a student will drop out of school.

We have to do more than offer these activities, though, because at-risk youth often do not feel connected to the school community. Counselors and other school personnel should invite, encourage, and facilitate youth participation. All school personnel must recognize the importance of positive leisure activities in developing resiliency. Extracurricular involvement must be seen as an integral part of the education experience that fosters resiliency and wellness.

Easing Grade Level Transitions

Students tend to drop out of school when they are making the transition between grades and school levels, such as between middle and high school. Schools can provide activities and services that prepare students for and support them through the transition. The counselor's role in this is paramount. Assistance with transitions and orientation of students, a traditional counselor role, fosters resiliency in students. Looping teachers with classes across grades is another way of dealing with transition problems (Lewis, Schaps, & Watson, 1995). Noddings (1995) encouraged this practice as a means of strengthening relationships. Small groups providing support for students who are retained a grade level are effective in countering the sense of loss and failure that students may experience when they are retained.

Together, these 10 characteristics of school programs serve as a guide for educators to increase resiliency in students who are at-risk for failure. School programs alone, however, will not foster resiliency to the extent desired. The environment beyond the school must be actively engaged as well (Waddock, 1995).

Resourcing and Creating Community

A child's behavior is influenced by many factors, only one of which is environment. Other factors include biological constitution, disposition, and developmental level. This last area—resourcing and creating community—is the major topic of this chapter. It focuses on the role of environment in fostering resilient behaviors.

Systems theory holds that behavior is affected by many interrelated systems. Thus, change in one subsystem (for example, the community) will reverberate throughout other interrelated systems including the classroom and schools. With Wang and Haertel's (1995) contention that resilience "provides a conceptual base for an intervention that calls for responsive classroom, school, and community environments" (p. 159), the importance of community joining with schools to build resilience in youth is clear. The counselors' coordination function facilitates this joining and places them in the role of *weaver of webs* and collaborative consultant (Keys, Bemak, Carpenter, & King-Sears, 1998).

One of the most successful means of encouraging resiliency is to create a school community that is positive and fosters a sense of belonging (Wang, Haertel, & Walberg, 1994). The African proverb says, "It takes a village to raise a child." In postmodern America the heart of that village is the school. A school has the opportunity to become the hub of a community that links and provides services through collaboration with external resources (businesses, volunteers, retirees, YMCAs and YWCAs, Boys/Girls Clubs, synagogues, mosques, and churches, as well as social-service agencies) that support and enhance everyone's efforts to rear healthy and whole children (Fowler & Corley, 1996). Resourcing and Creating Community provides for exploration of opportunities that schools offer to strengthen the proverbial village, through linking families and students to professional service providers and, perhaps more important, by creating a supportive and nurturing community by which students and families are connected in a caring manner (Lewis, Schaps, & Watson, 1995; Noddings, 1995; Wynne & Walberg, 1995).

Rationale for Creating Community

There is no better time than now for transforming communities to build resiliency in children and youth. Our society is on the edge of possibility. Our families are changing demographically, and technology has revolutionized the worlds of home and work. Yet the rise of poverty, crime, sexual promiscuity, drugs, and depression have made it difficult for families and schools to support and care for the nation's youth the way they once did. Zill and Nord (1994) and Waddock (1993) concluded that families today are less able to provide nurturing, supportive, safe, and secure environments where children can develop and learn. Communities must take stock and rearrange our resources to help children grow up to become responsible and actively productive members of this society (Dryfoos, 1994). With the intention of building both better learners, school personnel have an opportunity to lead the way as family and child advocates.

With a vision of social transformation, counselors and other educators can become partners not only in the development of a child but also in the preservation and development of the entire community (Booth & Dunn, 1996; Dryfoos, 1994). To achieve this, Haas (1993) suggested that schools must move away from the factory model of production with raw materials and move into a new era where schools adopt the metaphor of *family resource schools*—in which schools, as extensions of a child's family, provide the scaffolding for the child's growth that was once provided solely by relatives and neighbors. This will require a shift of attitudes about the roles of the school and of school personnel that must expand and evolve to meet the needs of the at-risk population. School counselors have been challenged to become advocates for school and community partnerships and to coordinate networks of resources for children and youth who are considered at-risk (Hart & Jacobi, 1992). Schools must go beyond the traditional "three Rs" and include the teaching and nurturing that parents have traditionally been expected to provide. Counselors and other school personnel must also reach out to parents through parent education, training, and support groups.

Although schools cannot be all things to all people, they must become more things to more people than they have in the past. Schools are in the unique position to help increase resiliency in children and youth by becoming part of a cohesive community that meets the needs of families of at-risk students. This is critical, not only for individual students and their families but also for the continued health and viability of our society. As an outgrowth of the National Commission on Children, Nickolas Hobbs (1975) wrote *The Futures of Children.* He stated, "Our failure to act today will only defer to the next generation the rising social, moral and financial costs of our neglect. Investing in our children is no longer a luxury, but a national imperative." This point is as appropriate today as it was in 1975, and the evidence of Hobbs' grave warning surrounds our cities and our people.

The presence of a support network is one of the most important factors in family adjustment during life-cycle changes and stresses. Schools can encourage support and should act as liaisons, linking at-risk students with public and private institutions, businesses, churches, retirees, and volunteers interested in and capable of providing services (Beck, 1994). The heart of service is in the relationship that is formed through interpersonal contact (Noddings, 1995). Schools can and should diagnose needs, collaborate and network, and share information as well as resources. They must also keep in mind that it is relationship that builds resiliency (Noddings, 1995). Mentoring, lunch buddies, Big Brothers/Big Sisters, tutoring by retirees, e-mail pen pals that link students with professors, and similar experiences will provide opportunities for the relationship building that fosters resilience (Rak & Patterson, 1996).

Schools must become part of the fabric that *gives back* to the community. Native American cultures emphasize giving back (Attnaeve, 1982), and those who give to others are held in highest regard. Service learning provides an opportunity for the school to connect with the community (Keith, 1997; Kleinbard, 1997). A class of adolescent students in a program for troubled youth might provide tutoring to kindergarten children who need to hear stories from supportive people. These same adolescents may be visited by senior citizens from the nearby community for retirees who share the experience of gardening. In this way all involved will benefit and realize the vital part they play in community life. In community we are inexorably linked with one another in ways that are critical, yet we forget the importance of sharing, community, and relationship—the human connection that gives meaning to our lives (Noddings, 1995). A gentler nation is aware of its potential and is in touch with its soul, connected across generations.

James Coleman (1987) concluded that the success students experience in parochial schools could be attributed to the crossing of generations encountered by religious organizations. "They are among the few in which the social capital of an adult community is available to children and youth." (p. 37). Therefore, community involvement is important for the success of children in school and as adults. Schools have to take a proactive stance to include citizens of all ages in meaningful relationships with children and youth, and members of the community must view themselves as central to the school's mission (Waddock, 1995).

At times, families need access to professional resources from the community. The goal of resourcing or referral is not to encourage family dependency on outside resources. Nor should families be expected to solve all their problems alone or be responsible for meeting all the needs of its members. Services are provided with the goal of reminding each family of its own resources so that, working together, they can draw out, through mutual clear and honest communication, the strengths, knowledge, and wisdom that are already there. The underlying belief here is reflected by the poet Gibran (1923) in the section from *The Prophet* titled "Teaching."

> No man can reveal to you aught but that which already lies half asleep in the dawning of your knowledge . . .
> If he is indeed wise he does not bid you enter the house of his wisdom, but rather leads you to the threshold of your own mind. . .
> For the vision of one man lends not its wings to another man. . . (pp. 56-57)

Counselors who assist families through referral to community resources from this frame of reference will develop important linkages and will foster resiliency-building in the process.

Frames of Reference

The counselor's understanding of the concepts of family resources and deficits will affect plans for, as well as interactions with, at-risk members. The individual and family may not be able to interpret the professional's attitude; however, when they deal with professionals who respect and view them as resourceful and consult with them as equal partners, trust is more likely to develop. To focus on the resources of an individual and family, the professional must assume that each has a wealth of assets that can be tapped (Dunst, Trivette, & Deal, 1994a). This does not mean that professionals ignore the family's deficits. Both resources and deficits can be acknowledged at the same time. The goal is to view the family's wholeness and strength.

Counselors must deal with and think about their frames of reference—how they view people in general, as well as how they view specific individuals. Discounting those who are at-risk and assuming that their lives are tenuous will lead to further losses and, in a subtle manner, may support self-fulfilling prophecies of those at-risk for failure in school or life (Rak & Patterson, 1996). If professionals' expectations for families who have children at risk are negative, they may miss the family resources as well as the possibilities the resources present for wholeness. Our society has had a jaundiced view of at-risk individuals and has focused for decades upon seeing deficits in those who have special needs—thereby failing to attend to the possibilities and resources.

The conceptualization of families as resourceful is an essential view with which to engage family members (Cameron & Vanderwoerd, 1997). When professionals view the family as resourceful and as a positive resource, they recognize that the need for additional resources is secondary and temporary. They also recognize that at certain times in the family's life cycle, the family may face an overload when attempting to meet demands. An appropriate analogy was presented by Imber-Black (1986): "The family has not suddenly become bankrupt in terms of its own resources, although its assets may be temporarily frozen or creating no interest" (p. 149).

A resource model of family functioning assumes that families continually create their own norms as they interact with history, culture, ethnicity, social class, politics, interpersonal relationships, individual quirks, and more. Counselors and other school professionals can frame their views of the family with this in mind and recognize the impact of context. Seeing context as significant, the professional is better able to make sense of family observations instead of seeing the family as abnormal. This focuses on the assets of the family while recognizing, but deemphasizing its deficits.

Sharing Information With Families

We provide the following information important to resourcing, focusing on areas in which school professionals serve as agents that link traditional and nontraditional families with supportive resources, thereby precluding their students from falling through the cracks (Greenawalt, 1994).

Helping individuals and family members not to be overly dependent upon outside resources is certainly good, but being independent does not mean having to meet all needs alone or within one's own family. The focus here is on sharing information that allows family members to learn more about family life and healthy communication and to know how to link with beneficial resources. Interdependence is the outgrowth of connection with others and builds the fabric of the community, which is relationship. This is a critical factor in producing resiliency.

Although sharing information with most families of at-risk students will present no difficulty, some will resist input from school professionals (Campbell, 1993). Some family members will consider it to be bordering on an invasion of privacy or indicative of perceived failure or inadequacy of the parent. Other parents may conjure up a racial, religious, or gender bias.

For example, in one family the suggestion that a child join a little League Team may be considered a positive intervention that fits the child's developmental level and offers a social outlet. In another family the same suggestion may be seen as squelching the child's natural creativity by requiring the child to take part in an organized sport rather than allowing exploration of unique physical and social needs. The professional who is aware of the uniqueness of families might recommend to the second family that members take time to play as a family and to explore each individual's creativity through interaction. Suzuki, a form of teaching a musical instrument that involves teaching the parent as well, or the family learning a foreign language together would fit such a family.

Resourcing

Not all at-risk families are dysfunctional; however, most would benefit from having resources available at times of increased stress. Assistance in resourcing can allow families to take advantage of their family and social networks, as well as free or low-cost social services. A support system is one of the most important factors in family adjustment to life-cycle changes and stresses. This support includes school-community resourcing, family resourcing, social systems resourcing, and external resourcing.

School-Community Resourcing

Characteristics of effective school and community programs are as follows, along with some suggestions for establishing effective services.

Schools as a Source of Support. Aside from the informal support that families receive from friends, relatives, and each other, school personnel are often the main source of support for families who need assistance (Burke & Cigno, 1996). Frequently, the schools are the first to recognize a problem and to contact the parent when a problem arises. Just a few of the challenges that students face and bring with them when they enter school are poverty, drug abuse, learning problems, health problems, child neglect and abuse, teen pregnancy, homelessness, and even single-parent families and two-parent families where both parents work. Thus, schools have become a place where basic education alone is not enough.

Unfortunately, a student's problems too often are left to the teacher or building principal and eventually are shuffled on from elementary to middle school or junior high and on to high school where a once preventable problem grows to crisis magnitude. Counselors have the necessary skills and training to ensure that families know about and benefit from the myriad services available in most communities.

Support Based on Need. The kinds of support services provided should depend on the family's desires and needs, the community resources available, and the specific challenges encountered. In today's complex society, families cannot meet all of their needs. Sooner or later, they will need and benefit from different kinds and levels of support. Although one might expect that two-parent, nonminority homes experience low stress and are able to cope, communicate, and parent effectively, this is not always the case (Allen, Brown, & Finlay, 1992). Whereas middle-income families are less likely to need financial help to pay for child care or health services, they can benefit from peer support or parenting classes as well as a number of other services matched to their needs.

Supportive School Programs. Among the human services located in or facilitated by the school, according to Dryfoos (1994), are school health teams, school-based dental health and general health clinics, mental health services, psychosocial counseling programs for substance abuse, teen pregnancy, and school failure, training in social skills and in parenting, assistance in occupational selection, mentoring programs, recreation and cultural enrichment classes, after-school centers for academic tutoring, and job training with links with businesses, universities, and nonprofit organizations. Programs show up in all shapes and sizes, reflecting the needs of the communities that they serve.

Programs involving senior citizens can be orchestrated or encouraged by counselors. Surrogate grandparents from the community paired with students can serve as tutors, special friends, group co-leaders, or lunch buddies. Nearby senior citizen residences are one source of referrals for a grandparent program.

Counselors can coordinate mentor programs (Christiansen, 1997). These programs could pair older students with younger ones, similar to the Big Brothers/Big Sisters programs, or pair professors from a neighboring teacher-training institution with students. Other sources for mentors include local businesses, service organizations, sororities/fraternities, and college students. Counselors can train mentors to use active listening skills, to listen for problems that might require professional intervention and referral, and to recognize new avenues for building resilience in children and youth throughout the community. In this role they serve as ambassadors within the community and beyond.

A worthwhile investment for schools is a family resource library in a room dedicated to family involvement. By defining a space for family members to gather and support their children's educational program and personal development, schools speak to the value of family involvement. A parent guidance advisory committee involves parents in meaningful ways with schools and provides another means of doing this. Involvement of and input from parents regarding the school environment, what programs and activities to include, and the school's mission and goals can facilitate the community building necessary for enhancing resiliency in students.

Counselors, school psychologists, and school social workers can organize and facilitate time-limited or ongoing support groups for parents. The nature of the groups will vary by community and other variables related to the children and families. Techniques such as enactment (mentioned later in this document) are powerful means of eliciting change in these groups.

Sibling group counseling is meaningful for siblings of children who are at-risk or have special needs. *Sibshops* (Meyer & Vadasy, 1994) is an excellent resource model for counselors to use when arranging and implementing sibling groups. Family retreats led by counselors with training in working with families allow family members the opportunity to get away from home to learn from other families as well as the professionals that facilitate the retreat. Family play group counseling led by counselors provides an avenue for increasing resiliency-building in families and healing wounds in a supportive and nonjudgmental environment. Teaching conflict resolution (Johnson, 1997) in group contexts is useful for families who need to develop their skills in dealing with intense feelings. Conflict resolution that is taught in schools and practiced in families and community settings will reinforce the skills and enhance resiliency-building beyond the school environment.

Counselors can generate many more ideas that encourage school-community resourcing. A planning committee that involves the counselor with representatives from students, family members, administration, and teachers can assume responsibility for generating, as well as orchestrating, practical means of providing school-community resources through needs assessment, program planning, and evaluation.

Prior to the opening of Saltonstall Elementary School, linkages with city officials, college faculty, and teachers were already in place. One feature that developed is the *Friday Club*. Every Friday community partners teach elementary students how to do a variety of things. For example, one club built, painted, wallpapered, and decorated doll houses. In another, students learned to play soccer. Meanwhile, teachers spent the 2 hours planning lessons (Fowler & Corley, 1996).

Sonnenblick (1997) described a middle-school program for girls identified as at-risk for dropping out and for membership in youth gangs. The program consisted of weekly club meetings and mentor relationships with school staff and some parents. It offered service activities and recreational events designed to promote personal growth and release from pressure to act "street-smart," impress boys, and deal with excessive family responsibility.

The Monticello, Arkansas, schools work with HIPPY (Home Instruction Program for Preschool Youngsters) to help parents develop social and interpersonal skills to reduce feelings of isolation (Greenawalt, 1994; Harvard Family Research Project, 1995). For example, parents of children entering kindergarten shared their feelings of inadequacy with the school counselor.

Schools in Indianapolis, Indiana, indicated that they wanted more contact with parents and more parent participation in the schools. Working with Parents In Touch (PIT), schools have set aside 20 minutes a day for parent-teacher conferences, created activity calendars to inform and make suggestions to parents, set up homework contracts, homework hotlines, call-in services, parent workshops, and even medical and dental services. Many parents have received other assistance through the various services the school system provides (Harvard Family Research Project, 1995).

Before schools can effectively begin to create programs and links to help students and their families, schools and school districts must decide what they want to achieve and provide. The possibilities abound, and counselors can assist in the planning process by serving along with other school personnel, parents, and community representatives on an advisory committee that assesses school/community needs and resources, establishes goals, and implements programs to promote community pride and improve school morale and climate.

According to the Harvard Family Research Project's *Raising Our Future* (1995), after 25 years of scientific research, Ramsey and Ramsey (1992, p. 5) determined that effective programs embody seven characteristics:

1. They start sooner and continue longer.

2. They increase the frequency of interactions with participants.

3. They give students direct learning experiences.

4. They provide for comprehensive services to students.

5. They take learning style into consideration for at-risk students.

6. They support students who are making a transition into elementary school.

7. They enhance cultural beliefs, traditions, and practices.

Weissbourd (1996) presented 11 principles for schools to use when working with vulnerable children. Counselors can support and help implement these principles in the school and community.

1. Emphasize academics that focus on results and academic achievements.

2. Respond to students' emotional/social challenges and material needs.

3. Develop a safe, orderly school environment.

4. Imbue students with high expectations across all areas of school functioning.

5. Collaborate with parents and children in a respectful manner, and when a problem develops, systemically view the roles of the student, family, community, and school.

6. Identify underlying causes of problems so negative interactions become cycles of success.

7. Share authority with parents and engender a sense of belonging; reaching out to all parents by creating experiences in which they can be involved meaningfully.

8. Engage the noncustodial parent and significant other adults in the child's life.

9. For administrators: Cull out the benefits of experienced teachers' wisdom, and find them the "time, support, and resources they need to work with struggling students" (p. 181), and foster teachers' professional development.

10. For administrators: Support counselors and nurses, and encourage all school staff members to support one another.

11. Form "effective partnerships with community services, businesses, and other community resources. These partnerships are designed to achieve specific goals that further children's academic achievements" (p. 181).

In school-community resourcing we have emphasized school personnel building resilience in students by utilizing strengths within the school. Today's circumstances demand that counselors adopt a systemic view and reach out to families and communities to build resilience in children.

Family Resourcing

Family resourcing encourages counselors to identify family strengths and builds on Weissbourd's principles of collaboration, highlighting the interdependence of systems. We initially define family resources, then provide information about four family resource areas that can be tapped during interactions with the family members. School personnel can catalog resources and problems for later use. *Cataloging* means tracking family patterns on a family-by-family basis. This allows for a greater use of family resources. Strategies for counselors to encourage the wise use of family resources are as follows.

Definition of Family Resources. Several types of family resources have been identified in the literature (Attneave & Verhulst, 1986; Dunst, Trivette, & Deal, 1994b; Hansen & Coopersmith, 1984; Hansen & Falicov, 1983; Karpel, 1986a). Karpel (1986b) defined family resources as "those individual and systemic characteristics among family members that promote coping and survival, limit destructive patterns, and enrich daily life" (p. 176).

Karpel's (1986b) first element of family resource is the *ability to access coping and survival techniques.* Families face a variety of predictable as well as unexpected stressors throughout the family life cycle. Families vary widely in their resources for promoting coping and survival (Pell & Cohen, 1995). Some families cope well with the challenges, while others struggle. Those who struggle with coping daily may benefit from family resourcing. Assistance can be a means of promoting resiliency in all family members.

Another element of family resources identified by Karpel (1986a) is the *ability of the family to limit destructive patterns.* This relates both to external stressors and to internal patterns such as attacking, demeaning, neglecting, or diminishing another. Limiting destructive patterns helps to prevent stressors from piling up (McCubbin & Patterson, 1982) within the family. Some families seem to resist destructive patterns, which Karpel (1986a) paralleled with immunological resistance. Examples of resistance are a wife's resisting her husband's invitation for a co-alcoholic marriage, parents exercising a clear hierarchy over an acting-out teenager, and a child's resistance to being triangulated into the parents' conflicts.

A third element of family resource relates to the *ability to enrich and enjoy daily life* (Karpel, 1986a). This element goes beyond dealing with problems and centers on life's more rewarding aspects—caring and sharing, satisfaction, and pleasure. The ability to bounce back—one characteristic of resiliency—is enhanced by the family's ability to enjoy simple aspects of daily life.

Karpel (1986a) expanded upon this three-element definition and described *personal resources* as well as *relational resources* in families. Examples of personal resources include self-respect, protectiveness, hope, tolerance, and affection. Relational resources include respect, reciprocity, reliability, repair, flexibility, family pride, and loops of interaction.

Personal and relational resources within families are affected by three characteristics: capacity, rules, and active efforts. For example, the relational resource of reciprocity, or give-and-take, in a family relates to how the family balances and holds fair play. Counselors can assess each family member's capacity for reciprocity and consider this in conjunction with the family rules (e.g., Dad is the disciplinarian). Finally, active efforts by family members to initiate and collaborate on reciprocity can be considered. Counselors, school social workers, and psychologists are the professionals most likely to look closely at these factors. Observations can be added to the catalog of family process, noting strengths and challenges faced by family members.

Areas of Family Resource. Imber-Black (1986) described four family resource areas that direct professionals' attention to the family's strengths as opposed to their deficits. The first area has to do with *religious, cultural, and racial identity.* McGoldrick, Giordano, and Pearce (1996) have addressed the issue of ethnicity and family therapy, and Carter (1995) has focused on the importance of racial identity.

Avoiding stereotypical thinking about people from other backgrounds is beneficial to healthy family-professional interactions. Counselors should be aware of their own values and any prejudices they may have. Looking for strengths in others' ethnic background is helpful, and being aware of differences is critical to avoid misinterpreting behavior. For example, Mexican-American families typically are cooperative rather than competitive. A counselor who tries to use a competitive strategy to motivate a Mexican-American child may get lackluster results that counselors might misunderstand. This child could easily be seen as unmotivated, whereas in truth the child might be easily motivated by a cooperative learning task. The cooperative task would serve as a resiliency-building strategy as well.

Counselors should observe family interactions with an eye toward recognizing and cataloging family identity, if any. Families also identify with religious groups, and these allegiances serve as a family resource. Some church groups have considerable resources that might be tapped in helping families. This linkage is important as schools reach out to community resources and form partnerships for mentoring and other resiliency-building programs.

A second area (Imber-Black, 1986) relates to the family's *inner language,* which identifies it as a family both to family members and to others. The professional should look for myths, metaphors, jokes, humor, and words or phrases with special meaning to the family members, note any examples, and use them at appropriate times. For example, a family may refer to itself as having "dogged determination." When the family is going through a particularly rough time, the counselor could provide support and encouragement in terms of the family members' own view of themselves by complimenting them on "hanging in there with dogged determination," a resiliency characteristic to be reinforced.

A third area of resource categorized by Imber-Black relates to *individual and family commitments, loyalties, or a sense of connections.* Counselors should be aware of and publicly recognize commitments and loyalties. Examples are a grandmother who takes over the custody and rearing of her unmarried teenage daughter's child, and a family that goes to all ends to be sure the wheelchair-bound child does not miss out on family outings. Counselors should validate family convictions about including everyone in the family fun, thus reinforcing several aspects of resiliency.

The fourth area (Imber-Black, 1986) relates to the *capacity of the family to interact with the outside world* in such a way that preserves and enhances its integrity as a family. The outside world is defined as everything beyond the family. Families have rules for dealing with the external world, beyond family, in the same way that rules develop for family relationships. Counselors should build upon family resources in dealing positively with people outside the family. School professionals are members of that outside world, and it is valuable to know how the family has interacted in the past with school professionals. If prior experiences with the schools have been negative, the current school professionals should attempt to engage the family members, which may mean overcoming negative expectations on both sides.

For example, former school professionals may have seen parents as recalcitrant. If the counselor views the family as having been protective rather than antagonistic, he or she will be better able to focus on the family's positive resources and functional survival skills for making it through an antagonistic situation.

Strategies. School professionals can assess, monitor, and reinforce all four areas of family resources. Again, when collaborating with any family, it is good to look for resources versus deficits (Malatchi, 1997). Everyone who has contact with the family of an at-risk student can contribute to cataloging. A file on each student is valuable, to which information on family resources can be added. The file can be divided into the resource areas described here or according to any other system that meets the needs of the counselor or other professional.

There is good reason to include family members in the process of recognizing their resources. Team meetings might include an agenda item on family resources. When family members attend meetings, professionals can observe the family's use of inner language, as well as how they interact with the outside world.

It is important not only to note but also to reinforce family resources. When counselors are in meetings with family members or in one-to-one interactions, they should take every opportunity to validate family resources related to resiliency. For example, a counselor might tell a mother, "I can see your son Timmy takes after the rest of your family when it comes to being gentle. I wish you had seen him with the new student from Iran."

It is also important to validate and encourage healthy family functioning that enhances resiliency. When spouses take a vacation together and tell the schools they will be out of town, school professionals should verbally reinforce their taking care of their marriage and encourage them not to worry about the child at school ("We can handle whatever might come up here").

The sibling subsystem also should be validated as a source of support and a valuable family resource. Too often, people think the siblings are in a rivalry. Counselors need to help frame existing or potential sibling relationships positively (Meyer & Vadasy, 1994; Powell & Gallagher, 1993; Seligman, 1991). Kahn (1986) has an excellent chapter about the sibling system with bonds of intensity, loyalty, and endurance. Knowing whether the family is either disengaged or enmeshed can also be helpful when making comments that might encourage balance and sibling support. When the family is disengaged, the school professional can facilitate alignment between siblings, fostering the resiliency-producing relationship bonds. For example: "I've noticed that you and your brother act quite differently, but it seems as though the two of you have had a similar experience in your family."

Dysfunctional family interaction patterns or roles, such as scapegoating (Satir, 1988), can be changed. For example, the professional might say, "It looks as if Sandy is the 'fall guy' in this family. I wonder if she might be bringing a fresh perspective instead?" Another dysfunctional role that can be transformed is that of *parentified* child, frequently the oldest daughter in families that are extremely stressed. Counselors can suggest the family allow the daughter an opportunity for extracurricular activities, thereby fostering resiliency. School professionals should not unwittingly reinforce *parentifying* (Nichols, 1996). For instance, comments about what a "great little mother" a child is are inappropriate.

Another resource of potential strength lies in the extended family. Family members may overlook the real possibilities the extended family has to offer. We can learn from African American families in which extended family members often pitch in, not only to care for but also to participate in, rearing the children in their families (Hines & Boyd-Franklin, 1996). The counselor can ask whether a grandparent, aunt, uncle, or other relative might be able to help with various functions. A simple suggestion that an unmarried aunt or uncle babysit once a week so that the parents could have time together might never have occurred to the family. Extended family members can serve as important role models for coping with stress and for increasing resiliency in children and youth.

Family retreats, family play-group counseling, and parent education groups can be implemented using flexible scheduling, with babysitting provided for infants and toddlers. When focusing on family as resource, the school professional can be creative and energizing. Many possibilities exist. It is up to the creative professional to make these possibilities real and to bring them to the school's attention.

Social Systems Resourcing

Cameron and Vanderwoerd (1997) defined social networks as "the actual, reccurring linkages between a focal person and significant others in her or his environment" (p. 27). Social support is from "instrumental, educational, social, and psychological assistance actually received by the focal person" (p. 27).

Extensive research shows that social support helps some individuals and families to cope better with a stressful event and improve health (Hobfoll & Stephens, 1990), life expectancy (Kennedy, Kiecolt-Glaser, & Glaser, 1990), and success on exams and other academic tasks (Goldsmith & Albrecht, 1993). Paradoxically, other evidence suggests that some forms of support may be detrimental (Kaplan & Toshima, 1990; Swann & Brown, 1990; Goldsmith, 1992). Advocating for continued social support, Burleson, Albrecht, and Sarason (1994) indicated that supportive communication can contribute in positive or negative ways to recovery from illness, coping with loss, managing chronic health problems, dealing with daily disruptions, performing tasks, and feeling good about themselves and their quality of life (p. xiii).

Families should be encouraged to pursue supportive relationships that reduce their stress and increase their well-being. Schools can help to facilitate social support by connecting people with others who face similar challenges or to people in their community who could serve as positive role models. The counselor, for example, could encourage designation of a room for families to meet with other families who share the same needs and with families who have already overcome similar obstacles. The room should be inviting, with careful attention to selecting the leaders that will facilitate the meetings. Counselors, social workers, and psychologists should all be particularly aware of the impact that social support networks have on individuals and families. Group co-leadership by a helping professional and a "veteran" successful parent can facilitate interaction and minimize the resistance of individuals who are defensive or mistrust professionals.

Researchers interested in at-risk families have written about social network interventions and the value of social support (Berger, 1984; Coopersmith, 1983; Dunst, Trivette, & Deal, 1994a; Dunst, Trivette, & Cross, 1986; Friedrich & Friedrich, 1981; Intagliata & Doyle, 1984; Kazak, 1987; Kazak & Marvin, 1984; Rueveni, 1979). Just as the resources of the immediate and extended family are valuable, so, too, are the resources of the family's social network.

Families that face a high level of stress will look to their social network for resources that enable them to reduce and better cope with that stress. Unfortunately, the social network may unwittingly add to the stress by providing contradictory and competing suggestions. One person may suggest a favorite intervention, and another might offer an diametrically opposing idea. This can be confusing. Thus social network interventions can be invaluable in getting all interested parties to understand and support realistic strategies.

Background. Systems theorists propose that social networks, with their attendant support, directly and indirectly influence attitudes, expectations, behavior, and knowledge of family members and other members of the network. Bronfenbrenner (1979) described ecological units or social networks topologically. He saw them as a nesting of concentric structures, one embedded within the other. The child and family are at the center. Broader ecological systems move out in concentric circles, to include relatives, friends, neighbors, and other acquaintances. Beyond that are larger social units (discussed under External Resourcing), encompassing the neighborhood mosques, churches, and synagogues, as well as social organizations, the workplace, play areas, and school.

Waddock (1993) also described ecological units or social networks topologically. She saw them as webs of influence outward from the center, where the child and school are center. Broader ecological systems move outward and include social workers, then the larger community where services are provided, then state policies, until at the outer edge of the web lies the nation and federal government. Counselors can serve as *web weavers* to develop linkages that promote resiliency-building for families and students between and among these systems.

Social systems theorists contend that these ecological units do not function in isolation but, rather, interact within and between levels. Thus, changes in one unit or subsystem will reverberate and impact upon other units or subsystems. When professionals understand this dynamic, reciprocal, systemic relationship, they will be more likely to plan appropriate interventions that promote resiliency by considering input from the school, the family, and the community, and its impact on students considered at-risk.

Definition of Social Support Systems. Social support networks are links among individuals and groups. These links relate to size, satisfaction, density, connectedness, and frequency of contacts. As Dunst, Trivette, and Cross (1986) indicated, "Social support is a multidimensional construct that includes physical and instrumental assistance, attitude transmission, resource and information sharing, and emotional and psychological support" (p. 403). They added that a consensus of social systems theorists view social support networks as serving the function of nurturing and sustaining links that support others daily as well as in times of need and crises.

Turner (1981) named social support as a component of psychological well-being. Although he did not study at-risk families, he did study four diverse populations, one of which was adults with hearing losses. He also traced research about social support and concluded that social support is most important in stressful circumstances. In his study, Turner adopted Cobb's (1976) view of social support, in which Turner related social support as providing information that result in people believing they are cared for and loved, esteemed and valued, and belong to a "network of communication and mutual obligation in which others can be counted on should the need arise" (pp. 358-359).

Findings and Strategies for Social Systems Resourcing. Social networks, with their attendant support, directly and indirectly influence the attitudes, expectations, behavior, and knowledge of family members and other members of the network alike. In this web of influence, counselors have the distinct opportunity, through the "collective anchoring of the individual life" (Haas, 1993, p. 215), to develop students by providing the tools that allow them to forge a tranquil, thriving, and equitable society.

The Harvard Family Research Project (1995) stated, "The heart of family support programs is the web of relationships connecting staff with families, parents with children, and parents with other parents" (p. 11). This study found that schools had to overcome some formidable obstacles including the negative images held toward schools, reaching families that are poor and isolated, and overcoming transportation and child-care barriers that make parents reluctant to leave their neighborhoods. Thus, counselors and other professionals must be willing to go into the communities to meet parents in their homes or, possibly, at a neutral establishment such as a library, mosque, church, synagogue, community center, park, or even a fast-food restaurant to strengthen relationships and to provide the necessary assistance.

As the Harvard Family Research Project (1995) found, outreach programs are complex and difficult. Professionals must be adept at disarming resistant and often dysfunctional attitudes and also able to convince the family of its need for assistance. A frame of reference that stresses the family's resources and ability to overcome challenges will facilitate this task. Many valuable concepts in family systems approaches can help counselors effectively share information with parents of at-risk and special-needs students, thereby promoting resiliency and reducing harmful stress.

A variety of findings presented in the literature on social network systems indicate the value of considering social systems as essential assets in reducing stress on family members. Dunst et al. (1986) examined effects of social support on parents of children with mental retardation and physical impairment, as well as developmentally at-risk children. These researchers were concerned with the impact of social support on "personal well-being, parental attitudes toward their child, family integrity, parental perceptions of child functioning, parent-child play opportunities and child behavior and development" (p. 403). Their findings supported the positive impact of social support systems on families having children with disabilities.

Kazak and Marvin (1984) studied stress and characteristics of social support networks of families with and without a child with a disability. They found that mothers are particularly subject to personal stress. Unlike previous research findings, they did not find a significant difference in the stress levels of marital dyads. They suggested that professionals view the differences between families (and their networks) as appropriate accommodations to raising a child with a disability. Specifically, they found both the overinvolvement of the mother and child and the peripheral role of the father in parenting to be appropriate and to be respected by professionals, "unless there is ample evidence that the marital relationship is impaired" (p. 75).

Kazak (1987) examined mothers and fathers of children with disabilities or chronic illnesses and compared them with matched parents of children without disabilities. She considered personal stress, marital satisfaction, and size and density of the social network. She found that only the mothers of the children with disabilities experienced higher levels of stress. Again, her findings indicated no differences in marital satisfaction. Finally, Kazak found that mothers of children with disabilities had higher-density social networks than comparison mothers.

Intagliata and Doyle (1984) examined social support for parents of children with developmental disabilities by training them in interpersonal problem-solving skills. From this pilot study, they concluded that enhanced problem-solving skills of these parents was relevant and could be a helpful intervention.

Friedrich and Friedrich (1981) compared parents of children with a disability with a control group of parents of children without disabilities. One of many measures included social support. They concluded that "an appropriate avenue of intervention might increase the availability of social support for these parents to help them cope with this additional stress" (p. 553).

Minuchin and Fishman (1981) described the technique of *enactment*. In enactment, people act out the problem as contrasted with simply talking about the problem in the family. For example, if a student is disobedient to the parents during a social systems networking session, the counselor might ask the parents what they plan to do. This allows the counselor to see the problem as it evolves naturally. It may also present an opportunity for the counselor to intervene while serving as a model for the whole social systems network.

Berger (1984) recommended the use of enactments in network interventions. He suggested creating a context in which those in attendance act differently toward one another. This helps when attempting to look at the family and social network as valuable resources: "Network interventions, then, are especially powerful contexts for the use of enactments that alter network members' definition of the handicapping condition or of what needs to be done about that condition" (p. 134).

Social support has a positive impact upon families with at-risk children. School professionals must consider this when relating to families (Rak & Patterson, 1996). Counselors, social workers, and psychologists in the schools should be particularly aware of the influence of social systems on building resilience.

External Resourcing

External resource networking helps families form supportive links with resources outside their family, school, or social network. This might include tapping into volunteer groups, social service agencies, support groups and counseling services.

A host of potentially valuable resources are available in every community and state, as well at the national level, which most professionals know about only generally. Every school should have a resource file that all professionals can consult in their efforts to provide resource information to families. As professionals learn about additional resources, they can add to the file. School professionals might even find resources beneficial for themselves or their families.

Each file should contain evaluation information, including feedback from family members who have used the resources. They can be asked to respond to a brief questionnaire covering their impressions and reactions to different resources. Space should be allotted for general comments from family members who have used the resource. If any school professionals have used a resource or know someone who has, they can add their comments to the evaluation. Neither parents nor professionals should be required to sign the questionnaire, nor should they quote or identify by name anyone receiving confidential services.

These files should be checked and purged at least once a year. Telephone numbers and contact people change regularly, as do opportunities for group as well as individual support. It is frustrating to hear of a resource that is no longer available. When this happens, parents may decide not to follow any other leads.

To generate a file, a group of professionals can get together and divide the workload and pool their findings. A search of resources in the community begins by contacting the local school board for brochures or information on agencies and services available to families. Then the community mental health center should be contacted for information on its services, as well as other resources with which the personnel are familiar. Community parks and recreation associations can also be contacted. Another source of services consists of local churches. The local United Way may also be a source of agencies that provide services and support, as well as a clearinghouse for agencies needing volunteer assistance.

Beyond the local community, professionals can contact state agencies such as the Department of Education for information on state-level services and opportunities for networking with families of at-risk and special-needs children. The division responsible for special education in the state should be contacted, along with the Department of Mental Health. The division on volunteerism within the state government may also be of service.

National agencies should be investigated. These are beneficial contacts for a variety of types of disabilities. Also, many organizations can be found through a national directory. Examples include the Association for Retarded Citizens (ARC), Learning Disabilities Association (LDA), and Bereaved Parents/Compassionate Friends. The textbook by Lambie (in press), on which this publication is based, contains a lengthy resource list in an appendix, which will be helpful in finding national resources.

References

Achilles, C. M. (1997). Small classes, big possibilities. *School Administrator, October,* pp. 6–15.

Achilles, C. M. (1996). Students achieve more in smaller classes. *Educational Leadership, 53,* 76–77.

Allen, M., Brown, P., & Finley, B. (1992). *Helping children by strengthening families: A look at family support programs.* Washington, DC: Children's Defense Fund.

Attneave, C. (1982). American Indians and Alaska Native families: Emigrants in their own homeland. In M. McGoldrick, J. K. Pearce, & J. Giordano (Eds.), *Ethnicity and family therapy* (pp. 55–82). New York: Guilford.

Attneave, C. L., & Verhulst, J. (1986). Teaching mental health professionals to see family strengths: Core network interventions in a hospital setting. In M. Karpel (Ed.), *Family resources* (pp. 259–271). New York: Guilford.

Barr, R. D., & Parrett, W. H. (1995). *Hope at last for at-risk youth.* Boston: Allyn & Bacon.

Beck, V. (1994). "Opportunity plus": A school and community based tutorial program for elementary students. *Elementary School Guidance and Counseling, 29,* 156–159.

Berger, M. (1984). Social network interventions for families that have a handicapped child. In J. Hansen & E.I. Coopersmith (Eds.), *Families with handicapped members* (pp. 127–136). Rockville, MD: Aspen.

Booth, A., & Dunn, J. F. (Eds.). (1996). *Family-school links: How do they affect educational outcomes?* Mahwah, NJ: Lawrence Erlbaum.

Bronfenbrenner, U. (1979). *The ecology of human development.* Cambridge, MA: Harvard University.

Burke, P., & Cigno, K. (1996), *Support for families: Helping children with learning disabilities.* Brookfield, VT: Ashgate.

Burleson, B. R., Albrecht, T. L., & Sarason, I. G. (Eds.). (1994). *Communication of social support: Messages, interactions, relationships, and community.* Thousand Oaks, CA: Sage.

Cameron, G., & Vanderwoerd, J. (1997). *Protecting children and supporting families: Promising programs and organizational realities.* Hawthorne, NY: Aldine de Gruyter.

Campbell, C. (1993). Strategies for reducing parent resistance to consultation in the schools. *Elementary School Guidance and Counseling, 28,* 83–91.

Carter, R. T. (1995). *The influence of race and racial identity in psychotherapy: Toward a racially inclusive model.* New York: John Wiley & Sons, Inc.

Christiansen, J. (1997). Helping teachers meet the needs of students at risk for failure. *Elementary School Guidance & Counseling, 31*(3), 204–210.

Cobb, S. (1976). Social support as a moderator of life stress. *Psychosomatic Medicine, 38,* 301–314.

Coburn, J., & Nelson, S. (1989). *Teachers do make a difference: What Indian graduates say about their school experience.* (ERIC Document Reproduction Service No. ED 306 071)

Coleman, J. A. (1987). Families and schools. *Educational Researcher, 16*(6), 32–38.

Coopersmith, E. I. (1983). The family and public service systems: An assessment method. In J. Hansen & E. Keene, (Eds.), *Diagnosis and assessment in family therapy* (pp. 83–100). Rockville, MD: Aspen.

Cowan, P. A., Cowan, C. P. & Schulz, M. S. (1996). Thinking about risk and resilience in families. In E. M. Hetherington & E. A. Blechman, (Eds.), *Stress, coping, and resiliency in children and families* (pp. 1–38). Mahwah, NJ: Lawrence Erlbaum.

Cuban, L. (1989). The "at-risk" label and the problem of urban school reform. *Phi Delta Kappan, 70,* 780–784.

Dryfoos, J. G. (1994). *Full-service schools: A revolution in health and social services for children, youth, and families.* San Francisco: Jossey-Bass.

Dunst, C. J., Trivette, C. M., & Deal, A. G. (1994a). Resource-based family-centered intervention practices. In C. J. Dunst, C. M. Trivette, & A. G. Deal (Eds.), *Supporting and strengthening families: Volume 1, Methods, strategies and practices* (pp. 140–151). Cambridge, MA: Brookline Books.

Dunst, C. J., Trivette, C. M., & Deal, A. G. (1994b). *Supporting and strengthening families: Volume 1. Methods, strategies and practices.* Cambridge, MA: Brookline Books.

Dunst, C. J., Trivette, C. M., & Cross, A. H. (1986). Mediating influences of social support: Personal, family, and child outcomes. *American Journal of Mental Deficiency, 90,* 403–417.

Edwards, D. L. (1995). The school counselor's role in helping teachers and students belong. *Elementary School Guidance & Counseling, 29*(3), 191–197.

Edwards, D. L., & Foster, M. A. (1995). Uniting the family and school systems: A process of empowering the school counselor. *School Counselor, 42*(4), 277–282.

Fewell, R. R. (1995). Early education for disabled and at-risk children. In M. C. Wang, M. C. Reynolds, & H. J. Walberg (Eds.), *Handbook of special and remedial education: Research and practice* (2d ed., pp. 37–60). New York: Elsevier Science.

Finn, J. D. (1998). *Class size and students at risk: What is known? What is next.* Washington, DC: U.S. Department of Education. (On-line www.ed.gov/offices/oeri/at-risk)

Fowler, R. C., & Corley, K. K. (1996). Linking families, building community. *Educational Leadership, 53*(7), 24–26.

Friedrich, W. N., & Friedrich, W. L. (1981). Psychosocial assets of parents of handicapped and nonhandicapped children. *American Journal of Mental Deficiency, 85,* 551–553.

Frymier, J. (1992). *Growing up is risky business, and schools are not to blame.* Bloomington, IN: Phi Delta Kappa.

Frymier, J., & Gansneder, B. (1989). The Phi Delta Kappa study of students at-risk. *Phi Delta Kappan, 71*(2), 142–146.

Garmezy, N., & Rutter, M. (Eds.). (1983). *Stress, coping, and development in children.* New York: McGraw-Hill.

Geary, P. A. (1988). *"Defying the odds?": Academic success among at-risk minority teenagers in an urban high school.* (ERIC Document Reproduction Service No. ED 296 055)

Gibran, K. (1923). *The prophet.* New York: Alfred E. Knopf.

Goldsmith, D. (1992). Managing conflicting goals in supportive interaction: An integrative theoretical framework. *Communication Research, 19,* 264–286.

Goldsmith, D., & Albrecht, T. L. (1993). The impact of supportive communication networks on test anxiety and performance. *Communication Education, 42,* 142–158.

Greenawalt II, C. E. (1994). Educational outreach programs. In C. E. Greenawalt (Ed.), *Educational innovation: An agenda to frame the future* (pp. 413–433). Lanham, MD: University Press of America.

Haas, T. (1993). School in communities: New ways to work together. In G. A. Smith (Ed.), *Public schools that work: Creating community* (pp. 215–245). New York: Rutledge.

Haggerty, R. J., Sherrod, L. R., Garmezy, N., & Rutter, M. (1994). *Stress, risk, and resilience in children and adolescents: Processes, mechanisms, and interventions.* Cambridge, UK: Cambridge University.

Hansen, J. C., & Coopersmith, E. I. (Eds.). (1984). *Families with handicapped members.* Rockville, MD: Aspen.

Hansen, J. C., & Falicov, C. J. (Eds.). (1983). *Cultural perspectives in family therapy.* Rockville, MD: Aspen.

Hart, P. J., & Jacobi, M. (1992). *From gatekeepers to advocate: Transforming the role of the school counselor.* New York: College Entrance Examination Board.

Harvard Family Research Project. (1995). *Raising our future: Families, schools, and communities joining together.* Cambridge, MA: Author.

Henderson, N., & Milstein, M. M. (1996). *Residence in schools: Making it happen for students and educators.* Thousand Oaks, CA: Corwin.

Henry, M. (1996). *Parent-school collaboration: Feminist organizational structure and school leadership.* Albany, NY: State University of New York.

Hetherington, E. M., & Blechman, E. A. (Eds.). (1996). *Stress, coping, and resiliency in children and families.* Mahwah, NJ: Lawrence Erlbaum.

Hines, P. M., & Boyd-Franklin, N. (1996). African American families. In M. McGoldrick, J. Giordano, & J. K. Pearce (Eds.), *Ethnicity and family therapy* (2d ed., pp. 66–84). New York: Guilford.

Hobbs, N. (1975). *The futures of children.* San Francisco: Jossey-Bass.

Hobfoll, S. E., & Stephens, M. A. P. (1990). Social support during extreme stress: Consequences and intervention. In B. R. Sarason, I. G. Sarason, & G. R. Pierce (Eds.), *Social support: An interactional view* (pp. 497–481). New York: John Wiley.

Imber-Black, E. (1986). Toward a resource model in systemic family therapy. In M. Karpel (Ed.), *Family resources: The hidden partner in family therapy* (pp. 148–174). New York: Guilford.

Intagliata, J., & Doyle, N. (1984). Enhancing social support for parents of developmentally disabled children: Training in interpersonal problem solving skills. *Mental Retardation, 22*(1), 4–11.

Jens, K. G., & Gordon, B. N. (1991). Understanding risk: Implications for tracking high-risk infants and making early service decisions. *International Journal of Disability, 38,* 211–224.

Johnson, D. (1997). *Reaching out: Interpersonal effectiveness and self-actualization* (6th ed.). Needham Heights, MA: Allyn & Bacon.

Johnson, D., & Johnson, R. (1994). *Learning together and alone: Cooperative, competitive, and individualistic learning.* Needham Heights: MA: Allyn & Bacon.

Joseph, J. M. (1994). *The resilient child: Preparing today's youth for tomorrow's world.* New York: Insight Books/Plenum.

Kahn, M. D. (1986). The sibling system: Bonds of intensity, loyalty, and endurance. In M. Karpel (Ed.), *Family resources: The hidden partner in family therapy* (pp. 235–258). New York: Guilford.

Kaplan, C. P., Turner, S., Norman, E., & Stillson, K. (1996). Promoting resilience strategies: A modified consultation model. *Social Work in Education, 18*(3), 158–168.

Kaplan, R. M., & Toshima, M. T. (1990). The functional effects of social relationships on chronic illness and disability. In B. R. Sarason, I. G. Sarason, & G. R. Pierce (Eds.), *Social support: An interactional view* (pp. 427–453). New York: John Wiley.

Karpel, M. (Ed.). (1986a). *Family resources: The hidden partner in family therapy.* New York: Guilford.

Karpel, M. (1986b). Testing, promoting, and preserving family resources: Beyond pathology and power. In M. Karpel (Ed.), *Family resources: The hidden partner in family therapy* (pp. 174–234). New York: Guilford.

Kazak, A. E. (1987). Families with disabled children: Stress and social networks in three samples. *Journal of Abnormal Child Psychology, 15,* 137–146.

Kazak, A. E., & Marvin, R. S. (1984). Differences, difficulties and adaptation: Stress and social networks in families with a handicapped child. *Family Relations, 33,* 66–77.

Keith, N. Z. (1997). Doing service projects in urban settings. In A. S. Waterman (Ed.), *Service-learning: Applications from the research.* Mahwah, NJ: Lawrence Erlbaum.

Kennedy, S., Kiecolt-Glaser, J. K., & Glaser, R. (1990). Social support, stress and the immune system. In B. R. Sarason, I. G. Sarason, & G. R. Pierce (Eds.), *Social support: An interactional view* (pp. 253–266). New York: John Wiley.

Keys, S. G., Bemak, F., Carpenter, S. L., & King-Sears, M. (1998). Collaborative consultant: A new role for counselors serving at-risk youths. *Journal of Counseling & Development, 76,* 123–133.

Kleinbard, P. (1997). Youth participation: Integrating youth into communities. In J. Schine, (Ed.), *Youth participation: Integrating youth into communities* (pp. 1–18). Chicago: University of Chicago.

Lambie, R. (In press). *Family systems within educational contexts: Understanding at-risk and special-needs students.* Denver: Love.

Lewis, C. C., Schaps, R., & Watson, M. (1995). Beyond the pendulum: Creating challenging and caring schools. *Phi Delta Kappan, 76,* 547–554.

Liontos, L. B. (1991). *Involving the families of at-risk youth in the educational process.* (ERIC Document Reproduction Service No. ED 328 946)

Malatchi, A. (1997). Family partnerships, belonging, and diversity. In L. Power-deFur and F. Orelove (Eds.), *Inclusive education: Practical implementation of the least restrictive environment* (pp. 91–115). Gaithersburg, MD: Aspen.

Masten, A. S. (1994). Resilience in individual development: Successful adaptation despite risk and adversity. In M. C. Wang & E. W. Gordon, *Educational resilience in inner-city America* (pp. 3–25). Mahwah, NJ: Lawrence Erlbaum.

McCubbin, H. I., & Patterson, J. (1982). Family adaptation to crises. In H. McCubbin, A. Cauble, & J. Patterson (Eds.), *Family stress, coping and social support.* Springfield, IL: Charles C Thomas.

McGoldrick, M., Giordano, J., & Pearce, J. (Eds.). (1996). *Ethnicity and family therapy.* New York: Guilford.

McMillan, J., & Reed, D. (1993). *Defying the odds: A study of resilient at-risk students.* Richmond, VA: Virginia Commonwealth University, Metropolitan Educational Research Consortium.

McMillan, J., & Reed, D. (1994). At-risk students and resiliency: Factors contributing to academic success. *Clearing House, 67*(3), 137–140.

Meyer, D. J., & Vadasy, P. F. (1994). *Sibshops: Workshops for siblings of children with special needs.* Baltimore, MD: Paul H. Brookes.

Minuchin, S., & Fishman, H. (1981). *Family therapy techniques.* Cambridge, MA: Harvard University.

Mullis, F., & Fincher, S. F. (1996). Using rituals to define the school community. *Elementary School Guidance & Counseling, 30,* 243–251.

Nichols, W. C. (1996). *Treating people in families: An integrative framework.* New York: Guilford.

Noddings, N. (1995). Teaching themes of care. *Phi Delta Kappan, 76*(9), 675–679.

Pell, E. C., & Cohen, E. P. (1995). Parents and advocacy systems: A family systems approach. In M. C. Wang, M. C. Reynolds, & H. J. Walberg (Eds.), *Handbook of special and remedial education: Research and Practice* (2d ed., pp. 371–392). New York: Elsevier Science.

Peng, S. S., Wang, M. C., & Walberg, H. J. (1992, April). *Resilient students in urban settings.* Paper presented at annual meeting of American Educational Research Association, San Francisco, CA.

Powell, T. H., & Gallagher, P. A. (1993). *Brothers and sisters: A special part of exceptional families* (2d ed.). Baltimore: Paul H. Brookes.

Rak, C. F., & Patterson, L. W. (1996). Promoting resilience in at-risk children. *Journal of Counseling & Development, 74*(4), 368–373.

Rhodes, W. A., & Brown, W. K. (1991). *Why some children succeed despite the odds.* New York: Praeger.

Rueveni, U. (1979). *Networking families in crisis: Intervention strategies with families and social networks.* New York: Human Sciences.

Rutter, M. (1994). Stress research: Accomplishments and tasks ahead. In R. J. Haggerty, L. R. Sherrod, N. Garmezy, & M. Rutter (Eds.), *Stress, risk, and resilience in children and adolescents: Processes, mechanisms, and interventions* (pp. 354–385). Cambridge, UK: Cambridge University.

Sagor, R. (1996). Building resiliency in students. *Educational Leadership, 54*(1), 38–43.

Satir, V. (1988). *The new peoplemaking.* Mountain View, CA: Science and Behavior Books.

Seligman, M. (1991). Siblings of disabled brothers and sisters. *The family with a handicapped child* (2d ed., pp. 181–201). Boston: Allyn and Bacon.

Sergiovanni, T. J. (1995). Small schools, great expectation. *Educational Leadership, 53*(3), 48–52.

Shepard, H. A. (1995). On the realization of human potential: A path with a heart. In D. Kolb, J. Osland, & I. Rubin (Eds.), *The organizational behavior reader* (6th ed., pp. 168–178). Englewood Cliffs, NJ: Prentice Hall.

Slavin, R. E., & Madden, N. (1989). What works for students at risk: A research synthesis. *Educational Leadership, 46*(5), 4–13.

Slavin, R. E., Madden, N. A., Dolan, L. J., & Wasik, B. A. (1996). *Every child, every school: Success for all.* Thousand Oaks, CA: Corwin.

Sonnenblick, M. D. (1997). The GALSS club: Promoting belonging among at-risk adolescent girls. *School Counselor, 44,* 243–245.

Sugai, G., & Lewis, T. J. (1996). Preferred and promising practices for social skills instruction. *Focus on Exceptional Children, 29*(4), 1–16.

Swann, W. B., Jr., & Brown, J. D. (1990). From self to health: Self verification and identity disruption. In B. R. Sarason, I. G. Sarason, & G. R. Pierce (Eds.), *Social support: An interactional view* (pp. 150–172). New York: John Wiley.

Trachtman, R. (1991). Early childhood education and child care: Issues of at-risk children and families. *Urban Education, 26*(1), 25–42.

Turner, R. (1981). Social support as a contingency in psychological well-being. *Journal of Health & Social Behavior, 22,* 357–367.

Waddock, S.A. (1993). The spider's web: Influences on school performance. *Business Horizons, 36*(5), 39–48.

Waddock, S. A. (1995). *Not by schools alone: Sharing responsibility for America's education reform.* Westport, CT: Praeger.

Wang, M. C., & Gordon, E. W. (Eds.). (1994). *Educational resilience in inner-city America: Challenges and prospects.* Hillsdale, NJ: Lawrence Erlbaum.

Wang, M. C., & Haertel, G. D. (1995). Educational resilience. In M. C. Wang, M. C. Reynolds, & H. J. Walberg (Eds.), *Handbook of special and remedial education: Research and practice* (2d ed., pp. 159–200). Hillsdale, NJ: Lawrence Erlbaum.

Wang, M. C., Haertel, G. D., & Walberg, H. J. (1994). Educational resilience in inner cities. In M. C. Wang & E. W. Gordon

(Eds.), *Educational resilience in inner-city America: Challenges and prospects* (pp. 45–72). Hillsdale, NJ: Lawrence Erlbaum.

Weissbourd, R. (1996). *The vulnerable child: What really hurts America's children and what we can do about it.* Reading, MA: Addison-Wesley.

Werner, E. E. (1984). Resilient children. *Young Children, 40*(1), 68–72.

Westfall, A., & Pisapia, J. (1994). Students who defy the odds: A study of resilient at-risk students. *Research Brief #18.* Richmond, VA: Virginia Commonwealth University, Metropolitan Education Research Consortium.

Wolin, S. , & Wolin, S. J. (1996). Beating the odds: Some kids who have been dealt a losing hand end up winning the game. What can we learn from them? *Learning, 25,*(1), 66–68.

Wolin, S. J., & Wolin, S. (1993). *The resilient self: How survivors of troubled families rise above adversity.* New York: Villard.

Wynne, E. A., & Walberg, H. J. (1995). The virtues of intimacy in education. *Educational Leadership, 53*(3), 53–54.

Yoder, D. I., Retish, E., & Wade, R. (1996). Service learning: Meeting student and community needs. *Teaching Exceptional Children, 28*(4), 14–18.

Young-Eisendrath, P. (1996). *The gifts of suffering: Finding insight, compassion, and renewal.* Reading, MA: Addison-Wesley.

Zill, N., & Nord, C. W. (1994). *Running in place: How American families are faring in a changing economy and an individualistic society.* Washington, DC: Child Trends.

Prevention of Substance Abuse Among Teenagers

Sharon E. Robinson-Kurpius

One hard, cold reality facing American society is that many teenagers are using and abusing chemical substances. This fact is accentuated by the public attention being given to adolescent substance abuse. For example, Nancy Reagan often spoke to kids, urging them to refuse to even try drugs. In addition, many famous movie and sports figures have become active in advising teens to stay away from drugs. Recognizing that teen drug use has become a national problem, Congress passed the *Drug-Free Schools and Community Act* of 1986, which for the first time gave the Department of Education $200 million for drug education in schools (Education Department starts school year, 1987).

According to statistics from the 13th annual survey of drug use by high school seniors, drug use for inhalants, phencyclidine (PCP, or angel dust), sedatives, amphetamines, and hallucinogens declined from 1986 to 1987, but the use of alcohol and cigarettes has not decreased (Money and high visibility, 1987). At some time, 67.2% of the seniors smoked cigarettes, and 92.2% consumed alcohol. Driving under the influence of alcohol has long been recognized as the leading cause of death among teenagers. In addition, research has shown that alcohol use is associated with 60% of all murders, 40% of all assaults, and 33% of all rapes and child molestings (Dept. of Health & Human Services, 1984; Tinklenberg, 1973).

In addition to alcohol and cigarettes, almost all adolescents have been exposed to illicit drugs, and a high percentage have experimented with them. According to Borton (1983), half of all 7th graders have been pressured to try marijuana. By 12th grade, about 57% have given in to this pressure (Johnston, O'Malley, & Bachman, 1984), and 5.5% use it daily. These statistics do not take into consideration those who have dropped out of high school and were even more likely to have used drugs. Use rates among seniors for other substances "used at some time in their life" include: alcohol (93%), stimulants (27%), cocaine (16%), hallucinogens (15%), sedatives or barbiturates (14%), inhalants (14%), tranquilizers (13%), opiates (non-heroin) (10%), LSD (9%), and amyl and butyl nitrates (8%) (Beschner, 1986, p. 2).

In spite of these statistics, little is known about the adolescent substance user. Perhaps examining this growing national problem from a variety of perspectives will facilitate our understanding of the issues involved in substance abuse.

Psychosocial Perspective

Jalali, Jalali, Crocette, and Turner (1981) classified adolescent users as experimenters, compulsive users, or floaters. Floaters alternate between experimenting with drugs and being compulsive users. Although experimenters may try drugs out of boredom or curiosity, in the hope of having fun, or in response to peer pressure, they typically use drugs in small amounts and infrequently. Usually they try only alcohol or marijuana, are aware of the difference between having fun and getting into danger, and typically do not develop serious drug problems.

A few unlucky teens, however, become compulsive users, and their lives and health will be at risk because of their drug abuse. For these youth, drugs are an escape. Generally, they have poor relationships with their parents, with their conventional peers, and with school personnel, and they have strong relationships with drug-using peers (Dembo, Blount, Schmeider, & Burgos, 1985). Intrapersonally these youth often experience self-derogation, depression, and alienation, which are acted out as rebelliousness, aggressiveness, independence, and risk-taking behaviors aimed at sensation seeking (Dembo et al., 1985). More and more of their time and energy is devoted to getting high, and they become connoisseurs of street drugs (Beschner, 1986). Although the data are not exact, between 4% and 5% of teenagers between the ages of 15 and 19 are estimated to use illicit drugs regularly. This represents about 1 million teenagers—a staggering number.

According to the Dembo et al. (1985) review of the literature on the etiology of drug use, of these million, the user who is white is most likely to be using alcohol or marijuana, or both. Ethnic minority youth (Black, Native American, and Hispanic) are more likely to use alcohol and drugs other than marijuana. Use seems to escalate until around age 19, when it declines. But the earlier the use starts, the greater is the potential for deviant behavior, self-derogation, and feeling rejected by family and peers. In response to feeling rejected, these individuals seek a social climate that accepts and supports drug use.

In a study of over 1,000 high school students, Newcomb, Chou, Bentler, and Huba (1988) found that the primary reason for using alcohol or cannabis (marijuana) was not the need for help to get through the day. The most prominent reasons were peer involvement and self-medication. Boys used drugs more frequently than girls and reported using drugs to enhance positive affect, creativity, and social cohesion. Older teens used drugs to reduce negative affect more than did younger teens. These results are especially important for school counselors in designing prevention programs for teens. The role of schools will be discussed in detail later.

Historical and Legal Perspective

A review of the political and legislative history of drugs reveals that substance abuse among adolescents is a relatively recent problem. In the early 1800s, the only drug-related law America had was the excise tax on whiskey. Although a regulatory tax was placed on opium in 1842, by 1875 opium dens were flourishing, and there were reports that young women and men from respectable families were being ruined. By 1914 an estimated 1 in every 400 Americans was addicted to opium or its derivatives.

Leading the fight against narcotics use, Dr. Alexander Wright drafted the *Harrison Act*, which outlawed heroin and put medical controls on other opiates and cocaine. In 1919 the Supreme Court upheld the Narcotics Division decree that providing any narcotic to an addict was not a legitimate medical purpose and physicians who did so were to be arrested. Between 1919 and 1929, 75,000 narcotics arrests were made, 25,000 of whom were physicians and druggists (Ray & Ksir, 1987).

During this period, Richard Pearson Hobson warned of demonic drug pushers and created the image of the dope fiend. His speeches and writings on teenage addiction led to passage of the *Marijuana Tax Act* in 1937; this brought marijuana under the same legal control as narcotics, with the same criminal penalties for sale or possession. Harry Anslinger, Director of the Federal Bureau of Narcotics, claimed that marijuana was the "assassin of youth" and that it caused insanity, murder, rape, and impotence (Mandel & Feldman, 1986). One of his most memorable images was of "rosy-cheeked, innocent girls, lured to inner-city neighborhoods by a misguided sense of excitement, waking up after smoking marijuana for the first time with the realization that they had been debauched by lower-class males" (Mandel & Feldman, 1986, p.23).

Heroin was gaining popularity among inner-city white youths in street gangs, and the young addict of the 1950s looked and behaved like the dope fiend earlier described by Hobson. To counteract the growth of heroin use, the *Narcotics Drug Control Act* of 1956 mandated tough penalties for every offense except first-offense possession and sanctioned the death penalty for anyone caught selling heroin to a minor.

With the 1960s came a shift in the type of drug used and a corresponding increase in drug usage. The 400 experts who participated in the 1962 Kennedy White House Conference on Drugs, and coined the term "drug abuse," indicated that the drug arena was characterized by inadequate information and misinformation, supported the use of civil commitment to allow medical treatment of drug abuse, and fostered the initiation of projects to address the social problems of delinquency and poverty.

Between 1964 and 1970, youths across America were becoming drug-conscious. Studies on LSD were conducted at Harvard, marijuana was openly smoked on many college campuses, and for the first time there were active pro-drug advocates (Mandel & Feldman, 1986). Drugs were used for "getting in touch" with oneself, for improved socialization, and for enhancing one's senses and realms of awareness. Young middle-class white youth had discovered the "information gap" (which some called the generation gap) between the reality of drugs and what they had been told (Mandel & Feldman, 1986).

By 1970, however, the flower children of 1967 had trouble coping with the drugs they had played with, and many were now burned-out speed freaks or heroin addicts. There were overdoses, admissions to emergency rooms, and bad trips. Between 1963 and 1969 the arrest of teens under age 18 for drug use increased four-fold. There was a flagrant "disregard of drug laws by large numbers of young people who were not all members of the under privileged and criminal classes" (Ray & Ksir, 1987, p. 42).

In 1969 Richard Nixon proclaimed a "War on Drugs" and increased the federal anti-drug budget from $40 million in 1969 to $750 million in 1973. Half was for law enforcement and half for treatment programs. The War on Drugs was an uphill battle, with drugs about equal to alcohol in popularity among adolescents. In many ways the use of drugs had been normalized; youth no longer saw drug use as deviant behavior. Indeed, many young men returning from Vietnam were addicted to drugs. During each year in the 1970s, however, 49% to 57% of those arrested for drugs were under age 21 (Mandel & Feldman, 1986).

The present law of the land, the *Controlled Substances Act* of 1970, expanded the role of Community Mental Health Centers and Public Health Service Hospitals in the treatment of drug abuse, authorized the development of drug education materials and workshops for professionals as well as school personnel, and established maximum penalties for manufacturing/distributing and for possession of drugs categorized into five schedules. For example, for a second offense of selling cocaine, the maximum prison term is 30 years, a fine up to $50,000, and six years' probation after release from prison (Ray & Ksir, 1987).

The drug-related arrest rate among young whites is declining and in 1983 was approximately half of the 1978 rate. In their study of seniors' use rates between 1978 and 1983, Johnston et al. (1984) reported decreases both in use of marijuana in the last 30 days (37% in 1978 and 25% in 1983) and in the daily use of marijuana (11% in 1978 and 5.5% in 1983). Similar decreases were found in use of sedatives, inhalants, tranquilizers, and hallucinogens. In contrast, the use of cocaine and stimulants has steadily increased.

Although youth may not be alarmed at someone smoking a joint or possessing several ounces of marijuana, the *Hutto v. Davis* (1982) ruling testifies to the feeling of those representing the nation. Davis was arrested for possession of 9 ounces of marijuana, was convicted on two counts of possession with intent to sell, and was sentenced to 40 years in jail. He appealed his sentence as being cruel and unusual punishment, but the U.S. Supreme Court ruled against him (Inciardi, 1986).

It is self-evident that everyone should know the drug laws of his or her state. The local library is a useful resource for state criminal codes and local drug laws. In addition, teens, their parents, and school personnel should be aware of the rights of minors who are arrested. As a result of *In re Gault* (1967), juveniles have a right to notice of the charges, a right to counsel, a right to confront and cross-examine witnesses, privilege against self-incrimination, a right to a transcript of the legal proceedings, and a right to an appellate review. Minors do *not* have a right to bail or to a jury trial.

The Psychophysiology of Drugs

In addition to knowing the psychosocial and legal perspectives of drug abuse, a basic understanding of how drugs affect the body is important. No matter what drug is taken—aspirin for a headache or cocaine to feel high—the drug must go through several phases: absorption, transportation, action, metabolization, and excretion. For some drugs these five phases occur in a predictable manner and in a short amount of time. For other substances, the process is erratic and can occur over an extended time.

Drugs are taken into the body in several different ways, the most common of which is oral. When drugs are swallowed, they are absorbed through the intestinal walls into the bloodstream. Alcohol, sedatives, and barbiturates, for instance, are taken orally. Marijuana, nicotine, and inhalants are smoked/inhaled and enter the bloodstream through the lungs. Heroin is injected directly into a vein. Snorting is the preferred method of taking cocaine, which is then absorbed through the mucous membranes.

The blood carries drugs to all parts of the body. Because *all* drugs have side-effects, physiological and behavioral reactions are not always predictable. The effects of a drug depend on many variables including the type, potency, and purity of the drug, the contaminant used to cut the drug, the user's personality, the social environment in which the drug is taken, and an individual's physiology, especially the nervous system.

It is evident that drugs interfere with the normal functioning of the nervous system as well as other organs in the body. When drugs are abused and overused and when drugs are combined, the effects can be deadly. The two greatest dangers are respiratory failure and cardiac arrest. Those who combine alcohol with sedatives, barbiturates, or tranquilizers are particularly at risk for respiratory failure; they will just stop breathing. No drug is free of toxic effects; some are minor, but others are deadly serious (Julien, 1978).

Alcohol, Marijuana, Cocaine, and Inhalants

Now that a variety of perspectives on substance abuse has been presented, it is time to focus on some of the drugs that adolescents abuse.

Alcohol

As previously noted, alcohol was the first drug regulated in the U.S. Since Prohibition was repealed in 1933, the trend has been to relax the laws on intoxicating beverages. With the steady increase in death resulting from driving while intoxicated (DWI), however, Congress authorized the withholding of federal highway funds from any state that did not raise its legal drinking age to 21 by 1986.

As Schonberg and Schnoll (1986) have pointed out, alcohol and marijuana are the drugs that adolescents frequently abuse. In 1983 at least 93% of a large national sample of seniors reported having drunk alcohol, 5.7% indicated daily drinking, and 41% claimed occasional hinging (Johnston et al., 1984).

When consumed, alcohol functions as a depressant. Because it is almost completely metabolized and the rate of oxidation is slow, alcohol has a long duration of action, half-life, which cannot be controlled (Ray & Ksir, 1987). At a blood alcohol level (BAL) of .05 percent, there is lower alertness, relaxing of inhibition, impaired judgment, and usually a sense of feeling good. As the BAL increases, judgment ability declines, reaction time slows, and both sensory and motor capabilities are impaired. Intoxication is officially reached at .20 BAL, a stupor is reached at .30, and .35 is the minimal level that can result in death from intoxication (Ray & Ksir, 1987). When a woman drinks heavily during pregnancy, the unborn baby can be at risk for fetal alcohol syndrome, which causes physical and behavioral abnormalities, and spontaneous abortions are twice as likely (Ray & Ksir, 1987).

Physical damage from alcohol use is rare in adolescents just because they probably have not been abusing it for a long enough time. With prolonged abuse, however, gastritis with hemorrhaging and inflammation of the pancreas can result (Schonberg & Schnoll, 1986). Bleeding, severe vomiting, and changes in the blood can result in hospitalization. Chronic alcoholism in adults can produce chronic liver disease, inflammation of various nerves, and impaired memory (Schonberg & Schnoll, 1986). Withdrawal symptoms for teens who have been heavy alcohol users include perspiring, agitation, brief seizures, tremors, and disorientation.

Alcohol is currently the most significant substance abuse agency among adolescents. It negatively affects cognitions, behaviors, and one's body and has been linked to increased crime, violence, and suicide. Heavy drinking by a teen who is pregnant can be dangerous for the baby and for the teenager herself.

Marijuana

Although marijuana is about equal to alcohol in popularity, even less is known about its effects. From 1937 to 1971 it was legally classified as a narcotic, and in large doses, it can produce hallucinogenic effects. Since the late 1960s, however, society has been far more concerned with the more potent and dangerous substances appearing on the black market than with marijuana.

Marijuana and hashish come from the cannabis plant and get their psychoactive effect from THC (tetrahydrocannabinol). Grades or types of marijuana include regular marijuana, which is 2% to 5% THC; sensimilla, which contains about 8% THC; and hashish, which can be up to 50% THC if made into hash oil.

When marijuana is smoked, the THC is absorbed rapidly into the blood. While having a sedative effect and causing an enjoyable dreamy high, marijuana is thought to alter the metabolization of serotonin and dopamine. Schonberg and Schnoll (1986) cite considerable research on the negative effects of marijuana on brain, cardiovascular, pulmonary, endocrine, and psychological functioning.

Causing short-term memory loss and depressing one's ability to learn, marijuana smoking has been linked to the "amotivational syndrome," in which smokers are lethargic, lack motivation, and are content to do nothing. This becomes a special concern for youth who use marijuana before or during the school day in that they are impairing both their desire and their ability to learn. The long half-life of marijuana means that daily smokers may be continually high because the marijuana is never out of their system, and this further contributes to the amotivational syndrome.

Many of the effects of smoking marijuana are similar to those of drinking alcohol. In addition to red eyes, there are lowered secretions of sex hormones, impaired motor coordination, reaction time, and sensory perception, and decreased ability to follow moving objects. With the poorer motor coordination and distorted time and distance perceptions, driving under the influence of marijuana presents the same safety risks as driving under the influence of alcohol. In fact, many consider marijuana to be the second leading cause of death or injury by car accidents among adolescents.

Although no current research indicates that a physical addiction to marijuana occurs, this may be because the existing research on the effects of marijuana is in its infant state. Chronic smoking of marijuana does impair air flow in and out of the lungs, and only long-term research will be able to verify the relationship between marijuana smoking and cancer.

Marijuana has many advocates, as well as many adversaries who believe they should publicize every evil related to marijuana, whether backed by research or not. Initial research has shown that its effects are not harmless, but neither are they devastating, and that the primary concern is for women using marijuana during pregnancy and for the psychosocial, educational, and physical development of adolescents who engage in daily heavy use. As Ray and Ksir (1987) have pointed out, there is no area of science in which emotion about the issue has played such a heavy and influential role as in the smoking of marijuana.

Cocaine

Stimulants, used to reverse mental and physical fatigue, are increasing in use among adolescents. Three well known categories of stimulants are caffeine, amphetamines, and cocaine. Cocaine, derived from the coca plant, has become the recreational drug of the 1980s. Crack (or "rock") is the street term for a smokable form of cocaine. Freebasing is the term for smoking the basic cocaine, derived from the salt, cocaine hydrochlorine. Taking cocaine results in an intense, short-lived high for a few moments and stimulation for 2 to 3 hours. This high and stimulation are followed by depression.

Any form of cocaine produces a powerful psychological addiction or dependence. The body quickly develops a tolerance for cocaine. Therefore, because cocaine is a short-acting drug, repeated administrations are needed to avoid withdrawal symptoms. Withdrawal includes the cocaine blues (dysphoria) and profound anguish (psychological depression). Large doses, or cocaine hinging, lead to a state of irritability, restlessness, and paranoia (Ray & Ksir, 1987). In severe cases, paranoid psychosis can result. When the drug is finally metabolized and excreted, long-lasting depression occurs. Fatalities do occur after either acute respiratory failure or circulatory collapse (Schonberg & Schnoll, 1986). The abstinence syndrome, which occurs in chronic users, is characterized by insomnia, depression, agitation, nausea, and headaches. The desire to remove these symptoms through drug readministration is highly potent, although the cocaine habit is very expensive.

In spite of the cost, cocaine abuse—particularly the use of crack—has become a major national concern. One indicator of the rapid increase in the use of crack is that in 1985 no calls to the national cocaine hotline (1-800-COCAINE) referred to crack; in mid-1986, one third of the calls were from crack addicts (Ray & Ksir, 1987). Whatever form of cocaine is taken, it is a dangerous, addictive drug.

Inhalants

Young adolescents between the ages of 11 and 15 are the primary users of inhalants, although use of inhalants has steadily declined with the increase in marijuana use. Airplane glue, gasoline, cleaning fluids, and aerosols are some of the compounds these young teenagers sniff. Each of these compounds contains volatile hydrocarbons that cause a strong, short-lived euphoric high. Symptoms of inhalant use include "lack of coordination, restlessness, excitement, confusion, disorientation, difficulty in walking (ataxia), delirium, and coma" (Schonberg & Schnoll, 1986, p 54). Repeated use can result in giddiness, dizziness, and hallucinations; long-term use can cause brain, liver, kidney, and nerve damage (Schonberg & Schnoll 1986). A syndrome called "sudden sniffing death" can occur when inhalant abuse is immediately followed by excessive exercise and stress. Teens may enjoy the giddy high that is connected with sniffing, but they again are playing with a potentially dangerous substance.

Prevention and Education

What most concerned adults are asking themselves is: How do we intervene to prevent teenagers from using drugs? How do we intervene to decrease or stop substance abuse that is already occurring? Two primary milieus for prevention and intervention are schools and the family. In addition, a variety of treatment programs address substance abuse.

Schools

The primary responsibility for substance abuse prevention and education has fallen on the public schools. Yet research (Goodstadt, 1980) has shown that just giving students drug education and information (often misinformation) has failed to deter drug use. During the 1970s, educators tried to fight drug abuse by employing affective education through the use of approaches such as Parent Effectiveness Training (Gordon, 1970), the DUSO kit (Dinkmeyer, 1973), and the Magic Circle technique (Ball, 1974). These seemed not to have a significant positive impact on adolescent drug use.

In 1982, Horan and Williams were able to demonstrate that general assertiveness training and drug-specific assertiveness training positively influenced junior high school students' willingness to use alcohol and marijuana. At a 3-year follow-up, these students reported less actual drug use and demonstrated higher levels of assertiveness.

What has evolved in the last decade is a variety of educational programs that attempt to address the teen drug problem. Nancy Reagan was the prime mover for the "Just Say No" approach, which tells kids to simply refuse to even try drugs. This, however, may be a very narrow approach to a multidimensional, complex problem.

Research on the effectiveness of the "Here's Looking at You Two" curriculum, which emphasizes increasing self-esteem, reducing peer influence, and providing drug information, has been promising (Swisher, Nesselroade, & Tatanish, 1985). Unlike the "Here's Looking at You Two" curriculum, most other curriculum packages either are not supported by empirical research or have not been systematically evaluated. A few of the commercially available drug intervention and prevention curricula that attempt to address the drug problem from multiple perspectives include:

1. *8:30 Monday Morning* (American Business Men's Research Foundation, Suite 1208, Michigan National Bank Tower, Lansing, MI 48933.) An alcohol prevention program for grades 7–12. Activities include alcohol-specific education and development of decision-making skills.

2. *Decision About Drinking: Alcohol Education Curriculum* (CASPAR, 226 Highland Ave., Somerville, MA 02143). Covers facts and attitudes about alcohol, reasons people drink, responsible decisions about drinking, alcoholism as a family illness, and more. Lesson plans for each grade level (3–12) include sequence of topics and behavioral objectives.

3. *Here's Looking at You Two* (Comprehensive Health Education Foundation, 20814 Pacific Highway South, Seattle, WA 98188). This curriculum is a merging of two projects of the Educational School District 121—"Here's Looking at You" (alcohol program) and "If Drugs Are the Answers, Who Knows the Questions?" Support materials, course outline, and activity guide for teachers are available.

4. *LIONS/Quest Program: Skill for Adolescence* (Quest National Center, 6655 Sharon Woods Blvd., Columbus, OH 43229, toll-free 1-200-446-2700). Positive prevention program for grades 6–8, focusing on 7 units, each with a wide variety

of classroom activities. The program provides detailed instruction for teaching the course and includes a student textbook, teacher manual, student workbook, and parent seminars. Local Lions' Clubs offer financial support for teacher training.

5. *The Drinking/Nondrinking Curriculum for Teachers* (James Snoddy, MSU/ Program CORK, 401 Erickson Hall, Lansing, MI 48824). Alcohol education program funded by Operation CORK and developed by Michigan State University for elementary school teachers. Consists of 17 individual modules grouped into four clusters. Four themes continue through all the modules: multicultural relationships, peer relationships, family relationships, and the range of drinking/nondrinking behaviors.

6. *Project PRIDE; Elementary Attitudes and Skills for Substance Abuse Prevention* (CODAC Behavioral Health Services, 151 S. Tucson Blvd., Suite 122, Tucson, AZ 85716). A comprehensive K–6 curriculum that includes lesson materials for each grade level, ongoing classroom activities, guidelines for school policy development, parent involvement and education, resource materials, and teacher inservice component.

7. *Children Are People* (Children Are People, Inc., 493 Selby Ave., St. Paul, MN 55102, 612/277–4031). A K–6 curriculum providing detailed lesson plans for teachers, with flexibility in how and when they are utilized. Key concepts covered include chemical use in society, emotional awareness, and social competency.

8. *"Just Say No" Clubs* (National Clearinghouse for Drug Abuse Information, P.O. Box 416, Kensington, MD 20795). Toll-free number, 1-800-847-6555, to assist K–8 students, teachers, parents, administrators, counselors, and youth group leaders to organize "Just Say No" clubs. A booklet on how to start a club is also available from the Clearinghouse.

Regardless of the school curriculum chosen or locally developed, it would seem appropriate that it attempt to address what research consistently has shown to be the primary factors in the etiology of substance abuse: peer use of illicit substances (Kandel & Yamaguchi, 1985), peer pressure (Brook, Whiteman, & Gordon, 1983; Brook, Whiteman, Gordon, Nomura, & Brook, 1986), early antisocial behavior (Hawkins, Lishner & Catalano, 1985), troubled families (Hawkins et al., 1985; Shore, 1985), and deficient intrapersonal qualities such as positive self-concept.

The Family

The role of the family in adolescent drug abuse has been widely recognized. Certain family characteristics place an adolescent at risk. Some of the most documented are the abusive family, the alcoholic family, a single-parent family, a family in which the children are latchkey children, a blended family, and a family with inconsistent limit-setting and rules for behavior.

Substance abuse does not just suddenly occur. It is often the result of many factors, including feelings of low self-esteem and inadequacy, ineffective coping skills, and poor decision-making skills. Most parents try to rear their children with love and caring, but too many teens have not learned to love themselves and how to cope with life's problems in a constructive way, and instead they turn to drugs to escape their problems. Glickman and Utada (1983) found a dramatic degree of conflict, misunderstanding, and disagreement between teens who were seriously involved in drugs and their parents. These teenagers reported that their parents objected to their friends (77%), were disappointed in them (69%), complained about them (64%), and did not trust them (63%). The quality of their relationship with their parents was poor, and communication was defensive and certainly not honest.

In 1984 the National Institute on Drug Abuse (NIDA) advised parents who suspect that their child is using drugs to tell the child about their concern and why the drug is harmful. In addition, they need to communicate that they are opposed to any drug use and that they intend to enforce that position. Parents have to be: *understanding* (I realize you're under a lot of pressure from friends to use drugs); *firm* (As your parent, I cannot allow you to engage in harmful activates); *self-examining* (Are my own alcohol and drug consumption habits exerting a bad influence on my child? (NIDA, 1984, pp. 4–5). What parents should *not* be is sarcastic, accusatory, sympathy-seeking, and self-blaming, because these behaviors tend to make a child defensive and likely to tune out the parent (NIDA, 1984).

A confrontation with a child regarding drugs can be difficult and charged with emotions; however, parents can control this by remaining calm, open, loving, and firm. Parents need to listen to their children and not just give advice. One of the keys to helping a child grow up is to teach him or her how to make responsible decisions, to accept the consequences of those decisions, and to love himself or herself. This cannot be accomplished quickly. It is a slow process that is nurtured by parental support, love, concern, and understanding.

Parents need to know the differences between firmness and punishment. Children respect fair limits that take into consideration their maturity and behaviors. Consistency in limit-setting helps a child understand the acceptable parameters for behavior and what consistently will earn approval or disapproval. Parents need to be in charge in a loving, supportive manner. Although adolescence is a time of seeking independence, autonomy, and self-identity, most teens still need and want a fair amount of parental direction along with the nurturing and caring.

Treatment Programs

If treatment rather than prevention is required, it often occurs in a more structured setting such as a treatment program. Treatment programs vary in the type of and setting for services provided. All programs make extensive use of group and individual therapy. They also "require some parental and/or familial involvement in the program and attempt to provide family counseling" in an effort to focus on the "underlying problems" in the family milieu (Kusnetz, 1986, p. 151). The more actively involved and supportive the family is, the greater is the chance of recovery for the substance abuser, if the abuser is motivated to stop his or her abuse.

The adolescents who have more successful treatment outcomes recognize that they have a problem and want to participate in the treatment (Kusnetz, 1986). Teenagers who have less successful outcomes tend to have been referred by the criminal justice system, have used drugs for a longer time and are more immersed in the drug culture, come from families in which the adults are substance abusers, and have histories of violence and gang involvement (Kusnetz, 1986). Regardless of the background of the abuser, however, motivation to change on the part of the teen and his or her family is the key to improvement.

Summary

Everyone has his or her own ideas on how to solve the drug problem. These vary from drug legalization to the execution of dealers. What we are doing now in our legal system is just not working. But strictly social interventions are not enough either. As mentioned previously, any intervention has to include multiple foci—not the least of which is the family (Daroff, Marks, & Friedman, 1986). In addition, teens and preteens need to receive accurate information on the effects of drugs—not just scare tactics designed to frighten them into avoiding drugs. This type of tactic perpetuates the "information gap" experienced by the counter-culture of the 1960s.

One role that the school can play is to provide adolescents with accurate information about the complexity of drug use and to teach them effective problem-solving skills so that they do not need to use drugs to make problems go away. In addition, whatever schools can do to enhance a child's self-love, self-respect, and assertiveness provides that child with some of the essential components for avoiding many of the different pressures to try drugs.

Adolescent drug abuse is not just a school problem, though. Parents, the community, adolescents, and school personnel all should be involved in finding ways to counteract drug abuse. One 2- or 3-hour assembly per year certainly is not enough. As Ingersoll and Orr (1988) have pointed out, the underlying basis for at-risk behaviors (substance abuse, sexually acting out, suicide, etc.) must be understood, and only then can an intervention matching the adolescent's needs be applied. To arrive at an effective, appropriate intervention, the ideas and commitment of all concerned with youth—not just school personnel—must be utilized. Just telling kids to say no is not enough.

References

Ball G. (1974). *Human development program: Level V activity guide.* La Mesa, CA: Human Development Training Institute.

Beschner, G. (1986). Understanding teenage drug use. In. G. Beschner & S. Friedman (Eds.), *Teen drug use* (pp. 1–18). Lexington, MA: D. C. Heath.

Borton, T. (1983, April 25). Pressure to try drugs, alcohol starts in early grades. *Weekly Reader.* Middletown, CT: Xerox Educational Publications.

Brook, J. S., Whiteman, M., & Gordon, A. S. (1983). Stages of drug use in adolescence: Personality, peer, and family correlates. *Developmental Psychology, 19,* 269–277.

Brook, J. S., Whiteman, M., Gordon, A. S., Nomura, C., & Brook, D. W. (1986). Onset of adolescent drinking: A longitudinal study of intrapersonal and interpersonal antecedents. *Advances in Alcohol & Substance Abuse, 5,* 91–110.

Daroff, L. H., Marks, S. J. & Friedman, A. S. (1986). Adolescent drug abuse: The parents' predicament. In G. Beschner & A. S. Friedman (Eds.), *Teen drug use.* Lexington, MA: D. C. Heath.

Dembo, R., Blount, W. R., Schmeider, J., & Burgos, W. (1985). Methodological and substantive issues involved in using the concept of risk in research into the etiology of drug use among adolescents. *Journal of Drug Issues, 15,* 537–553.

Department of Health and Human Services. (1984). *Alcohol and health: Fifth special report to the U.S. Congress* (Publication No. ADM 84–1291). Washington, DC: U.S. Government Printing Office.

Dinkmeyer, D. (1973). *Developing understanding of self and others—Manual.* Circle Pines, MN: American Guidance Service.

Education department starts school year with "Challenge" public service campaign (1987). *Substance Abuse Reports, 18*(16), 3–4.

Glickman, N., & Utada, A. (1983). *Characteristics of drug users in urban public high schools.* Rockville, MD: Project Report to National Institute on Drug Abuse. (Grant No. H81 DA 10657)

Goodstadt, M. S. (1980). Drug education—A turn on or a turn off? *Journal of Drug Education, 10*(2), 89–99.

Gordon, T. (1970). *P.E.T.: Parent effectiveness training.* New York: Wyden.

Hawkins, J. D., Lishner, D. M., & Catalano, R. F. (1985). Childhood predictors and the prevention of adolescent substance abuse. In C. L. Jones & R. J. Battejes (Eds.), Etiology of drug abuse: Implications for prevention. *NIDA Research Monographs 56,* 75–126.

Horan, J. J., & Williams, J. M. (1982). Longitudinal study of assertion training as a drug abuse prevention strategy. *American Educational Research Journal, 19*(3), 341–351.

Hutto v. Davis, 454 U.S. 370 (1982).

Inciardi, J. A. (1986). Getting busted for drugs. In G. Beschner & A. S. Friedman (Eds.), *Teen drug use.* Lexington, MA: D. C. Heath.

Ingersoll, G. M., & Orr, D. P. (1988). Adolescents at risk. *Counseling & Human Development, 20*(6), 1–8.

In re Gault, 387 U.S. 1 (1967).

Jalali, B., Jalali, M., Crocette, G., & Turner, F. (1981). Adolescents and drug use: Toward a more comprehensive approach. *American Journal of Orthopsychiatry, 51,* 1.

Johnston L., O'Malley, P., & Bachman, J. (1984). *Highlights from Drugs and American High School Students, 1975–1983.* Rockville, MD: U.S. Institute on Drug Abuse.

Julien, R. M. (1978). *A primer of drug action (2nd ed.).* San Francisco: W. H. Freeman.

Kandel, D. B., & Yamaguchi, K. (1985). Developmental patterns of the use of legal, illegal, and medically prescribed psychotropic drugs from adolescence to young adulthood. In C. L. Jones & R. J. Battejes (Eds.), Etiology of drug abuse: Implications for prevention. *NIDA Research Monographs 56,* 193–235,

Kusnetz, S. (1986). Services for adolescent substance abusers. In G. Beschner & A. S. Friedman (Eds.), *Teen drug use.* Lexington, MA: D. C. Heath.

Mandel J., & Feldman, H. W. (1986). The social history of teenage drug use. In G. Beschner & A. S. Friedman (Eds.), *Teen drug use.* Lexington, MA: D. C. Heath.

Money and high visibility add to power of "Just Say No" (1987). *Substance Abuse Reports, 18*(3), 2.

National Institute on Drug Abuse. (1984). *Parents: What you can do about drug abuse* (DHHS Publication Number ADM-1267). Washington, DC: NIDA, U.S. Government Printing Office.

Newcomb, M. D., Chou, C., Bentler, P. M., & Huba, G. J. (1988). Cognitive motivations for drug use among adolescents: Longitudinal tests of gender differences and predictors of change in drug use. *Journal of Counseling Psychology, 35*(4), 426–438.

Ray, O., & Ksir, C. (1987). *Drugs, society, and human behavior.* St. Louis: Times Mirror/Mosby College Publishing.

Schonberg, S. K., & Schnoll, S. H. (1986). Drugs and their effects on adolescent users. In G. Beschner & A. S. Friedman (Eds.), *Teen drug use.* Lexington, MA: D. C. Heath.

Shore, M. F. (1985). Correlates and concepts: Are we chasing our tails? In C. L. Jones & R. J. Battejes (Eds.), Etiology of drug abuse: Implications for prevention. *NIDA Research Monographs 56,* 127–135.

Swisher, J. D., Nesselroade, C., & Tatanish, C. (1985). "Here's Looking at You Two" is looking good: An experimental analysis. *Journal of Humanistic Education & Development, 23*(3), 111–119.

Tinklenberg, J. R. (1973). Alcohol and violence. In *Alcoholism: Progress in research & treatment.* New York: Academic Press.

Depression in Children and Adolescents

John W. Maag and Steven R. Forness

Depression in children and adolescents is a mood (affective) disorder whose magnitude and clinical importance has only recently permeated the concern of educators. Once considered exclusively the domain of psychiatrists, depression can and should be considered by school personnel in identification, assessment, and treatment (Reynolds, 1984). Unfortunately, professionals in special education have been slow to recognize that depression affects a wide range of school-related functioning (Maag & Rutherford, 1987, 1988). A survey by 47 nationally recognized experts in education of the behaviorally disordered, for instance, did not even mention depression as an important research issue in the field (Epstein & Cullinan, 1984). Youngsters with behavioral disorders are not the only handicapped group at risk for developing depression. Depression has been identified in children and adolescents with mild mental retardation, learning disabilities, and speech and language disorders (e.g., Cantwell & Baker, 1982; Reynolds & Miller, 1985; Stevenson & Romney, 1984).

Depression may be overlooked as a potentially important area of concern in special education, in part, because of its colloquial presence and associated ambiguity (Kendall, Hollon, Beck, Hammen, & Ingram, 1987). At one end of the spectrum, depression is a commonly used term to denote "feeling a little bummed out." At the other end of the spectrum, depression refers to a clinical syndrome or disorder. Kazdin (1990) provides the following distinction:

> As a *symptom*, depression refers to sad affect and as such is a common experience of everyday life. As a *syndrome* or *disorder*, depression refers to a group of symptoms that go together. Sadness may be part of a larger set of problems that include the loss of interest in activities, feelings of worthlessness, sleep disturbances, changes in appetite and others. (p. 121)

135

These distinctions are more than a matter of semantics—different definitions and uses of the label "depression" have important implications (Kendall et al., 1987). The syndrome of depression can be present, in secondary ways, in other disorders. For example, a schizophrenic individual may manifest depressive symptomatology without meeting diagnostic criteria for major mood disorder (American Psychiatric Association, 1987).

In this chapter we are providing only a brief overview of the current status of knowledge in the area of child and adolescent depression. For in-depth reviews, see Dolgan (1990), Kazdin (1990), and Reynolds (1985). We describe diagnostic criteria and identification procedures as well as assessment methodology and intervention strategies. The focus is on depression in handicapped populations in school settings and the implications for special educators.

Current Perspectives

For many years, controversy has surrounded the nature of depression in children and adolescents (Kaslow & Rehm, 1991). For example, conventional psychoanalytic doctrine postulates that depression cannot exist until the onset of adolescence and the development of the superego (Rie, 1966; Rochlin, 1959). A popular view during the 1970s reflected the belief that depression in children was "masked" and must be inferred from underlying behaviors such as hyperactivity, aggression, irritability, delinquency, and poor school performance, to name a few (e.g., Cytryn & McKnew, 1974; Malmquist, 1977). Lefkowitz and Burton (1978) suggested that depression represents a transitory developmental phenomenon which abates spontaneously without intervention; and Seifer, Nurcombe, Scioli, and Grapentine (1989) currently suggest that depression is but one symptom usually found in a pattern of other symptoms that seem to cluster together in children.

The current consensus among researchers and clinicians, however, is that depression in children and adolescents parallels that found in adults. Consequently, the diagnostic criteria for diagnosis of depression in adults also is appropriate and applicable to children and adolescents (Carlson & Cantwell, 1980; Chambers et al., 1985; Chiles, Miller, & Cox, 1980; Kashani, Barbero, & Bolander, 1981; Mitchell, McCauley, Burke, & Moss, 1988).

Diagnostic Criteria

The primary diagnostic system that researchers and clinicians currently use is the *Diagnostic and Statistical Manual for Mental Disorders—Revised* (DSM-III-R) (American Psychiatric Association, 1987). The DSM-III-R criteria for all mood disorders in adulthood, including depression, are applied to children as well. Although depression is a clinical condition that can be diagnosed in children, adolescents, and adults, its specific symptoms, associated features, and clinical course can vary as a

DSM-III-R Criteria for Major Depressive Disorder

At least five of the following symptoms must be present during the same 2-week period; at least one of the symptoms is either (1) depressed mood, or (2) loss of interest or pleasure.

- Depressed mood most of the day, nearly every day (either by subjective account; e.g., feels "down" or "low" or is observed by others to look sad or depressed)

- Loss of interest or pleasure in all or almost all activities nearly every day (either by subjective account or is observed by others to be apathetic)

- Significant weight loss or weight gain (when not dieting or binge-eating) (e.g., more than 5% of body weight in a month) or decrease or increase in appetite nearly every day (in children consider failure to make expected weight gains)

- Insomnia or hypersomnia nearly every day

- Psychomotor agitation or retardation nearly every day (observable by others, not merely subjective feelings of restlessness or being slowed down) (in children under 6, hypoactivity)

- Fatigue or loss of energy nearly every day

- Feelings of worthlessness or excessive or inappropriate guilt (either may be delusional) nearly every day (not merely self-reproach or guilt about being sick)

- Diminished ability to think or concentrate, or indecisiveness nearly every day (either by subjective account or observed by others)

- Thoughts that he or she would be better off dead or suicidal ideation, nearly every day; or suicide attempt

function of development (Kazdin, 1990). DSM-III-R provides a standardized nomenclature, but this system does not help to identify developmental differences. Cicchetti and Schneider-Rosen (1986) have suggested that depression becomes a problem when it interferes with social, cognitive, or emotional competencies necessary for the successful resolution of developmental tasks. A developmental perspective complements DSM-III-R criteria by providing a broader framework for understanding the nature of depression in children and adolescents (Carlson & Garber, 1986).

Depressive symptoms may be included in other types of disorders. Separation anxiety disorder, adjustment disorder with depressed mood, and uncomplicated bereavement are conditions associated with depressive symptoms such as sadness and loss of interest in usual activities. Severity, duration, and precipitants of the symptoms are major determinants of the type of depressive disorders diagnosed (Kazdin, 1990). A scheme depicting a continuum of mood disorders and selected differential problems is presented in Table 6.1.

Table 6.1   Classification Scheme for Mood Disturbances

PATHOLOGY	UNIPOLAR	BIPOLAR

Severe	Major depression:
	    Single episode*
	    Recurrent**
		Bipolar disorder:
		    Manic
		    Depressed
		    Mixed

Moderate	Dysthymia***	Cyclothymia***
Mild	Atypical depression	Atypical bipolar disorder

	Adjustment disorder:
	    Depressed mood
	    Withdrawal
		Adjustment disorder
		    with anxious mood

Differential	Schizophrenia Schizoaffective disorder Separation anxiety	Paranoia Schizoaffective disorder
Nonpathological	Demoralization Bereavement	(no equivalent)

*** Estimates are that more than 50% of individuals having a first single episode will eventually have recurrent episodes.
*** Major depression, recurrent, may predispose to development of bipolar disorder
*** Dysthymia and cyclothymia may predispose to development of a major mood disorder.

Distinctions should be made between depression and dysthymia. The latter is seen as relatively less severe but recurring over a longer period, often punctuated by periods of normal mood that may last for days or even weeks. Another important distinction is between unipolar and bipolar depressive disorders. Unipolar depressive disorders consist of continuous or intermittent periods of dysphoric mood or anhedonia (inability to have fun), whereas bipolar disorders involve alternating episodes of depression and inappropriate euphoria, excessive energy, grandiosity, impulsivity, and poor judgment (Rizzo & Zabel, 1988). Common conditions of both differential pathological and nonpathological origin are noted in Table 1 as well; the former are those of similar severity but different pathological nature, and the latter are within the range of normal emotional responses.

Little is known about manic conditions in children, as they are believed to be rare and difficult to diagnosis in this age group (Kovacs, 1989). Criteria for major depressive disorder and dysthymia generally are necessary in the diagnosis of bipolar disorder and cyclothymia, respectively, along with specific criteria for alternating manic features. It is interesting to speculate whether the episodic nature of a bipolar disorder could render an afflicted child ineligible for special education in that he or she would fail to meet consistently the criterion of a "pervasive mood of sadness or depression" even though bipolar disorder is possibly more debilitating than depression per se (Forness, 1988).

Subtypes of Childhood and Adolescent Depression

The classification scheme illustrated in Table 1 represents a continuum of mood disorders, from the DSM-III-R, that may be present in children and adolescents. Childhood depression can further be classified into several distinct subtypes, each positing a slightly different etiological base and, therefore, having implications for identification, assessment, and treatment (Maag & Rutherford, 1988). Different subtypes of depression are presented in Table 6.2.

Several important distinctions exist between each subtype. *Anaclitic depression*, also termed the "deprivation syndrome" (Spitz & Wolf, 1946), develops in an infant after loss of a caregiver and no provision of a substitute. *Reactive depression* differs from anaclitic depression in that loss of the caregiver does not invariably lead to anaclitic depression; poor parent-child relationships have the most impact on development of reactive depression (Abrahams & Whitlock, 1969). *Acute depression* develops in response to some traumatic event, such as the loss of a loved one, and the prognosis for recovery is good (Cytryn & McKnew, 1972). *Chronic depression*, in contrast, is more extreme and has no immediate precipitating events but is punctuated by repeated separations from the caregiver during early infancy. Finally, *endogenous depression* is thought to be genetic or biochemical in nature, and possibly related to learning disabilities in some children (Brumback & Stanton, 1983).

Table 6.2   Subtypes of Childhood and Adolescent Depression

SUBTYPE	CHARACTERISTICS
Anaclitic Depression	Loss of caregiver with no provision for a substitute; period of misery followed by loss of interest in environment.
Reactive Depression	Trauma or loss frequently accompanied by feelings of guilt for past failures; poor parent-child relationship is important factor.
Acute Depression	Onset occurs after some traumatic event; prognosis for recovery is good if relationship with caregiver is healthy.
Chronic Depression	Repeated separations from caregiver beginning in infancy; presence of depression in mother; no immediate precipitating event; periodic recurring emotional-depriving experiences; suicidal ideation early in childhood.
Endogenous Depression	Genetically or biochemically determined; no identifiable stressors; believed to exist, to some degree, throughout life of child; may reach psychotic or suicidal proportions.

Identification and Assessment

Upon examining prevalence figures of depression in children and adolescents, the importance for educators to identify this disorder becomes alarmingly apparent. The extent to which children and adolescents experience depressive symptomatology has been studied in school-based and clinical populations. Prevalence estimates usually are determined either through DSM-III diagnostic criteria or rating scales in which a score is translated into levels ranging from nondepressed to severely depressed (Reynolds, 1985). Because DSM-III focuses on clinical syndromes or symptom-clusters, prevalence estimates using this approach tend to be more conservative than those obtained for rating scales that provide only global indicators of symptom-severity. In fact, children obtaining rating scale scores in the severe range occasionally fail to meet DSM-III diagnostic criteria for depressive disorders (Kazdin, Colbus, & Rodgers, 1986).

Prevalence Estimates

Using DSM-III criteria, about 2% of school-based children (Kashani et al., 1983; Kashani & Simonds, 1979) and 10% to 20% of clinic-based children (Puig-Antich & Gittelman, 1982) have been diagnosed as depressed. When depression is identified using extreme scores on self report scales, between 2% and 17% of students attending general education school classes manifested moderate to severe levels of depressive symptomatology (Friedrich, Jacobs, & Reams, 1982; Kaplan, Hong, & Weinhold, 1984; Lefkowitz & Tesiny, 1985; Reynolds, 1983; Smucker, Craighead, Craighead, & Green, 1986; Teri, 1982a). Special education populations tend to have a much higher prevalence: Between 14% and 54% of learning disabled (LD) and seriously emotionally disturbed (SED) students manifested severe depressive symptomatology (Maag & Behrens, 1989a; Mattison et al., 1986; Stevenson & Romney, 1984).

A summary of selected prevalence studies is presented in Table 6.3. Only fairly recent studies employing large samples are included because they tend to be more accurate; however, considerable variability is evident, often depending on choice of diagnostic criteria and instrumentation.

Another reason prevalence estimates tend to be somewhat inchoate stems in part from the failure of researchers to consider variables such as gender and age. Gender differences in prevalence of depression usually do not surface until adolescence, when more females than males experience severe symptomatology (Angold, Weissman, John, Wickramaratne, Drusoff, 1991; Kashani et al., 1983; Lefkowitz & Tesiny, 1985; Lobovits & Handal, 1985; Mezzich & Mezzich, 1979; Reinherz et al., 1989; Reynolds, 1985). Similar results have been obtained with LD and SED adolescents; females are three times more likely to report severe depressive symptomatology than their male counterparts (Maag & Behrens, 1989b).

In regard to age, except for very young children (aged 1–6), who have low rates of depression (Kashani, Cantwell, Shekim, & Reid, 1982; Kashani, Ray, & Carlson, 1984), age differences in both handicapped and nonhandicapped populations tend

Table 6.3   Selected Prevalence Findings in Childhood and Adolescent
Depression

STUDY	SAMPLE TYPE	PERCENT DEPRESSED
School-Based General Education Samples		
Lefkowitz & Tesiny (1985)	3,020 3rd-, 4th-, & 5th-grade children, mean age 9.8	5.2%
Reynolds (1983)	2,874 adolescents, ages 13–18	7%
School-Based Special Education Samples		
Maag & Behrens (1989a)	465 LD and SED adolescents ages 12–18 attending resource programs	21%
Mattison et al. (1986)	109 students ages 6–18 referred for SED placement	18% (ages 6–12) 51% (ages 13–18)
Stevenson & Romney (1984)	103 LD students ages 8–13 attending resource programs	14%
Clinic-Based Samples		
Cantwell & Baker (1982)	600 children and adolescents ages 2–16 presented to a community clinic for speech and language evaluation	4%
Carlson & Cantwell (1980)	102 children and adolescents ages 7–17 presented for psychiatric evaluation to an outpatient department	58%
Colbert, Newman, Ney, & Young (1982)	282 children and adolescents ages 6–14 admitted to a child and family practice unit	54%

to be mediated by gender (e.g., Fleming & Offord, 1990; Maag & Behrens, 1989a; Rutter, 1986). Adolescents in general, however, seem to experience higher rates of depression than children do (Forness, 1988; Kazdin, 1990).

Educators' Perspectives on Depression

Given the unsettling prevalence of depression in schoolbased populations, educators clearly should play a strategic role in early identification. Youngsters spend more time in school than in most other structured settings outside the home, and their most consistent and extensive contact is with educators (Grob, Klein, & Eisen, 1983). Consequently, school personnel may be the first professionals to notice developing problems (Powers, 1979). To facilitate the identification process, school personnel must be knowledgeable of depression and sensitive to students who might exhibit it. Although school personnel possess some general knowledge of depression, they cleave to several misconceptions.

Maag, Rutherford, and Parks (1988) had a sample of regular education teachers, special education teachers, and school counselors complete a questionnaire assessing their ability to identify characteristics of depression. Their answers were coded into similar response categories and compared to information about depression drawn from empirical research. School counselors possessed the greatest knowledge of depression, whereas general and special educators identified only global characteristics. Of particular note, special educators tended to identify characteristics related to externalizing problems (e.g., disobedience, aggression) more frequently than internalizing problems (e.g., sadness, loneliness, crying). Externalizing behaviors tend to correlate more highly to depression scores for males, and internalizing problems and negative view of self correlate more highly with depression scores for females (Smucker et al., 1986). More males than females typically receive special education services, so the belief in masked depression should not be resurrected.

In a similar study, Clarizio and Payette (1990) surveyed school psychologists. Although the school psychologists in the study possessed considerable knowledge of depression, their responses diverged relative to the literature in two important areas. *First*, a substantial number of school psychologists believed that childhood depression was substantively different from adult depression. They almost unanimously agreed that masked depression exists, even though this conceptualization has been discounted for several years (Kaslow & Rehm, 1991). *Second*, projective techniques (e.g., TAT, sentence completion) were one of the most frequently named methods for assessing depression. This finding contradicts evidence that projective tests are not sensitive enough to identify specific psychiatric conditions in childhood, including depression (Gittelman, 1980).

More alarmingly, some evidence suggests that educators may respond more negatively to depressed students than to their nondepressed peers. Peterson, Wonderlich, Reaven, and Mullins (1987) had teachers rate their feelings in response to four films in which a child was portrayed as either depressed or nondepressed and as having experienced either high or low life stress. The children who were both depressed and stressed received the most negative reactions from educators; the children who were either depressed or stressed were viewed less negatively; and the children who were neither depressed nor stressed received the most positive reactions. Depression clearly influenced educators' responses in ways that could serve to maintain a child's depression. Educators who communicate less positive and more negative behavior to a depressed child may enhance feelings of low self-esteem, dysphoria, inadequacy, and helplessness.

Because the risk of suicide also is greatly heightened with depression (Myers et al., 1991), educators have a particular need to be sensitive to this disorder. Guetzloe (1989) discusses issues of suicidality in school settings.

Early Identification

Early identification of depressed children and adolescents in school settings is desirable, but Reynolds (1986a) recognized several factors that make this goal problematic:

1. Prevalence figures may be somewhat misleading as depressive symptomatology tends to be overendorsed on the first administration of a self-report measure of depression. A second administration of the same measure shortly thereafter may not show depressive symptomatology. What happens is that a specific event or stressor may trigger a depressive episode, which may account for many cases of depression identified in prevalence surveys.

2. School personnel often have difficulty identifying specific symptom clusters associated with depression. To complicate matters, secondary teachers have limited contact with students.

3. Depressed students rarely refer themselves for help.

4. Some parents deny that their child may be suffering from a mood disorder.

On the basis of findings from prevalence studies of depression in children and adolescents and the lack of self-referral, teacher referral, or parent referral, Reynolds (1986a) developed a three-stage screening program to identify depressed children and adolescents in school settings: (a) conducting large-group screening with self-report depression measures; (b) 3 to 6 weeks later retesting children who, on the basis of the large-group screening in Stage 1, meet cutoff score criteria for depression; and (c) conducting individual clinical interviews with children who manifest clinical levels of depression at both Stage 1 and Stage 2 evaluations.

Classroom teachers can conduct group assessment of students, utilizing a self-report depression measure appropriate for children or adolescents. Self-report is particularly important in assessing depression because primary symptoms such as sadness, feelings of worthlessness, and loss of interest in activities reflect subjective feelings and self-perceptions (Kazdin, 1990). Common self-report measures for children and adolescents are given in Table 6.4.

Reynolds (1986a) has suggested that teachers avoid telling students they are being tested for depression because this information may induce lower levels of mood awareness. Instead, students can be informed that the school is interested in how they are feeling about themselves. This information can be restated to students involved in a second screening. The second screening serves to weed out students who experienced a transient depressed mood during the initial screening or exaggerated their depressive symptomatology. During the last stage, individual clinical interviews are conducted with students who met depression criteria at both previous

Table 6.4 Commonly Used Measures for Childhood and Adolescent Depression

MEASURE	RESPONSE FORMAT	DESCRIPTION
Self-Report (Child)		
Children's Depression Inventory (Kovacs, 1985)	27 items, each rated on a 0–2 point scale	Derived from Beck Depression Inventory (Beck, Ward, Mendelson, Mock, & Erbaugh, 1961). Items reflect affective, cognitive, and behavioral symptoms.
Reynolds Child Depression Scale (Reynolds, 1986b)	30 items, each rated on a 1–5 point scale	Items selected to measure depression in school characteristics (e.g., suicide) are replaced by less severe behavior (e.g., hurting oneself).
Self-Report (Adolescent)		
Beck Depression Inventory (modified for adolescents) (Chiles et al., 1980)	33 items, each on a scale varying from 0 to 2, 3, or 4 points	Changes in language, not content of Beck Depression Inventory (Beck et al., 1961).
Reynolds Adolescent Depression Scale (Reynolds, 1986c)	30 items, each rated on a 4-point scale	Items derived from symptoms included in major, minor, and unipolar depression.
Clinical Interviews (Child)		
Bellevue Index of Depression (Petti, 1978)	40 items, each rated on a 4-point scale of severity and 3-point scale for duration	Administered separately to child, parents, and others; helpful to combine scores from different sources.
Children's Depression Rating Scale (Poznanski, Cook, & Carroll, 1979)	16 items scored after interview; symptoms rated on a 6-point scale for severity	Derived from Hamilton Depression Rating Scale (Hamilton, 1967) for adults. Administered also to parents and others to combine different sources.
Schedule for Affective Disorders for School-Age Children (Chambers et al., 1985)	Multiple items for mood disorders; depressive symptoms rated for degree of severity for scales varying in point values	Patterned after adult Schedule for Affective-Disorders (Endicott & Spitzer, 1978) based on Research Diagnostic Criteria (Spitzer, Endicott, & Robins, 1978). Parent and child are interviewed.
Clinical Interviews (Adolescent)		
Hamilton Depression Rating Scale (Hamilton, 1967)	17-item semi-structured interview with probes	Measures severity of depression and probes for psychotic symptoms; translates well for use with adolescents.
Research Diagnostic Criteria (Spitzer et al., 1978)	11 depression subtypes (e.g., simple, recurrent, unipolar, agitated)	Provides greater specificity than DSM classification; primarily used in research.

Note: For an in-depth review of the characteristics of individual assessment techniques, see Kazdin (1988).

stages. Common interview schedules also are presented in Table 4. Obtaining measures other than self-reports is important as some students consistently overestimate or underestimate depressive symptomatology or misinterpret items or response format.

To screen initially for only a single disorder may be neither desirable nor efficient sometimes, especially given limited resources in some school psychology or consulting services budgets. As an alternative to screening only for depression, Walker and Severson (1990) have developed a multi-stage procedure to screen for both internalizing and externalizing disorders. In this process, teachers are asked to nominate and rank order pupils who demonstrate characteristics of these broad-band disorders in their classroom (Stage 1) but then also rate only the top three pupils in each category on brief measures of adaptive and maladaptive behavior as well as on critical events or symptoms (Stage 2). A school psychologist then conducts brief observations of classroom attention and playground social interaction on two different occasions (Stage 3) for any pupils who exceed critical cutoff scores in the first two stages. Although this procedure is not specific to depression, it may identify children with a potential diagnosis of this disorder, which then can be verified using the techniques described above.

Depression-Related Characteristics

Depression influences a wide range of behavioral, cognitive, and affective functioning (Maag & Rutherford, 1987). Many depression-related characteristics vary as a function of developmental level (Kazdin, 1987). For example, infants have not acquired the ability to verbalize and have not experienced the world and therefore express depression through eating and sleeping disorders (Evans, Reinhart, & Succop, 1980). Because preschoolers are motor-oriented, much of their mood is expressed through behavior such as night terrors, enuresis, and encopresis. Older school-age children may become more outwardly aggressive, anxious, and antisocial (Kazdin, French, & Unis, 1983). Depression becomes more overt in adolescents as their better-developed conscience exacerbates feelings of guilt and low self-esteem (Teri, 1982b).

A number of salient characteristics correlate with, if not contribute directly to, depression. Although the range of domains is quite large, several key characteristics occur quite frequently with depression. For example, low self-esteem is likely to be part of the symptom picture of depression. Hopelessness, or negative expectations toward the future, correlates with depression, suicidal ideation and behavior, and low self-esteem (DiGangi, Behrens, & Maag, 1989; Kazdin, Rodgers, & Colbus, 1986).

In addition to cognitive disturbances, social skill deficits often are associated with depression (Helsel & Matson, 1984). Environmental events that induce stress can contribute to the development and maintenance of depression as well (Compas, 1987). These depression-related characteristics often reflect specific theoretical models of depression including social skill deficits, cognitive theory, learned helplessness theory, self-control deficits, and deficits in problem solving.

Descriptions of the relevant models are presented in Table 6.5. A number of measures focus on key areas related to depressive symptoms based on these theoretical models. Table 6.6 lists common measures that are used to assess areas central to current conceptual views of depression and convey areas reflecting specific theoretical models.

Categorizing Problems Associated With Depression

Based on current theoretical models, depression may result from social skill deficits, self-control deficits, learned helplessness attributions, or cognitive distortions or deficits. Interpersonal problem-solving skills contribute to both cognitive

Table 6.5 Theoretical Models Accounting for Depression

MODEL	DESCRIPTION
Social Skill Deficits	Depression results from a lack of social skills necessary to obtain reinforcement from the environment (Lewinsohn, 1974) Low rates of response-contingent positive reinforcement results in reduced activity levels. Punishing and aversive consequences (unpleasant outcomes) may result from person-environment interactions and lead to symptoms of depression.
Self-Control Model	Maladaptive or deficient self-regulatory processes in coping with stress cause depression (Rehm, 1977). Self-regulatory processes include self-monitoring, self-evaluation, and self-reinforcement. Individuals with self-regulatory deficits focus on negative events, set overly stringent criteria for evaluating their performance, and administer little reinforcement to themselves.
Learned Helplessness	Depression results from individuals' experiences and expectations that their responses do not influence events in their lives. Perfidious attributional style filters experiences in such a way as to produce deficits in affect, motivation, and self-esteem associated with depression (Abramson, Seligman, & Teasdale, 1978).
Cognitive Triad of Depression	Depressed individuals have a systematically negative bias in their thinking, which leads them to have a negative view of themselves, the world, and the future (Beck, 1967). Negative cognitions are considered to affect the individual's judgment about the world and interpersonal interactions, and to account for affective, motivational, and behavioral symptoms of depression.
Interpersonal Problem-Solving Deficits	Inability to generate alternative solutions to social problems, engage in means-end thinking, and make decisions exacerbate effects of negative events (Nezu, Nezu, & Perri, 1989). Depression emerges in response to problems of daily living.

Table 6.6 Common Measures for Assessing Depression-Related Characteristics

MEASURE	DESCRIPTION
Social Skills	
Matson Evaluation of Social Skills with Children (Matson, Rotatori, & Helsel, 1983)	Items pertain to social skills, assertiveness, jealousy, and impulsiveness as related to interpersonal interaction. Self-report and teacher-report forms rated on 5-point scale.
Walker-McConnell Scale of Social Competence and School Adjustment (Walker & McConnell, 1988)	Teacher-rated scale consisting of 43 descriptions of peer-related interpersonal social skills and adaptive behavior required for success within classroom instructional settings.
Cognition	
Children's Attributional Style Questionnaire (Seligman & Peterson, 1986)	Self-report measure consisting of 48 forced-choice items that permit assessment of three attributional dimensions considered important in a learned helplessness model of depression: internal-external characteristics, stable-unstable characteristics, and good-bad outcomes.
Children's Negative Cognitive Error Questionnaire (Leitenberg, Yost, & Carroll-Wilson, 1986)	Self-report measure consisting of 24 items presenting hypothetical situations or events followed by a statement about the event that reflects cognitive errors (catastrophizing, overgeneralizing, personalizing, and selective abstraction). Children rate degree of similarity to their own thoughts. This measure is based on Beck's cognitive therapy of depression.
Problem Solving	
Problem Solving Measure for Conflict (Lochman & Lampron, 1986)	Six means-end stories with each stem describing a problematic situation and a conclusion in which the problem was no longer occurring. Children provide the middle. Scores are based on children's responses on three content areas: verbal assertion, direct action, and physical aggression. This measure is based on Shure and Spivack's (1972) means-ends problem-solving test.
Simulated Problem Situations (Gesten et al., 1982)	Measures of children's natural problem-solving behavior when confronted with a simulated problem situation. Interactions between confederates and target children are observed. Scoring is based on number of alternative solutions generated, number of solution variants offered, number of irrelevant solutions generated, total number of solutions generated excluding irrelevant solutions, and effectiveness of solutions.
Stressful Events	
Life Events Checklist (Johnson & McCutcheon, 1980)	Self-report measure consisting of 46 items that list stressful events. Children indicate whether the event occurred in the past year, whether it was bad or good, and degree of impact on their lives.
Life Events Record (Coddington, 1972)	Stressful events varying as a function of age whose occurrence is rated according to life change units. Parents complete the form for young children; older children complete the scale themselves.

---

*Although many problem-solving measures have been reported in the literature, none are ideally suited for either research or practice (Butler & Meichenbaum, 1981).

(continued)

Table 6.6   (continued)

MEASURE	DESCRIPTION
Activities and Reinforcers Pleasure Scale for Children (Kazdin, 1989)	Children report on a 3-point scale the extent to which 39 items would make them happy. The instrument measures degree of anhedonia.
Adolescent Activities (Carey, Kelley, Buss, & Scott, 1986)	Adolescents rate the frequency of occurrence of 100 activities for degree of pleasantness and unpleasantness experienced during the last 2 weeks. The measure is based on Lewinsohn's work.
Children's Reinforcement Schedules (Cautela, Cautela, & Esonis, 1983)	Children identify events that can be used as reinforcers. Helpful as a method to assess pleasure children report in response to a variety of events.
Adolescent Reinforcement Survey Schedule (Cautela, 1981)	Parallels Children's Reinforcement Schedules.

and behavioral conceptualizations (Braswell & Kendall, 1988; Nezu, Nezu, & Perri, 1989). Systematically approaching and evaluating problem situations represents a general orientation common to most intervention approaches. In addition, environmental factors, such as inappropriate or absent reinforcement contingencies, inhibit expression of healthy and positive functioning or promote depression and related characteristics.

Figure 6.1 illustrates a four-category conceptualization of problems associated with depression. According to this model, depression can be conceptualized as resulting from social skill deficits, self-control deficits, cognitive distortions or deficits, and learned helplessness attributions. The presence of interpersonal problem-solving skills and environmental factors allows the categorization of depression for the basis of developing appropriate interventions. For example, poor social skills may result from erroneous problem solving or environmental factors. A child who is encouraged by his or her peers to participate in a game and is capable of performing the requisite behaviors but is unable to strategically select them probably indicates erroneous problem solving. Conversely, if the child lacks the behavioral requisites to participate in the game, social skill deficits may be targeted for intervention. Similarly, cognitive disturbances and misattributions may result from the child's inability to evaluate situations appropriately or perform the requisite behaviors.

Treatment of Childhood and Adolescent Depression

The model depicting problems associated with depression presented in Figure 1 can be used to develop intervention programs for depressed youth. When developing a

ENVIRONMENT INHIBITING SKILL ACQUISITION OR PERFORMANCE

Figure 6.1 Model for Determining the Nature of Depression Deficits

treatment program, the first consideration is whether depressive symptomatology represents a primary condition, (e.g., mood disorder) or is a byproduct of other behavior problems (Kaslow & Rehm, 1991). For example, youngsters who are hyperactive, aggressive, school phobic, or socially incompetent may experience depressive symptomatology and related dysfunctional cognitions as a result of these problems (Maag, Behrens, & DiGangi, 1991). If conventional treatments for these behavior problems are ineffective for ameliorating the primary problem and related depressive symptomatology, specific treatment strategies for depression should be employed.

Table 6.7 presents a summary of treatment approaches relative to theoretical models of depression. Intervention strategies generally reflect either behavioral or cognitive-behavioral orientations. Although techniques based on these models seem promising, only a few studies have investigated their efficacy with children and adolescents (see Maag, 1988a; Stark, 1990). In addition, Kazdin (1990) raises the issue of *comorbidity* (the individual meets criteria for more than one disorder). Several researchers have found that depression coexists with attention deficit disorders, conduct disorders, anxiety disorders, autism, and mental retardation (e.g, Anderson,

Table 6.7 Treatment Strategies Following Theoretical Models of Depression

MODEL	DESCRIPTION
Social Skill Strategies	Main strategies include shaping procedures that use adult reinforcement, modeling or combined modeling and reinforcement procedures, and direct training procedures to make use of the child's cognitive and verbal skills. Specific training techniques include instructions, modeling, role playing, rehearsal, feedback, and self-management techniques. Verbal-cognitive approaches emphasize teaching specific social skills and general problem-solving techniques.
Self-Control Strategies	Self-management strategies including self-monitoring, self-evaluation, self-reinforcement, and self-instruction would be appropriate for remediating self-control deficits. Intervention should take into account children's cognitive developmental capacities and require the practitioner to play an active role in effecting the desired change by utilizing action-oriented techniques and concrete tasks.
Helplessness Strategies	Strategies follow an attribution retraining conceptualization in which children are taught to take responsibility for their failure and to attribute success or failure to effort. Adaptive coping responses are substituted for attributions of helplessness.
Cognitive Strategies	Treatment focuses on determining the meaning of the child's nonverbal and verbal communication. Any distorted cognitions the child expresses must be challenged. Bestowing acceptance and affection are important, as is assigning tasks that ensure success experiences. Techniques are designed to help the child identify, reality-test, and modify distorted conceptualizations and dysfunctional attitudes and beliefs.

Williams, McGhee, & Silva, 1987; Bernstein, 1991; Bernstein & Garfinkel, 1986; Bird et al., 1988; Fendrich, Weissman, & Warner, 1991; Forness & Kavale, in press; McClellan, Rupert, Reichler, & Sylvester, 1990; Strauss, Last, Hersen, & Kazdin, 1988).

Ironically, the phenomenon of comorbidity has led some researchers to suggest that it may be more meaningful to conceptualize depression in terms of the broader classification of internalizing symptoms rather than the more specific symptomatology of depression, which is more difficult to distinguish (Wolfe et al., 1987). This finding is particularly germane to special educators, as problems of an internalizing nature tend to be frequent in children with learning problems (Thompson, 1986).

Determining Choice of Strategies

Given the range of deficits associated with depression, and their implications for treatment, it is important to determine which factor(s) seem most responsible for the development and maintenance of this disorder (Kaslow & Rehm, 1991). Attempting to assess youngsters' relative skills in each area is a tedious and exacting process. Nevertheless, to enhance treatment efficacy, intervention techniques should be matched to identified, specific problems (Maag, 1989).

In this regard, Kaslow and Rehm (1991) suggest sequencing potential intervention strategies and then making decisions on which ones to use in which order, depending on the results of assessment information. For example, if depression is secondary to a conduct or oppositional disorder, social skills training may be essential for the child to obtain an adequate level of response-contingent positive reinforcement in the environment. If the student's social skills are adequate, however, a more appropriate initial technique would be to modify the child's activity level.

Kaslow and Rehm (1991) also stressed the importance of eliciting overt behavior change prior to targeting cognitive factors, because overt behavior is easier to assess than self-reports of children's cognitions. In addition, obtaining an accurate sampling of the child's self-reported cognitions is easier once behavior has been modified. Figure 6.2 presents a modified version of the flowchart developed by Kaslow and Rehm (1991) for determining choice of intervention strategies. This figure is based on the need to accurately identify and define the problem using assessment measures previously described. Targets for intervention reflect three general areas: behavior, cognitive, and cognitive-behavioral. As with any aspect of depression in children and adolescents, care must be taken to modify intervention strategies based on the child's developmental level and level of cognitive, affective, and behavioral functioning (Cole & Kaslow, 1988).

Developing a Conceptual Model for Intervention

Although the treatment literature for childhood and adolescent depression is relatively sparse compared to other areas such as conduct disorders or attention deficit disorders, several new studies have investigated a variety of training techniques. Table 6.8 provides a summary of recent treatment studies for childhood and adolescent depression. One of the difficulties encountered when treating depression is organizing and integrating the various techniques into a structured training format (Maag, 1988a). Attempting to implement all available techniques would be cumbersome and time-consuming. Yet, many depressed youths exhibit a variety of deficits, and employing a single intervention technique may not be sufficient.

A comprehensive training format would provide a structured system for employing various techniques systematically. One conceptual format is offered in the stress inoculation training (SIT) paradigm. SIT is a multi-component intervention format that combines elements of didactic teaching, Socratic discussion, cognitive restructuring, problem solving, relaxation training, behavioral and imaginal rehearsal, self-monitoring, self-instruction, self-reinforcement, and environmental manipulation (Meichenbaum, 1985). SIT should not be viewed as a loose compendium of unrelated methods, but, rather, a set of interconnected techniques that can be combined in a systematic way.

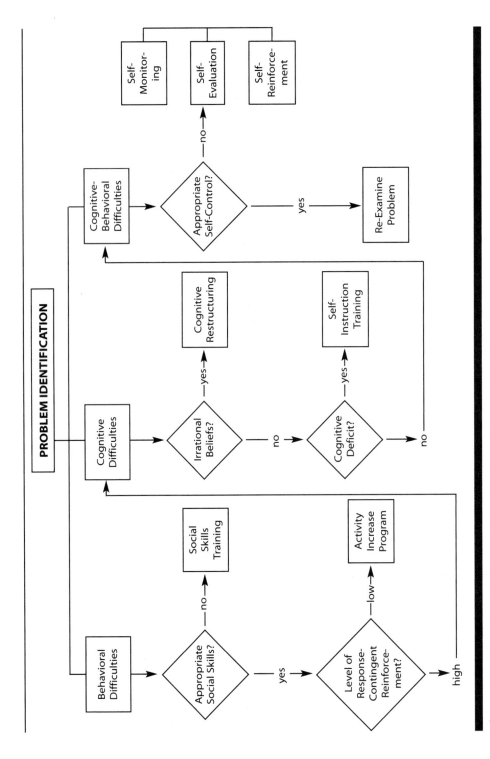

Figure 6.2 Flowchart for Determining Choice of Intervention Strategy

Table 6.8 Treatment Studies with Depressed Children and Adolescents

TREATMENT	STUDY	SAMPLE	FINDINGS
Social Skills Training	Calpin & Cincirpini (1978)	Two depressed inpatients (10-year-old girl, 11-year-old boy)	Improvement for both children on specific social skills (e.g., eye contact)
	Calpin & Kornblith (1977)	Four inpatient boys with aggressive behavior	Improvement of all boys on specific social skills (e.g., requests for new behaviors)
	Fine, Forth, Gilbert, & Haley (1991)	Five groups of 30 adolescent outpatients	Improvement to "nonclinical" levels on depression scales, but to a lesser degree than subjects receiving group therapy
	Frame, Matson, Sonis, Fialkov, & Kazdin (1982)	Borderline mentally retarded 10-year-old depressed male inpatient	Improvement on all target behaviors (e.g., inappropriate body position, lack of eye contact, poor speech quality)
	Petti, Bornstein, Delamater, & Conners (1980)	Chronically depressed 10½-year-old inpatient girl	Improvement on all target behaviors (e.g., eye contact, smiles, duration of speech)
	Matson et al. (1980)	Four depressed emotionally disturbed boys	Increased positive social responses on role-play scenarios for target behaviors (e.g., giving compliments)
	Schloss, Schloss, & Harris (1984)	Three depressed inpatient males	Improvement on five target behaviors (e.g., greets adult, maintains conversation, says goodbye)
Cognitive-Behavioral Interventions	Butler, Miezitis, Friedman, & Cole (1980)	56 fifth- and sixth-grade students	Decreases in depression for role-play and cognitive restructuring conditions; most improvement for role-play
	Maag (1988b)	56 adolescent inpatients	Decreases in depression and negative self-statement for subjects receiving stress inoculation training
	Reynolds & Coats (1986)	30 moderately depressed high school students	Decreases in depression and anxiety for subjects receiving either cognitive restructuring or relaxation training
	Stark, Kaslow, & Reynolds (1987)	29 fourth-, fifth-, and sixth-grade students	Decreases in depression for subjects receiving either self-control or problem-solving training

SIT is implemented in three phases: (a) *conceptualization;* (b) *skills acquisition and rehearsal;* and (c) *application and follow-through.* In Phase I, youngsters are educated about the causes, consequences, and alternative methods of handling depression. Phase II involves training youngsters in relevant skills for coping with depression. In Phase III, youngsters practice applying coping skills *in vitro* and *in vivo* during exposure to regulated doses of stressors that arouse but do not overwhelm their coping skills. SIT has been used to treat depression (Maag, 1988b) and for aggression and anger management (Feindler & Fremouw, 1983; Maag, Parks, & Rutherford, 1988) (see Maag, 1988a for an in-depth description of using stress inoculation training for treating depressed youths).

Pharmacological Treatment

Pharmacotherapy is an essential adjunct to behavioral and cognitive-behavioral interventions, particularly in cases with vegetive symptomatology and family history of mood disorders (Cantwell & Carlson, 1983; Gadow, 1986; Klein, Gittelman, Quitkin, & Rifkin, 1980). Five classes of psychotropics are used in depression; these are depicted in Table 6.9 in terms of their uses, side effects, and related considerations (see Gadow, 1986; Greist & Greist, 1979; Kazdin, 1990; and Petti, 1983 for reviews of pharmacological interventions). Imipramine seems to be the drug of choice for children and adolescents alike (Esman, 1981; Kashani, Shekim, & Reid, 1984; Petti & Law, 1982; Preskorn, Weller, & Weller, 1982; Puig-Antich, 1982); but other drugs, such as lithium and tegretol, are widely used for adolescents who have variant forms of mood disorders (Campbell, Schulman, & Rapoport, 1978; Kishimoto, Ogura, Hazama, & Inoue, 1983).

Although pharmacotherapy is prescribed by psychiatrists, school personnel should be aware of the types of drugs used and their potentially serious side effects. A classroom observation study documenting single-subject classroom effects of imipramine and lithium suggests important considerations for teachers (Forness, Akiyama, & Campana, 1984). Educators need to become much more involved in evaluating effects of such medication on classroom-based measures of treatment outcome (Forness & Kavale, 1988).

Integrating Treatment

Even as treatment of childhood and adolescent depression seems promising, factors external to the child should be considered. Because of parents' influence over their children, Kazdin (1990) suggests that family-based interventions should be incorporated into treatment programs. In this regard, teachers can play a pivotal role by cultivating positive relationships with parents. Positive parent-teacher relationships promote parental feedback to practitioners, enhance treatment outcomes, and extend positive effects of school programming into the home (Heward, Dardig, & Rossett, 1979).

In addition, parents can become trainers of their children by structuring activities and managing behavioral contingencies that promote participation in activities and social interaction (Kazdin, 1990). Parents have effectively implemented reinforcement and punishment techniques and taught prosocial behaviors to their children with externalizing behaviors (e.g., Kazdin, 1985; Patterson, 1982). Parent programs have resulted in decreases in maternal depression and increases in family cohesion (e.g., Eyberg & Robinson, 1982; Forehand, Wells, & Griest, 1980; Karoly & Rosenthal, 1977; Patterson & Fleischman, 1979).

School-based intervention adds several other dimensions as well. Many special educators already conduct social skills training and utilize other cognitive-behavioral techniques for working with aggressive and socially incompetent youngsters (Maag, 1990). Treating depression represents a natural extension of these responsibilities. Furthermore, peers can be recruited for the intervention process as they represent a resource for promoting entrapment (McConnell, 1987) of behaviors that may combat depression. Special educators, therefore, can play a vital role in the early identification, assessment, and treatment of depression.

Summary and Conclusion

Depression represents one of the most significant mental health problems facing children and adolescents. An emerging body of research addresses the nature and characteristics of this disorder in school-aged populations, but educators just recently have begun to address this problem. Part of the difficulty has been educators' lack of knowledge of this disorder and its impact on youngsters' functioning.

Early identification is considered essential, and schools should play an important role in this process. Assessment should focus not only on depressive symptomatology but also on related characteristics, such as social skills. Perhaps most important in treating depression from a school standpoint is that many special educators currently employ many of the intervention strategies that are effective for ameliorating depression for a variety of other conditions such as conduct and attentional disorders. Treatment can be enhanced by sequencing intervention techniques systematically and employing a structured training format.

No one intervention approach will be optimally effective with each youngster. Youngsters who have similar depressive symptomatology may vary greatly with respect to etiological factors, related characteristics, and environmental circumstances. For this reason, depression must be viewed from a holistic framework. This model should guide the development and implementation of treatment decisions. In sum, decisions regarding depression should be made on the basis of empirically based knowledge and the youngster's specific characteristics.

Table 6.9 Common Psychopharmacologic Medication Used with Depressed Children or Adolescents

TYPE (TRADE NAME)	INDICATION	DOSAGE*	THERAPEUTIC EFFECTS	SIDE EFFECTS	OTHER CONSIDERATIONS
Tricyclics: Imipramine (Tofranil)	Unipolar in children	10–175 mg	Improvement in vegetative symptoms at first, followed by improvement in mood some 3 or 4 weeks later	Dry mouth, drowsiness (especially Elavil), blurred vision, constipation, cardiac arrythmias (EKG monitoring is essential and over-dose in suicidal patients becomes a concern)	After offset of I month, discontinue gradually over 3 or more months (with-drawal symptoms mimic depression). Has been used to treat separation anxiety, hyperactivity, enuresis.
	Unipolar in adolescents	75–225 mg			
Amytriptyline (Elavil)	Unipolar in adolescents (little research with children)	45–110 mg			
Lithium Carbonate (Lithonate)	Bipolar in adolescents and occasion-ally in multiple episodes of unipolar	450–1800 mg	Improvement in symptoms in 4–10 days, with most of effect within first 2 weeks; "smooths" rather than elimi-nates symptoms, but early treatment may suppress recurrences	Nausea, drowsiness, thirst, frequent urination, hand tremor, possible cardiac or kidney problems	Small dose added to tricyclic medication during withdrawal as long-term prophylaxis against recurrence. Has been used to treat aggression.

(continued)

TYPE (TRADE NAME)	INDICATION	DOSAGE*	THERAPEUTIC EFFECTS	SIDE EFFECTS	OTHER CONSIDERATIONS
Monoamine Oxidase Inhibitors (Nardil)	Atypical depression in adolescents	30–60 mg	Gradual improvement over 1- to 3-week period	Nausea, dizziness, fainting, sleep disturbance and possible fatal reactions upon ingestion of certain cheese or yeast products	Used primarily in intractable conditions refractory to other drugs.
Carbamazepine (Tegretol)	Bipolar in adolescents, especially rapid-cycling	30–60 mg	Relatively more rapid onset of improvement	Nausea, drowsiness, weight loss, ataxia in instances, and possible toxic reactions with lithium	Primarily a seizure medication but has been used in lithium-resistant depression.
Fluoxetine Hydrochloride (Prozac)	Unipolar depression in adolescents	20–80 mg	Gradual improvement over 5–6 weeks (long-term effects have not been systematically studied)	Anxiety, nervousness, insomnia, weight loss, hypomania or mania, and seizures	Prozac has not been systematically studied for its potential for abuse, tolerance, or physical dependence

*These are doses in what have generally been considered as optimum levels and, in most cases, are determined on a mg/kg ratio based on body weight. Dosage levels vary widely, so these ranges should be considered with caution.

References

Abrahams, M. J., & Whitlock, F. A. (1969). Childhood experience and depression. *British Journal of Psychiatry, 115,* 883–888.

Abramson, L. Y., Seligman, M. E. P., & Teasdale, J. D. (1978). Learned helplessness in humans: Critique and reformulation. *Journal of Abnormal Psychology, 87,* 49–74.

American Psychiatric Association. (1987). *Diagnostic and statistical manual of mental disorders—Revised* (3rd ed.). Washington, DC: American Psychiatric Association.

Anderson, J. C., Williams, S., McGhee, R., & Silva, P. A. (1987). The prevalence of DSM-III disorders in pre-adolescent children: Prevalence in a large sample from the general population. *Archives of General Psychiatry, 44,* 69–76.

Angold, A., Weissman, M. M., John, K., Wickramaratne, P., & Drusoff, B. (1991). The effects of age and sex on depression ratings in children and adolescents. *Journal of the American Academy of Child and Adolescent Psychiatry, 30,* 67–74.

Beck, A. T. (1967). *Cognitive therapy and the emotional disorders.* New York: International Universities Press.

Beck, A. T., Ward, C. H., Mendelson, M., Mock, J., & Erbaugh, J. (1961). An inventory for measuring depression. *Archives of General Psychiatry, 4,* 53–63.

Bernstein, G. A. (1991). Comorbidity and severity of anxiety and depressive disorders in a clinic sample. *Journal of the American Academy of Child and Adolescent Psychiatry, 30,* 43–50.

Bernstein, G. A., & Garfinkel, D. B. (1986). School phobia: The overlap of affective and anxiety disorders. *Journal of the American Academy of Child Psychiatry, 25,* 235–241.

Bird, H. R., Canino, G., Rubio-Stipec, M., Gould, M. S., Ribera, J., Sesman, M., Woodbury, M., Huertas-Goldman, S., Pagan, A., Sanchez-Lacay, A., & Moscoso, M. (1988). Estimates of the prevalence of childhood maladjustment in a community survey of Puerto Rico: The use of combined measures. *Archives of General Psychiatry, 45,* 1120–1126.

Braswell, L., & Kendall, P. C. (1998). Cognitive-behavioral methods with children. In K. S. Dobson (Ed.), *Handbook of cognitive-behavioral therapies* (pp. 167–213). New York: Guilford.

Brumback, R. A., & Stanton, R. D. (1983). Learning disability and childhood depression. *American Journal of Orthopsychiatry, 53,* 269–281.

Butler, L., & Meichenbaum, D. (1981). The assessment of interpersonal problem-solving skills. In P. C. Kendall & S. D. Hollon (Eds.), *Assessment strategies for cognitive-behavioral interventions* (pp. 197–225). New York: Academic Press.

Butler, L., Miezitis, S., Friedman, R., & Cole, E. (1980). The effect of two school-based intervention programs on depressive symptoms in preadolescents. *American Education Research Journal, 17,* 111–119.

Calpin, J. P., & Cincirpini, P. M. (1978, May). A *multiple baseline analysis of social skills training in children.* Paper presented at Midwestern Association for Behavior Analysis, Chicago.

Calpin, J. P., & Kornblith, S. J. (1977). *Training of aggressive children in conflict resolution skills.* Paper presented at meeting of Association for the Advancement of Behavior Therapy, Chicago.

Campbell, M., Schulman, D., & Rapoport, J. L. (1978). The current status of lithium therapy in child and adolescent psychiatry. *Journal of Child Psychiatry, 17,* 717–720.

Cantwell, D. P., & Baker, L. (1982). Depression in children with speech, language, and learning disorders. *Journal of Children in Contemporary Society, 15,* 51–59.

Cantwell, D. P., & Carlson, G. A. (Eds.). (1983). *Affective disorders in childhood and adolescence: An update.* New York: Spectrum.

Carey, M. P., Kelley, M. L., Buss, R. R., & Scott, W. O. N. (1986). Relationship of activity of depression in adolescents: Development of the Adolescent Activities Checklist. *Journal of Consulting & Clinical Psychology, 54,* 320–322.

Carlson, G. A., & Cantwell, D. P. (1980). Unmasking depression in children and adolescents. *American Journal of Psychiatry, 137,* 445–449.

Carlson, G. A., & Garber, J. (1986). Developmental issues in the classification of depression in children. In M. Rutter, C. E. Izard, & P. B. Read (Eds.), *Depression in young people: Developmental and clinical perspectives* (pp. 399–435). New York: Guilford.

Cautela, J. R. (1981). *Behavior analysis forms for clinical intervention* (Vol. 2). Champaign, IL: Research Press.

Cautela, J. R., Cautela, J., & Esonis, S. (1983). *Forms for behavior analysis with children.* Champaign, IL: Research Press.

Chambers, W. J., Puig-Antich, J., Hirsch, M., Paez, P., Ambrosini, P. J., Tabrizi, M. A., & Davies, M. (1985). The assessment of affective disorders in children and adolescents by semistructured interview: Test-retest reliability. *Archives of General Psychiatry, 43,* 696–702.

Chiles, J. A., Miller, M. L., & Cox, G. B. (1980). Depression in an adolescent delinquent population. *Archives of General Psychiatry, 37,* 1179–1184.

Cicchetti, D., & Schneider-Rosen, K. (1986). An organizational approach to childhood depression. In M. Rutter, C. E. Izard, & P. B. Read (Eds.), *Depression in young people: Developmental and clinical perspectives* (pp. 71–134). New York: Guilford.

Clarizio, H. F., & Payette, K. (1990). A survey of school psychologists' perspectives and practices with childhood depression. *Psychology in the Schools, 27,* 57–63.

Coddington, R. D. (1972). The significance of life events as etiological factors in the diseases of children: A study of normal population. *Journal of Psychosomatic Research, 16,* 205–213.

Colbert, P., Newman, B., Ney, P., & Young, J. (1982). Learning disabilities as a symptom of depression in children. *Journal of Learning Disabilities, 15,* 333–336.

Cole, P. M., & Kaslow, N. J. (1988). Interactional and cognitive strategies for affect regulation: A developmental perspective on childhood depression. In L. B. Alloy (Ed.), *Cognitive processes in depression* (pp. 310–343). New York: Guilford.

Compas, B. E. (1987). Stress and life events during childhood and adolescence. *Clinical Psychology Review, 7,* 275–302.

Cytryn, L., & McKnew, D. H. (1972). Proposed classification of childhood depression. *American Journal of Psychiatry, 129,* 149–155.

Cytryn, L., & McKnew, D. H. (1974). Factors influencing the changing clinical expression of the depressive process in children. *American Journal of Psychiatry, 131,* 879–881.

DiGangi, S. A., Behrens, J. T., & Maag, J. W. (1989). Dimensions of depression: Factors associated with hopelessness and suicidal intent among special populations. In R. B. Rutherford, Jr., & S. A. DiGangi (Eds.), *Severe behavior disorders of children and youth* (Vol. 12, pp. 47–53). Reston, VA: Council for Children with Behavioral Disorders.

Dolgan, J. I. (1990). Depression in children. *Pediatric Annals, 19,* 45–50.

Endicott, J., & Spitzer, R. L. (1978). A diagnostic interview: The Schedule for Affective Disorders and Schizophrenia. *Archives of General Psychiatry, 35,* 837–944.

Epstein, M. H., & Cullinan, D. (1984). Research issues in behavior disorders: A national survey. *Behavioral Disorders, 10,* 56–59.

Esman, A. H. (1981). Appropriate use of psychotropics in adolescents. *Hospital, 12,* 49–60.

Evans, S., Reinhart, J., & Succop, R. (1980). Failure to thrive: A study of 45 children and their families. In S. Harrison & J. McDermott (Eds.), *New directions in childhood psychopathology.* New York: International Universities Press.

Eyberg, S. M., & Robinson, E. A. (1982). Parent-child interaction training: Effects of family functioning. *Journal of Clinical Child Psychology, 11,* 130–137.

Feindler, E. L., & Fremouw, W. (1983). Stress inoculation training for adolescent anger problems. In D. Meichenbaum & M. Jaremko (Eds.), *Stress reduction and prevention* (pp. 451–485). New York: Plenum.

Fendrich, M., Weissman, M. M., & Warner, V. (1991). Longitudinal assessment of major depression and anxiety disorders in children. *Journal of the American Academy of Child and Adolescent Psychiatry, 30,* 38–42.

Fine, S., Forth, A., Gilbert, M., & Haley, G. (1991). Group therapy for adolescent depressive disorder: A comparison of social skills and therapeutic support. *Journal of the American Academy of Child and Adolescent Psychiatry, 30,* 79–85.

Fleming, J. E., & Offord, D. R. (1990). Epidemiology of childhood depressive disorders: A critical review. *Journal of the American Academy of Child and Adolescent Psychiatry, 29,* 571–580.

Forehand, R., Wells, K. C., & Griest, D. L. (1980). AD examination of the social validity of a parent training program. *Behavior Therapy, 11,* 488–502.

Forness, S. R. (1988). School characteristics of children and adolescents with depression. In R. B. Rutherford, Jr., C. M. Nelson, & S. R. Forness (Eds.), *Bases of severe behavioral disorders in children and youth* (pp. 177–203). San Diego: College-Hill Press.

Forness, S. R., Akiyama, K., & Campana, K. (1984, November). *Problems in antidepressant medication and classroom performance.* Paper presented at Annual Conference on Severe Behavioral Disorders of Children and Youth, Tempe, AZ.

Forness, S. R., & Kavale, K. A. (1988). Psychopharmacologic treatment: A note on classroom effects. *Journal of Learning Disabilities, 21,* 144–147.

Forness, S. R., & Kavale, K. A. (in press). School identification and response to conduct disorders. In A. Duchnowski & R. Friedman *(Eds.), Conduct disorders: Research, practice, and issues.* Tampa: Florida Mental Health Research Institute.

Frame, C., Matson, J. L., Sonis, W. A., Fialkov, M. J., & Kazdin, A. E. (1982). Behavioral treatment of depression in a prepubertal child. *Journal of Behavior Therapy & Experimental Psychiatry, 13,* 239–243.

Friedrich, W., Jacobs, J., & Reams, R. (1982). Depression and suicidal ideation in early adolescents. *Journal of Youth and Adolescence, 11,* 403–407.

Gadow, K. D. (1986). *Children on medication: Volume 2. Epilepsy, emotional disturbance, and adolescent disorders.* San Diego: College-Hill Press.

Gesten, E. L., Rains, M. H., Rapkin, B. D., Weissberg, R. P., Flores de Apodaca, R., Cowen, E. L., & Bowen, R. (1982). Training children in social problem-solving competencies: A first and second took. *American Journal of Community Psychology, 10,* 95–115.

Gittelman, R. (1980). The role of psychological tests for differential diagnosis in child psychiatry. *Journal of the American Academy of Child Psychiatry, 19,* 413–438.

Greist, J. H., & Greist, T. H. (1979). *Antidepressant treatment: The essentials.* Baltimore: Williams and Wilkins.

Grob, M. C., Klein, A. A., & Eisen, S. V. (1983). The role of the high school professional in identifying and managing adolescent suicidal behavior. *Journal of Youth & Adolescence, 12,* 163–173.

Guetzloe, E. C. (1989). *Youth suicide: What the educator should know.* Reston, VA: Council for Exceptional Children.

Hamilton, M. (1967). Development of a rating scale for primary depressive illness. *British Journal of Social & Clinical Psychology, 6,* 278–296.

Helsel, W. J., & Matson, J. L. (1984). Assessment of depression in children: The internal structure of the Child

Depression Inventory (CDI). *Behaviour Research and Therapy, 22,* 289–298.

Heward, W. L., Dardig, J. C., & Rossett, A. (1979). *Working with parents of handicapped children.* Columbus, OH: Charles E. Merrill.

Johnson, J. H., & McCutcheon, S. M. (1980). Assessing life stress in older children and adolescents: Preliminary findings with the Life Events Checklist. In I. G. Sarason & C. D. Spielberger (Eds.), *Stress and anxiety* (Vol. 7, pp. 111–125). Washington, DC: Hemisphere.

Kaplan, S. L., Hong, G. K., & Weinhold, C. (1984). Epidemiology of depressive symptomatology in adolescents. *Journal of the American Academy of Child Psychiatry, 23,* 91–98.

Karoly, P., & Rosenthal, M. (1977). Training parents in behavior modification: Effects on perceptions of family interaction and deviant child behavior. *Behavior Therapy, 8,* 406–410.

Kashani, J. H., Barbero, G. J., & Bolander, F. D. (1981). Depression in hospitalized pediatric patients. *Journal of the American Academy of Child Psychiatry, 20,* 123–134.

Kashani, J. H., Cantwell, D. P., Shekim, W. O., & Reid, J. C. (1982). Major depressive disorder in children admitted to an inpatient community mental health center. *American Journal of Psychiatry, 139,* 671–672.

Kashani, J. H., McGee, R. O., Clarkson, S. E., Anderson, J. C., Walton, L. A., Williams, S., Silva, P. A., Robins, A. J., Cytryn, L., & McKnew, D. H. (1983). Depression in a sample of 9-year old children. *Archives of General Psychiatry, 40,* 1217–1223.

Kashani, J. H., Ray, J. S., & Carlson, G. A. (1984). Depression and depression-like states in preschool-age children in a child development unit. *American Journal of Psychiatry, 141,* 1397–1402.

Kashani, J. H., Shekim, W, O., & Reid, J. C. (1984). Amitriptyline in children with major depressive disorder: A double-blind crossover pilot study. *Journal of Child Psychiatry, 23,* 248–251.

Kashani, J. H., & Simonds, J. F. (1979). The incidence of depression in children. *American Journal of Psychiatry, 136,* 1203–1205.

Kaslow, N. J., & Rehm, L. P. (1991). Childhood depression. In R. J. Morris & T. R. Kratochwill (Eds.), *The practice of child therapy* (2nd ed., pp. 27–51). New York: Pergamon.

Kazdin, A. E. (1985). *Treatment of antisocial behavior in children and adolescents.* Homewood, IL: Dorsey.

Kazdin, A. E. (1987). Assessment of childhood depression: Current issues and strategies. *Behavioral Assessment, 9,* 291–319.

Kazdin, A. E. (1988). Childhood depression. In E. J. Mash & L. G. Terdal (Eds.), *Behavioral assessment of childhood disorders* (2nd ed., pp. 157–195). New York: Guilford.

Kazdin, A. E. (1989). Evaluation of the pleasure scale in the assessment of anhedonia in children. *Journal of the American Academy of Child and Adolescent Psychiatry, 28,* 364–372.

Kazdin, A. E. (1990). Childhood depression. *Journal of Child Psychology & Psychiatry, 31,* 121–160.

Kazdin, A. E., Colbus, D., & Rodgers, A. (1986). Assessment of depressive disorder among psychiatrically disturbed children. *Journal of Abnormal Child Psychology, 14,* 499–515.

Kazdin, A. E., French, A., & Unis, A. (1983). Child, mother, and father evaluations of depression in psychiatric inpatient children. *Journal of Abnormal Child Psychology, 11,* 167–180.

Kazdin, A. E., Rodgers, A., & Colbus, D. (1986). The Hopelessness Scale for Children: Psychometric characteristics and concurrent validity. *Journal of Consulting & Clinical Psychology, 54,* 241–245.

Kendall, P. C., Hollon, S. D., Beck, A. T., Hammen, C. L., & Ingram, R. E. (1987). Issues and recommendations regarding use of the Beck Depression Inventory. *Cognitive Therapy & Research, 11,* 289–299.

Kishimoto, A., Ogura, C., Hazama, H., & Inoue, H. (1983). Long-term prophylactic effects of carbamazepine in affective disorder. *British Journal of Psychiatry, 143,* 327–331.

Klein, D. F., Gittelman, R., Quitkin, F., & Rifkin, A. (1980). *Diagnosis and drug treatment of psychiatric disorders in adults and children* (2nd ed.). Baltimore: Williams and Wilkins.

Kovacs, M. (1985). The Children's Depression Inventory. *Psychopharmacology Bulletin, 21,* 995–998.

Kovacs, M. (1989). Affective disorder in children and adolescents. *American Psychologist, 44,* 209–215.

Lefkowitz, M. M., & Burton, N. (1978). Childhood depression: A critique of the concept. *Psychological Bulletin, 85,* 716–726.

Lefkowitz, M. M., & Tesiny, E. P. (1985). Depression in children: Prevalence and correlates. *Journal of Consulting & Clinical Psychology, 53,* 647–656.

Leitenberg, H., Yost, L. W., & Carroll-Wilson, M. (1986). Negative cognitive errors in children: Questionnaire development, normative data, and comparisons between children with and without self-reported symptoms of depression, low self-esteem, and evaluation anxiety. *Journal of Consulting & Clinical Psychology, 54,* 528–536.

Lewinsohn, P. N. (1974). Clinical and theoretical aspects of depression. In K. S. Calhoun, H. E. Adams, & K. M. Mitchell (Eds.), *Innovative treatment methods of psychopathology* (pp. 63–120). New York: Wiley.

Lobovits, D. A., & Handal, P. J. (1985). Childhood depression: Prevalence using DSM-III criteria and validity of parent and child depression scales. *Journal of Pediatric Psychology, 10,* 45–54.

Lochman, J. W., & Lampron, L. B. (1986). Situational Social problem-solving skills and self-esteem of aggressive and nonaggressive boys. *Journal of Abnormal Child Psychology, 13,* 527–538.

Maag, J. W. (1988a). Treatment of childhood and adolescent depression: Review and recommendations. In R. B. Rutherford, Jr., & J. W. Maag (Eds.), *Severe behavior disorders of children and youth* (Vol. 11, pp. 49–63). Reston, VA: Council for Children with Behavioral Disorders.

Maag, J. W. (1988b). *Treatment of adolescent depression with stress inoculation training.* Unpublished doctoral dissertation, Arizona State University, Tempe.

Maag, J. W. (1989). Assessment in social skills training: Methodological and conceptual issues for research and practice. *Remedial & Special Education, 10*(4), 6–17.

Maag, J. W. (1990). Social skills training in schools. *Special Services in the Schools, 6,* 1–19.

Maag, J. W., & Behrens, J. T. (1989a). Depression and cognitive self-statements of learning disabled and seriously emotionally disturbed adolescents. *Journal of Special Education, 23,* 17–27.

Maag, J. W., & Behrens, J. T. (1989b). Epidemiologic data on seriously emotionally disturbed and learning disabled adolescents reporting extreme depressive symptomatology. *Behavioral Disorders, 15,* 21–27.

Maag, J. W., Behrens, S. T., & DiGangi, S. A. (1991). Dysfunctional cognitions associated with adolescent depression: Findings across special populations. Manuscript submitted for publication.

Maag, J. W., Parks, B. T., & Rutherford, R. B., Jr. (1988). Generalization and behavior covariation of aggression in children receiving stress inoculation therapy. *Child & Family Behavior Therapy, 10,* 29–47.

Maag, J. W., & Rutherford, R. B., Jr. (1987). Behavioral and learning characteristics of childhood and adolescent depression: Implications for special educators. In S. Braaten, R. B. Rutherford, Jr., & J. W. Maag (Eds.), *Programming for adolescents with behavioral disorders* (Vol. 3, pp. 55–70). Reston, VA: Council for Children with Behavioral Disorders.

Maag, J. W., & Rutherford, R. B., Jr. (1988). Review and synthesis of three components for identifying depressed students.

In R. B. Rutherford, Jr., C. M. Nelson, & S. R. Forness (Eds.), *Bases of severe behavioral disorders in children and youth* (pp. 205–230). San Diego, CA: College-Hill Press.

Maag, J. W., Rutherford, R. B., Jr., & Parks, B. T. (1988). Secondary school professionals; ability to identify depression in adolescents. *Adolescence, 23,* 73–82.

Malmquist, C. P. (1977). Childhood depression: A clinical and behavioral perspective. In J. G. Schulterbrandt & A. Raskin (Eds.), *Depression in children: Diagnosis, treatment and conceptual models* (pp. 33–59). New York: Raven.

Matson, J. L., Esveldt-Dawson, K., Andraski, F., Ollendick, T. H., Petti, T. A., & Hersen, M. (1980). Observation and generalization effects of social skills training with emotionally disturbed children. *Behavior Therapy, 11,* 522–531.

Matson, J. L., Rotatori, A. F., & Helsel, W. J. (1983). Development of a rating scale to measure social skills in children: The Matson Evaluation of Social Skills with Youngsters (MESSY). *Behaviour Research and Therapy, 21,* 335–340.

Mattison, R. E., Humphrey, F. J., Kales, S. N., Handford, H. A., Finkenbinder, R. L., & Hernit, R. C. (1986). Psychiatric background and diagnoses of children evaluated for special class placement. *Journal of the American Academy of Child Psychiatry, 25,* 514–520.

McClellan, J. M., Rupert, M. P. M., Reichler, R. J., & Sylvester, C. E. (1990). Attention deficit disorder in children at risk for anxiety and depression. *Journal of the American Academy of Child and Adolescent Psychiatry, 29,* 534–539.

McConnell, S. R. (1987). Entrapment effects and the generalization and maintenance of social skills training for elementary school students with behavioral disorders. *Behavioral Disorders, 12,* 252–263.

Meichenbaum, D. (1985). *Stress inoculation training.* New York: Pergamon.

Mezzich, A. C., & Mezzich, J. E. (1979). Symptomatology of depression in adolescence. *Journal of Personality Assessment, 43,* 267–275.

Mitchell, J., McCauley, E., Burke, P. M., & Moss, S. J. (1988). Phenomenology of depression in children and adolescents. *Journal of the American Academy of Child and Adolescent Psychiatry, 27,* 12–20.

Myers, K., McCauley, E., Calderon, R., Mitchell, J., Burke, P., & Schloredt, K. (1991). Risks for suicidality in major depressive disorders. *Journal of the American Academy of Child and Adolescent Psychiatry, 30,* 86–94.

Nezu, A. M., Nezu, C. M., & Perri, M. G. (1989). *Problem-solving therapy for depression: Theory, research and clinical guidelines.* New York: Wiley.

Patterson, G. R. (1982). *Coercive family process.* Eugene, OR: Castalia.

Patterson, G. R., & Fleischman, M. J. (1979). Maintenance of treatment effects: Some considerations concerning family systems and follow-up data. *Behavior Therapy, 10,* 168–185.

Peterson, L., Wonderlich, S. A., Reaven, N. M., & Mullins, L. L. (1987). Adult educators' response to depression and stress in children. *Journal of Social & Clinical Psychology, 5,* 51–58.

Petti, T. A. (1978). Depression in hospitalized child psychiatry patients: Approaches to measuring depression. *Journal of the American Academy of Child Psychiatry, 22,* 11–21.

Petti, T. A. (1983). Imipramine in the treatment of depressed children. In D. P. Cantwell & G. A. Carlson (Eds.), *Affective disorders in childhood and adolescence: An update* (pp. 375–415). New York: Spectrum.

Petti, T. A., Bornstein, M., Delamater, A., & Conners, C. K. (1980). Evaluation and multimodal treatment of a depressed prepubertal girl. *Journal of the American Academy of Child Psychiatry, 19,* 690–702.

Petti, T. A., & Law, W. (1982). Imipramine treatment of depressed children: A double-blind pilot study. *Journal of Clinical Psychopharmacology, 2,* 107–110.

Powers, D. (1979). The teacher and the adolescent suicide threat. *Journal of School Health, 49,* 561–563.

Poznanski, E. O., Cook, S. C., & Carroll, B. J. (1979). A depression rating scale for children. *Pediatrics, 64,* 442–450.

Preskorn, S. H., Weller, E. B., & Weller, R. A. (1982). Depression in children: Relationship between plasma imipramine levels and response. *Journal of Clinical Psychiatry, 43,* 450–453.

Puig-Antich, J. (1982). Major depression and conduct disorder in prepuberty. *Journal of Child Psychiatry, 21,* 118–128.

Puig-Antich, J., & Gittelman, R. (1982). Depression in childhood and adolescence. In E. S. Paykel (Ed.), *Handbook of affective disorders* (pp. 379–392). New York: Guilford.

Rehm, L. P. (1977). A self-control model of depression. *Behavior Therapy, 8,* 787–804.

Reinherz, H. Z., Stewart-Berghauer, G., Pakiz, B., Frost, A. K., Moeykens, B. A., & Holmes, W. M. (1989). The relationship of early risk and current mediators to depressive symptomatology in adolescence. *Journal of the American Academy of Child and Adolescent Psychiatry, 28,* 942–947.

Reynolds, W. M. (1983, March). *Depression in adolescents: Measurement, epidemiology, and correlates.* Paper presented at annual meeting of National Association of School Psychologists, Detroit.

Reynolds, W. M. (1984). Depression in children and adolescents: Phenomenology, evaluation and treatment. *School Psychology Review, 13,* 171–182.

Reynolds, W. M. (1985). Depression in childhood and adolescence: Diagnosis, assessment, intervention strategies and research. In T. R. Kratochwill (Ed.), *Advances in school psychology* (Vol. 4, pp. 133–189). Hillsdale, NJ: Lawrence Erlbaum.

Reynolds, W. M. (1986a). A model for the screening and identification of depressed children and adolescents in school settings. *Professional School Psychology, 1,* 117–129.

Reynolds, W. M. (1986b). *Reynolds child depression scale.* Odessa, FL: Psychological Assessment Resources.

Reynolds, W. M. (1986c). *Reynolds adolescent depression scale.* Odessa, FL: Psychological Assessment Resources.

Reynolds, W. M., & Coats, K. I. (1986). A comparison of cognitive-behavioral therapy and relaxation training for the treatment of depression in adolescents. *Journal of Consulting & Clinical Psychology, 54,* 653–660.

Reynolds, W. M. & Miller, K. L. (1985). Depression and learned helplessness in mentally retarded and nonmentally retarded adolescents: An initial investigation. *Applied Research in Mental Retardation, 6,* 295–306.

Rie, H. E. (1966). Depression in childhood: A survey of some pertinent contributions. *Journal of the Academy of Child Psychiatry, 5,* 635–685.

Rizzo, J. V., & Zabel, R. H. (1988). *Educating children and adolescents with behavioral disorders: An integrative approach.* Boston: Allyn & Bacon.

Rochlin, G. (1959). The loss complex. *Journal of the American Psychoanalytic Association, 7,* 299–316.

Rutter, M. R. (1986). The developmental psychopathology of depression: Issues and perspectives. In M. R. Rutter, C. E. Izard, & P. B. Read (Eds.), *Depression in young people: Developmental and clinical perspectives* (pp. 3–30). New York: Guilford.

Schloss, P. J., Schloss, C. N., & Harris, L. (1984). A multiple baseline analysis of an interpersonal skills training program for depressed youth. *Behavioral Disorders, 9,* 182–188.

Seifer, R., Nurcombe, B., Scioli, A., & Grapentine, W. L. (1989). Is major depressive disorder in childhood a distinct diagnostic entity? *Journal of the American Academy of Child and Adolescent Psychiatry, 28,* 935–941.

Seligman, M. E. P., & Peterson, C. (1986). A learned helplessness perspective on childhood depression: Theory and research. In

M. Rutter, C. E. Izard, & P. B. Read (Eds.), *Depression in young people: Developmental and clinical perspectives* (pp. 223–249). New York: Guilford.

Shure, M. B., & Spivack, G. (1972). Means-ends thinking, adjustment and social class among elementary school-age children. *Journal of Consulting & Clinical Psychology, 38,* 348–353.

Smucker, M. R., Craighead, W. E., Craighead, L. W., & Green, B. J. (1986). Normative and reliability data for the Children's Depression Inventory. *Journal of Abnormal Child Psychology, 14,* 25–39.

Spitz, R. A., & Wolf, K. M. (1946). Anaclitic depression: An inquiry into the genesis of psychiatric conditions in early childhood. *Psychoanalytic Study of the Child, 2,* 313–341.

Spitzer, R. L., Endicott, J., & Robins, E. (1978). Research diagnostic criteria: Rationale and reliability. *Archives of General Psychiatry, 35,* 773–782.

Stark, K. D. (1990). *Childhood depression: School-based intervention.* New York: Guilford.

Stark, K. D., Kaslow, N. J., & Reynolds, W. M. (1987). A comparison of the relative efficacy of self-control therapy and a behavioral problem-solving therapy for depression in children. *Journal of Abnormal Child Psychology, 15,* 91–113.

Stevenson, D. T., & Romney, D. M. (1984). Depression in learning disabled children. *Journal of Learning Disabilities, 17,* 579–582.

Strauss, C. C., Last, C. G., Hersen, M., & Kazdin, A. E. (1988). Association between anxiety and depression in children and adolescents. *Journal of Abnormal Child Psychology, 16,* 57–68.

Teri, L. (1982a). The use of the Beck Depression Inventory with adolescents. *Journal of Abnormal Child Psychology, 10,* 277–282.

Teri, L. (1982b). Depression in adolescence: Its relationship to assertion and various aspects of self-image. *Journal of Clinical Child Psychology, 11,* 101–106.

Thompson, R. J. (1986). Behavior problems in children with developmental and learning disabilities. *International Academy of Research in Learning Disabilities Monograph Series, 3,* 1–125.

Walker, H. M., & McConnell, S. R. (1988). *Walker-McConnell Scale of Social Competence and School Adjustment.* Austin, TX: Pro-Ed.

Walker, H. M., & Severson, H. H. (1990). *Systematic screening for behavior disorders,* Longmont, CO: Sopris West.

Wolfe, V. V., Finch, A. J., Jr., Saylor, CA. F., Blount, R. L., Pallymeyer, T. P., & Carek, D. J. (1987). Negative affectivity in children: A multitrait-multimethod investigation. *Journal of Consulting & Clinical Psychology, 55,* 245–250.

Adolescent Suicide: Prevention and Intervention

Dave Capuzzi

A dolescent suicide has become a critical problem in the United States. Recent yearly estimates (Haffen & Frandsen, 1986) report as many as 400,000 attempts and 7,000 completions among the adolescent population in this country. The extent of the adolescent suicide problem is difficult to identify with an exact number because many suicides are confused as accidents or reported as accidents because of family embarrassment, religious beliefs, community discomfort, or denial of the adolescent suicide problem. During the last five years adolescent suicide has moved from being cited as the third leading cause of death among the 11- to 24-year age group to the second leading cause. Only accidents—quite often automobile accidents—rank higher.

Understanding the Problem

Myths About Adolescent Suicide

One of the first steps in developing an understanding of adolescent suicide is to identify the commonly believed myths regarding teenagers who attempt or complete the act of suicide. Some of the most typically cited misconceptions are discussed briefly in the following paragraphs.

- *Adolescents who talk about suicide never do it.* This is probably one of the most widely held misconceptions. In reality almost all suicidal adolescents have made an attempt (verbally or nonverbally—and usually verbally) to let someone else know that life seems too much to handle. A suicide attempt is a cry for help to identify options other than death that will decrease the pain of living. Verbal threats should always be taken seriously and never assumed to be only for the purpose of attracting attention or manipulating others.

■ *Suicide happens without warning.* Most suicidal adolescents leave numerous hints and warnings about their suicidal ideations and intentions. Clues can be verbal or in the form of suicidal gestures such as taking just a few sleeping pills or becoming accident-prone. Quite often the social support network of the suicide-prone adolescent is small. As stress escalates and options other than suicide seem few, suicidal adolescents may withdraw from an already small circle of friends, making it more difficult for others to notice warning signs.

■ *Adolescents from affluent families attempt or complete suicide more often than adolescents from poor families.* This, too, is a myth. Suicide is evenly divided among socioeconomic groups.

■ *Once an adolescent is suicidal, he or she is suicidal forever.* Most adolescents are suicidal for a limited time. In my experience, the 24- to 72-hour period around the peak of the "crisis" is the most dangerous. If counselors and other mental health practitioners can monitor this crisis period and then get the adolescent into regularly scheduled, long-term counseling/therapy, there is a strong possibility that another suicidal crisis will never occur. The more effort that is made to help an adolescent identify stressors and develop problem-solving skills during this post-suicidal crisis period and the more time that passes, the better is the prognosis.

■ *If an adolescent attempts suicide and survives, he or she will never make an additional attempt.* There is a difference between the adolescent who experiences a suicidal crisis but does not attempt it, as in the situation above, and the adolescent who actually tries to bring an end to life. An adolescent who carries through with an attempt has identified a plan, had access to the means, and maintained a high enough energy level to follow through. He or she knows that a second or third attempt would be in the realm of possibility. If counseling/therapy has not taken place or has not been successful during the period following the attempt, additional attempts may be made. Most likely, each follow-up attempt will become more lethal.

■ *Adolescents who commit suicide always leave notes.* Only a small percentage of adolescents who complete the act of suicide leave notes. This myth is common and is one of the reasons why many suicides are classified and reported as accidents by friends, family members, physicians, and investigating officers when suicide actually has taken place.

■ *Most adolescent suicides happen late at night.* This myth is not true for the simple reason that most suicidal adolescents actually want help. Mid to late morning and mid to late afternoon are the time periods when most attempts are made, since a family member or friend is more likely to be around to intervene than would be the case late at night.

■ *The word suicide should never be used when talking to adolescents, because using the word gives some adolescents the idea.* This is simply not true. One cannot put the idea of suicide into the mind of an adolescent who is not suicidal. If an adolescent is suicidal and the word "suicide" is voiced, it can invite him or her to verbalize feelings of despair and help establish rapport and trust. If a suicidal adolescent thinks someone knows that he or she is suicidal and realizes the person is afraid to broach the subject, it can bring the adolescent closer to the point of making an attempt by contributing to feelings of despair and helplessness.

■ *Every adolescent who attempts suicide is depressed.* Depression is a common component of the profile of a suicidal adolescent, but depression is not always a component. Many adolescents simply want to escape their present set of circumstances and do not have the problem-solving skills to cope more effectively, reduce stress, and work toward a more promising future.

■ *Suicide is hereditary.* Suicide, like physical and sexual abuse, tends to run in families, which has given rise to this myth. Although suicide is not genetically inherited, members of families do share the same emotional climate since parents model coping and stress management skills as well as a level of high or low self-esteem. The suicide of one family member tends to increase the risk among other family members that suicide will be viewed as an appropriate way to solve a problem or set of problems.

Causes of Adolescent Suicide

The causes of suicide among teenagers in the United States have been discussed by a number of experts (Haffen & Frandsen, 1986; Davis, 1983; Husain & Vandiver, 1984; Fairchild, 1986). The parameters commonly identified for consideration are (a) the adolescent struggle to develop and integrate a unique identity, (b) familial factors, and (c) environmental factors.

The Adolescent Experience

Early adolescence is second only to infancy in terms of physical growth and emotional development. It is a time during which many of the assumptions of childhood must be left behind as the demands and expectations of others increase with each stage of physical and sexual maturity bringing the adolescent closer to the world of "adults." Even though adolescents may look like young adults quite early, they cannot approach relationships and analyze life circumstances until they have had time to assess a number of areas. Rather than discussing the developmental tasks of adolescence in the traditional sense, the areas of adolescent development that seem to be factors in the development of suicidal tendencies in adolescents will be overviewed.

Self-esteem. In general, adolescents who become suicidal experience feelings of low self-esteem. These feelings have been present since early childhood, and such a young person may have been other-directed, rather than inner-directed, for a number of years prior to adolescence. Parents of adolescents such as these typically comment that their child seemed to lose control and judgment in the presence of peers, and that quite often they dreaded the arrival of their child's friends for an afternoon visit or a weekend stay.

Poor communication. Besides low self-esteem, many suicidal adolescents have developed a pattern of poor communication with parents, other adults and, quite often, friends. These adolescents never have been at ease with the prospect of sharing their feelings about parents, siblings, teachers, and friends. As time passes, it becomes easier and more acceptable simply to keep their feelings inside and experience frustration and discomfort than to attempt to deal with those feelings as they arise. Teachers, parents, and neighbors seldom have many verbal cues that relationships, circumstances, or expectations have been upsetting to these children.

Achievement orientation. In addition to low self-esteem and poor communication skills, suicide-prone adolescents may be quite achievement-oriented. Although it would be a mistake to assume that *all* achievement-oriented adolescents may become suicidal, experience with counseling the suicidal adolescent points to the realization that high achievement is one way to compensate for feelings of low self-worth. Achievement can be focused on any of a number of modalities—high grades, participation in athletic activities, developing a reputation as the "class clown," the best-dressed, most popular. All of these are ways to achieve prominence among peers.

Poor problem-solving skills. Poor problem-solving ability is also characteristic of many adolescents who become suicidal. This trait is usually observable prior to adolescence, epitomized by a lack of resourcefulness in generating options for solving a problem, coping with a difficult relationship, or planning for the future.

Narrow commitments. Lack of resourcefulness is particularly troublesome in conjunction with another trait that often is part of the developmental pattern of the suicidal adolescent—total commitment to a relationship or to a goal for the future. Suicidal adolescents often develop a tunnel-visioned perspective. A relationship may become so important that other friendships are dropped. A goal may begin to dominate every decision, allocation of time, and thoughts about the future. Commitment, total and unwavering, often becomes the theme for patterning daily, weekly, and monthly activities and priorities. When an important relationship ends or a goal becomes unachievable, self-esteem is lowered, feelings are kept secret and left unexpressed, achievement is roadblocked, and problem-solving skills are frozen in past and current maladaptive patterns, resulting in escalation of stress and anxiety.

High stress. Most suicidal adolescents have a history of high stress. As they move from childhood to adolescence and the demands of the peer group and the expectations of adults become even greater, they become even less resourceful in their ability to manage stress. During periods of high stress, they may spend more and more time considering the option of suicide and planning for the time, place, and means.

In addition to the above traits that contribute to an adolescent's inclination to consider, attempt, or complete the act of suicide, two other traits should be noted. In my experience, many (though not all) suicidal adolescents have a relatively small network of social support. Friendships that provide opportunities for self-disclosure may be lacking or few in number since the act of sharing feelings or thoughts is usually quite difficult. Finally, I believe that many suicidal adolescents have been bothered by feelings of guilt and not quite "measuring-up" for most of their lives. Adolescents who have low self-esteem and are other-directed usually are never quite satisfied with anything they do, say, or achieve and are likely to feel guilty about their perceived lack of "achievement."

Family Factors

A number of authors (Bigrar, Gauthier, Bouchard, & Jasse, 1966; Jacobziner, 1965; McAnarney, 1979; Otto, 1972; Truckman & Connon, 1962) have discussed family dis-organization as a characteristic of the families of suicidal adolescents. Divorce, death, unemployment, drug abuse, physical and sexual abuse, and mental illness are all factors contributing to disorganization. McAnarney (1979) stated that, "In societies where family ties are close, suicidal rates are low and conversely, where families are not close, suicidal rates are high." A number of family factors have become apparent to me as contributing causes of the adolescent suicide crisis in the United States.

Poor communication. In many families of adolescents who have attempted or completed suicide, family members seem to be lacking in communication. Families report that they have great difficulty communicating clearly and consistently with one another (whether between parents or between parent and child). Even when the family eats breakfast or dinner together, quite often the meal is eaten in silence or with family members' attention directed to a television program. Very often, parents have not modeled a positive, articulate communication style for their children to imitate and develop skills. Parents may have little knowledge of the tribulation their adolescent children experience, and adolescents may have difficulty talking with peers and siblings, while talking with parents may seem unthinkable.

Loss. Loss is something that requires a grieving and adjustment process before daily frustrations and responsibilities can be coped with as before. Losses involving dis-solution of the nuclear family because of divorce, death of a family member or close friend, termination of employment, changes in health status, or moves to a new community require the energy to develop changed perspectives and the problem-solving skills to make new beginnings or change life styles. Frequently, suicidal adolescents are from families that have experienced one or more major losses in the preceding one or two years.

Dual-career families. More and more American families are finding that two incomes are necessary to support a family. When both parents work, two adults may be bringing the stresses of employment back into the family system. In addition, time to accomplish household tasks, shop for groceries, schedule medical and dental appointments, and complete necessary errands is reduced. Parents may be too tired to spend as much time with their adolescent children as they would like or unable to give undivided attention to an adolescent at a time when he or she needs to talk.

Unless all family members are good at managing both time and stress, saying "no" to unnecessary work-related or other responsibilities, helping one another and meeting each other's needs at the time the needs arise, the family climate may be one of tension and lack of receptiveness. Adolescents may not think they can turn to family members for comfort and assistance.

Single parenting. The role of the single parent has long been characterized by escalated responsibility, lowered income, high stress, and lack of time. A single parent may be so busy attempting to make a home for his or her children that little time is allotted to the basics of a parent-child relationship. Many troubled adolescents come from single-parent homes.

Blended families. When two adults who have custody of the children from a previous marriage decide to form a new family, the dynamics of the family constellation can become quite complex. Some adolescents have great difficulty adjusting to a "substitute" parent, a new set of guidelines for behavior and discipline, additional siblings, less personal space, or a different home in a new neighborhood or community. Parents should be encouraged to seek family counseling when adolescent children show signs of depression and poor adjustment to the new family group.

Mid-life transition. Parents of adolescent children are usually between the ages of 35 and 50. As parents see their children mature to the point of looking like young adults, they may begin the process of assessing themselves as personalities and as partners. They may evaluate their careers and financial progress and begin thinking about employment changes. Issues between partners may surface or resurface if they were not dealt with earlier. Just at the time when children need more time and attention than ever, parents may be too focused on their own status and too concerned about "time running out" to notice and respond to the needs of their adolescent children.

Abuse. Families in which physical or sexual abuse is occurring or in which substance abuse is problematic may be at high-risk for adolescent suicide. Parents who are abusive of each other, themselves, or their children are typically low in self-esteem, stressed, poor communicators and problem-solvers, and financially distressed. Children of these parents have not been taught to feel good about themselves and to problem-solve effectively. During adolescence, escaping the pain of this type of family atmosphere or the self-deprecating viewpoint they have probably developed may become the most predominant motivation for suicide.

Environmental Factors

Adolescents may be concerned and upset about a number of trends in today's society.

Pressure to achieve. The pressure to achieve academically and vocationally in our culture is often felt keenly by today's adolescents. When families and teachers pressure teenagers to achieve, some may choose to commit suicide rather than to fail and disappoint others.

Mobility. Groups with the greatest amount of mobility are those living in central or rapidly changing portions of a city, immigrants, and families working for large companies that transfer them to different cities every few years (McAnarney, 1979). In addition, adolescents are more mobile than ever before because of improved public transportation and access to private vehicles. Families and their adolescent children often experience alienation, isolation, and loneliness when circumstances result in their changing communities or moving constantly from one neighborhood to another.

Uncertainty about the future. Many adolescents feel that school and work will only become more competitive and difficult. Many believe that they must prepare for a much lower standard of living than that of their parents because of the escalating costs of housing, utilities, automobiles, and so on in relation to the slower rise in salaries. Some are afraid that no matter how much effort they exert, they already are destined for failure and, perhaps, should not even make a try at life.

Graduation from high school. Although high school students often complain about the expectations of teachers, principals, and school boards and talk frequently about the anticipated joys of finishing school, many teenagers are threatened by the approach of high school graduation. For many, graduation symbolizes the transition to young manhood or womanhood and the initiation of a life more independent of other family members. Even though adolescents tell friends, family members, and other adults that they can hardly wait to finish secondary school and that they have everything under control for later, they may be quite apprehensive. The transition to the next stage of development can be a period of extremely high stress.

Nuclear threat. Most of today's young people are totally aware of the reality that no nation or component of the world community can be independent or safe from the actions, and the consequences of those actions, of another country. The recent nuclear accident in Chernobyl and resultant radioactive fallout reinforces the fact that no one will be safe during a nuclear war no matter where nuclear detonation takes place. Some adolescents cite these observations as reasons for "opting out."

Drug abuse. The United States is experiencing an epidemic of drug use and abuse. Opportunities to experiment with marijuana, alcohol, and other drugs are presented to fifth and sixth graders in most school districts. Pressure from peers, a mistaken sense of autonomy and feeling of well-being, and lack of funding to provide school-based prevention, intervention, and after-care programs often result in heavy use and abuse of drugs during the early high school years. Since problem-solving ability, self-esteem, and communication skills—which already may be inadequate—are never enhanced through drug use, suicide-prone adolescents usually become even higher risks as drug experimentation and dependency increase.

Approaches to Prevention

The Role of Families and Friends

In addition to understanding the myths connected with adolescent suicide, as well as the impacts of adolescence as a developmental stage and of certain familial and social factors, family members and friends should familiarize themselves with the signs and symptoms of impending suicide. The four following areas should be assessed by anyone concerned about the welfare of an adolescent child or teenage friend: changes in behavior, verbal cues, themes or preoccupations in thinking, and personality traits.

Noticing Changes in Behavior

In general, any behavior that is decided change for a particular adolescent should be noted. Warning signs include: sudden drops in grades for a good student; difficulty with concentration; loss of interest in friends, hobbies, or goals; changes in patterns of sleeping and eating; experimentation with marijuana, alcohol, and other drugs; lack of cooperation at school or at home; running away; and sexual promiscuity.

Depression is also a symptom of an impending suicidal crisis. When depression, combined with other behavior changes, occurs repeatedly, for periods lasting longer than a week, it is a cause for concern. Family members and friends should realize that when an adolescent who has been struggling with periodic depressive episodes suddenly improves, the possibility of a suicide attempt or completion may be imminent. It is not logical for an adolescent who has seemed troubled for some time to change overnight. Quite often an abrupt change in emotional tenor results after the individual has made the decision about when and how to make a suicide attempt.

Listening for Verbal Cues

Changes in behavior, such as the ones described above, also may be accompanied by a number of verbal warnings. Always listen for statements such as the following:

- I can't go on.
- I'm going to kill myself.
- I wish I were dead.
- I'm not the person I used to be.
- The only way out is to die.
- You won't be seeing me around any more.
- You're going to regret how you've treated me.
- Life is too much to put up with.
- Life has no meaning any more.
- I'm getting out.
- I'm tired.
- If (such and such) happens, I'll kill myself.
- If (such and such) doesn't happen, I'll kill myself.
- I'm going home.
- Here, take this (cassette, jewelry, etc.); I won't be needing it any more.

Although the "language" of adolescents varies from year to year and from one part of the country to another, the above statements convey the meaning that adolescents communicate as their stress and discomfort make suicide seem like an acceptable problem-solving option. Statements similar to the ones listed above invite additional disclosure and description of the person's circumstances and feelings.

Listening for Themes or Preoccupations in Thinking

Themes or preoccupations also seem to dominate the thinking pattern of young persons who are contemplating suicide. Although suicidal adolescents often have difficulty sharing feelings and thoughts, self-disclosure should be encouraged for the following themes:

- Wanting to escape from a situation that seems intolerable (e.g., physical abuse, difficulty at school, drugs, lack of friends).
- Wanting to join a friend or family member who has died.
- Wanting to gain the attention of others.
- Wanting to manipulate others.
- Wanting to be punished.
- Wanting to avoid being punished.
- Wanting to control when death will occur.
- Wanting to end a seemingly unresolvable conflict.
- Wanting to become a martyr for a cause.
- Wanting to punish the survivors.
- Wanting revenge.

Noticing Personality Traits

Traits that often characterize suicidal adolescents were discussed earlier. Low self-esteem, poor communication skills, high achievement orientation, poor problem-solving skills, total commitment to a relationship or a goal, high stress, small social support networks, and feelings of guilt should all be noted, especially if they are observed in conjunction with behavior changes, verbal cues, and preoccupations that could serve as motivations for a suicide attempt.

The Role of School Counselors

Suicide prevention measures can and should be taken at the elementary level and continue through middle and high school years. Traits such as low self-esteem, weak problem-solving ability, high stress, and poor communication skills are noticeable in first and second graders. At this level, counseling programs can be initiated for the purpose of enhancing self-esteem or improving communication skills. These services can be continued or begun at middle and high school levels as well. Because these traits are so often part of the profile of suicidal adolescents, early intervention and prevention would seem essential.

Further, counselors who work with students in grades five through twelve can provide information about the signs and symptoms of an impending suicidal crisis through classroom presentations on the topic. These presentations should be direct (the word "suicide" should be used) and should focus upon encouraging students who are concerned about themselves or their friends to ask for assistance. Students should be made aware that when they are concerned about a friend, someone in the school, as well as the friend's parent or parents, should be alerted. The reason for involvement outside of the family is that parents, when told that their child is in difficulty and may be suicidal, often react in the same way as parents who are told that a child is using or abusing drugs—with denial or anger.

Faculty/staff and administration must participate in inservice education on the topic of preventing adolescent suicide prior to presenting programs to students. Not only must school personnel understand the dynamics of the suicidal adolescent, but they also must be sensitive to the necessity of being able to provide or refer a person to counseling services quickly so that attempted suicides can be averted.

Approaching Crisis Management

When called upon to assist an adolescent who is suspected of being in a suicidal crisis, the counselor can take a number of steps to ascertain the severity of the crisis and the lethality or risk that must be monitored.

1. *Be a good listener.* Understanding and respect must be conveyed for everything that is being shared by the young person. Whatever the circumstances, concerns, and feelings are, they are, for this client, reality. Counselors must begin with reality as perceived by the client even if the counselor would not interpret the circumstances in the same way.

2. *Be nonjudgmental.* If an adolescent is suicidal, he or she may have great difficulty communicating the thoughts and feelings that have led to the current feelings of desperation and hopelessness. Rapport cannot be built through comments such as, "You can't be thinking such thoughts," "It's against the teachings of your religion" or, "It would be such an embarrassment to your family."

3. *Be supportive.* When talking with an adolescent who may be at risk, it is important to be reassuring. This does not mean that the counselor should convey messages such as, "Things aren't really that bad" (for the client, things *are* bad) or "The situation will take care of itself" (circumstances usually do not become better without effort on the part of both client and counselor). Being supportive *does* mean that the counselor communicates understanding, reinforces the client for seeking assistance, and outlines some counseling options for the near future. (If the client is experiencing a high level of stress and suicidal preoccupation, counseling will not be effective until the crisis subsides.)

4. *Ask questions to assess lethality.* The following questions will help determine the degree of risk:

■ *What has happened to make life so difficult?* The more circumstances the client describes, the higher is the risk.

■ *Are you thinking of suicide?* Use the word suicide. Doing so will not put the idea of suicide into the thoughts of an adolescent who is not suicidal. Being direct will let the client know that the counselor has listened, is concerned, and is interested in helping.

■ *Do you have a suicide plan?* The more specific the client is about the method, the time, the place, and who will or will not be nearby, the higher is the risk. If the client describes using pills, a gun, a knife, or other specific means, ask if he or she has that item in a pocket or purse, and require that the suicide "weapon" be left with you. (Firearms and highly lethal items, however, should be handled by the police.) Most clients will cooperate since they are most likely at low point, "other-directed," and responsive to taking directions from a trusted adult.

■ *How much do you want to live?* The more difficulty the client has in giving reasons for continuing with life, the higher is the risk.

■ *How much do you want to die?* The more the client discusses ending life, the higher is the risk.

■ *When you think about suicide, how often do these periods of suicidal preoccupation occur, how intense are they, and how long do the periods last?* The more frequent the episodes, the more dysfunctional is the client's behavior during periods of intense preoccupation, and the longer the preoccupation, the more lethal is the situation for the client. Frequent episodes of suicidal preoccupation that are lasting longer and longer mean that the periods of preoccupation with suicidal thoughts are moving closer together and consuming more and more of the client's time.

■ *Have you ever attempted suicide in the past?* If the answer is yes, the client is more lethal. In that case, ask: *How long ago was that attempt?* The more recent the attempt, the greater is the current risk.

■ *Has a family member, neighbor, or friend ever attempted or completed suicide?* If the answer is yes, the client is more lethal because he or she may have learned or come to believe that suicide is an acceptable form of decision making.

■ *On a scale of 1 to 10, with 1 being low and 10 being high, what is the number that depicts the probability that you will attempt suicide?* The higher the number, the higher is the lethality.

■ *Is there anyone to stop you?* This question is extremely important for two reasons. First, if the client has a difficult time identifying a friend, family member, or respected adult who would be worth living for, the risk is higher than if as few as one or two people are named. Second, it is important to obtain specific information about the people identified in response to this question. Names, addresses, phone numbers, and the nature of the current or past relationship may be needed to organize a suicide watch.

5. *Remember the meaning of* crisis management. The word crisis means that the situation is not normal or usual because the adolescent you are concerned about is self-destructive. The word *management* means that, for a short time (24 to 72 hours), the client must be directed and monitored. Definite steps must be taken to safeguard the client's well-being, and these steps must be explicated in an assertive, direct manner while conveying concern and empathy. If a young person were in an accident that resulted in life-threatening physical injury and loss of consciousness, paramedics and hospital emergency room physicians and nurses would take decisive action without the permission of the patient to save the patient's life. Managing a suicidal crisis is no different.

6. *Make a decision relative to needed interventions.* If, as a result of the counselor's assessment, the risk factor or lethality is judged to be high, the counselor should develop a management plan to follow until the crisis subsides and long-term counseling can be initiated. If the client is in proximity to a hospital with a psychiatric unit, hospital personnel can undertake additional assessment to determine if hospitalization for a 2- or 3-day period is advisable. Often, if a client has not been eating and sleeping or does not have family or friends to provide a suicide watch, a brief hospital stay will facilitate subsiding of the crisis to the point at which counseling can be initiated.

   If hospital services are not available in the community and the counselor believes the risk is high, a suicide watch should be organized by contacting the individuals that the client has identified in response to the question: "Is there anyone to stop you?" After receiving instructions from the counselor, family members and friends should take turns staying with the client until the crisis has subsided and counseling has begun. Under no circumstances should an adolescent in crisis leave the counselor's office until arrangements have been made to monitor the client at all times. Contacting friends and family does break confidentiality, but it does not violate ethical codes of professional groups such as the American Association for Counseling and Development and the American Psychological Association. These steps must be taken to potentially save the client's life.

   At times a written contract can be developed with the client, to be used along with a suicide watch (or in place of a suicide watch if the risk is low). The contract should specify activities, time with friends, and the like to which the client will commit, along with phone numbers of individuals to contact if preoccupation with suicide begins again.

   A high-risk adolescent never should be left unmonitored, and the counselor should not assume that the client will have the initiative and energy to arrange and arrive for needed counseling when the crisis has subsided enough for counseling to be beneficial. This means that the counselor must be willing to cancel appointments and other scheduled activities to assist if no one else is available to be of support to the client.

7. *Be flexible enough to work with colleagues or crisis center staff.* Responding to a suicidal adolescent and assessing lethality requires patience, energy, and decision making. If another colleague has received training in crisis management, that colleague could help to make an assessment and decide upon the most appropriate crisis management plan. Or it may be necessary to call upon a local crisis center to provide assistance. This is especially true if a suicidal adolescent is on the telephone and someone needs to go to the caller's location to remove firearms, provide transportation to a hospital, or other intervention. The crisis center staff can help determine whether to involve the police and whether emergency medical assistance may be needed prior to arrival at a hospital emergency room.

After a suicidal crisis has subsided, the services of an agency counselor or private practitioner may be necessary to provide follow-up counseling on a consistent and rather long-term basis. Never assume responsibilities that you do not have the expertise to carry through with or the time to provide.

Providing Follow-Up or Post-Vention Services

As many as six to 10 people are affected, on a long-term basis, for each adolescent suicide attempt or completion. Therefore, planning and offering either individual or group ("survivor group") counseling experiences for family members and friends of the suicide victim or attempter is necessary. On a short-term basis, hundreds of people, if not entire communities, may be in need of assistance ranging from information about the dynamics of suicide to individual or group counseling.

In a school setting, providing information about suicide and offering counseling assistance as a follow-up to an actual suicide are appropriate measures. If an adolescent who has attempted suicide is returning to the same classrooms in the same school, however, suicide prevention programs should not be provided for the first time until a few months have passed, so that the returning student will not be focused upon. But individual or group counseling still can be provided for those who seem to need to talk about their feelings related to the suicide attempt of one of their peers.

Members of both school and community groups must realize that the end of a period of suicidal crisis or the return of an adolescent who has made an unsuccessful attempt does not signify the end of responsibility of school and community groups to provide counseling assistance. The only hope for improved mental health of the adolescent is long-term counseling focused upon overcoming low self-esteem and other traits so that life and its options can be viewed differently.

An adolescent who attempts suicide is reaching out for the help that can be provided only in the context of the helping relationship. School and community groups must plan, network, and fund services to cope with the increasing problem of adolescent suicide in the same way that provisions are made for interventions related to physical and sexual abuse and drug abuse. Family members and friends must affirm the self-worth of all adolescents by being sensitive to their developing individuality, as well as the stresses of the complex, changing society of which they are a part. Only then will the promise of a new tomorrow become the reality of today.

References

Bigrar, J., Gauthier, Y., Bouchard, C., & Jasse, Y. (1966). On the depressive illness in childhood: Suicidal attempts in adolescent girls. A preliminary study. *Canadian Psychiatric Association Journal, 11* (Supplement), 275–282.

Davis, P. A. (1983). *Suicidal adolescents.* Springfield, IL: Charles C Thomas.

Fairchild, T. N. (1986). Suicide intervention. In T. N. Fairchild (Ed.), *Crisis intervention strategies for school-based helpers* (pp. 321–369). Springfield, IL: Charles C Thomas.

Haffen, B. Q., & Frandsen, K. J. (1986). *Youth suicide: Depression and loneliness.* Provo, UT: Behavioral Health Associates.

Husain, S. A., & Vandiver, T. (1984). *Suicide in children and adolescents.* New York: SP Medical and Scientific Books.

Jacobziner, H. (1965). Attempted suicides in adolescents by poisoning. *Journal of the American Medical Association, 191*(1), 101–105.

McAnarney, E. R. (1979). Adolescent and young adult suicide in the United States— A reflection of societal unrest? *Adolescence, 14*(56), 765–774.

Otto, U. (1972). Suicidal acts by children and adolescents: A follow-up study. *Acta Psychiatrica Scandinavica, 233* (Supplement), 5–123.

Truckman, J., & Connon, H. E. (1962). Attempted suicides in adolescents. *American Journal of Psychiatry, 119*(3), 228–232.

Uncovering the Hidden Causes of Bullying and School Violence

Barry K. Weinhold

ecause the bulk of the iceberg that the Titanic hit on April 14, 1912, was invisible to the ship's captain, this great ship sank to the bottom of the ocean. On April 20, 1999, our great nation also hit a largely invisible iceberg at Columbine High School. Since then, the public eye has been focused on the tip of this metaphoric iceberg, known as the "culture of violence." In trying to find ways to avoid further school violence, the larger culture of violence remains hidden from our collective view. Unless this nation changes its course, it surely is headed for more collisions with this invisible iceberg that can cause the deaths of many more innocent people.

Ever since the Columbine tragedy, people have been asking, "How could this have happened?" and "What can we do to prevent it from happening again?" Much of the public commentary about the causes of the Columbine massacre has been directed at assigning blame and finding quick-fix solutions. What might be more useful is uncovering the hidden causes of this tragedy and developing long-range primary prevention strategies to deal with these hidden causes. The goals of this chapter are to (a) examine the hidden elements of the culture of violence that were present in the Columbine tragedy, (b) expose the pervasive nature of bullying and school violence, (c) show how school violence is only a small part of a larger pattern of violence that is fed by the culture of violence, and (d) describe effective long-range prevention methods that address the hidden elements of the culture of violence.

What Is the Culture of Violence?

The most visible forms of the culture of violence that make up the tip of the iceberg of violence are

- youth violence
- domestic violence
- road rage
- gang violence
- hate crimes
- community crime and violence
- global conflict and war.

Ample evidence documents the increasingly negative effects of the culture of violence. For example, juvenile crime is up 47 percent nationally, and almost 3 million violent crimes occur annually at or near schools. The number of violent crimes committed by youth is expected to double by the year 2010 (Perry, 1996a). Similar increases have occurred in reported cases of child abuse and domestic violence (Portner, 1997). According to Sebastian (1996), half of all married women will experience some form of violence from their partners during their marriage and more than one-third are beaten repeatedly.

Feeding this rapidly growing culture of violence is the prevalence of violence on television and in movies and interactive videos. The World Wrestling Federation (WWF), which sponsors professional wrestling matches, particularly glorifies violence by portraying bullies as heroes. Teachers report the influence of WWF wrestling on their students, describing a marked increase in the number of children imitating aggressive WWF gestures and behaviors at school. Many of these teachers also report that parents are becoming more threatening and intimidating toward the teachers when they come to school to complain about something they think is unfair.

Public opinion surveys show that violence in the schools is the number-one education-related concern of Americans (Adler & Springen, 1999). Many schools have adopted get tough policies to deal with violence in the schools. These include initiating zero-tolerance policies, installing metal detectors, hiring more police to patrol the halls, and placing video cameras in school buildings for increased surveillance.

The Hidden Elements in the Culture of Violence

The culture of violence has at least six hidden elements that point toward the occurrence of more Columbine-type shootings:

1. A dominator value system that supports violence

2. An over-focus on negative behaviors

3. The pervasiveness of bullying behavior

4. Collective denial of the effects of bullying behavior

5. The role of post-tramatic stress disorder (PTSD) in the perpetration of violence

6. The effects of parental neglect and emotional abandonment on children.

In this chapter I will address each one of these relatively hidden elements of the culture of violence and describe effective primary prevention methods for dealing with these underlying causes of violence.

A Dominator Value System That Supports Violence

What supports this pervasive culture of violence is a system of dominator values (Weinhold & Weinhold, 2000). These values are behind the increase in aggressive and bullying behaviors. Those who live by these dominator values:

- Use power plays involving violence, threats of violence, intimidation, and exploitation to get their way and to bully others.
- Have little regard for the rights, needs, or even the lives of others, particularly if they see these others as a threat.
- Exploit the needs and rights of others when they perceive them as having less power, status or influence, including women, children, and minorities.
- Are on the defensive and never admit mistakes.
- Blame others for causing their problems.
- Believe that "might makes right."

As evidence of the widespread influence of the dominator system, a study reported that one in three women worldwide has been beaten, raped, or somehow mistreated by men (Heise, Ellsberg, & Gottemoeller, 1999). Dominator values are so tightly woven into the fabric of our culture that they are virtually invisible. For example, most Americans agreed with the United States' bombing of Iraq and Kosovo, even though they knew that thousands of innocent civilians were being killed.

Dominator values are actively promoted by the sports and entertainment industries. For example, hardly anyone even questions the gratuitous violence in wrestling matches sponsored by the World Wrestling Federation or World Championship Wrestling. These matches have some of the highest ratings on cable television. Regular television channels are no better, with daytime shows exemplifying dominator values, such as the Jerry Springer and Jenny Jones programs, commanding huge ratings. Movies such as *The Terminator* glorify violence and pack the theaters. Violent video games such as *Doom* had considerable influence on Eric Harris and Dylan Klebold, the Columbine killers. Violence is a profitable business. Unless these values are changed or supplanted by kinder and more humane values, the culture of violence will continue to grow and flourish in the United States, further undermining all of our democratic institutions.

As a counter balance to the dominator value system is another value system that some call the "humanistic or democratic value system" (Eisler, 1987). Those who espouse these values are people who:

■ Strive to resolve their conflicts with others in peaceful, nonviolent ways so everyone gets their needs met.

■ Use the "rule of law" and seek common ground to settle racial, cultural, religious, and political disputes.

■ Understand cultural relativity and are able to show tolerance and respect toward people of different cultures.

■ Seek equalitarian relationships based on mutual respect, trust, and caring.

■ Admit mistakes and strive to learn from them.

■ Take responsibility for their actions.

These are the values of democracy that we strive to teach our children, but dominator values are undermining the very foundation of our democracy. The dominator value system lurks behind all domestic violence, child abuse, elder abuse, workplace violence, school violence, road rage, hate crimes, and wars.

Over-Focus on Negative Behaviors

Much of people's behavior is motivated by a desire to meet the basic needs for recognition, attention and approval. Over the past 6 years, I visited more than 100 schools, and asked students and faculty members the following question: "Is it easier for you to get noticed or get attention in this school by doing something positive or something negative?" Almost 100 percent of them have replied "negative" (Weinhold, 1999a). This consistent feedback from children and faculty members indicates that children and adults adapt and learn to use negative behaviors to meet their need for recognition because their positive behaviors usually go unnoticed. This is not just a school problem. If someone were to ask the same question of kids in families or workers in companies or in organizations such as the military, they likely would get the same answer.

This focus on negativity is hidden below the tip of our social iceberg and supports the visible culture of violence that we see in the media. For example, have you ever noticed how characters on television sitcoms get the most audience laughter when they make a mistake? This culture of negativity in schools, families, the workplace, and the highway creates an overall climate that breeds violence.

A basic law of psychology says: "What you pay attention to is what you are going to get more of." If we focus too much of our attention on negative behaviors and not enough on positive behaviors, negative behavior will increase. An overwhelmingly negative school climate is damaging to the self-esteem of kids. For example, when kids in kindergarten were asked if they like themselves, 95 percent or more said "yes." By fourth grade, the percentage of these kids who reported liking themselves was down to 60 percent. By eighth grade, the percentage was down to 40 percent, and by twelfth grade, it was down to 5 percent (Weinhold, 1999a).

Columbine High School was no exception. At this upper middle-class suburban high school, every student who was the least bit insecure about himself or herself was worried about being different in some way. A senior girl at Columbine summed it up: "It's a rat race inside the school to see who's going to be more popular. Everybody's thinking: 'Am I going to look cool for the popular kids? Are they going to accept me?'" Another student said, "With all the animosity between the various social groups at Columbine, something like this was bound to happen" (Dube, 1999).

Pervasiveness of Bullying

From firsthand accounts (Dube, 1999; Prendergast, 1999) and from the killers' own videos (Gibbs & Roche, 1999), we know that Harris and Klebold were repeatedly bullied and subjected to verbal put-downs, leading to their plan of violent revenge. Initially, the role of bullying in the Columbine killings was played down. The role of bullying in the Columbine shootings is discussed in more detail later in this chapter.

Bullying is the most common form of violence in our society, and it is what drives the culture of violence. Dominating males and females bully people whom they perceive as weaker and less powerful. Men bully their female partners, women bully their children, older children bully their younger siblings, and younger children bully their pets.

Bruce Perry (1996b) calls this phenomenon the "vortex of violence." He says that violence always travels from the strongest to the weakest or from the most powerful to the least powerful. Known as the *talionic response*, it is part of the adage in the Bible, "an eye for an eye and a tooth for a tooth" (Weinhold, 1991). Men and women who are adult bullies are violent toward less powerful men and women. Men who are adult bullies are violent toward less powerful women. Women who are bullies commit the most violence against children. Older children who bully are the most violent toward younger children. Younger children who have been bullied take it out on their pets. Young children, who are at the bottom of this vortex, often do not have anyone to pass it on to, so they absorb it, accumulate it, and wait until they are old enough, big enough, or strong enough to erupt in some dramatic way that hurts other people.

Bullying in Schools

Although more than 97 percent of U. S. schools report having some sort of violence-prevention program, very few of them are effective, according to the U. S. Department of Education. In a study of the top 84 violence-prevention programs, only 10 were seen as effective (Lederer & Varela, 1998). Less than 10% of the nation's 85,000 public schools have comprehensive school-based mental-health services for kids (Joseph, 1999). Most of the violence-prevention initiatives and studies of the causes of violence, not just those dealing with bullying or school violence, focus on violence of a specific type—family violence, school violence, gang violence, and so on. They do not understand the interrelatedness of the culture of violence, and they usually start too late.

Few programs feature early intervention and primary prevention even though primary prevention programs cost significantly less and are far more effective. Most people are inclined to wait until the problem is acute, and then they try to fix it. In addition, few programs look at the culture of violence for the underlying causes of bullying and school violence. Many homes actually instill in their children dominator values that support bullying and school violence. Instead, we need to instill partnership values in our schools to counter some of the dominator values that kids bring with them to school. Using reactive and shortsighted approaches to try to prevent violence is like trying to avoid hitting an iceberg by rearranging the deck chairs on the Titanic. It has no effect on the outcome.

What is bullying? There is some confusion about what constitutes bullying. Bullying is defined as something that someone repeatedly does or says to gain power over or to dominate another person. The following are some typical examples of bullying:

■ name calling, put-downs, cruel teasing

■ saying or writing nasty things about others

■ deliberately excluding certain people from activities

■ not talking to certain people

■ threatening others with bodily harm

■ taking or damaging others' things

■ hitting or kicking

■ making people do things they don't want to do.

Among several kinds of bullies are the following (Marano, 1995).

1. *Proactive bullies* need no provocation and are naturally more aggressive toward others. This group frequently has poor social and relational skills and compensates for this lack of skills by picking on others.

2. *Reactive bullies* often are victimized by other bullies and then retaliate by becoming bullies as well.

3. *Provocative victims* provoke fights or aggressive encounters with others. They are quick to become oppositional or defiant and cry or display exaggerated responses in conflict situations. This group is mostly rejected by their peers and has the fewest friends.

It is often difficult for even peers to identify who are the bullies and who are the victims because the vortex of violence is so prevalent and so many participate in it (Paulk et al., 1999).

Brown's Broken Toy Project

Tom Brown (1999), the founder of the Broken Toy Project and conductor of school workshops on bullying, asked kids to describe bullying. Here is what they told him, in their own words:

- new kids
- fat kids
- skinny kids
- boys that "suck" in sports
- boys that act like "fags"
- lesbians
- kids who are smart
- kids who are dumb
- geeks
- computer-freaks
- kids who wear geeky out-of-style clothes
- kids who stink and smell
- teacher's pets
- kids with unkempt hair
- retarded kids
- kids who talk funny
- kids who walk funny
- minority kids
- kids in wheelchairs
- kids who get good grades
- kids who get poor grades
- girls with blonde hair
- kids with curly hair
- kids with freckles
- kids with funny looking ears or noses
- kids with diseases

As you can see from this list, just about any kid in school could become a target of a bully. All they have to do is be different in some way that causes them to stand out.

The kids in Tom Brown's study were explicit about *where* kids get bullied. They said:

the bus
the bathroom
the halls
recess
P.E. class

When Tom Brown asked the students why they thought bullies picked on other kids, the students gave the following answers:

They have low self-esteem.
Other kids egg them on.
For attention.
They're mean and don't care about other kids' feelings.
It's cool. You get a lot of friends when you're a bully.

Tom Brown's kids were explicit about why they don't tell grown-ups about bullying incidents:

Fear of a parent or guardian going to school and yelling at the bullies or teachers or principal.
Fear of being told to fight back when they have no desire to fight back.
Shame.
Not wanting to scare or worry their parents.

Tom's kids indicated that they got mixed messages from grown-ups:

Fight back.
Walk away.
Tell your teacher.
Quit being a baby. Start taking up for yourself.

The kids gave their reasons why kids are afraid to confront bullies:

You get instant retaliation.
You get ganged up on by bullies and their friends.
You get in trouble with the school.
You get a reputation of being a bully yourself.
The bully's older brother or sister will get after you.
You might hurt the bully and get sued or in trouble with the police.

When Tom Brown asked kids what three things kids usually do when they see someone being bullied, he got an answer that is at the heart of why bullying persists. The students said:

Run over and watch.
Run over and watch.
Run over and watch.

What keeps bullying going isn't just the bullies and the victims. It is also the bystanders who watch the incidents of bullying and do nothing to stop them. Bystanders provide an audience for the bully and give bullies the peer attention they crave. Any intervention designed to stop bullying must address the role of the bystanders.

What do kids do when they are bullied? Again Tom Brown's kids told it like it is:

Walk or run away.
Get a teacher to help.
Use humor.
Tell the bully to leave you alone.
Yell to attract a lot of attention.

Brown (1999) summarized some of the most ineffective methods that educators use to deal with bullying:

Punish both the bully and the victim.
Look the other way; ignore bullying behavior, passing it off as horseplay or kids being kids.
Bring the bully and the victim together in one room and ask the bully if he or she has been bullying the victim.
Tell the victim to quit being a crybaby and start standing up for himself or herself.
Tell the victim to make better friends.
Tell the victim to quit tattling on other kids.
Punish the bully without any attempt to resolve the situation—for example, setting up a meeting between the bully and a counselor or someone else who can talk to this student without coming off as a threat.
Yell at either or both the victim and the bully in front of other children.
Show an educational film dealing with bullying without processing the contents of the film before or afterward.
Spend money to bring an anti-bullying program into a school without doing follow-up activities.

Brown (1999) summarized his research by saying, "This is what I hear from children everywhere I go to present my program. It doesn't matter what kind of school or if the child is a first or a sixth grader. Kids know exactly what is going on."

Olweus's Research on Bullying

Dan Olweus (Olweus, 1994), from the University of Bergen in Norway, did an extensive study of bullying. Here are his definition and conclusions:

Bullying occurs when one or more persons deliberately and repeatedly try to hurt another person through words or actions. Relevant conclusions are:

■ Bullying is an act of violence, and it is against the law.

■ The bully's ultimate goal is to achieve domination and control over another person.

■ Bullies often are not good students and have academic problems in school, such as a learning disability.

■ Bullies often lack power in their own lives and compensate for it by dominating others.

■ Children who bully become adults who bully unless they receive help.

■ Bullying is a cry for help.

Why is bullying important to us?

1. *All school violence begins with bullying.* All serious school violence starts with seemingly innocent bullying or put-downs which eventually can escalate into violence involving guns or knives. The lack of respect for another person's human rights—the most common factor in all criminal behavior—begins with school bullying. Schools that do not deal with bullying when it first appears can become a breeding ground for criminal behavior and pose a serious threat to public safety.

2. *Serious school violence is on the increase.* One of the first cases of school violence to reach the national press occurred in 1994. Fifteen-year-old Brian, from Woodstock, Georgia, cried out in his school classroom, "I can't take this any more," and then, with a single gunshot, ended his life. After his death, his parents and the school officials learned that Brian had been the victim of repeated harassment, humiliation, and bullying at school. Actually, since 1992, there have been 250 violent deaths in schools that involved multiple victims, culminating with the Columbine massacre (Joseph, 1999).

The great majority of these deaths occurred in cities and towns with populations of under 80,000 people, showing us that there is no safe place for our kids. Almost all the killers were white males from relatively affluent families, not gang-members or teens from the inner city. In virtually every school shooting, bullying has been a factor. As in the Columbine shootings, most of the students who committed these violent crimes were "reactive bullies" who finally decided to get revenge against the other bullies who had picked on them.

Some of the other school shootings that involved bullying are as follows.

Feb. 2, 1996:   Two male students in Moses Lake, Washington, were shot to death by a 14-year-old male honor student who had been the target of repeated bullying by those students.

Mar. 24, 1998: An 11-year-old boy and a 13-year-old boy shot and killed four girls and a female teacher in a Jonesboro, Arkansas, middle school. They had made repeated threats to others in the school about their intent to do violence, but they were ignored. The 13-year-old was described as a bully.

Sept. 1998:   Two school outcasts in Green River, Wyoming, 18-year-old Cody Bradley and 16-year-old David Taylor, who were ostracized and

	bullied by other students, stabbed and killed a 17-year-old boy who they said stole Bradley's girlfriend, and then they shot themselves a day later in a suicide pact.
Oct. 1998:	A 12-year-old middle-school student from Woodstock, Georgia, was beaten up by a known 15-year-old bully as he got off the bus at school. The victim went into a coma and a few days later was taken off life support.
Nov. 1998:	Five Burlington, Wisconsin, boys were arrested for plotting the deaths of their teachers, administrators, and the other students who they said were picking on them. They told school officials that the other students "treated them like trash."

3. *Bullying was at the root of the Columbine massacre.* We must learn the lessons of the Columbine massacre if we are to prevent it from happening again. The group of Columbine students identified as the "trenchcoat mafia," which included Eric Harris and Dylan Klebold, was harassed, bullied and put down daily for years. This practice was initiated by a clique of student athletes and later joined many other Columbine students.

Every day when Harris and Klebold came to school, they were met at the door by a group of students who harassed them by pouring orange juice on their trenchcoats so they would have to wear the sticky stuff all day. Harris, Klebold, and others in this group who were bullied tried to sneak into school through a side door or back door to avoid this daily ritual. They also were harassed in the hallways and cafeteria and were called names. Frequently the football players would throw a body block on them, knocking them into the lockers or the wall, and call them "dirt bags" or "dirt balls." One 15-year-old Columbine student said, "It must have been hell for them" (Dube, 1999).

Time magazine (Gibbs & Roche, 1999) quoted a 255-pound defensive lineman at Columbine as saying,

> Columbine is a clean, good place except for those rejects. Sure, we teased them. But what do you expect with kids who come to school with weird hairdos and horns on their hats? It's not just the jocks; the whole school's disgusted with them. They're a bunch of homos, grabbing each other's private parts. If you want to get rid of someone, usually you tease 'em. So the whole school would call them homos, and when they did something sick, we'd tell them, "You're sick and that's wrong."

Even though this happened in front of many students and teachers, no one tried to stop it. The killers wore weird clothing to call attention to themselves and even wore armbands that said, "I hate people." As they opened fire on their classmates, Harris and Klebold were heard to say, "This is for all the people who made fun of us all these years" (Dube, 1999).

Notwithstanding their obvious cries for help, no one gave these boys the kind of attention they really needed. They were very bright and very lonely, yet no one seemed to try to redirect their behavior in more positive ways. Further, cliques like those that bullied and harassed Harris and Klebold at Columbine High School exist in every school in this country. In most schools, the athletes are at the top of the heap. They act out the dominator behaviors that many school athletic programs highly value.

Killing is a learned behavior. Children don't naturally kill. They learn it from their experience of violence in their home and, most pervasively, from violence as entertainment on television, in the movies, and by playing interactive video games. Killing requires the availability of weapons and training because there is a built-in aversion to killing one's own kind. Law enforcement and military personnel know this because they have to go through rigorous training before they are able to shoot someone, if necessary. And then they are trained not to kill but, instead, to maim or disarm a dangerous person with a weapon (Grossman, 1998).

Research on the effects of television is clear. In nations or regions where television is introduced for the first time, the murder rate doubles within 15 years. The American Medical Association concluded that long-term childhood exposure to television is a causal factor behind approximately half of the violent crimes committed in the United States, or about 10,000 homicides, 70,000 rapes, and 700,000 injurious assaults (Grossman, 1996).

David Grossman (1998) said:

> The result is a phenomenon that functions much like AIDS, which I call AVIDS—Acquired Violence Immune Deficiency Syndrome. AIDS has never killed anybody. It destroys your immune system, and then other diseases that shouldn't kill you become fatal. Television violence by itself does not kill you. It destroys your violence immune system and conditions you to derive pleasure from violence. And once you are at close range with another human being and its time for you to pull that trigger, Acquired Violence Immune Deficiency Syndrome can destroy your midbrain resistance. (p. 36)

Further, violent video games are teaching our children how to shoot to kill with increasing accuracy. In the Jonesboro, Arkansas, killings, one boy had no experience shooting guns and the other had only some experience in shooting guns. Yet, they fired 27 shots from 100 yards and hit 15 people. That's pretty good shooting. Why were they so good? They both had played violent video games for hours at a time that taught them how to hit targets. Video games train kids to shoot a gun to kill someone (Grossman, 1998).

On a dare from a friend, a 15-year-old boy in South Carolina tried to rob a local convenience store. In the process, he reflexively shot and killed the clerk. From 6 feet away, he pointed a snub-nosed .38-caliber pistol at the back of the clerk's head, and when the clerk turned around to face the boy, the boy shot the clerk right between the eyes. This boy had spent hundreds of hours playing video games, learning to point and shoot, point and shoot. When asked why he did it, the boy replied, "I don't know. It was a mistake. It wasn't supposed to happen" (Grossman, 1998).

Those who have been in the military or law-enforcement know that the correct option is often not to shoot. But when kids put their quarter in a video machine, their intention is to shoot to kill. In a video game, there is always a stimulus that sets them off and instructs them to start shooting.

In the case of the 15-year-old boy in South Carolina—he said he got excited and scared when the convenience clerk turned around; his heart rate went up; the flow of adrenaline closed down his forebrain, he panicked and reflexively he did what he was conditioned to do: He pulled the trigger, shooting just as accurately as he had done hundreds of times before when he was playing video games. Our children are learning to kill and to enjoy it (Grossman, 1998).

Here are some additional statistics:

- 60 percent of men on TV dramas are depicted in violent scenes; 11% are killers (Grossman, 1998).

- In the media in general, the majority of victims are women and children (Grossman, 1998).

- 20 percent of suburban high-school students endorsed the idea of shooting someone "who has stolen something from you" (Grossman, 1996).

Bullying is pervasive in most schools. Some statistics that bear this out are:

- Half of all violence against teenagers occurs in school buildings, on school property, or on the street in the vicinity of the school. Most begins as bullying or put-downs (NIDR, 1999).

- The National School Safety Center estimates that more than 525,000 attacks, shakedowns, and robberies occur per month in public secondary schools in the United States (Weinhold & Weinhold, 1998).

- The National Education Association estimates that 160,000 students miss school every day (totaling 28 million missed days per year), because of fear of attack or intimidation by a bully (Fried & Fried, 1996).

- Students receive an average of 213 verbal put-downs per week, or 30 per day (Fried, personal communication, 1996).

- In a survey of 558 students in a Midwestern middle school, the researchers found that 80 percent of the students had engaged in bullying behaviors in the previous 30 days (Espelage et al., 1999).

- 80 to 90 percent of adolescents report some form of victimization from a bully at school (Espelage et al., 1999).

- 90 percent of all students thought that bullying caused social, emotional, or academic problems for the students who were bullied (Weinhold & Weinhold, 2000).

- 69 percent of all students believe that schools respond poorly to bullying and victimization (Weinhold & Weinhold, 2000).

How does bullying differ from grade to grade? (Olweus, 1994).

■ Bullying occurs in every grade, but it happens most frequently in grades 4 through 8.

■ Bullying usually starts as teasing and put-downs with younger bullies and then becomes more physical and more violent as bullies get older.

■ Bullies can be easily identified in each grade by the sixth week of the school year.

■ Potential bullies can be easily identified as early as preschool if we recognize the early warning signs.

How does bullying differ between boys and girls? (Saunders, 1997).

■ Boys tend to use direct physical and verbal attacks to bully others.

■ Girls tend to use more indirect, subtle, and social methods such as exclusion, manipulation, and spreading rumors.

■ Boys tend to bully other boys (80 percent) and girls (60 percent).

■ Boys are more likely than girls to be both perpetrators and victims of aggressive physical and verbal bullying by peers.

■ In middle-school, girls who mature early are often bullied and sexually harassed by boys.

■ Girls tend to bully only other girls.

■ Boys usually bully alone, and girls bully in groups.

Bullying Outside of School

How pervasive is bullying outside of schools? Considering that bullying is a hidden part of the overall culture of violence that is supported by dominator values, you can see that it occurs almost everywhere—at home, at work, and on the road.

At home, some key points in bullying are as follows.

■ Older siblings often bully their younger brothers and sisters.

■ Bullies and victims of bullying often grow up to become batterers. Adult perpetrators of domestic violence often have been identified as bullies or victims of bullying while they were in school (Straus & Gelles, 1988).

Bullying occurs in the workplace as well. Bully OnLine (1999) reported the results of a study, as follows.

■ Bullies at school who get away with it often become serial bullies at work.

■ Children who get bullied at school tend to become targets for bullying at work.

■ More than one million U. S. workers are assaulted annually.

■ The most common reasons people are bullied on the job are that they are good at their job and they are popular with other employees (the workplace bully is driven by jealousy and envy).

- In the United Kingdom, one in three people leave their job because of bullying.
- The same study showed that 53 percent of UK employees have been bullied during their working life.

Road rage has become recognized in recent years. Nerenberg (1999) reported the following:

- Road rage is another form of bullying.
- In 1996, 28,000 Americans died because of aggressive driving.
- There are 2 billion episodes of road rage per year in the United States.
- Violent incidents of road rage have increased 51 percent over the last five years.

Collective Denial About Effects of Bullying

The most common way that schools deal with bullying is to ignore it. Many teachers don't see anything wrong with bullying. One Columbine student reported, "Teachers would see them push someone into a locker, and they'd just ignore it" (Prendergast, 1999). A junior at Columbine said, "I can't believe the faculty couldn't figure it out. It was so obvious that something was wrong" (Dube, 1999). In another study, teachers were able to identify only 10 percent of the students who reported being a victim of a bully (Paulk et. al., 1999). A prevailing attitude among some teachers is that those who get bullied probably had it coming to them. In families, fewer than one in 10 incidents of bullying involving suspected child abuse or domestic violence ever get reported, and of the incidents that are reported, few are ever investigated and almost none result in any criminal charges (Weinhold, 1991).

How does bullying differ from normal peer conflicts? The collective denial is supported by misconceptions about how bullying situations differ from normal peer conflicts. There is a big difference between these situations (Weinhold, 1999a). A bullying situation has six defining factors:

- *Intent to harm.* The perpetrator finds pleasure in taunting or trying to dominate the victim and continues even when the victim's distress is obvious.
- *Intensity and duration.* The bullying continues over a long period and the extent of bullying is damaging to the self-esteem of the victim.
- *Power of the bully.* The bully has power over the victim because of age, strength, size, or gender.
- *Vulnerability of the victim.* The victim is more sensitive to teasing, cannot adequately defend himself or herself, and has physical or psychological qualities that make him or her more prone to victimization.
- *Lack of support.* The victim feels isolated and exposed. Often, the victim is afraid to report the bullying for fear of retaliation.
- *Consequences.* Damage to the victim's self-esteem is longlasting and leads the victim to markedly withdraw from school or, conversely, to become aggressive.

In a normal peer conflict situation, in contrast, none of these elements is present. Those who are involved in a normal peer conflict

- do not insist on getting their own way.
- give reasons why they disagree.
- apologize or offer win-win suggestions.
- are free to bargain and negotiate to get their needs met.
- can change the topic and walk away.

Effects of Bullying

What are the short-term effects of bullying in our schools? Here are some examples of the immediate or short-term effects of bullying in schools:

- 10 percent of students who drop out of school do so because of repeated bullying (Weinhold & Weinhold, 1998).
- 20 percent of all high school students surveyed report avoiding the restrooms out of a fear of being bullied (NIDR, 1999).
- In the United States, about 2 million teenagers carry guns, knives, clubs, and razors (NIDR, 1999).
- As many as 135,000 take these weapons to school (NIDR, 1999).
- Nearly one-third of the students have heard a classmate threaten to kill someone (Langer, 1999).
- 78 percent who knew of the threats to kill someone said they didn't report them to an adult (Langer, 1999).
- 40 percent of high school students say there are potentially violent cliques at their school (Langer, 1999).
- One in five of the students say they personally know a classmate who has brought a gun to school (Langer, 1999).
- Of those who knew a classmate who brought a gun to school, 83 percent say they did not report it to an adult (Langer, 1999).
- 54 percent of the students say it would be easy for them to get a gun (One student said it was as easy as buying candy at the corner store) (Langer, 1999).
- 67 percent say it would be easy for them to make a bomb (Langer, 1999).

What are the known long-term effects of bullying? Some of the conclusions of the Olweus (1993, 1994) studies are:

Studies on Those Who Are Bullied (Olweus, 1993)

- Being bullied during middle school is predictive of low self-esteem 10 years later.

■ By age 23, children who were bullied in middle school were more depressed and had lower self-esteem than their peers who had not been bullied.

■ Bullied children feel more isolated than their peers, who often reject them out of fear that they, too, will become a target of bullies if they are seen with targeted students.

■ Being bullied can lead to suicide.

■ Some victims of bullies resort to eventual violent retaliation against the bully.

Studies on the Bullies Themselves (Olweus, 1994)

■ By age 23, about 60 percent of the boys identified as bullies in middle school had at least one conviction of a crime, and 35 percent to 40 percent had three or more convictions.

■ 50 percent of all identified school bullies became criminals as adults.

■ Bullies at age 8 are three times more likely to be convicted of a crime by age 30.

■ Bullies are less likely than nonbullies to finish college or locate a good job.

Why do children bully and put others down? There is a clash between the old and the new thinking on the causes of bullying and school violence. The new thinking is based on the recent research findings cited in this chapter. Table 8.1 presents a comparison.

Causes of Bullying

If we are going to eliminate the causes of bullying, a multitude of risk factors have to be addressed. Consider the following risk factors.

Family factors

■ The home is the most violent place in the United States (Straus, 1994).

■ Children from violent homes are three to four times more likely to become bullies. Contrary to popular belief, most of the violence directed at young children in the home comes from the mother and older siblings (Straus & Gelles, 1988).

■ Three primary predictive family factors are (Weinhold & Weinhold, 2000):

— a lack of solid bonding/attachment with the young child.

— poor supervision and neglect of the child's needs.

— acceptance and modeling of aggressive or bullying behaviors by parents or older siblings.

■ Few early identification and intervention programs are available to help young children who show aggressive tendencies.

Table 8.1   Conventional Versus New Thinking

CONVENTIONAL THINKING	NEW THINKING
Bullying is genetic. Bullies are born that way.	Bullying is shaped by early childhood experiences.
Bullies should just be expelled.	Bullying is a cry for help.
Bullying is normal kids' behavior.	Bullying is a symptom of untreated trauma.
Bullying is harmless.	Bullying is traumatic for those being bullied.
Bullies will grow out of it.	Without intervention, bullying leads to further violence.
Bullies are influenced by peer modeling.	Bullies are influenced more by media and family modeling.
Watching violence on TV or movies is harmless.	TV and movie violence traumatizes kids.
Violent video games are harmless fantasy.	Traumatized kids can't separate reality and fantasy.

Personality factors

- Children with an impulsive temperament are more inclined to develop into bullies (Olweus, 1994).

- Bullies often have attachment disorders (Weinhold, 1999).

- Boys who are physically bigger or stronger than peers of the same age are more likely to become bullies (Olweus, 1993).

- Bullies like to be in charge, dominate, and assert their power. They like to win at any cost (Olweus, 1993).

- Bullies crave attention, so they show off and act tough to get it from peers (Olweus, 1994).

- Bullies lack empathy for their victims and have difficulty feeling compassion (Olweus, 1993).

- Bullies believe that the victim provoked the attack and deserves the consequences (Olweus, 1994).

- Bullying is a cry for help (Olweus, 1994).

School Factors

- The amount of adult supervision is directly tied to the frequency and severity of bullying in schools (Saunders, 1997).

- A negative school climate where negative behavior gets most of the attention encourages the formation of cliques and bullying (Espelage et al., 1999).

- Some teachers threaten, tease, shame, or intimidate students to maintain control of their classroom (Olweus, 1994).

- 25 percent of teachers see nothing wrong with bullying and put-downs. Schools often condone this behavior and do nothing to prevent bullying and put-downs (Olweus, 1994).

- The learning environment can be poisoned by bullying and put-downs, raising the fear and anxiety of all students (Johnson & Johnson, 1995).

- Early identification and intervention programs are lacking. Bullies can be identified as early as preschool (Olweus, 1994).

Community Factors (Hawkins, Catalano et al., 1992).

- Schools in poor urban neighborhoods experience more violence in and around schools.

- People feel less safe in neighborhoods that show evidence of crack houses, drug dealing, and related violence. This spills over into the neighborhood schools, where there is more drug-dealing and related violence.

- Schools located in neighborhoods with high turnover mobility and transiency also have more bullying.

- State and local policies about early prevention, identification, and intervention are lacking.

Role of PTSD and Trauma as a Hidden Cause of Violence

A book on conflict resolution, *Conflict Resolution: The Partnership Way* (Weinhold & Weinhold, 2000) presents research indicating that most conflict situations involve stimulus conditions that remind those involved of previously unresolved conflicts and traumas. In a conflict situation, people frequently show symptoms resembling a post-traumatic stress reaction, or when they witness violent conflicts involving others, they may actually regress to an earlier trauma or conflict. They are actually existing in two realities at once, and usually they are unaware of why they are reacting the way they are.

Symptoms of PTSD

Clinical symptoms of post-traumatic stress disorder (PTSD) (APA, 1996) are as follows:

- *Reexperiencing old traumas*—Recurrent and intrusive recollections, distressing dreams, flashbacks, intense reactions to ordinary events.

- *Persistent avoidance of triggering situations and a "numbing" effect on general responsiveness*—Compulsive efforts to avoid people, thoughts, or feelings that arouse memories, depression, or detachment from others; a restricted range of affect.

- *Increased hypervigilence*—Difficulty sleeping, irritability and outbursts of anger, difficulty concentrating; an exaggerated startle response.

Activation of the Adrenal Stress Response

Another effect of repeated exposure to conflict and violence is that people become desensitized to violence. When I give talks on violence, I typically ask members of the audience to raise their hand if they have personally witnessed violence or if they were the victim of violence. Typically, about one-third of the audience members raise a hand. To not have witnessed any violence, they would not have seen a violent television show or a violent movie and would not have seen anyone in the family, workplace, highway, school, or neighborhood being violent. Highly unlikely! Why did they not raise their hand then?

They likely had to dissociate so they could cope with the amount of violence they were exposed to. At the same time, they remain in a constant hypervigilent state to avoid being triggered by memories of past violence. If people are in a persistent hyperaroused state, adrenal horomones are flowing through their bloodstream, and they are likely to fight, flee, or freeze if the current conflict situation contains even the slightest hint of an earlier conflict situation that they did not resolve. These classic adrenal stress reactions are wired into us to help us deal with situations in which we perceive danger. We don't even have to think about it (Weinhold & Weinhold, 2000).

When bullies pick on others, they likely have been triggered into the fight mode of the adrenal stress reaction. They hope they can discharge the accumulated fear, anger, and hurt from an earlier traumatic incident by picking on those they perceive as weaker. Untreated symptoms of PTSD may be a major factor in why people own more than 250 million guns in the United States. They just don't feel safe.

Accompanying the fear of violent encounters is a companion factor that causes people to be attracted to and fascinated by violence. The natural learning style of humans is to repeat a behavior until it is learned or understood or the trauma is healed. Freud called this *repetition compulsion*. Thus, we are drawn to what we fear. That is why so many people like to watch violent events, such as wrestling and seem to enjoy being scared out of their wits by violence on TV and in the movies.

People actually seem to be addicted to violence at the same time they are still trying to understand and heal what happened to them when they were traumatized by it during early childhood. Children see violence on TV and it traumatizes them. They then either compulsively try to stay away from anything that might remind them of this kind of violence and at the same time are drawn to it (Weinhold & Weinhold, 2000).

Parental Neglect and Emotional Abandonment of Our Children

In Ken Magid's and Carol McKelvey's book *High Risk: Children Without a Conscience* (1989), they state that severely abused and neglected children will grow up to become violence-seeking adults unless there is an intervention in their lives before age 16. These authors estimate that up to 20 million adults fall in this category and the numbers are growing more rapidly than the population. They advise that we must do a better job of protecting these children and intervening in the lives of young children who exhibit symptoms of attachment disorder. If we don't, Magid predicts that "soon there will be more of them than us and then we will be in real trouble" (Magid, 1992).

Research by Dr. Bruce Perry of Baylor College of Medicine (1996a, 1996b) has pointed to a particular family environment that will turn a normal child into a killer. He uncovered the effects on the brain of repeated stress caused by abuse, neglect, or terror, which cause physical and maybe permanent changes in young children. He found that the constant flood of adrenaline causes the brain to reset the brain's alarm system on an almost constant hair-trigger alert. Children who are constantly exposed to abuse or who witness the abuse of others, such as a sibling or a parent, can also cause their brains' system of adrenal stress horomones to become unresponsive.

These are the high-risk kids that Magid is talking about. They have antisocial personalities and typically have a low heart rate and impaired emotional sensitivity including a lack of empathy. They often kill or torture animals (Begley, 1999).

A Profile of the Character-Disturbed Child

Cline (1979) was one of the first to profile the characteristics of a high-risk child who has an attachment disorder. He listed the following characteristics:

■ Lack of ability to give and receive affection.

■ Self-destructive behavior.

■ Cruelty to others.

■ Phoniness.

■ Severe problems with stealing, hoarding, and gorging on food.

■ Marked control problems.

■ Lack of long-term friends.

■ Abnormalities in eye contact.

The three types of maternal attachments are: secure, avoidant, and anxious/ambivalent. Campos, Barrett, et al. (1983), found that 62 percent of infants are securely attached, 23 percent are avoidant, and 15 percent are insecure/ambivalent. The type of early attachment a child has causes him or her to develop what is called an internal "working model" of the world (Ainsworth, 1989; Bowlby, 1988). There are also three identifiable sub-types of avoidantly attached children: (a) the lying bully who blames others; (b) the shy, dissociated loner who seems emotionally flat, and (c) the obviously disturbed child with repetitive twitches and tics who day-dreams and shows little interest in his or her environment. The two ambivalent sub-types are: (a) the fidgety, impulsive child with poor concentration who is tense and easily upset by his or her failures, and (b) the fearful, hypersensitive, clingy child who lacks initiative and gives up easily (Karen, 1998).

The *DSM-IV* (APA, 1996) has updated these characteristics in its diagnosis of a "Conduct Disorder." This diagnosis applies to anyone under 18 years of age, and for those over 18, it usually is called an Antisocial Personality Disorder. The symptoms are as follows:

Aggression toward people and animals:

■ Often bullies, threatens, or intimidates others.

■ Often initiates physical fights.

■ Has used a weapon that can cause serious physical harm to others.

■ Has been physically cruel to people.

■ Has been physically cruel to animals.

■ Has stolen while confronting a victim.

■ Has forced someone into sexual activity.

Destruction of property:

■ Has deliberately engaged in fire-setting with the intention of causing serious damage.

■ Has deliberately destroyed others' property (other than by fire-setting).

Deceitfulness or theft:

■ Has broken into someone else's house, building, or car.

■ Often lies to obtain goods or favors or to avoid obligations.

■ Has stolen items of nontrivial value without confronting a victim.

Serious violations of rules:

■ Often stays out at night despite parental prohibitions, beginning before 13 years of age.

■ Has run away from home overnight at least twice while living in parental or parental surrogate home.

■ Is often truant from school, beginning before 13 years of age.

To be diagnosed with this disorder, a persistent pattern of three or more of these behaviors must be present over the past 12 months, with the presence of at least one of the behaviors for the past 3 months. Most of these behaviors are similar to the ones that Cline found in his study on the effects of poor bonding and attachment. Clearly, parental neglect, abuse, and emotional abandonment play an important role in creating the internal "working model" of these kinds of young people. If we are going to stop bullying and school violence as well as the rest of the antisocial behaviors of children and adults, we have to help parents achieve a secure bond or attachment with their children.

In addition, Perry's research has indicated that parents who are withdrawn and remote, neglectful and passive or depressed, are at risk of causing their child's brain to stop developing. Perry found that neglect impairs the development of the brain's cortex, where feelings of belonging and attachment occur. According to Perry, these neglected kids desperately need positive adult attention to compensate for the lack of attention or negative attention they received early in life from their parents or family members (Perry, 1996b).

Violato and Russell (1994) conducted a Canadian meta-analysis of 88 published research studies on the effects of nonmaternal care on the development of infants and young children. They found that if the mother is gone for more than 20 hours a week, it can seriously affect the social-emotional, behavioral development and maternal attachment of infants and young children. Lero, Goelman, et al. (1992) found that 70 percent of Canadian mothers with children under 6 years old are working fulltime. In the United States, the figure is estimated to be 75 percent. This form of neglect has serious implications for our national policy of federal and state support for daycare so mothers can work.

Other research has confirmed that once the internal working model of the world is formed in early childhood, it persists into adulthood virtually unchanged (Pearson, Cowen, et al. 1993). Krause and Haverkamp (1996) summarize the research this way:

Existing research does suggest that the bond between parent and child is likely to remain in effect across the life span and plays an important role in later life parent-child relations. (pp. 85–86)

From their meta-analysis cited above, Violato and Russell (1994) concluded that the absence of the mother for more than 20 hours per week during infancy and early childhood increases the prevalence of insecure/ambivalent attachments by approximately 50 percent.

Developmental Trauma

As a part of the author's research on conflict resolution, he has identified the presence of developmental traumas during early childhood as the main cause of a later fear of or fascination with violence. These traumas often are caused more by neglect than abuse and, therefore, are harder to identify because "nothing happened," except that the child's needs were neglected and the significant adults disconnected from them (Weinhold & Weinhold, 2000).

The following are the usual causes of developmental traumas (Weinhold & Weinhold, 2000):

- Child abuse, neglect, or emotional abandonment during the first 2 years of life.
- Disruptions in the normal sequence of development.
- Prolonged or repeated separations between mother and child during early bonding because of illness.
- Daily small disconnects between mother and child.
- Repeated encroachment of the child's physical, psychological, and emotional boundaries.
- A lack of understanding of the child's needs.
- Lack of support for safe exploratory behavior.
- Using the child to satisfy the parent's needs.

This research (Weinhold & Weinhold, 2000) has shown that developmental traumas may be the cause of the following problems:

- Developmental delays—"late-bloomers."
- Attachment disorders (ambivalent or anxious/avoidant).
- Attention deficit/hyperactive disorder.
- Cognitive impairment because of cognitive neglect.
- Primitive problem-solving strategies that involve use of violence.
- Dissociation in females.
- Aggressive, impulsive, reactive, and hyperactive behaviors in males.

The author of *Real Boys* (Pollack, 1998), says that when parents or other adults disconnect from young boys, the boys learn to suffer in silence and, rather than crying tears, they eventually "cry bullets." This fits with the description of events in the lives of Eric Harris and Dylan Klebold. Their pent-up abandonment rage, exacerbated by the marginalization at school, discharged through violence. By studying brain scans, Perry found that neglected children had more damage to the cognitive functions of their brain than did abused children. The brain actually atrophies when it isn't stimulated enough. Another of Perry's findings is that children who were traumatized early in life develop more primitive, less mature styles of conflict resolution. They tend to be more impulsive, more easily triggered by stimulus events, and less likely to consider the consequences of their actions. Looked at through this lens, bullying can be seen as adapting to the effects of early traumas and using bullying as a protective mechanism to try to feel safe again (Perry, 1996b).

Conclusions from this research can be summarized as follows (Weinhold & Weinhold, 2000):

- Many bullies and victims of bullying show classic signs of PTSD and possibly suffer from the effects of the neglect of their basic attachment needs early in life.

- Bullying incidents usually begin with a triggering event that leads to a traumatic reenactment of previous unresolved developmental traumas or conflicts experienced by the bully or the victim, or both.

- Bullies and victims need counseling that teaches them trauma-reduction techniques and conflict-resolution skills, and provides them with the positive attention they missed in their early childhood experiences.

The Kindness Campaign: A Primary Prevention Program To Curb Bullying and School Violence

The Kindness Campaign was started in July 1994 under the National Program for the Study and Prevention of Youth and Family Violence at the University of Colorado at Colorado Springs. It was designed as a primary prevention program to address the rising tide of violence among youth, in families, and in schools. Though the National Program receives in-kind support from the university, it depends upon grants and contributions from individuals and corporations. The Kindness Campaign is based on the idea that the best way to eliminate a negative behavior (bullying, put-downs, aggressive behaviors) is by focusing everyone's attention on the opposite of these behaviors: kindness. The program addresses each of the hidden elements of the culture of violence. Below is a summary of how the Kindness Campaign addresses these hidden elements and the results achieved thus far.

Promoting Humanistic Values

The predominant message of the Kindness Campaign is that domination and violence can be stopped if schools and communities use their resources to promote humanistic values such as kindness, respect for the law, peaceful resolution of conflicts, and understanding and tolerance of differences. The campaign's co-sponsor, the local CBS television affiliate, conducted a random sample interview of its viewers in late 1994 and found that 75% of its viewers believed the Campaign was having a positive impact on the community (Weinhold, 1996). Since then, the Kindness Campaign has co-sponsored many community events designed to build common ground and increase understanding and tolerance. These events include an Annual Interfaith Celebration of Kindness and neighborhood ceremonies to recognize the positive activities of residents.

Kindness Campaign programs have been started in more than 105 schools, reaching over 70,000 students in Colorado Springs. Ten other U.S. cities have adopted the Kindness Campaign in their community and schools. As a result of the efforts of the Kindness Campaign's programs, in 1997 the city of Colorado Springs was one of three U.S. cities to be named a "Community of Kindness."

Creating a Positive School and Community Climate

More than 105 area schools have used the Kindness Campaign to improve their school climate. Their results indicate that children who get more recognition for positive behaviors don't have to bully others or wear trench coats to get attention. The Kindness Campaign has produced a curriculum guide, *Spreading Kindness: A Program Guide for Preventing Peer Violence in Schools,* which contains 154 activities for schools to use in designing their own program.

One suggested activity shows how to develop a school Kindness Code that would include the following:

1. "We will say and do kind things to others in this school."

2. "We will recognize the kind things that other people say and do."

3. "We will help those who are having trouble being kind."

In most schools that started the Kindness Campaign, student to student put-downs dropped significantly. One elementary school reduced put-downs by 94 percent after the Kindness Campaign was introduced (Weinhold, 1999a).

Reducing Bullying and Aggressive Behaviors

When bullies see other kids getting recognized for positive behaviors, they begin exhibiting more positive behaviors. In three different middle schools where the Kindness Campaign was introduced, discipline referrals to the office dropped by more than 30 percent. The Kindness Campaign's Creating Kind and Safe Schools program helps schools develop an anti-bullying policy. Faculty and students learn about the negative effects of bullying and then collaborate to create a schoolwide anti-bullying policy. Such a policy might include the following:

1. "Teachers and staff agree to confront all incidents of bullying and put-downs that they see."

2. "Students agree to help those being bullied or put down by speaking out and/or getting adult help."

3. "All students, faculty and staff agree to include everyone in their activities. No one is marginalized."

Dealing With Student Traumas

One of the best ways to deal with untreated trauma is the use of peer mediation programs and schoolwide conflict-resolution classes. Peer mediation involves identifying a group of students, who are selected for their leadership and interpersonal qualities, to become identified as peer mediators. These peer mediators are trained to intervene in peer-conflict situations, where they attempt to get the parties to resolve their conflict peacefully or get adult help, if necessary. This helps prevent peer conflicts from escalating into more aggressive actions. They are trained to approach students engaged in a peer conflict and to offer to help them mediate the conflict.

Usually the agreement is that if the parties can resolve the conflict to everyone's satisfaction, the matter is ended. If not, the peer mediator takes the parties to see a teacher, a counselor, or an administrator, who then will intervene. In combination with a conflict-resolution curriculum, peer mediation helps prevent peer conflicts from escalating and helps prevent bullying. Again, excellent peer-mediation training materials are available on the market. More than 8,500 of the some 85,000 schools in the United States teach conflict resolution to all students (NIDR, 1999).

Research (Johnson & Johnson, 1995) shows that a conflict-resolution curriculum in the schools:

■ decreases physical violence in the school,

■ leads to less disruptive behavior,

■ improves academic performance,

■ empowers kids to solve their own problems, and

■ increases student leadership.

Developing Cooperative Learning Methods to Resolve Conflicts

Many schools have found that, by adding cooperative learning to their curriculum, they are able to reduce bullying and related school violence. In the 1960s, David and Roger Johnson (1995) from the University of Minnesota created a cooperative learning program called Teaching Students to be Peacemakers. This K–12 program has been operating for more than 30 years and teaches all students:

■ to recognize what is a conflict and what is not a conflict,

■ to negotiate win-win solutions to conflicts, and

■ to help mediate schoolmates' conflicts.

After conducting numerous research studies to determine the effectiveness of this program, they found that it resulted in a schoolwide discipline program focused on empowering students to regulate and control their own and their classmates' actions. As a result of this program, when a conflict occurred, the students involved would first try to negotiate a resolution. If that failed, they would ask a classmate to help mediate the conflict. If that failed, they would ask a teacher to help mediate the conflict. If that failed, the teacher would be asked to arbitrate the conflict. If that failed, they would ask the principal to help mediate the conflict, and if that failed, they would have the principal arbitrate the conflict (Johnson & Johnson, 1995).

In addition, teachers and counselors need to be trained to identify the symptoms of PTSD and how to intervene effectively in these cases. I have developed training materials and, through the Kindness Campaign, offer inservices and train teachers and counselors in these skills. The whole field of traumatology has had a number of breakthroughs that have led to the development of new trauma reduction techniques that school counselors and teachers can learn to use when they encounter students who are experiencing symptoms of PTSD (Weinhold & Weinhold, 2000).

Addressing Parental Abuse and Neglect

The Kindness Campaign has produced an activity guide for parents, *Raising Kind Kids: An Activity Guide for Fostering Kindness in Families* (Weinhold, 1999b). This guide contains 25 family-kindness activities that parents can use to instill more kindness into their families. Working through the PTAs in schools, the Kindness Campaign offers inservices to parents who want to increase their ability to relate to their children in positive ways. In addition, the Kindness Campaign has produced a guide for preschools, *Kind Beginnings: An Activity Guide for Fostering Kindness in Preschools* (Weinhold, 2000). This activity guide contains 36 field-tested activities that preschool teachers can utilize to teach young children how to be kind and respectful toward each other.

Businesses Adopting a Kind and Safe School

One of the main intervention programs of the Kindness Campaign in schools is the Adopt a Kind and Safe School project. Area businesses that are interested in helping make area schools kinder and safer for the children of their employees have "adopted" schools. The business donates funds for the Kindness Campaign to work intensively with their adopted school to create a positive learning climate and put in place an anti-bullying policy. The business also arranges for its employees to volunteer at the school as aides or tutors in the classroom. The Kindness Campaign conducts inservices with the faculty and students, plans school assemblies, and installs follow-up evaluation procedures. An outline of the process that the Kindness Campaign uses to deliver this program follows.

   I. Conduct a needs assessment.
      A. Determine what is needed to make this a kind and safe school.
      B. Meet with faculty and students.
      C. Develop a contract with the school to provide the program it needs.
  II. Establish the Kindness Campaign to change the overall school climate.
      A. Conduct inservices with faculty and staff.
      B. Select a Kindness Committee and School Coordinator(s).
      C. Help committee design program to meet school needs (Utilize the Program Guide: *Spreading Kindness*).
      D. Organize kick-off assembly for the students.
      E. Do follow-up consultation with faculty and students.
      F. Start Kind Kids Council(s).
      G. Conduct ongoing evaluation of outcomes.

III. Create an all-school policy on bullying and put-downs.
   A. Conduct student and teacher survey/needs assessment.
   B. Do inservice for faculty and staff.
   C. Design classroom activities for students.
   D. Develop classroom and school rules.
   E. Do follow-up in-service/consultation.
   F. Design and conduct ongoing evaluation (formative and summative).

IV. Help the school establish primary prevention/school safety methods (optional).
   A. Help establish a peer mediation program.
   B. Help establish a conflict-resolution curriculum for all students.
   C. Help create an emergency disaster plan.
   D. Help create an overall school safety plan.

V. Conduct in-service trainings (optional).
   A. Trauma Reduction Techniques for Counselors and Teachers.
   B. Understanding Gender Differences: Real Boys and Real Girls.
   C. High-Risk Kids: Early Identification and Intervention.
   D. Kids' Rights: The Legal Rights of Children to Protection Against Violence.
   E. Conflict Resolution/Peer Mediation Training.

VI. Provide other services, if needed. Sometimes schools need help with special projects such as designing a better system to deal with students who are disruptive. The Kindness Campaign has designed community and school service programs as an alternative to school suspension.

VII. Help develop long-term cooperative relationships between the school and the business sponsor. The Kindness Campaign staff attempts to encourage the development of a cooperative, long-term relationship between the school and the business. This varies with each school and business. Most businesses arrange to have their employees volunteer at the school they have adopted. Some tutor or read to students who don't get much help at home, and others assist the teacher in the classroom in various ways. Some businesses encourage their adopted schools to provide them with a wish list of equipment or supplies that the school needs and then, if possible, the business provides it.

VIII. Develop programs for the business employees and their families. This is a vital link in the Adopt a Kind and Safe School project. Here, the staff of the Kindness Campaign offers inservice training to the employees of the businesses that have adopted a school. These programs include parenting classes for employees who have families, teaching them how to discipline using kindness and nonthreatening methods. An ambulance company was noticing that its employees were suffering from vicarious trauma and burn-out because of their daily exposure to traumatic and crisis situations. The staff of the Kindness Campaign offered to teach the employees how to recognize their own trauma symptoms and then teach them practical trauma reduction techniques that they could use with each other and with themselves.

Will we wake-up in time? George Kennan, former Secretary of State, likened the American public to a sleeping dinosaur. He said every now and then something would disturb the dinosaur and it would wake up and flail about, trying to find who or what was to blame for waking it up. In the process, it would destroy or damage much of its surroundings. Finding no one to blame, it would go back to sleep.

It seems to me that we are in danger of having a repeat of the Columbine shootings. We may say, "It isn't going to happen here, so we don't have to worry" or, "We can't seem to find who is to blame." So we may go back to sleep until something wakes us up again. I assure you that the next time will be an even more dramatic wake-up call.

The Cost of Failure to Act

Unless we take action to deal with the hidden elements of the culture of violence, the problem will get worse. We will see some of the following:

■ The dropout rate as a result of bullying will continue to rise. (It is currently 10 percent.)

■ The number of high school students who are afraid to go to restrooms at school will increase. (It is now 20 percent of high school students.)

■ The number of kids who report being bullied will increase. (Currently it is 80 to 90 percent among middle school students.)

■ The number of kids who stay home to avoid bullying will increase. (Currently, 162,000 students stay home each day because they are afraid to go to school.)

■ More short-sighted, reactive solutions, such as installing metal detectors, hiring more police to patrol the halls, and putting in more surveillance cameras, will be tried with no tangible results.

■ More school shootings will occur. (64 percent of adults believe it will happen in their own community.)

■ The government will be forced to intervene and pass restrictive legislation holding schools and parents legally accountable. (A description of a first attempt at this is presented below.)

Bullying and Human Rights

Bill and Rita Head, Georgia parents of a 15-year-old who shot himself in front of his classmates after suffering repeated bullying, have proposed new legislation to better protect our children. As a result, a bill was introduced into the Georgia State Legislature that amends the Georgia Criminal Code to give children the same protection under the law that persons 21 years old and older have.

Currently, the Criminal Code in Georgia, as well as some other states, excludes children from protection under the law concerning five types of violent behavior: simple assaults, simple battery, battery, stalking, and using so called "fighting words" or engaging in disorderly conduct. The Heads also want mandatory posting of the rights of children under the law in all schools and mandatory reporting of violations of these laws by the teachers (Brown, 1999).

This is an attempt to classify bullying and put-downs as violations of the rights of children "to be secure and protected from fear, intimidation and physical harm caused by the activities of violent groups and individuals." This represents an intriguing proposal because, using the standard definitions of assaults and battery, stalking, fighting words, bullying, and put-downs are violations of human rights under the laws that cover adults. The same human rights clearly should be extended to children and youth under 21 years of age. This would get the attention of school officials who until now have essentially turned their backs on bullying and put-downs. If such a law had existed in Colorado, the Columbine shootings would not have occurred. The Juvenile Code in Colorado covers these five categories of violent behavior, but it does not call for posting these laws in schools and it does not call for mandatory reporting by teachers. You might check on the Criminal Code in your state.

Summary

Hidden aspects of the culture of violence that keep it going include the dominator value system, an over-focus on negativity, the pervasiveness of bullying, collective denial of the effects of bullying, the presence of PTSD, and an increase of parental abuse and neglect. These hidden factors must be addressed if we are going to change the culture of violence. The Kindness Campaign is an effective primary prevention program that addresses these hidden elements of the culture of violence in schools and communities.

References

Adler, J. & Springen, K. (1999). How to fight back. *Newsweek,* May 3, 1999, p. 37.

Ainsworth, M. (1989). Attachments beyond infancy. *American Psychologist, 44,* 709–716.

American Psychiatric Association (APA). (1996). *The diagnostic and statistical manual (DSM-IV), (4th ed.).* Washington, DC: American Psychiatric Association Press.

Begley, S. (1999). Why the young kill. *Newsweek,* May 3, 1999 p. 32–37.

Bowlby, J. (1988). *A secure base: Parent-child attachment and healthy human development.* London: Routledge.

Brown, T. (1999, January 18). *The bullying reference,* 1(4), Zanesville, OH: The Broken

Toy Project. Retrieved February 6, 1999 from World Wide Web: http:/members. tripod.com/-Ghoul2x/Bully1.html

Brown T. (1999). *The broken toy project.* 846 1/2 McIntire Ave. Zanesville, OH, 43701.

Bully OnLine. (1999). *Web Site of the UK National Workplace Bullying Advice Line.* URL: <www.successunlimited.co.uk/ costs.htm>

Campos, J., Barrett, K., et al. (1983). Socioemotional development. In M. M. Haith & J. J. Campos (Eds.), *Handbook of child psychology: Vol. 2. Infancy and psychobiology.* New York: Wiley, pp. 783–915.

Cline, F. (1979). *Understanding and treating the severely disturbed child.* Evergreen, CO: Evergreen Consultants in Human Behavior.

Dube, J. (1999). High school hell. *ABC NEWS.com,* April 24, 1999, p. 1.

Eisler, R. (1987). *The chalice and the blade.* San Francisco: Harper & Row.

Espelage, D., et al., (1999, Aug.). Interviews with middle school students: Bullying, victimization, and contextual factors. Presentation at American Psychological Association Annual Conference, Boston, Aug. 21.

Fried, S., & Fried, P. (1996). *Bullies and victims: Helping your child survive the schoolyard battlefield.* New York: M. Evans & Co.

Gibbs, N., & Roche, T. (1999). The Columbine tapes. *Time,* 154 (25), 40–51.

Grossman, D. (1996). *On killing: The psychological cost of learning to kill in war and society.* New York: Little, Brown & Co.

Grossman, D. (1998). Trained to kill. *Christianity Today,* Aug. 10, 1998, pp. 31–39.

Hawkins, D., Catalano, R., et al. (1992). *Communities that care: Action for drug abuse prevention.* San Francisco: Jossey-Bass.

Heise, L., Ellsberg, M., & Gottemoeller, M. (1999, Dec.). *Ending violence against women.* (Population Reports, Series L, No. 11). Baltimore: Johns Hopkins University, School of Public Health, Population Information Program.

Johnson, D. W., & Johnson, R. (1995). *Teaching students to be peacemakers.* Edina: MN: Interaction Book Co.

Joseph, J. (1999). Sugar, spice and ready to kill. *ABCNEWS.com,* April 28, 1999, pp. 1–2.

Karen, R. (1998). *Becoming attached.* New York: Oxford University Press.

Krause, A. & Haverkamp, B. (1996). Attachment in adult child-older parent relationships: Research, theory, and practice. *Journal of Counseling & Development, 75,* 83–92.

Langer, G. (1999). Students report violent peers. *ABCNEWS.com,* April 26, 1999, pp. 1–2.

Lederer, L., & Varela, S. (1998). *Safe schools, safe students: A guide to violence prevention strategies.* Washington DC: Substance Abuse & Mental Health Services Administration.

Lero, D., Golman, H., et al. (1992). *Parental work patterns and childcare needs* (Catalogue 89-529E) Ottawa: Canadian National Child Care Study.

Magid, K., & McKelvey, C. (1989). *High risk: Children without a conscience.* New York: Bantam Books.

Marano, H., (1995). Big. bad. bully. *Psychology Today,* 28, 50–68.

National Institute for Dispute Resolution. (1999). *Conflict resolution education facts.* URL: <www.CRFnet.org>

Nerenberg, A. (1999). *Road rage.* Web Site URL: <www.roadragenerenberg.com>

Olweus, D. (1993). Victimization by peers: Antecedents and long-term consequences. In K. H. Rubin & J. B. Asendorf (Eds.), *Social withdrawal, inhibition, and shyness in childhood.* Hillside, NJ: Erlbaum.

Olweus, D. (1994). *Bullying at school: What we know and what we can do.* Oxford, UK: Blackwell Publishers.

Paulk, D. et al. (1999). Teacher, peer and self-nominations of bullies and victims of bullying. Presentation at American Psychological Association Annual Conference, Boston, August 21, 1999.

Pearson, J., Cowen, P., et al. (1993). Adult attachment and adult child-older parent relationships. *American Journal of Orthopsychiatry*, 63, 606–613.

Perry, B. (1996a). Aggression and violence: The neurobiology of experience. *AACAP Developmentor*. Spring.

Perry, B. (1996b). Neurodevelopmental adaptations to violence: How children survive the intergenerational vortex of violence. In *Violence and childhood trauma: Understanding and responding to the effects of violence on young children*. Cleveland, OH: Gund Foundation Publishers, 66–80.

Pollack, W. (1998). *Real boys*. New York: Random House.

Portner, J. (1997). Zero-tolerance laws getting a second look. *Education Week on the Web*, March 26.

Prendergast, A. (1999). Doom rules. *Denver Westword*. August 5–11, 1999, pp. 1–16. URL: <westword.com>.

Saunders, C. (1997). When push comes to shove: Dealing with bullies requires adult supervision. *Our Children*, March/April.

Sebastian, S. J. (1996). Domestic violence. In A. L. Harwood-Nuss (Ed.): *Emergency medicine—A comprehensive study guide* (4th ed.). New York: McGraw Hill.

Straus, M. (1994). *Beating the devil out of them*. New York: Lexington Books.

Straus, M & Gelles, R. (1988). How violent are American families? Estimates from the national family violence resurvey and other studies. In G. Hotaling, et al. (Eds.), *Family abuse and its consequences: New directions in research*.

U. S. Department of Education, National Center for Educational Statistics, *Principal/school disciplinarian survey on school violence* (1997). (Fast Response Survey System, and FRSS 63). Washington, DC: Government Printing Office.

Weinhold, B. (1991). *Breaking free of addictive family relationships*. Walpole, NH: Stillpoint Publishing.

Weinhold, B. (Ed.) (1996). *Spreading kindness: A program guide for reducing youth violence in the schools*. Colorado Springs, CO: Kindness Campaign.

Weinhold, B. (1999a). Bullying and school violence. *Counseling Today*, 42(4), 14.

Weinhold, B. (1999b). *Raising kind kids: An activity guide for fostering kindness in families*. Colorado Springs, CO: Kindness Campaign.

Weinhold, B. (Ed.). (2000). *Kind beginnings: An activity guide for fostering kindness in pre-schools*. Colorado Springs, CO: Kindness Campaign.

Weinhold, B. & Weinhold, J. (1998). Conflict resolution: The partnership way in schools. *Counseling & Human Development*, 30 (7), 1–12.

Weinhold, B. & Weinhold, J. (2000). *Conflict resolution: The partnership way*. Denver: Love Publishing.

Teaching Children to Care Rather Than Kill

Radha J. Horton-Parker

*I*t's a typical April morning, and school has begun like always at Columbine High School. With thoughts of graduation, summer vacation, and the vast tomorrow that seems to stretch out endlessly before them, students laugh and converse as the day proceeds. But soon carefree laughter is transformed into terror and tears as two students, armed with guns and grenades, enter the school and begin the massacre that will end the tomorrows of 15 individuals.

The tragedy in Littleton, Colorado, which brought immediate reactions of shock and disbelief, has begun to awaken us from the complacency that predominates in our culture. Although violence prevails in movies and video games, popular music is replete with hate-filled lyrics, guns are readily available, and bomb-making recipes abound on the Internet, we never expect our children to commit murder. Yet, when two teenagers from affluent homes with apparently caring parents went on a killing spree in a nice, suburban high school, few of us were spared the realization that major changes are needed in our society.

Although controversy abounds about what should be done, nearly everyone agrees that we must do *something*. Legislation regarding gun control, censorship in the media, greater control of the Internet, fining parents for children's misdeeds, and increased security in the schools all have been proposed as possible solutions. On a more therapeutic note, mental health professionals have advocated diagnostic procedures to identify students who may be at risk of violent behavior, as well as counseling interventions to help alienated students fit in better with their peers.

Even though these ideas have merit, a more efficacious strategy might be to engage in primary prevention in early childhood rather than remediation in adolescence. One untapped resource is the potential of humanistic parenting to engender prosocial behavior in children. *Prosocial behavior,* defined as action intended to benefit others without the expectation of an external reward (Eisenberg, 1988), contrasts with aggression, defined as "behavior aimed at harming another person" (Perry, Perry, & Boldizar, 1990, p. 135). Dave Sanders, the teacher and coach who lost his life while protecting his students during the Columbine massacre, is perhaps the ultimate exemplar of prosocial behavior. In contrast, the student assassins represent extreme cases of aggression.

The key to understanding why some individuals selflessly help their fellow humans while others murder them might be found in early childhood. Much evidence suggests that parents—who serve as children's first models—can be instrumental in assisting children to develop the ability to act thoughtfully and kindly toward others (Eisenberg, 1992). Parental influence is so powerful that one longitudinal study found that 36% of the variance in adult levels of empathy could be explained by the child-rearing practices that the participants had experienced in early childhood (Koestner, Franz, & Weinberger, 1990). This is especially significant in that a meta-analysis of the research revealed that empathy and sympathy were correlated positively with prosocial behavior (Eisenberg & Miller, 1987).

Thus, a firm foundation of prosocial behavior, established when children are young, could be essential to curbing violence in the adolescent years. Perhaps, if parents acquire basic skills in humanistic parenting, today's affectionate toddlers with teddy bears will be deterred from becoming tomorrow's maleficent teens with grenades. The purpose of this chapter is to provide information that counselors can use to assist parents in developing practices that will lead to lifelong prosocial outcomes in young children.

Our Culture of Violence

Striking insights into the psychology of extreme interpersonal violence have emerged with the advent of a new field of study, "killology." The foremost authority in this field is Lt. Col. Dave Grossman (1996), a former professor of psychology at West Point and author of the best-selling book, *On Killing*. Grossman maintains that just as AIDS breaks down the body's immune system and leaves it vulnerable to disease, so does constant exposure to rampant violence in the media and video games break down children's natural aversion to killing, effectively "taking off the safety catch" that keeps fatal aggression psychologically in check.

To support his theories, Grossman recounts the history of the development of techniques by military psychologists to increase the kill rate of soldiers. Definitive evidence collected after the end of World War II showed that only 15% to 20% of combat infantry were willing to fire their weapons. Appalled by these findings, military psychologists began seeking and implementing new training strategies to engender a greater willingness to kill in soldiers. The needed strategies were discovered and successfully applied. The fire rate of infantry in Korea rose to 50%, and to more than 90% in Vietnam.

Military trainers accomplished their magic by using three tools: operant conditioning, classical conditioning, and social learning, focusing on the imitation of role models. Soldiers are classically conditioned by being made to view films depicting people being injured or killed in increasingly violent ways. As a result, they become able to disassociate themselves emotionally from the fear or revulsion that arises in empathy for another person being hurt or abused. Operant strategies include the use of *human-shaped* pop-up targets on firing ranges and other life-like simulated situations. Soldiers trained in this way learn to target and shoot reflexively, bypassing any potential rational inhibitions, as they are reinforced by seeing their bullets make their marks.

Finally, we can credit the well known stereotype of the drill sergeant as a heroic, ultra-capable, invincible role model for the social learning component of the initiatives we are discussing. Boot camp was redesigned to be an ever more efficient initiatory rite of passage through which the neophyte soldier's previous value system is stripped away and replaced with a new ethos in which devastating physical aggression and unconditional obedience become the new foundations of self-worth. These qualities are incarnate in the drill sergeant, who becomes a role model and a surrogate father, brother, and even mother to the troops.

Grossman argues convincingly that the same conditioning techniques used successfully by the military to train soldiers to kill are present in the films, music, television programs, and video games that children regularly watch. Hyper-violent films provide an example of classical conditioning at work. The films themselves vie with each other to portray mutilation and murder in ever more graphic detail. Repeated exposure to incrementally more gruesome imagery inevitably desensitizes children and weakens their natural aversion to seeing others harmed. In a kind of *Clockwork Orange* reverse scenario, the enjoyment that derives from sitting in the comfort of a movie theater munching popcorn and enjoying the company of friends becomes paired with the aggression they are witnessing so that observing violence actually comes to evoke a pleasurable state by association.

Similarly, the principles of operant conditioning are powerfully active in children who immerse themselves in the world of violent video games. As children learn to fire weapons reflexively at pop-up villains, they receive instant reinforcement from seeing characters' heads blown off—or worse. As with films, violent video games tend to incorporate increasingly realistic weapons, wounds, and associated trauma. In some cases, the targets are not bug-eyed monsters but, instead, normal human beings, and the child plays the role of an assassin or a monster.

Through this sort of visual programming, children not only develop "automaticity" and learn to see the world through a gunsight, but they also can actually sharpen their shooting skills. Police officers and FBI agents both utilize the same training procedures to develop combat readiness. So effective is this training that "shoot/no shoot" programming was introduced to constrain collateral violence created by officers who receive such training. Of course, video games enjoin no such restraints.

Finally, as children watch powerful action heros successfully defeat their foes, they learn that violence is a rewarding and effective way of problem-solving.

Because media characters often are shown killing others for minor slights, youth learn that murder is an acceptable response to injustice, imagined or perceived.

Grossman (1996) also offers readers a thoughtful reappraisal of the actual extent of youth violence occurring in our society. Between 1985 and 1991, the homicide rates for males 15 to 19 years of age increased 154%, with homicide the second leading cause of death for all males in this age group and the first leading cause of death in Black males. As shocking as these statistics are, things actually are significantly worse than they appear. Grossman points out that advanced medical capabilities, such as resuscitation technology, save the lives of many persons who certainly would have died in the past. Grossman cites UCLA professor James Q. Wilson's estimate that if trauma care were the same now as in 1957, the homicide rate would be close to three times what statistics reflect now.

Even though the youth violence rate is higher in the United States than in any other industrialized nation, most industrialized nations having a similar level of media violence have witnessed parallel increases in teen violent activity. The one significant exception to this rapid rise in youth aggression is Japan. Although Japanese children partake of the same violent media influences as other youth, a protective "bubble" immunizes them from acting out the aggression they observe. The key to this phenomenon is theorized to be the incredibly strong sense of interdependence between the individual and the family and social structure that is intrinsic to Japanese culture. Japanese children are taught to engage in prosocial behavior from an early age, and that lesson is reinforced at every stage of life. Perhaps by strengthening our families and helping parents learn to influence their children positively, we, too, may turn the tide of violence in our society.

Parenting Styles

Because fads in parenting come and go, parents and counselors often are left wondering what methods actually lead to the most desirable outcomes in children. The answers may lie in Diana Baumrind's ground-breaking research showing that parenting styles significantly impact children's behavior in ways that may be permanent.

In her landmark study, Baumrind (1967) observed children in a nursery school for 14 weeks. Based on their differing patterns of behavior, she categorized the youngsters into three groups: energetic-friendly children, conflicted-irritable children, and impulsive-aggressive children. Baumrind then interviewed the children's parents and observed them interacting with their children in home and laboratory settings.

On the basis of these observations, Baumrind identified three styles of parenting that appeared to be associated with the differing behavioral patterns in children. She labeled these three parenting styles as authoritarian, permissive, and authoritative. In a longitudinal study of the children from early childhood through adolescence,

Baumrind (1991) found that these three parenting styles were associated with specific outcomes, which will be described in the following section.

Using Baumrind's typology of authoritarian, permissive, and authoritative parenting styles as a basis, Maccoby and Martin (1983) added a fourth category—indifferent parenting—and proposed that the four parenting styles could be distinguished by the relative balance of control/ demandingness and warmth/responsiveness present in each.

1. *Control/demandingness* refers to the extent to which parents set high standards and exert firm control to ensure that their children exhibit mature behavior. This continuum represents the extent to which parents insist that their children perform developmentally appropriate tasks that require increasing social and cognitive competence.

2. Warmth/responsiveness refers to the extent to which parents convey affection and acceptance in their communication and are responsive to their children's feelings and needs. This continuum relates to the parental warmth and responsiveness so critical to forming attachment bonds in infancy and in maintaining loving, trusting relationships with children as they mature.

The following description of the four parenting styles is based on the models of Baumrind (1967) and of Maccoby and Martin (1983). Figure 9.1 depicts these styles.

Authoritarian Parents

In the Sutter home, the parents like to think that they "run a tight ship." Frank and Miriam Sutter are strict disciplinarians and do not allow any divergence from the expected norms of behavior. When faced with any resistance from their children, the Sutters quickly exert pressure to produce the desired result. "Do it now or else" is often stated in their home, and the children intimately know that the "else" means either a spanking or a sojourn in their rooms for an extended time. When the children occasionally ask their parents why they have to do something, the inevitable reply is "because we said so," and the children then are told to "just stop complaining and do what we say."

Authoritarian parents are high in control/demandingness, but low in the humanistic qualities of warmth/responsiveness. These parents set rigid standards, demand unquestioning compliance, and allow no opportunities for their children to articulate any concerns they have about their parents' expectations. The parents show little warmth or respect in interactions with their children, and parental authority is absolute. Punishment follows quickly when their children disobey orders, and even though the children might have legitimate needs that are not being met, divergent views are not allowed expression.

Baumrind (1967) found the authoritarian parenting style to be correlated with the child behavioral pattern identified as *conflicted-irritable*. In nursery school, the children of authoritarian parents appeared unhappy, withdrawn, mistrustful, and

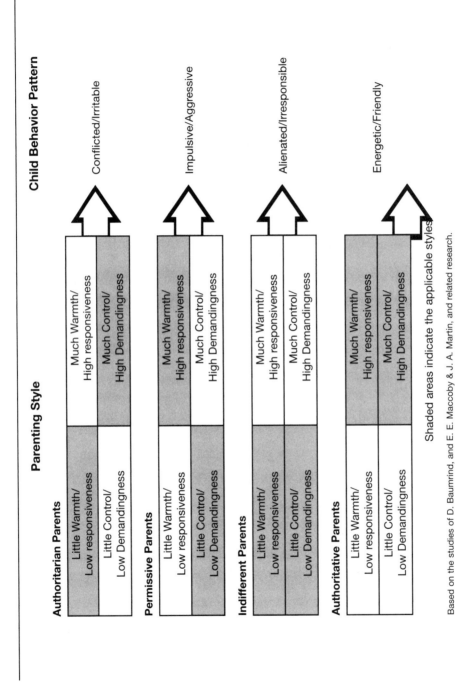

Figure 9.1 Parenting Styles Related to Child Behavior Patterns

socially anxious. When frustrated with their playmates, these preschoolers often responded with hostility. The negative impact of authoritarian parenting did not end when the last days of childhood had passed, but instead extended into adolescence. The effects were more pronounced for boys than girls. The adolescent sons of authoritarian parents were socially incompetent, unfriendly, and lacking in initiative and self-confidence (Baumrind, 1991).

Other studies also suggested that authoritarian parenting produced children with low self-esteem who lacked self-confidence and spontaneity (Coopersmith, 1967; Lamborn, Mounts, Steinberg, & Dornbusch, 1991; Lempers, Clark-Lempers, & Simons, 1989). Adolescents from authoritarian homes were obedient but lacking in competence (Steinberg, 1990). When corporal punishment was employed as a central component of authoritarian parenting, the results were especially detrimental. Children developed aggressive behaviors themselves when they were exposed to spanking and other harsh disciplinary practices (Dodge, Bates, & Pettit, 1990; Weiss, Dodge, Bates, & Pettit, 1992).

Permissive Parents

The Jenkins family is at the end of the continuum opposite from the Sutters. Fran and Jake Jenkins allow their children total freedom and shower them with compliments and praise. These parents rarely discipline or set limits for their children and, instead, encourage them to do whatever they wish. The children face no real consequences for failing to fulfill parental requests and often are unaware that their parents have any expectations for them other than to be themselves.

In situations in which one of the Jenkins children is asked to help with a household task, the child typically objects ("I can't. I'm busy playing this video game, and I can't stop.") When the child resists, the parents usually just do the chore themselves so their child can continue to play. Sometimes they even say, "Don't worry about it, honey. You're busy, so we'll take care of it. Go ahead and finish your game."

As this illustration shows, permissive parenting contrasts starkly with authoritarian parenting in that it is low in control/demandingness but high in warmth/responsiveness. Permissive parents offer unconditional love and acceptance but fail to provide adequate guidelines for mature, responsible behavior. Instead, they allow children to have greater freedom than is appropriate for their developmental levels and permit them to make choices that require more maturity than they possess.

Although permissive parents often believe that they are nurturing their children's growth, they could be unintentionally cultivating their children's self-indulgence and fostering a lack of social concern. By showering youngsters with unlimited material possessions and expecting nothing in return, some permissive parents think they are teaching their children to be correspondingly generous and loving. In reality, they likely are teaching their children to think only of themselves. Because this approach affords so little structure or consistency, prosocial behavior in children is not a likely outcome of permissive parenting.

Baumrind (1967) noted that the preschoolers of permissive parents exhibited the behavioral pattern categorized as *impulsive-aggressive*. These children not only had difficulty controlling their impulses but also exhibited highly immature behavior. Lacking confidence in themselves, they were extremely demanding and dependent on adults (Baumrind, 1971). Although some of the children were creative and friendly, others were socially inept. They frequently gave up when they encountered any frustration in their nursery school tasks and became aggressive when other children's needs conflicted with their own. Later research showed that adolescents from permissive homes were likely to be self-confident but to have higher levels of substance abuse and more problems in school (Steinberg, 1990).

Authoritative Parents

Ike and Samantha Freeman clearly state what they want their children to do and how they expect them to behave. The children know that disobedience will have consequences directly related to their misbehavior. Sometimes, however, the children have valid reasons for being excused from doing expected tasks or for asking for special considerations. In these cases, the children voice their concerns, and their parents listen respectfully.

Recently one of the Freeman children asked to be allowed to stay up an hour and a half later than her customary bedtime on a school night to watch a television show about a topic she had studied in her science class. Although Ike and Samantha recognized their daughter's interest as being legitimate, they let her know that they thought it was important for her to get adequate rest. After discussing the issue, the Freemans agreed that everyone's needs would be met if the parents were to tape the show and let the daughter watch it immediately after school the next day. Although this solution meant that Ike had to make an unplanned trip to the store to purchase a blank videotape, everyone was satisfied with the outcome.

Unlike the former two parenting styles, authoritative parenting is high in both control/demandingness and warmth/responsiveness. The Freemans could have flatly denied their daughter's request and said, "You know the rules—go to bed," as the Sutters would have. Or the Freemans could have given in to whatever their daughter wished to do and said, "Sure, sweetie—we wouldn't want you to miss your show," as the Jenkinses would have. The Freemans, however, chose the authoritative approach of maintaining their parental authority while also ensuring that their daughter felt respected and that her concerns were adequately addressed. Authoritative parents set firm limits for children's behavior and also exhibit warmth and flexibility in responding to their children's needs while encouraging them to be involved in problem solving.

The children of authoritative parents exhibited the behavioral pattern that Baumrind (1967) labeled as *energetic-friendly*. Of all the children in the nursery school, this type was found to be the most well adjusted. These preschoolers showed friendliness, confidence, self-control, and high achievement. In addition, they appeared to be happy and were less likely than their peers to engage in disruptive and defiant behaviors. For these reasons, the authoritative approach is associated with the best outcomes for children. As adolescents, the children of authoritative parents continued to exhibit these positive qualities (Baumrind, 1991). Other studies have yielded similar findings, showing that children experience the most positive outcomes when parents practice child-centered patterns of discipline accompanied by clearly communicated demands, careful monitoring, and an atmosphere of acceptance (Maccoby, 1984; Maccoby & Martin, 1983).

Indifferent Parents

The Schmidts pay little attention to their children. Struggling to survive on their meager incomes, they worry more about having enough money to pay for groceries and rent than about what their children are doing. George and Bertha each work two part-time jobs with schedules that change from week to week, so their children often are left at home alone. Sometimes a teenage girl from the neighborhood watches the children, but when she is not available, the Schmidts have their own 10-year-old son attend to his four siblings.

Because their jobs are so demanding and frequently require them to work late-night shifts, George and Bertha are easily irritated when their children attempt to get their attention. The parents often respond angrily if their children make requests, as happened recently when the 5-year-old asked her mother to help her remove a splinter from her finger. Trying to get a few hours rest before going to her second job, Bertha looked at her daughter and said, "Go away. Can't you see I'm trying to sleep?" No one else was around at the time, so the daughter did go away—and began walking to her grandmother's house, 3 miles away. Concerned neighbors saw the little girl walking alone on the road and called Child Protective Services.

Indifferent parenting lies at the opposite end of the continuum from the authoritative style because it is low in both control/demandingness and warmth/responsiveness. Although Baumrind did not study this group, Maccoby and Martin (1983) described indifferent parents as being both lax in discipline and lacking in warmth. These parents show little concern for their children's welfare, are disengaged from parenting, and do not monitor their children's behavior. As a result of this parental neglect, children fail to form attachment bonds and suffer from social incompetence and low self-esteem. Indifferent parental behavior has been linked to children's noncompliance, aggression, delinquency, truancy, precocious sexuality, and alcohol problems in adolescence and adulthood (Lamborn, Mounts, Steinberg, & Dornbusch, 1991; Patterson, 1982; Pulkkinen, 1982). We therefore could describe the child behavior pattern resulting from indifferent parenting as *alienated/irresponsible*. The children of indifferent parents generally have the worst outcomes of all.

The Need for Humanistic Parenting

Because authoritative parenting has been associated with the best and most prosocial outcomes in children, counselors might help to prevent violence indirectly in the teen years by teaching parents how to interact skillfully with their children authoritatively in early childhood. Learning humanistic, authoritative parenting techniques will enable parents to respond to their children's needs respectfully while setting high behavioral standards and maintaining firm control. This balance of control and respect should provide a firm foundation for fostering positive outcomes in children and for building trusting parent-child relationships that will endure throughout the turbulence of adolescence.

Skillful parenting is not guaranteed by virtue of being able to successfully procreate. Although most parents probably have good intentions toward their children, people tend to adopt a child-rearing style similar to that of their own parents—which may or may not be conducive to helping children learn to care about others as well as themselves. More than in the past, effective parenting is critically needed.

In the remainder of this chapter, I will attempt to address the parenting-skills deficit so prevalent in our society today by presenting ideas that counselors can share with parents to promote prosocial behavior in children. The approach, which I call humanistic parenting, consists of strategies drawn from behavioral research and popular parent-training programs that adopt an authoritative child-rearing style (Horton-Parker, 1998). These humanistic parenting techniques, which can be imparted to parents via workshops, counseling sessions, and newsletters, should provide a solid basis for prosocial behavior as children mature. Because I believe that workshops can be especially beneficial for parent training, I also will include some ideas for activities that counselors can use with parents in a large-group setting.

Before introducing the techniques of humanistic parenting, I would like to point out several points. First, although I use the term "parent" throughout this chapter, it is meant to refer to any adult serving in a parental or caregiving role to a child. Because families come in many forms today, "parents" refers to any individuals serving in a parental capacity, regardless of whether they are biologically or legally related to the children they are rearing.

A second note concerns the exclusive emphasis I have placed on parenting in early childhood. Although all of the techniques contained in this chapter can be adapted with older children, my focus is on parenting the very young. Because early childhood is critical to future development, I believe that counselors can have the most impact by helping parents become more effective during children's formative years. Finding that prevention is preferable to remediation, I encourage counselors to work with the parents of preschoolers to help them develop trusting, loving parent-child relationships and exert consistent, firm control while their children are still highly receptive.

Teaching Children to Care: Humanistic Parenting

Components of humanistic parenting include respectful communication, passive listening, using I-messages, setting limits, giving choices, catching children being good, confronting misbehavior, applying logical consequences, using time-out, conducting family meetings, and conveying love.

Respectful Communication

Mental health professionals sometimes suggest that parents speak to their children as though they were their best friends. Conversely, it is interesting to consider how it might be if we spoke to our best friends as though they were our children. The following dialogue is an imaginary conversation with a couple, Mike and Judy, who have come for dinner:

> So you finally arrived! Do you have any idea what time it is? We had about given up on you two. Mike, don't you ever wear your watch? Maybe you think you can just show up any time you please. Well, think again! Now go wash your hands and we'll be ready to eat. Judy, don't drip water on the floor like you did last time. We're tired of cleaning up your mess. Mike, remember to put the toilet seat down after you use it. This isn't a bus station..
>
> Okay, dinner is served! Come to the table and have a seat. Oh, Judy, don't sit there. You and Mike can't sit next to each other tonight because you might get into another fight. We're sitting between you two so you'll stay out of trouble. You know you can't make it through a whole meal without ruining it for everyone with your bickering. Judy, wipe that nasty look off your face and do what you're told. We don't want any complaints about the seating arrangement.
>
> We're so glad you could come, since we haven't seen you for a while. Mike, how do you like your new job? Make sure that you don't oversleep too often and lose this one like you did the last one. It's about time for you to grow up and be responsible! Judy, you had said you were going on a diet. How's that going? You know, you could actually be quite pretty if you weren't so overweight!
>
> Mike, please pass the gravy. Oh, no! You spilled it again. You're such a klutz! Why do you always have to be so clumsy? Judy, what's your problem? Stop glaring at us and try to be pleasant for once in your life.
>
> Who's ready for dessert? None for you, Mike, until you finish the rest of your spinach. Judy, you may have a small piece of pie, but go easy on the ice cream, or you'll never stop looking like a big, fat pig!
>
> Well, you two certainly haven't had much to say this evening. You'd better just go home and go to bed. Come back when you can behave more like ladies and gentlemen!

This humorous example illustrates the less than respectful manner in which parents communicate with their children. While not intending to hurt their children, many parents issue directives in ways that sometimes are demeaning or insensitive to children's feelings. Disrespectful communication does not convey the warmth and responsiveness that are essential ingredients of humanistic parenting.

In contrast, when parents listen empathically and communicate respectfully, children not only feel loved and valued but also have the opportunity to observe empathy in action as their parents demonstrate. Because children imitate much of what they witness in their parents, they likely will acquire the ability to respond empathically and respectfully themselves simply by emulating that behavior. On the other hand, parental responses such as threatening, commanding, lecturing, and name-calling create roadblocks to communication and produce defensiveness in children by conveying a lack of acceptance. The following scenario exemplifies the differences in parental responding to children's expressed feelings:

When Christy Sutter came crying to her mother because her baby brother had bitten her again, Mrs. Sutter responded, "Don't be such a baby yourself. He doesn't know any better, so just ignore him and stop whining."

When a similar situation occurred in the Freeman home, however, it met with a very different response. Mrs. Freeman stopped what she was doing to listen to her daughter and replied, "That must have really hurt when he bit you, and I can tell you're frustrated because this isn't the first time he's done it. Can you tell me more about what happened?"

Passive Listening

To avoid creating roadblocks to communication, Gordon (1970) recommends that parents use passive listening (silence), verbal and nonverbal acknowledgment responses (nodding, "uh-huh"), door openers ("Could you tell me more?" "How do you feel about that?"), and active listening, which demonstrates accurate empathy by reflecting both the content and the affect of the child's message (e.g., "You're disappointed that we can't afford to buy you that game."). Empathic listening validates children's feelings and enables them to assume responsibility for their own emotions.

I-Messages

Learning to use I-messages rather than you-messages is beneficial in communicating with children. Gordon (1970) offers a simple formula for constructing effective I-messages: "When you _____, I feel _____ because _____" The first blank is to be filled in with the child's *behavior*, the second with the *emotion* the parent experiences in conjunction with the given behavior, and the third with the *reason* the parent feels that way. For example, a parent might say, "When you interrupt me while I'm talking, I feel frustrated because I don't get to finish what I'm saying." This message is likely to be far more productive than other remarks that could be said to the child, such as "Shut up when I'm talking," or "Be quiet, blabbermouth!"

Setting Limits

In addition to responding to children warmly and respectfully, authoritative parenting involves setting clear behavioral limits that provide structure and consistency.

Parents should be kind and firm in their interactions with children while clearly communicating behavioral expectations (Nelson, Lott, & Glenn, 1993). Behavioral expectations should be appropriate to children's developmental stages, and it is normal for children to test the limits as they strive for increased autonomy (Brazelton, 1992).

For example, although a 6-year-old would be expected to know that hitting another child is wrong, a 2-year-old might hit playmates as a way of getting their attention or as a means of social interaction. Although limits should be set with both children, parental reaction to the 2-year-old should take into account that the child's behavior might have been exploratory rather than hostile in nature.

When setting limits, parents should state clearly what constitutes unacceptable behavior, as well as what substitute behavior will be accepted (Ginott, 1971). For example, telling the 6-year-old, "Other children are not for hitting, but you may hit this pillow if you are angry," provides clear guidelines for what will and will not be accepted. Similarly, the 2-year-old might be instructed, "Playmates are not for hitting, but you can touch them gently like a butterfly if you want to say hi or get them to look at you."

Giving Choices

To honor and nurture children's growing sense of autonomy, parents should allow children to choose between at least two acceptable alternatives whenever possible (Ginott, 1971; Nelson et al., 1993). With very young children, the choices have to be limited—for example, "You may come and eat dinner when you are called, or you may wait until breakfast tomorrow to eat." Giving children choices enables them to assume responsibility and to learn that choices have consequences.

Catching Them Being Good

Rather than waiting for children to misbehave and reprimanding them, noticing children's appropriate behavior and praising them is more effective. When children receive positive reinforcement, such as parental approval, for appropriate behavior, they are more likely to increase the behavior and to develop high self-esteem. Parents can easily show approval for their children's behavior through words, such as "Good job!" and gestures, such as a gentle touch, loving hug, approving smile, or friendly wink.

If the given behavior is prosocial in nature, parents might articulate to the child *why* his or her actions were desirable. For example, a father might say to his son, "I really liked the way you just helped your little sister pick up her toys, because that let her know that you care about her."

Confronting Misbehavior

A common mistake that parents make is talking too much and taking too many opportunities to remind their children about what they are expected to do. As many mothers have painfully discovered, children quickly learn to ignore nagging parents as though they were noisy gnats. For this reason, it is more effective for parents to follow through on enforcing rules by taking kind, firm action than by engaging in incessant nagging or punishing (Nelson et al., 1993).

For example, if a young child refuses to stop playing outside and come inside when called, the parent could simply state, "Time to come in," and take the child by the hand into the house. If the child resists, the parent could provide a limited choice, such as, "We need to get ready to go to your grandmother's house, so would you rather get dressed first or pack your toys?"

As mentioned previously, I-messages are also helpful for parents to let children know how their behavior is affecting others (Gordon, 1970; Popkin, 1993). For example, a parent might say, "When you don't come when I call you, I feel annoyed because I have to stop what I'm doing to go and get you."

Using Logical Consequences

When children misbehave discipline is required, and parents must decide what to do. Although punishment sometimes brings an end to a given undesirable behavior, it often is accompanied by unwanted side effects. For example, when his mother yells at him for spitting on his older sibling who has called him a nasty name, a little boy might stop ejecting saliva on his big sister but might smash her porcelain horse instead. Corporal punishment, such as spanking, can be detrimental because children could learn to imitate the aggression they have experienced as they interact with others. Even subtle forms of punishment, such as ridicule and humiliation, can damage the parent/child relationship and destroy trust.

A viable method of discipline that avoids the negative effects of punishment is logical consequences. Logical consequences are actions that logically follow from the child's behavior but that are not arbitrarily punitive (Dinkmeyer & McKay, 1973; Popkin, 1993; Nelson, 1987; Nelson et al., 1993).

To be effective, logical consequences must be composed of the "three *R's*": They must be directly *related* to the child's behavior, *respectful* of the child, and *reasonable* to both child and parent (Nelson et al., 1993).

For example, if a child draws a picture on the wall with a crayon after being told that paper is for drawing, a logical consequence would be for the child to help scrub the markings off the wall. This logical consequence is related directly to the child's misbehavior and is respectful and reasonable. On the other hand, sentencing the child to a week without television for this transgression would not be related to the offense, to call the child "a moron who thinks he's Picasso" would not be respectful, and to expect the child to wash all the walls in the entire house would not be reasonable.

Logical consequences can be especially effective if parents enlist children's help in planning them before misbehavior occurs. When children are involved directly in discussing what the consequences should be for not doing what is expected, they will be much less likely to feel that they are being punished unfairly when consequences are applied. For example, a parent might ask a child, "What should be a logical consequence for splashing water on the floor as you play with your toys in the bathtub?"

Using Time-Out

When children are actively engaging in misbehavior, time-out is another disciplinary strategy that parents can employ. Time-out typically consists of removing the child from the situation in which the problematic behavior is occurring, for a short time appropriate to the child's developmental level. The child could be placed in a separate room or simply asked to sit in a chair in the same room in a designated spot away from where he or she was misbehaving.

Time-out also may consist of the parent withdrawing his or her attention from the child for a specific period. Four minutes was found to be an effective length of time for 4- to 6-year-olds, and a longer duration of up to 30 minutes could be used with older children (Howard, 1996; Roberts & Powers, 1990). Parents should explain that the purpose of time-out is to give children a chance to calm down, and that they can return when they have worked through some of their feelings and are more in control of their behavior (Nelson et al., 1993). Time-outs must be brief, and expressions of affection are important when children return. A hug and a caring message will let children know that they are loved but that they must develop the ability to behave appropriately. For example, parents might say, "I love you, but I can't let you do this. Someday you'll learn to stop yourself, and then I won't need to stop you" (Brazelton, 1992, p. 253).

Conducting Family Meetings

Weekly family meetings provide an invaluable means of addressing issues and allowing family members to brainstorm solutions to family problems. Because these meetings should be democratic in nature, leadership rotates from week to week, and all family members are allowed to raise issues. Solutions are reached by consensus rather than by majority vote, and each person in the group is allowed to give input and play an essential role in the decision-making process (Nelson, 1987; Nelson et al., 1993).

Family meetings also can be used to discuss the tasks that have to be accomplished during the week and to delegate responsibilities for attending to household chores (Eyre & Eyre, 1994). The main purpose of family meetings, however, should be to address issues that arise in the family and to resolve conflicts between family members rather than simply assigning chores (Dreikurs, 1968). For example, a family meeting might focus on a younger child's resentment that an older sibling is allowed more freedom or an older child's frustration with a younger sibling always demanding to tag along.

Conveying Love

Finally, parents must let children know that they are deeply loved and valued so they will develop high self-esteem (Brazelton, 1992). Each child should receive some special time alone with each parent every week (Nelson et al., 1993). The quality of the time spent together is more important than its quantity.

Family rituals provide an excellent means for busy parents to maximize limited time with their children and to achieve high-quality interactions with them (Parker, 1999; Parker & Horton, 1996). The rituals may be simple or elaborate, and may be short and occur daily or longer and reserved for special occasions or unique needs. Reading a bedtime story, giving a goodbye kiss, and saying "Good morning—I love you!" are all simple rituals that parents can perform daily to strengthen their bonds with their children. Other rituals, such as attending religious services or having Sunday dinner together, can be conducted at certain times during the week; and seasonal rituals, such as going trick-or-treating or exploding fireworks, might happen just once a year.

In addition to developing rituals to celebrate special events, such as birthdays and holidays, parents can create rituals to address family issues, such as dealing with grief, facing transitions, and healing from emotional wounds. For example, planting a tree to celebrate the birthday of a recently deceased loved one can help to alleviate some of the pain the family is experiencing and allow family members to express their feelings and support one another. Although family rituals might seem insignificant at the time, they often comprise some of our most lasting and important childhood memories and can be a powerful means of conveying love.

Teaching Children to Engage in Prosocial Behavior

In addition to adopting a humanistic parenting style, parents can employ specific strategies to promote prosocial behavior in children. The development of prosocial behavior can be cultivated through a variety of methods, such as modeling, induction, didactic instruction, and assigning responsibility for tasks.

Modeling

One of the best ways by which parents can help children learn to treat others with care and respect is to demonstrate these behaviors themselves. Research has shown that children exposed to models that demonstrated altruistic behavior were more likely to exhibit similar behaviors themselves, especially if the children were given an explanation for *why* the behavior was performed and that the act was done to help another person in distress (Yarrow, Scott, & Waxler, 1973). For example, the caregiver could say to the child, "He's upset because he spilled his drink and doesn't have any more, so I'm going to help him feel better by giving him some of mine."

In addition to observing models who demonstrate altruistic behaviors and giving a verbal rationale for doing them, children need to be allowed to practice these behaviors themselves. One study showed that 12-month-old infants were more likely to share things with their mothers if they had been exposed previously to models who both shared objects with them and asked them to share in return (Hay & Murray, 1982). By asking children to share back with them, parents also teach children about the reciprocal nature of relationships.

When considering the effects of modeling on children's development, another issue that must be addressed is the influence of the media. Some television shows with altruistic models, such as Mr. Rogers, have been found to increase prosocial behavior in children (Huston et al., 1992). Unfortunately, however, children have many more opportunities to observe aggression than altruism in the media, and the influence of viewing violence begins early. Research shows that children as young as 15 months of age copy the aggressive acts of television characters (Centerwall, 1992). Young children are especially vulnerable to the effects of viewing violence because of their limited conceptual understanding of what actually is happening and the consequences of the action. For example, aggressive characters might appear to be attractive and powerful to young children who do not recognize the antisocial ramifications of their behavior. Similarly, the true impact of action figures killing others might have little meaning for preschoolers who do not understand either the finality of death or the fictional nature of the characters.

For these reasons, parents have to carefully monitor the shows children watch and the video games they play. All shows and games that consist primarily of gratuitous violence should be avoided, as they have the potential to teach children to behave aggressively and callously toward others. Even shows that are mostly acceptable sometimes contain momentary displays of aggression. Parents can counteract some of the negative influence of such media violence by watching the shows with their children and discussing with them the impact of the characters' actions on others and their own feelings.

Induction

Just as parents need to provide a verbal explanation while modeling altruistic behaviors, giving a verbal rationale is also helpful as they apply discipline for their children's antisocial actions. Induction refers to the the act of explaining the consequences of actions and suggesting solutions to interpersonal dilemmas. This promotes the development of children's inductive reasoning and expands their capacity to understand how their behavior impacts others and to empathize. For example, a mother might say to her young child, "When you hit me, it hurts and I don't like being with you when you hurt me. I'm going away from you until you can stop hitting me." The mother's explanation allows the child to understand that hitting causes pain to another person, and thus to develop empathy.

Because the ability to empathize with others is a prerequisite to altruism, induction provides a foundation for prosocial behavior. Many studies have confirmed the positive relationship between parental inductions and prosocial behavior in children (Brody & Schaffer, 1982; Dekovic & Janssens, 1992; Karylowski, 1982; Krevans & Gibbs, 1996; Moore & Eisenberg, 1984; Radke-Yarrow, Zahn-Waxler, & Chapman, 1983).

Didactic Instruction

Although lecturing children does not often bring the desired results, parents may find that providing them with moral instruction does foster prosocial behavior. One study showed that children as young as 15 to 20 months of age were more likely to show sympathy toward or attempt to help another child in distress when their mothers frequently explained to them how their behaviors affect other children (Zahn-Waxler, Radke-Yarrow, & King, 1979). Several other studies suggest that moral instruction such as, "You ought to make a get-well card to help your aunt feel better because she's very sick," can be as effective as modeling in eliciting prosocial behavior in children (Grusec, Saas-Korsaak, & Simutis, 1978; Rice & Grusec, 1975).

Didactic instruction is most effective when parents verbalize reasons for acting altruistically that evoke empathy or sympathy in children, and least effective when parents use coercive overtones or threats to pressure children. In the above example, pointing out the aunt's sickness is likely to evoke the child's sympathy and lead to prosocial behavior. In contrast, telling the child, "You'd better make a get-well card for your aunt or no television tonight," is likely to lead to resistance and to elicit little regard for the aunt's welfare.

Assigning Responsibility for Tasks

Another strategy that parents can use to nurture prosocial behavior is to make their children responsible for household tasks at a young age. Cross-cultural research in India, Kenya, Japan, Mexico, and the Philippines indicates that children from societies that make youth responsible for major domestic tasks, such as caring for younger siblings, develop more prosocial behaviors than their peers in cultures that do not promote such active involvement (Whiting & Edwards, 1988). By assisting others, children learn to think of themselves as helpful people and to develop increased prosocial behavior (Eisenberg et al., 1987).

In the process of carrying out family tasks, children discover how others feel, experience reinforcement such as parental approval, develop a sense of personal competence, and acquire a repertoire of prosocial skills they can use in the future (Eisenberg & Murphy, 1995). On the other hand, children who are given few responsibilities are more likely to have an underdeveloped ability to be helpful and to recognize the needs and rights of others.

Parents can foster children's aptitude for altruism and concern for others by establishing routines in which all family members participate in doing chores. Routines can be planned in the weekly family meeting, and visual aids, such as a pictorial chart on the refrigerator, can be used to remind each person of his or her tasks (Nelson, Lott, & Glenn, 1993). For example, the family can set up a house-cleaning routine in which each person is in charge of specific tasks, such as vacuuming, dusting, washing windows, and mopping floors.

Routines can be especially beneficial for children if the whole family performs the tasks together at a designated time during the week. Working together with parents and siblings not only helps to ensure that the tasks are accomplished but also promotes a sense of family unity and esprit de corps. Through this group effort, children can learn the tremendous value of assisting others to achieve the common good.

A common question that parents have concerns the types of tasks young children can be assigned. Children's chores must be age-appropriate, but even preschoolers can participate in family routines and be responsible for a variety of tasks (Nelson et al., 1993). For example:

■ 2- to 3-year-olds can do simple chores such as putting away their toys, sweeping the floor, folding socks, putting magazines in a rack, helping put groceries on lower shelves, unloading utensils from the dishwasher, clearing their own place at the table, and dressing themselves

■ 4-year-olds can put groceries away, dust furniture, feed pets, bring in the mail, prepare cold cereal, and help with tasks such as vacuuming, making the beds, filling the dishwasher, and yardwork

■ 5-year-olds can accomplish more advanced tasks, such as cleaning their rooms, scrubbing sinks and toilets, cleaning mirrors and windows, taking out garbage, making their own sandwiches, folding clean clothes and putting them away, and helping with meal planning and grocery shopping.

As children grow and mature, the variety of tasks they can be assigned expands, and they can be expected to assume more responsibility in performing family routines.

A Workshop for Parents

Although many avenues can be pursued in providing information to parents—such as written materials, family counseling sessions, and consultation—I particularly like working with parents using a workshop format. The educational nature of workshops reduces much of the stigma associated with asking for help and also provides a means for parents to see that others have similar concerns. Parenting sometimes is a lonely proposition, and parents can easily inflict guilt on themselves by assuming that everyone else knows how to do it right while they continue to struggle.

The length and format of parenting workshops should be determined by the needs of the participants, but conducting more than one session may be desirable.

After attending a parenting workshop, parents can benefit from participating in support groups to reinforce each other as they practice the skills they have acquired.

In beginning the parenting workshop, I like to mention that it seems somewhat ironic that we must pass both written and performance tests to drive a car, yet no prerequisites or requirements prepare us for functioning in perhaps the most important and difficult role there is—being a parent. I emphasize that none of us are born knowing how to be perfect parents and that most of us probably are prepared inadequately for the challenges that seem to arise constantly. I then commend them for seeking help and for wanting to become better at what they do.

To introduce the topic of parenting styles, I ask parents to think about their own parents' child-rearing practices. Questions to be considered might include:

How do you feel about the way you were raised?

How strict were your parents?

What means of discipline did they use?

How did you feel about your parents when they disciplined you?

How consistently did they apply discipline?

How did each parent's method of discipline compare and contrast with each other?

What were their expectations regarding your behavior?

How responsive were they to your issues?

To what extent were you able to confide in your parents and feel understood?

Which parent were you more likely to confide in, and why?

What were some of the things you liked about the way you were parented?

If you could have changed anything about the parenting you received, what would it have been? Why would you have changed that?"

Finally, I like to ask, "How much similarity is there between how you were raised and the way that you are trying to parent your children?"

By considering questions like the above, parents begin to gain insight into the impact of parenting practices on children from a personal perspective. Sharing these perceptions with others in small groups provides a valuable means of gaining first-hand information about varying child-rearing styles and to discover that others have had quite different experiences. For partners to realize that some of their difficulties in disciplining their children stem from their own experiences in their families-of-origin can be illuminating.

In processing the information derived from this exercise, I point out that although certain forms of harsh discipline can control misbehavior effectively, these can have lasting adverse emotional consequences for children. Similarly, lack of parental control might seem desirable as a child but could have a less than positive impact on a child's overall development. Some adults who were reared by strict parents veer toward extreme permissiveness with their own children, which results in a lack of balance not unlike that of their parents.

After presenting a description of the parenting approaches and asking parents to consider which style their family-of-origin resembles and which is most like their own, I begin to explore the issue of discipline. Parents are asked to volunteer examples of misbehavior that they have found to be challenging to change in their children. In discussing these problem behaviors, I like to have them give a brief description of a specific incident in which the misbehavior occurred, what the parent did to change the behavior, and how the child responded to the disciplinary action. The behavior, the disciplinary action, and the child's response can be listed on a flipchart. After parents have volunteered a number of examples, they can be asked, "How satisfied were you with the outcome of your disciplinary action?" I then tell parents that we will return to these examples later.

As I present the techniques of humanistic parenting, I give parents opportunities to practice skills such as empathic listening, using I-messages, and giving choices in dyads or small groups. Handouts with scenarios can be provided, and the attendees can be asked to practice responding using the skills they have just learned. Brainstorming logical consequences for various problem behaviors is another excellent exercise that the workshop participants can practice with others in a small group. Their responses have to be processed so that the logical consequences adhere to the 3 Rs and are not punitive in nature.

To introduce the strategies for developing prosocial behavior, I first ask parents how they were taught to consider the needs of others and to act kindly toward them. I then ask them to volunteer any examples of altruistic behavior they have observed in their children. I also inquire if they have any ideas regarding what prompted each instance of altruism and, if so, how the parent responded. At this point, I reemphasize the importance of catching children being good and reinforcing desirable behavior, especially if it is prosocial in nature.

After concluding the discussion regarding engendering prosocial behavior, I return to the examples of misbehavior on the flipchart. Parents can be asked to use the skills they have practiced and the information they have received to brainstorm alternative ideas for dealing with each incident listed on the chart. The possible solutions and their probability for success can be processed with the whole group and fine-tuned to achieve the best possible outcome. Finally, parents can be asked to use what they have learned in the workshop to develop and commit to a simple plan to address at least one parenting issue they have encountered with their children.

Conclusion

Parents—who are children's first models—are key to instilling altruistic attitudes and prosocial behaviors in the generation of tomorrow. When parents provide a nurturing environment that abounds with both limits and love, children not only learn the art of relationship but also have opportunities to accept responsibility for their own behaviors and to develop high self-esteem.

The respectful and caring interactions that parents have with their children offer a blueprint for these youngsters to use as they develop their own modes of relating to others. By helping children understand the impact of their actions on others and develop empathy for others' distress, parents can help to prevent their children from committing travesties such as the one that occurred at Columbine High School. The isolation and alienation that fuel such desperate acts of interpersonal destruction can be displaced by the altruism and self-respect that enable us all to live up to our highest potential.

References

Baumrind, D. (1967). Child care practices anteceding three patterns of preschool behavior. *Genetic Psychology Monographs, 75,* 43–88.

Baumrind, D. (1971). Current patterns of parental authority. *Developmental Psychology Monograph, 4,* 1–103.

Baumrind, D. (1991). The influence of parenting style on adolescent competence and substance use. *Journal of Early Adolescence, 11,* 56–95.

Bombeck, E. (1974). Etiquette lesson. *The Reader's Digest.*

Brazelton, T. B. (1992). *Touchpoints: Your child's emotional and behavioral development.* New York: Addison-Wesley.

Brody, G. H., & Schaffer, D. R. (1982). Contributions of parents and peers to children's moral socialization. *Developmental Review, 2,* 31–75.

Centerwall, B. S. (1992). Children, television, and violence. In Schwartz, D. F. (Ed.), *Children and violence* (Report of the 23rd Ross Roundtable on Critical Approaches to Common Pediatrics Problems. Columbus, OH: Ross Laboratories.

Coopersmith, S. (1967). *The antecedents of self-esteem.* San Francisco: Freeman.

Dekovic, M., & Janssens, J. M. A. M. (1992). Parents' child-rearing style and child's sociometric status. *Developmental Psychology, 28,* 925–932.

Dinkmeyer, D., & McKay, G. (1973). *Raising a responsible child: Practical steps to successful family relationships.* New York: Simon & Schuster.

Dodge, K. A., Bates, J. E., & Pettit, G. D. (1990). Mechanisms in the cycle of violence. *Science, 250,* 1678–1683.

Dreikurs, R. (1968). *The new approach to discipline.* New York: Dutton.

Eisenberg, N. (1988). The development of prosocial and aggressive behavior. In M. E. Lamb & M. H. Bornstein (Eds.), *Developmental psychology: An advanced textbook* (pp. 461-495). Hillsdale, NJ: Lawrence Erlbaum Associates.

Eisenberg, N. (1992). *The caring child.* Cambridge, MA: Harvard University Press.

Eisenberg, N., & Miller, P. A. (1987). The relation of empathy to prosocial and related behavior. *Psychological Bulletin, 101,* 91–119.

Eisenberg, N., & Murphy, B. (1995). Parenting and children's moral development. In M. H. Bornstein (Ed.), *Handbook of parenting* (Vol. 4, pp. 227–257). Mahweh, NJ: Lawrence Erlbaum Associates.

Eisenberg, N., Shell, R., Pasternack, J., Lennon, R., Belber, R., & Mathy, R. M. (1987). Prosocial development in middle childhood: A longitudinal study. *Developmental Psychology, 23,* 712–718.

Eyre, L., & Eyre, R. (1994). *Teaching your children responsibility.* New York: Simon & Schuster.

Ginott, H. G. (1971). *Between parent and child: New solutions to old problems.* New York: Macmillan.

Gordon, T. (1970). *Parent effectiveness training.* New York: Wyden.

Grossman, D. G. (1996). *On killing.* Boston: Back Bay Books.

Grusec, J. E., Saas-Kortsaak, P., & Simutis, Z. M. (1978). The role of example and moral exhortation in the training of altruism. *Child Development, 49,* 920–923.

Hay, D. F. & Murray, P. (1982). Giving and requesting: Social facilitation of infants' offers to adults. *Infant Behavior and Development, 5,* 310–310.

Horton-Parker, R. (1998). Teaching children to care: Engendering prosocial behavior through humanistic parenting. *Journal of Humanistic Education and Development, 37,* 66–77.

Howard, B. (1996). The short- and long-term consequences of corporal punishment. *Pediatrics, 98,* 809–817.

Huston, A. C.. Donnerstein, E., Fairchild, H., Feshbach, N. D., Katz, P. A., Murray, J. P., Rubenstein, E. A., Wilcox, B. L., & Zuckerman, D. (1992) *Big world, small screen: The role of television in American society.* Lincoln, MN: University of Minnesota Press.

Karylowski, J. (1982). Doing good to feel good versus doing good to make others feel good: Some child-rearing antecedents. *School Psychology International, 3,* 149–156.

Koestner, R., Franz, C., & Weinberger, J. (1990). The family origins of empathic concern: A 26-year longitudinal study. *Journal of Personality & Social Psychology, 58,* 709–717.

Krevans, J. & Gibbs, J. C. (1996). Parents' use of inductive discipline: Relations to children's empathy and prosocial behavior. *Child Development, 67,* 3263–3277.

Lamborn, S. D., Mounts, N. S., Steinberg, L., & Dornbusch, S. M. (1991). Patterns of competence and adjustment among adolescents from authoritative, authoritarian, indulgent, and neglectful families. *Child Development, 62,* 1049–1065.

Lempers, J. D., Clark-Lempers, D., & Simons, R. (1989). Economic hardship, parenting, and distress in adolescence. *Child Development, 60,* 25–39.

Maccoby, E. E. (1984). Socialization and developmental change. *Child Development, 55,* 317–328.

Maccoby, E. E., & Martin, J. A. (1983). Socialization in the context of the family: Parent-child interaction. In P. H. Mussen (Series Ed.) & E. M. Hetherington (Vol. Ed.), *Handbook of child psychology: Vol. 4. Socialization, personality, and social development* (4th ed., pp. 1–101). New York: Wiley.

Moore, B., & Eisenberg, N. (1984). The development of altruism. In G. Whitehurst (Ed.), *Annals in Child Development* (Vol. 1, pp. 107–174). New York: JSI Press.

Nelson, J. (1987). *Positive discipline.* New York: Ballantine Books.

Nelson, J., Lott, L., & Glenn, H. S. (1993). *Positive discipline A Z: 1001 solutions to everyday parenting problems.* Rocklin, CA: Prima Publishing.

Parker, R. (1999). The art of blessing: Teaching parents to construct rituals. *Professional School Counseling, 2,* 218–225.

Parker, R., & Horton, H. S. (1996). A typology of ritual: Paradigms for healing and empowerment. *Counseling & Values, 40,* 82–97.

Patterson, G. R. (1982). *Corrective family process.* Eugene, OR: Castalia.

Perry, D. G., Perry, L. C., & Boldizar, J. P. (1990). Learning of aggression. In M. Lewis & S. Miller (Eds.), *Handbook of developmental psychopathology.* New York: Plenum.

Popkin, M. (1993). *Active parenting today.* Marietta, GA: Active Parenting Publishers.

Pulkkinen, L. (1982). Self-control and continuity in childhood delayed adolescence. In P. Baltes & O. Brim (Eds.), *Lifespan development and behavior* (Vol. 4, pp. 64–107). New York: Academic Press.

Radke-Yarrow, M., Zahn-Waxler, C., & Chapman, M. (1983). Prosocial dispositions and behavior. In P. H. Mussen

(Series Ed.) & E. M. Hetherington (Vol. Ed.), *Handbook of child psychology: Vol. 4. Socialization, personality, and social development* (pp. 469–545). New York: Wiley.

Rice, M. E. & Grusec, J. E. (1975). Saying and doing: Effects on observer performance. *Journal of Personality and Social Psychology, 32,* 584–593.

Roberts, M. W., & Powers, S. W. (1990). Adjusting chair timeout enforcement procedures for oppositional children. *Behavior Therapy, 21,* 257–271.

Steinberg, L. D. (1990). Interdependence in the family: Autonomy, conflict, and harmony in the parent-adolescent relationship. In S. S. Feldman & G. R. Elliot (Eds.), *At the threshold: The developing adolescent* (pp. 255–276). Cambridge, MA: Harvard University Press.

Weiss, B., Dodge, K. A., Bates, J. E., & Pettit, G. S. (1992). Some consequences of early harsh discipline: Child aggression and a maladaptive social information processing style. *Child Development, 63,* 1321–1335.

Whiting, B. B., & Edwards, C. P. (1988). *Children of different worlds: The formation of social behavior.* Cambridge, MA: Harvard University Press.

Yarrow, M. R., Scott, P. M., & Waxler, C. Z. (1973). Learning concern for others. *Developmental Psychology, 8,* 240–260.

Zahn-Waxler, C., Radke-Yarrow, M., & King, R. (1979). Child rearing and children's prosocial initiations toward victims of distress. *Child Development, 50,* 319–330.

Family Issues and Interventions

Jon Carlson and Judith A. Lewis

In our present-day civilization people are not well prepared for cooperation. Our training has been too much towards individual success, towards considering what we can get out of life rather than what we can give to it.

—Alfred Adler

The family has been called "the crucible of identity." The sense of personal integration and coherence Erikson (1981) saw as the major achievement of adolescence depends in large part on the social, intellectual, and emotional development that is fostered within family relationships.

Family life, which for infants and children is typically marked by gentle care and appreciation, often becomes a battleground during the teenage years. Parents who had been almost worshiped become the objects of resentment and suspicion. Teenagers are in the process of busily carving out a niche and trying to figure out where they belong, how to feel important, and how to belong. When teenagers carve out niches, parents often dig in their heels. They are determined to survive this crisis and often feel bitter, angry, and confused—on the one hand they feel like surrendering, and on the other hand they feel like creating all-out warfare. The teenage years often translate into a collision course in the home.

The teen years are a time of rapid physical, psychological, cognitive, and social changes that affect not only the teens but all family members. Teenagers begin to look toward their friends more than ever before to formulate their identities and to try to develop feelings of belonging and worth. Those friends can become either the allies of parents or the parents' competitors as the parents work to influence their children in appropriate, responsible ways. Teenagers often feel uncertainty about some important issues, such as identity, self-importance, self-value, sex roles, belonging, and status. Parenting is a formidable job in the teenage years, and when parenting becomes complicated as a result of divorce, remarriage, or marital problems, the entire situation can become chaotic and filled with conflict.

People often think that the problem with teenagers and their parents is, simply, the generation gap. This belief is an oversimplification and is consistently challenged by research. The real problem in parent-teen relationships—as with all human relationships—is the failure to talk, listen, and try to understand another's point of view. Teenagers often go through the turmoil of adolescence much better than their parents do. They are anxious to make this transition to adulthood, to become independent and self-reliant. But many parents are not willing to let them go.

Surprisingly, more than 8 of 10 teenagers report that they can, at least sometimes, talk with their parents. Even more surprising, research shows that most adolescents want to share more of their lives and feelings with their parents, even though they might not know how (Dinkmeyer, McKay, Dinkmeyer, Dinkmeyer, & Carlson, 1985). Teenagers want to use their parents as sounding boards for new ideas and feelings. They do not want approval or agreement; they simply want their parents to listen. In talking with their parents, teenagers want understanding and involvement. They are in the process of learning how to think for themselves. Although this process can be frustrating for parents, the end product—a mature, self-reliant adult—is surely worth a little agony.

The real key to communicating with young people is a readiness to listen and care about what *they* say, even when one does not agree. For parents, listening is easy when teenagers parrot their beliefs. The hard part is accepting the teens' right to argue, disagree, and speak out against one's tightly held views. If parents want to have open communication with teenagers, they cannot belittle their teens' opinions. Teenagers are testing not only their parents' reactions but also their own, and the response the parents give will determine, to a large extent, the kind of relationship the teens will have with their parents.

Compromise is important, as it gives teenagers credit for knowing something. Rather than lecturing, judging, and criticizing, it is important to show respect. Teenagers will let parents and other adults know if they need more advice or more input. Parents should try to learn to offer advice without demanding that it be followed. Although teenagers tend to prefer talking with their mothers, the power of their contact with fathers should not be underestimated.

In Chapter 10, Jon Carlson and Dan Fullmer provide a rationale for working with families and the fundamental principles that should be followed when intervening in the family system. They describe the positive strengths oriented model as the treatment of choice with adolescents. Models that emphasize criticism and exploration of weaknesses lead to resistance. Professionals who understand family dynamics and adolescent development also understand the wisdom, and in fact necessity, of a growth-centered intervention.

In Chapter 11, Bonnie Robson discusses the impact of changing family patterns on teenagers. She presents many statistics on divorce and shows how divorce creates both positive and negative aspects for adolescents. For example, following the divorce of their parents, teens have increased responsibility, but they suffer many disadvantages in psychosocial and other areas. She presents several specific methods of intervention and ways of modifying family patterns that children and teens experience. The chapter points out the great need for using preventive methods in these changing times.

Family mediation, an intervention that can reduce the deleterious effects of traditional adversarial divorce and other family life-cycle conflicts, is discussed next. Charles Huber, Barry Mascari, and Aviva Sanders-Mascari describe family mediation as a form of negotiation and conflict resolution in which a third party aids the disputing parties in making mutual decisions. Proactive solutions to predictable, universal problems help families avoid situations that may hinder normal development or add stress to teenagers' world of turmoil and change.

According to Richard and Bree Hayes, divorce, remarriage, and stepfamilies are becoming more and more commonplace, and stepfamilies should be recognized as having their own unique interpersonal relationships and concerns. If not addressed, the issues unique to these families can create stress, unhappiness, and conflict. These authors offer insight into and understanding of this type of family arrangement.

Ann Vernon begins her chapter with a vignette that portrays how having accurate information on adolescent development can lead to a counselor's reformulation of adolescent problems and behavior. According to Vernon, it is imperative for counselors to consider developmental factors in problem conceptualization and treatment. In this chapter, she describes developmental characteristics and their implications for counseling and consulting.

In Chapter 15, Tom Sayger and Arthur Horne describe the family counseling practice with children and adolescents. The authors make a strong case for the benefits of working with children in the family context. They caution that this modality is not effective in every situation and provide guidelines for when and how to use it effectively.

Jon Carlson and Len Sperry end this section with an overview of the many societal changes that have occurred in recent years and their implications for counseling. Many of the counseling profession's ideas about theory, research, and practice are rooted in a world that no longer exists. Carlson and Sperry assess the societal trends and present specific recommendations for how counseling must change.

References

Dinkmeyer, D., McKay, G. D., Dinkmeyer, D., Dinkmeyer, J., & Carlson, J. (1985). *PREP for effective family living*. Circle Pines, MN: American Guidance Services.

Erikson, E. H. (1981). *Youth and challenge*. New York: Norton.

Family Counseling-Consultation: Principles for Growth

Jon Carlson and Dan Fuller

The national barometer of mental health seems to be dropping at an ever accelerating rate as more and more people become symptom-ridden victims of stress. Psychoses, neuroses, high blood pressure, ulcers, backaches, headaches, nervous tics and bodily discomforts are all commonplace. In today's world of emphasis on technology and change, this situation seems to be changing—for the worse. Preventive interventions are not occurring, and remedial efforts are still producing a 50% chance of recovery—the same percentage as no treatment at all. This is a time when humans must decide to live a healthy life or have a new car; to have a body or be a body; to continue to just exist or to begin to live and grow.

Typical mental health treatment (i.e., counseling, therapy, analysis) involves reducing, or *shrinking,* the symptoms of the injured, sick or identified patient. Research, however, indicates that this procedure is, for the most part, inefficient (in terms of money, resources and time usage) and largely ineffective (especially in terms of permanent rather than short-term changes). This situation need not be. Approaches to mental health that are anchored in *expanding* our educational and growth-centered perspectives produce effective, efficient, and permanent mental health. These approaches practice equality and collaboration, center upon complete systems rather than elemental analysis, and flow or work with the natural flow of living in a Tao or "Watercourse Way" (Watts & Huang, 1975).

Research indicates that the family is the prime source for the establishment of healthy and "growthful" living,* as well as the breeding ground for our pathology. Human development is a lifelong process, and growth can be facilitated or arrested at any stage. The family plays a major role in personality formation and development,

---

*"Growthful" living is more than just healthy living. White (1973) claims counseling should not have chosen the metaphor or paradigm of health. The metaphor of what is the best way to live, or values advocacy paradigm, would more accurately define the counseling mission.

and we are just now realizing its lifelong importance. According to Burton White (1976),

> "it appears that the nuclear family is, for most children, their first and most important educational delivery system. Yet we as a nation, for many understandable reasons . . . continue to fail to equip families to do the job." (p. 5)

The counseling profession has not been effective in helping people. Research does not seem to support our traditional and current paradigms. The purpose here is to acquaint the reader with the rationale, essential principles, and constructs of family counseling-consultation; provide a description of a healthy and "growthful" family; present a set of directions of how to use a strengths-oriented educational approach with families; and discuss how school guidance counselors can use these ideas.

Rationale for Family Work

Although family counseling has been in existence for some time, it has come into prominence in both professional and public eyes over the past three decades or so. Its recognition and acceptance have resulted from a growing awareness that individuals cannot be responsible for all the problems they encounter, many of which come from outside pressures and influences, including the family and the social environment. Even the problems of children are typically a result of family interaction and are best dealt with through family counseling.

There is no one model or pattern for conducting family counseling. The approach is dependent upon the problems, the conditions surrounding them, and the counselor's theoretical orientation. But several basic universal principles are important for all family work.

General systems theory (Bertalanffy, 1968) applies the principle of synergy*. Extending the principle to family practice, it is claimed that if one family member changes behavior, all other family members need to change enough to cope with the new conditions, especially the emotional climate in the family network. Fullmer's (1971) relationships theory of behavior focuses on the relationship definition between the family members (mother-son, father-daughter, sibling peer group, symbiotic parent-child, friendship). The basic principle is that behavior is the expression of each individual's personal experience of meaning acted out of the relationship definition perceived by each significant other in the dyad.

Adlerian, or individual, psychology has a well developed system for family work. The primary focus for application has been on child-rearing practices. The central principle treats the individual's behavior as goal-directed. The child's goal

---

*Synergy is defined as "the whole is more than the sum of the parts."

is to achieve a place of importance in his or her environment. The motivation principle is a will to belong or to find a meaningful place in society. The variety of approaches* continues to grow, as does the number of counselors using the family network as the target for counseling.

Principles Used in Family Work

The foundation on which behavior is based can be expressed in principles that represent the key components in the family counseling-consulting model described herein. The principles incorporate motivation, needs, communication, identity, and power. The principles are given equal insight even though there may be a differential impact in any given context. The counselor, through understanding of the following principles, can learn to understand, communicate, and facilitate effectively within a family context.

Principle 1:
Context Is Fundamental to Meaning

The concept of "context" is simply the setting one is in. Given your behavior in an elevator, look quickly at your behavior in your bedroom. How are the two alike? How are they different? Notice your emotional response when you imagine yourself making love in the elevator! What you feel is what we refer to as "meaning." This principle can be seen within a family setting in which a child is encouraged to fight at home but not at school; where the wife is sensuous when the lights are out and frigid when the lights are on; using loose and colorful language when eating at home and being sent to the car when using these words in a public restaurant. The behaviors are the same, but the meanings or feelings are different.

Meaning has feelings because it is tied to the emotional system, the basis of the relationship system. What you feel is the way communication takes place within your family context. Processing one's own feelings is what leads to meaning. Feelings of anger, joy, sadness, elation, sorrow, and so on determine the meaning of the event. Feelings are the connection between the emotional system (myself) and the relationship system (others) (Bowen, 1971). *Your perception is what you are going to do about it.*

Principle 2:
Relationships Are Substance and Behavior Is Form

The concept of relationship refers to the complex feelings one gets when faced with an enemy, as contrasted with a friend. The enemy relationship feels like flight or

---

*Family treatment systems are of two types: those which treat the individual, and those which treat the systems or group life situation or context.

fight, but the friendship feels warm and free. Our behavior in each instance serves to express the meaning we are experiencing. The form may vary for each instance, but undoubtedly we will each display a consistent pattern of behavior with latitude for unique variation. *How you feel is how you act.* The "why" of your feeling is relationship definition.

When someone does things for someone else, the message may be "I love and care for you" or "I'll dominate and trap you," depending upon the relationship. Relationship is substance, and behavior is form. A parent may agree to participate in family counseling (behavior) one week to placate or "butter you up" in order to *control,* and he or she may not agree to participate the next week to show you who is boss and to *control.* Although the relationship remains unchanged, the behavior is different.

Principle 3:
Patterns of Behavior Repeat Themselves in Cycles

The concept of patterns of behavior is derived from the redundance in communication created by a person repeating herself or himself over and over again and receiving acceptable results. The redundant behavior can be either verbal or nonverbal, both verbal and nonverbal, or contextual-verbal/nonverbal. Take a quick imaginary trip through your past 48 hours. What do you find? It is typical for a counselor to be doing the same thing at a given moment of time each day. Nobel Prize winners Konrad Lorenz (1965) and Nikko Tinbergen (1951) have observed that much of the motor behavior of any species can be described by specifying only a few dozen fixed action patterns. Your schedule is a concrete example of redundant patterns of behavior. What is stable is predictable. *What is unstable is unpredictable. Redundance in pattern is the predictable way of life.*

One specific example of our consistent patterns can be found in the "buzz phrases" (Sperry & Hess, 1974) we frequently and automatically use in conversation. Buzz phrases are simply words, explanations, exclamations, or questions that a person uses consistently. In fact, some people actually can be identified with one or more of their buzz phrases. Researchers have found that from one half to two thirds of a person's verbalizations may be reduced to 15 to 30 buzz phrases. The buzz phrases, of course, relate to the person's dominant goal. Some possible buzz phrases associated with certain goals (Sperry, 1975, p. 24) are:

Buzz Phrase	Goal
"How do you like my . . ."	Attention or
"Have you ever gone to . . ."	Elevation
"I'll bet you didn't know . . ."	
"If this job's too hard for you . . ."	Power or
"I want it done *this* (my) way . . ."	Control
"Who does he think he is?"	

Buzz Phrase	Goal
"Just you wait and see!" "It's impossible to get anything through his thick skull."	Revenge
"Well, I didn't volunteer for this job anyway." "I'll try, but I know that I can't do it."	Inadequacy
"Remember how things used to be . . ." "Say, what did you do over the weekend?"	Time Wasting
"Don't get so excited, it's nothing." "There must be *something* we can do about it?"	Peace Making
"Wow, that's really something!" "I might as well try it; I've done everything else."	Excitement

We take this concept into a family and quickly map the individual patterns. Frequently it becomes immediately apparent where the conflicts are likely to happen. The myriad of familial problems recurs in a predictable fashion as the same action chains or patterns are triggered. Each family is like an individual in that it has a characteristic way or pattern of generating conflict. Your action chain is another way to see how your relationships are defined.

Principle 4:
Action Chains Express Definition and Relationships

The concept of an action chain (Hall, 1976) comes from observing what you do following a given cue or stimulus. All behaviors actually consist of sequences, or chains of behaviors. The links in the chains are each composed of simpler behavioral components. For example, the behavior "going to bed" can be broken down into a set of component behaviors: proceeding to the bedroom; taking off clothes; putting on sleeping attire; using bathroom and toilet facilities; saying goodnight to spouse; turning out light; getting into bed.

Each of these component behaviors could be broken down into even smaller components. Taking off clothes, for instance, may be composed of: untying right shoe; reaching down and removing shoe with hands; untying left shoe; reaching down and removing left shoe; removing right sock; removing left sock; removing pants; removing sweater; removing shirt; removing underwear; removing jewelry. *You are chained to your routine of actions.*

Chains are learned by taking simple behaviors already in the individual's repertoire and combining them into more complex behaviors. Each behavior in a chain has a dual function—serving as a reinforcer for the previous response and a stimulus for the preceding one. The action chain utilized will depend on what a situation means to the individual. For example, if someone gives you a compliment, you probably will activate an action chain that passes it on to someone else at the first opportunity. If someone gives you a put-down, you probably will activate an action chain that passes it on to someone else. The action chain will express the meaning each experience has for you, completing the communication of your definition of relationship with the sender.

Principle 5:
Families From a Particular Culture Will
Display Similar Behavior in a Given Context

Context is the manifestation of culture parameters or rules for the way it is supposed to be. *What I do is natural because it is culturally correct. What you do is unnatural because it is culturally incorrect.* A family teaches children the culture of which it is a part. The family is an entire culture on a small scale (microcosm). Rarely does a given family master a culture's entire rule system; thus, each family represents a particularly unique pattern in a given culture.

Because each family emphasizes unique patterns and symbols, the range of microcosm equals the number of families in the culture. Yet, each family resembles each other family within a given culture in the global dimensions such as language, values, attitudes, and basic patterns of behavior. This phenomenon provides the basic rationale for working with multiple families in groups. The healthy family is able to accommodate the wide range of differences encountered in other families without losing its own uniqueness.

Context as a concept defines meaning to an individual in any given situation. The culture's rules for "the way it is supposed to be" form the person's emotional system, complete with physiological and biochemical consequences. The way you feel in a given situation is the manifestation of the principle. The "human potential movement" claimed feelings could be the basis of behavior. The fallacy is in omission of the fact that each individual can create a new context and, therefore, new feelings by his or her own initiative.

Principle 6:
People Learn Social Behaviors All at Once,
in Gestalts, Not in Pieces

The context in social behavior may be more important than the specifics of what is learned. The conditions under which you come into your learning (knowledge and behavior) may be more important than the context of the learning (Loukes, 1964). *It is not what you do; it is the way you do it.*

For example, think of what is learned about sex if you are raped as your initial experience. Or think of the child who learns toilet behavior from a mother who always rewards successful execution with candy. The context may teach many values in addition to the central content of the learning experience. The counselor's attitude toward the family will set the tone for what will occur. For example, the first few minutes of contact between people, according to Zunin and Zunin (1972), usually determine whether or not a successful relationship will develop. The counselor's prejudgments in regard to prejudices, values, and attitudes influence the depth of subsequent interactions.

Principle 7:
The Healthy Family Solves Problems Through Support and Trust From Within the Group

The power of the family bond endures because no matter when you go to your family, they will take you in. No other human group has approached that characteristic functioning in the families of the world. After more than 50 years in the kibbutz, for example, the grandparents relate to the children in much the same way as in most extended families—with a strong emotional bond.

The strong emotional bond is the base for a healthy family. The family bond helps to solve problems because it is the source of support and the essence of trust. With this emotional base, a healthy family can use the most effective means of problem solution and conflict resolution. The most effective means for solving problems is to redefine the family's relationship to the source of the problem. This can be done by stepping outside the context containing the problem. Communications experts call it *meta-communicating*. Essentially, the process requires each participant in any encounter to step outside the frame or context and look at the larger stage or picture. *The view from out here is different from the view from within.* The counseling process centers on helping families learn this method in order to become self-healing.

Principle 8:
Encouragement Is Fundamental to Creative Behavior

A person must gain the courage to violate his or her own rules for behaving if he or she is to achieve new behavior (Bateson, 1972). Learning is fun if the risk is manageable. If the risk is too great, the result is traumatic. Pathology in behavior frequently is generated by the anxiety or fear of failure. Failure is the deterrent to foolishness. To risk, to go beyond what you know and can predict the consequences of, requires you to violate your rules of safety. Whenever you violate your rules and survive the pathology generated, you stand to learn in significant terms or degrees.

Bateson (1972) calls this *trans-contextual learning.* You begin in context A and wind up in context B. Transpersonal experience is similar in social learning terms. You are as usual in context A; then a transformation happens (you learn something new) and find yourself changed and living in context B: I left home at age 20. Five years later I returned home to visit. Home was different, though the same people were there. My experience of home was from the perceptions in context B. I cannot go home again in terms of the old context A perceptions. Experience is altered by the new perception achieved in context B.

This process has to be anchored in a stable, secure setting. Individuals and their families gain security through understanding and accepting their assets and where they are in life. *Tell me what is right with me—not what is wrong.* Security does not result from a diagnosis of liabilities or a concentration on one's problems or weaknesses. This results in insecurity, discouragement, depression, and failure.

The counselor should model encouraging behavior, identify existing strengths in the family, and facilitate activities that increase the possibilities of future encouraging behaviors. The counselor should make frequent use of confrontation—not confronting individuals with their mistakes but, rather, with their strengths. Research has not shown much support for negative confrontation (Berenson & Mitchell, 1974) but strongly supports positive changes resulting from the use of positive confrontation (Jacobs & Spradlin, 1974; Lieberman, Yalom, & Miles, 1972).

Principle 9:
Overemphasis on Individual Achievement
Leads to Erosion of Basic Support Within Families

A social system that produces a Howard Hughes, Albert Einstein, Henry Ford, B. F. Skinner, William Douglas, Tom Dooley, and Muhammed Ali will have a powerful emphasis upon individual achievement.

The price society pays for outstanding individual achievement is ultimate destruction of the basic social support system, the family group. Slater (1974), in *Earthwalk,* believes that this will lead to ultimate destruction of the world. You can decide for yourself if the price is right. The counselor has to be constantly aware of keeping a balance between individual and family achievement. This same balance is necessary for our survival in larger or world affairs (Slater, 1974).

Principle 10:
People Do Not Change;
They Become More and More Like Themselves

In a healthy environment this principle is true. In a traditional environment the principle is modified to read: People do not change; they become less and less like themselves. The shrinking, correcting, evaluating paradigm leads to reductionism, almost to zero or nothingness. The person, for example, may feel a void or nothingness and powerlessness. Contrast this unhealthy condition with the growth paradigm that encourages people to become more and more like themselves. *Happiness is finding more and more where there used to be less and less.*

Competencies Necessary for
Healthy and "Growthful" Family Life

Family competencies are defined as *those vital elements responsible for maintaining the growth and health of the family unit.* To help teach people to become healthy and "growthful," we have to know what we want to teach. Imagine a math teacher teaching a unit on algebra without being too sure what equations are, or a mechanic instructing on computerization in cars without knowledge of those systems. Yet, this sometimes seems to be the situation in mental health. We previously have had little agreement on standards of growthful living for an individual, let alone a family.

The following are among the essential competencies for healthy and "growthful" family life. These are not isolated variables but, rather, form clusters, constellations, and chains that are dynamic, fluid, interrelated, and variable at different stages in a family's life cycle (Otto, 1975, p. 11):

■ *Uniqueness* of each member is allowed to develop.

■ The constructive use of *power* is facilitated, and each member learns to achieve intellectually, socially and emotionally.

■ *Flexibility,* and *creative coping* with the ever changing environment, is a must. The ability to adapt to each other's needs creates a collaborative environment.

■ Accurate *communication* among all members of the family is fostered.

■ An atmosphere of *belonging* is essential to the healthy family. The family should represent a stronghold where changing needs can be met, a system in which individual problems can be resolved conjointly.

■ A supportive climate that provides enough *security* for family members to attempt various endeavors is healthy for both the family and its members.

■ *Democratic principles* of family management are an additional competency.

■ Frequent use of *feedback* and *feedforward* helps members assess themselves and grow.

■ *Problem solving* and *decision making* are needed for healthy living.

■ The use of *consequences* and *consistency* in everyday family interactions is also regarded as a competency.

Otto (1975) believes there are "primary strength clusters" in a family that should be nourished, developed, and expanded throughout the life-span of a family. He thinks that these clusters have a great deal to do with a family's adaptability, resiliency, and optimum functioning. A partial list includes:

■ The capacity to give love, affection and support to each other.

■ Open communication and listening.

■ The ability to give encouragement.

■ Each helping the other to develop his or her unique potential.

- Capacity for understanding.
- Sensitivity to each other.
- Empathy.
- Fostering curiosity, creativity, and the spirit of adventure.

The family counselor-consultant can learn to encourage primary strength clusters, or positive "action chains," and facilitate their continued development through teaching family members this process. By encouraging appropriate segments of these chains, the entire chain is affected and "strength syndromes" are created. Table 1 demonstrates how to encourage specific behaviors and how these behaviors are linked to bigger action chains or clusters.

The Strengths-Oriented Education Model

The use of a strengths-oriented model in education and in family living has many ramifications. The single element most significant to behavior change for any individual is a *new life situation.* The introduction of family and group counseling has created situational changes that have led to more opportunity for new expectations and, consequently, new behavior. *Encouragement* is the second element significant to a strengths-oriented education model. New life situations create anxiety. Anxiety must be counterbalanced by *hope.* Hope comes from the encouragement to risk oneself in a new situation. In contrast to the prevailing weaknesses model, the strengths

Table 10.1 Encouragement of Action Chains

POSITIVE BEHAVIOR	POSITIVE MENTAL HEALTH PRINCIPLE OR LARGER ACTION CHAIN	FACILITATIVE RESPONSE
Doing a job that is yours.	Social interest or concern for others.	"I like the way you see a job that needs to be done and do it!"
Waking up with a smile and making a nice remark (e.g.,"good morning").	Encourages others and demonstrates ability and willingness to live cooperatively.	"You sure seem to know how to make me smile."
Asking for other family members' opinions.	Democratic decision making.	"It feels good to be a part of the family and to know that what I have to say matters to you."

model does not require one to retool. You are OK as you are—just give it a try. The task is to get the other person to try to act in a new situation. If he or she does, the public reinforcement helps maintain the new relationship definition and the new self-definition acquired. It even becomes difficult to go back to the previous behavior. As long as a situation in life does not change, the tendency is to maintain the familiar behavior. The same is true for changed behavior, but the new situation must become stable.

Weaknesses make us losers. Strengths make us winners. In the strengths-oriented model, relationships are made (tamed) and maintained over time. The rules we live by create the situation or define the relationships in which we behave. Strengths make us OK. Weaknesses make us not OK. If I am OK, I can try to imitate new behavior demonstrated in an old situation. I am free to create new behavior in a new situation. If I am not OK, none of the above is likely to happen.

To be a winner, it is necessary to have rules to live by that permit exercise or expansion and, consequently, growth. To be a loser, it is necessary to have rules to live by that require "exorcise" or shrinkage by casting out or reducing the not OK part of yourself. Win or lose, the myth of unchangeability in humans persists. Evidence is legion that the situation in which people find themselves influences their behavior more than do their inner traits of personality (Weisstein, 1970; Bakker, 1975). Cohen (1953), Milgram (1965), and Zimbardo (1971) have each concluded that the situation influences behavior beyond the personal expectations of the individual. Thus, the unpredictability of human behavior has persisted.

Counseling and education have given lip service to the idea that we should begin with a person wherever he or she is. To start where the person is constitutes the cardinal rule for a strengths-oriented education model. There will be no chance to bring the client up to grade level or put him or her back into his or her mythical group. The person must be treated as unique, and new situations must be created for him or her to learn and grow. When this was done in our Peer Counselor-Consultant Training Program (Fullmer, 1976), the new behavior the students were able to create made the significant difference in the way they saw themselves. Low self-esteem became an aspiration to post-high school training in the spirit of a winner, where prior to training, the despair of losing prevailed. *Peer counseling training* is one way to actualize a strengths-oriented *education model* in a school.

Applications for School Counselors

There are two models or systems for the work of a counselor with families. The first is aimed at skill development for parents (Carlson & Faiber, 1976). And a second system or model of family counseling/consulting forms the basis for the following examples of group counseling that school counselors can use. These selected family counseling/consulting cases indicate how the 10 stated principles are applied. To change behavior, the life situation has to be changed, encouraged, and stabilized.

The aim is to change the life situation or family system. Thus, individuals will behave in new ways.

Rationale

School counselors do not always have skills to work with families, because few school counselors have permission to enter this domain. Role statements separate home and school. Professional counselors have debated the legitimacy of whether they have the right to go into the home. The real issue, however, is whether we have an obligation to help in the most effective manner available.

Most school counselors deal on the periphery of family work, however, through parent conferencing and involvement with home problems that students carry with them to school. But these marginal approaches bring marginal results, as the real issues are being overlooked. Through switching the focus to direct family work, permanent change can take place. Individuals learn to become more creative and more understanding, to communicate better with the world in general, and to learn to live and work with other people. School counselors traditionally have been non-effective because they have searched for inner traits when they should have been looking for the social context.

CASE 1

The school counselor was experienced in family counseling and consulting. The case involved the family of a seventh grade girl in a suburban setting. The presenting complaint concerned disruptive behavior and deterioration in behavior generally, especially in school achievement. Because her teachers found no obvious reasons, the counselor invited the parents to come in for an information session. During the initial session with the family, several items of information were disclosed. The most significant change in the life situation in the family was the fact that the father, 41, has just lost his job that had provided the family with a very comfortable living. A check of dates between daughter's change in behavior at school and the father's job situation confirmed that the girl's behavior change came a short time after father lost his job.

Several of the 10 principles are apparent in this case. The relationship between father and daughter was very robust (Principle 2). Principle 4 claims that action chains express definitions of behavior. The heavy emphasis on individual achievement in the family (Principle 9) seemed to have intensified the daughter's reaction.

The case was successfully handled through encouraging (Principle 8) the family members to assess their individual and family strengths and to develop ways of communicating to each other what pleases them. The family came for three additional sessions. During the family counseling, the daughter learned of resources in her family (both financial and psychological) of which she had been unaware. A new pattern of behavior was proposed to meet and stabilize the new situation. The girl's school work improved, and she modified her behavior in a new, more acceptable fashion.

Man's behavior is not primarily determined by unchangeable personality traits or other essential characteristics; on the contrary, his behavior is extremely changeable as a function of the situation in which he finds himself. Change the situation and the person's behavior will change. If one wants to predict his behavior, it is more important to know the situation than the person. (Weisstein, 1970)

Through dealing with the entire family, permanent direct change can occur. Secondary gains are felt by the community and school as their social context is changed when the "new" family ripples out.

CASE 2

The counselor decided to try family counseling with a case referred by a teacher of a first-grade boy. The counselor had used parent conferences before, but this was the first time she tried to convene the entire family to help.

As stated in the referral, the boy was unable to handle social interaction without becoming panicky. Sometimes he would withdraw, and other times he would become hyperactive. In either mood it was difficult to reach him and to help him restore the balance of normal affect. During each event, he was unable to participate with the group in the room or on the playground. He had been removed from a private school a week earlier for similar behavior.

The public school he attends is not in his neighborhood because of the existing busing quotas in his district. Consequently, the boy, in his second month of school, has to attempt to make it under adverse conditions. The child has the additional drawbacks of being from a disadvantaged community and being ethnically different from the majority of children in his class. His new school is in an affluent neighborhood.

The counselor began by using the family counseling/consultation method of asking for help from outside resource persons. She started with the boy's mother. The boy, from a single-parent family, has older siblings and one younger brother. None of the other school-age children have any reported difficulties in school. The counselor visited the mother at home because she did not have private transportation. The counselor was welcomed into the home but experienced the impact of being out of her familiar context because of cultural "differentness" (Principle 5). She had to learn from the mother what behavior was appropriate. The mother displayed strengths and a depth of understanding that initially proved disarming to the counselor, until she realized that her first impression of the case came out of her own culture and was inappropriate.

There is a happy ending, but it didn't come easily. Time was required to bridge the cultural gap. The new learning for each participant, including the counselor, teacher, and student peers, came with application of Principle 1, that new context(s) supplied new meaning(s). Principle 2 was applied when the counselor came to the mother for help to gain understanding of the new situation. The action chain forged by the counselor defined the relationship with the mother as one of mutual trust, and the reciprocity of the helping relationship flourished. For the counselor, Principle 6 fits the learning she needed for new social behavior.

Through family counseling/consultation, some individuals who could not be reached with other methods are helped. Individuals experience dissonance as previous behaviors no longer work when contexts are modified. Many ineffectual responses are reinforced and, though somewhat troublesome, accepted.

Methods

Counselors may choose from any or all of the following suggested interventions.

Family Education

A family education program is a formal learning experience that teaches families in a didactic setting how to live in a healthy fashion. Topics might include communication, family planning and decision making, conflict resolution, family activities and recreation, vacations, stages of family development, encouragement, sex, and birth order.

Family Demonstration Model

Each week a different family volunteers to receive counseling on normal problems in front of an audience. The counselor uses this format to teach or educate all present. From any given group about 80% to 90% of the parents can make direct use of the information that the family in focus receives (Christensen, 1972, p. 129).

Family Involvement Communication System (FICS)

The FICS model provides a human relations "umbrella" approach for parent and teacher input and participation in a school guidance program. This system uses a variety of strategies to enhance the educational growth of children by providing information and assistance to families who are experiencing normal and problematic growth (Shelton & Dobson, 1973).

Multiple-Family Group Counseling (MFGC)

MFGC is a short-term, relatively new form of treatment in which several families are brought together in weekly group sessions. MFGC combines the advantages of group therapy and family counseling, and increases the counselor's effectiveness and the size of the population reached (Sauber, 1971)

Family Counseling

Assisting families with normal or abnormal problems is an important counselor function. Treatment involving the family unit directly affects the situation in which an individual lives rather than dealing with the "identified patient." Treating the living unit rather than the "symptom bearer" has proven effective for problems of different types and magnitudes.

Others

Among additional strategies available to counselors:

- Refer to outside sources—psychologists, mental health centers, clergy.
- Establish a community-wide family clinic where several professionals volunteer their services on a minimal or no-fee basis. Lay people, paraprofessionals, or graduate students may intern under a professional's supervision.
- Offer family life education courses for junior and senior high school students.
- Prepare newsletters and other printed materials that provide information and activities to help families with "normal" problems (e. g., caring, sharing, thinking positively, communicating, recreation, finances).
- Provide parent and couples counseling and education to develop strong relationship and management skills.
- Give group counseling and education for mothers (Carlson & Golding, 1976).

School counselors who choose to do family work are initially confronted with the problem of *when*. Once the importance of doing family work is clearly understood by the counselor and communicated to administrators, alternatives become available. Scheduling conferences during lunch time, early morning hours, evenings, and weekends offers more options for working parents. Some counselors arrange for the school to be open during evenings and weekends to conduct family work.

Summary

Family counseling/consulting is an effective process that counselors should utilize. A wide variety of theoretical approaches and techniques is available. Procedures that focus on strengths and encouragement are the most successful.

CHECKLIST OF HEALTHY FAMILY CHAINS OR STRENGTHS

	Never				Repeatedly
1. Regular periods of relaxation, recreation, and rest are scheduled.	1	2	3	4	5
2. Positive feedback and encouragement are noted frequently.	1	2	3	4	5
3. In daily conversation, assets are included more than liabilities.	1	2	3	4	5
4. Family activities are frequently scheduled, and family has a lot of fun together (many common interests).	1	2	3	4	5
5. Decision making is done in a democratic fashion.	1	2	3	4	5
6. Communication among family members is accurate (includes facts and feelings).	1	2	3	4	5
7. Family problems are dealt with as they come up—never staying at odds long (willing to forgive) or burying problems.	1	2	3	4	5
8. Family work responsibilities are divided in a fair and equitable fashion.	1	2	3	4	5
9. Sharing daily experiences is done on a regular basis and with respect.	1	2	3	4	5
10. Rules are made cooperatively.	1	2	3	4	5
11. Personal goals and family goals are interfaced in an agreeable fashion (a sense of mission).	1	2	3	4	5
12. The family's physical needs are provided for.	1	2	3	4	5
13. The family's spiritual needs are provided for.	1	2	3	4	5
14. The family's emotional needs are provided for.	1	2	3	4	5
15. Support of family members and security are ever present— a liking/loving caring for each other, freedom of expression.	1	2	3	4	5
16. Growth-producing relationships and experiences are initiated and maintained both within and without the family.	1	2	3	4	5
17. Constructive and responsible community involvement is created and maintained.	1	2	3	4	5
18. Growth is evidenced through and with children.	1	2	3	4	5
19. The family has the ability for self-help, as well as to accept outside help when appropriate.	1	2	3	4	5
20. The family uses "injuries" and "crises" from which to grow.	1	2	3	4	5
21. Family members have time together and time alone.	1	2	3	4	5
22. The family has a good circle of friends.	1	2	3	4	5
23. Good humor is valued.	1	2	3	4	5
24. Family finances are understood and agreed upon.	1	2	3	4	5
25. The family has good food and nutrition patterns.	1	2	3	4	5
26. Family traditions and celebrations are celebrated.	1	2	3	4	5
27. Family members share respect for self and each other and are sensitive to each other's needs.	1	2	3	4	5
28. The family has the ability to plan ahead rather than react.	1	2	3	4	5

References

Bakker, C. B. (1975). Why people don't change. *Psychotherapy, 12*(2), 164–172.

Bateson, G. (1972). *Steps to an ecology of mind.* New York: Ballantine.

Berenson, B. G., & Mitchell, K. M. (1974). *Confrontation for better or worse.* Amherst, MA: HRD Press.

Bernard, H. W, & Fullmer, D. W. (1977). *Principles of guidance: A basic text* (2nd ed.) New York: T. Y. Crowell.

Bertalanffy, L. Von. (1968). *General system theory: Foundations, development, application.* New York: Braziller.

Bowen, M. (1971). The use of family therapy in clinical practice. In J. Haley (Ed.), *Changing families* (pp. 159–192). New York: Grune & Stratton.

Carlson, J., & Faiber, B. R. (1976). Necessary skills for parenting. *Focus on Guidance, 8*(7), 1–12.

Carlson, J., & Golding, G. (1976). A school initiated group counseling program for mothers. Available from Human Resources Development Center, 1110 University Ave., Suite 308, Honolulu, HI 96814. (mimeo).

Christensen, O. C. (1972). Family education: A model for consultation. *Elementary School Guidance & Counseling, 7*(2), 121–129.

Cohen, E. A. (1953). *Human behavior in the concentration camp.* New York: Grosset & Dunlap.

Fullmer, D. W. (1971). *Counseling: Group theory and system.* Scranton, PA: Intext.

Fullmer, D. W. (1976). Peer counselor-consultant training manual. Honolulu: Department of Education.

Fullmer, D. W. (1976). Family consultation. In Gazda, G. (Ed.), *Theories and methods of group counseling in the schools.* Springfield, IL: Charles C. Thomas.

Hall, E. T. (1976). *Beyond culture.* Garden City, NY: Anchor Press/Doubleday.

Jacobs, A., & Spradlin, W. (1974). *The group as agent of change.* New York: Behavioral Publications.

Lieberman, M. A., Yalom, I. D., & Miles, M. B. (1972). *Encounter groups: First facts.* New York: Basic Books.

Lorenz, K. (1965). *Evaluation and modification of behavior.* Chicago: University of Chicago Press.

Loukes, H. (1964). Passport to maturity. *Phi Delta Kappan, 46,* 54–57.

Milgram, S. (1965). Liberating effects of group pressure. *Journal of personality & Social Psychology, 1,* 127–134.

Otto, H. A. (1975). *The use of family strengths concepts and methods in family life education.* Beverly Hills, CA: Holistic Press.

Sauber, S. R. (1971). Multiple family group counseling. *Personnel & Guidance Journal, 49*(6), 459–465.

Shelton, J. E., & Dobson, R. L. (1973). FICS: An expanded view of counselor-consultation. *Elementary School Guidance & Counseling, 7*(3), 210–215.

Slater, P. (1974). *Earthwalk.* New York: Bantam.

Sperry, L. (1975). *Developing skills in contact counseling: A workbook.* Reading, MA: Addison-Wesley.

Sperry, L., & Hess, L. R. (1974). *Contact counseling: A workbook.* Reading, MA: Addison-Wesley.

Tinbergen, N. (1951). *The study of instinct.* Fairlawn, NJ: Oxford University Press.

Watts, A. & Huang, A. C-H. (1975). *Tao: The watercourse way.* New York: Pantheon.

Weisstein, N., (1970). Kinder, kuche, kinche as scientific law: Psychology constructs in the female. In R. Morgan (Ed.), *Sisterhood is powerful.* New York: Vintage Books.

White, B. (1976). Exploring the origins of human competence. *APA Monitor, 7*(4), 4–5.

White, R. (1973). The concept of a healthy personality: What do we really mean? *Counseling Psychologist, 4*(2), 3–12.

Zimbardo, P. G. (1971, October 25). *The psychological power and pathology of imprisonment.* Statement prepared for the U. S. House of Representatives Committee on the Judiciary (Subcommittee No. 3, R. Kastenmeier, Chairman: Hearings on Prison Reform).

Zunin, L., & Zunin, N. (1972). *Contact: The first four minutes.* Los Angeles: Nash.

Changing Family Patterns: Development Impacts on Children

Bonnie E. Robson

Today, children are likely to grow up experiencing more than one family pattern. The traditional structure of a family unit or household as a set of parents and children and possibly other blood relatives has been replaced by a multitude of possible family patterns. These include single parents, widowed, separated, divorced, adoptive, or selective families, and blended or remarried families, as well as the adoptive or biological two-parent families with intact first marriages.

Recently the interest of researchers, counselors, and the general public has focused on the effects of various patterns on individuals within the family. This chapter explores the impact of the change from one type of family structure to another on the development of children. It focuses on which developmental styles or coping strategies and which environmental supports potentiate healthy adaptation to a change in family pattern. Using this knowledge, counselors can exert a positive influence on the process of normal development in ameliorating or preventing maladaptive responses.

The Probability of Change in Family Pattern

Most children who have lived in more than one family pattern have experienced parental separation or divorce (Bane, 1979; Norton & Glick, 1979). Since 1972, in the United States, more than one million children under age 18 have been affected each year by their parents' divorce (Carter & Glick, 1976) (although not all marital separations end in legal divorce proceedings). An estimated 40%–50% of children born in the 1980s will spend some time in a single-parent home (Hetherington, 1979; Statistics Canada, 1983).

By the end of the 1980s, almost half of Canadian families and 45% of American families will be of the remarried form (Visher & Visher, 1982). This prediction is not surprising given that 80% of divorced men and 75% of divorced women remarry (widowed persons are much less likely to remarry) (Morrison & Thompson-Guppy, 1985). These statistics suggest that 25% of all children will be part of a remarried family; others will live with parents who are in a blended common-law union. Although the latter is not remarriage, the children will be required to form a relationship with an adult in the stepparent role. Even this readjustment is not the end of the divorce process for some children, as 47% of second marriages eventually dissolve (Morrison & Thompson-Guppy, 1985) and the children of these parents must adapt once more.

Parental Marital Status Effects

That children of divorce are over-represented in psychiatric populations has been known for almost two decades (Kalter, 1977; McDermott, 1970). These children show higher rates of delinquency and antisocial behavior, more neurotic symptoms, depression, conduct disorders, and habit formations such as sleep disturbances than do children in intact homes (McDermott, 1970; Morrison, 1974; Schoettle & Cantwell, 1980). In non-clinic populations the reported maladaptations are numerous. The children are more dependent, disobedient, aggressive, whining, demanding, and unaffectionate (McDermott, 1970). Hetherington, Cox, and Cox (1978) reported that children with divorced parents have generalized feelings of anxiety and helplessness and lower self-esteem. They perform less well on a variety of social and adjustment indices (Guidubaldi & Perry, 1985).

In interviewing 703 children from separated, divorced, and remarried families, Brady, Bray, and Zeeb (1986) found that they differed in both type and degree of problems. Although differences between children with separated parents and children with divorced parents were not significant, the children with separated parents showed more immature behavior, tensions, hyperactivity, and sleep disturbances. Children from remarried families "were found to demonstrate more behavior problems as characterized by conduct problems and hyperactive behavior" (p. 409).

Demographic Variables

In a 6-year follow-up of 60 children of divorcing parents who were compared with 64 children of non-divorcing parents, Hetherington, Cox, and Cox (1985) found that divorce had more adverse long-term effects on boys. Remarriage of the custodial parent was found to be associated with an increase in behavioral problems for girls and a decrease in problems for boys. Further, stability of the problem behaviors was found to be related to the gender of the children. "Early aggressive and antisocial behavior is more predictive of later behavior problems and lack of social competence than is early withdrawal and anxiety. Moreover, early externalizing behavior in girls, perhaps because it is less frequent and viewed as less sex appropriate, is the best predictor of later socially inept behavior" (p. 529). They suggested that these gender differences may be more prominent in younger children.

Brady, Bray, and Zeeb (1986) failed to find any significant interaction among parental marital status and the child's age and sex. Similarly, other studies have not found gender to be correlated significantly with divorce adjustment (Kalter, 1977; Kurdek, Blisk, & Siesky, 1981; Saucier & Ambert, 1986). In a psychiatric population McDermott (1970) found that the proportion of male to female patients was generally equivalent.

Firstborn children, who might feel more responsible for their parents and younger siblings, may experience more stress. The youngest child may have difficulty in later adolescence in identity formation and leaving home to pursue a career if leaving home means abandoning his or her single parent.

Studies of non-clinic populations have suggested that the child's age or specific developmental phase at the time of parental separation is related to the quality as well as the severity of the reaction (Kalter & Rembar, 1981; Wallerstein & Kelly, 1980). Further, the child's age appears to be related to adjustment to the divorce (Kurdek, Blisk, & Siesky, 1981; McDermott, 1970). Generally the younger the child is, the more vulnerable he or she appears to be, because younger children show the most behavioral disturbance (Brady, Bray, & Zeeb, 1986; Hetherington, Cox, & Cox, 1978; Kalter, 1977; Wallerstein & Kelly, 1980).

Developmental Reactions

The child's developmental stage at the time of parental separation appears to be related to the reaction (Hetherington, Cox, & Cox, 1985; Wallerstein & Kelly, 1980; Robson, 1980, 1985). Thus, the following descriptions of the common reactions are divided into age-related (but not age-specific) groupings.

Infants and Preschool Children (0–5)

Following parental separation children under age 5 tend to regress in their development, showing feeding difficulties, toileting problems including soiling, smearing, and enuresis, and frequently disturbed sleeping patterns. Preschool and kindergarten children show, among other symptoms, intense separation anxiety manifested as fear that they will be left alone or abandoned by both parents.

The intensity of this reaction has two possible explanations. These children understand, albeit simplistically, that their parents no longer love each other; they are no longer living together. They reason that if this can happen to their parents, they, too, can be abandoned. An alternate explanation is that having lost one parent, they already have experienced abandonment. Fearing that they will be abandoned by the other parent, they regress to more childish behavior, recalling that when they were babies, they were loved and cared for and in close proximity to both of their parents.

Early responses of anger, fear, depression, and guilt are common in children in this age group. Preschoolers repeatedly state that they miss the non-resident parent. Although these statements may anger the custodial parent, he or she should be helped to realize that this expression of loss does not mean the child loves the resident parent any less—rather, that the child wishes for both parents to be together again.

A child in this age group can develop an attachment to other parental figures and may come to view a resident stepparent as a psychological parent. This result can lead to ongoing discord between the biological parents, with subsequent negative effects on the child.

School-Age Children: Younger (6–8), Older (9–11)

Open denial of the separation or of any difficulties with the separation are frequent findings in early school-aged children. Initially, parents may report that the child is adjusting well, but underlying feelings may not be readily apparent. As one illustration, Virginia, while drawing a picture of her father on the playroom blackboard, announced, "When he's not home, I pretend he's at work and it's okay. When I see him, then I'm sad." Thus, despite the denial, they view the separation as a profound loss. If these children are symptomatic, they appear depressed with anxious mood. They may be extremely hard to control and often have temper tantrums.

To differentiate the vulnerable from the invulnerable in this age group may be difficult for the counselor. The high-risk group appears to express more of a sense of guilt for having caused the separation. Nightmares are common. In addition, refusal to go to school, school failure, and unexplained illnesses are not uncommon.

School refusal may indicate a child who, in the intermediate phase of the divorce process, 6 months to a year after the initial separation, is attempting to get the parents back together. Parents who are concerned about their child's sudden change in behavior sometimes meet to discuss what should be done. This, however, reinforces the behavior and confirms for the child that his or her actions can bring the parents back together. Hence, negative behavior patterns may escalate. Despite the remarriage of one or both parents, children of 7 or 8 remain hopeful that their parents will reunite. For some children these fantasies persist as long as 10 years after the separation (Wallerstein, 1984).

Shock, surprise, denial, incredulity, and disbelief are characteristic of children within the older school-age group. This makes sense when we recall that these children adhere strongly to a sense of fair play. Rules are based on a strong identification with parental guidelines. When parents separate, the image of an all-knowing, all-good, ideal parent is destroyed, and children in this developmental phase can become intensely angry—usually at the non-resident parent. Once their initial anger subsides, they may assume that their parents are still angry with each other. Thus, they are vulnerable to a propaganda game in which they will accept, without question, bitter or false statements by one parent about the other.

Children in this developmental stage experience loyalty conflicts but fail to express them openly. They may attempt to resolve the conflict by becoming excessively dependent on one parent while completely rejecting the other. Susan, who is 9 years old, is unable to go out without her mother. She does not play with friends after school, preferring her mother's company. When the mother and daughter were interviewed, they sat huddled together on a coach. To pry them apart—even to get them to sit in separate chairs—was difficult at first.

These children frequently become enmeshed of their own volition in the custody struggle, and some hang on for years to the image of one parent as all good and the other parent as all bad. Some children engaged in the custody battle are permitted to read court transcripts and even testify on behalf of one parent. They are forced into a position of rejecting not only the other parent's behavior but also all those parts of that parent with which they had previously identified.

Shortly after his parent's separation, Kurt, who previously had shared an interest in soccer with his father, dropped the team despite his obvious enjoyment of the sport. This perceived need to reject all parts of one's life that were associated with the "other" parent can result in a lowered self-image and a concomitant decrease in level of functioning, both socially and academically.

Children in this age group may show anger at the time of a parent's remarriage. Anger that may have been directed at the non-custodial parent may be displaced onto the new marital partner. This can severely disrupt integration of the new family unit (Weiss, 1975).

Adolescents (13–18)

Parental divorce in adolescence can accelerate growth toward maturity, with many adolescents taking on more responsibility than their peers (Robson, 1980). This observation led many people to assert that the adolescent personality was minimally affected by divorce (Reinhard, 1977). If the spurt comes too early, however, it can intensify normal adolescent developmental conflicts and result in a premature attempt at mastery or a pseudo-adolescence (Wallerstein & Kelly, 1980).

Hetherington (1972) has found that adolescent girls, fatherless through separation, tend to change in their interactions with males. They seek attention from men and demonstrate early heterosexual behavior, as compared with the daughters of widows, who tend to be more inhibited around men.

After surveying 1,519 high school students from three different districts, Saucier and Ambert (1986) found that adolescents from divorced families were most disadvantaged on a wide range of psychosocial variables. These included mental health, subjective reporting of their school performance, and perceptions of their life in the future, their parents, and their environment. Those authors also found that boys of widowed parents were more disadvantaged than girls but found no striking difference between boys and girls with divorced parents.

Without conventional support systems and parental guidance, the independent capacity to make judgments and to establish interpersonal relationships is weakened. Lack of parental discipline, which is perceived as emotional withdrawal, is often a crucial factor constituting a further loss and an increased sense of abandonment.

College Students (18–22)

Only recently have young adults been considered when taking a developmental approach to the reactions of offspring to their parents' divorce or remarriage. Cooney, Smyer, Gunhild, Hagestad, and Klock (1986) studied 18 male and 21 female university students whose parents had been divorced 3 years or less. The authors found that in this age group the girls were more likely to experience the divorce as initially stressful.

The students appeared to lack networks, both formal and informal, and only 14% sought formal counseling. This low utilization rate may have been because of a lack of services or a lack of awareness of the availability of services. Entry into a university, with the loss of former peer support systems accompanied by the stress of an unfamiliar environment, is reported to delay adjustment to the parental separation. "The occurrence of multiple transitions was an important issue in the divorce experience in this age group" (Cooney et al., 1986, p. 473). The authors reported that this does not apply to all of the students because some found that living away from home provided protection from enmeshment in the family crisis.

Fifty percent of males and 62% of females reported a change in their relationship with their parents (Cooney et al., 1986). The women seemed more polarized in their post-separation parental relationships and experienced a deteriorating relationship with their fathers.

These are extremely important findings because the quality of relationships cannot be accounted for by custody decisions, as they might be with younger children. Although two-thirds of the college students experienced anger directed at one or both parents, they were equally worried about their parents' future. More students reported being worried about their mothers' ability to cope with independent living situations.

A study of 400 18- and 19-year-old college students revealed that those with divorced or separated parents were anxious about their own future marriages (Robson, 1985). They were less likely to want children. If they planned to marry, they thought they should delay it until they were older—perhaps in their late 20s. More of the students reported that they planned to live with their partners prior to marriage because of their anxiety that their own marriage might end in divorce. Wallerstein and Kelly (1980) reported similar concerns in their interviews with younger adolescents.

Role of the Counselor

From the preceding discussion of the severity and extent of typical reactions of children to their parents' separation, one can readily agree with Hetherington, Cox, and Cox, (1978) that every family breakdown has its victim or victims. The results of Wallerstein's (1980) study are troubling. It revealed that one-third of the children were still distressed and intensely unhappy 5 years after their parents' separation. Of course, two-thirds of the children were coping well and described as emotionally healthy.

Thus, some children cope, and some do not. Viewing divorce as an inevitable disaster may be only one perspective; the divorce process might encourage healthy development for some children. This is not to suggest that these "invulnerable" children have escaped unscathed but, rather, that they may experience the divorce as a growth enhancing process albeit a painful and initially distressing event.

Primary Prevention

Education

Educational programs designed to enhance adjustment fit well with Caplan's (1964) definition of primary prevention as a ". . . community concept. It involves lowering the rate of new cases of mental disorder in a population over a certain period by counteracting harmful circumstances before they have had a chance to produce illness. It seeks to reduce the risk for a whole population" (p. 26). In this instance the population at risk consists of children who are exposed to parental separation and divorce. In discussing children's adjustment, Kurdek, Blisk, and Siesky (1981) stated that:

> Adjustment involves cultural beliefs, values and attitudes surrounding modem family life (the macro system), both the stability of the post divorce environment and the social supports available to the restructured single parent family (the exo system), the nature of the family interaction in the pre and post separation periods (the micro system), and the child's individual psychological competencies for dealing with stress (the ontogenic system). (p. 569)

The literature contains few reports of community intervention strategies designed to correct cultural misperceptions and attitudes (which might be stated as programming directed at the macro system). Educational programming may be in the forms of *bibliotherapy, programs, public forums, information events, individual parent education groups, group education for children, formal school curriculum, and education for professionals.* Gardner (1979) strongly advocated that educators be involved in all aspects of the divorce process.

Rubin and Price (1979) have recommended education within the school system as a preventive measure that can counteract the perpetuation of divorce in families. This type of intervention is especially important for married teenagers, because we know that this group is at high risk for marriage dissolution. By actively working with this population to further knowledge and problem-solving skills, a higher marital success rate may be ensured.

Warren and Amara (1984) found that parenting groups for custodial parents that begin after legal divorce proceedings are more effective than groups offered immediately after the separation. They further reported that participants in these 6-week groups who benefited most were the parents who had reported the greatest post-divorce stress.

Structured, educationally oriented groups exclusively for children of separated and divorced parents, either within the nursery or primary schools or within community centers and public libraries, have been recommended (Boren, 1983; Fine, 1982; Kurdek, Blisk, & Siesky, 1981; Nevins, 1981; Robson, 1982; Tableman, 1981). These community or non-clinic groups appear to be more effective when they are highly structured and when they adhere to a specific curriculum. Many organizations offer family-oriented parallel group programs similar to the program proposed by Isaacs and Levin (1984).

Freeman (1984) stated that children who participated in an 8-week semi-structured educational group were significantly better adjusted than their wait-listed controls. They showed improved in-classroom behavior, and their parents reported that they were more achievement-oriented. They had developed more specific coping repertoires and responses to stress.

In one unique program Crossman and Adams (1980) used crisis theory and social facilitation programs with preschool children. This intervention was based on the assumption that children of divorce need adult-child interaction in addition to that provided by the mother, to mediate the negative consequences of having only one parent available. In a carefully designed double control study, preschool children with separated parents made marked gains in locus of control and intelligence testing.

Legislation

Most recommendations for legislative changes advocate uniform state laws to avoid child snatching by a non-custodial parent. Others suggest changes to involve children in determining custody and visitation and to promote the concept of no-fault divorce (Atwell, Moore, Nielsen, & Levite, 1984; Payne & Dimock, 1983).

Conciliation counseling may assist families through the legal procedures surrounding a divorce and can help reduce adverse effects (Cleveland & Irvin, 1982; Lebowitz, 1983). Similarly, family mediation can simplify the procedures by proper preparation of the couple for the legalities. A full description of the place of family mediation in the divorce process is described by Haber, Mascari, and Sanders-Mascari (1983).

Much has been written about the best arrangements for custody and visitation of children. In recent years several states have followed the example of California in awarding joint custody as the preferred mode of custody. Joint custody acknowledges the continuation of parenting rights, responsibility, and duties of both parents but does not dictate place of residence or visiting and access practices. Wallerstein and Kelly (1980), Clingempeel and Reppucci (1982), and Steinman (1981) recommend joint custody, while Nehls and Morsenbesser (1980) and Goldstein, Freud, and Solnit (1973) caution against its overuse.

In examining 414 consecutive cases of divorce Ilfeld, Ilfeld, and Alexander (1982) found a significant decrease in relitigation rates when joint custody was awarded. This is not surprising when one considers that a requirement for successful joint custody is the ability to negotiate. In 18 cases the joint custody award was made over the opposition of both parents, and their relitigation rate was the same as when sole custody was awarded.

Is joint custody the best alternative? Certainly some children find a joint custody arrangement that requires frequent changes of residence unsettling and anxiety provoking (Steinman, 1981). In conclusion, joint custody can work, but it is not effective in all cases.

Direct Intervention

Early identification

To be most effective, programs should be provided first for children and adolescents who are at high risk for maladaptive responses to their parents' separation. The previously described research indicated that the children more at risk are boys (Hetherington, Cox, & Cox, 1985), children with poor academic achievement (Rutter, 1979), first-born children (Despert, 1962), and children whose parents are only recently separated (Wallerstein, 1980).

Several researchers (Chess, Thomas, Korn, Mittleman, & Cohen, 1983; Ellison, 1983; Rutter, 1971) have implicated ongoing parental discord as a high risk factor for maladaptive patterns. Alternatively, children and adolescents who had a supportive peer group and were able to rely on their custodial parent and siblings were less vulnerable (Kalter, 1977; Robson, Homatidis, Johnson, & Orlando, 1986).

The quality and availability of support services, both before and after the separation, appear to differentiate the vulnerable and the invulnerable. Because vulnerable children make less use of their families for support and rely more heavily on fewer friends who also are more likely to have separated parents, peer support groups for these children would seen to be an efficacious preventive program.

School-Based Supportive Group Programs

The education of teachers, administrative personnel, and parents can provide a firm basis for the success of school-based group programs. Supportive groups that are moderately structured and time-limited seem to constitute ideal programming for adolescence and late latency (ages ± 10–12) children for the reasons indicated earlier (Rubin & Price, 1979). During these group sessions, children often project and portray their parents as mean, selfish, abusive, and violent. Ultimately, the parents do emerge as having strengths as well as weaknesses.

Children's divorce groups led by elementary school counselors have been found to be extremely successful (Wilkinson & Bleck, 1976). This type of group, which is based on a developmental model of counseling and includes play activities and crafts, is synopsized by developmental phase in Table 11.1. From personal experience, common themes of these groups are loneliness, fears of separation or abandonment, and feelings of guilt.

While acknowledging that preventive programs based on a crisis intervention model can be effective initially, Kalter, Pickar, and Lesowitz (1984) believe that children go through a reworking of "nodal developmental points." They caution that divorce should be viewed not as a single life event but, rather, as a process. Thus, they recommend that groups within the school setting should assist children "to negotiate more effectively the developmental tasks associated with both divorce and post-divorce experiences" (p. 614). Although they worked with students in grades 5 and 6, they also recommend groups for students at other nodal developmental points and possibly at the point of entry or leaving junior or senior high school and as preparation for college or university entrance.

Themes that emerge for students of about 10–12 years are anxiety over parental fighting, loyalty conflicts, worry about custody decisions, loss of family and loss or partial loss of the father, worry and anger about parents' dating, and concern about stepparents' discipline (Kalter et al., 1984). In adolescent school-based groups, anxiety-charged issues include marital infidelity and family violence. Teens express fear about parents' dating—and about parents who are not socially active. Adolescents feel an increased sense of responsibility and guilt if the parent is not socially active, but when the parent expresses a wish to remarry, the adolescent is concerned about having to revert from the adult position that he or she currently occupies back into a child role.

In addition, anxieties about homosexuality are increased during adolescence. Although this is a normal developmental fear during adolescence, it appears to be increased among students with divorced parents. They express fears about disturbed gender identity formation as a result of living with only one parent—particularly if that parent has preferred an opposite-sex child. Not being of the preferred gender is an issue for both males and females.

Discussion of loyalties is prominent in group sessions when holidays and vacations are imminent—especially summer and Christmas. Girls' groups tend to confirm research demonstrating lower self-concept among girls whose parents are separated (Parish & Taylor, 1979). A persistent theme in girls' groups was that they felt deprived of a normal teenage life and that they felt abnormal and unlike their peers.

An advantage of students participating in school-based groups is the opportunity to observe participants more closely in peer interactions. Close observation can enable the counselor to select students who might benefit from a more individualized approach or who might warrant referral to a clinical setting for treatment.

School-based groups, compared with community-based groups, are less likely to require parallel parent groups. Adolescent groups prefer not to have parents regularly involved, and groups may be more productive when they are free from direct parental interference. To participate actively and openly, adolescents need to be reassured about confidentiality.

Family or Individual Counseling

Reviewing the literature that deals with disruption of the family unit, there are few reports advocating a family approach. Beal (1979) has recommended family counseling as a preventive measure. Multiple family group therapy, as employed by Messinger, Walters, and Freeman (1978), promotes change and realignment with the family.

Parental *support,* not education, is recommended to assist very young children in adapting to separation and divorce of their parents. As Rutter (1971) pointed out, a good relationship with one parent can be highly preventive of later difficulties. Parents who participate in parent support groups report improved self-esteem as they acquire better parental coping skills (Kessler, 1978; Thiessen, Avery, & Joanning, 1980). And if they feel more positive about their own skills, they are likely to have improved relationships with their children.

Parents of preschoolers need support in maintaining appropriate limits in the face of their child's often extreme regression. Parents who already are stressed may become intensely angry and displace their anger at the failure of the marriage onto their preschoolers. If the child is encopretic and smearing or crying and stating repeatedly that he or she wants the absent parent, the resident parent is likely to get even angrier. Preschoolers need to cope with the separation cognitively, but 80% of them are given no explanation for the loss or partial loss of one parent (Wallerstein, 1980).

When parent counseling alone is insufficient to promote security and reassurance, filial therapy, in which the parent is trained to interact in a therapeutic-like play session with the child, is recommended. Filial therapy is especially helpful when a child appears to have an ambivalent attachment to the resident parent and an anxious avoidant attachment to the non-resident parent (Robson, 1982).

Individual secondary prevention or treatment programs should be oriented to the child's developmental phase. Individually oriented programs usually are reserved for secondary prevention or treatment of symptomatic children. One exception is the specific high-risk population of children "kidnapped" by their non-custodial parent. Individual counseling is recommended with these children to avoid post-traumatic stress syndrome, which is specific to this group (Terr, 1983).

Early school-aged children seem to respond extremely well to individual play therapy sessions in which issues of the "neurosis of abandonment," as defined by Anthony (1974), can be represented symbolically. Play therapy assists the child in achieving mastery of the stressful situation by repetition of the feared event in the play situation. Short-term play therapy, supported by frequent visiting with the non-resident father, has been extremely effective in reducing boys' anxiety symptoms such as nightmares or fears of robbers, murderers, or monsters.

Table 11.1 School-Based Groups for Children of Separation or Divorce

DEVELOPMENTAL PHASE	EARLY SCHOOL AGE (6–8)	LATENCY (8–12, 9–11)	EARLY ADOLESCENT (13–15)	MIDDLE AND LATE ADOLESCENT (15–18) (18–22)
Symptoms	Pervasive sadness, crying, suffering, experience loss. Fearful nightmares. Guilt. Reconciliation desired.	Shock and surprise. Intense anger. Blaming and rejecting one parent. Dependency conflicts.	Shock, not surprise. Pain, "loss of family." Anger at loss. Pseudo-maturity. Acting-out, delinquency, promiscuity.	
Group Size	5–6	5–7	5–6	6–8
Sex	Both sexes	Same sex	Same sex	Both sexes
Length of Time	1 hour	1–1½ hours	1 hour	1–1½ hours
Setting	One room. Table, chairs around it. Carpeted floor space.	Two rooms — group room and activity space. Sturdy chairs.	Group room. Video playback and taping. Sturdy chairs.	Group room. Avoid swivel chairs. Lamps, pictures. Regular seating, coffee tables.
Equipment, Supplies, and Materials	Pillows, craft supplies, paper, scissors, glue, crayons, etc. Simple games— Bingo, Twister, ET, Simon Says, Star Wars, Candyland, Plasticine, Polaroid camera, display area.	Indoor/outdoor sports— floor hockey, soccer, softballs. Film. Dress-up materials, hats, bells, make-up Polaroid camera, craft supplies, string, paper, cooking supplies.	Suggestion box. Paper, pens. Films. Simple dress-up props, collage materials. Soda pop.	Pop, coffee, tea. (15–18) No refreshments. (18–22)
	Juice, milk, cookies.	Juice, milk, cookies.		
Activities	Individual—crafts or games(2 per session) plus refreshment time (start with snack).	One per session— alternate large motor with quieter. End with refreshment.	Films, guest speakers, videodrama, discussion. Refreshments available at outset.	Discussion. Refreshments available at outset. (15–18)

Counselor Activity	Group preparation. Interpretation of positive transference. Avoid splitting. Modeling. Individual in group. Structure, rules, boundaries, Coaching. Rules—listen when someone is talking, stay in room, keep hands off others and others' work.	Coaching approach. Interpret group process during planning. Define boundaries. Provide security. Stimulate ideas, topics. Promote group cohesion, psychodrama.	Focus on group process. Define boundaries. Assist in maintaining structure and focus. Role play. Participate. Relate group to reality.	Group as whole. Use reasoning. Use events to develop group insights. Use modeling. Allow for verbal confrontation with adult. Relate group to reality.
Parent Involvement	Regular contact (once a week/ once a month).	Group meetings irregular, discussed with group. Parents available to transport and wait for children if necessary. Parent groups.	Initially 6–8 weeks.	As indicated; not necessary.
Goals	Have peer support. Reduce anxiety. Reduce unrealistic or catastrophic expectations of adults. Link feelings with language. Help child focus on individual needs. Improve concentration and school motivation through improved self-image.	Have peer support. Reduce guilt. See both sides of parents. Gain insight. Improve behavior. Control, reduce impulsiveness. Improve self-image. Improve interpersonal skills.	See both sides of parents. Tolerate ambivalence. Not use alcohol and drugs for loneliness. Improve self-image. Gain insight.	Share and care. Foster cohesion and confrontation in supportive environment. Develop capacity to resolve conflicts in school and family. Develop hope for future. Improve self-esteem.
Themes	Loneliness. Guilt. Being left out. Abandonment.	Anger. Blame. Rights and fair play. Intolerance of mistakes. Sadness linked with anger.	Hostility. Violence. Rejection. Too much responsibility too soon. Hunger and pain.	Loneliness. Fear of future. Existential anxiety. Loss of adolescence. Sexuality.

Clinical Group Counseling Programs

More symptomatic older children and adolescents in clinic settings similar to those in school-based programs appear to respond well to group therapy. Older school-aged children have a tendency to take sides and become embroiled in parental conflict and intractable custody disputes (Robson, 1982). In this situation, family counseling with the unfavored parent and the child or children is imperative. Separate individual counseling for the favored (usually the custodial) parent is recommended in conjunction with family counseling. The custodial parent must be helped to overcome his or her own anger and resentment at the situation and to support the children in a more reality-oriented approach to visitation.

Adolescents who show more severe reactions, such as acting-out through delinquent behavior or promiscuity or marked withdrawal, can benefit from an intensive psychotherapeutic group experience, which may protect them from developing a personality disorder. The creative drama and videotape playback employed in these groups increases the individual's awareness, facilitates expression of fantasy and feelings, and promotes problem solving (Stirtzinger & Robson, 1985).

The video playback technique is unique in that it allows the adolescent to both invest in the process and maintain a safe distance. In light of these adolescents' loss of alliance with parents and their difficulty in forming a treatment alliance, video playback allows each group member to maintain a sense of control. It allows the adolescent to be an active participant either as part of the audience or as the director of a drama. Thus, the individual is permitted to identify with the group in a role function rather than as a dependent patient.

Creative drama can be viewed as a complex form of play. The adolescent is developmentally intermediate between needing the discharge of play and the ability to bind and delay inherent in talking therapy. Creative drama is intermediate between concrete, symbolic play with toys and personal revelation. It permits displacement on the characters.

In my experience with early adolescent clinic groups, family violence seems to be portrayed with increasing frequency. In client dramatizations fathers set themselves on fire and threaten the family with guns, while mothers take overdoses or suddenly abandon the family. There is much sex stereotyping, often linked with violence and anger (Robson, 1986).

Confusion over the cause of separation and the need to blame is captured in plays about family conflicts. In these plays parents frequently are portrayed as fighting over their adolescent's behavior—such as failing to clean up his or her room or not finishing homework or getting into trouble at school. Portrayal of the parents' continued fighting may represent an ambivalent wish to have the parents reunite. Fathers usually are blamed for the break-up; mothers are viewed as stupid and inadequate. Stepmothers typically are seen in the classic Cinderella sense. Parents who remarry often bear another child, so expression of the theme of being "replaced" by an infant also is common in these groups.

The older adolescent clinic groups, in my experience, tend to be more metaphorical. Through discussion these adolescents rework their understanding of their parents' separation, issues of dating, or the loss of a boyfriend or girlfriend. These themes may reflect a greater sense of parents as individuals with needs of their own. Dramatized solutions to the dilemmas, however, are at times magical and childish, with the main character suddenly becoming a famous rock star, lawyer, or journalist—an individual who goes into the world successfully, needing help from no one.

Families sometimes are portrayed as arguing endlessly with no resolution, but later themes frequently involve asking for and receiving help. A loss of discipline may represent the loss of the family as a unit. The adolescent's strivings for independence and identity can be intensified in an attempt to seek the appropriate discipline. A struggle that extends beyond the family unit into the community suggests that the parent (or both parents) needs support and guidance in providing consistency and structure. Individual counseling for the single custodial parent or separate counseling with the same counselor for both the resident and the non-resident parent may be indicated.

Conclusion

The percentage of students in elementary, secondary, and even postsecondary schools who recently have experienced a change in their family pattern is increasing. This demands the development of more innovative, preventive programming for the students affected. This programming is vital if counselors are to ward off maladaptive responses in later years and help both adults and children cope with changing family patterns.

References

Anthony, E. J. (1974). Children at risk from divorce: A review. In E. J. Anthony & C. Koupernik, *The child in his family* (pp. 461–477). New York: Wiley.

Atwell, A. E., Moore, U. S., Nielsen, E., & Levite, Z. (1984). Effects of joint custody on children. *Bulletin of American Academy of Psychiatric Law, 12,* 149–157.

Bane, M. J. (1979). Marital disruption and the lives of children. In G. Levinger & O. C. Moles (Eds.), *Divorce and Separation* (pp. 276–286). New York: Basic Books.

Beal, E. W (1979). Children of divorce: A family systems perspective. *Journal of Social Issues, 35,* 140–154.

Boren, R. (1983). The therapeutic effects of a school-based intervention program for children of the divorced. *Dissertation Abstracts International, 43* (12-A), 3811–3812.

Brady, C. P., Bray, J. H., & Zeeb, L. (1986). Behavior problems of clinic children: Relation to parental marital status, age and sex of child. *American Journal of Orthopsychiatry, 56,* 399–412.

Caplan, G. (1964). *Principles of preventive psychiatry.* New York: Basic Books.

Carter, H., & Glick, P. E. (1976). *Marriage and divorce: A social and economic study.* Cambridge, MA: Harvard University Press.

Chess, S., Thomas, A., Korn, S., Mittleman, M., & Cohen, J. (1983). Early parental attitudes, divorce and separation and adult outcomes: Findings of a longitudinal study. *Journal of American Academy of Child Psychiatry, 22*(1), 47–51.

Cleveland, M., & Irvin, K. (1982). Custody resolution counselling: An alternative intervention. *Journal of Marital & Family Therapy, 8,* 105–111.

Clingempeel, G. W, & Reppucci, N. D. (1982). Joint custody after divorce: Major issues and goals for research. *Psychology Bulletin, 92,* 102–127.

Cooney, T. M., Smyer, M. A., Hagestad, G. O., & Klock, R. (1986). Parental divorce in young adulthood: Some preliminary findings. *American Journal of Orthopsychiatry, 56,* 470–477.

Crossman, S. M., & Adams, G. R. (1980). Divorce, single parenting and child development, *Journal of Psychology, 106,* 205–217.

Despert, J. (1962). *Children of divorce.* New York: Doubleday.

Ellison, E. S. (1983). Issues concerning parental harmony and children's psychosocial adjustment. *American Journal of Orthopsychiatry, 53*(1), 73–80.

Fine, S. (1982). Children in divorce, custody and access situations: The contribution of the mental health professional. *Journal of Child Psychology & Psychiatry, 21,* 353–361.

Freeman, R. (1984). *Children in families experiencing separation and divorce: An investigation of the effects of brief intervention.* Toronto: Family Service Association of Metropolitan Toronto Press.

Gardner, R. A. (1979). Social, legal and therapeutic changes that should lessen the traumatic effects of divorce on children. *Journal of the American Academy of Psychoanalysis, 6,* 231–247.

Goldstein, J., Freud, A., & Solnit, A. J. (1973). *Beyond the best interest of the child.* New York: Free Press.

Guidubaldi, J., & Perry, J. D. (1985). Divorce and mental health sequelae for children: A two year follow-up of a nationwide sample. *Journal of American Academy of Child Psychiatry, 24,* 531–537.

Haber, C. H., Mascari, J. B., & Sanders-Mascari, A. (1983). Family mediation: An idea whose time has come. *Counseling & Human Development, 16*(3), 1–16.

Hetherington, E. M. (1972). Effects of father absence on the personality development in adolescent daughters. *Developmental Psychology, 7,* 313–326.

Hetherington, E. M. (1979). Divorce: A child's perspective. *American Journal of Psychiatry, 34,* 851–858.

Hetherington, E. M., Cox, M., & Cox, R. (1978). The aftermath of divorce. In J. Stevens & M. Mathews (Eds.), *Mother-child relations.* Washington, DC: National Association for the Education of Young Children.

Hetherington, E. M., Cox, M., & Cox, R. (1985). Long term effects of divorce and remarriage on the adjustment of children. *Journal of American Academy of Child Psychiatry, 24,* 518–530.

Ilfeld, F. W., Jr., Ilfeld, H. Z., & Alexander, J. R. (1982). Does joint custody work? A first look at outcome data of relitigation. *American Journal of Psychiatry, 139,* 62–66.

Isaacs, M. B., & Levin, I. R. (1984). Who's in my family? A longitudinal study of drawings of children of divorce. *Journal of Divorce, 7,* 1–20.

Kalter, N. (1977). Children of divorce in an out-patient psychiatric population. *American Journal of Orthopsychiatry, 47,*40–51.

Kalter, N., Pickar, J., & Lesowitz, M. (1984). School-based developmental facilitation groups for children of divorce: A preventive intervention. *American Journal of Orthopsychiatry, 54,* 613–623.

Kalter, N., & Rembar, J. (1981). The significance of child's age at the time of parental divorce. *American Journal of Orthopsychiatry, 51,* 85–100.

Kessler, S. (1978). Building skills in divorce adjustment groups. *Journal of Divorce, 2,* 209–216.

Kurdek, L. A., Blisk, D., & Siesky, A. (1981). Correlates of children's long-term adjustment to their parents' divorce. *Developmental Psychology, 17,* 565–579.

Lebowitz, M. L. (1983). The organization and utilization of child-focused facility for divorcing, single-parent and remarried families. *Conciliation Courses Review, 21,* 99–104.

McDermott, J. R. (1970). Divorce and its psychiatric sequelae in children. *Archives of General Psychiatry, 23,* 421–427.

Messinger, L., Walters, K. N., & Freeman, S. J. J. (1978). Preparation for remarriage following divorce: The use of group technique. *American Journal of Orthopsychiatry, 48,* 263–272.

Morrison, J. (1974). Parental divorce as a factor in childhood psychiatric illness. *Comprehensive Psychiatry, 15,* 95–102,

Morrison, K., & Thompson-Guppy, A. (1985). *Stepmothers: Exploring the myth.* Ottawa: Canadian Council on Social Development.

Nehls, N., & Morsenbesser, M. (1980). Joint custody: An exploration of the issues. *Family Process, 19,* 117–125.

Nevins, V J. (1981). Evaluation of effectiveness of a group treatment intervention with children of divorce. *Dissertation Abstracts International, 42* (2-B), 781.

Norton, A. M., & Glick, P. S. (1979). Marital instability in America. In G. Levinger & O. C. Moles (Eds.), *Divorce and separation* (pp. 6–19). New York: Basic Books.

Parish, T. S., & Taylor, J. C. (1979). The impact of divorce and subsequent father absence on children's and adolescents' self concepts. *Journal of Youth & Adolescence, 8,* 427–432.

Payne, J. D., & Dimock, J. L. (1983). Legal and psychiatric approaches to marriage breakdown or divorce. *Psychiatric Journal University of Ottawa, 8,* 189–197.

Reinhard, D. (1977). The reaction of adolescent boys and girls to the divorce of their parents. *Journal of Clinical Child Psychology, 6,* 21–23.

Robson, B. (1980). *My parents are divorced, too.* New York: Everest House.

Robson, B. E. (1982). A developmental approach to the treatment of children of divorcing families. In L. Messinger (Ed.), *Therapy with remarriage families* (pp. 59–78). Rockville, MD: Aspen Systems Corp.

Robson, B. (1985). Marriage concepts of older adolescents. *Canadian Journal of Psychiatry, 30,* 169–172.

Robson, B. E. (1986). School-based groups for children and adolescents of divorce. *Canadian Home Economics Journal, 36,* 13–22.

Robson, B., Homatides, G., Johnson, L., & Orlando, F. (1986). *Toronto family study.* Toronto: Toronto Board of Education Publication.

Rubin, L. D., & Price, J. H. (1979). Divorce and its effects on children. *Journal of School Health, 49,* 552–559.

Rutter, M. (1971). Parent-child separation: Psychological effects on the children. *Journal of Child Psychology & Psychology, 12,* 233–260.

Rutter, M. (1979). Invulnerability or why some children are not damaged by stress. In S. J. Shamsie (Ed.), *New directions in children's mental health* (pp. 53–75). New York: Spectrum.

Saucier, J., & Ambert, A. (1986). Adolescents' perception of self and of immediate environment by parental marital status: A controlled study. *Canadian Journal of Psychiatry, 31,* 505–512.

Schoettle, J. C., & Cantwell, D. P. (1980). Children of divorce: Demographic variables, symptoms and diagnoses. *Journal of American Academy of Child Psychiatry, 9,* 453–476.

Statistics Canada. (1983). *Divorce: Law and the family in Canada.* Ottawa: Ministry of Supply & Services.

Steinman, S. (1981). The experience of children in joint custody arrangement: A reprint of a study. *American Journal of Orthopsychiatry, 51,* 403–414.

Stirtzinger, R., & Robson, B. (1985). Videodrama and the observing ego. *Journal of Small Group Behaviour, 16*(4), 539–548.

Tableman, B. (1981). Overview of programs to prevent mental health problems of children. *Public Health Reports, 96,* 38–44.

Terr, L. C. (1983). Childsnatching: A new epidemic of an ancient malady. *Journal of Pediatrics, 103,* 151–156.

Thiessen, J. D., Avery, A. W., & Joanning, H. (1980). Facilitating post divorce adjustment among women: A communication skills training approach. *Journal of Divorce, 4,* 4–22.

Visher, E. B., & Visher, J. S. (1982). Step families in the 1980's. In L. Messinger (Ed)., *Therapy with remarriage families* (pp. 105–119). Rockville, MD: Aspen Systems Corp.

Wallerstein, J. S. (1980). The impact of divorce on children. *Psychiatric Clinics of North America, 3,* 455–468.

Wallerstein, J. S. (1984). Children of divorce: Preliminary report of a ten year follow-up of young children. American *Journal of Orthopsychiatry, 54,* 444–458.

Wallerstein, J. S., & Kelly, J. B. (1980). *Surviving the breakup: How children and parents cope with divorce.* New York: Basic Books.

Warren, N. J., & Amara, I. A. (1984). Educational groups for single parents: The parenting after divorce programs. *Journal of divorce, 8*(2), 79–96.

Weiss, R. S. (1975). *Marital separation.* New York: Basic Books.

Wilkinson, G. S., & Bleck, R. T. (1976). Children's divorce groups. *Elementary School Guidance & Counseling, 11,* 205–213.

Family Mediation: An Idea Whose Time Has Come

Charles H. Huber, J. Barry Mascari, and Aviva Sanders-Mascari

Family mediation is one of the most rapidly growing movements today for facilitating more favorable family relations. Its growth may parallel society's search for a new sense of community where the healthy survival of the family, in whatever form, takes precedence over the search for individual satisfaction. Or perhaps the increased use of legal action in recent years accompanied by the seemingly constant display of intimate family concerns in the public arena has pushed society too far (Vroom, Fassett, & Wakefield, 1982). Whatever the basis, professionals and the public alike have a growing realization that family mediation can resolve family conflicts in an equitable and more sensitive manner.

Mediation is a form of negotiation and conflict resolution in which the disputing parties are aided by a third party in making mutual decisions. The mediator does not exert decision-making power on the issue(s) in dispute. As such, family mediation maintains decision-making power with those it most directly affects—the family members themselves. It fosters a cooperative sharing of power that results in positively transformed rather than negatively severed relationships. The attraction of the mediation process for settling family disputes is obvious and is being applied to a wide range of issues throughout the family life cycle. Some of these issues are briefly identified and illustrated in Figure 12.1.

Theoretical Foundations

Family mediation draws practitioners from a wide spectrum of professional backgrounds. Each has contributed somewhat differently to the practice of family mediation as it exists today. Coogler (1978) described family mediation as "an art in its early stages of development" (p. 79). The greater portion of research efforts on

Mediation Along the Family Life Cycle

Pre-Marital Mediation
Mediators are helping couples draw up marriage agreements prior to the ceremony. This "ounce of prevention" can help ensure a more stable marriage.

Disabled and Handicapped
Stress often occurs in families caring for disabled or handicapped members. Counselors are using mediation to resolve some of the resulting conflicts.

Teenage Pregnancy
Struggles often arise over situations involving unmarried pregnant teenagers. Mediation can assist in resolving the conflicts between parents and child.

Homosexuals
Gay couples ending a relationship often have many of the same conflicts that divorcing couples do. The legal system does not necessarily provide a forum, so mediation can be valuable in resolving disputes.

Unmarried Cohabitants
At least one campus mediation service handles disputes between nonmarried couples who live together and seek a solution other than separation.

Teenagers and Parents
Numerous conflicts arise between parents and their adolescent children. Parent-teenager disputes often involve power struggles, and mediation can help restore relative peace to these households.

Runaways
Mediation is being used to bring together runaways and their families, and to resolve their conflicts out of court. Mediators are also helping to resolve family differences caused by juvenile drug abusers.

Relocation
New comprehensive relocation services use mediation to resolve the conflicts brought to the surface by a family move, such as problems related to dual careers, care of dependents, adolescent anxieties and emotional problems.

Domestic Violence
Mediation is helpful in the area of spouse abuse, particularly with first-time abusers.

Separation and Divorce
Property settlements and support payments are often the two areas of greatest contention in separation and divorce disputes. Mediation helps the couple to separate emotional issues from financial decisions.

Custody and Visitation
Mediation allows for more flexible and finely tailored child custody arrangements than those resulting from the adversarial process. Couples often reach cooperative joint custody agreements.

Retirement
Mediation services can help settle disputes at retirement time, such as when a husband might want to move to Florida just when his wife is embarking on a new career.

The Elderly vs. Their Middle-Aged Children
With the elderly population increasing, more and more conflicts are arising when older people can no longer care for themselves. Mediators help families to reach decisions about institutional versus home care.

Wills and Estate Planning
Mediation is useful when families disagree over estate plans. It also cuts costs when family members are contesting the execution of a relative's will.

Figure 12.1 Some Issues in Family Mediation

conflict resolution have been carried out only in the last 15 years, and family mediation is still somewhat of a pioneering application of that research.

Although family mediation as an identifiable professional practice is a relatively new phenomenon, many mental health and legal professionals claim that they have been doing it for some time. To a certain extent, they are correct. Therapists who assist families in restructuring during times of change, conflict, or crisis may be involved in a form of mediation. Those utilizing problem-solving strategies or task-oriented interventions are especially likely to crisscross the seemingly ambiguous boundary between therapy and mediation.

Court judges in pre-trial conferences often actively advocate that adversary family members and their attorneys attempt to arrive at a mutually amicable agreement outside of court, if possible. Lawyers may be operating in a mediating capacity when they agree that a proposed settlement is fair and each believes it to be in the best interest of his or her client. In these contexts, however, the professional has a role that takes precedence over his or her role as a mediator, and the mediating process is simply a tactic to further the goals of another process (Girdner, 1983). The actual dynamics of family mediation are specific unto themselves when a professional is engaged as a mediator for the sole purpose of mediation.

Conflict Resolution vs. Conflict Cessation

Mediation involves the resolution of conflict, not merely the cessation of it. Cessation of conflict is frequently mistaken for conflict resolution. Consider the following example:

> Sarah, 15 years old and pregnant, had strong personal convictions about abortion and believed it to be morally wrong. Her parents—actually more concerned about what the community would think of them as Sarah's condition became increasingly evident—provided her with many reasons why an abortion was the "best" alternative. Sarah, dependent and unassertive, followed their advice. Not really agreeing with that course of action, she later underwent a long period of therapy to deal with the guilt and depression she experienced as a result.

Without full and mutual participation in the decision-making process by all involved, actual resolution of a dispute may not be achieved. Some family members, like Sarah, are overwhelmed by others' seemingly more powerful positions. Often, finding themselves in a disadvantageous position, individuals simply withdraw—but fully intend to resume the controversy when conditions are more favorable. Others respond by passively accepting whatever terms are thrust upon them, with absolutely no expectation of complying with them. In none of these instances is resolution reached.

Decision-making can be viewed as an unequal, superior-inferior relationship wherein one party (the superior) decides, while another (the inferior) is given little or no role in the process—only the outcome; or, alternatively, as a mutual venture in which all concerned contribute to the process and take responsibility in any outcome decided upon (Huber, 1981). Mediation seeks to make decision making "mutual" and its results mutually acceptable. This has a dramatic impact upon the way in which decisions are made and adhered to, as well as the emotional aftereffects experienced.

Coogler (1978) proposed that six conditions be present for true conflict resolution to occur:

1. The physical well-being of each party involved is maintained during negotiations and in the resolution reached.

2. Each party maintains its feelings of self-worth during the negotiating process and in the resolution itself.

3. All involved parties are respected and tolerated as persons, but with the understanding that this need not imply approval of others' morals or values.

4. All relevant facts, available options, and technical information are considered and used in reaching any resolution.

5. The consequences of each available option are considered by all parties before any resolution is agreed upon.

6. The resolution that is reached is agreed to by all parties even though other choices were available.

The Structures of Family Mediation

Coogler further proposed that these six conditions suggest a specific structure that fosters resolution of conflict rather than merely controlling or ending it. He identified a coherent integration of three separate structures as being the essence of family mediation (Coogler, 1978): the procedural structure, the value structure, and the psychological structure.

The Procedural Structure

The procedural structure gives order to the mediation process. It presents all involved with a clear and common framework from which to function. It provides the means by which the factual and technical information needed for assessing alternatives becomes available to family members. The procedural structure identifies issues to be considered, schedules regular times for negotiations, establishes a neutral territory in which mediation is conducted, and gives the mediator the power to see that all parties follow agreed-to rules. Coogler (1978) cautioned that the procedural structure be kept simple so that family members need not devote excessive efforts to understanding it or, conversely, be encouraged by its complexity and resulting confusion to manipulate it to their advantage.

The Value Structure

The value structure establishes basic ethical standards of fairness to be followed during mediation. Family members should be told that these standards constitute the framework of an elementary sense of fairness. The standards cannot be expected to satisfy everyone's personal idiosyncratic conceptualizations of what is just. The intent is to project a common value structure that can be comprehended by all concerned and seen as fairly applicable to them rather than to try to provide a procedure for meeting every test of fairness—which would be fruitless.

The Psychological Structure

The psychological structure creates a setting wherein the physical and emotional needs of family members are sufficiently met so they can make optimal use of their decision-making capabilities. The mediator's understanding of group and family dynamics, and accompanying skills for creating a favorable working environment, provide the basis for the psychological structure. The procedural and value structures also contribute significantly to an appropriate psychological structure by creating a context that facilitates a fair and equitable resolution of conflict.

Mediation Models

Mediation as a means of conflict resolution has been employed since the earliest recorded history. Traditionally, the extended family has been the primary mediating institution. Similarly, the church has played a large role in helping families deal with internal conflicts. The local minister, rabbi, or parish priest has been called upon frequently to help family members mutually resolve problems. Family friends likewise have often been a source of objective advice and support.

Although these and similar forms of mediation have been present, their informal character has facilitated little objective evaluation and scientific development of the process. Examination of the professional literature reveals surprisingly little information. In an analytic review of research on the process of mediation, Wall (1981) stated that "mediation remains understudied, less than understood, and unrefined" (p. 157). The emphasis has been on the characteristics and techniques of mediators and on the content of disputes rather than on the process itself (Girdner, 1983).

In most forms of mediation, practices have been established largely by the "unwritten law" of custom rather than specified procedures. Most mediators have learned by "on-the-job experience," and most have come to mediation from another field quite by accident. Mediators who have developed their own style have written about their experience in an anecdotal fashion, but research still lags (Coogler, Weber, & McKenny, 1979).

Gulliver (1979) proposed a cyclical and developmental model for understanding the process of mutual decision making in negotiated settlements. This model provides one concentrated focus that ties together the common threads used to define varying forms of interaction as being mediation. The cyclical aspects of Gulliver's model refer to the information sharing and learning that take place during the course of family mediation. The developmental aspects illustrate an overview of the family mediation process as it progresses from the time at which a disagreement becomes a dispute to its final outcome.

Family members come to mediation with often vague and inconsistent expectations that must be continually revised throughout the course of mediation efforts. Each member is expected to convey information about his or her demands, desires, strengths, and weaknesses, as well as to process similar forms of data from the other members and the mediator. Throughout this repetitive process of information exchange, family members and the mediator must learn to progressively adjust their expectations and preferences in order to make clearly understood and common choices. Thus, *mediation is a dynamic interactive process that facilitates change through clarification and discovery* (Girdner, 1983). This cycle repeats itself over and over as mediation proceeds from beginning to end.

A Typical Sequence of Mediation

When family members elect to come to mediation, they are mutually recognizing some dispute they need to work on together to resolve. Shortly, however, a shift from coordinated to antagonistic positions occurs as family members move from agreeing on mediation to disagreeing about the issues in dispute. This can involve disagreement about the issues themselves or the order in which they are to be considered. With the mediator's assistance the family members seek agreement regarding the boundaries of their dispute and the agenda to be followed. The mediator explains that it is his or her responsibility to give them information about various options so they can make more informed decisions. The mediator stresses, however, that the final outcomes will be of their own making.

Agreement on the agenda is normally followed by an antagonistic phase wherein family members communicate, often in rather extreme terms, their preferences and present positions. This is not a period during which solutions are considered but, rather, a phase in which symbolic issues and declarations are used to emphasize personally held positions. These can include open or veiled threats, or absolutistic statements about what one is willing to accept. The mediator's interventions are critically important in this phase. He or she must identify underlying overlapping interests and points of agreement. Otherwise family members may reach an impasse, refusing to move from an entrenched position.

For example, the mediator might acknowledge family members' mutual concern about constant arguing and fighting and ask them if they would like to know more about the potential future effects of their continuing conflict and possibly consider the types of arrangements that have created more cooperative circumstances for other families. In this manner, the emphasis is shifted from individual personalities and positions to the shared problem. Specific potential outcomes are raised and discussed. As family members are helped to further clarify their preferences and positions, they revise them and begin brainstorming various possibilities. Family members are urged to consider options in terms of what they would perceive to be realistically workable for them. *The mediator clarifies communication, identifies overlapping interests, and reinforces cooperative interactions.*

Frequently, the mediator may have to refocus a problem. Before actual agreement can be reached, family members, with the mediator's assistance, must establish a range of acceptable outcomes, further clarify the more difficult issues, and examine possible trade-offs. During the final bargaining, the mediator proposes suggestions that would lead to an integrated outcome. A positive momentum evolves as successful coordination and agreements accumulate, leading family members to see that a mutually acceptable resolution is possible. The final agreement is followed by closure to the mediation process.

Throughout this process the mediator's role is that of "an advocate of the process of discussion and bargaining rather than an advocate of a particular settlement" (Trombetta, 1982, p. 69). The mediation process seeks to facilitate the orientation of family members and their efforts toward one another in arriving at a mutual solution. It helps them "achieve a new and shared perception of their relationship, a perception that will redirect their attitudes and dispositions toward one another" (Fuller, 1971, p. 325).

Preparing to Mediate—Changing Hats

Mediation is not psychotherapy. It may, of course, be therapeutic in many ways, but it should have no pretense of providing therapy. The mediator must learn to "change hats" from his or her primary function (as psychologist, counselor, family therapist, police officer, etc.) to that of mediator. Unlike clinical counseling or psychotherapy, *mediation is a nonexploratory process.* The mediator's role is not to change a family relationship but, rather, to help members resolve the concrete issues that have brought them to mediation (Vroom, 1983).

The mediator should keep in mind that his or her goal is to help family members reach *their* goal. Irrational beliefs, minor pathology, or neurotic behavior may become obvious, but these must be left alone unless they are interfering in the mediation process. The subtle art of intervening in disruptive interchanges among family members as a mediator and not as, for example, a trained mental health professional often takes time to master. Without this competency, mediators can get lost in issues and never facilitate family members in achieving a solution.

Circumstances calling for therapeutic intervention are best approached through referral for concurrent treatment by a mental health professional. Thus, the mediator might share the following with the family members:

> "My role is that of a mediator and not a therapist. It is my responsibility, however, to provide you with objective feedback that might be helpful to you during this

mediation as well as in your future. For some reason, you all are having a great deal of difficulty objectively hearing what each other is saying. Emotions seem too often to be getting out of control. It might be best to seek the additional assistance of a mental health or family counselor."

Before seeking to mediate any family dispute, acquiring some formal training is advisable. The effective mediator must be competent in many skills. The mediator must be able to train and facilitate family members in negotiation—focusing, clarifying, bargaining, and compromising on important issues. Being able to create open, receptive communication channels is critical. Family members also must be aided in identifying general principles rather than simply specifying their demands.

Allowing family members to state fixed demands without understanding the general principles or underlying motives behind the demands results in "blind bargaining." In contrast, *principled negotiation* helps all sides see and understand others' positions and viewpoints and the real issues involved. These real issues are usually not what family members are actually disputing but, rather, an underlying principle of personal involvement on each participant's part—who is right, who is being treated unfairly, the desire to win, threats to personal status, prestige, or superiority (Huber, 1981). Increased give-and-take and real resolution can take place only if these principles are brought to awareness and considered. *Getting to Yes* (Fisher & Ury, 1982) is an excellent source explaining the key points of principled negotiation.

Family members are often heard to say, "Why do we need to mediate with you? It seems like a simple enough process." In a gentle way, family members should be told that if they had the skills to work out their differences on their own, they would not need formal mediation assistance. The mediator should stress to the family that mediation is not only an isolated problem-solving experience but also a training program in which skills are being learned for future use. In one research investigation of family mediation efforts, the conclusion noted as most critical was "participants' increased confidence about their ability to solve problems given a new orientation for resolving future concerns on their own" (Pearson & Thoennes, 1982).

An initial contact with a family is not the time to consider "changing hats." Advanced preparation in both attitude and skills application is necessary before taking on the role of a mediator. Readings, workshops, association with an experienced mentor, and participation in a peer supervision group are ideal ways of acquiring the knowledge base and mind set to facilitate the family mediation process.

The Mediation Process

The mediation process we follow in our work with families has 10 steps:

1. Referral.
2. Orientation and clarification.

3. Identification of principles and prioritization of demands.

4. Negotiations: Initial demands.

5. Negotiations: Early bargaining.

6. Negotiations: Investigating options.

7. Negotiations: Narrowing differences and trading.

8. Tentative agreement and revisions.

9. Memorandum of understanding.

10. Termination and follow-up.

Mediation is a fluid process, and the steps presented here can represent, but do not necessarily correspond to, specific sessions. Normally, more than one step of the process is accomplished at a session, depending upon the specific portion of the mediation involved. Also, the chronology of the process may be changed occasionally to meet the individual needs of certain families. Although a universal process of mediation can be described, the process should be applied idiosyncratically to individual families as it will be affected by the particular needs of a specific family (Haynes, 1982).

Referral

The typical mediation case is normally referred from the court, an involved community agency, or knowledgeable professional colleague. The initial contact with a family is usually by telephone. The mediator should be prepared to provide a brief overview of mediation without going into great depth—especially if only one family member is initiating the contact. If this occurs, the mediator should request to speak to all involved parties *before* the intake meeting. In this way, the idea of mutuality and balance is established at the very onset (Haynes, 1982). An initial screening should be conducted by telephone so that a more relevant referral, if indicated, can be made immediately. If mediation appears appropriate, the first appointment is set.

Orientation and Clarification

Orientation and clarification take place in the initial intake session. The mediator's responsibility in this session focuses on a number of tasks: establishing his or her credibility, setting a positive tone, explaining the process and the mediator's role, clarifying family members' expectations, establishing empathy, and determining participants' readiness for mediation efforts (Haynes, 1981).

Family mediation is still relatively new to referring professionals and the public alike. Therefore, the mediator must fully educate family members about the mediation process. After sharing the scope, function, goals, and other pertinent details of the mediation process before it formally begins, the mediator should request that family members sign an "Engagement Letter" outlining the parameters of the process, as well as arrangements relating to fees, co-mediators, and the like. Copies should be distributed to all concerned parties to further ensure everyone's understanding of the process.

After introducing the Engagement Letter, the mediator must help family members become aware of the family issues that have heretofore gone unaddressed. This ability to help the family "focus" is an important skill that enables family members to interpret their current conflict as a potential reflection or symptom of more serious dysfunction. Often, families come to mediation as a "premature referral." Too much dysfunction is present for mediation to effectively proceed. In cases like this, the mediator should recommend that the family seek therapeutic assistance either concurrently with, or prior to, beginning mediation efforts.

Engaging reluctant family members can create another issue that must be addressed in the intake session. The mediator must "sell" the positive and immediate, as well as the long-term problem-solving potential that mediation can have. Many persons entering mediation have a history of poor or ineffective experiences with professional "helpers." The family members have been termed resistant, blamed for lack of progress, or led to feel responsible and guilty for not achieving any concrete solutions to their problems. Providing a positive connotation through reframing the current conflict ("This crisis is a sure signal that your family wants positive change to take place") often helps to draw in all the family members.

> Marie and her mother were reluctant to participate in mediation—very angry and hostile toward each other—knowing that nothing up to this time had worked for them. Both expected further failure and felt helpless. Getting basic information and identifying each party's beliefs about what was happening was impossible because the other would openly disagree and begin yelling. The mediator met with each of them individually and suggested that the conflict and their responses to it were most helpful in calling attention to the problems at hand. The mediator also "joined" empathically with each of them, explaining that "it must be difficult to live with (Mom/Marie), and you have done an admirable job. . . ."
>
> This family had experienced extreme conflict, with Marie throwing scissors at her mother just prior to the session. Development of "ground rules" was imperative. Using the leverage of the Juvenile Justice System (and lock-up), a simple agreement for no violence, with built-in options such as punching the bed, was created. The mediator placed the demand for no violence, and the parties agreed. They were relieved of the sense of losing that they would have felt from giving in to one another. The mediator accomplished this by going from room to room, meeting with Marie and her mother, separately, shuttling information back and forth.

During the intake session the mediator also must elicit initial clarification of issues. The mediator should listen carefully to all the family members and actively question the relevant information presented. For example, in working with Marie and her mother, the mother had a series of complaints about Marie coming home late, swearing, staying on the telephone, and other "smaller" issues. If the mediator were to similarly focus on these smaller events, the major issues would be missed.

In this case, these issues related to the disregard of rules and basic challenges to the mother's power.

Successful orientation and clarification in the intake session will therefore establish:

- a win-win atmosphere with no "bad guy."

- an atmosphere of equality, but with a clear sense of the mediator's power to prevent imbalance in the participants' bargaining abilities.

- a sense that the mediator emphasized and believes that *each* family member has valid, legitimate demands.

- the belief that resolution is possible.

- a clearer understanding of the major issues involved.

- a summary of agreements or beliefs common to all parties.

Identification of Principles and Prioritization of Demands

During the intake session specific issues were identified. If these were to remain the focus of mediation, a stalemate would likely occur quickly. Basic principles underlying these issues must be brought to awareness if any movement is to occur when negotiations begin in the next step of the process. In addition, each family member must develop a sense of priorities. Frequently, family members employ a linear priority system in which every action carries the same weight.

> Marie's mother would seek to ground Marie or even call the police if Marie came in late, played her stereo too loud, or visited a friend whom her mother disapproved of. Whatever the offense, the mother's reaction was the same.

In identifying principles, the mediator seeks to facilitate family members' comprehension of their basic belief systems and the principles that guide them. Before beginning any in-depth discussion of demands, the mediator assists family members in formulating principled demands. Initial complaints are reconsidered with a goal of identifying general principles underlying them—the result being more relevant, pointed demands. Table 12.1 illustrates this process, as experienced in part by Marie and her mother.

When specific demands based on principles have been adequately identified, each party must rank them. This prioritization is done individually and in private, although the mediator's assistance is strongly urged. The list of initial demands can be substantial. It may present a picture so imposing to other family members (in the upcoming step of the process) that they immediately feel a sense of defeat. The mediator might help by discussing with each family member the issues being prioritized—before their presentation—making sure that only major issues are noted, with a focus on underlying general principles.

Family members who have a prioritized list of principled demands will be better able to negotiate. They can enter negotiations with a clearer sense of what is

Table 12.1 The Formulation of Principled Demands

	FROM COMPLAINTS	TO PRINCIPLES	TO DEMANDS
Mrs. S.:	I want Marie to stop disobeying me. She totally disregards every rule I establish. I want her to come in early, clean her room, do what I say …	What is most important is that Marie is safe. Also, it is important that she know that I am her parent. Her room is not really that significant to me.	Marie should call me if she will be late. I want her to acknowledge that I am her parent and she must listen to me.
Marie:	I hate my mother. All she wants to do is put restrictions on me and not allow me to grow up and have my own friends. I want to make my own rules.	I think I'm old enough to participate in making my own rules and should be allowed to pick my friends.	Mom should let me discuss rules instead of assuming that I have to agree with her because she is older and is my mother.

important to them, what they *must* have to be satisfied, and what they are willing to give up. This knowledge encourages active participation and increases the probability that individual family members will be satisfied with their final agreement.

Negotiations: Initial Demands

"Negotiations" as an overall descriptor constitutes the next four steps of the mediation process, beginning with negotiations regarding initial demands. The various components are difficult to separate in terms of actual time and number of sessions. These portions of the process may repeat themselves throughout the entire process until the Memorandum of Understanding is firmly agreed to.

Before beginning each session—during the negotiations' portions of the process especially—the mediator must summarize and recap for family members the events of the preceding session and highlight any agreements made. Following this opening ritual, movement directly into specific negotiations' concerns flows much easier.

> "During our previous session, Mrs. S., you said that you wanted . . . from Marie and, Marie, you said you believed that. . . ." (An agreement was reached during that session, so the mediator also highlights the points of agreement, providing a sense of positive movement and accomplishment.) "In addition, Marie acknowledged that she realizes you (Mrs. S.) do worry about her and agreed with you that she will make a telephone call when she is going to be late."

In considering initial demands, each family member is given a limited time to present his or her list of demands that have been compiled privately (usually with the mediator's assistance) in the previous step. Even though each party knows his or her own priority order, the demands should be presented with equal importance.

During this period, the mediator should request clarification of any demands that generate puzzled looks from fellow family members, prevent immediate discussion of any demand at this point in time, and block "put downs" by one party toward another's demands. For reference purposes, the mediator might list the demands, in simplified form as they are presented, on a blackboard or large newsprint so all can look at them simultaneously.

After the demands are presented and listed for all to see, the mediator should help family members take note of similar demands or common areas of concern. Different views about the same issue will present conflicts that must be addressed. By focusing on the principles of each family member underlying his or her demands, greater movement and flexibility can be attained. In the case of initial demands presented by Marie and her mother, the mediator rearranged the initial list of demands, placing similar issues across from each other to better focus on the degree of difference between Marie and her mother on the same issue. Relevant principles motivating Marie and her mother in their demands were also requested and noted at this time. This revised list is illustrated in Table 12.2.

In the case of parent-child conflicts, the process of identifying accompanying principles often has a remarkably positive effect on each party. Children, especially, gain from hearing the beliefs their parents hold about issues or demands that have been longstanding areas of conflict. Frequently, this simple sharing in itself can unlock a diehard dispute by "demystifying" the importance of calling home or getting good grades in school.

Once the initial list of demands is prepared, recorded, and rearranged by the mediator, if appropriate, family members are ready to bargain, based on the priorities that were individually established in the previous step of the mediation process.

Negotiations: Early Bargaining

Although family members are called upon to "bargain" daily, they surprisingly are often ill prepared to do so with each other. Children bargain with their friends over what games they will play and activities they will mutually participate in. Parents commonly bargain at the local fruit and vegetable stand or discuss what is a fair price for a used car in a give-and-take process similar to mediation. Yet, this procedure within the family is frequently "foreign."

At this point in the mediation, the mediator may have to demonstrate how to bargain. Especially in families with intense conflict or longstanding mistrust on the part of all parties, some "leading" must be done. Borrowing a technique from labor mediation, the mediator meets with each party separately. During these individually oriented sessions, the mediator plays each party off the other(s) by "speculating" about what the other side might accept, remembering, of course, to not influence family members toward a direction they may truly not want. The major function of this phase of the mediation process is to create enough movement and reference to specific principles that family members will develop their own suggestions as to how and what they will proceed to bargain.

Table 12.2 Initial Demands and Underlying Principles

MRS. S.	MARIE
■ Stay away from "undesirable" friend. (An adult friend might sway your opinion/challenge my authority; *I* want to be your friend.)	■ Visit friend Mom dislikes. (An adult friend can give me different ideas about areas I'm uncomfortable talking about with Mom.)
■ Call if you are going to be late. (I worry that something might have happened to you.)	
■ Follow *my* rules. (Mothers are supposed to be the ultimate authority; kids should listen.)	■ Participate in making rules. (I'm old enough to have a say in rules that apply to me.)
■ Keep your room clean. (Sloppy rooms are not good; you need to learn to be clean as a kid.)	
■ No telephone calls after 10 p.m. (Late calls wake up the rest of the family.)	■ Telephone use any time. (I like to talk to my friends about dates, etc. If I have to be in for curfew, at least I can use the phone.)
■ Go to school every day and get good grades. (Marie oversleeps; if she keeps going this way, she won't amount to anything.)	■ Stop being nagged about grades and school. (No matter what I do, it isn't good enough; I like school but hate to get up.)
■ Come in at stated times: 9 p.m. weekdays and 10 p.m. weekends. (I'm responsible for your safety; something might happen at night. I worry.)	■ Come in 10 p.m. weekdays and be allowed out later on weekends and special occasions. (When my brother was my age, he had later hours; my friends stay out until this time.)

Negotiations: Investigating Options

All through the mediation process, the mediator has actually been helping family members focus on potential options available to solve their concerns. Now that family members have identified the items of most importance and the personal principles behind them, made their initial demands, and begun to consider how they will bargain, they have effectively narrowed their own options. They are now locked into working around specific problems and finding solutions that have previously eluded them. At this point, potential options are investigated in a way that will enable family members to narrow their differences and trade, using the options available to them.

A common deficiency among families in conflict is their failure to investigate or create different options for resolving mutual problems. One means mediators have for preparing family members to expand their outlook is to instill the belief that what has not worked in the past will not work now. Parents, in particular, hold on to methods that are ineffective or inappropriate with their children. The mediator can demonstrate, through questioning, that their present mode of interacting is not working; otherwise they would not be here. Staying with that mode will only continue to undermine cooperative family relationships and lead to further disagreements on additional issues.

New options for resolving differences must be developed and explored. If family members describe themselves as being stuck or continue to consider only one or two ideas, the mediator must tactfully probe these blockages. Questions that focus back on the principle behind the demand often lead family members to their own discovery of new options; for example, "Are you telling me that this is the *only* way to solve this problem?" The mediator should encourage family members to create a long list of options, no matter how ridiculous. "Brainstorming"!—simply listing potential options to be evaluated later—can be valuable in leading to mutually acceptable ideas.

Many times family members stop themselves from creating options—not because they do not exist or cannot be identified but because members would rather not see these options exist. Confronting family members who withdraw into a "turtle-in-the-shell" style of problem solving will encourage them to consider new options even if they don't like them. For example, with reference to Table 13.2, Marie's mother originally acted as if the only option available to prevent late-night calls from Marie's friends from interrupting the family's sleep were to make a rule: "No phone use after 10 p.m." She was unwilling to come up with alternative solutions. The mediator confronted her inflexible stance. The list eventually developed (see Table 12.3) might contain a number of presently unacceptable alternatives, but it did encourage her toward more creative thinking.

This creativeness often is translated into a willingness to develop increased flexibility, and it frequently gives rise to humor stemming from the absurd possibilities available. Embroiled in conflict, many family members take everything, regardless of how insignificant or minor, with great seriousness. Being able to laugh at what they previously saw as serious can indicate real progress.

When an impasse exists regarding options, the mediator can utilize self-disclosure and appropriately mention similar situations that he or she has worked with in the past: "One family I mediated with had a similar stalemate and came up with. . . ." Showing how other families have resolved their disputes makes family members feel that they are not alone. Framed properly, suggestions of this nature can facilitate identification with the case example and learning by modeling. If the mediator cannot think of a relevant previous example to propose, a hypothetical one created to fit the situation is appropriate.

Homework assignments can be another helpful tool for investigating options. Assigning family members the task of writing at least five options each for solving a particular problem usually results in a list that did not exist before. If family members decide to work together to create options, this is most facilitative to the

Table 12.3 Some Brainstorming Options For Phone Use

PROBLEM	CURRENT OPTION	CREATIVE OPTIONS
Late telephone calls interrupt family's sleep.	No phone use after 10 p.m.	1. Make only outgoing calls. 2. Put phone in Marie's room. 3. Get bell silencer on phone. 4. Store phone in insulated bag. 5. Remove phone from home. 6. Put light instead of bell on phone. 7. Buy family members headsets to block sound.

mediation. Other family members have consulted friends or other relatives in search of options. These interchanges, too, facilitate cooperative problem-solving interactions. The mediator must emphasize that homework is *required*. By forcing family members to consider doing something they may find distasteful, they are not choosing to do it; the mediator is "directing" them to do it. Participants may use this as an excuse to give up some of their responsibility. But they can regain it when they complete their assignment.

Negotiations: Narrowing Differences and Trading

Family members usually want to achieve their objectives without giving up anything. The work of the previous steps of the process—setting priorities, early bargaining considerations, and investigating options—should have caused participants to begin to think that if any agreement is to be realized, they must give up some things or, at the very least, change their expectations. Now is the time to make these necessary concessions.

For example, parents often expect their children to change while they themselves refuse to give ground on issues. Gentle reminders such as, "You've been living in less than desirable conditions with your daughter, and I'm sure you're ready to try something new" can help create a more positive mind set. In more difficult cases, the mediator can meet individually with family members, encouraging movement by carrying options back and forth and suggesting a "deal" for them. Although this is a "gamey" technique, it is often quite successful.

> With Marie and her mother, neither would budge unless the major objectives of both were met. It was suggested alternatively to both mother and daughter that if they were to accept one of the other's first-priority items, the other would be willing to give in on a demand.

Most trading is done, and resultant trade-offs made and accepted, in "package" form. In focusing on singular areas of disagreement, settling a dispute is often much more difficult than considering total packages. The package that Marie and her mother arrived at is illustrated in Table 12.4.

Tentative Agreement and Revisions

Once family members agree to a tentative package, a rough draft of the areas of agreement can be set forth. Presenting the family members with a typewritten draft on which they can make corrections, and eventually sign, is preferable to simply summarizing the agreement by reading it to them. (Younger children, too, should be given a written copy even though they may need the mediator's assistance in reviewing it.)

Having tangible evidence of their efforts to review and critique provides participants with a sense of accomplishment and power. They are now taking responsibility for refining what their agreement will actually be like. Any concerns raised in this step of the process are dealt with by recycling to relevant previous procedures. Once this step is completed, the formal Memorandum of Understanding can be prepared.

Memorandum of Understanding

Preparing a written document of what the family members have already agreed to is relatively easy. The Memorandum of Understanding should be written in simple, clear language and at a level that all family members can readily understand. They will likely have to refer to the agreement in the future and ought to be able to understand it completely without assistance. Incorporating the language the family members themselves have used to characterize their problems and solutions is usually best. This is especially important for keeping children involved in understanding and maintaining the agreement (Wixted, 1982). Also, by keeping language plain and

Table 12.4 A Trading Package

MRS. S.'S PRIORITIES	MARIE'S PRIORITIES
1. Follow my rules.	1. Visit friend Mom dislikes.
2. Call if you'll be late.	2. Use telephone anytime.
3. Go to school every day.	3. Stop being nagged about school.
4. Don't be late; come in at stated times.	4. Revised curfew: Weekends.

CONCESSIONS BY MRS. S.	CONCESSIONS BY MARIE
— Stay away from friend.	— Participate in making rules.
— Keep room clean.	— 10 p.m. curfew weekdays.
— No telephone calls after 10 p.m.	
— 10 p.m. curfew on weekends.	

simple and items behaviorally oriented, family members have a yardstick by which to measure compliance and, ultimately, the success of their agreement.

Although the mediator and the family members know that the document is an *agreement,* the mediator is advised to use the term "Memorandum of Understanding." Family members tend to see the final agreement more significantly when it has this formalized title. In addition, if the mediation is part of a court-sanctioned program or agency, this is the preferred descriptor for the document presented to a judge for approval.

Figure 12.2 gives an example of a Memorandum of Understanding. Note that a remediation clause is added to the basic agreement. This simple clause can prevent future disputes from adding to an already clogged court calendar or overwhelmed social service agency client load. Reentry into mediation efforts forms a preventive first step.

Termination and Follow-up

Family members who have signed the Memorandum of Understanding have worked out with the mediator and each other a most significant agreement—to seek new paths of conflict resolution. As noted earlier, the most important part of this process might simply be learning and experiencing the process itself. Agreements are only as good as the family members' willingness to adhere to them. The mediator should monitor agreements for a time, by telephone, brief follow-up "progress" sessions, or mail, as a gentle reminder that the mediator (and system) is watching and really cares about the ultimate outcome of the mediation.

Ethics and Ethical Issues

Even though family mediation services are becoming increasingly available, certain basic questions remain (Vroom, 1983). How does a consumer find a qualified mediator? How do members of the mental health or legal profession refer a family to a mediator they know is competent? Currently, no licensing or certification requirements for family mediators are in force to provide any objective clues to a mediator's skill level.

Without any organized certifying procedure, both consumers and professionals making referrals would do well to consider a code of ethics to which a mediator might subscribe. Codification of principles of ethics is an important benchmark in the development of any professional field. It speaks to the willingness of professionals to take responsibility for protecting their clientele and, equally important, it defines the boundaries, standards, and legitimate purposes of any endeavors entered into (Margulies, 1982). We adhere to a code adapted from the Canons of Ethics developed by the New Jersey Council on Divorce Mediation (Margulies, 1982) and applied to our practice of family mediation. This code, with accompanying explanatory comments, is presented in the appendix.

This agreement by and between Mrs. S. and her daughter, Marie, was developed with full knowledge and participation by both of us on May 19, 1983. We have developed this agreement as outlined below to reduce conflict and continue to enjoy the good parts of our relationship. We agree to the following:

1. Marie will be allowed to choose and visit her own friends. Mrs. S's prior approval is required for overnight stays with friends.
2. Marie agrees to discourage her friends from calling her at home after 10 pm and before 7 am. She will be allowed to make outgoing calls during these times.
3. Marie agrees to call home if she will be late. If she does not call, her curfew will be shortened for the following night, at a ratio of two (2) minutes for every one (1) minute she was late.
4. Mrs. S. agrees not to be responsible for waking Marie up on school days and Marie will wake up on her own and attend school regularly.
5. The established curfew will be 9 pm weekdays and 11 pm weekends for Marie as long as she informs Mrs. S. of her destination.
6. A subsequent set of rules will be appended to this agreement.

In the event of any dispute arising out of this agreement, we agree that prior to directing the problem to the Court, we will first attempt to settle the dispute through the use of mediation services.

Signed this 19 Day of May, 1983.

_____

_____   _____
                                             Aviva Sanders-Mascari, Mediator

cc: Juvenile Court Clerk
       Mrs. S.
       Marie
       File

Figure 12.2 Memorandum of Understanding

The ethical principles identified here are only a beginning. As the field of family mediation continues to grow as a professional practice, these basic principles will have to be expanded, and additional principles will have to be developed.

Future Implications

Forecasting the future course of family mediation suggests some obvious trends already under way and some others representing our "crystal ball gazing." As family mediation becomes increasingly recognized as an effective alternative for resolving family conflicts, referrals will increase. This will undoubtedly swell the ranks of mediators in independent practice, as well as increase the number of agencies that include family mediation as a core service. Many professionals are already beginning to identify family mediation as their area of speciality.

Professional schools have begun to offer courses, as well as degree programs, in family mediation. For example, Vroom (1983) has reported that courses in family mediation are being offered at the University of Illinois and the University of Iowa; a curriculum in family mediation has been developed in the Department of Human Development at the University of Maryland's College of Education; and a 2-year graduate certification in family mediation is being contemplated at Catholic University in Washington, DC.

Although family mediation will likely not be a cure-all for society's ills, it has the potential to drastically influence the way Americans interact. The influence of mediation on the American family, if popularly embraced, will undoubtedly serve to further democratize and encourage egalitarian family relationships and, with that, the skills and understandings to create a more egalitarian society. Small, formerly powerless groups and persons will be able to truly be heard, and thus, realistically negotiate with powerful groups, individuals, and institutions.

More research will be done to answer the questions that are now beginning to be asked. What is required to be an effective family mediator? Who is best suited to mediate family disputes? What form of training and how much is necessary to produce effective family mediators? Ethical questions that are now in the gray areas will become clearer and resolved.

What was once said about banks could one day be said about family mediators—that "there is one on every street corner." Only time will tell. One thing is clearly affirmable: Family mediation is not another fad; it is an idea whose time has come. And American families are benefiting from it.

A Caveat: Divorce Mediation

One of the major areas of practice currently within the family mediation movement is divorce mediation. All the components identified and discussed in this article are similar in divorce mediation, with one notable addition necessary. Mediators facilitating divorce mediations must have specific technical and legal knowledge and resources at their command to a degree not needed for most family mediation efforts. Consultation with attorneys, accountants, and similar professionals relevant to a divorce settlement are an integral part of the former. The interface of law and mediation, especially, must be clearly understood. State domestic relations laws must be fully comprehended, because agreements reached by a divorcing couple through mediation eventually will be translated into a formal legal document drawn up by a relevant professional.

Readers who are interested in investigating divorce mediation are referred to *Structured Mediation in Divorce Settlements* (Coogler, 1978) and *Divorce Mediation: A Practical Guide for Therapists and Counselors* (Haynes, 1981), two seminal works on the intricacies of this particular process.

References

Coogler, O. J. (1978). *Structured mediation in divorce settlements.* Lexington, MA: Lexington Books.

Coogler, O. J., Weber, R. E., & McKenny, F. C. (1979). Divorce mediation: A means of facilitating divorce and adjustment. *Family Coordinator, 28,* 255–259.

Fisher, R., & Ury, W. (1982). *Getting to yes.* Boston: Houghton-Mifflin.

Fuller, L. (1971). Mediation: Its forms and functions. *Southern California Law Review, 44,* 305–339.

Girdner, L. K. (1983, March). *Adjudication and mediation: A comparison of custody decision-making processes involving third parties.* Paper presented at the National Conference on Peacemaking and Conflict Resolution, Athens, GA.

Gulliver, P. H. (1979). *Disputes and negotiations: A cross-cultural perspective.* New York: Academic Press.

Haynes, J. (1981). *Divorce mediation: A practical guide for therapists and counselors.* New York: Springer.

Haynes, J. (1982). A conceptual model of the process of family mediation: Implications for training. *American Journal of Family Therapy, 10,* 5–16.

Huber, C. H. (1981). An Adlerian approach to marital counseling. *Counseling & Human Development, 14,* 1–16.

Margulies, S. L. (1982). *Ethical principles of divorce mediation.* Montclair, NJ: New Jersey Council on Divorce Mediation.

Pearson, J., & Thoennes, N. (1982). Divorce mediation: Strengths and weaknesses over time. In H. Davidson, L. Ray, & R. Horowitz (Eds.), *Alternative means of family dispute resolution.* Washington, DC: American Bar Association.

Trombetta, D. (1982). Custody evaluation and custody mediation: A comparison of two dispute interventions. *Journal of Divorce, 6,* 65–75.

Vroom, P. (1983). The anomalous profession: Some bumpy going for the divorce mediation movement. *Family Therapy Networker, 7,* 38–42.

Vroom, P., Fassett, D., & Wakefield, R. A. (1982). Winning through mediation: Divorce without losers. *Futurist, 16,* 28–34.

Wall, J. (1981). Mediation: An analysis, review and proposed research. *Journal of Conflict Resolution, 25,* 157–180.

Wixted, S. (1982). The children's hearings project: A mediation program for children and families. In H. Davidson, L. Ray, & R. Horowitz (Eds.), *Alternative means of family dispute resolution.* Washington, DC: American Bar Association.

Appendix

Ethical Principles of Family Mediation

I. Within the mediation process, the mediator shall remain impartial at all times and not represent any one party.

This Principle is the basis for the impartiality a mediator must bring to the process, as well as the basis for the integrity of mediation as mediation, not legal representation, not therapy, not arbitration, not anything else.

Mediators may, and at times should, share generic information based upon objective facts of which they are aware. Mediators may share this information with clients in order to inform clients about the consequences of proposals as an aid to informed decision making. The essence of this Principle is to protect and emphasize the mediator's stance as an impartial facilitator with a role to play that is discrete from those taken by professionals engaged in traditional modes of dispute resolution.

II. The mediator shall not mediate in instances where he or she has previously treated, counseled, or represented one or more of the clients.

This Principle is an outgrowth of the strict necessity of impartiality on the part of mediators, and their avoidance of conflict or the appearance of conflict. By elevating this requirement to the status of an Ethical Principle, the absolute independence and impartiality of mediators, both in substance and in appearance, are promoted.

III. The mediator shall use an Engagement Letter in connection with each mediation.

Mediation is a process still new enough to professionals and the public at large that mediators have an educative responsibility to state clearly and in plain language the scope, function and goals, and other pertinent details of the mediation process before it begins, and in writing. Clients shall sign, and each keep a copy of, the Engagement Letter so that there will be no question regarding each person's understanding of the process. In the letter, any fee arrangements shall be clearly stated, including fee arrangements respecting co-mediators.

IV. The mediator shall encourage the parties to consult with outside experts whenever appropriate during the mediation process.

The mediator shall be alert to the necessity for accurate answers to any questions that arise during the mediation process by encouraging clients to seek the service of relevant professionals who can provide information germane to informed decision making. The mediator shall stay apprised of available professionals by maintaining an ongoing list of competent persons in appropriate disciplines.

V. Subject to the requirements of law, the mediator shall retain confidentiality of the clients.

Any testimonial privilege attached to mediation, whether under the statutes, rules of evidence, or judicial opinion, is unknown. Notwithstanding, the mediator has an ethical obligation to preserve client confidentiality at all times within his or her control.

As a corollary, the mediator shall undertake to maintain confidentiality in the storage and disposal of records accumulated in the course of mediation. Further, to the extent that the mediator intends to refer to particular cases in published material or lectures, he or she shall expressly refrain from revealing any information that will identify individual clients, and shall obtain any appropriate releases.

VI. The mediator shall maintain knowledge of current professional information related to the services he or she provides.

The mediator has a serious responsibility, expressly recognized by this Principle, to engage in continuing education relevant to legal and societal changes and developments affecting the mediation process. The mediator shall participate in appropriate ongoing professional education such as seminars, workshops, and peer supervision (where possible), and shall keep current his or her professional affiliations and adhere generally to a high standard of competence.

Adapted from "Ethical Principles of divorce Mediation" by S. L. Margulies (Montclair, NJ: New Jersey Council on Divorce Mediation, 1982).

Remarriage Families: Counseling Parents and Their Children

Richard L. Hayes and Bree A. Hayes

B y the year 1990 one of every three children under the age of 18 in the United States is projected to spend a portion of his or her life living with a single parent (Glick, 1979). Given that 80% of divorced persons remarry within 4 to 5 years, and that 60% of them have children, single-parent and remarriage families will comprise nearly 45% of all families (Visher & Visher, 1982). As a consequence of these changes, more people are expected to be living in a second marriage than in a first marriage by the end of this century (Duberman, 1975). Recognizing that these figures represent large amounts of loss and pain—much of which will go unresolved—one can easily understand why 40% of second marriages end in divorce in the first four years, with the likelihood of another divorce increasing when children from a previous marriage are present (Becker, Landes, & Michael, 1977).

This statistical picture suggests that most of us will have close contact with persons who have divorced (at least once) *and* remarried. Moreover, these persons are likely to be living with children other than their own, or with a person some of whose children will be living with someone else. Yet, despite the prevalence of this family structure, the portrait of the American family continues to present Mom, Dad, and *their* children as living together in marital bliss. One might say that the nuclear family remains the standard but not the norm.

What will be required during the remainder of this century is to develop new traditions that set more realistic standards for families to follow. Counselors can play an important role in the development of these new traditions. This article presents an overview of the unique challenges that face remarriage families, and suggestions as to how counselors can help these parents and their children deal more realistically with the challenges facing them.

What Do We Mean by Remarriage Families?

Despite calls from some researchers for counselors to broaden their views of accept-able family structures (Ahrons, 1981), the rapid increase in families resulting from the merger of two preexisting families has left the profession without a common vocabulary to describe the phenomenon. Traditionally, these families had been called *stepfamilies,* but many writers have abandoned the term in reaction to its long historical use as what Bernard (1956) has called a "smear word." *Blended, recoupled, reconstituted, merged, reorganized,* and *restructured* have emerged as more sympathetic and descriptive titles.

Although the term *restructured* captures an essential element of these families, it describes single-parent, foster-parent, and adoptive-parent families as well. For purposes of this article, we have used the term *remarriage family* to refer to families that are formed as the result of a marriage between two partners, at least one of whom has been previously married. This type of family is considered a specific type of restructured family. Even though remarriage families may and do arise without children, the concern here will be with remarriage families that include at least one child from the outset.

A Present Born of the Past

To point out that one must first have been married before one can be remarried may seem so obvious as to be unworthy of mention. Nonetheless, critical to understanding the remarriage family is to recognize its origins in the losses of prior marital relationships. Unresolved losses play significant roles in the lives of remarriage family members and can profoundly limit subsequent developmental progress (Hayes, 1984). Members of remarriage families must each resolve the losses associated with dissolution of previous family structures as a prelude to creating a successful remarriage family.

Parents must resolve the losses associated not only with the old marriage, but also with their *expectations* for marriage, and then with the passing of their single-parent status. As Garfield (1980) has pointed out, those who divorce must attend to a number of developmental tasks in dealing with resolution of loss. These include self-acceptance, acceptance of new roles and responsibilities, renegotiating roles and relationships with family and friends, and transforming the relationship with the former spouse.

Unlike death or abandonment, only the relationship—not the person—is lost through divorce. Often, former spouses continue to influence the lives of those who remarry, especially when children are involved. Spouses who have resolved former marital losses appear better prepared for remarriage than those who have not (Messinger, Walker, & Freeman, 1978).

Counselors working with remarriage families must evaluate the extent to which unresolved mourning is exerting an influence on the current situation. Clients then must be encouraged to work through, rather than around, previous losses and to accept the reality of former losses. Bowlby (1980) noted that widowed spouses were healthier if they continued to speak with their spouses in fantasy rather than to let go of the relationship. This method for resolving mourning suggests that remarriage clients may do better to transform existing relationships to more productive ones rather than to deny the loss, especially when those former spouses are living and in frequent contact with the client. Because clients may be reluctant to raise these issues in front of the current spouse, counselors should be sensitive to and aware of the need to schedule some sessions with spouses individually.

As complicated as divorce and remarriage appear to an adult, to the child these changes present "a cognitive puzzle [that brings] dissonance and inconsistency to the child's social and affective world. To deal with loss and to rearrange the disrupted perceptions demand time and energy that must be withdrawn from the work of the schoolroom and from social interaction with peers" (Hess & Camara, 1979, p. 82). The cycle of attachments and losses that attends the history of a remarriage family disrupts the child's normal developmental progress. Familiar schemes of family and the social order must be reconstructed as the child attempts to form workable solutions to the problem of forming attachments to many different people.

In working with families, Huntington (1982, pp. 27–28) encouraged counselors to consider a number of transactional factors associated with attachment, divorce, and remarriage:

1. For the child:
   - the child's cognitive and emotional assimilation and understanding of the divorce and the subsequent remarriage.
   - personality traits, flexibility, temperament, tolerance for stress, handling of affect, adaptive behaviors, and areas of competence.
   - developmental level and prior developmental tasks accomplished.
   - the sex of the child and siblings.

2. For the parent:
   - each parent's emotional health or relative narcissistic injury.
   - the effects of being a single parent: in terms of the economy, on discipline and order, emotionally, and practically, in terms of child-care arrangements and the like.
   - the remaining bonds with the ex-spouse; the desire to continue the battle or to resolve it.
   - remarriage and the quality of that new relationship; the dynamics are very different for the cases in which both parents remain single, either custodial parent remarries, or both remarry.

3. For the parent-child relationship:
   - quality of total family interrelationships, prior to and after divorce, parental needs for the child for emotional support.
   - loyalty conflicts.
   - custody and visitation battles and agreements.
   - the effects of parental absence directly on the child and indirectly via the impact on the remaining parent.

4. For the context:
   - the life event changes that coincide with divorce.
   - outside supports and support networks—social groups, extended family, and so on.
   - economic realities.
   - prior and current levels of discord—conflict prior to and after divorce, the changes over time; divorce does not set people in concrete—the outcome is not predetermined.

Myths and Expectations

Myths serve as powerful half-truths that crystallize our thinking and actions around important social issues, the most important of which may be the family (see Capaldi & McRae, 1979; Coleman & Ganong, 1985; Einstein, 1982; Lewis, 1980; Schulman, 1972; Visher & Visher, 1979). Early in their lives children are introduced to the folklore about stepfamilies as hostile environments. Taking heed of the warning to avoid these entanglements, children are sent happily to bed, secure in the knowledge that they are safe in the care of their natural and biological parents. As Mead (cited in Thies, 1977) noted, "Each American child learns, early and in terror, that his whole security depends on that single set of parents" (p. 60).

This notion—that to love anyone else as your mother or father means that you are being disloyal to them—has been called the *loyalty myth* (Lewis, 1980). Not infrequently, children in remarriage families believe, and often rightfully, that their biological parent will be angry or hurt if the children express any affection toward the stepparent. The frightening experiences of Snow White, Cinderella, and Hansel and Gretel serve as cogent remainders of the importance attached to keeping the family intact and avoiding contact with persons who would presume to take the place of one's parents.

The term *step* actually comes from the Anglo-Saxon *astepan,* "to deprive," from which came *stepchild,* "a bereaved child or orphan" (Simon, 1964, p. 19). Despite their prevalence, remarriage families continue to be the object of popular derision, viewed as led by parents who have deprived their children of a *normal* family life and who are somehow *out of step* with the natural order of things.

The myth of the *wicked stepparent* is balanced by the myth of *instant love*. Because two adults love one another and choose to become marriage partners is no guarantee they will love each other's children or that the children will love them in return. Yet this expectation, perhaps more than any other, is the source of a substantial amount of the stress generated in remarriage families. More to the point is the realization that love takes time to grow and must be nurtured. Parents and children do have a right to expect that they will be treated with respect; they must not expect, however, that this will be easy or instantaneous.

The modem antidote to the fairy tale presentation is the equally engaging myth that remarriage families are really no different than nuclear families. Television's "Brady Bunch" blissfully combined a father and his three sons with a mother and her three daughters with the housekeeper Alice. Together they encountered the problems common to original families but met few of the problems encountered by remarriage families.

The major difference between original and remarriage families is in the structure of their relationships (Capaldi & McRae, 1979; Jones, 1978; Kompara, 1980; Nelson & Nelson, 1982). Consider that two people can have one relationship with each other. Add another person, and three people now have a system characterized by three relationships (see Figure 13.1). It is little wonder that a new baby in the home creates stress in a previously stabilized relationship. Add another child, and the number of relationships doubles to six—confirming many parents' observation that two children are far more work than they had originally anticipated. Using the formula $[n^2-n]/2 = R$ (where n equals the number of people and R equals the number of relationships between them), the Brady Bunch, with its 9 members (including Alice), has 36 relationships ($[81–9]/2$) with which to contend.

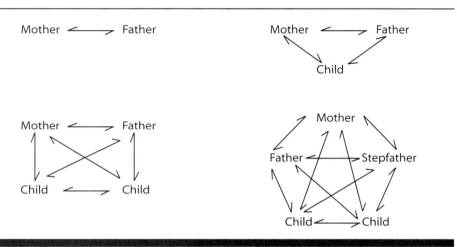

Figure 13.1 Relationships Between Family Members In Selected Family Structures

Beyond the obvious note that members of remarriage families are not necessarily related biologically, stress is created by the division of loyalties between separate but related nuclear families (Ahrons & Perlmutter, 1982). The presence of other parents and grandparents, as well as stepgrandparents, and unresolved feelings from the past, continue to remind family members of their previous family history. Add these members to the 9 above and the number swells to 19, if all parents and grandparents are living, neither absent spouse remarries or has other children, and Alice's parents stay out of the family. (Actually we never hear about these people on "The Brady Bunch.") The number of relationships that this not-so-unusual remarriage family must form is an overwhelming 171!

Remarriage families, at least at first, have a family but no history. More than any single thing remarriage families need, but don't yet have, is time together. Clearly love is not something that stepparents ought to expect instantly.

A final myth that characterizes the expectations of remarriage families is the *take away myth* (Lewis, 1980), so-called because those who accept it believe that the stepparent will take away the love of the child or the parent. So, too, the custodial parent may see the continued involvement of absent parents with their children as undermining the stepparent's relationship with the children. Of course, love is not a fixed pie to he divided among those who want a share, but the significance of a myth is its power to shape the believer's reality.

Concerns of Remarriage Families

In our experience in working with remarriage families, not the least important of which has been our own, we have found a set of concerns that arise recurrently in our discussions. These concerns, which have been described in varying detail by other authors (Brady & Ambler, 1982; Crohn, Sager, Brown, Rodstein, & Walker, 1982; Skeen, Covi, & Robinson, 1985; Visher & Visher, 1978), can be grouped under four general categories: roles and relationships, feelings and fantasies, rules and regulations, and external forces.

Roles and Relationships

The instability of remarriage families is exacerbated by the lack of positive, institutionalized roles for each of the members to play. Because more than one half of remarriage families formed after divorce include stepfathers (Rallings, 1976), the task of dealing with the spouse's children more often falls to men than to women. Socialized to be in charge, men find themselves in the awkward position of enforcing discipline when they have no apparent authority. In remarriage families wherein stepfathers set consistent limits, however, and when the mother welcomed his support, the stepchildren (especially boys) generally functioned better than did children in single-parent families or conflicted, non-divorced families (Hetherington, Cox, &

Cox, 1982). Stem (cited in Skeen, Covi, & Robinson, 1985) suggested that "stepfathers are more likely to be successful disciplinarians when taking a slow, gentle, flexible approach and develop a friendship to foster the child's participation, instead of trying to control the child through authoritarian means" (p. 122).

Women, on the other hand, have been socialized toward fulfilling the needs of others as their primary obligation in life. Placed in the role of stepmother, the woman often tries to take on the burdens of the entire family and finds herself rearing his children. Duberman (1975) reported that women were far less likely than men to achieve a good relationship with their stepchildren. Although reports are mixed on whether older or younger women have less difficulty as stepmothers, there is agreement that younger children have better relationships with their stepmothers than do adolescents (Draughton, 1975; Duberman, 1973; Wallerstein & Kelly, 1980). In general, the younger the child is at the time of divorce, the more likely the child is to accept the stepparent (Hetherington et al., 1982; Santrock, 1972; Wallerstein & Kelly, 1980).

A final difficulty that stepparents encounter is their ambiguous legal status. Although stepparents are considered in loco parentis—and thereby have all the rights, duties, and obligations of the biological parents—their assumption of the role is voluntary and may be terminated at will (Wald, 1981). As well, the rights of the stepparent toward the stepchild, regardless of whether that parent provides support for the child, are unclear and vary from one court ruling to another (Kargman, 1983).

Sibling rivalries are typical in any family. In families with a common history, territorial battles often are resolved on the basis of privilege of age. In remarriage families, however, each dispute provides an occasion for rekindling old memories.

After an extensive review of the literature, Skeen, Covi, and Robinson (1985) concluded that "stepsibling relationships are crucial to the success of stepfamilies . . . [and although] in most cases the presence of stepsiblings makes the marriage much more complex . . . the better the relationships between stepsiblings, the better the total family integration" (p. 122). In addition, when couples choose to have children of their own following the remarriage, relationships among all the children are more likely to be harmonious, although some children from former marriages may feel left out of the new relationship (Brooks, cited in Skeen, Covi, & Robinson, 1985, p. 122). As remarriage families grow in their relationships with one another, the children report feelings of divided loyalties—uncomfortable feelings that often are vented as anger directed at the stepparent (Einstein, 1982)—as each move toward the "new" family threatens to separate them from the "old."

Perlmutter, Engel, and Sage (1982) have suggested that sexual boundaries loosen in remarriage families. Without the usual time to develop deeper parent-child relationships, and devoid of the customary biological and legal prescriptions against sexual contact, stepfamilies become stimulating places sexually, especially for adolescents (Visher & Visher, 1979). "In biological families, children often consider their parents as nonsexual beings" (Visher & Visher, 1982, p. 117), while in remarriage families sexual desires can be heightened, increasing anxiety and disrupting already fragile relationships. Anger may mask attempts to cope with the situation, further compounding the difficulties in developing meaningful relationships. Although sexual abuse by males accounts for more than 80% of reported cases (Berliner cited in Skeen, Covi, & Robinson, 1985), no clear data support the notion that stepfathers are any more or less involved in incestuous relationships with their stepdaughters than are biological parents (Meiselman, 1978).

Feelings and Fantasies

As noted earlier, myths play an important role in the lives of remarriage families, especially to the extent to which those families are dysfunctional. Because the remarriage family begins with children and without a history, these myths provide an instant history that projects at least a sort of reality to which the members can react. The inevitable disappointments that result are a direct consequence of the experience of the remarriage family to live up (or down) to the various members' expectations. For example, the wicked stepmother turns out to be less wicked and more likeable (if not loveable) than expected by the children, while the stepmother comes to grips with the reality that she is less perfect and her stepchildren less adoring than she had thought they might be.

The consequence of members' failed expectations are feelings of disappointment. Some turn this feeling outward in anger or resentment directed at any convenient target. Disappointment turned inward becomes guilt. Although these expectations remain unidentified, they continue to go unmet and set up a recurring cycle of guilt and resentment (Einstein, 1982).

Rules and Regulations

Stepparents appear to take one of three approaches to the discipline issue (Capaldi & McRae, 1979; Skeen, Covi, & Robinson, 1985). Some remain inattentive and disengaged from the relationship, giving the natural parent little support or encouragement. Others become very actively involved, tending to be overly restrictive—especially stepfathers with stepsons. And some remain tentative, as if "walking on eggshells," paralyzed by the anticipation of feeling guilty if they do or don't do this or that just right.

Of course, none of these strategies is particularly successful because each acts to inhibit the development of an open and trusting relationship between the stepparent and the stepchild. Instead, the struggle degenerates into a series of contests in which neither participant emerges with the respect each attempts to get from the other. Remarriage couples do not have the luxury of time to develop shared ideas on discipline as they did in their original families before the children were born. Because these couples must develop a relationship with each other and with their children at the same time, Capaldi and McRae (1979) advocate a cooperative approach to discipline that acknowledges the rights of all parties.

External Forces

Because parents divorce each other and not their children (Duncan & Duncan, 1979), the degree to which the absent parent accepts the fact of the remarriage family has a significant impact on its chances for success. Research indicates that the greater is the amount of contact between the absent parent and the child, the less is the disruption in the parent-child relationship, and thus less stress in the remarriage family (Greif, 1982). The more limited is the contact between absent parents and their children, the more precious does that time become, such that both parties are reluctant to say goodbye as they court one another to extend the visit.

Despite the "common assumption that diminishing a child's relationship with a biological parent promotes the development of a relationship with the same-sexed parent, . . . children often feel as though an unequal distribution of their time with each parent is reflective of their having been made to choose the stepparent over the absent biological parent" (Greif, 1982, p. 53). Instead, Greif suggested that shared parenting after divorce may protect the remarriage family system by decreasing the experience of loss, blunting the potential for conflicting loyalties, and mitigating competition between adults.

Beyond the instability introduced by the relative involvement of the absent parent in the affairs of the remarriage family, persons whom Bohannan (1970) called *quasi-kin* are present. These relatives of relatives, so to speak, create an extended network of additional expectations that complicate an already ambiguous social structure. As Clingempeel (cited in Skeen, Covi, & Robinson, 1985) reported, people from remarriage families in which only the wife had children from a previous marriage showed higher marital quality than did people from more complex families. Further, people who maintained only moderate, as opposed to high or low, contact with quasi-kin showed better marital quality.

Given that the predominant proportion of children affected by divorce and remarriage is of school age, the school, its policies, and the people who work there have a substantial effect on the success of remarriage families. Visher and Visher (1979) believe that effect is largely negative, serving to reinforce stereotypes and exacerbate conflicts in the family. In particular, the school's role in observing customs such as Mother's Day or Father's Day, holding father-son banquets, limiting seating at school functions or graduations to selected family members, and sending notices and report cards to only one set of parents all serve to increase stress and miscommunication between parents.

Developmental Tasks of Remarriage Families

More than anything, remarriage families appear to be characterized by a greater reliance on fantasy and hopes in their interactions (Schulman, 1972), greater expectations for themselves and acknowledgment by their stepchildren (Visher & Visher, 1979), and the lack of a commonly shared history (Goldner, 1982) than is the case with natural parents in original families. Because remarriage families start with children and yet have had no time to build a history, the family must deal with the tasks required of more mature families while possessing the skills of a family just starting out. Because they lack a common set of experiences, remarriage families hold limited or unrealistic expectations that paralyze them into inaction or galvanize them into a reaction against people or events they little understand.

Developmental tasks that are important for remarriage families to accomplish include clarifying roles and developing realistic expectations, setting reasonable limits and establishing a pattern of appropriate discipline, and liberalizing the boundaries between families by acknowledging the nature of shifting alliances. Most importantly, the family must begin to shape its own traditions and to acknowledge the development of its own history. Turnbull and Turnbull (1983) have suggested 10 guidelines that parents in remarriage families might follow in resolving some of their inevitable conflicts:

1. Provide neutral territory.
2. Don't try to fit a preconceived role.
3. Set limits and enforce them.
4. Allow an outlet for feelings by the children for natural parents.
5. Expect ambivalence.
6. Avoid mealtime misery.
7. Don't expect love.
8. Don't take all the responsibility. The child has some, too.
9. Be patient.
10. Maintain the primacy of the marital relationship.

What Can Counselors Do?

Counselors working with remarriage families can help by:

— encouraging family members to relinquish myths they may hold about the remarriage family.

— helping members to understand the entire family system, its differences from their past families, and the involvement of non-family members in the system.

— teaching members more effective communication skills.

— helping members, especially children, to mourn the loss of previous relationships and encouraging the development of new relationships.

— providing a forum in which members can work out their relationships with one another and with quasi-kin, especially the absent parent.

— offering structured programs of parent training and lists of readings that family members can use as self-instructional devices.

— informing members of the latest research findings and clinical evidence that may be helpful to them in the reorganization process.

— identifying the tasks of parenting and the relationships that are necessary to enact those roles.

— running groups for remarriage parents in the community or for stepchildren in the schools.

In closing this section, these questions by Kirby (1979) are offered for remarriage families:

■ What evidence is present to indicate that each family member will feel secure in the merged family?

■ What are illustrations of how the merged family will gain strength from the usual cultural conditions imposed?

■ Under what conditions have the merged family members demonstrated open family discussions?

■ When have we as parents cooperatively reinforced predictable consequences in the children?

■ What are our attitudes toward seeking professional help in working with the children?

■ What are the role expectations of the various merged family members?

The Future for Remarriage Families

Remarriage is coming to be recognized as a normal developmental phase in an increasingly complex family life cycle (Goldner, 1982). As such, remarriage families represent a normal adaptation to changing social conditions. Recognizing that more complex internal organizations are better able to withstand the threats posed to them by outside forces, remarriage families may provide just the family structure necessary to prepare members for survival in the multicultural, interdependent, global society of the future. Indeed, its differences from the nuclear family of recent American tradition may be the very strength of the remarriage family.

Certainly members of remarriage families have made notable contributions to our history. Unlike the remarriage families of fable, those of George Washington, Abraham Lincoln, Nancy Reagan, and Jacqueline Onassis are all reported to have been nurturing environments that encouraged greatness in their members. In a nation where some fear that the family may be failing, it just may be that the society around it fails to appreciate the vitality of the family's evolution in this period of transition.

References

Ahrons, C. R. (1981). The continuing co-parental relationship between divorced spouses. *American Journal of Orthopsychiatry, 51,* 415–428.

Ahrons, C. R., & Perlmutter, M. S. (1982). The relationship between former spouses: A fundamental subsystem in the remarriage family. In L. Messinger (Ed.), *Therapy with remarriage families* (pp. 31–47). Rockville, MD: Aspen Systems Corp.

Becker, G. S., Landes, E. M., & Michael, R. T. (1977). An economic analysis of marital instability. *Journal of Political Economy, 85,* 1141–1187.

Bernard, J. (1956). *Remarriage: A study of marriage.* New York: Dryden.

Bohannan, P (Ed.) (1970). *Divorce and after.* New York: Doubleday.

Bowlby, J. (1980). *Attachment and loss* (Vol. 3). New York: Basic Books.

Brady, C. A., & Ambler, J. (1982). Use of group educational techniques with remarried couples. In L. Messinger (Ed.), *Therapy with remarriage families* (pp. 145–157). Rockville, MD: Aspen Systems Corp.

Capaldi, F., & McRae, B. (1979). *Stepfamilies: A cooperative responsibility.* New York: New Viewpoints/Vision Books.

Coleman, M., & Ganong, L. (1985). Remarriage myths: Implications for the helping professions. *Journal of Counseling & Development, 64,* 116–120.

Crohn, H., Sager, C., Brown, H., Rodstein, E., & Walker, L. (1982). A basis for understanding and treating the remarried family. In L. Messinger (Ed.), *Therapy with remarriage families* (pp. 159–186). Rockville, MD: Aspen Systems Corp.

Draughton, M. (1975). Step-mother's model of identification in relation to mourning in the child. *Psychological Reports, 36,* 183–189.

Duberman, L. (1973). Step-kin relationships. *Journal of Marriage & The Family, 35,* 283–292.

Duberman, L. (1975). *The reconstituted family: A study of remarried couples and their children.* Chicago: Nelson-Hall.

Duncan, T. R., & Duncan, D. (1979). *You're divorced, but your children aren't.* Englewood Cliffs, NJ: Prentice-Hall.

Einstein, E. (1982). *The stepfamily.* New York: Macmillan.

Garfield, R. (1980). The decision to remarry. *Journal of Divorce, 4,* 1–10.

Glick, P. C. (1979). Children of divorced parents in demographic perspective. *Journal of Social Issues, 35,* 170–182.

Goldner, V. (1982). Remarriage family: Structure, system, future. In L. Messinger (Ed.), *Therapy with remarriage families* (pp. 187–206). Rockville, MD: Aspen Systems Corp.

Greif, J. B. (1982). The father-child relationship subsequent to divorce. In L. Messinger (Ed.), *Therapy with remarriage families* (pp. 47–57). Rockville, MD: Aspen Systems Corp.

Hayes, R. (1984, November). Coping with loss: A developmental approach to helping children and youth. *Counseling & Human Development, 17*(3), 1–12.

Hess, R., & Camara, K. A. (1980). Post-divorce relationships as mediating factors in the consequences of divorce for children. *Journal of Social Issues, 35*(4), 79–96.

Hetherington, E. M., Cox, M., & Cox, R. (1982). Effects of divorce on parents and children. In M. E. Lamb (Ed.), *Nontraditional families* (pp. 233–288). Hillside, NJ: Erlbaum.

Huntington, D. S. (1982). Attachment loss and divorce: A reconsideration of the concepts. In L. Messinger (Ed.), *Therapy with remarriage families* (pp. 17–29). Rockville, MD: Aspen Systems Corp.

Jones, S. M. (1978). Divorce and remarriage: A new beginning; a new set of problems. *Journal of Divorce, 2,* 217–227.

Kargman, M. W. (1983). Stepchild support obligations of stepparents. *Family Relations, 32,* 321–328.

Kirby, J. (1979). *Second family.* Muncie, IN: Accelerated Development.

Kompara, D. R. (1980). Difficulties in the socialization process of stepparenting. *Family Relations, 29,* 69–73.

Lewis, H. C. (1980). *All about families: The second time around.* Atlanta: Peachtree Publishers.

Meiselman, K. (1978). *Incest.* San Francisco: Jossey-Bass.

Messinger, L., Walker, K. N., & Freeman, S. J. (1978). Preparation for remarriage following divorce. *American Journal of Orthopsychiatry, 48,* 263–272.

Nelson, M., & Nelson, G. (1982). Problems of equity in a reconstituted family: A social exchange analysis. *Family Relations, 31,* 223–231.

Perlmutter, L. H., Engel, T., & Sage, C. J. (1982). The incest taboo: Loosened sexual boundaries in remarried families. *Journal of Sex & Marital Therapy, 8,* 83–96.

Rallings, E. M. (1976). The special role of stepfather. *Family Coordinator, 25,* 445–449.

Santrock, J. W. (1972). The relations of type and onset of father absence to cognitive development. *Child Development, 43,* 455–469.

Schulman, G. L. (1972). Myths that intrude on the adaptation of the stepfamily. *Social Casework, 53,* 131–139.

Simon, A. W. (1964). *Stepchild in the family.* New York: Odyssey Press.

Skeen, P., Covi, R., & Robinson, B. (1985). Stepfamilies: A review of the literature with suggestions for practitioners. *Journal of Counseling & Development, 64,* 121–125.

Thies, J. M. (1977, Summer). Beyond divorce: The impact of remarriage on children. *Journal of Clinical Child Psychology, 6,* 59–61.

Turnbull, S. K., & Turnbull, J. M. (1983, April). To dream the impossible dream: An agenda for discussion with stepparents. *Family Relations,* 227–230.

Visher, E. B., & Visher, J. S. (1978). Major areas of difficulty for stepparent couples. *International Journal of Family Counseling, 6,* 70–80.

Visher, E. B., & Visher, J. S. (1979). *Stepfamilies: A guide to working with stepparents and stepchildren.* New York: Brunner/Mazel.

Visher, E. B., & Visher, J. S. (1982). Stepfamilies in the 1980s. In L. Messinger (Ed.), *Therapy with remarriage families* (pp. 105–119). Rockville, MD: Aspen Systems Corp.

Wald, E. (1981). *The remarried family: Challenge and promise.* New York: Family Service Association of America.

Wallerstein, J. S., & Kelly, J. B. (1980). *Surviving the break-up: How children actually cope with divorce.* New York: Basic Books.

Working With Children, Adolescents, and Their Parents: Practical Application of Developmental Theory

Ann Vernon

A single-parent father and his 15-year-old son arrived for an appointment with a mental health counselor. The father told the counselor that he and his son Kevin had recently begun to have some major arguments about curfew and chores. They both wanted to address these problems before they escalated. The counselor had previously seen Kevin for school performance and sibling relationship issues and had experienced him as a "good" kid who was concerned about his grades but had to work hard to keep them up. And, although he had trouble controlling his temper when his younger brother did things that annoyed him, he had learned new ways to handle his anger and frustration and their relationship had improved considerably.

As the father and son described their recent conflict, it became apparent to the counselor that the father was seeing his son's refusal to do assigned chores as defiance and was assuming that this defiant behavior would begin to surface in other areas. When the counselor asked Kevin to share his perspective, she began to sense that while this adolescent didn't necessarily like doing chores, the real issue was the arbitrary way in which his dad was instructing him to do them. Kevin also told the counselor that he resented the fact that his curfew was earlier than most of his friends' curfews, but admitted that he hadn't talked to his dad about this because he assumed it wouldn't do any good. Instead, he sometimes stayed out later and then argued with Dad when he was grounded for being late.

Based on what her clients had shared, the counselor felt that many of the problems they were experiencing were a result of the difficulties inherent in the transition from childhood to adolescence. She explained that significant changes occur in parent–child relationships during this period and shared that adolescents are naturally struggling to achieve independence and need the opportunity to make some of their own decisions. Therefore, when parents tell their children what, when, and how to do things, adolescents hear this as a command and feel like they are being treated as children who aren't responsible enough to make any decisions. The counselor assured the father that this didn't mean his son shouldn't assume responsibility, but indicated that there would probably be less defiance if he phrased his request in a way that allowed Kevin to take more control of the task. She also explained that, at this age, many adolescents assume things without checking them out and don't have the cognitive ability to carefully analyze situations and anticipate consequences. Therefore, it was normal for Kevin to assume that his dad wouldn't negotiate on curfew and to take matters into his own hands by just staying out.

With this information about adolescent development, Kevin's father was able to reframe the issue of defiance and recognize that his son was attempting to assert his independence, which is normal at this age. At this point Kevin and his father were able to work out a contract for chores and curfew, with reasonable timelines and consequences if Kevin failed to do what was agreed upon.

As this vignette illustrates, knowledge about developmental characteristics is essential in assessment and intervention with children, adolescents, and their parents. Without this perspective, problems can be easily misconstrued. If parents fail to take into account what is normal at each stage of development, they may assume that the symptom they see is indicative of something more pervasive.

Helping professionals acknowledge the importance of incorporating a developmental perspective into the counseling process with clients of all ages. However, much of the emphasis on applying developmental theory to counseling children has been in comprehensive counseling programs that focus on prevention through classroom and small-group work, rather than assessment and intervention in individual counseling (Vernon, 1993). Although the preventive focus is extremely important, it is also critical to consider developmental factors in problem conceptualization, in designing or selecting age-appropriate assessment instruments, and in developing interventions that take into account the developmental capabilities of the child. In addition, because adult models of assessment and treatment cannot be extrapolated to young clients, knowledge of development is essential in selecting appropriate interventions to engage children in the counseling process.

A further application is to use knowledge about developmental norms and competencies in consultation with parents. If parents have a better understanding about what to expect with their children at various stages of development, they have a better perspective from which to assess symptoms that they may see as problematic.

The purpose of this article is to describe developmental characteristics of children ages 4 to 18, with specific emphasis on applications in individual counseling and consulting.

Developmental Characteristics of Early Childhood

Physical Development

To the 4- and 5-year-old preschooler, the world can be a fascinating place. In their imaginations, anything is possible. Ordinary playrooms transform into museums, and imaginary friends are frequent dinner-table guests. Typical preschoolers are curious, energetic, and eager.

Growth is slower during the preschool years, and gross motor skills such as running, jumping, throwing, and climbing improve dramatically during this period (Berger & Thompson, 1991). Fine motor skills are more difficult to develop. Gradually 4- and 5-year-olds lose their baby fat, so that by age 6 their body proportions are similar to those of an adult. Because growth is slower, it is not uncommon for preschoolers to have smaller appetites.

Cognitive Development

Preoperational thinking characterizes preschoolers' cognitive development (Bee, 1992; Santrock & Yussen, 1992). Although they are beginning to reason more logically, if they are asked to think about familiar things in a familiar context, they still base their problem-solving on what they hear or see rather than logical reasoning. They also have difficulty with abstract concepts such as divorce and death (Garbarino & Stott, 1989).

Also characteristic of their cognitive style is *centration* (Berger & Thompson, 1991). Centration refers to the tendency to center on their perceptions, or on one aspect of the situation, rather than on a broader view. This interferes with their ability to understand cause and effect and makes it difficult for them to see that the same object or situation can have two identities. For example, it is hard for many preschoolers to realize that their teacher could also be a parent.

Animism and *artificialism* are two other aspects of preschoolers' thinking (Vernon & Al-Mabuk, in press). Animism is when children attribute lifelike qualities to inanimate objects (comforting a doll when it falls). Artificialism is the belief that someone causes natural phenomena, such as a 4-year-old thinking that rain occurs because fire fighters are spraying water from the sky. Both of these characteristics contribute to the child's ability to engage in make-believe during play.

Language is another important aspect of intellectual development during this period. By age 5, children can understand almost anything if it is explained to them in context and if the examples are specific (Berger & Thompson, 1991). They have difficulty with abstract nouns and concepts such as time and space, as characterized by the frequent question, "Are we there yet?"

Self-Development

Preschoolers are very egocentric, assuming that everyone thinks and feels as they do. They find it difficult to see things from another's perspective. This egocentrism is also reflected in their excessive use of "my" and "mine." Their self-esteem is quite high, and they tend to overestimate their abilities, thinking that they are competent in everything (Harter, 1983). This is advantageous during this period when there are so many new tasks to master. With each mastery, their sense of competence increases.

Another self-development issue relates to their self-control, which increases during this period. Preschoolers are better at modifying and controlling their own impulses and are not as frustrated and intolerant if their needs are not met immediately (Sarafino & Armstrong, 1986).

Developing initiative is another important self-development task. As they enter preschool, they face more challenges and assume more responsibilities. In turn, they increase their self-initiated behaviors.

Social Development

Play serves an extremely important function for children at this age. Most of the play for 4-year-olds is associative; that is, they interact and share but do not actually seem to be playing the same game. By age 5, they begin to be more cooperative—taking turns, creating games, and elaborating on activities (Charlesworth, 1983).

Selman (1980) noted that children at this age do not understand give and take and are most likely to be quite egocentric and unable to see another child's point of view. They also have difficulty understanding intentionality, so they may respond inappropriately to others' behavior because they misinterpret it.

Gender differences are quite apparent at this age. Boys more readily engage in rough, noisy, aggressive play; girls are more nurturing and cooperative (LeFrancois, 1992).

Emotional Development

Although their vocabularies are expanding, preschoolers still have a rather limited vocabulary for expressing how they feel. As a result, feelings are often expressed behaviorally. According to Harter and Buddin (1987), it is very difficult for children at this age to understand that it is possible to have simultaneous emotions about a situation. However, they can understand the concept of experiencing different emotions at different times.

Toward the end of the preschool period, children develop a better understanding of why someone is upset, and they begin to respond verbally or physically to others' emotions. Their understanding of other peoples' emotions is limited by their perception, and they tend to focus on the most obvious aspects of an emotional situation, such as being mad, happy, or sad (Vernon & Al-Mabuk, in press).

Applications in Counseling and Consulting

Mental health professionals working with 4- and 5-year-olds need to tailor assessment and intervention strategies to the developmental level of their clients. They also need to remain cognizant of the child's physical, intellectual, social, emotional, and self-development characteristics during the assessment and intervention process. Because the attention span of children at this age is limited, practitioners should use a variety of techniques to engage their young clients. They should also use very concrete approaches because the children's ability to remember concepts is enhanced if they can manipulate objects, have a visual representation of the concept, or engage in some form of play to help them resolve issues.

Following is a description of several typical problems characteristic of the preschool child, along with specific examples of developmentally appropriate interventions for a typical problem. Information to share with parents is also included.

Typical Problems Experienced During Early Childhood

The social and emotional development of preschoolers may be manifested in their difficulty engaging in cooperative play; they may also experience problems getting along because of their limited ability to understand give and take or to see situations other than from their own egocentric perspective. In addition, young children take things quite literally. Elkind (1991) shared the example of a young child who refused to go home from preschool because he was going to meet his new "half brother." After discussing his fear, it became apparent that he actually thought he would be seeing half of a brother! This type of thinking is very characteristic and not unlike many of the other fears and uncertainties 4- and 5-year-olds experience because of their preoperational thinking: fear of dark rooms, noises at night, monsters, or bad people (Robinson, Rotter, Fey, & Robinson, 1991). In addition, they may be hesitant to leave the house to play in the yard, visit a friend, or be left at preschool because they are afraid of separation from a parent.

It is important to remember that while these are typical problems that many preschoolers will experience to some degree, there are many other situational problems such as death, divorce, abuse, or other serious events that affect the lives of children. Keep in mind that the way they process these situations is directly related to their developmental capabilities.

A Typical Problem and Possible Interventions

Five-year-old Joshua had recently started refusing to go outdoors to play in the yard. This was confusing to his parents because until the past month, he had shown no hesitation at all in playing in the neighborhood with his friends. They were not aware of any traumatic incident that had occurred when he had been playing outside, nor did they see any other problematic symptoms. They asked the school counselor for help.

The counselor first reassured the parents that this is not an uncommon problem for children at this age because they have vivid imaginations, take things literally, and have limited abilities to process concepts. She explained to them that she would first attempt to determine specifically what Joshua was afraid of and then develop some interventions to help him deal with the problem.

In working with Joshua, the counselor first had him draw a picture of himself playing in the yard. He readily drew himself with several friends playing in the sand pile. The counselor told him that she knew he didn't want to play outside much anymore and asked if he was afraid of something in the yard. At first he denied this by saying that it was too cold outside or that his friends couldn't play, so the counselor read him a book, *Dark Closets and Voices in the Night* (Colman, 1991), to help normalize fears. At this point Joshua did admit that he was a little scared to go outside but couldn't verbalize why, so the counselor asked Joshua to draw a picture to show what he thought might happen. Based on the picture, it appeared that he was afraid that there were "bogeymen" hiding in the trees and that they would come out and hurt him.

The counselor wanted to empower Joshua to handle this fear, as well as others he might experience. She used a combination of self-talk, puppet play, and empowerment strategies to specifically address the imaginative fear, which seemed very real to this 5-year-old.

First, she asked Joshua if he could think of anything that he could put in the yard or on the fence that might scare the bogeymen away. After some brainstorming, he and the counselor decided that he could make scary masks to hang around the yard. The counselor also knew that he had a dog, so she suggested that Joshua put up a sign that said, "This is a bogeyman guard dog." Next, the counselor helped Joshua generate some statements he could say to himself when he was going outside: "My dog will scare them away." "The masks will scare them away." "Even if they aren't scared away, my friends are there with me and we can protect each other." She also suggested that Joshua buy a whistle that he could blow to alert his parents if he felt threatened. Finally, the counselor had Joshua use puppets to act out different ways he could react if he thought he saw a bogeyman in the yard.

In conferring with the parents, the counselor again stressed that this seemed to be a normal problem for a child his age and that they might even see some of this fear transferred to monsters in the room at bedtime. She emphasized that these fears do seem very real and probable to a young child and cautioned them to take the fear seriously and not let siblings tease him about it. They were asked to help Joshua rehearse his self-talk and make his masks. If these interventions were unsuccessful, new approaches could be tried.

As this case illustrates, the problem was conceptualized by taking into account how children at this age experience the world and process experiences. Interventions were concrete and addressed the problem in a variety of ways.

Developmental Characteristics of Middle Childhood

Physical Development

During this period, ages 6 to 11, growth is relatively stable. Children grow taller, their body proportions change, and their muscles grow stronger (Lowrey, 1986). Due to the slow rate of growth, children have a high degree of self-control over their bodies. They can master most motor skills and become adept at running, skipping, jumping, and riding a bike. By the end of this period, there is a major improvement in their fine motor skills as well.

Depending on the rate of maturity, it is not at all uncommon to see some 10- and 11-year-olds entering puberty. Height and weight growth spurts also begin at different times for different children, contributing to self-consciousness and embarrassment.

Cognitive Development

According to Piaget (1967), a transitional period between preoperational and concrete operational thought occurs between the ages of 5 and 7. By age 8, children are definitely concrete operational thinkers. As a result, they are able to understand reversibility, reciprocity, identity, and classification. They begin to apply these principles in a variety of contexts, such as friendships, rules in games, and team play (Vernon, 1993).

During this period of development, their thinking becomes more logical and their problem-solving abilities are enhanced. However, because they are concrete thinkers, they still cannot reason abstractly or consider possibilities, which influences the way they approach situations. For example, if their best friend doesn't sit by them, they logically assume that they did something that made the friend angry, rather than consider a variety of other possibilities.

School-age children learn best by questioning, exploring, and doing (Flavell, 1985). Their language development continues; they can understand more abstract concepts and use vocabulary in more sophisticated ways (Berger & Thompson, 1991).

Self-Development

Children's self-understanding expands during this period. They are able to describe themselves in terms of several competencies at once: "I am short, a good reader, and a fast runner." They are also beginning to develop more of an internal locus of control (Collins, 1984).

As they enter school and begin to compare themselves to others, they become self-critical, feel inferior, and may experience a decrease in self-esteem (Ruble, Boggiano, Feldman, & Loebl, 1980). They may be more inhibited about trying new things and are sensitive to feedback from peers. As they become aware of their specific areas of competence, they may experience self-confidence or self-doubt (Newman & Newman, 1991).

Social Development

Socialization with peers is a major issue during the school-age years. Acceptance in a group and having a "best friend" contribute to children's sense of competence. As they learn to deal with peer pressure, rejection, approval, and conformity, they begin to formulate values, behaviors, and beliefs that facilitate their social development (Berger & Thompson, 1991).

Friendships serve other important functions. Through association with peers, children learn to develop a broader view of the world, to experiment with ideas and roles, and to learn important interaction skills. As they participate in activities, they learn to cooperate and compromise, to make and break rules, to assume roles as leaders and followers, and to understand others' points of view (Vernon & Al-Mabuk, in press).

By age 7, children begin to outgrow their egocentrism and adopt more prosocial behaviors. As they develop the ability to see things from another's perspective, they also become more adept at interpreting social cues and evaluating input (Hartup, 1984). As a result, they become better able to resolve conflicts and solve social problems.

Emotional Development

During the school-age years, children begin to experience more complex emotions such as guilt, shame, or pride. They are also increasingly aware that people are capable of experiencing more than one emotion at once. They are more adept at hiding their emotions when they don't want to hurt someone's feelings (Fischer & Bullock, 1984).

Generally children at this age are more sensitive, more empathic, and better able to recognize and communicate their feelings to others. They realize that feelings can change and that they are not the cause of another person's discomfort (Carroll & Steward, 1984). Because they are experiencing many new situations, anxiety over school performance or peer inclusion is not uncommon (Vernon, 1993).

Applications in Counseling and Consulting

Middle childhood spans a number of years in which there are many "firsts," particularly those associated with school and friends. Although it is a period of relatively stable growth, mental health professionals need to keep in mind that children in the concrete stage of development are limited in their abilities to think logically and to see possibilities. Despite the gradual enhancement of their problem-solving abilities, they continue to need adult guidance in consistently applying their skills to common problems.

Professionals working with this age group should continue to employ concrete interventions to help children resolve problems. Bibliotherapy, art activities, puppets, role-play, and games are very appropriate for this age group.

Typical Problems Experienced During Middle Childhood

Youngs (1985) identified several typical concerns that children this age experience. In particular, she noted issues surrounding peer approval: being chosen last for a team, fear of not being liked, fear of being ridiculed or disapproved of by classmates, or fear of losing a friend. In addition, children worry about school performance, passing to the next grade, or being disciplined by the teacher. As they get older, appearance and emerging sexuality issues become concerns.

Once again, these are typical concerns experienced in varying degrees by most school-age children. Unfortunately, far too many young children today have more serious situational problems, such as growing up in abusive or alcoholic homes, living in poverty, or dealing with difficult adjustments to parental divorce and remarriage. These children must deal with the more serious situational problems in addition to the challenges of dealing with normal growing up. Mental health professionals need to design interventions that are concrete in nature in order to engage the child in the problem-solving process. With school-age children, simply talking about the problem is generally not an effective process (Vernon, 1993).

A Typical Problem and Possible Interventions

Nine-year-old Jennifer asked to see the school counselor because she was afraid to take tests. Although she was a good student, she became so anxious prior to and during a test that she sometimes missed school on the day of the test or felt sick to her stomach at school as the test time approached. Jennifer tended to be very self-critical and was very hard on herself if she didn't get a perfect score.

In order to get a more accurate assessment of the problem, the counselor asked Jennifer to describe:

▪ what she is thinking prior to taking a test

▪ what she is feeling physically prior to taking a test

▪ what she imagines will happen

▪ how she feels emotionally before and during the test.

The counselor also asked her to share what she had tried to do to solve the problem.

Based on what this young client shared, the counselor confirmed her hypothesis that Jennifer was very perfectionistic and looked at the test-taking situation as an "all or nothing, pass/fail" event. In addition, she always imagined the worst, even though she seldom received less than a perfect score. This sort of absolutistic thinking is not uncommon for children at this age, but it is important to help them see the range of possibilities. To help with this, the counselor placed a strip of masking tape on the floor and placed notecard markers from one end of the line to the other in this order:

1. Fail by getting everything wrong.

2. Get a bad grade and miss a lot.

3. Get an average grade and miss quite a few.

4. Get a very high grade but still miss a few.

5. Get the top grade and not miss any.

Next she asked Jennifer to stand on the spot that represented where she stood with her test scores most of the time. Then she asked her to stand on the spot that represented where she was if she didn't get a perfect score. As the counselor had expected, Jennifer stood at the far end of the line (top grade, not miss any) and at the next level down.

The counselor gave Jennifer two pairs of old glasses. She told her that the first pair were the "doom-and-gloom" glasses and that when she put them on she would imagine only terrible things happening when she took a test. She asked Jennifer to verbalize those thoughts while the counselor recorded them. Next, she asked her to put on the "rose-colored" glasses. When she had these glasses on, things would look very good. The counselor asked Jennifer to verbalize her thoughts when she wore the rose-colored glasses. She explained to Jennifer that since she had never failed a test before, nor had she ever gotten an average or below-average grade, that she probably didn't need to wear the "doom-and-gloom glasses." She pointed out that if Jennifer pretended to put on the rose-colored glasses before each test, she could say positive things to herself, such as, "Since I usually do very well, why should I even think that I won't do well this time?" "Even if I got a few wrong, does this mean I'm a stupid kid?" "If I get too nervous, I'll worry too much and make myself sick, but if I just work hard, I'll probably do O.K." After the counselor modeled these rational self-statements to Jennifer, they generated a few more together and put them on notecards for Jennifer to look at prior to taking a test.

As a final intervention, the counselor taught Jennifer some relaxation exercises that she could use prior to taking a test from *The Second Centering Book* (Hendricks & Roberts, 1977). The counselor also had her interview her sister, her father, and her grandmother. She and Jennifer generated interview questions, which related to a time they had made a mistake, whether they had ever scored less than perfect on an exam, and identifying individual strengths and weaknesses. This activity helped Jennifer see that other people had strong and weak areas, that they also made mistakes, and that they had scored less than perfect on a test and it hadn't been a catastrophe.

To Jennifer's parents, the counselor explained that it was normal for Jennifer to feel more pressure at school because she was more aware of her performance in relation to others. She emphasized the importance of sharing some of their "less than perfect" experiences with Jennifer, of reinforcing her efforts rather than the final grade, and of helping her avoid thinking the absolute worst by looking at her "track record" of performance. She also recommended that they read Jennifer the story "The Less Than Perfect Prince" from *Color Us Rational* (Waters, 1979), a story about a prince who learns that he and the world can't be perfect. She also explained the relaxation exercises so that the parents could help their daughter use them at home the day of her test.

Developmental Characteristics of Early Adolescence

Physical Development

With the exception of infancy, physical changes occur more rapidly during early adolescence (ages 11 to 14) than at any other point in the life span (Dusek, 1991). The increased production of sex hormones and the changes associated with puberty begin at about age 11 for females and at about age 13 for males. At this time, maturation of the reproductive system, the appearance of secondary sex characteristics (breast enlargement, pubic hair, voice change), and a growth spurt occur. This growth spurt can last approximately 3 years and begins about 2 years earlier in girls than in boys (Malina, 1991).

Children in this age group vary tremendously in their rate of maturation, which results in self-consciousness and anxiety. Both males and females will be clumsy and uncoordinated for a period of time because the size of their hands and feet may be disproportionate to other body parts. In addition, their rate of physical change affects how they see themselves. Early adolescents want to be like everyone else and are painfully aware of appearing awkward or different. Because they don't want others to see their bodies, "locker-room phobia" is common during this period of development (Baumrind, 1987).

The physical and hormonal changes characteristic of early adolescence can be very confusing. Sexual thoughts and feelings abound, often accompanied by feelings of shame and guilt. Young adolescents are curious about sex and wonder if others feel the same way they do. Straightforward information about sex is extremely critical prior to and during early adolescence.

Cognitive Development

During early adolescence, the shift from concrete to formal operational thinking begins. Although this change begins at about age 11, it is not attained until the ages of 15 to 20 (Schave & Schave, 1989). As they move into more formal operational thinking, adolescents begin to think more abstractly, develop the ability to hypothesize, and can mentally manipulate more than two categories of variables simultaneously (Newman & Newman, 1991). Although they can also reason more logically and predict consequences of events, they do not always apply these skills to themselves. In other words, they may apply their skill in logic to their work in mathematics, but they may not logically assume that if they stay out past their curfew they might be grounded (Vernon, 1993).

According to Schave and Schave (1989), the shift from concrete to formal operational thinking is "the most drastic and dramatic change in cognition that occurs in anyone's life" (p.7). With these new abilities, young adolescents are able to detect inconsistencies, think about future changes, see possibilities, think of logical rebuttals, and hypothesize about the logical sequence of events (Newman & Newman, 1991). It is important to remember that considerable variability exists in the degree to which formal operational thinking is attained and in the consistency with which it is applied during early adolescence. Because it is easy to assume they are capable of more mature cognitive thought than they actually are, working with members of this population can be confusing.

Self-Development

The tasks of self-definition and integration begin during early adolescence (Dusek, 1991). As adolescents engage in their self-development search, they push for autonomy. Elkind (1984) noted that although they strive for independence, they are still immature and lack life experience. These contrasts, coupled with their cognitive, physical, and pubertal changes, leave them very vulnerable. As a result, they may show increased dependency, which can be very confusing to them and to the adults involved in their lives.

In some ways, young adolescents contradict themselves. They want to be unique, yet they want to look like everyone else. They are very self-conscious, assuming that everyone is looking at them or thinking about them. Elkind (1988) termed this belief that others are as concerned with us as we are the "imaginary audience." As a result of this type of thinking, early adolescents fantasize about how others will react to them, becoming oversensitive about their performance and appearance. Because they feel awkward and ugly, self-esteem usually decreases during this period of development (Baumrind, 1987).

Adolescents can also be very egocentric, seeing themselves as more important than they really are or assuming that no one else experiences things the way they do (Berger & Thompson, 1991). They also assume that because they are unique, they are also invulnerable. Elkind (1984) labeled this the "personal fable"—because adolescents believe they are special, they think bad things can happen to others but not to them. The personal fable accounts for self-deprecating as well as self-aggrandizing behavior, in which the adolescent assumes that he or she will be heroic and world famous.

Social Development

Because young adolescents look to peers as a source of support, they are very sensitive and vulnerable to peer humiliation (Vernon & Al-Mabuk, in press). Peers play an increasingly significant role in their lives and are an important part of the socialization process. The need to belong is very strong, which also means that young adolescents have to learn to contend with peer pressure and decisions about which group to associate with. It is during this period that cliques and distinct groups emerge, with specific "rules" about how to dress and behave.

As adolescents mature, their relationships become more complex. Because it is still difficult for some adolescents to step outside themselves and look at their own behavior objectively, they may behave obnoxiously. This, in turn, influences how others respond to them. They also continue to have difficulty taking others' viewpoints into account because they are still preoccupied with their own needs (Newman, 1985).

Emotional Development

Many early adolescents ride an emotional roller coaster during this developmental stage. Moodiness, accompanied by emotional outbursts, is common. Troublesome emotions such as anxiety, shame, guilt, depression, and anger also occur more frequently (Adelson & Doehrman, 1980).

Because these negative emotions can be overwhelming and cause adolescents to feel very vulnerable, they often mask these feelings of fear and vulnerability with anger, which typically distances people and often results in increased conflict as adults react to the anger and fail to recognize the true feelings behind it.

The increased intensity of emotions permeates all aspects of life. Early adolescents feel anxious about what is happening to them, but because many are unable to think abstractly, they tend to view things from an "either-or" perspective. They don't make good choices about how to deal with the anxiety because they are unable to generate alternatives. This may result in more anxiety, guilt, or shame.

It is particularly important that adults who interact with young adolescents recognize their emotional vulnerability and not exacerbate the problems by reacting insensitively.

Applications in Counseling and Consulting

Working with young adolescents can be challenging because it is often difficult to get at the underlying feelings they mask with their anger, apathy, or acting out. Mental health professionals need to remember that because the attainment of formal operational thinking occurs gradually, many of the problem behaviors occur as a result of incompetencies in thinking and reasoning. This is sometimes easy to overlook because the rapid achievement of physical maturity leads adults to assume that adolescents are more mature than they actually are.

Although many significant changes occur during early adolescence, many researchers contend that what the adolescent experiences is part of a normal, healthy, developmental process (Berger & Thompson, 1991; Newman, 1985; Schave & Schave, 1989). Furthermore, the majority of adolescents do not resort to drug dependence, delinquent acting-out, school failure, sexual promiscuity, or other self-destructive behaviors (Steinberg & Levine, 1987). That is not to say that early adolescents don't have worries and experience problems.

Typical Problems Experienced During Early Adolescence

Young adolescents are easily overwhelmed by their feelings, and many of their problems result from their inability to deal effectively with these feelings. Because they tend to be oversensitive, they overreact to relationship issues with friends and parents. They worry excessively about how they look, how they act, and whether they belong. They also have concerns about dealing with their own sexuality.

Adults often overreact to adolescent behavior and assume that their illogical actions are intentional. This creates additional problems for adolescents, and they may respond with defiance or withdrawal. Mental health professionals working with adolescents need to remember that concrete strategies may still be necessary to help them look at cause and effect, alternative behaviors, and long-range implications.

A Typical Problem and Possible Interventions

Cory's mother referred him to a counselor at a local mental health center because the school had called to inform her that he had skipped school for the last 5 days. Although she had to leave for work before it was time for Cory to go to school, school attendance had never been a problem in the past. His mother indicated that he seemed happy at home and had several friends. He had struggled some with his studies in the seventh grade but generally got average grades. There had been no major changes in his life other than the transition to junior high last year.

When the counselor saw Cory for the first time, he immediately noticed that although Cory was very tall, his feet and hands were still too big for his body, making him appear clumsy and awkward. He had a fair amount of acne and seemed somewhat immature compared with other eighth-graders this counselor had worked with. Cory didn't deny skipping school but wasn't willing to talk about why. In an attempt to elicit more information, the counselor asked Cory to complete the following unfinished sentences:

1. When I go to school, I feel _____.

2. The part of the school day I like best is _____.

3. The part of the school day I like least is _____.

4. The subject I like best is _____.

5. The subject that is easiest for me is _____.

6. The subject I like least is _____.

7. The subject that is hardest for me is _____.

8. If I could change something about school, I would change _____.

9. Other kids in this school _____.

10. Teachers in this school _____.

Cory's responses to these questions appeared to indicate two problem areas: speech class and physical education. The counselor hypothesized that Cory was overly sensitive about his body and didn't want to undress in the locker room after physical education. He also assumed that Cory wanted to skip speech class because he was self-conscious about getting up in front of 25 other students to give a speech.

After some discussion, Cory admitted that he felt self-conscious in these classes. The counselor explained the concept of the "imaginary audience" to him and assured him that these were typical concerns that other classmates were probably experiencing as well. He asked Cory to assess how helpful skipping school had been in dealing with these problems and consequently obtained a commitment from him to work on more productive ways to handle the situation.

The counselor adapted an activity called "Magnify" (Pincus, 1990). In this adaptation several events were listed and Cory was instructed to magnify their importance by turning them into catastrophes. For example:

1. You walk to the front of the room to give a speech. Catastrophic thought: _____.

2. You go into the locker room to change for physical education. Catastrophic thought: _____.

After Cory identified the worst case scenario, the counselor taught him to look at the probable situation by adapting "Getting Straight Our Magnifications" (Pincus, 1990).

You walk to the front of the room to give a speech.

Best case scenario:_____

Worst case scenario:_____

Probable scenario:_____

By identifying best, worst, and probable outcomes and identifying his catastrophic thoughts for several different situations, Cory began to dispute some of his anxieties about his speech and physical education classes. Next, the counselor helped Cory develop self-statements to deal with the anxiety:

■ Even though it seems like everyone is looking at me when I give a speech, probably only a few people are, and that's not the end of the world.

■ If I mess up when I'm giving a speech, I'm not a total jerk.

■ If I'm embarrassed to undress in physical education, other kids probably are too, so it's not worth skipping school over.

Following these activities, Cory and the counselor again looked at the consequences of skipping school and generated alternative ways he could handle the situation if he felt nervous again. The counselor recommended that he read *Changes and Choices: A Junior High Survival Guide* (McCoy, 1989) to help him see that the thoughts and feelings he experienced were normal. Together they drew up a contract for school attendance.

In consulting with Cory's mother, the counselor explained the concept of the imaginary audience and assured her that her son's solution to the problem no doubt seemed very logical to him due to the cognitive incompetencies characteristic at this stage of development. He suggested that the mother might visit with the speech teacher to discuss the possibility of utilizing small groups for some of the speech activities because students wouldn't feel as anxious about performing for fewer classmates. Finally, he praised the mother for being firm about school attendance, yet at the same time trying to understand why Cory had chosen to behave as he had.

Developmental Characteristics of Mid-Adolescence

Physical Development

Depending on when the early adolescent entered puberty, physical development for 15- to 18-year-olds may continue at a rather rapid rate or may gradually slow down. Since males generally lag behind females in the rate of physical development, females often tower over males until this trend is reversed in mid-adolescence (Berger & Thompson, 1991).

Generally, by mid-adolescence, females have achieved full breast growth, have started to menstruate, and have developed pubic hair. Males experience a lowering of their voices at about age 15, and facial hair appears approximately a year later (Newman & Newman, 1991).

Sexual urges are very strong during mid-adolescence. This can evoke anxiety for adolescents and their parents. Sexuality is one way to try out "grown up" behaviors, but many adolescents don't think about the possibly serious consequences, such as sexually transmitted diseases or pregnancy (Vernon & Al-Mabuk, in press). Although most teenagers aren't obsessed by sex and don't have intercourse on a regular basis, good sex education is imperative (Steinberg & Levine, 1990).

Cognitive Development

Formal operational thinking continues to develop during mid-adolescence, allowing 15- to 18-year-olds to think and behave in significantly different ways. For example, as they develop the ability to think more abstractly, they can hypothesize, think about the future, and are less likely to conceptualize everything in either-or terms because their thought processes are more flexible. They are capable of pondering and philosophizing about moral, social, and political issues. They are better able to distinguish the concrete and real from the abstract and possible (Dusek, 1991; Sroufe & Cooper, 1988).

Although their cognitive abilities have improved considerably since early adolescence, mid-adolescents are still likely to be inconsistent in their thinking and behavior. While they might be able to see alternatives, they still may lack the experience or self-understanding to make appropriate choices.

Self-Development

Along with achieving independence, preoccupation with their identities is a primary focus for teens at this stage of development. This process of finding themselves involves establishing a vocational, political, social, sexual, moral, and religious identity (Erikson, 1968). They do this by trying on various roles and responsibilities; engaging in discussions; observing adults and peers; speculating about possibilities; dreaming about the future; and doing a lot of self-questioning, experimenting, and exploring. This may be a period when they spend more time alone, contemplating ideas and trying to clarify their values, beliefs, and direction in life.

Mid-adolescents are generally more self-confident and do not have to look like carbon copies of their peers. In fact, they may do the opposite, dying their hair green if someone else's is red or wearing quirky clothes from secondhand stores to "make a statement." This self-assertion extends to other areas as well. Mid-adolescents are more capable of resisting peer pressure due to increased self-confidence and the ability to look beyond the immediate present and speculate about long-term consequences.

According to Baumrind (1987), much of what happens in terms of self-development at this stage depends on the degree to which the individual has attained formal operational thinking and his or her level of self-esteem.

Social Development

Peer relationships continue to be very important during this stage of development. The increased time spent with peers serves several important functions: to try out various roles, to learn to tolerate individual differences as they come in contact with people with different values and lifestyles, and to prepare themselves for adult interactions as they formulate more intimate relationships (Dusek, 1991).

If they have attained formal operational thinking, adolescents approach relationships with more wisdom and maturity. They are not as dependent on friends for emotional support, and by the end of this period they begin to select friendships based on compatibility and shared experiences as well as on what they can contribute to the relationship (O'Brien & Bierman, 1988).

Intimate friendships increase during mid-adolescence, which helps teens develop more social sensitivity. As they become less egocentric, they are better able to recognize and deal with the shortcomings in relationships. As a result, friendship patterns become more stable and less exclusive (Dusek, 1991). There is also more dating and sexual experimentation during this period (Newman & Newman, 1991).

Emotional Development

As they attain formal operational thinking, adolescents are not as overwhelmed by their emotions and subsequently experience less rapid mood fluctuations. Fifteen- to 18-year-olds tend to be less defensive and are more capable of expressing their emotions rather than acting them out behaviorally (Vernon & Al-Mabuk, in press).

Many adolescents experience loneliness and ambivalence toward the end of this developmental stage. They may be gradually growing away from their friends as their needs and interests change. As high school graduation approaches, they may be apprehensive about the future. Some experience self-doubt and insecurity if they compare themselves to peers or realize that they don't have the skills or ability to qualify for a particular job or postsecondary education.

Adolescents are better able to deal with emotionally charged issues if they have developed formal operational thinking skills. As a result, they are not as impulsive or likely to behave irrationally or erratically in response to emotional upset. Bear in mind that the wide variation in how adolescents manage emotions results from their different levels of cognitive maturation.

Applications in Counseling and Consulting

Counseling the mid-adolescent is easier than working with the 11- to 14-year-old, but a lot depends on the degree to which the adolescent has obtained formal operational thinking. In general, the older adolescent does not feel as vulnerable, is better able to express feelings, and is more willing to be in counseling. That is not to say that all older adolescents are this way; a lot depends on the nature of the problem and the personality of the adolescent.

For the most part they are better able to verbally express themselves, and it is easy to assume that concepts don't need to be reinforced in concrete ways. Because adolescents vary in their rate of maturation and because some are visual rather than auditory learners, it is still very appropriate to use activities to help illustrate points. Use of short homework assignments such as bibliotherapy or journalizing is very helpful for this age group.

Typical Problems Experienced During Mid-Adolescence

Although the emotional turbulence lessens to a large degree during mid-adolescence, a new set of circumstances arises that can create problems for 15- to 18-year-olds. Specifically, adolescents at this age are dealing with more complex relationships that may involve sexual intimacy and with decisions about their future. According to Youngs (1985), teenagers at this age worry about getting enough out of high school to prepare them for life. They also express confusion about career choices and worry about money. Relationships with family may be strained as they push for more autonomy, and yet they may have anxiety about being too independent.

Mid-adolescence serves as a "stepping stone" to the young adult world, in which there are even greater challenges and new opportunities. This can be an exciting time, but it can also create anxiety. Mental health professionals working with adolescents need to be aware of this ambivalence and of the fact that by age 18 most will be making significant transitions involving changes in roles, relationships, routine, and assessment of self.

A Typical Problem and Possible Interventions

Stacie, 17, initiated contact with the school counselor to discuss her relationship with her boyfriend. According to Stacie, the relationship had been very good for the first few months, but lately they had been arguing so much that she was afraid Matt would break up with her. Whenever they went out, she constantly wanted reassurance that he cared about her, which irritated him. When she persisted, he ignored her. If he didn't call when he said he would, she got anxious and was upset if he didn't return her phone calls right away. She was certain he was seeing other girls and assumed that there was something wrong with her. Her response to this situation was to sit home and wait for his phone calls, call his friends to see where he was, and stay awake at night thinking about the situation. She felt depressed and anxious.

In talking with Stacie further, it appeared that the majority of arguments occurred because Stacie wanted to spend all her time with Matt and he insisted on having some space. Stacie expressed concern about what he would do if he wasn't with her, so the counselor had her make a list of all the things that could happen. In the next column, she asked Stacie to put a check next to the things that she could prove had happened. Once this was completed, the counselor explained that there was a difference between probability and possibility and that one way of distinguishing between these was to look at past evidence. For example, it was possible that Matt could take out another girl, but to her knowledge had he ever done this? It was possible that he could get killed in a car accident, but had he ever driven recklessly or while drunk when she had been with him? The counselor instructed Stacie to use this type of questioning to deal with her anxiety about things that could happen but seemed unlikely based on past history and information about Matt.

Next the counselor discussed issues of control in the relationship. She tied some strings to her arms and legs and asked Stacie to pull on them. The harder Stacie pulled, the more the counselor resisted. They discussed the fact that Stacie's attempts to control Matt would probably drive him away, which Stacie acknowledged had happened once already. To help her deal with this, the counselor had Stacie make a list of things she could say to herself when she felt like she wanted to control her boyfriend, such as "Will it do more harm than good to control?" "What's the worst thing that could happen if I don't control him?" "Can I really control another person?"

As Stacie talked about the relationship, it also seemed that there were times when Stacie wasn't being controlling but that Matt was not treating her with respect. The counselor gave Stacie some handouts on personal rights and assertion and explained the concepts to her. They then role-played assertive and nonassertive responses to some issues that Stacie had generated.

When Stacie left the session, she admitted feeling less anxious and indicated she had several things she could work on to help her deal with this relationship issue.

Conclusion

The intent of this article was to provide helping professionals with characteristics of children and adolescents across several dimensions of physical, cognitive, social, emotional, and self-development. This information can be used several ways in assessment and intervention. In assessment, it can serve as a barometer to indicate how a child is progressing relative to normal developmental guidelines. This barometer serves an extremely important function because without it parents and professionals can easily misconstrue or misdiagnose problems. With this information they have a general sense of what's "normal." In addition, knowledge about developmental characteristics is essential in selecting or designing appropriate assessment strategies for the child's developmental stage.

Developmental knowledge is also exceptionally critical in designing effective interventions. Children and adolescents don't respond to the same counseling approaches that work with adults. Because children's attention spans are more limited—at least until adolescence—helping professionals must be more creative and use visual and kinesthetic as well as auditory methods. Games, art activities, play, simulation activities, music, and drama are all examples of interventions that take into consideration the developmental capabilities of the child or adolescent.

Although extensive coverage of consultation could not be provided within the limited scope of this article, the examples with the preschooler, elementary-aged child, and young adolescent demonstrate the significance of sharing information about development with parents. Helping professionals can readily apply the same concept with teachers or other professionals to help them better understand characteristic behaviors and typical problems experienced by a particular age group. In addition, it is very important to share how development affects children's abilities to comprehend concepts, which in turn has an impact on their behavior. Far too often parents and teachers think children (and adolescents in particular) are being obnoxious, when in fact they are acting that way because that is the only way they know to process information in the given situation.

Growing up is challenging. In addition to the normal developmental issues identified in this article, children in today's society have other significant concerns with which to deal. Helping professionals who are well-grounded in developmental theory will be better equipped to understand how young clients process information and how to most effectively work with them to facilitate resolution of typical problems as well as more serious situational problems.

References

Adelson, J., & Doehrman, M. J. (1980). The psychodynamic approach to adolescence. In J. Adelson (Ed.), *Handbook of adolescent psychology* (pp. 99–116). New York: Wiley.

Baumrind, D. (1987). A developmental perspective on adolescent risk-taking in contemporary America. In C. D. Irwin (Ed.), *Adolescent social behavior and health* (pp. 93–125). San Francisco: Jossey-Bass.

Bee, H. (1992). *The developing child*. New York: HarperCollins.

Berger, K., & Thompson, R. (1991). *The developing person through childhood and adolescence*. New York: Worth.

Carroll, J., & Steward, M. (1984). The role of cognitive development in children's understanding of their own feelings. *Child Development, 55*, 1486–1492.

Charlesworth, R. (1983). *Understanding child development*. Albany, NY: Delmar.

Collins, W. A. (Ed.). (1984). *Development during middle childhood: The years from six to twelve*. Washington, DC: National Academy Press.

Colman, P. (1991). *Dark closets and noises in the night*. Mahwah, NJ: Paulist Press.

Dusek, J. B. (1991). *Adolescent development and behavior*. Englewood Cliffs, NJ: Prentice Hall.

Elkind, D. (1984). *All grown up and no place to go: Teenagers in crisis*. Reading, MA: Addison-Wesley.

Elkind, D. (1988). *The hurried child: Growing up too fast too soon*. Reading, MA: Addison-Wesley.

Elkind, D. (1991). Development in early childhood. *Elementary School Guidance and Counseling, 26*, 12–21.

Erikson, E. (1968). *Identity: Youth and crisis*. New York: Norton.

Fischer, K. W., & Bullock, D. (1984). Cognitive development in school-age children: Conclusions and new directions. In W. A. Collins (Ed.), *Development during middle childhood: The years from six to twelve* (pp. 70–146). Washington, DC: National Academy Press.

Flavell, J. H. (1985). *Cognitive development* (2nd ed.). Englewood Cliffs, NJ: Prentice Hall.

Garbarino, J., & Stott, F. (1989). *What children can tell us*. San Francisco: Jossey-Bass.

Harter, S. (1983). Developmental perspectives on the self-system. In. P. H. Mussen (Series Ed.) and E. M. Heatherington (Vol. Ed.), *Handbook of child psychology, Vol. 4: Socialization, personality, and social development* (pp. 275–385). New York: Wiley.

Harter, S., & Buddin, B. J. (1987). Children's understanding of the simultaneity of two emotions: A five-stage developmental acquisition sequence. *Developmental Psychology, 23*, 388–399.

Hartup, W. W. (1984). In W. A. Collins (Ed.), *Development during middle childhood: The years from six to twelve* (pp. 240–282). Washington, DC: National Academy Press.

Hendricks, G., & Roberts, T. B. (1977). *The second centering book: More awareness activities for children, parents, and teachers*. Englewood Cliffs, NJ: Prentice Hall.

LeFrancois, G. R. (1992). *Of children: An introduction to child development*. Belmont, CA: Wadsworth.

Lowrey, G. H. (1986). *Growth and development of children* (8th ed.). Chicago: Year Book Medical Publishers.

Malina, R. M. (1991). Growth spurt, adolescent. In R. M. Lerner, A. C. Petersen, & J. Brooks-Gunn (Eds.), *Encyclopedia of adolescence* (pp. 244–289). New York: Garland.

McCoy, K. (1989). *Changes and choices: A junior high survival guide*. New York: Perigee Press.

Newman, B. M., & Newman, P. R. (1991). *Development through life: A psychological approach*. Pacific Grove, CA: Brooks/Cole.

Newman, J. (1985). Adolescents: Why they can be so obnoxious. *Adolescence, 79*, 635–646.

O'Brien, S. F. & Bierman, K. L. (1988). Conceptions and perceived influence of peer groups: Interviews with preadolescents and adolescents. *Child Development, 59*, 1360–1365.

Piaget, J. (1967). *Six psychological studies*. New York: Random House.

Pincus, D. (1990). *Feeling good about yourself*. Carthage, IL: The Good Apple.

Robinson, E. H., Rotter, J. C., Fey, M. A., & Robinson, S. L. (1991). Children's fears: Toward a preventive model. *The School Counselor, 38*, 187–192.

Ruble, D., Boggiano, A., Feldman, N., & Loebl, J. (1980). A developmental analysis of the role of social comparison in self-evaluation. *Developmental Psychology, 16,* 105–115.

Santrock, J., & Yussen, S. (1992). *Child development: An introduction.* Dubuque, IA: William C. Brown.

Sarafino, E. P., & Armstrong, J. W. (1986). *Child and adolescent development.* St. Paul, MN: West.

Schave, D., & Schave, B. (1989). *Early adolescence and the search for self: A developmental perspective.* New York: Praeger.

Selman, R. (1980). *The growth of interpersonal understanding: Developmental and clinical analyses.* New York: Academic Press.

Sroufe, L. A., & Cooper, R. G. (1988). *Child development: Its nature and course.* New York: Knopf.

Steinberg, L. D., & Levine, A. (1987). *You and your adolescent.* New York: Harper Perennial.

Steinberg, L. D., & Levine, A. (1990). *You and your adolescent: A parent's guide for ages 10 to 20.* New York: Harper & Row.

Vernon, A. (1993). *Developmental assessment and intervention with children and adolescents.* Alexandria, VA: American Counseling Association.

Vernon, A., & Al-Mabuk, R. (in press). *What growing up is all about: A practical guide to help parents understand children and adolescents.* Champaign, IL: Research Press.

Waters, V. (1979). *Color us rational.* New York: Institute for Rational Living.

Youngs, B. (1985). *Stress in children.* New York: Arbor House.

Family Counseling With Children: Attending to the Children in Our Midst

Thomas V. Sayger
and Arthur M. Horne

onducting family counseling when a child is present can be a humbling experience for even the most skilled professional. Providing family counseling with children requires a "fourth generation" professional, in which skills and knowledge of individual child psychology must be blended equally with skills and knowledge of family dynamics and functioning (Kaslow & Racusin, 1990). Therefore, in the field of child-focused family therapy, we find professionals who retain identities (e.g., counseling psychologist, child clinical psychologist, child psychiatrist) that, at least in part, lie outside the traditional boundaries of family psychology.

Counseling children automatically directs our clinical attention to an ecological perspective in which we explore the interaction of the child with his or her immediate social environment, the family (Garbarino, 1993). Clinicians, however, also must examine the interplay of social systems in the environment that shape the child's experience (e.g., school, society, culture). Children who are identified for counseling, in essence, may be experiencing the traumas of living in an ecological system that is threatening, dysfunctional, and unhealthy. The child's ability to relate stories of his or her experiences with the family therapist is imperative and may provide insights into the child's cognitive abilities and level of self- and social awareness.

Some researchers and clinicians have doubts about the effectiveness of family therapy for addressing clinical issues in general, notwithstanding those related to a child's mental health needs. Most family therapy models have major limitations because they fail to appreciate the importance of key variables that pertain to individual family members and to extrafamilial systems, do not consider important individual developmental issues that should influence the therapist's understanding of the problems and choice of intervention strategies, and rarely utilize proven intervention strategies derived from other treatment models (Henggeler & Borduin, 1990).

According to some professionals, even the terminology of family therapy can elicit negative connotations. Professionals offering family counseling might best perceive their role as consultant rather than treater, therapist, or healer (Johnson, 1993). Subscribing to a position that labels clients as "disturbed," "pathological," or "dysfunctional" can be a disempowering frame of reference that discourages children and families considering their counseling options.

An empowerment position that focuses on clients strengths and resources implies that families and children are people with problems to be addressed, not individuals in need of repair. Empowering families and children entails helping them gain accurate information and access to community resources (e.g., financial assistance, child or respite care, transportation, medical assistance), developing coping skills for managing difficult behaviors or communicating with school personnel, and identifying and establishing a social support network (e.g., prevention programs, extended family/friends networking, parent support groups, individual counseling). Most clinicians agree that family therapy should have therapeutic and healing effects; however, beliefs and language that attribute virtually every emotional or behavior problem of children to parental pathogenesis can become offensive to many parents in the same way that gender-biased or ethnic-biased language can be offensive to women, men, or members of ethnic groups (Johnson, 1993).

Clinical practice with regard to child mental health concerns entails an understanding of the contribution of many different systems (i.e., biological, cultural, economic, political, organizational, legal) to family interactions and the overall quality of family life. Professionals also must be knowledgeable of laws, policies, procedures, and programs that relate to the needs and concerns of families of children with mental and emotional disorders. Parents want family therapists to share what they know about the etiology of emotional and mental disorders of childhood based on current research and the research evidence regarding the effectiveness of different treatment approaches. Professionals must have knowledge about parental views of counseling services, attitudes, and behaviors and be aware of possible connections between counseling ideologies, attitudes, and behaviors that parents view as problematic or contradictory to their beliefs and values. Finally, family therapists must be knowledgeable about the goals and activities of parent support groups and the experiences and needs of siblings of children with emotional and mental disorders (Johnson, 1993).

Clearly, family relationships do not take place in a vacuum. They are affected by biological, cultural, economic, and political dynamics. So, although Bowen (1985) viewed the family as the unit of illness and consequently the unit of treatment, current thinking in child mental health stresses the effects of macrosystems (i.e., dominant culture, governments, mass media) on the quality of family life. When conducting family counseling with children, the family therapist must not forget that any changes effected in treatment will be only as successful as the family's or child's ability to implement those changes in society as a whole.

Why Family Therapy?

Combrinck-Graham (1989) wrote that the family is the child's primary resource system. She envisioned the child's world as a series of concentric circles in which the child is the center, encircled by the nuclear family, which is encircled by the mental health system, and so on. From this perspective it makes sense to assume that children will be most affected, at least during their early developmental stages, by the immediate family, which filters all information from surrounding systems (e.g., the community, culture).

Given that the mental health system in general may have little direct impact (or even contact) with the child, directing specific interventions toward the family system seems plausible and perhaps even desirable. Family therapists often are faced with a dilemma, however, because many families request help for one member whom they view as having individual problems that belong to that person and not to the family as a whole (Nichols & Everett, 1986). When the presenting problem is focused on a child who displays difficulties and disturbances of the kind referred to as symptomatic (e.g., depression, delinquency, school phobia), the family therapist must decide whether that child or other children should be invited to the initial session.

When Garbarino (1993) was asked the question "What do we need to know?" he answered, "It depends on what we want to do" (p. 9). Children referred for clinical services may be traumatized by their life events and have memory problems and distorted information. The family therapist has to be able to help children tell their story and must be sensitive to children's needs to construct a narrative of self and family experiences that meets their emotional needs and is consistent with their cognitive resources.

Families as systems strive to maintain balance or homeostasis. In this way an individual family member (many times the child) may be sacrificed or may sacrifice himself or herself to maintain the system's balance. For example, a child may engage in behaviors that he or she knows will elicit abuse to keep the father from abusing the mother, which may lead to dissolution of the family. The therapist's goal is to facilitate change in which a healthy family balance is maintained by eliminating abuse and developing effective communication patterns (Walker, Bonner & Kaufman, 1988).

Children typically are excluded from family therapy if the therapist deems that the child needs to be protected or if specific information may hurt the child (e.g., parental sexual relations, marital difficulties). Children also may be excluded from family therapy because the therapist has difficulty addressing adult and child modes of interacting at the same time (Chasin & White, 1989). In addition, children may be excluded from therapy if the counselor deems it theoretically inappropriate or determines that the key to the problem and its solution lie in the parental subsystem.

Recalling her experiences as a child playing musical chairs, Hoffman (1993) noted having feelings of exclusion (music is playing, children are having fun, the music stops, someone is kicked out of the game). Are we playing musical chairs with children in the family therapy process if we choose to exclude them from the process because we define them as symptom carriers and assert the belief of accentuating the parental hierarchy as having more importance than the child subsystem? Perhaps clinicians should be adding chairs to our family therapy game of musical chairs as Hoffman suggested, so each family members feels of equal value.

Patterson (1975) suggested that siblings of aggressive children should also be included in any treatment program. Children change their parents, just as parents contribute to changes in their children. In addition, Framo (1992) noted that when a family presents a child as the problem, he works with the whole family, or subgroups of the family, until the symptomatic child has been defocused and the symptoms either have disappeared or have been alleviated. Then, if the parents are motivated, Framo works on the marital relationship, as he views most children's symptoms as a metaphor for the parent's marriage. Framo stated that some of the parents who originally came to therapy out of concern for a child become interested in working out some of their own issues with the family of origin, particularly when the parents recognize that they are repeating with their own children their parents' patterns of parenting.

The primary issues of conducting family therapy with children seem to center on child or family development, psychopathology, and treatment orientation and its history of effectiveness with specific client issues (Combrinck-Graham, 1989). When viewing families, clinicians should reframe their thinking to one in which families are seen as relationship matrices and the primary unit of child development and, therefore, treatment (Chasin & White, 1989).

Issues of Development

The main issue to be addressed in family therapy with children centers on individual adult or child development needs and family development (Zilbach, 1989). Evaluating and understanding a behavior problem in a child as existing apart from the important relationships of his or her life is not possible (Allen, 1990). The child must be understood from the point at which he or she is in his or her own development and how the child is reacting to deal with this experience.

Child Development

To achieve healthy growth and development, we generally believe, children need a warm, loving, and stable home environment (Thompson & Rudolph, 1992). Social crises (e.g., unemployment, poverty, faltering educational systems, latchkey households) and changing value systems (e.g., gender role identities, sexual freedom) have challenged the stability of home environments for children. The high-risk child's better functioning seems to be associated, in part, with maternal warmth, a warm, active, and balanced family interaction, and healthy and benign parental attributions toward the child (Wynne, Jones, & Al-Khayyal, 1982). Morris ct al. (1988) found that fathers of aggressive boys reported eight times more negative thoughts about their child and more negative thoughts about their family than fathers of well behaved boys. "Healthy communication" on the part of parents is important in promoting healthy adjustment in children, particularly by providing children a model for developing the cognitive capacities of attending, focusing, remaining on task, and communicating ideas and feelings clearly and directly (Wynne et al., 1982).

In developing clinical interventions for children in the family context, individual techniques and family techniques and modes can be used conjointly. Several treatment goal areas are available to explore when counseling children (Gibson, Mitchell, & Basile, 1993). These goal areas include:

1. *Developmental*, assisting children to meet and advance their general human growth and development.

2. *Preventive*, helping children avoid some undesired outcome.

3. *Enhancement*, helping children to further develop or identify their special skills and abilities.

4. *Remedial*, overcoming or treating an undesirable development.

5. *Exploratory*, examining options, testing skills, and trying new and different activities.

6. *Reinforcement*, helping children recognize that what they are doing, thinking, and feeling is okay.

7. *Cognitive*, encouraging children to enjoy the learning process and its intrinsic rewards.

8. *Physiological*, helping children acquire the habits of good health.

9. *Psychological*, developing effective social interaction skills, learning to understand emotions, and developing a positive self-concept.

10. *Protective*, ensuring that children can experience the fun, joy, and happiness of being a child.

Young children tend to be trial-and-error learners, are egocentric, and use mental images and imagination, thinking in pictures. Prior to age 7, children also are typically capable of understanding simple rules but often see them as being unchangeable (Thompson & Rudolph, 1992). When counselors are working with preschool or early elementary school children, they should use short sentences in keeping with the length of a child's statements, should use names instead of pronouns, should use the child's terms and words, should ask the child to repeat your message instead of asking "do you understand?", should rephrase, not repeat, questions children do not understand, and should not respond to every answer with another question (Garbarino & Stott, 1989). Because preschoolers and other young children tend to be literal, the counselor should not overinterpret answers a child might give. Encouraging children to expand on their answers might be accomplished by providing short summaries or simply acknowledging the child's responses.

With children ages 5 and younger, the best therapeutic approach is to hold discussions in tandem with play activities, encourage them, tell or read stories that teach, and point out children's strengths to help them develop a sense of self-worth (Gibson, Mitchell, & Basile, 1993). When working with somewhat older children (e.g., ages 7–11 years), a different set of developmental issues arises. Children in this age group are much more active thinkers and are beginning to understand their feelings more fully. These children tend to have high energy levels, be more self-critical, lack self-confidence, and are not comfortable with being singled out for praise. They also are apt to be more social, are moving away from parents as the central focus of their lives to establishing peer group activities, typically are more verbal, and have greater capacities for concentration.

Whereas sessions with very young children should be limited to 20–25 minutes, sessions with pre-adolescent children can be 40–45 minutes long. As children get older, play activities in the counseling sessions become less useful and the traditional verbal approaches can be used more extensively. Pre-adolescent children should experience the feeling of being "understood," and activities such as values clarification, modeling, bibliotherapy, and focusing on more cognitively and affectively complex tasks are more appropriate.

With all children, the school environment becomes a primary system within which they interact. Therefore, the counselor should expect to hear complaints about teachers, principals, or other children. Pre-adolescent children in particular may be unintentionally rude, fidgety, talk quickly and in an animated fashion, and have a roaming memory. To deal with these issues in session, the family counselor should interject direct leads that focus upon the specific problem.

In sum, the task is to determine if the child is having experiences or behaving in ways that are consistent with their developmental stage. As a cautionary note, the family counselor should guard against the tendency to treat children as "little adults." Children typically have different interests, behaviors, and cognitive abilities than adults and should be treated as unique individuals with challenges specific to their development both in and outside the family system.

Family Development

The family life cycle at the time young children are present requires accepting the new generation of members into the system (McGoldrick & Carter, 1982). Second-order changes require adjusting the marital relationship to make space for children, taking on parenting roles, and realigning relationships with extended family to include parenting and grandparenting roles. This stage requires that adults now move up a generation and become caregivers to the younger generation.

When parents cannot make this shift, they may struggle with each other about taking responsibility or refuse to behave as parents to their children. Often parents are unable to set limits and exert the required authority, or they lack the patience to allow their children to express themselves as they develop. Family therapy might reframe the situation to help parents view themselves as part of a new generational level with specific responsibilities and tasks in relation to the next level of the family life cycle.

Changing family systems present the family therapist with a major challenge in addressing family development issues. An increase in teenage pregnancy and subsequent multigenerational family households, increasing divorce rates and consequent single-parent households, dual-career families and latchkey children, and the rising rate of children living in poverty all present the family therapist (and society) with difficult challenges and add to our confusion in attempting to understand the family life cycle.

Multigenerational families organize themselves in different ways (Chase-Lansdale, 1993). Young mothers may be the primary parents of their children, with grandmothers as supportive, background figures. On the other hand, grandmothers may be in charge of the family, with young mothers and grandchildren treated as siblings. Or co-parenting may occur, wherein mothers and grandmothers share childrearing and child care and coordinate parenting tasks.

Two-parent, two-earner families face two major challenges: marital discord and child care. The stress of maintaining the household and providing child care can place a strain on even the most highly functioning parent. Because of these multiple stressors, marital arguments, lack of time together, and faltering communication, the marital dyad is at high risk for dysfunction. These families need to find ways to divide tasks, set aside time for family meetings, develop times for shared activities as a couple, parent-child, and family, and maintain open lines of communication.

The growing divorce rate has presented the family system with a variety of problems, including poverty and unemployment, custodial versus noncustodial parenting, stepfamilies and stepparenting, and systems that place the child in a tug-of-war between the two parents. Some children living in poverty-related risk conditions do manage to develop in a healthy pattern (Chase-Lansdale, 1993). This resiliency seems to be embedded in the child's internal resources, such as an easy temperament, average or above-average intelligence, and sociability; a good relationship with at least one member of the family; and adequate social support outside the family. Chase-Lansdale argued that these children are not given enough credit for their abilities to make sense of their complex social world or how they derive strength from certain experiences and overcome multiple life stressors.

Noncustodial (usually father) parent research suggests that loss of access to the father has been associated with greater problems in children's adjustment to divorce, and loss of access to their children has been associated with more dissatisfaction and problems for fathers (Goldsmith, 1982). Active, continuing involvement between fathers and children has been linked to successful adaptation to other subsystems, such as the co-parental subsystem and the one-parent household. Involvement and engagement of the father are likely to be crucial when dealing with a two-parent family, whether that be a bioparent family or stepparent family, and in divorced families with noncustodial or joint-custodial fathers. The family therapist should always monitor the relationships between the various subsystems, their boundaries and relative power, and the manner in which the presenting problem is embedded within them (Goldsmith, 1982; Sager et al., 1983).

Cultural Relevancy

Using and developing culturally relevant interventions are important because most of the minority cultures in the United States share a primary emphasis on the importance of the family (Isaacs & Benjamin, 1991). In Native American, African-American, Hispanic-American, and Asian-American families the role of extended family members and support individuals (e.g., grandparents, friends, shamans, religious leaders) may be accentuated. These individuals within the social support or kinship network may have been delegated specific parenting functions within the family. In addition, strong family orientations typically override loyalty to other institutions and, consistent with the ecological perspective, the family and its cultural identity may play the primary role in determining objects of loyalty.

In the dominant American culture the family generally is conceptualized as the parents having ultimate authority over the child. In ethnic minority cultures families tend to be built around eldership, so even when parents are present, the ultimate authority may reside with a grandmother, an elder uncle, a tribal leader, or others the family recognizes as having the greatest wisdom and respect. A thorough understanding of the roles various family members play, as well as an articulation of the family values, especially as they relate to childrearing practices, are critical to the assessment process in determining family development issues and the direction of family therapy interventions.

With respect to their cultural styles, families can be classified on a traditionalism-modernism dimension (Ramirez, 1991). Modern lifestyles and belief systems encourage separation from family and community early in life. Modern orientations to socialization emphasize individual competition, and science is accorded great importance in explaining the mysteries of life. Traditional lifestyles, on the other hand, emphasize close ties to family and community throughout life. Traditional orientations stress cooperation and give spiritualism more importance in explaining life events. Clearly, cultural identity plays a significant role in determining family boundaries, values, beliefs, attitudes, and behaviors and, as such, should be assessed and incorporated directly into the family counseling process.

Psychopathology

Many children experience psychological distress and may receive a clinical diagnosis (Rapoport & Ismond, 1990). Perhaps the most common diagnostic category is that of disruptive behavior disorder (attention deficit hyperactivity, conduct, or oppositional defiance) (Horne & Sayger, 1990). Other diagnostic categories include anxiety disorders, depression, body function disorders such as enuresis and enco-presis, tic disorders, and personality disorders, to name a few. We do not attempt to discuss all of these disorders in this article but, rather, to simply touch on the role of family in the development of childhood psychopathology.

Combrinck-Graham (1989) has come to the conclusion that dysfunction in chil-dren may be understood more usefully as a part of patterns of family interaction and, in some cases, family interactions with larger systems. For Bowen (1985) pathology takes a multigenerational twist in which psychopathology results from each genera-tion's unsuccessful attempt to achieve differentiation. He discusses the conceptual-ization of schizophrenia as a three-generation development characterized by high levels of immaturity and intense early attachments to the mother.

If a child has a serious psychological problem, the parent becomes overinvested in the child, fails to achieve differentiation for self, and blocks the child's attempts at achieving differentiation (Sayger, 1992b). The Bowen systems family therapist focuses on an available family strength to achieve a more stable family structure and works toward helping the parent maintain a more definitive position in relating to the child.

The bottom line for family therapists who determine that the child referred for treatment has a pathology is to select the treatment regimen that has shown the most success in dealing with that issue. Often the family therapist works with children who are taking medication for a disorder by stressing adherence to the medical reg-imen, developing appropriate social or behavioral skills, and addressing the family's concern regarding the disorder or any one of a number of concerns with which the family and child are being confronted.

Treatment Orientation

Multiproblem families tend not to benefit from traditional mental health treatment, have multiple problems with several symptomatic members, and utilize foster place-ment and institutionalization at a higher rate than other families (Zarski & Fluharty, 1992). Therapists working with families at risk for child placement can help these families by positively reframing stressful events related to the child at risk and encouraging any efforts by the parents to learn alternative coping styles. Social class, poverty, and associated problems may contribute significantly to the presenting problems of families in treatment. Therapists should explore alternative models for the most effective matching of family to treatment. Matching is needed to ensure that the unique characteristics of children and families are taken into consideration prior to intervention (Zarski & Fluharty, 1992).

Weltner (1985) asserted that therapeutic style also has to be matched to the fam-ily need and identified four levels of family functioning:

Level I   Families dealing with life and death issues and ineffective parenting. By mobilizing support for the ineffective parenting system, the family is bet-ter able to deal with the life stresses at hand.

Level II   Families facing issues of establishing authority and setting limits. The parental system is unable to maintain sufficient control over family members, and this threatens the stability of the entire family. The family intervention should focus upon surveying family strengths and resources and developing a system coalition that is strong enough to offer sufficient authority.

Level III   Families with a structure and style that seems to be working and a mixture of coping mechanisms to which they are committed and attempt to pass on to their children. Working with these families involves changing ingrained patterns and dealing with the expected resistance to these changes.

Level IV   Families concerned with the fine art of living. Thoughts, feelings, and memories usually become the focus of clinical work. Interventions tend to have insight-oriented goals with more sensitive awareness of the world of relations and understanding of legacies and heritage. Psychoanalytic techniques, along with family sculptures or imaging, work best with these families.

Chasin and White (1989) offered the following criteria for conducting effective family therapy with children:

1. Use constructive family activities in therapy.

2. Assume that parents are in charge of the family, and encourage, not undermine, this role.

3. Stress clear structure for sessions, clear rules and expectations for addressing discipline and safety, and personal rights of individual participants.

Chasin and White also noted that children are more frequently excluded than included in family therapy even though including children makes them available to the therapist for direct intervention, and full understanding of the family cannot be achieved if some members are known only by hearsay.

Strategic Family Therapy

Strategic family therapies seem best suited to families that want symptom relief. This approach has had considerable success with families that have had negative experiences in counseling in the past and resist therapy because the focus is placed immediately on communication strategies and interactions. Because most strategic family therapies are brief, this form of counseling also has been accepted widely by the professional mental health community.

Strategic family therapists believe that families present symptoms that metaphorically represent some other problem. A mother's abuse of her son, for example, may be representative in part of the emotional and psychological neglect she experiences when her husband is drinking (Walker et al., 1988). Watzlawick, Weakland, and Fisch (1974) saw problems occurring from wrong attempts at changing ordinary difficulties. Segal (1982) described these "wrong" attempts as following one of four patterns:

1. Family members attempt to solve their problem by being "spontaneous deliberately." A scenario for "curing" insomnia might be to lie in bed until you fall asleep. This places the individual in a paradoxical trap by attempting to force a specific behavior. Substance abusers force themselves not to drink, and overeaters force themselves not to eat.

2. Family members attempt to find a "no-risk" solution when some risk is inevitable. In responding to a fear of failure or rejection, the child or parent tries too hard or gets "stuck" when trying to resolve the issue.

3. Family members attempt to achieve agreement through arguing. In attempting to discuss and share their feelings, children and their parents become overly sensitive and create problems where none exist.

4. A child or parent attempts to attract attention by attempting to be left alone. A parent, for example, might withdraw from a situation when he or she feels personally attacked or not respected.

When utilizing a strategic family therapy approach with families in which the child is the identified client, the therapist first attempts to determine who the child is protecting and in what way (Madanes, 1981). The therapy is planned in stages, and the therapist decides on an intervention that will change the family organization to one with a single hierarchy in which the parents have the superior position. Specific interventions usually are either straightforward or paradoxical directives to family members to do something in and out of the session with the goal of changing the interaction patterns of family members. The strategic family therapist makes no direct attempt to make family members aware of how communication takes place. If the problem can be resolved without the family's knowing how or why, that is satisfactory. As the client's problem increases in severity, however, knowledge of the rationale for change could be helpful in improving success and client satisfaction (Szykula, Sayger, Morris, & Sudweeks, 1987).

Madanes (1984) presented four paradoxical directives that seem most amenable to family therapy with children. Paradoxical interventions, or prescribing the symptom, encourages a person to perform the symptom, thus emphasizing that the symptomatic behavior is under the person's control.

In the first directive the counselor prescribes *pretending of the symptom*. In this scenario parents request their child to pretend to have the presenting problem. The parents then criticize the performance and make sure the pretending is accurate. Then, when the child presents the real problem, the parents are to behave as they usually do. For example, a child may be asked to pretend to have a temper tantrum while the parents evaluate the performance. Parents must be careful to evaluate in a caring and affectionate manner and avoid hostility. In most cases the therapist does not expect the performance to occur, and the family or child will realize that he or she does have control over the problem.

The second directive prescribes *a reversal in the family hierarchy*. Most problems are seen as stemming from incongruent hierarchies, usually the marital hierarchy, in which either the husband or the wife has more power with regard to intimacy, affection, or decision making. Two common extensions of imbalances in power are: (a) a child's behavior protecting the weaker parent by distracting the stronger parent from direct attacks; (b) the child's problem representing an arena for parental fighting that is less threatening than the parent's real dispute (e.g., fighting about a child's misbehavior rather than a parental lack of sexual intimacy).

Strategic interventions frequently involve rebalancing the marital hierarchy. For example, the parent with lesser power is placed in charge of implementing the directives and the parent with more power serves as expert consultant. Prescribing a reversal of the family hierarchy is a directive that puts the children in charge of the parents. This approach is appropriate when the parents present themselves as incompetent, helpless, and unable to take charge of their children, and at the same time complain that the children are out of control. This directive also can be used with children who are shy and withdrawn or rebellious. For example, children might be instructed to discuss what they would have their parents do if they were in charge of their parents' happiness. This technique is meant to tap in to the child's sense of humor and the natural caring between children and parents.

The third directive involves *asking parents to prescribe the presenting problem or the symbolic representation of the presenting problem*. Parents are asked to request that the child purposefully display the presenting problem. During the child's performance the parents supervise the child and see that he or she does it correctly. For a child with a fire-setting problem, the prescription is that the child is to set fires under the parents' supervision. Later, this behavior is to be replaced by the parents' and child's performing more constructive activities. Hypothetically, this paradoxical intervention addresses the part of the parent-child interaction in which the child helplessly persists in the disturbing behavior while the parents helplessly insist that it should end but are unable to stop it.

The fourth directive entails *prescribing who will have the presenting problem*. In essence, this directive consists of prescribing the symptom but changing who will have it. Strategic family therapists might employ this intervention with more severe problems, such as delinquency, depression, drug or alcohol use, antisocial behavior, or bizarre communication. The underlying hypothesis for this technique is that the presenting problem is distracting the family from conflict with a family member in a way that is benevolent and prevents resolution of the original conflict. For example, an acting-out child might be the family problem for a depressed father in that the antisocial behavior takes the family's focus away from the father's problem. Consequently, by asking another family member to be the "family problem," family members are expected to rebel against this task and progress to a discussion of the "real" family problem.

Sayger (1992b) reviewed two other techniques associated with strategic family therapy:

■ *Benevolent sabotage.* In this technique the counselor tells the child or parent to "go slow" or warns of impending danger if improvement occurs, thus emphasizing the consequences of behavior. Examples of benevolent sabotage are parents' apologizing for the consequences that occur "accidentally" to the child (e.g., not being able to find a favorite shirt after the parent cleans the child's room, being locked out after curfew).

■ *Reframing.* To attempt to change the conceptual or emotional tone of a situation, the counselor suggests a different frame of reference. For example, a child who is demanding of his or her parent's attention may be seen as an irritating, bothersome brat. A strategic reframe might suggest that the child values the parent's attention so highly that he or she is willing to go to extreme lengths to obtain it. Consequently, the parent's frame of reference changes from one of irritation and disgust to one of expression of respect and love.

In presenting a case of a child experiencing night terrors, Madanes (1981) reported that the initial session was directed at obtaining information on the specific scenario of night terrors (e.g., family history, sleep patterns, antecedent events). During session the child was instructed to demonstrate the night terror and the mother was asked to think of causes of the behavior. In this instance the child's night terrors centered on a burglar who was harming the mother. The strategic therapist envisioned the purpose of the night terrors as the child's attempt to protect the mother from the burglar because the mother, hearing her child's cries, would awaken and go to the child's room. In the rest of the treatment scenario, family members were to pretend the symptom every evening, the mother would wake up the child and all other family members, and a sibling kept notes on each family member's performance. Finally, the therapist attempted to strengthen the relationship between the child and the mother's live-in partner and conducted an individual session with the child to change the "night terror burglar" to a more positive vision. The treatment ended when the child began to be involved more actively with other children and the night terrors ceased.

Structural Family Therapy

Rather than focusing on power, structural family therapists emphasize structural aspects of the family (Minuchin, 1974). They interest themselves with intergenerational boundaries and with the formation of alliances and coalitions. Structural therapists believe that difficulties are most likely to arise during critical points in the life cycle. Structural family therapy seems most suited to families that are disorganized, authoritarian, and unmotivated (Sayger, 1992b).

Structural therapy has its roots in crisis intervention and treatment of chronically dysfunctional, inner-city, delinquent, and psychotic families. During critical stages of development, parents who have established nurturing patterns must modify those patterns and develop appropriate methods of maintaining control while encouraging growth during this cycle of family life (Minuchin & Fishman, 1981). New patterns must be explored and stabilized in all family subsystems (e.g., parent-child, sibling, couple, individual), and when children go off to school, for example, the family must learn to relate to a new, well organized, highly significant system. As children grow and learn that their friends' families operate by different, and usually more fair (at least according to the child), rules, the family has to negotiate adjustments, changing some rules and developing new boundaries between parents and children.

Dysfunctional patterns arise most often when generational boundaries are unclear or absent. The classic dysfunctional family structure is *enmeshed* (over-involved) at one end of the spectrum and *disengaged* (uninvolved) at the other. Dysfunction or underfunction, exists when families experiencing stress increase the rigidity of their interactional patterns and boundaries and resist exploring alternative actions. The unit of intervention for the structural family therapist is the family subsystem. Therapy begins with construction of a family map that describes the family structure in terms of its subsystems, the family hierarchy or organization, family relationships and their boundaries, and the family's transactional processes (e.g., coalitions, detouring). The goal of therapy is to unbalance the family members so a new, more adaptive family organization can be achieved. Healthy family functioning is attained when the family demonstrates an ability to adapt to both internal and external stressors.

In the case of physical abuse (Walker et al., 1988), a structural explanation for its occurrence in a family might highlight disengagement of the father and enmeshment of the mother and child. Furthermore, it might be suggested that the mother covertly precipitates the child's acting out, which necessitates the father's presence at home to discipline the child, thereby increasing the father's involvement in the family but also angering the father and increasing the probability of abuse. Structural family therapists attempt to elicit, during a session, a behavior as close as possible to the problem behavior. In this way the therapist has a first-hand opportunity to observe the process of family interaction around this issue. An attempt then should be made to facilitate change in the family's structure. The therapist might either reframe a crucial element of the process or direct family members to respond in a different way. For example, reframing the child's behavior as helpful in keeping the father involved in the family may pave the way to asking the father to suggest more appropriate ways that the child can continue to involve him.

Behavioral/Cognitive/Social Learning Family Therapy

Behavioral/cognitive therapists believe that family dysfunction can be related to some combination of an individual's behaviors, thoughts, and feelings and the environment's response. Behavioral family therapists assume that family dysfunction develops through erosion of positive reinforcement control and is maintained by reciprocal aversive control. Families are viewed as systems of interbehaving people, and a child's behavior is reinforced and maintained by environmental factors.

According to Horne (1991), behavioral family therapy is a systematic method of assessing family interactions, developing intervention strategies, and evaluating change. Behavioral family therapy emphasizes the functional analysis of behavior and, as such, develops highly specific and empirically based treatment methods (Sayger, Horne, & Glaser, 1993). This analysis includes observing behavior, obtaining a baseline assessment of rate and frequency of behaviors, identifying consequences, and altering consequences to change the behavior. According to behavioral family therapists, humans attempt to maximize the pleasurable consequences of their behavior while minimizing the aversive consequences (Horne & Sayger, 1990). As the ratio of costs to benefits increases in a relationship, the more likely is the occurrence of dysfunction.

Family dysfunction is seen as an interpersonal phenomenon resulting from coercive or reciprocal relationships. When family relationships are maintained and controlled through aversive, negatively reinforcing reactions, the relationship is deemed coercive. In situations in which family members maintain their relationships through equitable and mutual positive reinforcement, the relationship is deemed reciprocal (Patterson, 1982). Deviant behavior, therefore, is seen not as crazy, illogical, or dysfunctional but, rather, as an appropriate response to the contingencies in that system. Conceptualization and treatment are focused in the here-and-now as the problem is redefined in interactional-systemic terms, complete with an understanding of the antecedents and consequences of behavior as well as the circularity of the antecedents and consequences for maintaining the dysfunctional system (Horne & Sayger, 1990).

Believing that all family members are doing the best they can, given their circumstances and previous learning experiences, the behavioral family therapist attempts to construct a therapeutic environment in which family members feel safe and comfortable in discussing their concerns (Fleischman, Horne, & Arthur, 1983). Based upon the premise that interpersonal problems often arise from faulty or inadequate learning, the behavioral family therapist accentuates skills training procedures to prevent and solve family problems. Skills taught in therapy include communication, problem solving, negotiation, parenting and child management, self-control, and relationship enrichment.

Sayger (1992a, pp. 16, 36) suggested the following component for treating families with conduct problem children:

A. Prepare the family for a successful outcome.

    1. Set specific, realistic, and achievable goals.

    2. Communicate your belief that the family can change and successfully resolve its problems.

    3. Assess and implement strategies to alter environmental barriers to the client's success.

4. Focus on and accentuate the family's strengths and positive qualities.

5. Elicit cooperation of school personnel and/or social service agency workers.

B. Help family members gain control of their life situation by instituting and teaching strategies to help parents and children repudiate self-defeating thoughts.

C. Identify primary behavioral problems and instruct parents in remedial strategies of discipline (e.g. time-out, loss of privileges, Premack principle).

D. Instruct family members in effective strategies of communication to establish and maintain effective family interactions.

1. Check for the family's level of mastery over new skills.

2. Generalize newly learned skills to other problem areas/settings.

3. Schedule booster sessions to review and assess the family's continued use of effective problem-solving strategies.

A behavioral conceptualization of physical abuse might include identification of skill deficits (e.g., child management skills or communication skills between the couple), unrealistic developmental expectations, feelings (e.g., anxiety), and difficulties in response to environmental stressors (e.g., child-care demands, financial stress). The process of therapy includes modifying behavior or cognition, or both, to facilitate change, prompting further behavioral change to enhance social interaction and facilitating cognitive integration of the true meaning of these changes to ensure that the changes are maintained (Walker et al., 1988).

Behavioral approaches have been demonstrated to be effective in treating a broad range of problems including sexual dysfunction, somaticism, phobias, depression, marital conflict, and child conduct (Sayger, 1992b). Behavioral family therapy's strong adherence to scientific methods and evaluation makes it the most researched approach to family therapy. Because it emphasizes a systematic, structured, assessment-based approach to treatment, it lends itself to both outcome and process research. Behavioral family therapy is the treatment of choice for child conduct problems (Olson, Russell, & Sprenkle, 1980). A combination of family therapy and cognitive therapy may be the most effective approach for working with eating disorders (Weltner, 1985).

Object Relations Family Therapy

Object relations theorists believe that humans have a fundamental drive to be in a relationship. Conducting family therapy from this perspective emphasizes the assessment of developmental levels, defense and anxiety, and transference and countertransference. Common therapeutic strategies include sequencing individual and couples therapies with family therapy and incorporating play with childrearing families. At birth, the child seeks to form an attachment with the mother and becomes vulnerable to her responses. The child's attitudes toward family members and eventually others is determined largely by the gratification or frustration of these needs.

Unhappiness and dysfunction are seen as rooted primarily in the past, existing unconsciously, and operative in both the client's intrapersonal and interpersonal world.

Therapy begins by developing a caring environment in which family members can feel safe and make themselves "known" to the therapist (Luepnitz, 1988). Therapy attempts to help family members understand each other better and open up choices to the family that allow them to be less disconnected from their family context. The process of "remembering" aims to enable family members to review and reexperience what is troublesome, to bring repressed material into consciousness, explore feelings and attitudes, and break up dysfunctional patterns of intrapsychic reacting and interpersonal interacting (Luepnitz, 1988; Scharff & Scharff, 1987). Change, therefore, is achieved via analysis and a process of confrontation, clarification, interpretation, and working through.

People with interpersonal problems are holding onto expectations consistent with childhood (Skynner, 1976). The immediate goal of object relations family therapy is not to resolve the problem but, rather, to progress through the current developmental phase of the family with an improved ability to work together, self-differentiate, and meet the individual needs of its members. As growth occurs, the goals of family therapy from this perspective change. The goal of treatment for individual family members is individuation and ego integration. From the interpersonal perspective the aim is to enable family members to interact as whole persons on the basis of current realities. Once each family member achieves a heightened level of individuation, individuals will be better equipped to make important choices (e.g., mate selection, vocation) based on reality, consciousness, and needs versus unmet, unconscious childhood deficiency needs.

In practice, infants, toddlers, and play-age children are included in treatment so that their contribution to the family system can be observed. Excluding children from the therapeutic process can lead to invalid perceptions of family dynamics, and difficulties in children cannot be detected early if all family members are not seen. Including children in treatment completes the whole picture of the family that is essential to analysis (Scharff & Scharff, 1987). Typically, children between ages 3 and 10 do not seem to understand family defenses and frequently blurt out family "secrets." Similarly, the impact of parental arguments regarding the child is readily visible by watching the child's response. In addition, object relations family therapists frequently utilize play interventions to access the child's internal world, in which play is seen as a normal, age-appropriate way for children to deal with anxiety. In clinical situations play also can serve as a way for the child to feel more comfortable.

Scharff and Scharff (1987) presented a case of a predelinquent, 11-year-old, adopted boy and his family. The child was characterized as argumentative, stated that he hated his family, and was particularly upset with his father and the family's religious orientation. During sessions the child drew violent pictures, many of which depicted deaths and murders of family members, and he played "smuggling" games. The therapist noted that the family members were discussing angry feelings while the child was making his drawings. Using the child's drawings as an intervention strategy, the therapist discussed how the family drawings represented how family members felt they were being treated by each other. This intervention resulted in the family's gaining insight into its family system and becoming gentler and kinder in interactions with one another. The child, likewise, gave up his aggressive tendencies and came to feel a part of a more caring and nurturing family system.

Because object relations family therapy focuses on personal and spiritual growth (Weltner, 1985), it is well suited to families who can tolerate its slower pace, higher cost, and lack of powerful shaping interventions on the therapist's part. This therapeutic approach is geared much more toward creating a deep and warm experience of human contact than toward removing symptoms. Therefore, object relations therapy may best be matched with families at Level IV (Weltner, 1985).

Integrated Family Therapy

Assessment in integrated family therapy should attempt to understand the individual child, other family members, and their reciprocal interactions (Kaslow & Racusin, 1990). The focus is on the psychological symptomatology and functioning of each family member across cognitive, affective, interpersonal, adaptive behavior, and family domains. Incorporating a developmental perspective, integrationist family therapists strive to understand family functioning in the context of normative expectations for the individual's and the family's stage of development.

Depressive symptomatology in the child may be understood as a reflection of family dysfunction. In some families with a depressed child, the child experiencing sadness, helplessness, and low self-esteem attempts to elicit nurturant caregiving and relief from other family members, who, because of their own depression and low self-esteem and the negative moods the child's depression induces in them, often can provide only a form of caregiving characterized by alternating overprotection and rejection. Because it fails to address the child's needs, this form of caregiving reinforces the child's depression, which further engenders a sense of inadequacy in the other family members, who in turn may become more critical, hostile, or withdrawn and thus sustain the cycle of depression in the family.

In other families with depressed children, parents exhibit ambivalence over a child's achievement born out of their own narcissistic needs to keep the child dependent. The parents in these families express mixed expectations for success and failure but actually may provide concrete reinforcement only for the child's failure to achieve. Interventions address the needs of all family members by helping them to identify these problematic patterns and their origins and by facilitating the development of alternative interactional patterns leading out of the depressive cycle. Kaslow and Racusin (1990) see the field of family psychology as consolidating its movement toward an integrationist perspective, drawing more fully upon contributions from object relations theory, family systems theory, cognitive-behavioral psychology, developmental psychopathology, and biological psychiatry.

Play Therapy

Incorporating play therapy into family therapy approaches has been done with varying levels of success. In part, professionals providing family therapy services may have no formal training in child development, child therapy, or specific play therapy concepts. Our training programs seem to have placed a much greater emphasis on adult development and the marital/parental system than on understanding children. In this chapter we have attempted to provide some of this developmental information as it relates to conducting family therapy with children. In addition, many professionals simply do not have the space or funds to develop and furnish a play room.

Chasin and White (1989) identified three categories of play activities that they suggest incorporating into family therapy with young children. Play interventions can be defined on three continua: (a) involved-distanced; (b) directed-nondirected; and (c) imaginative-factual.

1. *Involved play* incorporates child role plays or puppets and requires other family members to become actively engaged in the play activity. Typically this mode of play therapy results in a high level of energy and works well with families because adults and children alike can communicate through actions instead of talk.

2. *Distanced play* involves the child playing with objects (e.g., drawing materials, dolls, clay) in the presence or absence of family members, but not actively involving their participation.

3. *Directed play* requires the child to draw a picture of some specific person or thing or to enact a given scene or play a given role. For example, you have just broken one of your mother's favorite lamps and are sitting at the dinner table. You play yourself and your brother is Mom. What would happen?

4. *Nondirected play* is characterized by giving the child drawing materials or a box of play materials and instructing him or her to draw whatever he or she pleases.

5. *Factual play* involves the documentation of actions and feelings of real people as they are now or realistically could be in the future ("Sally, you be your daughter, and John, you be the doctor. Show us what will happen at her check-up next week").

6. *Imaginative play* is exemplified by free drawing while the adults converse. Through these drawings children might express their concerns about the family that otherwise might not be expressed.

Clearly, involved, directed, and factual play provide access to more specific events and processes that the child and other family members experience. In contrast, distanced, nondirected, and imaginative play allow children to create their own structure and call for interpretation of intrapsychic phenomena. Depending upon the clinician's orientation, each form of play therapy can provide useful and insightful information about families and the children in them.

Parting Comments

Depending upon the needs of the family and the child, the therapist must decide whether to include or exclude the child. If the child is to be included, decisions have to be made as to what has to be done. When asked what we do with children in family therapy, we quote Garbarino (1993): "It depends." It depends upon whether the child is the identified patient. It depends on one's theoretical orientation. It depends on the appropriate training and knowledge to work with children. It depends on space and funds to furnish a play room. It depends on the treatment of choice for the client concern. It depends on professional commitment to provide the most effective treatment possible for encouraging client growth and happiness.

References

Allen, F. H. (1990). Participation in therapy. In C. Schaefer (Ed.), *The therapeutic use of child's play* (pp. 535–542). Northvale, NJ: Jason Aronson.

Bowen, M. (1985). *Family therapy in clinical practice*. Northvale, NJ: Jason Aronson.

Chase-Lansdale, P. L. (1993). The impact of poverty on family processes. *Child, Youth & Family Services Quarterly, 16*, 5–8.

Chasin, R., & White, T. B. (1989). The child in family therapy: Guidelines for active engagement across the age span. In L. Combrinck-Graham (Ed.), *Children in family contexts: Perspectives on treatment* (pp. 5–25). New York: Guilford Press.

Combrinck-Graham, L. (Ed.). (1989). *Children in family contexts: Perspectives on treatment*. New York: Guilford Press.

Fleischman, M. J., Horne, A. M., & Arthur, J. L. (1983). *Troubled families: A treatment approach*. Champaign, IL: Research Press.

Framo, J. L. (1992). *Family-of origin therapy: An intergenerational approach*. New York: Brunner/Mazel.

Garbarino, J. (1993). Childhood: What do we need to know? *Childhood: A Global Journal of Child Research, 1*, 1–10.

Garbarino, J., & Stott, R. (1989). *What children can tell us*. San Francisco: Jossey-Bass.

Gibson, R. L., Mitchell, M. H., & Basile, S. K. (1993). *Counseling children in the elementary school: A comprehensive approach*. Boston: Allyn & Bacon.

Goldsmith, J. (1982). The postdivorce family system. In F. Walsh (Ed.), *Normal family processes* (pp. 297–330). New York: Guilford Press.

Henggeler, S. W., & Borduin, C. M. (1990). *Family therapy and beyond: A multisystemic approach to treating the behavior problems of children and adolescents*. Pacific Grove, CA: Brooks/Cole.

Hoffman, J. (1993). Musical chairs. *Simi Valley Church of Religious Science Newsletter,* September/October, p. 4.

Horne, A. M. (1991). Social learning family therapy. In A. M. Horne & J. L. Passmore (Eds.), *Family counseling and therapy* (2nd ed., pp. 463–496). Itasca, IL: F. E. Peacock.

Horne, A. M., & Sayger, T. V. (1990). *Treating conduct and oppositional defiant disorders in children*. New York: Pergamon Press.

Isaacs, M. R., & Benjamin, M. P. (1991). *Towards a culturally competent system of care: Volume 2. Programs which utilize culturally competent principles*. Washington, DC: CASSP Technical Assistance Center, Georgetown University Child Development Center.

Johnson, H. C. (1993). Family issues and interventions. In H. C. Johnson (Ed.), *Child mental health in the 1990s: Curricula for graduate and undergraduate professional education*. Washington, DC: U. S. Department of Health and Human Services, Center for Mental Health Services.

Kaslow, N. J., & Racusin, G. R. (1990). Depressed children and their families: An integrationist approach. In F. W. Kaslow (Ed.), *Voices in family psychology* (Vol. 2., pp. 194–216). Newbury Park, CA: Sage.

Luepnitz, D. A. (1988). *The family interpreted: Feminist theory in clinical practice*. New York: Basic Books.

Madanes, C. (1981). *Strategic family therapy*. San Francisco: Jossey-Bass.

Madanes, C. (1984). *Behind the one-way mirror: Advances in the practice of strategic therapy*. San Francisco: Jossey-Bass.

McGoldrick, M., & Carter, E. A. (1982). The family life cycle. In F. Walsh (Ed.), *Normal family processes* (pp. 167–195). New York: Guilford Press.

Minuchin, S. (1974). *Families and family therapy*. Cambridge, MA: Harvard University Press.

Minuchin, S., & Fishman, H. C. (1981). *Family therapy techniques*. Cambridge, MA: Harvard University Press.

Morris, P. W., Horne, A. M., Jessell, J. C., Passmore, J. L., Walker, J. M., & Sayger, T. V. (1988). Behavioral and cognitive characteristics of fathers of aggressive and well-behaved boys. *Journal of Cognitive Psychotherapy: An International Quarterly, 2*, 251–265.

Nichols, W. C., & Everett, C. A. (1986). *Systemic family therapy: An integrative approach*. New York: Guilford Press.

Olson, D. H., Russell, C. S., & Sprenkle, D. H. (1980). Marital and family therapy: A decade review. *Journal of Marriage & the Family, 42*, 973–993.

Patterson, G. R. (1975). *Families: Applications of social learning to family life*. Champaign, IL: Research Press.

Patterson, G. R. (1982). *Coercive family process*. Eugene, OR: Castalia.

Ramirez, M., III. (1991). *Psychotherapy and counseling with minorities: A cognitive approach to individual and cultural differences*. New York: Pergamon Press.

Rapoport, J. L., & Ismond, D. R. (1990). *DSM–III–R training guide for diagnosis of childhood disorders*. New York: Brunner/Mazel.

Sager, C. J., Brown, H. S., Crohn, H., Engel, T., Rodstein, E., & Walker, L. (1983). *Treating the remarried family*. New York: Brunner/Mazel.

Sayger, T. V. (1992a). Children with conduct disorders and their families: Discovering the sources for change. *Family Psychologist, 8*, 16, 36.

Sayger, T. V. (1992b). Family psychology and therapy. In C. E. Walker & M. C. Roberts (Eds.), *Handbook of clinical child psychology* (2nd ed., pp. 783–807). New York: John Wiley & Sons.

Sayger, T. V., Horne, A. M., & Glaser, B. A. (1993). Marital satisfaction and social learning family therapy for child conduct problems: Generalization of treatment effects. *Journal of Marital & Family Therapy, 19*, 393–402.

Scharff, D. E., & Scharff, J. S. (1987). *Object relations family therapy*. Northvale, NJ: Jason Aronson.

Segal, L. (1982). Brief family therapy. In A. M. Horne & M. M. Ohlsen (Eds.), *Family counseling and therapy* (pp. 276–301). Itasca, IL: F. E. Peacock.

Skynner, A. C. R. (1976). *Systems of family and marital psychotherapy*. New York: Brunner/Mazel.

Szykula, S. A. (1989). Child-focused paradoxical psychotherapy: Reframing the behavioral picture for therapeutic change. In L. M. Ascher (Ed.), *Therapeutic paradox* (pp. 340–377). New York: Guilford Press.

Szykula, S. A., Sayger, T. V., Morris, S. B., & Sudweeks, C. (1987). Child-focused behavior and strategic therapies: Outcome comparisons. *Psychotherapy, 24S,* 546–551.

Thompson, C. L, & Rudolph, L. B. (1992). *Counseling children.* Pacific Grove, CA: Brooks/Cole.

Walker, C. E., Bonner, B. L., & Kaufman, K. L. (1988). *The physically and sexually abused child: Evaluation and treatment.* New York: Pergamon Press.

Watzlawick, P., Weakland, J., & Fisch, R. (1974). *Change: Principles of problem formation and problem resolution.* New York: Norton.

Weltner, J. (1985). Matchmaking: Choosing the appropriate therapy for families at various levels of pathology. In M. P. Mirkin & S. L. Koman (Eds.), *Handbook of adolescents and family therapy* (pp. 39–53). New York: Gardner Press.

Wynne, L. C., Jones, J. E., & Al-Khayyal, M. (1982). Healthy family communication patterns: Observations in families "at risk" for psychopathology. In F. Walsh (Ed.), *Normal family processes* (pp. 142–164). New York: Guilford Press.

Zarski, J. J., & Fluharty, L. B. (1992). Treating emotionally disturbed youth: A comparison of home-based and outpatient interventions. *Contemporary Family Therapy: An International Journal, 14,* 335–350.

Zilbach, J. J. (1989). The family life cycle: A framework for understanding children in family therapy. In L. Combrinck-Graham (Ed.), *Children in family contexts: Perspectives on treatment* (pp. 46–66). New York: Guilford Press.

The Future of Families: New Challenges for Couples and Family Therapy

Jon Carlson and Len Sperry

Prologue

As I ponder how to begin an essay on the future of families, a temptation arises to describe my own Midwestern upbringing. It hopefully will provide a point of reference for what is to follow.

My family was an American one with a mom and a dad and four children, two boys and two girls (of course). My parents were of the hard-working, rags-to-riches type. Dad worked, and Mom stayed home and raised the family in our segregated suburb. We took vacations, had a summer house and a boat, were involved in church, sports, and music, and were among the first families to own a TV. This seemed to be the way things were supposed to be. We learned the rules and developed expectations for what our future families would be like.

Here is my family today: My brother was treated for alcoholism, one sister was divorced after 25 years in an abusive marriage, and the other sister has refused to speak to any member of the family for more than 15 years. My children and the children of my siblings are mostly grown now and have families of their own. They have experienced things such as divorce, treatment for cocaine use, home-schooling, life in a fundamental religious commune, foreign adoption, cohabitation, death from AIDS, juvenile diabetes, and unemployment. It's amazing how what is "normal "has changed.

—Jon Carlson

■ ■ ■

Counseling and therapy with couples and families always has been a challenge, and the future promises more of the same. Presently, marriage and family therapists are treating marital conflict, conduct disorders of children and teens, anorexia and bulimia, depression, sexual dysfunction, schizophrenia, drug addiction, personality disorders, and other problems. The question, "Is marital and family therapy effective?" has been replaced by, "Just how pervasive is the effect of the family upon our life? What other mental, physical, and behavioral challenges can be treated successfully?" This charter issue of *Family Counseling and Therapy* explores the future family landscape. Family counseling likely will be an occupation in high demand in the year 2010 (Maushard, 1990).

Trends

Family structure and composition have been changing for years. At the same time, marriage and family therapy has not responded with changed paradigms or interventions. Treatment is based largely on the concept of the traditional nuclear family. This is an institution that is now an ever declining minority. The new reality of family life is the topic of discussion here.

Status of Women

Even the traditional family unit has seen fundamental changes. Not long ago, husbands brought home the bacon and wives cooked it. Today, only 22% of married-couple households contain a male breadwinner and a female homemaker, a dramatic decline from 61% in 1960. A new division of labor has taken place, reinforced by the closing gap between men's and women's earnings (Riche, 1991, p. 44).

Women have entered the workforce because the family needs additional income or women are the only support for their families. It is hoped that the status of women will continue to improve through policy development and that this will lead to an improved quality in family life. If this increase in status, however, results in a decline in men's status, it will lay the groundwork for future conflict.

Status of Children

Today's children are living a childhood of firsts. They are the first daycare generation; the first truly multicultural generation; the first generation to grow up in the electronic bubble, the environment defined by computers and new forms of television; the first post-sexual revolution generation; the first generation for which nature is more abstraction than reality; the first generation to grow up in new kinds of dispersed deconcentrated cities, not quite urban, rural, or suburban. The combination of these forces has produced a dynamic process. Childhood today is defined by the expansion of experience and the contraction of positive adult contact (Louv, 1990, p. 5).

As a result of this situation, children and adults tend to pass one another with little contact, creating loneliness for both. Despite this reality, more young adults are remaining with their parents longer. In 1960, 43% of 20- to 24-year-olds were living with their parents, and by 1988, 55% were (Glick, 1990).

Family Violence

> Over 6 million children and 3 million spouses are severely assaulted each year. Physical abuse is a major threat to American families. Those who are not physically injured are often injured psychologically. How can families be the most loving and supportive social institution and also the most violent? (Straus, 1990, p. 26)

Abuse is demoralizing and undermines self-esteem, leading to basic distrust of other people. It often is at the root of divorce and is manifested in children's running away and becoming involved in drugs, prostitution, and crime. It is encouraging to note that both child abuse and spouse abuse are decreasing. This is largely a result of programs such as shelters for battered women, treatment programs for abusing parents, and enforcement of national and statewide policies. It often has been implied that male dominance is the fundamental cause of abuse, especially spouse abuse. Laws clearly may stop physical abuse. Psychological abuse, however, may continue until national policies on equality are accepted. The causes of family violence, not just the casualties, have to be addressed (Keen, 1992).

Substance Abuse

Drug use and addiction permeate American life. Although this is not a policy, it seems to be accepted, as many Americans are addicted to what are called "soft" or legal drugs. Alcohol, drugs, and nicotine continue to create major health problems among the young. Research shows that life expectancy continues to rise except for young Americans, and these deaths often are related to substance abuse. When we look at the high percentages of usage among young adults, the potential for continued substance abuse seems great. The implications are great, as things such as crime rate and violence often are related to substance abuse.

Many experts believe an all-out war against the abuse of drugs is necessary to stop the current drug and alcohol epidemic. Although some changes certainly have occurred, a solution seems to be far away. The family component in drug abuse is now becoming better understood, as researchers are interpreting and debating how drug abuse may be related to certain family types and how it is being passed from one generation to another. Today's buzzword "co-dependency" is a positive sign that the broader impact of substance use is better understood (Bradshaw, 1988; Lawson & Lawson, 1991; Stanton & Todd, 1982; Steinglass, 1987).

More Blended and Stepfamilies

Families today consist of nuclear families, singlehood, nonmarital heterosexual and homosexual cohabitation, single-parent families, remarried and stepfamilies, foster and adoptive families, childless families, nonsecretive extramarital relationships, and multi-adult households. The expanding diversity of family forms implies that more individuals will experience family change over their life cycle than in previous generations. These diverse family forms will become more prevalent, emphasizing individual needs and choices. A wide variety of marriages with and without children will form American households of the future. Race, class, and gender will remain important variables in predicting the frequency of the various family forms. Counselors and therapists must learn to recognize the complexity and variety of family forms as divorce, remarriage, and stepfamily relationships tend to create emotion-laden experiences and legal dilemmas for the immediate and extended family members alike (Zinn & Eitzen, 1987).

Remarriage forms a different kind of marriage system, one in which children live with one biological parent and stepparent, or divide their family life between a maternal home and a paternal home. Yet we hold on to a traditional concept of the "normal" family—the intact "Dick and Jane" with both parents and their biological children living together. The model that we learned for first marriages and family life does not apply to second marriages and their families.

Nonbiological (Chosen) Families

Along with the previous trend, nonbiological families will be seen in the large number of people who claim families (i.e., chosen families) other than their biological roots as their home. This has prompted some to consider defining "family" by the frequency of interactions rather than on a genetic basis. A company now in Tokyo, called Japan Efficiency, specializes in renting out "families" to elderly citizens who have no offspring or whose own families are unable to visit them. One afternoon of "human warmth" with pretend kin—a son, daughter-in-law, and grandchild—sets grandma and grandpa back about $350 (Blackwell, Blackwell, Guccione, & Kohut, 1992).

Multicultural Factors

Models of marital quality and healthy family life will have to involve new awareness that incorporates ideas from an increasingly diverse culture. More single life, divorce, and stepparent families will be characteristic of Blacks and Hispanics. Lower-class families will have high divorce rates. Women will more often be single parents. In the 21st century the United States will emerge as a nation with greater ethnic diversity; a projected distribution of 33% of the population will be people of color. The highest concentration of ethnic families will be of Hispanic origin, followed by Blacks, Asians, and Native Americans (McCubbin, 1990).

Further research will be needed on resilient families among ethnic groups, the impact of social policy and programs upon cultural and ethnic values, health and mental health of ethnic families, the role of ethnic communal ties in family preservation and survival, and processes of family adaptation to social change in ethnic families. For example, Hispanics and Asians tend to have larger, more extended families living together than do other Americans, but they will be subject to the same longterm economic forces, and these forces tend to mean that the family will continue to change.

Family Size

Women today bear an average of fewer than two children, compared to nearly three in 1965. Married couples with children are still declining as the share of all households. As people learn that they can support themselves and their children, they will have less need to depend on one another. As this economic evolution replaces communal values with individual ones, the family lifespan shortens, and people will have even fewer children.

Research shows that, with increasing education, women have fewer children, and a gap is widening between families in which the mother has less education and more children and families in which the mother has more education but fewer children. Unless policy tends to affect this, these trends will polarize tomorrow's families both economically and psychologically. A minority will grow up in small families with economic and educational advantages, but their parents will spend more money on them than time with them. Many young adults will come from larger families with potentially attentive mothers, but they will have fewer educational and economic opportunities.

Career-Driven Marriage

Demographic studies reveal that work is the major focus of most individuals' lives and that love and friendship needs are more likely to be met in the job environment than anywhere else (Sperry & Carlson, 1991b). Although the idea of a two-paycheck couple is not new, the idea of a dual-career couple is. The "career" designation indicates the partners' pursuit of a goal-directed work choice. This change leaves women torn between traditional roles and the desire to earn, and often necessity of earning, a wage. Only with the recent appearance of a compassionate marriage model have we been able to imagine relationships wherein each partner can have goals of equal importance. Overwork and overload are common complaints in most relationships, and these phenomena are compounded in the dual-career couple. The greater burden seems to fall on the wife because of her traditional role in addition to her career role (Goldenberg & Goldenberg, 1984).

Counselors have to understand the new social context in which people are living, and those who do not will miss the ability and opportunity to intervene effectively. Other challenging variations of the career-driven couple are the commuting couple, the military couple, the executive couple, and the family business couple (Sperry & Carlson, 1991b).

Men's Roles Must Change

Although the fact that men's role must be changed seems obvious, it is often over-looked. The recent popularity of the books *Fire in the Belly* and *Iron John* highlight the interest in the "new" masculinity. Men can no longer be the "strong, silent providers" but must instead learn to be more balanced and capable of a full range of emotions. Pittman (1985) talks about the complex process in which gender roles are learned. He provides a clear discussion of just how difficult it is to degenderize people.

> Men, even at their most villainous are usually just trying to be masculine, and never feel masculine enough. So at every crisis point, they just try to act more masculine. (p. 32)

As men become more and more powerless in their own lives, they are given more and more media images of excessive, caricatured masculinity with which to identify. This disparity between their real lives and the macho images of masculinity perpetrated by the media confuses and confounds many men. Gender role stereotypes seem to pathologize both men and women and will need to be removed carefully by therapists through both policy changes and direct interventions.

Family Support Services

Family support services will increase. Housekeeping and childcare have come to the fore, among others, in traditional services once performed by family members. Many families will need both childcare and eldercare simultaneously. The avenues for family involvement are changing from physically based to socially and emotionally based.

Less Educated, Lower-Functioning Mental Health Clients

Family structure and composition have been changing for years, as has the psychological treatment population. Psychologists have been trained to, and prefer to work with, YAVIS clients: young, attractive, verbal, intelligent, and successful. This population characteristically and without external intervention is able to form a positive therapeutic relationship and often improves with minimal or no intervention. The YAVIS population is in contrast to the new breed of psychotherapy client, the HOUND: homely, old, unattractive, nonverbal, and dumb. This is a population that psychologists have not been trained or compelled to treat (Garfield & Bergen, 1986).

In addition, mental health services were once thought of as services for the wealthy only. Mental health services, however, have become more accessible to everyone. Services are more available than ever before and are often free, low-cost, or covered by health insurance. Marriage and family counselors have not adequately responded with changed paradigms or interventions. Treatment continues to be based on the concept of the traditional, high-functioning nuclear family. Therefore, new paradigms will have to be developed (Carlson & Sperry, 1992).

Mandated Treatment

Mental health services at one time were sought by people who wanted to change their lives. With changing society and family, much treatment now has become court-ordered and mandated. No longer is the mental health treatment population voluntary, socioeconomically advanced, well educated, and functional. This significantly changes the rules of treatment—rules that were designed and developed for this population. Compulsory clients are different and require different methods of treatment, assessment, and intervention (Huber, 1992).

Less Interest in Children

The 1990s and the first decade of the 21st century are the baby boomers' family years. This movement tends to model self-orientation, mobility, and independence at the expense of other essential family qualities. People in this generation will not be as interested in their children as their parents were. They will tend to be much more interested in themselves and their own lives and needs. Therefore, many families will not have healthy homes and will not be rearing children responsibly and effectively. This has deep implications for future multiproblem families.

   The world of today and tomorrow is becoming more and more complex. Simultaneously, problems will occur in groups. Drug abuse, suicide, alcoholism, divorce, teenage pregnancy, violence, crime, and sexual abuse all tend to interact. Interventions must focus on the factors related to the intergenerational transmission of individual and family behavior patterns. Interventions have to take place at a program and policy level, together with treatment strategies that deal with the multiplicity of problems.

Complex Multiproblem World

Many families do not have healthy homes and are not rearing their children in responsible and effective ways. This situation has to change, as these families become the roots of future problems in the intergenerational transmission of individual behavior and family patterns. The increasing rates of drug abuse, suicide, alcoholism, divorce, teenage pregnancy, and violence are rooted in high-risk families. These multiproblem homes require unique solutions. The unique character of each family calls for a unique intervention. Despite the apparent external view of an extremely troubled family, most of the family members feel familiar and comfortable living in this type of setting. Programs must deal with the remedial issues identified and also have a preventive focus that helps families nurture altruism, stability, and interdependence.

Older and Multigenerational Population

Americans are aging. By 1996, 7.5 million Americans will be over age 80 (Dychtwald, 1989). Many elderly people are outliving younger family members and are without a support system of caregivers. If current statistics hold, we will have as many as five generations living at one time, and children will comprise only one of these generations. Many older people are therefore being left alone. The stereotypes of aging must be recognized and abandoned as older adults become healthier with increasing years (Sperry & Carlson, 1991a). Fries and Carpo (1981) predicted that, with foreseeable advances in science and improvements in health care, most people can remain relatively healthy until age 85 or so and that almost all deaths will occur between ages 85 and 90.

Gay and Lesbian Couples

The stigma toward gay and lesbian couples will lessen. Ten percent of the people in North America currently self-identify themselves as gay or lesbian. Gays will organize and create intimate kinship networks called "chosen families." Rather than being organized through marriage and childrearing, these chosen families are characterized by fluid boundaries, eclectic composition, and relatively little differentiation between erotic and nonerotic friendships. They are not structured by hierarchies of gender and age unless there are children. Most gay families will last only one generation (Bernstein, 1992).

Adoption

Legal adoption will continue at current rates. As nuclear families begin to change, however, the number of nonbiological family members will increase. Although these unions are unlikely to be legally based, they will function as if they were biological or fully vested family members.

Fertility

Infertility and childlessness will be virtually eliminated. With advanced technology and medicine, anyone who wishes to have children will be able to (Schwartz, 1991).

Loss

Loss will be viewed differently. With increasing world changes, people will accept change and loss as an essential part of life. What is normal and acceptable in terms of grieving and loss will be understood better with further research. Behavior that has been viewed as unhealthy and dysfunctional will be understood as normal and adaptive (Walsh & McGoldrick, 1991).

Workplace

The workplace will become an extension of family. Employers can no longer expect workers to give priority to the job without giving help to their families. Further commitment will include parental leave, dependent care support, counseling and education, relocation assistance, and flexible work hours. In previous generations, workers worked with their family, and they worked in family-run businesses and community stores. Although this has changed greatly, the role of work as an extension of the family continues.

With the technology revolution and the further development of computer-based communication, many more people will be working in their home environment rather than going away from the home to work. This will put further stress upon the home as the boundaries between home and work become enmeshed.

Health Care and Issues

Health problems are largely preventable through public health programs for promoting health, reducing risk, and providing services for poor and disadvantaged people. The family's role in health protection and promotion is integral. Strategies must be developed for reducing health risks by improving family behaviors. Families continue to provide most of the day-to-day services and costs of caring for the chronically or acutely ill. Health providers must become more sensitive to this role of the family.

Before the 1980s, acquired immune deficiency syndrome (AIDS) was virtually unknown. As of 1989, more than 100,000 cases had been reported in the United States. By 1992, an estimated 365,000 people will have been diagnosed with AIDS. The numbers and types of families in which a member has HIV, the consequences for these families, and the implications have yet to receive sufficient attention.

Divorce

Most marriages do not last a lifetime. We live in a society in which more marriages end in divorce than by death of a spouse. Divorce has become a reality. According to recent researchers, about two thirds of all new marriages will end in some form of dissolution, and between 40% and 50% of the children born in the 1970s and 1980s will experience parental divorce. Divorce is no longer considered abnormal or to be avoided at all costs. By accepting divorce as a reality, families are seen as in transition or fluid rather than permanent. This change can have both positive and negative effects.

Remarriage

Remarriage after divorce forms a different kind of marriage system, one in which children live with one biological parent and one stepparent or divide their family life between a maternal home and a paternal home.

Researchers are finding that the effects of divorce span generations. The first generation of children for whom divorced parents were common are now becoming adults, and they are a new breed. On the average, children of divorced parents are less educated than others their age and are less likely to graduate from high school than are children of similar backgrounds who grow up in intact families. Children of divorce leave home earlier than others, but not to form families of their own. They are far more likely than their peers to cohabit before they marry, and when they do marry, they also are more likely to divorce.

Single Parenting and Problems

In the future, more than half the children in the United States are expected to be in single-parent families. This has serious implications for all members of the helping professions. The five basic types of single parents are widowed, divorced, separated, never married, and the adopting parent. Specific strategies are needed to help this population. Counselors have to be able to deal with communication and traditional family problems and also must understand the special demands on time and money and support resources available. Although the tendency for single parents to move into new marital relationships is great, research shows this often compounds problems rather than leading to resolution. Counseling must help people to change in a relationship rather than to find a different partner.

Cohabitation and Alternative Family Forms

Cohabitation and alternative family forms will increase. Cohabiting couples have increased in number, as have the numbers of children born to unmarried mothers. Having babies seems to be back in popularity, but to assume that marriage will come back with them is risky. Many employed women do not need a marriage to rear children and therefore are choosing cohabitation. Cohabiting households can look like a family from the outside—they can consist of a man and a woman and children—but on the inside they may function differently than a married couple with children. Cohabiting couples share housework more equally than married couples do, but they tend to share childcare less. Children usually belong to and are cared for by the women. The foundation for cohabitation resides more out of economic issues than those of romance.

Commonplace Psychoeducation

Training programs in marriage, family, and parenting skills will become common. They will be offered by counselors as part of therapy and also will be offered through self-help and lay leader programs. The goal will be to increase the marital and family quality that now is lacking, with an emphasis on examining how our educational system does or does not prepare us to be socially competent citizens, spouses, and parents. Programs like *PREP for Effective Living* (Dinkmeyer, McKay,

Dinkmeyer, Dinkmeyer, & Carlson, 1985) will impart these skills to a pre-adult population. The assumption that people succeed at marriage, family, and parenting automatically is absolutely not supported. To have a successful marriage, people need to learn a large number of skills (Dinkmeyer & Carlson, 1984).

Interest in Quality

More and more people are downshifting (Saltzman, 1991). In the 1980s people seemed to embrace the notion of a fast track as the surest path to success. Today and in the near future, a new breed of career trendsetters, the "downshifters," are taking control of their careers rather than allowing their careers to control them. These people are not dropouts. They're not giving up the intellectual, emotional, and financial rewards of professional success. Instead, they're learning to limit their careers to devote more time to their families, communities, and their own needs beyond work. Many Americans will work hard at "downward mobility" (Edmondson, 1991).

Family Finances/Financial Concerns

Money problems are pervasive family concerns. Most families have more needs and wants than financial resources. Traditionally counselors have not dealt directly with these issues, but they must do so now. Financial issues tend to exacerbate marital and parent-child conflicts. In a time when recession, mortgage foreclosures, bankruptcy, and other negative financial outcomes are prevalent, sound family economic management can be helpful. Shared economic decision making in families seems to be on the rise, largely because of increases in dual-earner households. Couples are having a difficult time dealing with the upward spiral of family standards that continues to demand more vehicles, bigger houses, consumer conveniences, continued education, and services. This often results in less savings and larger debt and has a negative impact on quality childcare.

Many interesting assessment issues will have to be addressed to better understand economic situations and how mental health professionals can intervene. "What is the effect of economic problems on family relationships?" and "who needs family assistance?" require answers.

Increasing Gender Sensitivity

The experience of family life varies considerably according to gender. The major issue of all family counseling may well rest in these gender differences. For example, dual-earner families entail three jobs: the husband's work, the wife's work, and the family work. Women in all social classes do the bulk of the family work. Women tend to be paid less than men, are affected more negatively by divorce, are more likely to be poor, and are more often the victims of physical violence. Approaches to mental health tend to be male-dominated and therefore perpetuate these problems. Alleviating problems involving gender differences will require not only new procedures and techniques but also better formulation of treatment and understanding of problems.

Faced with these trends and changes, professionals and the general population have divided into two groups. The *pessimists* believe these changes in the American family are destructive and prevent the family from carrying out its functions of childrearing and providing stability for adult life. This group calls for a return to the traditional values of commitment and responsibility. The *optimists,* on the other hand, view the family as an institution that is not declining but, rather, is showing its flexibility and resilience. This group believes that traditional family structures were too male-dominated and conformity-oriented to allow for growth and that they no longer are appropriate today. Regardless of the position, most people still reside within a family. According to Dougherty (1992):

> The world is now more oriented to individual options, particularly for women, and the family has changed accordingly. From this point of view, the main problems faced by contemporary families can be traced to the failure of society to accept that the "Leave It to Beaver" family is a dinosaur and to provide adequate support for the variety of post-Beaver families that now dominate the landscape. (pp. 32–34)

Dougherty believes a third orientation is emerging. It agrees with the pessimists that the family is in trouble and a transformation of values is needed; it also agrees with the optimists that changes in family structure are inevitable and here to stay, and that both old and new family forms should receive more community support. Dougherty believes that families at the beginning of the 20th century could be called *institutional families* and their chief value was *responsibility.* In the mid-1920s the component marriage and the psychological family shifted to a chief value of *satisfaction.* Now we have moved to the pluralistic family with its chief family value of *flexibility.* This form includes responsibility and satisfaction as well as flexibility. According to Dougherty:

> This completes a century-long trek toward liberation of the individual, particularly women and children, from the oppressive features of the traditional family. The pluralistic family offers individuals freedom to create the family forms that fit their changing needs over life's course with little stigma about failing to conform to a single family structure and value system. (p. 35)

Family Rules and Systems

As a result of these changes in the therapeutic landscape, the need to clearly formulate problems becomes apparent. Counselors need to understand the purpose of a family and what the family tasks are. Some of the most critical are (Walsh, 1991):

■ *Teaching/learning.* The family is the major vehicle for communicating forms of knowledge and skills.

- *Support.* Physical and emotional support are basic to the growth of all family members.

- *Stability.* Set patterns of behavior can provide structure in our confusing and changing world.

- *Mutuality/privacy.* Mutuality refers to the family's working together toward common goals. Each member, however, also needs private time and space to grow as an individual.

- *Independence/dependence.* This task leads to the gradual development of more and more independent behavior.

- *Defining expectations.* The establishment of reasonable short- and long-term goals is essential for orderly development.

- *Problem-solving.* Developing a problem-solving process with both flexibility and openness is important.

The family therapist of the future will have to take an integrated approach to helping others. Two helpful frameworks are found in family systems theory and structural family therapy. These concepts likely will form the basis for integrated intervention strategies.

Family Systems Theory

Family systems theorists conceptualize the family as an open system that functions in relation to its broader social/cultural context and evolves over the life cycle. Families operate according to rules and principles that apply to all systems (Bertalanffy, 1968; Miller, 1978; Walsh, 1982):

1. *Circular causality.* A family system can be defined as *a group of individuals interrelated so that a change in any one member affects other individuals and the group as a whole.* This in turn affects the first individual in a circular chain of influence. Every action in this sequence is also a reaction. Causality is thus seen as circular rather than linear.

2. *Nonsummativity.* The family as a whole is greater than the sum of its parts, and it cannot be described simply by summing up characteristics of individual members. The family organization and interactional patterns involve an interlocking of the behaviors of its members.

3. *Equifinality.* According to the principle of equifinality, the same origin may lead to different outcomes and the same outcome may result from different origins. Watzlawick, Beavin, and Jackson (1967) refer to the error or genetic fallacy in confusing origin with significance in determining outcome. Rather, they assert, the influence of initial conditions or events will be outweighed by the impact of the family organization—its ongoing interactional patterns and responses to stress. Thus, one family may be disabled and another family may rally in

response to the same crisis. Or two well-functioning families may have evolved from quite different circumstances.

4. *Communication.* All behavior is regarded as communication transmitting interpersonal messages. Every communication has two functions: a *content* (report) aspect conveying factual information, opinions, or feelings; and a *relationship* (command) aspect that, in conveying how the information is to be taken, defines the nature of the relationship (Ruesch & Bateson, 1951). In an ongoing relationship this definition cannot be left unclear without pathological consequences. Families stabilize the process of defining relationships through mutual agreements or family rules.

   Family therapists need to be aware of not just the communication process but also *perception.* Often, people send clear and concise messages, but these messages are perceived inaccurately. A breakdown in perception, according to Walsh and Wood (1983), is more common (90%) than poor communication (50%). Communication is the transmission of a message in any verbal or nonverbal manner, and perception is the act of receiving the message. These two processes have to be considered separately. Clear communication is possible without accurate perception; however, clear perception is not likely without clear communication.

5. *Family rules.* Relationship rules, both implicit and explicit, organize family interaction and maintain a stable system by prescribing and limiting members' behavior. They provide expectations about roles, actions, and consequences that guide family life. Through the *redundancy principle,* a family tends to interact in repetitive sequences so that family operations are governed by a relatively small set of patterned and predictable rules. Families develop different lifestyles based on their family rules.

6. *Homeostasis.* To maintain a steady, stable state in the ongoing interaction system, norms are delimited and enforced by homeostatic mechanisms. All family members contribute to the homeostatic balance through a mutually reinforcing feedback loop, such as in complementarity or reciprocal behavior. Too great a deviation from the family norm may be counteracted in the negative feedback process, to regulate tension and restore the family equilibrium or homeostasis.

7. *Morphogenesis.* At the same time, flexibility is required for a family to adapt to internal and external change. Internally, the family must reorganize in response to developmental challenges as its members and the family as a whole move through the life cycle. A shift of rules is required to go from one developmental stage to the next as new phase-appropriate needs and tasks demand new norms and options.

From a systems perspective, individual dysfunction also is seen as symptomatic of current family dysfunction. Even if an individual's functioning and development are pathological, the symptoms may be functional and adaptive within the family context. The individual's problem may function as a homeostatic regulator, restoring family stability by expressing and deflecting family tension. Psychopathology is defined as a relationship problem (Haley, 1970). The individual's symptomatic behavior is seen as embedded in a dysfunctional interaction pattern.

Regardless of the origin of symptoms, given the circular nature of causality, the family's response is the readjustment or recovery of the individual symptom bearer. Dysfunctional family systems tend to maintain or reinforce the symptoms in ongoing interactional processes. If the dysfunctional relationship pattern is not altered, symptoms may shift from one member to another.

Structural Family Therapy

In addition to systems concepts, we have found the ideas of structural family therapy (Minuchin, 1974) useful. This approach stresses the importance of family organization on functioning of the family unit. Minuchin contends that all families have problems and that the difference between a healthy and an unhealthy family is the way they contend with these problems. Minuchin tries to help families function effectively and accomplish their goals. He believes this is accomplished through clear subsystems and boundaries: A functional family has to be flexible enough to change, yet rigid enough to know who is in charge.

This approach focuses upon subsystems organized around family functions. The family decides who will participate and who will be excluded in these subsystems. The possible combinations of family members into subsystems are infinite; however, it is helpful to concentrate on the three major subunits of the family: marital or adult, parental, and sibling (Walsh, 1991). Intragenerational alliances, according to this approach, are more functional than intergenerational ones.

1. The *marital subunit* is composed of adult family members bonded by emotional, sexual, or economic factors. This may encompass relationships ranging from the husband and wife in a nuclear or remarried family to the single parent and a lover. The subunit is the source of adult need satisfaction in the functional family.

2. The *parental subunit* is the governing body of the family. It is the source of decision making, goal setting, and nurturance for the entire unit. This subunit usually consists of the mother and father or any surrogate for these roles.

3. The *sibling subunit* consists of children of the family. This unit is, in a sense, the training ground of the family. In the functional family, this unit provides education, support, and guidance appropriate to the developmental levels of all individuals involved.

Minuchin described family boundaries as an important part of the family structure. The family system has to protect itself from and be open to outside influences from extended family and societal institutions. These clear boundaries allow the two-way flow of information and activity between the family and the outside world. Diffuse boundaries provide little protection from outside forces. Rigid boundaries, on the other hand, provide too much protection and shut out any outside influence.

Role responsibility is another aspect of a sound family structure. A role is defined as *the identity a family member assumes,* either temporarily or permanently, to complete certain tasks. According to Walsh (1991), responsibility is an aspect of the family's teaching/learning task. *Expectations* have to be clear, mutual, realistic, specific, and consistent. A complete *follow-through* is necessary, with clear, mutual, realistic, specific, and consistent *consequences.* The family clearly defines and articulates individual expectations. The responsibilities are age-appropriate and realistic. All members contribute to the definitions of their roles. In addition, each member accepts responsibility for his or her assigned duties. If the expectations are fulfilled, there are positive emotional, physical, or material consequences. When they are not followed through, negative consequences accrue.

Assumptions for Treatment

In the early days of counseling, identifying with a certain school of therapy was important. Now this is less so. Identifying what should be done and how to move a family toward healthier living is more important. Beavers (1990) developed the following global assumptions regarding families (pp. xii–xiii):

1. Family functioning in terms of systemic qualities of relationships, communication, and exchange takes precedence over form or typology. Attempting to identify or label clinical typologies of symptomatic families (such as the "schizophrenogenic family") yields little useful information. Instead, functional and behavioral qualities of the unique system must be assessed.

2. Family competence ranging from healthy family functioning to severely dysfunctional is viewed along a progressive continuum rather than in categorical typologies. This helps us assume a potential for growth and adaptation in all families.

3. Families at similar competence levels may show different functional styles of relating and interacting. Further, most competent families are able to balance and shift their functioning styles to match developmental changes.

4. The successful therapist achieves an understanding of the presenting family and subtly alters factors such as therapeutic orientation, power differential, and operating styles to join the family and catalyze its growth.

5. The successful therapist appreciates the hierarchical structure of interacting systems within and surrounding the family, ranging from the biological/cellular through the individual to higher-order systems, including extended family and the larger social network. Although direct intervention with any specific level or all levels may not be necessary in a given case, ignoring potentially important biochemical, neurological, or larger system influences may lead to failure.

6. Individual treatment for relationship difficulties including, but not limited to, marital or parent-child relationships is often ineffective and complicating.

Utilizing these guidelines, family counselors can offer effective treatment. No two families are alike. Therefore, successful therapists need to have principles and guidelines such as these to underlie their ideographic interventions.

Assessment

Assessing family functioning as an ongoing system is difficult and complicated. Counselors often have to untangle the present and temporary situation, collect family histories extending over several generations, understand the purposes of the presenting problems, and essentially sort out the labyrinth of potentially useful data (Reiss, 1980). Reiss suggests several pathways for assessment available to counselors:

■ Whether to adopt a cross-sectional or a developmental view.

■ Whether to conduct a family-based or an environmental-based inquiry.

■ Whether to adopt a crisis or character orientation.

■ Whether to focus on family pathology or on family competence.

■ Whether to emphasize underlying family themes or observable behavioral events.

How individual counselors make these choices is probably related to their theoretical orientation, counseling style, the family being appraised, and what the counselor wants to learn. We have found that a systematic way to collect the multitude of information available is helpful. The counselor might use the genogram (McGoldrick & Gerson, 1985), the circumplex model (Olson, Russell, & Sprenkle, 1989), the Beavers system model of rating family competence (Beavers & Boeller, 1983), or the McMaster model of family coping skills (Westley & Epstein, 1969). In addition, counselors should utilize a clinical interview to find clues to the following (Goldenberg & Goldenberg, 1990, p. 69):

■ Why is the family seeking help now?

■ What are the sources of stress on this family?

■ Who has the symptom?

■ How severe is the symptom?

■ Is the symptom chronic or acute?

■ Why this person?

■ When did the symptom first begin, and who is most affected by it?

■ What function does the symptom serve for family stability?

■ How often, when, and under what circumstances does the symptom occur?

■ Are interactive patterns discernible that may relate to the onset or termination of symptomatic behavior?

- Is an enmeshed or disengaged family system operating?
- What is the current level of family functioning?
- Are noticeable alliances or coalitions operating?
- How permeable are the boundaries between subsystems?
- In what manner and with what degree of success has the family dealt with this or other problems in the past?
- Has the family sought professional help before? If so, with what degrees of success?
- How adaptable or rigid is the family?
- How receptive is the family to help?
- What apparent family interactive patterns are related to perpetuation of this problem?

Healthy and Normal Families

Counselors can be easily taken up with the various degrees of family dysfunction, but to set meaningful treatment goals, we also must understand what is normal and healthy. What is normal and healthy, however, means different things to different people, depending on their frame of reference. The definition also is changing as the aforementioned statistics highlight. Normality often is defined in four different ways (Walsh, 1982):

1. *Asymptomatic family functioning.* "Normal" can be defined as having no problems or symptoms. Many people believe if no symptoms are present, a person is healthy.

2. *Optimal family functioning.* In this context, "normal" is defined as accomplishing several positive ideal characteristics. Optimally functioning families are viewed at the top of a continuum, with average or asymptomatic families in the midrange and severely dysfunctional families at the lower end.

3. *Average family functioning.* A family is viewed as normal from this perspective if it fits a pattern that is typical or average compared to most other families.

4. *Transactional family process.* In this view, what is normal is defined in temporal and social context, and it varies with the internal and external demands that require adaptation over the course of the family life cycle.

On May 10, 1990, leading experts convened in Washington, DC, to identify successful families and to overview the various constructs and measurements of what an effective family is. From this meeting, the researchers identified nine characteristics that form the basis of a strong, healthy family (Krysan, Moore, & Zill, 1990):

1. *Adaptability.* This dimension refers to the family's ability to accommodate to predictable life-cycle changes and also to stressful events. This capability is

related to external resources, as well as to good communication and other internal family processes.

2. *Commitment to family.* This commitment involves recognition of individual worth and acceptance of the value of the family as a unit.

3. *Communication.* A pattern of clear, open, and frequent communication is one of the characteristics of healthy families most often cited.

4. *Encouragement of individuals.* This dimension refers to the family's ability to engender a sense of belonging and at the same time encourage individual development.

5. *Expression of appreciation.* Extending appreciation means consistently doing things that are positive for the other person simply for his or her sake.

6. *Religious/spiritual orientation.* Many researchers list religiosity or spirituality among the characteristics of healthy families, although no consensus exists regarding the specific aspects of religion that are important to functioning.

7. *Social connectedness.* A connection with the larger society, extended family, friends, and neighbors, and participation in community activities typically makes available external resources to assist the family in adapting and coping.

8. *Clear roles.* In a clear and flexible role structure, family members know their roles and responsibilities and thus are able to function effectively in times of crisis as well as during normal times.

9. *Shared time.* Shared time means that family members devote both quality and quantity time to the extent that this is enjoyable for family members.

Counselors, we hope, will understand the characteristics of effective, successful families and will use these as goals to help families move forward to higher levels of functioning.

Treatment

Marriage and family life (childrearing patterns) have become so complex that even generalities are difficult to state. Earlier family analyses were made as if these differences did not exist. Only first marriages with children were used as a standard of normal and preferred. This scenario now is useful only for a minority of people. The time to define a normal or typical family is long past, if it ever really did exist. Today's families are most notable in terms of their variety and diversity. No single structure or set of interactional patterns can be identified as right or healthy for all families. If any one generalization can be made about a healthy family, it is that the family can accomplish its own goals and those of its members. Family counseling then must focus on helping each client system to be successful in its own terms.

The changes in procedures present a complicated situation, one that requires new methods to handle information and to formulate treatment. Traditional tools such as genograms have to be modified to accommodate blended and nonbiological families. Computers will be needed to handle the volume of data and to retain it in a useful form.

Professional turf wars will continue as to who will work with families—psychiatrists, social workers, counselors, psychologists, or marriage and family therapists. Professional organizations such as ACME (Affiliated Council for Marriage Enrichment), AAMFT (American Association for Marriage and Family Therapy), IAMFC (International Association of Marriage and Family Counselors), APA (American Psychological Association) Division 43, AFTA (American Family Therapy Association), NCFR (National Council on Family Relations) will expand. Treatment will be provided on three levels: primary, secondary, and tertiary. Each of the professional organizations tends to concentrate on a certain area. Primary intervention involves prevention, secondary intervention involves more education and training, and tertiary intervention primarily consists of therapy and treatment of dysfunction. Table 16.1 shows the focal points of the major professional organizations.

Treatment in the future will tend to be brief, of a biopsychosocial nature, and tailored specifically to each family. Traditional methods of treatment developed on YAVIS (young, attractive, verbal, intelligent, successful) clientele will no longer work (Carlson & Sperry, 1992). HOUND (homely, old, ugly, nonverbal, dumb) clientele are becoming much more common. Employer-sponsored health benefits may be increased to include some form of coverage for marriage and family problems as changes in the DSM-IV necessitate.

Marriage and family counseling/therapy has now become firmly established, both clinically and politically. The future decades are likely to produce some interesting changes and significant movements within this field. The practice of marriage and family therapy likely will be influenced as Gurman and Kniskern (1992) predict. These predictions seem to sum up our prior facts and discussion.

1. The practice of marital and family therapy will be shaped by insurance reimbursement policies far more than in the past. Therapy will be brief, entailing more clearly defined treatment goals and utilizing psychoeducational methods.

Table 16.1 Treatment Emphases by Professional Organization

	PRIMARY	SECONDARY	TERTIARY
IAMFC	X	X	X
ACME	X		
AAMFT			X
APA			X
AFTA			X
NCFR		X	

2. Marital and family therapy will be characterized by much less purity of treatment formats and clinical methods. Clinicians will continue to use integrated or technical eclecticism in providing family and couple services.

3. Family therapists will become more involved in the treatment of certain psychiatric disorders. Research continues to point to several areas, such as schizophrenia and adolescent conduct problems, indicating couple and family therapy as the treatment of choice.

4. Family therapists will pay much more attention to the therapist/patient/family relationship. Recent literature has addressed the effect of the family on the disease process, and even more will occur in the future. The patient/family relationship will be addressed in terms of the therapeutic change-inducing potential of these relationships in and of themselves via the impact of empathic understanding, being actively concerned, and demonstrating genuine warmth.

5. Couple and family therapy will undergo a major shift toward providing treatment that has a research base. A noticeable increase in programmatic changes in clinical services will likely occur as a result of quantitative research findings. No longer can therapists use methods that "feel right." Counselors and psychologists will join with medical doctors and dentists and be compelled to use only research-supported treatments.

Changes in the family structure also have made decision making more difficult, and family decisions must be made jointly, requiring cooperation among all family members. This shift calls for a cooperative therapy environment characterized by modeling and teaching cooperation.

Summary

Today's counselors face new relationship combinations and challenges. Traditional methods of assessment and intervention based upon treatment for individual clients or models developed for traditional families are no longer appropriate. Most counselors have been trained in dealing with problematic individuals. In today's world, however, we must deal with couples, entire families, and a variety of combinations such as stepfamilies, single people living alone, childless families, mothers with out-of-wedlock children, and so on. Counselors are confronted by couples who are trying to decide if they should be together or remain together or separate. Counselors have to figure out if they are doing pre-marriage counseling, marriage counseling, divorce counseling, family counseling, or individual counseling.

Counselors are facing issues that didn't exist or were uncommon during their own upbringing. Child custody between divorced parents, stepfamilies living with "yours, mine, and ours" children, and the impact of two-career couples are just a few of the possible challenges today's counselors must be prepared for. These and the other issues discussed in this essay require distinct counseling strategies. We no longer can refer to what was once a "typical" American family; we have to consider a variety of "typical" families.

The face of the American family has changed remarkably over the past few decades. These changes have made successful marriage, healthy childrearing, and the ability to maintain strong, lifelong bonds more difficult than ever.

References

Beavers, W. R., (1990). *Successful families.* New York: W. W. Norton.

Beavers, W. R., & Boeller, M. N. (1983). Family models: Comparing and contrasting the Olson circumplex with the Beavers Model. *Family Process, 22,* 85–98.

Bernstein, A. (1992). The love that dares to speak its name. *AFTA Newsletter, 49,* 12–16.

Bertalanffy, von, L. (1968). *General systems theory: Foundation, development, applications.* New York: Braziller.

Blackwell, J., Blackwell, M., Guccione, B., & Kohut, J. (1992). Out: Closing comments. *Spin, 8*(6), 124.

Bly, R. (1990). *Iron John.* Boston: Addison-Wesley.

Bradshaw, J. (1988). *Healing the shame that binds you.* Deerfield Beach, FL: Health Communications.

Carlson, J. (1992). Rediscovering healthy families. *Topics in Family Psychology and Counseling, 1*(1), 1–90.

Carlson, J., & Sperry, L. (1992). YAVIS vs. HOUND. *Family Psychologist, 8*(3), 17–19.

Dinkmeyer, D., & Carlson, J. (1984). *Time for a better marriage.* Circle Pines, MN: American Guidance Service.

Dinkmeyer, D., McKay, G. D., Dinkmeyer, D. Jr., Dinkmeyer, J. S., & Carlson, J. (1985). *PREP for effective family living.* Circle Pines, MN: American Guidance Service.

Dougherty, W. J. (1992). Private lives, public values. *Psychology Today,* May/June, pp. 32–82.

Dychtwald, K. (1989). *Age wave.* Los Angeles: Jeremy P. Tarcher.

Edmondson, B. (1991). Remaking a living. *Utne Reader, 46,* 66–77.

Fries, J., & Carpo, L. (1981). *Vitality and aging.* San Francisco: Freeman.

Garfield, S. L., & Bergen, A. E. (Eds.). (1986). *Handbook of psychotherapy and behavior change.* New York: John Wiley.

Glick, P. C. (1990). Marriage and family trends. In D. H. Olson and M. K. Hanson (Eds.), *2001: Preparing families for the future.* Minneapolis: National Council on Family Relations.

Goldenberg, H., & Goldenberg, I. (1990). *Counseling today's families.* Pacific Grove, CA: Brooks/Cole.

Goldenberg, I., & Goldenberg, H. (1984). Treating the dual career couple. *American Journal of Family Therapy, 12,* 29–37.

Gurman, A. S., & Kniskern, D. P. (1992). The future of marital and family therapy. *Psychotherapy, 29*(1), 65–71.

Haley, J. (1970). Approaches to family therapy. *International Journal of Psychiatry, 9,* 233–242.

Huber, C. H. (1992). Compulsory family counseling. *Topics in Family Psychology and Counseling, 1*(2), 1–81.

Keen, S. (1991). *Fire in the belly: On being man.* New York: Bantam Books.

Keen, S. (1992). *Can we end the battle between the sexes?* Keynote Address, American Family Therapy Association Annual Conference, Amelia Island, Florida, June 20.

Krysan, M., Moore, K. A., & Zill, N. (1990). *Identifying successful families: An overview of constructs and selected measures*. Washington, DC: Child Trends.

Lawson, A., & Lawson, G. (Eds.). (1991). *Family dynamics of addiction quarterly*. Frederick, MD: Aspen Publishers.

Louv, R. (*1990). Childhood's future: Listening to the American family. New hope for the next generation*. Boston: Houghton Mifflin.

Maushard, M. (1990, March 25). New family forms seen. *The Milwaukee Journal*, p. 6.

McCubbin, H. (1990). Ethnic and mixed race families. In D. H. Olson & M. K. Hanson (Eds.). *2001: Preparing families for the future*. Minneapolis: National Council on Family Relations.

McGoldrick, M., & Gerson, R. (1985). *Genograms in family assessment*. New York: W. W. Norton.

Miller, J. G. (1978). *Living systems*. New York: McGraw-Hill.

Minuchin, S. (1974). *Families and family therapy*. Cambridge, MA: Harvard University Press.

Olson, D., Russell, C. S., & Sprenkle, D. H. (Eds.). (1989). *Circumplex model: Systematic assessment and treatment of families*. New York: Haworth.

Pittman, F. (1985). Gender myths: When does gender become pathology? *The Family Therapy Networker, 9–6*, 24–33.

Reiss, D. (1980). Pathways to assessing the family: Some choice points and a sample route. In C. K. Hofling & J. M. Lewis (Eds.). *The family: Evaluation and treatment*. New York: Brunner/Mazel.

Riche, M. F. (1991). The future of the family. *American Demographics,* March, pp. 44–46.

Ruesch, J., & Bateson, G. (1951*). Communication: The social matrix of psychiatry*. New York: Norton.

Saltzman, A. (1991). *Downshifting: Reinventing success on a slower track*. New York: Harper Collins.

Schwartz, L. L. (1991). *Alternatives to infertility*. New York: Brunner/Mazel.

Sperry, L., & Carlson, J. (1991a). The family psychologist as futurist: Some facts and challenges. *Family Psychologist, 7*(2), 30–38.

Sperry, L., & Carlson, J. (1991b). The work-centered couple. *Family Psychologist, 7*(4), 19–21.

Stanton, M. D., & Todd, P. C. (1982). *The family therapy of drug addiction*. New York: Guilford Press.

Steinglass, P. (1987). *The alcoholic family*. New York: Basic Books.

Strauss, M. A. (1990). Family violence. In D. H. Olson & M. K. Hanson (Eds.). *2001: Preparing families for the future*. Minneapolis: National Council on Family Relations.

Walsh, F. (1982). *Normal families*. New York: Guilford Press.

Walsh, F., & McGoldrick, M. (Eds.). (1991). *Living beyond loss: Death in the family*. New York: W. W. Norton.

Walsh, W. M. (1991*). Case studies in family therapy: An integrated approach*. Needham Heights, MA: Allyn & Bacon.

Walsh, W. M., & Wood, J. I. (1983). Family assessment: Bridging the gap between theory, research, and practice. *American Health Counselors Journal, 5*, 111–120.

Watzlawick, P., Beavin, J., & Jackson, D. D. (1967). Pragmatics of human communication. New York: Norton.

Westley, W. A., & Epstein, N. B. (1969). *The silent majority*. San Francisco: Jossey-Bass.

Zinn, M. B., & Eitzen, D. S. (1987). *Diversity in American families*. New York: Harper & Row.

School Issues and Interventions

Jon Carlson and Judith Lewis

The junior and senior high schools have a major influence on adolescents. Unfortunately, their impact is not always positive. For most teenagers, school is a "necessary evil" with one primary benefit: It is a prime place for socializing. No other nonfamily setting consumes so much of their time, involves so much attention, or demands so much effort. They often view the actual process of formalized classroom activity as secondary to social aspects. The way in which students feel about their school experience is determined largely by their teachers' opinions. Parents often suggest that adolescents ignore their teachers' shortcomings and concentrate on the subject matter, but this is hard to accept, as everything in a classroom is filtered through the teacher's personality.

What can be done about teenagers who are turned off to school and learning, who are disinterested, who are not working up to their capabilities? The first step is to uncover the reason. In most cases, however, there is not a simple answer. Sometimes parents themselves are at fault. With the best intentions in the world, parents tell their children, "You have to learn to do things you don't like to do," and all too often schoolwork falls into this category. Parents foster this attitude because they want their teenagers to realize that schoolwork must take precedence over hobbies and pleasurable activities, but these words can backfire if their children attend school with the attitude that they are doing so at sacrifice of all pleasure and fun.

In schools, as in other settings, counselors have trouble providing effective services in today's world. The confusion, uncertainty, and alienation that young people experience today derive from problems that past generations did not face. Increases in adolescent depression and suicide, drug and alcohol use, and the growing number of single-parent families present staggering issues for our society. In addition, today's counselors are affected by social conditions that did not, to the same degree, touch professionals of the past, such as the effects of unemployment (and underemployment), the rising rate of adult alcoholism, and the alarming prevalence of child abuse. These social conditions, as well as crime, violence, socioeconomic inequalities, and the public's disillusionment with the quality of education in general, have contributed to a disaffected view of counseling services in the school.

Because of these conditions, today's counselors must be more active; they must be willing to experiment and must realize that traditional counselor roles and strategies will not alleviate these problems. Although counseling techniques for young people have been improving over the years, many strategies that have consistently not worked have not yet been discarded. Of course, discarding ideas and theories that one has learned in training from respected teachers is not easy.

In Chapter 17, Patricia Gallagher and Linda Satter describe a comprehensive high school that promotes a positive and supportive environment. This is accomplished by involving students, faculty, and the community in a variety of prevention and intervention activities that respond to students' needs. A safer environment is imperative before any other counseling interventions can occur.

Barry and Janae Weinhold present conflict-resolution methods and curriculum. The program is entitled the "Partnership Way" and is designed to address the psychological and social conditions that foster conflict. This program also helps to fuel safe environments in school.

Despite all the improvements in modern life, conflicts still persist. The results of the 26th annual Gallup poll (Elan, Rose, & Gallup, 1994) reveal that Americans view fighting, violence, and gangs, along with discipline, as the primary issues facing today's schools. David and Roger Johnson assert that students must be taught to be peacemakers if schools are to be places where quality education occurs. In this chapter they describe how to create a peacemaker program and further enhance the safety of the school.

In Chapter 20, Elsie Moore discusses inequalities in education and how counselors can help minority youngsters achieve. According to Moore, teenagers from minority backgrounds have lost performance because of low expectations. Cultural differences are evaluated incorrectly and misunderstood, impacting learning and achievement. Minority children are often relegated (sometimes voluntarily) to inferior positions. IQ scores, achievement tests, and other culturally loaded forms of assessment label minority students as not being as capable as others. Moore provides suggestions for counteracting these problems.

In Chapter 21, Walter Bera and Fran Sepler describe how sexual harassment, a major problem in today's secondary schools, can be dealt with in the school setting. According to these authors, secondary school systems can become important arenas for teaching problem solving; how to take risks; how to be courageous; how to stick up for others; how to step into situations that others may say are not anyone else's business; and, finally, how to tolerate another's honest and inadvertent mistakes.

In Chapter 22, Robert L. Wren points out that most schools do not have a plan of action for what to do in the event of the death of a student, a faculty member, or an administrator. Adolescents should be informed about the topic of death and comfortable discussing it. With regard to death education, Wren describes developmental issues, grieving, interventions, resources, and organizational issues.

Beverly Johns and John Keenan discuss how counselors can help schools handle traumatic events. They provide general guidelines for dealing with traumatic crises in schools and procedures to follow in the event of the death of a student or staff member or the potential death of a student.

In Chapter 24, Larry Brendtro and Steven Van Bockern support psychoeducational approaches for meeting the diverse needs of troubled adolescents. The notion of providing training rather than treatment seems to encourage the discouraged.

In the final chapter, Peter Leone, Matthew Mayer, Kimber Melmgren, and Sheri Meisel examine issues related to school violence and disruption. They have created practical violence prevention initiatives and guidelines for parents, teachers, and administrators.

References

Elam, S., Rose, L. & Gallup, A. (1974). The 26th annual Gallup poll of the public's attitudes toward the public school. *Phi Delta Kappa, 76,* 41-56.

Promoting a Safe School Environment Through a Schoolwide Wellness Program

Patricia A. Gallagher
and Linda S. Satter

When school officials have metal detectors at school entrances for weapon checks, conduct random drug testing of athletes, use breathalyzers to detect alcohol, inspect lockers, forbid pagers and cell telephones, and install video cameras in buses, they are doing so to protect youth from injury and tragedy. "Although some safety measures may need to be in place, this approach cannot be at the forefront of safe school plans" (Lantieri, 1997, p. 157).

A balance can be created between promoting safe school environments through inspection practices and surveillance equipment and presenting a comprehensive wellness program that promotes a positive and supportive environment. School curricula should be taught by competent and caring teachers who provide students with experiences in problem solving and decision making strategies and opportunities to practice responsibility and respect. Teachers need to involve students as active participants and collaborators in program activities and extracurricular experiences to help them undertake commitments that encourage and reinforce kinder and gentler relationships.

IMPACT is such a program. It is a comprehensive high school program that promotes a positive and supportive environment by involving students, faculty, and the community in a variety of prevention, collaboration, and intervention activities in response to students' needs. The long-range goal of the program is to equip students with essential skills to be healthy adults.

Origin of the Total Wellness Program

The program at North Kansas City High School (NKCHS), a small community adjacent to Kansas City, Missouri, grew out of an incentive grant written by the building principal to secure funding for safe-school training. The grant enabled eight of her teachers and some from area high schools to complete 36 hours of professional training through the Baptist Medical Center in Kansas City, Missouri.

The training is referred to as a student assistance program. Student assistance programs became prominent in the middle 1970s as an approach to addressing the growing problems related to adolescents' use and abuse of alcohol and other drugs. Over the years, advocates of student assistance programs realized that substance abuse is the result of, and is accompanied by, many problems. These include parental drinking or substance abuse, family frustrations with rearing children in today's culture, teenage depression and suicide, teen pregnancy, sexually transmitted diseases, divorce, and nicotine addictions.

As a result, the original training expanded to address the many and varied issues affecting adolescents today. It taught the adult learners the roles they can play to improve the school climate, promote students' self-image, and provide a home base where students can go to get help. As such, the program emphasized a comprehensive program designed to meet adolescents' needs. It also encouraged participants to find and network with human and community resources to assist the youth and their families. Essentially, the program teaches the value of enabling.

From its "humble" beginning, which focused on keeping kids in and drugs out of school, IMPACT expanded each year with the addition of innovative programs to meet the needs of safety in the school and community. Currently, IMPACT is a total wellness and awareness program that provides students with a support network of peers, teachers, parents, and school and community programs. It is designed to recognize troubling trends and respond to societal changes that can consume the lives of youth and drive some from the education system. The ultimate outcome is to provide students with the necessary skills to be healthy adults.

When the initial group of North Kansas City High School teachers returned from their student assistance training, they reported their experiences at a faculty meeting. Their enthusiasm for what could be done at the school was contagious and encouraged other colleagues to become part of this new wellness program. Now when new faculty members arrive at the school, they are encouraged to take the training offered at Baptist Medical Center.

Students learn about the program's activities during registration and the freshmen orientation session. Throughout the school year posters and announcements are made inviting students to join.

Block-scheduling arrangements give students and staff members interested in the IMPACT program opportunities for participation. This scheduling allows students to meet their seven classes on Monday and four 85-minute classes from Tuesday through Friday. Two of these classes are designated as seminar times encompassing a variety of activities. For example, students can use seminar time to plan skits, organize events, and present lessons to children in nearby elementary and middle schools. Teachers are assigned to five classes, two planning periods, and three extra-duty assignments. Teachers can fulfill their extra-duty requirements by acting as sponsors for an IMPACT program.

The Current Wellness Program

IMPACT consists of two major components: a "participation" and a "helping" component. The *participation component* is composed of a variety of student activities that include SAVE, peer mediation, Impact Improv, SADD, Hi-Step, PAL, high school heroes, and TRY. The *helping component* includes PATHS, a student's resource officer services, individual counseling, community counseling services, conflict-resolution meetings, support groups, ethical decision-making and problem-solving workshops, teen institute, and referral services to outside agencies. The following descriptions will reveal an interconnection between these two major components of the wellness program.

In addition, there is a complementary relationship between IMPACT and the school discipline policies and procedures. For example, peer mediation may be an alternative to suspension or arrest. If word reaches IMPACT that a potential fight may erupt, the likely violators can be offered a mediation session that potentially can prevent a suspension or arrest. Peer mediation also has been used after an incident that resulted in disciplinary action. In this case, mediation assists the violators to think ahead to acceptable responses if a similar incident, temptation, or problem should arise.

Participation Component

SAVE

Students Against Violence Everywhere is a group of concerned students who work closely with local police departments and community agencies to find ways to decrease violence in the schools and communities. The program was designed to address violence in the high schools and to carry the message that school is a safe environment. At first it was concerned with six topics: gangs, cliques, weapons, students feeling like outcasts, racial problems, and drugs.

SAVE began in 1991 when the Kansas City, Missouri, Police Department decided that a comprehensive program was needed to make the school environment safer. Faculty members at the four high schools within two school districts in the North Patrol Division of Kansas City, Missouri, were asked to provide a group of students that the police could talk to about violence in their schools. The students gave their perceptions of violence in the schools, and recommendations on how to combat it.

Students from each grade level in each high school were brought together to discuss the problem of violence in the area's high schools and to design a program that would address the problem. They suggested that the following three committees be formed to help carry out a series of activities as outlined below:

■ a Student Steering Committee, composed of three students from each of the four high schools

■ an Administration Committee made up of representatives from law enforcement, the school administration, social service agencies; IMPACT coordinators from the four high schools who represented the teachers, and juvenile justice officers

■ an Advisory Committee composed of community leaders.

Once the committees had been established, the following 10 activities were recommended as a means to address violence in the schools.

1. *Mediation.* Students were to be trained to serve as mediators to handle disputes between fellow students.

2. *Police.* Uniformed police were to be present in the school to interact with the students and to enforce the laws. The officer would instruct, counsel, and arrest.

3. *Disciplinary procedures.* The police would be called and appropriate action taken when students commit acts of violence in schools. Students would be disciplined by assigning them jobs at the school, such as assisting the custodians in cleaning the school or in the community, such as working at the city's recycling center. Suspension from school was not seen as punitive. Therefore, detention periods were recommended during the offender's free time, such as Friday nights and Saturday mornings.

4. *Family counseling.* Services were to be made available to families needing counseling assistance. This would include problem counseling for the students and assistance for parents who were having difficulty with parenting skills.

5. *Awareness.* As an initial effort to change some destructive attitudes of students and adults, it was recommended that publicity be generated about SAVE and the causes of violence in the schools.

6. *Teen hotline.* A hotline was to be established. Through the hotline, individuals could notify school administrators and the police about illegal activity, such as students carrying weapons and engaging in gang activity.

7. *Legislation.* Legislation was recommended for holding parents accountable for the weapons they have in their homes.

8. *Student body.* A cross-section of the student body was to give suggestions to students with disciplinary problems.

9. *Activity night.* Occasional nights were to be designated for dances at a neutral place for all high school students.

10. *Questionnaire.* A questionnaire was to be developed and distributed to all students to secure their perceptions of violence in their school and to solicit suggestions on how to combat violence. This was to be the basis for further program development.

As an initial step, the Student Steering Committee developed a questionnaire and gave it to each student in the four high schools. More than 4,000 students responded. The questionnaire and responses are shown in Figure 17.1.

Students Against Violence Everywhere

1. Do you think violence is a problem in your school?
   Total Responses = 2386   Yes = 654 (27%)   No = 1732 (73%)

2. Do you think your safety is threatened at your school?
   Total Responses = 2380   Yes = 308 (13%)   No = 2072 (87%)

3. Do you think the administration takes proper measures in handling violence?
   Total Responses = 2322   Yes = 1441 (62%)   No = 881 (38%)

4. Would you rather discuss your problem with trained peers than the administration?
   Total Responses = 2272   Yes = 1450 (64%)   No = 822 (36%)

5. Have you personally experienced a violent confrontation while in school?
   Total Responses = 2326   Yes = 651 (28%)   No = 1675 (72%)

6. Do you think weapons are a problem at your school?
   Total Responses = 2302   Yes = 438 (19%)   No = 1864 (81%)

7. Do you think a lot of violence starts with racism?
   Total Responses = 2311   Yes = 1522 (66%)   No = 789 (34%)

8. What do you think is a leading cause of violence in your school?
   A. Broken Relationships   = 684 (17%)
   B. Sports Competition   = 482 (12%)
   C. Drugs and Alcohol   = 669 (17%)   Total Responses = 4054
   D. Racism   =1526 (38%)
   E. Sexual Harassment/Date Rape   = 357 (9%)
   F. Other   = 336 (7%)

9. How do you think violence can be prevented in your school?
   A. Harsher Punishments   = 949 (45%)
   B. Uniformed Police Officers   = 539 (26%)   Total Responses = 2093
   C. Other   = 605 (29%)

10. Where do you think violence originates?
    A. Home   =1347 (41%)
    B. School   = 941 (28%)
    C. Work   = 203 (6%)   Total Responses = 3315
    D. Television   = 565 (17%)
    E. Other   = 259 (8%)

Figure 17.1   Results of Questionnaire

After the responses to the questionnaire were analyzed, the Student Steering Committee, faculty, school administrators, IMPACT coordinators, law enforcement personnel, and social service agencies proceeded to implement their safe school programs. North Kansas City High School implemented the following.

■ A faculty member teaches students to mediate disputes between peers. This peer mediation enables students to negotiate differences before they escalate. The training also covers information on racial and cultural differences.

■ A uniformed police officer is present. The officer is available to teach in the classrooms, assists in counseling sessions with students, and serves as a liaison between the school and outside agencies, such as the county juvenile justice personnel. In addition, the officer takes reports and makes necessary arrests.

- A disciplinary procedure requires parent involvement and alternative solutions to after-school detention periods. Detentions are on Friday from 2:40 p.m. to 5:00 p.m. Parents or guardians are asked to check their child into the detention period.

- A process enables students to work out personal problems and directs students and their parents to family counseling. A youth and family service agency provides services including counseling, a place for runaways, and a girl's home. The program offers a 24-hour hotline for personal problems. The telephone number is displayed on a SAVE poster.

- Displays of SAVE posters and SAVE certificates for participating classrooms endorse the SAVE concept. The poster, designed by a student, contains two telephone numbers: one number for personal problem counseling and the other for reporting illegal activity.

- A method has been established to report illegal activity. Students call to report illegal activity anonymously. The Kansas City Crime Commission, staffs the telephone number, and contacts the appropriate school administrator to report the information. When necessary, the school administrator works with the police to address the activity.

- Mandatory reporting of violent activities is required. Missouri Code, Chapter 12.3, requires that certain crimes be reported to the police; therefore, every school has to report violent crimes to the police who would handle each case on its merit. During a meeting, representatives from the juvenile justice system informed the students, police, IMPACT coordinators, and administrators about prosecution for juvenile crimes.

- A curriculum that addresses violence is in place. The material promotes a decrease of dating/domestic violence and abuse of children and their families. In addition, it advocates prevention in educational videos and during lectures and discussions. The program is designed to promote (a) effective interpersonal communication skills, (b) conflict resolution in a peaceful manner, (c) self-awareness and appropriate identification and expression of feelings, and (d) awareness and understanding of the dynamics of abusive relationships. The program is taught by classroom teachers who have been trained at a facility for abused children and adults.

The SAVE program is reviewed annually. When the first year ended, new Steering Committee members were selected to replace graduated seniors. In addition, a brochure was designed to describe the SAVE programs. Funding was secured from an advertising agency and a printing company to have a brochure printed for every student in the four high schools.

Among the comments of SAVE students is the following from a junior who plays varsity football and plays golf. He said the program had a direct effect upon him by helping curb his tendency to get involved in fights.

> I had a short quick temper. I've learned to control it and realize there is no point giving into violent behavior. I have other solutions and ways out. I will back off.

Another student shared his experiences:

SAVE has given me the opportunity to voice my opinion of how we should deal with the growing amount of violence. Not only have I told my ideas, but I see them going into effect.

Peer Mediation

Peer mediators are students who, with adult supervision, help resolve disputes between students. Issues that create disputes include rumors, threats, name-calling, fighting, and loss of property. Peer mediators are selected for their abilities of fairness, reliability, and good communication. In addition to training in effective communication techniques, problem solving, and critical thinking skills, they are taught a conflict resolution approach wherein disputants have the chance to sit face-to-face and talk uninterrupted so each side of the dispute is heard.

As the outside persons who lead the discussion, peer mediators do not take sides, and they keep all information confidential. After the disputants relate their versions of the incident the mediators define the problem. Then the mediators and disputants brainstorm options to resolve the conflicts and write them on the Brainstorming Worksheet form (Figure 17.2). They discuss what could have been done differently, what they can do to solve the immediate dispute, and what options they could choose if a similar problem should arise again in the future. When a solution is reached and agreed upon, it is written on the Peer Mediation Agreement Form (Figure 17.3), which the disputants and the mediators sign.

After the conflict resolution session, the peer mediators are responsible for completing a self-evaluation form designed to encourage the student's mastery of the mediation skills (Figure 17.4). Mediators receive feedback and support throughout their work with peers.

A peer mediator, who was the senior class president, wrestler, and down lineman for the football team, said he believes that involvement in athletics is a healthy outlet for potentially aggressive behavior:

I'm not a fighter. When I see a fight, I think there are other ways out. I like to help people and look for reasonable solutions for problems. There are a lot of things we can do through peer mediation.

Impact IMPROV

Impact IMPROV is a group of students who perform skits with wellness themes to preschool, elementary, middle school, and high school students. IMPROV students receive education in drug and alcohol abuse, family dysfunction, peer pressure, dating issues, eating disorders, and other social ills. Then they and a teacher work together to plan skits on requested topics. After the students give a performance, they ask questions of the audience to initiate dialogue. For example, at a day care center where the students performed *Stranger Danger,* the 4-year-olds were asked to

Brainstorming Worksheet

List all the possible options.

▲ What could be done to resolve this dispute?

▲ What other possibilities can you think of?

▲ In the future, what could you do differently?

1. _____

2. _____

3. _____

4. _____

5. _____

6. _____

7. _____

8. _____

9. _____

10. _____

Figure 17.2   Brainstorming Worksheet

identify the stranger in the performance. They were asked why they should not go with strangers and were asked what they would do if a stranger were to approach them.

IMPROV activities have been effective in that they not only keep everyone's attention but also elicit great conversations. One of the actresses said,

> We enjoy performing for our audiences. It makes us feel that we're helping them solve their problems. In return it makes us feel better.

IMPROV activities are described in a brochure circulated to the elementary schools and in verbal communications with civic groups. Requests for performances

Peer Mediation Agreement

Peer mediator _____ Date _____

Briefly describe the conflict: _____

_____

_____

_____

_____

_____

Type of conflict (check one) ☐ Rumor   ☐ Threat   ☐ Name-calling   ☐ Fighting

☐ Loss of property   ☐ Other (specify) _____

The students whose signatures appear below met with a peer mediator and with the assistance of the mediator reached the following agreement.

Disputant_____

Agrees to_____

_____

_____

Disputant_____

Agrees to_____

_____

_____

We have made and signed this agreement because we believe it resolves the issue(s) between us.

_____   _____
Disputant signature   Disputant signature

_____   _____
Peer mediator signature   Length of mediation (minutes)

Figure 17.3   Peer Mediation Form

come from elementary counselors, teachers, day care centers, civic groups such as the Rotary, church groups, and PTAs. During a given year, IMPROV performed at four elementary schools during each of five lunchtimes. In addition, the group does after-school, breakfast, evening, and weekend performances. Requests are now coming in from other cities and school districts.

Thank-you notes have come from preschool children, parents, teachers and community members. The group has become very popular. Demands for after-school performance have become so extensive that IMPROV has been included in the school's Drama II class.

Peer Mediator Self-Evaluation

Peer mediator _____ Date _____

Directions: Place a checkmark (✓) by each step where you did quality work. Place an asterisk (*) by each step where you think the quality could improve.

☐ Step 1: Open the session

☐ Step 2: Gather information

☐ Step 3: Focus on common interests

☐ Step 4: Create options

☐ Step 5: Evaluate options and choose a solution

☐ Step 6: Write the agreement and close

1. What did you do well?

2. If you could do this mediation again, what might you do differently?

3. Were certain steps more difficult for you than others? If so, what could you do to strengthen these steps?

4. Do you have any other concerns or questions?

Staff supervisor_____ Date _____

Comments:

Figure 17.4   Peer Mediation Self-Evaluation

SADD

Students Against Destructive Decisions (formerly known as students against drunk drivers) is a program designed to raise students' awareness of the dangers of drinking and driving. To reinforce its message, the group engages in a number of activities throughout the academic year. For example, in May SADD presents a skit to demonstrate the risks of drinking and driving. During a mock scene, members of SADD wear "fatal vision" goggles that simulate the effects of alcohol by impairing their ability to walk a straight line.

In a docudrama held outdoors, police, medical technicians, squad cars, and ambulances join the SADD group for a DWI mock car accident. The emergency personnel attend to the accident victims, and the police question the witnesses to highlight the consequences of drinking. After the audience has watched the scene, they wear "fatal vision" goggles to learn firsthand how vision, coordination, driving skills, and mental judgment become impaired after drinking. Thus, the potential for fatal consequences becomes very real. The goggles give students the opportunity to understand the dangers of alcohol and drug ingestion without actually experimenting with them.

SADD members also send birthday cards, with a quarter enclosed, to sophomores when they turn 16. Students are encouraged to use the money to call home for a ride if they have been drinking. A week in the fall is designated Red Ribbon Week. This is a time when students are asked to wear red ribbons to remind everybody of the dangers of drinking and driving. During this week SADD also places small white crosses on the school grounds to demonstrate how many teenagers die daily in alcohol-related deaths. During Christmas week the student body is encouraged to stay safe over the holidays.

Hi-Step

High School-Taught Elementary Program is a cross-age teaching program in which high school students teach fourth graders about peer pressure, conflict mediation, drug and alcohol abuse, and relationships. Two faculty members sponsor the program.

Because Hi-Steppers are viewed as role models for the younger students, candidates are carefully screened. They are chosen for having good academic records and an interest in helping fourth grade students grow emotionally and socially.

Hi-Step students receive their training during late winter and early spring. They attend an 8-hour training session to become familiar with the characteristics of fourth graders, learn to investigate topics, plan activities, and learn to write lesson plans. After their training, Hi-Step participants develop six lessons. Students meet with one of the sponsors weekly during seminar time to review their lessons, receive feedback, and practice with the other students in their group.

After the six lessons are ready, the group is assigned to an elementary school. Hi-Steppers are responsible for meeting with the fourth grade teachers and setting up times to meet with their classes. For this purpose, the Hi-Steppers have permission to leave high school during the seminar times. They have time to arrive at their assigned elementary school and teach the hour-long lessons with their accompanying activities, and return before their own academic periods begin.

Although publicity for the program is done in the classrooms through the school's television channel and posted flyers, the most compelling publicity comes from the enthusiastic Hi-Steppers. Telephone calls start coming in October of the year preceding the performance.

Hi-Step experiences are great for the high school students who have a career interest in teaching or social services and for the fourth graders who have met teenage models. Hi-Step students tell how important they feel when they meet the fourth graders at the mall and are introduced to the parents.

The president of the Hi-Steppers summarized the group's intentions:

> If we reach one child, giving them the courage to do what is right, then we've met our goal. We want kids to know that their high school years can be a great time in their lives if they make the right decisions, and we help them to realize what those good decisions are. Most of all, we want them to know that we care.

PAL

Peers Always Listen (PAL) provides a group of students to whom other students can talk. PALS make a commitment to do what they can to encourage a positive and supportive atmosphere at the school. PALS do not give advice but, instead, listen and try to help their peers sort out their feelings. Consequently, all PALs receive training in assertive listening skills. They learn that emotion can be "energy" in motion and that the best way to defuse an emotional moment is to give the excited student an opportunity to "let the air out." They accomplished this by listening attentively. A student who is "highly charged" may talk only in syllables or phrases. A PAL listens until the peer is able to express himself or herself coherently. PALs are committed to the positive action of listening with care.

PALs also take part in other IMPACT programs such as SADD and IMPROVS. They tutor, distribute, and hang red ribbons for Red Ribbon Week and participate in activities that have the potential to improve the school atmosphere. They welcome new students and help them adjust to school.

One of the latest activities to be included in PAL is to spend some seminar time in a special day school for students who have behavior disorders. PALs engage in nonacademic tasks such as playing board games, shooting baskets, and making crafts. They have been well received by the students and teachers alike.

A PALs participant stated,

> The group teaches students how to be more aware of their peers' feelings and about themselves. It introduced me to many new students like myself who are interested in the well-being of their classmates. The training teaches great people skills.

High School Heroes

High School Heroes is a group of students who teach a tobacco prevention program to fourth, fifth and sixth graders, sponsored by the American Lung Association. This organization prepares the students to be peer educators regarding the forces that influence children's decisions to smoke or not to smoke. In preparation for their roles, the High School Heroes learn about the immediate effects of smoking, how to reinforce positive attitudes about being a nonsmoker, how to make specific decisions, and how to use the refusal skills necessary to resist pressures to smoke. They also learn how to lead a discussion about the respiratory system that includes a demonstration of the effects of smoking.

The American Lung Association recommends that the Heroes program be used as part of a health curriculum to enhance the existing substance abuse program. The Association provides a guide with activities for tobacco education. After the Heroes complete their training, they work in groups of five to prepare a 1-hour tobacco education lesson. After completing their lesson work, they contact fourth-, fifth-, and sixth-grade teachers to set up times for delivering their lesson.

The Lung Association suggests that peer education can have a significant influence on students' knowledge and attitudes about smoking. They believe their training can have an impact on high school students' leadership skills and can reinforce positive attitudes about being a nonsmoker.

TRY

Teaching and Reaching Youth (TRY) is composed of parents and community members from business, police, the service agencies, and education. Its main purpose is to engage the community in focusing on developing knowledge, attitudes, and skills concerning tobacco, alcohol and other drug abuse, and related wellness issues. Specific efforts familiarize the community with state laws, school district policy, and local ordinances relating to these topics. The group's mission is to promote physical and mental wellness in young people through community involvement.

TRY recognizes that youth can be at risk when drugs and alcohol are present during social events. It knows that some students will be pressured by peers to participate. Therefore, one of its programs is Safe Homes for Teens, in which information is sent to parents to secure their support in providing safe homes for student parties. Safe Homes provides homes free of drugs and alcohol. Safe Home parents have access to other committed parents who have pledged to support this cause. TRY has also met with hotel and motel managers requesting that they deny room reservations to prom students who seek accommodations for their parties.

TRY has provided some of the financial support for a popular annual youth activity, school lock-in, in which the SAVE group is also involved. A lock-in provides a safe environment, such as a community center, for a night of social activities that include music, dancing, basketball, swimming, gameroom fun, food, and non-alcoholic beverages.

Some of TRY's other activities include sponsorship of Red Ribbon Week with a community kick-off rally. The group purchases ribbons to tie on utility poles and trees, and yard signs caring the message Drug Free and Proud throughout the city. TRY also sponsors community PIE (Parent Informational Evenings) nights. Here, speakers from the community share information about current topics—for example, the issue of methadone laboratories and what to do about their accessibility to the youth. Methadone labs, for some reason, are prevalent in the surrounding area; hence the need to address the situation.

Helping Component

PATHS

Practical and Academic Transitions to High School (PATHS) is a 3-week summer course designed to prepare eighth graders for a smooth transition to high school. During this course incoming students receive an orientation to the school and community and participate in a special curriculum that promotes student bonding and thematic learning.

For the development phase of PATHS, the building principal recruited a group of teachers interested in the PATHS concept. They developed the summer program, an environment in which students making the transition from middle school to high school could feel more secure and successful. The principal presented the idea to the central office and received funding for the 3-week program.

Two faculty members became co-directors of PATHS. They were joined by four teachers, an instructional assistant, and an attendance secretary to develop the summer program's activities. Peer helpers representing a diverse student population were also selected to give special presentations to middle school students, the potential participants for the summer program.

Peer helpers serve as tutors, conflict mediators, teacher assistants, and hall monitors. They operate the school store during the breaks, are group leaders in the homerooms, and run errands.

In the first PATHS program in 1994 four middle schools enrolled 91 students. They received one-half elective credit for attending all the sessions and completing assignments. The five peer helpers received credit also. The 3-week program began with student bonding activities that continued into week two and week three, which focused on thematic learning.

Week 1. The main objective of the first week was to encourage the students to bond as a team and to become oriented to the school and community. The activities were as follows:

■ *The Challenge* consisted of high and low rope courses designed to teach cooperation, communication, peer support, team building, and self-confidence through a series of well supervised physical challenges. Students spent a full day off campus at an adventure site in the woods.

■ *Being Successful* focused on characteristics that successful people have in common. These include being responsible, hard-working, and team players, as well as going the extra mile. Students became acquainted with successful peers and guest speakers who taught the school's expectations for its students. They were asked to reflect and write about someone whom they considered successful. In addition, they were instructed in the components of peer mediation leading to win/win situations.

■ *Community Orientation* involved students in a picture-taking walking tour of North Kansas City. Students learned about aspects of the city including its history, architecture, and culture. The mayor welcomed the students and discussed city government. When the students returned from the day's adventures, they worked together to develop a travel brochure of the city.

■ *School Orientation* familiarized the students with traditions of the high school. The students went on a walking tour of the campus and learned the buildings and locations of departments. Course offerings, transcripts, school rules, and expectations were discussed. Students became acquainted with the school planner, which they are responsible to keep during their freshmen year.

■ *Diversity Training* was presented by Anytown USA, a program sponsored by the Council of Christians and Jews. It begins with participatory situations for students to experience being different, such as having the disability of blindness, deafness, or confinement in a wheelchair. These are followed by decision-making activities that promote an understanding of and appreciation for diversity of people in the community and school. The experiences encourage positive self-image, communication skills, leadership ability, male/female perceptions, police/ youth relations, racial understanding, cultural awareness, and family and peer relationships.

Week 2 and Week 3. A thematic learning experience focused on the music industry and provided continuity throughout the second and third weeks. A music theme was selected because of its appeal to the adolescents. Students attended three classes per day. At the end of each day, students assembled in the auditorium to participate in musical enrichment. A variety of musical groups performed, and students responded to and critiqued the performances. Three specific academic areas were imbedded in the learning: mathematics, communication, and study skills and are described as follows.

■ *The Mathematical Skill Program* invited the students to use their skills to manage a band. They were responsible for scheduling performance events, figuring time cards, using charts and graphs to record number of performances and the time schedules, mapping travel routes, and writing paychecks. Students were scheduled individually to work in the Computer Curriculum Corporation, a programmed learning of computer use for the development of math skills.

■ *The Communication Skills Program* prepared students to read, discuss, and analyze music reviews. Students wrote critiques of the musical performances they heard in the afternoon. They practiced proofreading skills and oral presentation of their work. They engaged in an art activity by making a collage around the theme of music.

■ *The Study Skills Program* familiarized the students with teacher expectations. Students were taught techniques for previewing lessons and learning the value of understanding each section. Techniques for oral and written reviews also were taught and applied to the materials they were using in the thematic unit. Test-taking skills were presented. Instruction included the teaching of skills required to pass verbal, multiple-choice, and essay tests successfully. Students also were exposed to the assessment procedures the faculty used for grading assignments.

PATHS participants get together several times during the academic year. They have plays, speakers, and casual conversation periods to talk about how school life is going. The Peer Helpers have initiated many informal one-on-one meetings with the freshmen.

School Resource Officer

The School Resource Officer is available to assist students with various legal concerns. These concerns have been about abusive parents, abusive boyfriends, DUI arrests, traffic tickets, and probation contingencies.

The School Resource Officer program, begun in Phoenix, Arizona, in the mid-1980s, has been adopted by some police departments throughout the United States. The duties of the School Resource Officer in the IMPACT program are as follows:

1. To be a resource to instructional units to students on issues related to a basic understanding of the law and the role of law enforcement.

2. To be a resource for instruction to students on issues related to violence, prevention of violence, and personal safety.

3. To facilitate individual and small-group discussions based on material presented in class, or other topics such as date rape, driving while intoxicated, and automobile accidents relevant to student/officer interests. These groups take place during school time or outside of school time.

4. To hold conferences with students to assist them with problems regarding alcohol, other drugs, law enforcement, crime prevention, or personal safety.

5. To meet with students and make referrals to community agencies that offer assistance to youth and their families.

6. To provide informational services to the staff on issues related to alcohol and other drugs, the law, violence, gangs, safety and security.

7. To provide faculty training on skills related to violence prevention, violence diffusion, creation and maintenance of a safe environment.

8. To meet and interact with the Student Steering and Administrative Committees to assist them in any of the programs or legislative issues that SAVE is pursuing.

The SRO commented at the conclusion of his 4 years in the school.

My job as an SRO has been a very rewarding period of my law enforcement career. I've been able to interact with, educate, and positively influence more kids over time than many officers do throughout a career. Since the inception of my role, the number of fights, gang activity, thefts, and drug-related cases has consistently declined. An SRO should be mandatory for every middle school and high school. The value of a safe school environment and the positive law enforcement presence cannot be overstated. SROs are a necessity in schools today. They not only assist in maintaining a safe school environment but also help in building responsible adults.

Operation Drug Dog

In 1997 the entire community took a proactive position on the drug issue by purchasing Twiko, a black Belgian Malinois dog, born and trained in the Netherlands for police work. His specialty is sniffing for drugs, especially marijuana, cocaine, heroin, and methamphetamines. Twiko became part of the community as a result of a campaign spearheaded by a trio of adults—the School Resource Officer, the IMPACT coordinator, and a mathematics teacher.

Although drug reduction efforts had been established in the school and community, not all drugs are found because they are concealed so easily. Teachers had been concerned about the prevalence of drugs in the community and how it was reflected in the school. Some students were returning "high" from open lunch and some were passing drugs on school grounds. At a faculty meeting the teachers said, "We're sick of losing students to drugs." The School Resource Officer, dedicated to the students' welfare, was adamant about finding ways, in addition to his work, to eliminate drugs from the school. The SRO, the IMPACT coordinator, and a mathematics teacher approached the school administration, police chief, community organizations, and city council regarding a plan, "Operation Drug Dog." They received approval, but not financial support, for the plan.

The School Resource Officer searched for other communities that had raised the $20,000 required to cover the cost of the dog, his training, travel, kennel and cage, the travel lodging and training of the officer (who is not the SRO) assigned to Twiko. After finding a community that issued stock to raise funds, the trio decided to use that approach for fundraising. Stock was sold to individuals, including students and senior citizens, civic organizations, and corporations, for $10, $25, and $100, respectively. Within 4 months the funds had been raised. The dog was purchased and trained with the officer. Then Twiko arrived to live in the community that owns him.

After his arrival each contributor was presented with a stock certificate and a photograph of Twiko with his officer. Their duties include night patrols, searching for drugs at sporting events, and random visits to the high school. There Twiko is treated to plenty of petting and attention. He is successful in sniffing out drugs, even minute amounts.

Counseling Services

Counseling services are available for individuals and groups during school hours and with a variety of community agencies. Students are referred by parents, teachers, friends, and self-referrals to the IMPACT coordinator, who devotes all her time to the role. Reasons for referrals include suspected drug and alcohol abuse, poor or failing grades, eating disorders, pregnancy, abuse, depression, and suicidal tendencies. When a student discusses a problem with the IMPACT coordinator, it is followed by an appraisal relevant to the type of support that will be needed. This may include school support, a community referral, a support group, or professional counseling.

The IMPACT coordinator contacts others, such as the parents, teachers, or community personnel, to gather pertinent information that will be useful in an intervention and treatment plan. If a student receives services outside the school, the coordinator is in contact with the agency to facilitate communications and coordinate everyone's efforts. In addition, if the student spends time in a treatment facility, the coordinator notifies the student's teacher, collects homework, and maintains communication between the agencies.

One student commented,

> Being sent for treatment saved my life because it helped me realize that I did have things to live for and look forward to when I'm older.

A parent noted,

> I really appreciate your efforts, your compassion, and your understanding during all of this with my daughter. We have been down a long, rocky road, and without the support of others like you, I don't think the ending of this story would have turned out nearly so well.

The IMPACT coordinator has seen a change in students' attitudes about getting help with their problems.

> It's no longer "un-cool" to talk about having problems. In fact, I can see where students have become more comfortable about dealing with their issues. I can't think of anything more important than the emotional well-being of our youth. If students aren't ready emotionally, they are never going to get it together academically.

Grief Counseling

Grief counseling became prominent in 1995, when the staff at NKCHS and other high schools throughout the United States recognized changes in the emotional health of students after traumatic events. Fatal and near-fatal injuries from accidents and acts of violence, as well as serious illness, were touching students' lives. When adolescents suffer grief from the loss, injury, or illness of someone they love, the emotional experience affects their behavior and can affect academic performance. They are particularly vulnerable to loss. "Grief is a keen and complex emotional experience that includes fear, anger, relief, despair, peace, guilt, numbness, agitation, and sorrow" (Naierman, 1997, p. 62). As students go through the stages of bereavement, they do not always know that others are having similar experiences. In an effort to reach out to the students, NKCHS established guidelines to help the students heal. A plan was written describing an organized way to respond to a crisis.

During the time when the committee was working on the plan, a tragedy occurred: Four students were killed in an automobile accident. The developing guidelines were immediately put into operation, subsequently reviewed, and changes made. The IMPACT coordinator contacts community agencies for their support and obtains trained teachers to lead support groups. The guidelines delineate duties between the administrative team and the counseling team, and the lines of communication to students, staff, parents, community agencies, and the media. The teams provide crisis counseling and crisis rooms as long as they are needed. All activities are documented on a checklist for the management of a traumatic event.

Data and Results of IMPACT

The success of IMPACT is revealed informally by the participants in their comments cited throughout this article. In addition to these statements, data records for the number of student fights and student conflicts reveal a decline in student to student confrontations. Data on peer mediation illustrate an increase in the number of sessions. Figures 17.5 and 17.6 present these data. It is reasonable to assume that the following variables contributed to the decline of fighting: (a) the SAVE program had been initiated in the 1993-94 school year; (b) the peer mediation program was initiated in 1994-95; (c) a school resource officer was assigned to the school; and (d) a zero-tolerance policy relevant to fighting was implemented in the 1995-96 school year.

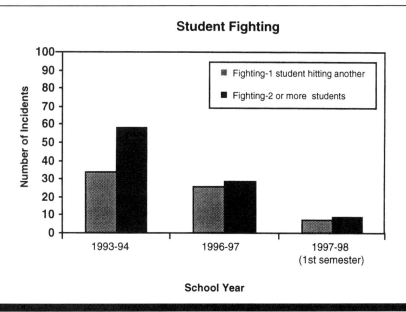

Figure 17.5   Number of Student Fights

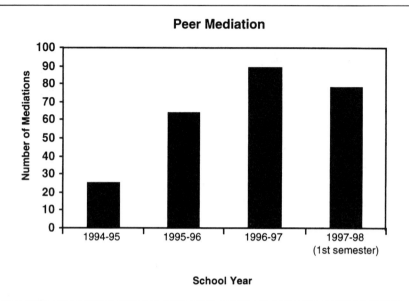

Figure 17.6   Number of Peer Mediation Sessions

Summary

One midwestern high school is taking proactive, constructive steps to protect students and strengthen their relationships with their peers, the faculty, and the community. The IMPACT program focuses on the importance of improving the entire school environment as a significant way to enhance students' wellness and safety. When students, faculty, and community members nourish inviting relationships, caring communities develop. Schools that implement only measures such as metal detectors, student identification badges, and locker inspections have confined themselves to solutions that are problematic. If, on the other hand, schools include practices that promote cooperation, teach conflict resolution, highlight the value of service to others, encourage empathy, and promote belonging and trust, they truly create safe schools.

References

Lantieri, L. (1997). From punishment to prevention: Educating the heart. *Reclaiming Children and Youth.* 6:(3).

Naierman, N. (1997). Reaching out to grieving students. *Educational Leadership. 55* (2).

We thank the many persons who have contributed to the success of IMPACT, the schoolwide wellness program, especially Evelyn Matthys, IMPACT coordinator for North Kansas City School District; Dr. Vicki Baker, Associate Superintendent of North Kansas City School District; Debbie Burns, Special Education Teacher; Rob Russell, School Resource Officer; IMPACT Care Team; IMPACT Student Participants; Bob Kelly and John Admire, Baptist Medical Center, Kansas City, Missouri.

Appendix

Demographics of NKCHS

North Kansas City High School (NKCHS) is one of three high schools serving the North Kansas City School District, which includes 20 elementary schools and four middle schools. The school is located in the small town of North Kansas City; therefore, most of the students are residents of the surrounding areas. The school district is north of the business and financial nucleus of metropolitan Kansas City, Missouri. It is a campus-style facility composed of five separate buildings, the oldest of which was constructed in 1925.

The population represents nearly a complete cross-section of socioeconomic groups. Primary employers of the parents include the major airport, federal and state government agencies, automobile, electronic, paint, and agriculture industries.

The school has 1,400 students. The ethnic make-up of the school is 90% caucasian; the minority populations are represented equally by African American, Asian American, and Latin/Hispanic American cultures.

The school is a Missouri A+ school. A major benefit of this designation is that students who plan to attend a Missouri 2-year community college or vocational school after graduation may be eligible for State-reimbursed fees, books, and tuition. To be eligible, a student must complete the standards for graduation set by the school. In addition, the student must (a) have attended an A+ school for at least 3 years, (b) maintain 95% attendance, (c) have a 2.5 grade-point average on a 4.0 scale, (d) complete 50 hours of unpaid tutoring or mentoring, and (e) maintain good citizenship.

Conflict Resolution: The Partnership Way in Schools

Barry K. Weinhold
and Janae B. Weinhold

onflicts between students, teachers, and other school personnel have long been a part of the school experience, but the tragic results of the recent shooting sprees by enraged students have brought that conflict more sharply into focus. One half of all violence against teenagers occurs in school buildings, on school property, or on the streets in the vicinity of schools (NIDR, 1998). Rarely has the time been better for a school to institute conflict resolution methods and curricula. The Partnership Way, which was developed by the authors, is designed to address the psychological and social conditions that foster conflict. This model is unique in that it embraces conflict and encourages those involved to see themselves as partners who can help resolve conflicts at their source.

The Partnership Way can be used to help individuals, including children, develop skills to maintain an internal sense of "object constancy" and hold themselves as objects of worth even when feeling rejected or unworthy during conflicts. These skills include "I'm okay, you're okay" thinking that discourages *splitting* behaviors (which divide people or groups into "good" and "bad") and looking for three options or choices when resolving conflicts.

Professionals who work in school settings bring with them the residue of developmental trauma, such as incomplete psychosocial tasks and unmet developmental needs from their individual, couple, family, and work relationships. These unresolved developmental issues will eventually surface as conflicts containing Drama Triangle (persecutor, rescuer, and victim) dynamics within schools, neighborhoods, and community organizations. When people overreact during in-school, conflicts they are probably experiencing symptoms of post-traumatic stress. (See Figure 18.1 for information useful in identifying the impact of developmental trauma in school settings.) With the Partnership Way, that behavior is not judged; rather it is viewed from a compassionate and understanding perspective. The Partnership Way teaches

SYMPTOMS OF DEVELOPMENTAL TRAUMAS	DEVELOPMENTAL ISSUES	SUGGESTED INTERVENTIONS
Clinging, an obvious need to touch or be touched, shy, regressive behaviors, whining, helplessness, watching others rather than participating, dependent in relationships with others, tendency to be lethargic and low energy	*Incomplete bonding with another person* Trauma during the first year of life that has damaged the child's ability to bond, including: premature separation from mother; repeated separation from mother; too many different caregivers	Spend extra time, recruit help with tasks, listen to and support feelings ("You look like you are sad"), give unconditional responses ("I like you"), provide mirroring ("I see you...")
Suspicious, sneaky, little self-disclosure, few friends, lying, secretive, belligerent, high-risk behaviors	*Poorly developed sense of basic trust* Impaired ability to trust due to abuse or threat of abuse, physical trauma such as a surgery or medical procedures, particularly during the first two months of life	Encourage them to trust their own feelings and responses, teach them effective ways to determine the trustworthiness of others
Putting objects in their mouths, chewing pencils and erasers, talking incessantly, acting-out to get attention, smoking, drinking, using drugs, gum chewing, nail biting, excessive snacking	*Unsatisfied oral needs* Trauma during period between the ages of four and six months that disrupts the period of oral bonding between the child and mother	Confront inappropriate behavior, support "okayness" and problem solving, set reasonable limits, give positive reinforcement on appropriate behaviors
Not respecting property, feelings, and rights of others; not keeping agreements; minor shoplifting; interrupting; name calling; not taking responsibility but blaming others; touching others inappropriately	*Lack of respect for personal boundaries, personal boundaries not respected by parents* Lack of developmentally appropriate limits during the second year of life, inhibiting the child's abilities to accept external authority and to develop boundaries and consequences	Set reasonable, clearly defined limits that are enforced consistently; arrange logical and natural consequences
Have trouble taking compliments, over-personalizing issues, moodiness, short attention span, attempting to be different in behavior and dress	*Difficulty in separating self from others* Trauma during the period between six and eight months during the critical stage of symbiosis between the mother and child	Encourage independent thinking and acting, give feedback on personal uniqueness

Behaviors	Developmental Trauma	Intervention
Withdrawal from activities involving any physical risk, reluctance to try new things, fear of failure, perfectionism, procrastination, easily confused	*Poor object constancy, weak self-image* Trauma during period between two and four months of age that disrupts the first stage of self-development and inhibits building the foundation of self-esteem	Arrange safe exploratory learning activities, encourage risk-taking, reframe "mistakes" into "learning"
Exaggerations, grandiosity, black-and-white thinking, comparative thinking, daredevil acts, impulsiveness	*Weak cause and effect thinking, stuck in the "splitting" stage of separation* Trauma during period between 12 and 18 months of age when child is in the "splitting" stage of development, leaving a residue of narcissistic behaviors	Help arrange logical and natural consequences to behaviors, help with identification of good and bad qualities in situations and people
Denial, saying "I can't" and "I don't know," agitating, escalating, not thinking, reacting without thinking	*Failure to develop effective ways to explore their world, lack of self-confidence* Trauma during between period of 8 and 10 months of age when the child typically begins exploring	Avoid rescuing, support problem solving, cheerlead ("You can do it"), encourage appropriate risk-taking
Use of control, intimidation, manipulation, and games to get needs met, blaming others, avoiding responsibilities, low tolerance for frustration, poor coordination, bullying younger peers	*Lack of personal power, failure to develop skills in autonomy* Trauma during period between 12 and 18 months of age when child is in the "splitting" stage of development, leaving a residue of narcissistic behaviors	Mediate disputes, positive support for independent action
Poor impulse control, inability to follow through, inability to delay gratification, poor personal hygiene, inability to handle resources such as time and money effectively, poor planning, last-minute cramming, sloppy or messy homework	*Lack of self-management and mastery skills* Trauma during the first year of life that inhibits the child's development of an internal regulating structure	Teach skills In structuring time and preparing budgets, encourage better self-care, empower by mirroring effective self-management behaviors

Figure 18.1 Skill Practice Exercise: Identifying Developmental Traumas at the Source of Student Conflicts

individuals to avoid getting "triggered" in school or neighborhood conflicts and to develop a compassionate attitude toward themselves and their reactions to others and subsequent events.

The Nature of School Conflict and How To Deal With It

Although conflict has, unfortunately, become an accepted fact in public school life, most students do not know how to resolve conflicts in nonviolent or cooperative ways. If students are taught to resolve conflicts effectively, they can live more productive lives, as well as avoiding the drastic and life-threatening action seen in the news. There are two ways to incorporate conflict resolution training in schools. The first is training students as conflict mediators to help other students resolve conflicts at school. The other is to offer a K-12 curriculum in conflict resolution for all students. A combination of these two approaches is the most effective way to insure that all students learn how to resolve conflicts nonviolently and from a win-win perspective.

Even with the trend toward teaching students conflict resolution skills, there seems to be a breakdown in civility among our young people and a sharp increase of peer violence. Student-to-student put-downs have become more cruel and hurtful, as well as more common. In addition, there is a growing group of children and youth who wish to dominate, intimidate, or bully other students, either to gain the attention of others or to pass on the vicious cycle of cruelty from experiences of being dominated, intimidated, or bullied by their parents or older siblings. Schools also become battlegrounds for rival gangs who vie for control in order to sell drugs to students. School officials often do not know how to cope with these challenges.

Public schools have become the largest purchasers of metal detectors. Many now hire guards to patrol their hallways. The most effective way to address these problems is mobilizing everyone in the school to work cooperatively to end the violence. Some schools have developed zero-tolerance policies that make it impossible for bullying and criminal behavior to exist in the schools. These same zero-tolerance policies can be extended into neighborhoods and communities.

How Conflict Resolution Can Stem the Rise of Peer Violence

The tremendous amount of peer violence and conflict in schools is often manifested as bullying and put-downs. Teachers and parents too often look the other way when children fight with each other. The tendency is to "let them fight it out." While this policy may prevent rescuing behaviors, "innocent" fighting, bullying and put-downs can severely traumatize a child. The average child receives 213 put-downs a week or 30 per day. Three out of four students report being bullied at school. Each month, over 525,000 students are victims of attacks, shakedowns, and robberies while at school (Fried & Fried, 1996). Getting away with bullying behavior doesn't bode well for the perpetrator either. More than 50% of all schoolyard bullies end up in prison.

Peer violence is far more pervasive than youth violence in gangs and perhaps even more pervasive than domestic violence. Peer violence is first learned at home. Children who experience violence at home often go to school and treat their peers violently. Schools have become the battleground for releasing pent-up anger and rage. Violence, furthermore, can erupt over little things, such as the way one person looks at another.

There are many different kinds of conflicts that occur daily in school: teasing, bullying, fighting, pushing, and shoving. Bullies often roam the schools looking for smaller kids to pick on, shake down, harass, beat up, or intimidate. Bullying behavior is one of the most destructive forms of school conflict.

Skill Practice Exercise: Identifying Developmental Traumas as the Source of Student Conflicts

1. Study the chart in Figure 18.1 and make sure everyone understands it.
2. Discuss how it could be used in a school or agency that deals with children and youth.
3. Divide into small groups of 4-6 persons. Take turns role-playing a student who is displaying one of the symptoms listed below. The rest of the group is asked to try different ways to confront this behavior.
4. Discuss each role-play situation and evaluate the effectiveness of the confrontation. Discuss the results in the large group.

Addressing Bullying Behaviors in Schools

The problem of bullying behavior in schools has been around for a long time, and very little has been done to correct it. Children feel afraid to report it to school officials. Even when they do report it, adults usually fail to help them. Teachers and administrators often have difficulty distinguishing the boundary between true bullying behavior and normal peer conflict. Many teachers believe children should learn to resolve their own differences and are reluctant to rescue. Many children do not report bullying traumas because they fear they will be branded "snitches" and incite further retaliation by the bullies. These victims of violence and aggression feel isolated, fearful, and alone. Here are some facts about bullying behavior (Fried & Fried, 1996; Garrity et al., 1994):

■ Three-out-of-four students from non-urban schools report being bullied during their school career.

- Ninety percent of all students felt that being bullied caused lasting social, emotional, or academic problems.
- Sixty percent of victims report being bullied by boys; 40% were bullied by girls.
- Bullying is reported as most severe in grades 7-9, followed by grades 9-12.
- Sixty-nine percent of all students believe that schools respond poorly to bullying and victimization.
- Ridiculing/teasing, verbal harassment, and practical jokes are the most frequently reported forms of bullying. Physical attacks are reported less frequently.
- Forty-four percent of teachers believe disruptive school behaviors are getting worse.
- Each month, over 525,000 students are victims of attacks, shakedowns, and robberies while at school.
- One out of five high school students report avoiding restrooms out of a fear for their safety.
- Ten percent of those who drop out of school do so because of repeated bullying.
- Both bullies and victims have problems later in life related to their experiences.
- Everyone plays a role in allowing bullying behavior to go on and everyone can play a role in helping to stop the problem.

The following strategies have proven to be effective:

- Teach the students effective strategies to stop bullying behavior.
- Train the faculty to recognize and effectively intervene in bullying situations.
- Establish school/classroom rules for reporting and eliminating bullying behavior.
- Develop programs for recognition of prosocial behaviors.
- Create peer mediation programs.
- Teach conflict resolution skills to all students and faculty.

Preventing School Conflicts

Although most of the attention goes into trying to contain current conflict situations, it is just as important to work to prevent conflict. There are three basic kinds of prevention programs: primary, secondary, and tertiary. School-based intervention programs such as cooperative learning are an example of a primary prevention program. Cooperative learning has proven to be very effective in dealing with high-risk kids prone to violent conflicts. If begun early, children can learn quickly and effectively to use nonviolent means for resolving their conflicts. These skills help children feel safe and powerful without resorting to guns, gangs, and violence. In 1997, the

National Institute for Dispute Resolution estimated that there are over 8,500 school-based conflict resolution programs in the United States (NIDR, 1998).

Primary Prevention

These programs encourage interventions prior to the appearance of a problem and provide a pleasurable experience as part of the intervention. When people are engaged in pleasurable or kind acts, the hypothalamus gland secrets endorphins that inhibit the release of "substance P," a brain chemical that communicates pain to the brain. Linking desired positive social behaviors with the biological secretion of a neurochemical can help build a new psychophysiological structure for behavior patterns (Kotulak, 1996). Primary prevention programs in schools provide supportive services to all members of the school community without focusing on a target group that has been identified as in conflict or at risk of conflict. Peer mediation programs, conflict resolution skills training for all K-12 students, and a cooperative learning curriculum are examples of primary prevention programs in schools.

Secondary Prevention

These programs intervene after a problem has begun and provide supportive services to target groups already identified as having conflicts or at risk of having conflicts. A program that offers support services to students who have been active in school fights is an example of secondary prevention. One such program assigns youths to community service rather than at-home suspension with the hope of giving them experiences that change their attitudes and behaviors. Other examples include the creation of zero-tolerance policies on bullying.

Tertiary Prevention

Services for those who have gotten into academic difficulty and can be rehabilitated are tertiary prevention programs. An example of this is alternative high schools for students who have dropped out of school and then decided to return.

Some Successful Prevention Programs

This section identifies programs used by schools to help identify the source of conflicts, create direct communication dynamics, and prevent triangulation. These programs utilize components such as psychoeducation, individual empowerment, skill development. and peer mediation from the Partnership Way. Programs that focus on prevention are critical for teaching children to resolve conflicts nonviolently.

The growing problem of peer violence has been a catalyst for the expansion of conflict resolution and peer mediation curricula in schools. Over 8,500 schools in the United States are now using one or both of these kinds of programs (NIDR, 1998).

Peer Mediation

Peer mediation is designed to teach students how to help each other resolve conflicts nonviolently and effectively. One peer mediation program for resolving conflicts involves training a group of elementary-school or middle-school students to serve as the school's conflict managers. Peer mediators often wear a special sweatshirt, T-shirt, button, or some kind of tag to identify them. Peer mediators facilitate every-day school conflicts by bringing together the individuals in conflict to resolve the issues peacefully and honorably. A conflict manager who sees a conflict starting can approach the students involved and offer mediation services. The students in conflict are free to refuse this offer. If they do accept it, the peer mediator establishes ground rules for the students to use in working through their conflict.

Peer mediator training usually includes skills in conflict analysis, active listening, interest-based bargaining, and facilitation. Advanced training content includes more experiential activities, including structured experiences, role-playing, and simulations. Ongoing in-service training is also a part of this program. Peer mediators meet regularly with their trainers or coaches to discuss how they handled specific situations and get feedback on how they might improve their efforts.

Most schools that have adopted peer mediation programs believe they are effective. To get the most benefit from peer mediation programs, however, schools need to teach all students conflict resolution skills. Many large city school districts, including Chicago, New York, and Kansas City, have mandated teaching conflict resolution in their K-12 curricula. Teachers in school districts that have not yet mandated conflict resolution skills training can still do much to create a peaceful classroom (see Figures 18.2 and 18.3).

Conflict Resolution Curricula

In his book, *Creative Conflict Resolution,* Kreidler (1984) lists the five qualities of a peaceful classroom:

1. *Cooperation.* Children learn to work together, trust and help each other, and share with each other.

2. *Communication.* Students learn to ask directly for what they want, rather than acting out or whining to get attention. They also learn how to listen sensitively.

3. *Tolerance.* Students learn to show respect and appreciation for differences. They learn to understand racial, religious, and other forms of prejudice and how to deal with it.

4. *Positive emotional expression.* Students learn to express feelings, particularly anger and frustration, in ways that are not aggressive or destructive. Students also develop impulse control.

5. Conflict resolution. In the peaceful classroom students learn win-win methods for resolving conflicts.

The following skill practice exercise is designed to help the students in this course better understand the role and functions of a peer mediator operating in a school.

1. Divide into small groups of 4 to 5 students and brainstorm a list of typical school conflicts where mediators could be helpful in facilitating a win-win resolution.
2. Each small group reports on what they have found and a larger list is developed containing all the ideas.
3. The class then decides which of the typical conflicts to use in their skill practice session.
4. Using the mediation process in Figure 18.3, review the steps to make sure everyone understands them.
5. Select two small group members to role-play one of the typical conflict situations and two other members to be the peer mediators. Any additional small group members should serve as process observers and give feedback after each role-play.
6. While the two students role-play the school conflict, the mediators need to follow the mediation process and attempt to get the students to resolve their conflict.
7. Rotate the roles so that each member of the small group gets to play all the roles.
8. Discuss the results in your small group and in the large group class.

Figure 18.2 Skill Practice Exercise: What Is the Role of the Peer Mediator?

Kreidler is quick to point out that a peaceful classroom climate will not eliminate all conflicts, but will reduce them by providing effective methods of dealing with them when they arise. He also contrasts the peaceful classroom with one where conflict erupts on a regular basis. He groups the causes of conflict into six categories:

1. *A competitive atmosphere.* Students learn to work against each other rather than cooperate. They develop an attitude of everyone for himself or herself and do not learn how to work together in groups. They lack trust in the teacher and their classmates.

2. *An intolerant atmosphere.* Students are unfriendly, critical, unsupportive, and intolerant. Conflicts arise out of friction between cliques, from scapegoating, from intolerance of racial and cultural differences, because of resentment toward those who are successful, and from feelings of loneliness and isolation.

3. *Poor communication.* Students attempt to get their needs met by acting out and fighting and escalate incidents into conflicts because of misperceptions.

1. **The Mediator Monologue:**

   Intervene and ask if the parties would like some help in resolving their conflict.
   If the answer is "yes," then explain the mediation process.
   Explain the mediator's role and confidentiality.
   Explain the ground rules:

A. Parties agree to resolve the conflict themselves with the mediator's help.
B. No name calling or put-downs.
C. Do not interrupt and listen to each other.
D. Tell the truth.
E. Ask each student if they want to use mediation to help resolve their conflict.

2. **Opening Statements:**
   — Ask student # 1 what happened and how they feel.
   — Ask student # 2 what happened and how they feel.
   — Use active listening to reflect back the content and feelings.

3. **Reframe the Problem:**
   — Summarize the conflict in neutral terms.
   — Get agreement on what the conflict involves.

4. **Explore Interests:**
   — Ask student # I what is most important for them in a solution.
   — Ask student # 2 what is most important for them in a solution.
   — Ask student # I what would make them feel better or happier.
   — Ask student # 2 what would make them feel better or happier.

5. **Invent Options:**
   — Ask student # 1 to give possible solutions they would like.
   — Ask student # 2 to give possible solutions they would like.

6. **Choose the Best Option:**
   — Help the students pick what they agree is the best option.
   — If the option they select is not clear to you, ask clarifying questions.
   — Write down the option they agreed to and have them sign it.
   — Specify any consequences if they don't keep the agreement.

Figure 18.3 Skill Practice Exercise: The Peer Mediation Process

4. *Inappropriate expressions of emotion.* Students use conflicts as a way to express their feelings. They lack assertive ways to express feelings of anger and frustration and skills in impulse control.

5. *Lack of conflict resolution skills.* Students deficient in effective win-win conflict resolution skills are unable to respond effectively in conflict situations. Without skill training, students often resort to the aggressive or violent models of conflict resolution they see on television and at the movies.

6. *The misuse of power by the teacher.* Stressed-out teachers who feel out of control often misuse their power to cope with their stress and feelings of disempowerment. They may place irrational or unreasonable expectations on certain students who annoy them, create rigid rules, or use authoritarian methods that create an atmosphere of fear and mistrust.

A Curriculum to Prevent Violent Youth Conflicts

One of the most highly regarded conflict resolution curricula was developed in 1994 by the Education Development Center in Newton, MA, as the result of a collaborative study. Called Aggressors, Victims and Bystanders, (Slaby, et al., 1994) it is designed for grades 7 to 12 as part of a comprehensive school health curriculum. It is delivered in 45-minute class segments and contains a teacher's guide plus student activities and handouts. This curriculum has three main assumptions:

1. Fighting is not a viable way to resolve conflicts.

2. Adolescents can learn skills to resolve conflicts in nonviolent ways.

3. Conflict resolution skills will enhance the safety of students and help everyone maintain self-respect and the respect of others.

The backbone of the curriculum is a four-step "Think-First" model. It teaches students how to think, what to think, and how to develop a cool-headed approach in conflict situations. A unique aspect of this program is that it doesn't just focus on the aggressor's role in starting or preventing conflicts. It also emphasizes the roles of the bystander and the victim in preventing violent conflict. This approach correlates with the Drama Triangle aspect of the Partnership Way and its interchanging roles of Persecutor, Rescuer, and Victim.

Bully-Proofing Schools

Other primary and secondary peer violence prevention programs have targeted bullying behavior. Aggressive and antisocial behavior is easy to spot and easy to treat, if caught early enough. One of the most effective programs to stop bullying behavior is the Bully-Proofing Program (1995) developed in Colorado. (Garrity, et al., 1995)

This comprehensive curriculum targets elementary schools as early-intervention targets. Developed by a team of consultants in the Cherry Creek Schools in suburban Denver, the curriculum has three primary strategies:

1. Develop school-wide no-bullying policies.

2. Train the faculty and staff on effective implementation of the policy.

3. Train all the students in the school to deal with bullying behavior.

Olweus (1991) found that the single most effective way to stop bullying behavior in schools is to teach the adults to recognize bullying behavior and train them to stop it. Children look to adults for help in combating bullying. It is surprising how many teachers cannot recognize bullying behaviors or know when and where their help is needed. If they do recognize the problem, few know how to make effective interventions.

A key to teacher involvement in prevention programs is awareness of their own personal style of conflict resolution. This helps them correlate it with appropriate interventions for bullying situations. Teachers can quickly see how their style may not be effective in all conflict situations. For example, a teacher who is more of a compromiser or an accommodator might have trouble intervening in bullying situations such as physical fighting that requires a more directive approach. The Bully-Proofing Program suggests that teachers expand their personal style of conflict resolution and team up with other teachers whose style complements theirs.

The implementation part of this program involves developing classroom rules that parallel the overall school discipline policy and teaching students how to cope with bullying. In addition to these classroom interventions, the program also includes materials to help counselors work more intensively with students, either individually or in small groups, who are frequent victims of bullying. It also includes strategies for working directly with bullies to change their behaviors.

Dealing with bullying students themselves is another important intervention. Without intervention, these behaviors will get worse. In a study in Norway, Olweus (1991) discovered that 60% of the boys who were identified as bullies in the second grade were convicted of a felony by age 24. An American longitudinal study by Eron (1987) showed that aggressive behavior rarely changed over the course of his 22-year study. The more aggressive a boy was at age eight, the greater the chances he would be in trouble with the law as an adult. In addition, he was less likely to have finished college or secured a job. Aggressive girls were more likely to use aggressive methods of punishing their children when they became mothers. The children of these mothers were also more likely to become bullies. Eron says, "Early intervention is critical" (p. 14).

Samenow (1984, 1989) found that aggressive antisocial youth use faulty thinking to justify their actions. These thinking errors include the following:

1. "Life is a one-way street—my way."

2. "1 should be number one immediately."

1. Discuss "what is bullying?" Get examples from the students.
2. Introduce the idea that if everyone sticks together, no one is left out and a bully can't isolate and pick on anyone.
3. Discuss the difference between tattling and getting adult help. Make sure they understand that it is not tattling when they help someone who is in danger.
4. Present and discuss the following classroom rules about bullying:
   - We agree that no student in the class will be permitted to bully any other student.
   - We agree that we will come to the aid of any student being bullied by telling a bully to stop and by getting help from an adult.
   - We agree not to exclude any student from an activity in school or on the playground and make sure to include all students in our activities at school.
5. Post the rules in the classroom.

Figure 18.4   Skill Practice Exercise: Developing Classroom Rules to Deal with Bullying Behavior

   3. "It's not my fault."
   4. "If someone disagrees with me, they are putting me down."

These kind of thinking errors are characteristic of people who are wounded by severe developmental trauma. These individuals probably suffer from unresolved abuse and neglect inflicted during early childhood that impacts their adolescent behavior. Table 18.1 identifies some of the common errors in thinking of people who haven't completed the counter-dependent stage of development. Teachers, counselors, and parents can confront children and adolescents in these errors in thinking in ways that can help correct these errors and promote responsible behavior.

Some of these errors in thinking are symptoms of Reactive Attachment Disorder and the presence of antisocial behavior. Many of these children are misdiagnosed with Attention Deficit Disorder. Studies show that the earlier these symptoms are addressed, the better the chances are that these disorders will not occur. Magid and McKelvey (1987) say that if a child is not treated by age sixteen it is difficult and perhaps impossible to reverse the effects of the early trauma. The only solution is to "warehouse" them. Many untreated youth and adults are already warehoused in our country's jails and prisons or locked residential adolescent treatment facilities.

As indicated in the research, bullying students can be identified early in their school years and given individual help. According to Lewis (1992), the early

Table 18.1   Behavioral and Affective At-Risk Factors Among Junior High School Students

Thinking Errors Related to Developmental Traumas	Healthy Ways to Deal With Students who Have These Thinking Errors
"I am a victim." "He started it." "I couldn't help it." "it is their fault."	Do not accept these excuses. Focus on the individual, e. g., what he or she did that contributed to the problem.
"I can't do it." Tries to avoid responsibility by claiming it is impossible to accomplish anything.	Respond with, "'I can't' usually means 'I won't.'" Ask why they are refusing to do this.
"I didn't know that would hurt you." They do not think how their actions affect others.	Say, "When you do this, I lose my trust in you and don't want to be with you. Will you change your behavior?" Ask, "How would you feel if someone did that to you?"
"I don't understand why you feel that way." They have little empathy for others. Very egocentric.	Ask, "How would you feel if someone did that to you?" Tell them your feelings.
"I'm bored" (and it's your fault). These people engage in self-pity. They may develop psychosomatic aches and pains as avoidance defenses.	Say, "Boredom is anger without enthusiasm." Ask what or who are the sources of blame and excuses. Point out natural consequences of their anger.
"I forgot to do it. So what!" Does not keep agreements, does not want to be held responsible for breaking them. Looks for excuses, blames circumstances for broken agreements.	Point out that people remember what they want to remember. Ask them to explain why they forget and to examine the real reasons. Give logical consequences. Ask how they feel when others break agreements.
"I am entitled to it, so if you don't give it to me, I'll take it." They expect others to do what they want them to do. No respect for property of others. Makes demands on others. Righteous attitude.	Give logical consequences for not respecting the property of others. Point out that they are not entitled to use the property of others without permission.
"You can't trust people." These individuals are emotional loners and have little trust or loyalty to anyone. Blame others for breaking trust but really are saying, "I can't trust you."	Give specific examples of behaviors that make it difficult to trust. Confront any betrayal of trust. Insist that trust be earned.

"If I think so, it will happen." Have unrealistic expectations and "magical thinking," which is often grandiose, with no understanding of how to accomplish goals.	Get them to provide a step-by-step plan and point out any missing steps. Help them to state their expectations, prepare for disappointment.
"I assumed you knew what I wanted." Make unwarranted assumptions and are angry when others don't agree. They don't find the facts or truth and blame others when things go wrong.	Point out their unwarranted assumptions and ask them to check them against the facts. If they don't know how to find the facts, help them learn.
"I am right and you are wrong." Prideful, refuse to back down, even on small points. Will not admit mistakes. Pride usually covers up shame. Egotistical.	Help them find a third alternative to black-and-white, either/or ways of thinking. Admit a mistake to them when you make one and request they do the same. Ask what they learned from their mistakes.
"I didn't know that would happen." They lack the ability to plan ahead or to make long-range plans.	Ask for a step-by-step plan and help them think ahead at each step. Show how advanced planning can prevent unpleasant events.
"If I do that, I will be a _____." Definitions of success and failure are grandiose. Failure is seen as something less than being first. Uses either/or thinking.	Help them see grades of success and failure. Teach that mistakes are just new kinds of learning. Help them define success and failure from a self-reference point.
"You are just trying to put me down." Feel put down if even the smallest things don't go their way. Personalizes feedback from others. Feels criticized by others.	Help them learn from mistakes. Show them how their behavior drew criticism and then how to evaluate the criticism.
"I'm not afraid of anything." Denial of fear. Uses false bravado to cover up fear. Sees fear as a weakness.	Tell them that acknowledging fear can be a sign of strength. Help them understand the sources of their fear.
"I don't get mad, I get even." Uses revenge to act out hurts. Uses attacks, intimidation, sarcasm, or threats to get their way. Anger may also be expressed passively or indirectly.	Help them realize that the function of anger is to let them know what they want. Also show how anger covers fear and help them identify their fears.
"I need to be in charge." These people try to dominate others through power and skills and control. They have to win at all costs.	Confront every attempt to use power over others. Help them learn partnering, show how dominating others doesn't get them what they really want.

warning signals are impulsivity, hypersensitivity, and erroneous thinking. Garrity, et al., (1995) list the following early warning signs that teachers can easily observe:

- Irritability, impatience, and moodiness from an early age.
- A tendency to perceive hostile intent of others even when it isn't there.
- A tendency to retaliate quickly for genuine or imagined threats.
- Trouble identifying feelings; acts them out rather than communicating them.
- Inability to recognize one's own pain or the pain of others.
- An abusive or neglectful home environment.

A Cooperative Learning Curriculum

The Partnership Model suggests that the school years between ages six and eighteen are the years to learn about cooperation and develop interdependence. This is the research finding of brothers David W. and Roger T. Johnson, pioneers in the development of cooperative learning curriculum materials and programs for the schools. The Johnsons have created theory, research, and application materials to develop interdependent thinking and behavior in students to facilitate social interdependence. They identify three key components for teaching social interdependence: competitive learning situations, individualistic learning situations, and cooperative learning situations. Their research, which reveals the limits of competitive and individualistic learning, indicates that cooperative learning produces:

- higher achievement
- more caring, supportive, and committed relationships
- greater psychological health, social competence, and self-esteem

In the 1960s, the Johnsons developed an effective conflict resolution model called the *Teaching Students to be Peacemakers Program* (Johnson & Johnson, 1987). It is a K-12 conflict resolution training program based on the principles of cooperative learning. The goal of the program is to teach all students to be peacemakers. They have implemented this program in the United States and other parts of the world. The program has six steps:

1. *Create a cooperative context for resolving conflicts.* Teach students to recognize the importance of their long-term interdependence when resolving conflicts. De-emphasize the need to win and emphasize the need to resolve the conflict for mutual benefit.

2. *Teach students how to recognize what is and what is not a conflict.* Many students hold misconceptions about conflict, based on what they see on television or in the movies. They do not see the positive gains from successful conflict resolution, such as laughter, insight, learning, and closer relationships.

3. *Teach students a specific, concrete procedure for negotiating agreements.* Students need a step-by-step method they can use to resolve conflicts without damaging their relationships. Telling students to "talk it out" or "solve your problem" is not enough.

4. *Teach students to use a concrete and specific mediation procedure.* Students need to be taught how to mediate their classmates' conflicts. They are given 30 hours of specific training on recognizing conflict, negotiation skills, and mediation skills.

5. *Implement the program.* Working in pairs, initially, student mediators help other students mediate conflicts. These roles are rotated so that all students get a chance to be a mediator.

6. *Continue weekly training in negotiation and mediation procedures throughout the first through twelfth grades.* This helps everyone refine and upgrade their skills. The students learn that to become competent in conflict resolution takes years of practice.

Unlike many similar programs, the Johnsons conducted extensive research, using ten different studies to document the effectiveness of their program in different schools. They found the following results (Johnson and Johnson, 1995):

1. In urban schools, most of the conflicts referred to student mediators involved physical and verbal violence. In suburban schools, most conflicts centered on possessions and access to resources, preferences about what to do, playground issues, and turn-taking.

2. Untrained students would almost always strive to win in a conflict situation, while those trained in peacemaking focused on maximizing joint outcomes.

3. The number of discipline problems dropped by 60% and referrals to the principal's office dropped about 95%.

4. Untrained students held generally negative attitudes toward conflict, while trained students held more positive attitudes toward conflict.

David and Roger Johnson's cooperative learning approach is now used widely in schools in this country to provide a counterbalance to the competitive and individualistic learning that is so prevalent in our public schools. There have been many criticisms of cooperative learning by some educators, who often do not understand the negative impact of competitive and individualistic models and who do not know how to facilitate effective cooperative learning activities. As many high-tech businesses adopt project team structures, the value of cooperative learning as an important job skill for the Information Age has increased. Schools are being encouraged to use more cooperative learning strategies to better prepare their students for living in a shrinking, increasingly more interdependent world.

1. Divide into small groups of five or six people.
2. Brainstorm as many ways as you can think of to teach each of the nine types of interdependence described earlier in this chapter.
3. Select what you as a group decide are your best ideas.
4. Each small group gives a report to the class on their ideas of how to teach the different types of interdependence.

As a variation, the large group could utilize one or more of the suggested activities to develop more interdependence in the class.

Figure 18.5   Self-Awareness Exercise: Positive Interdependence Brainstorming

They cite five causes of resistance to cooperative learning by educators and others:

1. Confusion about what makes cooperative learning groups work.

2. The patterns of isolation created by organizational barriers to cooperation.

3. A false social norm of "rugged individualism."

4. The risk that educators perceive because the groups might fail.

5. That using cooperative learning groups requires disciplined action by teachers for which they can be held accountable.

At the core of David and Roger Johnson's program on cooperative learning is the concept of positive interdependence (see Figure 18.5). The Johnsons' program of cooperative learning focuses directly on how to teach this vital skill. This program identifies and describes nine different types of activities that develop positive interdependence in children and youth (Johnson, Johnson, & Holubec, 1993). These nine types of activities are described briefly below:

Positive Goal Interdependence: Activities are arranged so that students can achieve their learning goals only if all the members of their learning group also attain their goals. Members of a learning group develop their learning goals in a way that helps everyone achieve the goals.

Positive Reward Interdependence: Each learning group member receives the same reward for completing an assignment. A joint reward is given for a successful group effort.

Positive Resource Interdependence: Each group member is given only a portion of the information, resources, or materials needed to complete a task. The group members have to work cooperatively in order to complete their task.

Positive Task Interdependence: Learning tasks are arranged so that the actions of one group member have to be completed before the next group member can complete his or her part.

Positive Role Interdependence: Each group member is assigned complementary and interconnected roles that are necessary to complete a group task.

Positive Identity Interdependence: The learning group creates its own identity through a name, flag, motto, song, or poem.

Positive Outside Enemy Interdependence: Nothing will bring a group of people together more quickly than an outside force that they must overcome in order to be successful. Creating external opposition promotes this.

Positive Fantasy Interdependence: The group task is to imagine that they are in a life-or-death situation and must cooperate in order to survive.

Environment Interdependence: Group members are bound together by a physical environment in some way. For example, having to work in a confined area that they have to rearrange in order to work most effectively.

The Kindness Campaign: A Primary Prevention Program

The Kindness Campaign is a primary prevention program that reinforces empathic, prosocial rather than antisocial behaviors (Weinhold, 1996 a & b). It is designed to create a positive school and community climate where antisocial behavior cannot thrive. The motto of the Kindness Campaign is "Spread Kindness-It's Contagious"©. The goals of the Kindness Campaign are:

1. To restore a sense of community and neighborliness that we seem to have forgotten and

2. To prevent the spread of violence that has taken hold in many parts of our schools, community, state, and nation.

Spreading kindness is up to everyone, and it can be fun and rewarding. Anyone can participate in this campaign to stop the spread of violence, hatred, and unkindness by remembering to do small daily acts of kindness for ourselves, our family, friends, neighbors, school mates, work mates, strangers, those who are sick or in need, and anyone else we meet.

This campaign reconfirms the important principle of interdependency and the responsibility to act kindly towards one's self as well as towards others. The attitude of kindness begins with first being kind to one's self because it is difficult to be kind to others when one's own heart is empty of kindness. True kindness comes from having a compassionate heart. It takes countless small daily acts of kindness to create an atmosphere of compassion necessary to transform a mass of separate individuals into a kind, caring community.

The Kindness Campaign is designed to provide simple recognition for daily acts of kindness. Many acts of kindness go unrecognized, while acts of violence are quickly recognized, perhaps even over-recognized by the media. The best way to eliminate violence is to reinforce its opposite: kindness. When you sign a pledge card, you are given a button that says "Spread Kindness—It's Contagious." A person who witnesses another person committing an act of kindness gives their button to this person to acknowledge this act. As they give away their button, they ask the recipient to pass on the button when they witness another act of kindness. In this way, kindness can spread quickly to help build a kind, caring school or community.

The Kindness Campaign is spreading rapidly in Colorado Springs schools. Many use *Spreading Kindness* (Weinhold, 1996a), a program guide developed for elementary and middle schools. Participating schools typically report an immediate 30% or more drop in discipline referrals after beginning the campaign. Longer term results show a 26% drop. Put-downs are also drastically reduced, with reports of up to 94% in several schools. Reports of bullying behavior and violent conflicts also drop sharply in participating schools.

Primary prevention programs that use kindness, mediation, and conflict resolution are slowly transforming the country's schools and providing more and more people with foundation skills in win-win conflict resolution skills. As the positive results of these efforts become more apparent to everyone, Resolution will literally become the "Fourth W" in our nation's schools.

References

Eron, L. (1987). Aggression through the ages. *School Safety.* Fall, 12-16.

Fried, S., & Fried, P. (1996). *Bullies and victims: Helping your child survive the school yard battlefield.* New York: M. Evans and Company, Inc.

Garrity, C., et al. (1995). *Bully proofing your school: A comprehensive approach for elementary schools.* Longmont, CO: Sopris West.

Johnson, D. W., & Johnson, R. (1987). *Creative Conflict.* Edina, MN: Interaction Book Company.

Johnson, D. W., & Johnson, R. T. (1995). *Teaching students to be peacemakers.* Edina, MN: Interaction Book Company.

Johnson, D. W., Johnson, R. T., & Holubec, E. J. (1993). *Circles of learning: Cooperation in the classroom* (6th ed.). Edina, MN: Interaction Book Company.

Kotulak, R. (1996). *Inside the brain.* Kansas City, MO: Andrews and McMeel.

Kreidler, W. J. (1984). *Creative conflict resolution.* Glenview, IL: Scott Foresman and Company.

Lewis, D. 0. (1992). From abuse to violence: Psycho-physiological consequences of maltreatment. Journal of American Academy of Child and Adolescent Psychiatry, 31, 383-391.

Magid, K., & McKelvey, C. (1987). *High risk: Children without a conscience.* New York: Bantam Books.

National Institute for Dispute Resolution. (1998). Conflict resolution education facts. WWWURL:http//www.CREmet.org.

Oliveus, D. (1991). Bully/victim problems among school children: Basic facts and effects of a school based intervention program. In D. Peple and K. Rubin (Eds.), *The development and treatment of childhood aggression,* Hillsdale, NJ: Lawrence Erlbaum.

Samenow, S. (1984). *Inside the criminal mind.* New York: Random House.

Samenow, S. (1989). *Before it's too late: Why some kids get into trouble and what parents can do about it.* New York: Random House.

Slaby, R., Wilson-Brewer, R., & Dach, K. (1994). *Aggressors, victims and bystanders: Thinking and acting to prevent violence.* Newton, MA: Educational Development Center, Inc.

Weinhold, B. (Ed.) (1996a). *Spreading kindness: A program guide for reducing youth violence in the schools.* Colorado Springs, CO: The Kindness Campaign.

Weinhold, B. (1996b). *Building a community of kindness: A community organizer's guide to the Kindness Campaign.* Colorado Springs, CO: The Kindness Campaign.

Peacemakers: Teaching Students to Resolve Their Own and Schoolmates' Conflicts

David W. Johnson
and Roger T. Johnson

"Joshua was chasing Octavia. He pushed her down and she kicked him."

"Jane was going to beat up Joan after school. They were spitting in each other's face and calling each other names."

"Tom shoved Cameron up against the lockers and threatened him. Cameron said he's going to bring a knife to school tomorrow to get even."

Schools are filled with conflicts. Considerable instructional, administrative, and learning efforts are lost because students and faculty often manage their conflicts poorly. The frequency and severity of conflicts seem to be increasing, and for the first time, the category "fighting, violence, and gangs" is tied with "lack of discipline" for the number-one problem confronting local public schools (Elam, Rose, & Gallup, 1994). Conflicts will not go away. Students are clearly fascinated by and drawn to conflicts. They like to start them, watch them, hear about them, and discuss them. To make schools orderly and peaceful places in which high quality education can take place, conflicts must be managed constructively without physical or verbal violence. To do so, students must be taught to be peacemakers.

How Conflicts Can Be of Value

A number of points can help clarify the value of conflicts. *First*, conflicts are inevitable. You might as well try to stop the earth from turning on its axis as to try to eliminate conflicts from your life. No matter what you do, conflicts arise. *Second*, conflicts are desirable if they are managed constructively. *Conflicts occur whenever people have goals they care about and are involved in relationships they value.* The absence of conflict often signals a dysfunctional situation wherein neither the goals nor the relationship is valued. Conflict often signals a commitment to the goals and the relationship. This commitment fuels an engagement in conflict that can lead to either constructive or destructive outcomes. On the destructive side, conflicts can (a) create anger, hostility, lasting animosity, and even violence, (b) result in pain and sadness, and (c) end in divorce, lawsuits, and war. There is nothing pretty about a conflict gone wrong. On the positive side, conflicts are constructive when (a) all disputants are satisfied with the outcome (the agreement maximizes joint benefits and allows all participants to achieve their goals and, therefore, everyone goes away satisfied and pleased), (b) the relationship between the disputants is strengthened and improved (disputants are better able to work together and have more respect, trust, and liking for each other), and (c) disputants are able to resolve future conflicts constructively.

Besides these direct outcomes, conflicts have value in a number of other ways. Conflicts:

1. *Focus attention on problems that have to be solved.* Conflicts energize and motivate us to solve our problems.

2. *Clarify who you are and what your values are.* Through conflicts, your identity is developed.

3. *Clarify how you need to change.* Conflicts clarify and highlight patterns of behavior that are dysfunctional.

4. *Help you understand who the other person is and what his or her values are.* Conflicts clarify the identity of your friends and acquaintances.

5. *Strengthen relationships by increasing your confidence that the two of you can resolve your disagreements.* Every time a serious conflict is resolved constructively, the relationship becomes less fragile and more able to withstand crises and problems.

6. *Keep the relationship clear of irritations and resentments so positive feelings can be experienced fully.* A good conflict may do a lot to resolve the small tensions of interacting with others.

7. *Release emotions (such as anger, anxiety, insecurity, and sadness) that, if kept inside, make us mentally sick.* A conflict a day keeps depression away!

8. *Clarify what you care about, are committed to, and value.* You only fight over wants and goals you value. And you fight much more frequently and intensely with people you value and care about. The more committed you are to your goals, and the more committed you are to the other person, the more frequent and intense are the conflicts.

9. *Add fun, enjoyment, excitement, and variety to your life.* Being in a conflict reduces boredom, gives you new goals, motivates you to take action, and stimulates interest. Life would be incredibly boring in the absence of conflict.

Third, what determines whether a conflict is constructive or destructive are the procedures taken to manage the conflict. To manage conflicts with skill, finesse, and grace, you need:

1. To understand the procedures for managing conflicts constructively. Further, everyone involved must understand and use the same procedures. Different individuals often have quite different ideas about how to manage conflicts. Some rely on physical dominance through threats and violence. Others use verbal attack, the cold shoulder, giving in, or getting even. When two individuals involved in a conflict are using different procedures, chaos results. If conflicts are to be managed constructively, everyone has to use the same procedures to resolve them. Because the procedures for resolving conflicts constructively are *not* learned in most families or from television, movies, or novels, students must learn them at school.

2. The opportunity to practice, practice, practice the procedures to gain real skill and expertise in their use. Resolving conflicts takes great skill and considerable practice. Schools need to emphasize overlearning of the conflict resolution procedures by having students practice the procedures again and again.

3. Norms and values to encourage and support use of the procedures. Just because people know how to manage conflicts constructively does not mean that they will do so. As long as school norms emphasize working alone and valuing "winners," students will "go for the win" in a conflict rather than by trying to solve the problem.

Based on these points (conflicts are inevitable, a sign of commitment, and potentially constructive), schools are advised to welcome and face conflicts rather than to avoid and repress conflicts. To do so, students need to learn how to be peacemakers.

Teaching Students to Be Peacemakers Program

We began the *Teaching Students to Be Peacemakers Program* in the 1960s. It originated from:

1. Our research on integrative negotiations (Johnson, 1967), perspective taking in conflict situations (Johnson, 1967, 1971a), conflict resolution in the school (Johnson, 1970, 1971b; Johnson, Johnson, & Johnson, 1976), communication in conflict situations (Johnson, 1974), and constructive conflict (Johnson, 1970; Johnson & Johnson, 1979).

2. Our development of social interdependence theory (Deutsch, 1949; Lewin, 1951; Johnson, 1970; Johnson & Johnson, 1989; Watson & Johnson, 1972).

3. Our training of elementary, junior-high, high-school and college students and adults in how to manage conflicts constructively (Johnson, 1970, 1972/1993, 1978/1991, 1983; Johnson & Johnson, 1975/1994a). Besides regular students,

teachers, and administrators, we taught delinquents, runaways, drug-abusers, and married couples in therapy how to manage their conflicts more constructively.

The Teaching Students to Be Peacemakers Program is a 12-year spiral program in which students learn increasingly sophisticated negotiation and mediation procedures (Johnson & Johnson, 1995b, 1995c). *It focuses on teaching all students in a school to be peacemakers.* We have implemented the peacemaker program in schools throughout North America, Europe, and several countries in Asia, Central and South America, the Middle East, and Africa.

The Teaching Students to Be Peacemakers Program has six steps.

1. *Create a cooperative context.* Considerable evidence and practical experience demonstrate that when individuals are in competition, they will strive for a "win" in conflicts and not try to solve the problem. A problem-solving approach requires the disputants to recognize their long-term interdependence and the need to maintain effective working relationships with each other—conditions that exist only in a cooperative context.

2. *Teach students to recognize when a conflict is and is not occurring.* Many students see conflicts as always involving anger, hostility, and violence and do not recognize conflicts as such when they lead to laughter, insight, learning, and problem solving.

3. *Teach students a concrete and specific procedure for negotiating agreements.* Everyone involved can thus achieve their goals while maintaining or even improving the quality of their relationship. Telling students to "be nice" or "talk it out," or "solve your problem" is not enough.

4. *Teach students to use a concrete and specific mediation procedure.* Give them enough practice in using this procedure to develop some expertise. If students are to mediate their schoolmates' conflicts, they must know how to do so. This initial training of the nature of conflict and how to negotiate and mediate usually consists of approximately 30 half-hour lessons.

5. *Implement the peer mediation program.* Working in pairs, at first, mediators are made available to help schoolmates negotiate more effectively. The mediator's role is rotated so each student is a mediator.

6. *Continue the training in negotiation and mediation procedures weekly throughout first through twelfth grades* to refine and upgrade students' skills. To become competent in resolving conflicts takes years and years. Any thought that a few hours of training is enough to ensure constructive conflict management is terribly misguided.

Each of these steps will be discussed in more detail in the following pages.

Creating a Cooperative Context

In beginning a conflict resolution and peer mediation program, we have to focus on the total school environment and create an awareness of students' interdependence and interaction. A conflict resolution program should seek to do more than change individual behavior. Instead, it should transform the total school environment into a learning community in which students live by a credo of nonviolence and problem solving. In addition, students need to recognize that they manage conflicts in long-term, ongoing relationships in a different way than they do in ad hoc, one-time, temporary relationships. In ongoing, long-term relationships, the future of the relationship has to be taken into account along with the interests of each disputant. Schools involve long-term, ongoing, interdependent relationships and, therefore, conflicts should be managed accordingly.

If conflicts are to be managed constructively, they must occur in a cooperative, not a competitive, context. Attempting to teach students to manage conflicts constructively makes little sense if the school is structured so students are pitted against each other in competition for scarce rewards (such as teacher attention and grades of "A") and students have to defeat each other to get what they want. In competition, rewards are restricted to the few who perform the best (Johnson & Johnson, 1989). Competitors typically have a short-term time orientation and focus all their energies on winning with little or no paid to the long-term interest in maintaining good relationships. Competitors tend to avoid communicating with each other, misperceive each other's position and motivations, be suspicious of each other, deny the legitimacy of others' needs and feelings, and see the situation only from their own perspective.

For conflicts to be resolved constructively, a cooperative context must be established. A cooperative context entails setting mutual goals that all participants are committed to achieving (Deutsch, 1973; Johnson & Johnson, 1989). Cooperators tend to seek outcomes that are beneficial to everyone involved. Cooperators typically have a long-term time orientation and focus their energies both on achieving goals and on maintaining good working relationships with others. Communication is apt to be frequent, complete, and accurate, with each person interested in informing the other as well as being informed. Cooperators are more likely to perceive other participants' positions and motivations accurately. Because they tend to trust and like each other, they usually are willing to respond helpfully to each other's wants, needs, and requests. Cooperators tend to recognize the legitimacy of each other's interests and search for a solution that accommodates the needs of both sides. Conflicts are more likely to be defined as mutual problems to be solved in ways that benefit everyone involved.

A cooperative context is established most easily by structuring the majority of learning situations cooperatively (Johnson & Johnson, 1989; Johnson, Johnson, & Holubec, 1993). Students should spend most of the day working together in cooperative learning groups so their ongoing interdependence and need for future interaction are clear. Hundreds of studies indicate that cooperative learning, compared to competitive and individualistic learning, tends to promote greater effort to achieve (which includes retention, higher-level reasoning, process gain, intrinsic motivation, achievement motivation, transfer), more positive relationships among students (including students who are heterogeneous in terms of ethnicity, gender, culture, and achievement as well as academic and personal social support), and greater psychological adjustment (encompassing psychological health, self-esteem, and social competence) (Johnson & Johnson, 1989). Because cooperative learning has considerable benefits, most teachers should welcome the opportunity to create a cooperative context that will enhance the success of conflict resolution programs.

When conflict resolution and peer mediation programs are implemented in the existing competitive/individualistic context of schools, their effectiveness can be compromised severely (Johnson & Johnson, 1975/1994b, 1995c). When the context and the procedures used to manage the conflict are congruent (an integrative procedure used in a cooperative context or a distributive procedure used in a competitive context), conflicts tend to be managed constructively. When the context and the conflict resolution procedures are incongruent (an integrative procedure used in a competitive context or a distributive procedure used in a cooperative context), destructive outcomes tend to result. To teach students how to seek solutions to problems rather than to strive for a "win," educators must create a cooperative context in the classroom and school.

Once a cooperative context has been established, students may be taught directly to recognize conflicts when they occur. Then they are able to learn the procedures and skills required to manage conflicts constructively.

Teaching Students What Is and Is Not a Conflict

Most of the diverse conflict resolution programs in schools are either cadre or total student body programs. In the *cadre approach*, a few students are trained to serve as peer mediators for the entire school. In the *total student body approach*, every student learns how to manage conflicts constructively by negotiating agreements and mediating schoolmates' conflicts. The responsibility for peer mediation is rotated throughout the entire student body (or class) so every student gains experience as a mediator. The greater number of students trained in how to negotiate and mediate, the greater is the number of conflicts that may be managed constructively in the school.

Whether training a cadre or an entire class or student body, teaching students what is and is not a conflict is an important early step in conflict management training. Students generally have a *negativity bias*, in which they tend to view conflicts as involving anger and violence and, therefore, tend to overestimate the frequency of conflicts involving anger and violence and underestimate the incidents of actual conflicts. The most common types of conflicts in schools are verbal harassments (name-calling, insults), verbal arguments, rumors and gossip, physical fights, and dating/relationship issues. Although physical and verbal aggression may be more frequent in urban than in suburban schools, it almost never involves serious altercations or violations of law. The first part of the Teaching Students to be Peacemakers Program, therefore, is to teach students what is and is not a conflict so they can become aware of (a) how they manage their conflicts and (b) how to manage conflicts constructively. Once students understand what is and is not a conflict, they are taught how to negotiate constructive resolutions to conflicts and how to mediate the conflicts of their peers.

Teaching Students to Negotiate

The best way I know how to defeat an enemy is to make him a friend.

(Abraham Lincoln)

The heart of conflict resolution training is teaching students how to negotiate constructive resolutions to their conflicts. *All* students in all schools need to learn how to negotiate (and mediate). *Negotiation* is a process by which people try to work out a settlement when they (a) have both shared and opposing interests and (b) want to come to an agreement (Johnson & Johnson, 1994). The two types of negotiations are *distributive* or "win-lose" (in which one person benefits only if the opponent agrees to make a concession) and *integrative* or problem solving (in which disputants work together to create an agreement that benefits everyone involved). Only in very limited conflicts involving ad hoc, one-time relationships are win-lose negotiations appropriate. In ongoing relationships that have a future as well as a present, an integrative approach to negotiations is the only constructive alternative. The steps in using problem solving negotiations are (Johnson & Johnson, 1995b, 1995c):

1. *Describing what you want.* "I want to use the book now." This means using good communication skills and defining the conflict as a small and specific mutual problem.

2. *Describing how you feel.* "I'm frustrated." Disputants must understand how they feel and communicate it openly and clearly.

3. *Describing the reasons for your wants and feelings.* "You have been using the book for the past hour. If I don't get to use the book soon, my report won't be done on time. It's frustrating to have to wait so long." This includes expressing cooperative intentions, listening carefully, separating interests from positions, and differentiating before trying to integrate the two sets of interests.

4. *Taking the other's perspective and summarizing your understanding of what the other person wants, how the other person feels, and the reasons underlying both.* "My understanding of you is . . ." This includes understanding the perspective of the opposing disputant and being able to see the problem from both perspectives simultaneously.

5. *Inventing three optional plans that maximize joint benefits.* "Plan A is . . ., Plan B is . . ., Plan C is . . ." This requires inventing creative options to solve the problem.

6. *Choosing one plan and formalizing the agreement with a hand shake.* "Let's agree on Plan B!" A wise agreement is fair to all disputants and is based on principles. It maximizes joint benefits and strengthens disputants' ability to work together cooperatively and resolve conflicts constructively in the future. It specifies how each disputant should act in the future and how the agreement will be reviewed and renegotiated if it does not work.

Students need to practice this procedure again and again until it becomes an automatic habit. If students have to stop and think what they should do, it may be too late to manage the conflicts constructively. Overlearning the integrative negotiation procedure is needed so it is available for use in conflicts with intense emotions such as fear and anger. Students need to overlearn the negotiation procedure and become skillful in its use in relatively easy situations before they can be expected to use it to resolve emotionally charged conflicts. Mediation, furthermore, is easier and more effective when all students are skilled in integrative negotiating procedures.

Teaching Students to Mediate Schoolmates' Conflicts

A soft answer turneth away wrath. (Bible)

When students cannot negotiate a constructive resolution to their conflicts successfully, peer mediators should be available. *In the Teaching Students to Be Peacemakers Program, all students are taught the procedures and skills they need to mediate their classmates' conflicts of interests* (Johnson & Johnson, 1995c). A *mediator* is a neutral person who helps two or more people resolve their conflict, usually by negotiating an integrative agreement. The mediator has no formal power over either disputant. A mediator does *not* tell disputants what to do or decide who is right and who is wrong. When you mediate, you stand in the middle and help disputants go through each step of problem-solving negotiations so they reach an agreement that is fair, just, and workable.

Mediation usually is contrasted with arbitration. *Arbitration* is the submission of a dispute to a disinterested third party (such as a teacher or a principal) who makes a final and binding judgment as to how the conflict will be resolved. Mediation consists of four steps (Johnson & Johnson, 1995c):

1. *End hostilities*. The mediator ensures that disputants end hostilities and disputants cool off. Usually the disputants ask the mediator for help. In some cases the mediator may see a dispute taking place and ask if he or she can be of service. In rare instances the mediator may have to get a teacher or an administrator to break up a fight. The mediator must be sure that all disputants are emotionally capable of problem solving and conflict resolution. If disputants are too angry to problem solve, they must cool down before mediation begins.

2. *Ensure that disputants are committed to the mediation process*. The mediator introduces the process of mediation and sets the ground rules to ensure that disputants are committed to the mediation process and ready to negotiate in good faith. The mediator first introduces him- or herself. The mediator then asks the disputants if they want to solve the problem and does not proceed until both answer "yes." Then the mediator explains:

   ■ "Mediation is voluntary. My role is to help you find a solution to your conflict that is acceptable to both of you."

   ■ "I'm neutral. I won't take sides or attempt to decide who is right or wrong. I'll help you decide how to solve the conflict."

■ "Each person will have the chance to state his or her view of the conflict without interruption."

■ "The rules you must agree to are (1) agree to solve the problem, (2) no name calling, (3) do not interrupt, (4) be as honest as you can, (5) if you agree to a solution, you must abide by it (you must do what you have agreed to do), and (6) anything said in mediation is confidential (you, the mediator, will not tell anyone what is said)."

3. *Help disputants negotiate successfully with each other.* The mediator carefully takes the disputants through the negotiation procedure by helping disputants:

■ Define the conflict by having disputants jointly define the conflict by asking each disputant, "What happened, what do you want, how do you feel?" The mediator paraphrases what each disputant says when necessary to demonstrate that the mediator is listening to and understanding what the disputants are saying and when the mediator believes the other disputant does not understand clearly what the other person is saying. The mediator also enlarges the shadow of the future by highlighting the ways the disputants will have to work cooperatively with each other in the future.

■ Exchange reasons for their positions by helping the disputants present their reasons and the rationale for their positions and understand the differences between their positions. The mediator keeps disputants focused on the issue, not on peripheral issues such as their anger toward each other, equalizes power between the disputants, recognizes disputants' constructive behaviors during negotiations, and reframes the issue by helping disputants change their perspectives.

■ Reverse perspectives so that each person is able to present the other's position and feelings to the other's satisfaction. The mediator also may role play the conflict and switch roles at critical points.

■ Invent at least three options that maximize joint outcomes and leave disputants feeling they have benefited. The mediator encourages creative thinking.

4. *Formalize the agreement.* Reach a wise agreement and shake hands to formalize it. The mediator helps disputants weigh the advantages and disadvantages of each alternative and select the one they wish to implement. The disputants sign a Mediation Report Form to formalize their commitment to implement the agreement and abide by its conditions. The mediator becomes the keeper of the contract and checks back with the disputants a day or so later to see if the agreement is working.

Table 19.1 summarizes the steps in mediation and offers possible mediator statements.

If mediation by peers fails, the teacher mediates the conflict. If teacher mediation fails, the teacher arbitrates by deciding who is right and who is wrong. If that fails, the principal mediates the conflict. If that fails, the principal arbitrates. Teaching all students negotiation and mediation procedures and skills and implementing a

Table 19.1 Steps to Mediation

STEPS	POSSIBLE STATEMENTS
End hostilities	"Would you like a mediator?"
Ensure commitment to mediation	"You must follow four rules."
Facilitate negotiations	"How do you feel?"
Formalize the agreement	"Are you willing to sign the agreement?"

peer mediation program results in a schoolwide discipline program that empowers students to regulate and control their own and their classmates' actions. Teachers and administrators are then freed to spend more of their energies on instruction.

Implementing the Peacemaker Program

If civilization is to survive, we must cultivate the science of human relationships— the ability of all peoples, of all kinds, to live together, in the same world, at peace.

(Franklin Delano Roosevelt)

Once students understand how to negotiate and mediate, the teacher implements the Peacemaker program. Each day the teacher selects two class members to serve as official mediators. Any conflicts that students cannot resolve themselves are referred to the mediators. The mediators wear official T-shirts, patrol the playground and lunchroom, and are available to mediate any conflicts that arise in the classroom or school. The role of mediator is rotated so all students in the class or school serve as mediators an equal amount of time. At first students mediate in pairs. This ensures that shy and nonverbal students get the same amount of experience as more extroverted and verbally fluent students. Mediating classmates' conflicts is perhaps the most effective way of teaching students the need for the skillful use of each step in the negotiation procedure.

The processes of negotiation and mediation allow students to practice joint decision making within a structure that emphasizes a solution/settlement acceptable to all parties involved and, therefore, is fair. Students are given the power to decide the outcome (within the constraints of school policy and the law) and solve a joint problem. For a settlement to be reached, they take responsibility for their conflict. Negotiation and mediation are self-empowering. These procedures enable students to make decisions about issues and conflicts that affect their own lives rather than have a decision imposed on them by teachers and administrators.

Continuing Lessons to Refine and Upgrade Students' Skills

Booster sessions are needed throughout the year to maintain the use of the negotiation and mediation procedures. Gaining real expertise in resolving conflicts constructively takes years and years of training and practice. It may even take a whole lifetime. A few hours of training clearly is not sufficient to teach students how to negotiate or mediate skillfully. The initial Peacemaker training is not enough to create highly skilled negotiators and mediators. At least twice a week or so, students should receive further training or practice in negotiating and mediating. The Teaching Students to Be Peacemakers Program is intended to be a 12-year spiral program that is retaught each year at a more sophisticated and complex level.

One of the most natural ways to integrate negotiation and mediation training into the fabric of school life is to integrate it into academic lessons. Literature, history, and science involve conflict. Almost any lesson in these subject areas can be modified to include role-playing situations in which the negotiation or mediation procedures are used. In our recent research, for example, we have integrated the Peacemaker training into English literature units involving a novel. Each of the major conflicts in the novel was used to teach the negotiation or mediation procedures, and all students role played how to use the procedures to resolve the conflicts in the novel constructively. With some training, teachers can integrate the Peacemaker program readily into academic units.

Research on Peacemaker Program

We have conducted more than 10 studies on the effectiveness of the Teaching Students to Be Peacemakers Program (Johnson & Johnson, 1995d; Johnson, Johnson, & Stevahn, 1995). The studies focused on peer mediation programs in elementary, middle school, and high school settings. The programs were evaluated over a period of several months to a year. The schools were in urban and suburban school districts. Students varied from lower to upper middle class socioeconomically and were from diverse ethnic and cultural backgrounds. Mediators were drawn from a wide variety of ethnic backgrounds. The studies were carefully controlled field-experimental studies with high internal and external validity. The research addressed the following series of questions:

■ *How often do conflicts among students occur, and what are the most commonly occurring conflicts?* The findings indicate that students engage in conflicts daily. In the suburban schools studied, most of the conflicts reported centered on the possession and access to resources, preferences about what to do, playground issues, and turn-taking. Some conflicts involved physical and verbal aggression. In the urban elementary school studied, the vast majority of conflicts referred to mediation involved physical and verbal violence.

- *Before training, what strategies did students use to manage their conflicts?* Before training, students generally managed their conflicts through trying to win by (a) forcing the other to concede (either by overpowering the other disputant or by asking the teacher to force the other to give in) or (b) withdrawing from the conflict and the other person. One of the teachers stated in her log, "Before training, students viewed conflict as fights that always resulted in a winner and a loser. To avoid such an unpleasant situation, they usually placed the responsibility for resolving conflicts on me, the teacher." Students seem to lack all knowledge of how to engage in problem-solving, integrative negotiations.

- *Was the Peacemaker training successful in teaching students the negotiation and mediation procedures?* After the Peacemaker training, the students knew the negotiation and mediation procedures and retained their knowledge up to 7 months after the training ended.

- *Could students apply the negotiation and mediation procedures to conflicts?* For all three types of measures used, students were able to apply the negotiation and mediation procedures to a variety of conflicts.

- *Do students transfer the negotiation and mediation procedures to nonclassroom and nonschool situations?* Our studies demonstrated that students did in fact use the negotiation and mediation procedures in the hallways, lunchroom, and playground. In addition, students used the procedures in family settings.

- *When given the option, would students engage in "win-lose" or problem-solving negotiations?* Following the Peacemaker training, students were placed in a negotiation situation in which they could either try to win or maximize joint outcomes. Untrained students almost always strive to win. Most trained students, on the other hand, focused on maximizing joint outcomes.

- *Does the Peacemaker training increase students' academic achievement?* In three of our studies, we integrated the Peacemaker training into English literature units. While studying a novel, students also learned the negotiation and mediation procedures and used them to understand the dynamics among the major characters. The students were given an achievement test following the end of the unit and again several months later. The results indicated that the students who received the integrated training achieved significantly higher on the achievement and retention tests than did students who spent all their time studying the novel without learning the conflict resolution procedures.

- *Does the Peacemaker training result in fewer discipline problems that have to be managed by the teacher and the administration?* In our studies the number of discipline problems the teacher had to deal with decreased by about 60 percent, and referrals to the principal dropped about 95 percent.

- *Does the Peacemaker training result in more positive attitudes toward conflict?* Untrained students uniformly had negative attitudes toward conflicts. After training, students had more positive attitudes toward conflict. Teachers and administrators and parents perceived the peacemaker program to be constructive and helpful. Many parents whose children were not part of the project requested that their children receive the training next year, and a number of parents requested that they receive the training themselves so they could use the procedures to improve conflict management within the family.

Overall, these findings provide considerable empirical validation of the effectiveness of the Peacemaker program and of conflict resolution and peer mediation training in general.

School Discipline Program

Classroom and school discipline programs may be classified on a dimension from a basis in giving external rewards and punishments that control and manage student behavior to a basis in teaching students the competencies and skills required to resolve their interpersonal conflicts constructively, cope with stress and adversity, and behave in appropriate and constructive ways. At one end of the continuum, the focus is on the faculty and staff controlling and managing student behavior. At the other end of the continuum, the focus is on students regulating their own and their peers' actions.

Most discipline programs are clustered at end of the continuum in which adults administer external rewards and punishment. Thus, the faculty has to monitor student behavior, determine whether it is or is not within the bounds of acceptability, and force students to terminate inappropriate actions. When the infractions are minor, the staff often arbitrates ("The pencil belongs to Mary; Jane be quiet and sit down") or cajoles students to end hostilities ("Let's forgive and forget"; "Shake hands and be friends"). If that does not work, students may be sent to the principal's office for a stern but cursory lecture about the value of getting along, a threat that if the conflict continues, more drastic action will ensue, and a final admonition to "Go and fight no more." If that does not work, time-out rooms may be used. Eventually, some students are suspended or expelled from school. Such programs teach students that adults or authority figures are needed to resolve conflicts. These programs cost a great deal in instructional and administrative time and work only as long as students are under surveillance. Students are not empowered. Adults may become more skillful in how to control students, but students do not learn the procedures, skills, and attitudes required to resolve conflicts constructively in their personal lives at home, in school, at work, and in the community.

At the other end of the continuum are programs aimed at teaching students self-responsibility and self-regulation. *Self-regulation* is the ability to act in socially approved ways in the absence of external monitors. It is the ability to initiate and cease activities according to situational demands. Self-regulation is a central and significant hallmark of cognitive and social development. To regulate their behavior, students must monitor their own behavior, assess situations and take other people's perspectives to make judgments as to which behaviors are appropriate, and master the procedures and skills required to engage in the desired behavior. In interaction with other people, students have to monitor, modify, refine, and change how they behave in order to act appropriately and competently.

If students are to learn how to regulate their behavior they must have opportunities to (a) make decisions regarding how to behave, and (b) follow through on the decisions made. Allowing students to be joint architects in matters affecting them promotes feelings of control and autonomy. Then teachers and administrators can concentrate on instruction rather than control.

Structuring Academic Controversies

In addition to implementing the Teaching Students to Be Peacemakers Program, faculty may use intellectual, academic conflicts as an inherent part of the instructional program to increase student achievement, higher-level reasoning, motivation to learn, and conflict skills (Johnson & Johnson, 1995a). *Academic controversy* exists when one student's ideas, information, conclusions, theories, and opinions are incompatible with those of another student, and the two seek to reach an agreement. Over the past 25 years, we (with colleagues such as Dean Tjosvold and Karl Smith) have developed a theory of controversy, tested it by conducting more than 20 experimental and field-experimental studies, developed a series of curriculum units on energy and environmental issues structured for academic controversies, and trained teachers to use academic controversies in schools and colleges throughout the United States, Canada, and a number of other countries (Johnson & Johnson, 1979, 1989, 1995a).

Structuring academic controversy into learning situations results in students learning that conflicts are potentially constructive and even enjoyable. The procedure for structuring academic controversies is to have students follow these steps:

1. Prepare scholarly positions on an academic issue.
2. Advocate these positions.
3. Refute the opposing positions while rebutting criticisms of their position.
4. View the issue from both perspectives.
5. Come to a consensus about their "best reasoned judgment" based on a synthesis of the two positions.

Participating in academic controversies teaches students how to (a) prepare, present, and defend a position, (b) take an opposing perspective, (c) make creative, high-quality decisions that integrate the best information and reasoning from both sides, and (d) engage in a set of social skills such as "criticizing ideas without criticizing people." Similar to cooperative learning, the use of academic controversy may be welcomed by educators because it results in improved student achievement, critical thinking, higher-level reasoning, intrinsic motivation to learn, and a number of other important educational outcomes (Johnson & Johnson, 1979, 1989, 1995a).

Engaging in academic controversies demonstrates the value of conflict and promotes positive attitudes toward engaging in conflict. The skills learned in controversy support and reinforce the skills used in negotiation and mediation. A detailed program to train teachers in how to structure academic controversies to ensure that all students are intellectually challenged within the classroom is presented in Creative Controversy: Intellectual Challenge in the Classroom (Johnson & Johnson, 1995c).

Creating a Conflict-Positive School

Schools do not become orderly and peaceful places in which high-quality education can take place by suppressing the occurrence of conflicts among students. For a variety of reasons, many students want to engage in conflicts. In interviewing inner-city, seventh grade, lower-class, minority students in New York City, Opotow (1991) found that the students perceived fights as being more constructive than destructive.

The students viewed fights as necessary and desirable to maintain valued social norms, deter harmful behavior, provide protection from victimization, provide gains in status, increase self-awareness, clarify personal identity, clarify others' identities, clarify dominance hierarchies, initiate friendships, and provide enjoyable and entertaining experiences. The students reported that in conflicts they found opportunities for (a) modifying the status quo and the behavior of troublesome peers, (b) increasing self-protection, social advancement, personal worth, interpersonal insight, conflict resolution, and excitement, (c) providing heroic drama that generated an oral history of danger, heroism, and good versus evil, and (d) providing moral discourse and clarification of values and codes of behavior. Opotow concluded that these inner-city seventh graders were fascinated clearly by and drawn to conflicts. They liked to start conflicts, watch them, hear about them, and discuss them. Telling students not to fight obviously is not an effective strategy to pursue.

Schools are much better advised to seek an orderly and safe learning environment by encouraging conflicts and their constructive management. A *conflict-positive school* is one where conflicts are encouraged and managed constructively to maximize their potential in enhancing the quality of teaching, learning, and school life in general (Johnson & Johnson, 1995c). Conflicts are not the problem; they are part of the solution and should be a pervasive part of school life. Conflicts not only are inevitable, but also, *when they are managed constructively,* they are healthy and valuable and revitalize and rejuvenate the school. Conflicts can be constructive and valuable.

To summarize:

- Conflicts can increase achievement and long-term retention of academic material.
- Conflicts are the key to using higher-level cognitive and moral reasoning and healthy cognitive, social, and psychological development.
- Conflicts focus attention on problems that have to be solved and energize us to solve them.
- Conflicts clarify who you are, what your values are, what you care about and are committed to, and how you may need to change.
- Conflicts help you understand who the other person is and what his or her values are.
- Conflicts strengthen relationships by increasing your confidence that the two of you can resolve your disagreements and by keeping the relationship clear of irritations and resentments so that positive feelings can be experienced fully.
- Conflicts can release anger, anxiety, insecurity, and sadness that, if kept inside, makes us mentally sick.
- Conflicts can be fun.

What determines whether conflicts result in these positive outcomes is how skillfully students (and faculty) use the integrative negotiation and mediation procedures.

A Life-Long Advantage

A number of recent research studies have found that executives in high-level positions spend much of their time dealing with conflicts. The more skillful they are at doing so, the more successful their careers. Because conflicts occur continually, and because so many people are so unskilled in managing conflicts, teaching students how to resolve conflicts constructively is one of the best investments schools can make.

Once learned, conflict skills go with students to every situation and every relationship. Students do not have to manage every conflict constructively, but the ability to do so should be in their repertoire. Knowing how to resolve conflicts with skill and grace will give students a developmental advantage and increase their future academic and career success, improve the quality of relationships with friends, colleagues, and family, and generally enhance their lifelong happiness.

Summary and Conclusions

The frequency of conflicts is not the problem facing schools. In many cases schools are too conflict-avoidant and need to increase the frequency with which conflicts occur among students and between students and faculty. Conflict has many positive outcomes that cannot occur unless conflict is encouraged. The problem facing schools is how to manage conflicts in constructive and healthy ways. The major barrier to solving this problem is students' lack of effective skills in conflict resolution. Students do use procedures for managing conflicts, but often these procedures are not constructive and not shared by all classmates. The many different methods of managing conflicts within classrooms create some chaos in how conflicts are managed. This is especially true when students are from different cultural, ethnic, social class, and language backgrounds. Life in schools gets easier when *all* students (and staff members) use the same set of negotiation and mediation procedures in managing conflicts.

When students are taught how to negotiate and are given opportunities to mediate their classmates' conflicts, they are given the tools to (a) regulate their behavior through self-monitoring, (b) judge what is appropriate given the situation and the perspective of the other person, and (c) modify how they behave accordingly. Students then have the opportunity to resolve their dispute themselves, in mutually satisfactory ways, without having to engage a teacher's attention. This empowers the students and reduces the demands on teachers and administrators, who then are able to devote less time to establishing and maintaining control over students and spend more time on instruction.

Teaching *all* students negotiation and mediation procedures and skills and implementing a peer mediation program results in a schoolwide discipline program focused on empowering students to regulate and control their own and their classmates' actions. When a conflict occurs, the students involved first try to negotiate a resolution. If that fails, a classmate mediates their conflict. If that fails, the teacher attempts to mediate the conflict. If that fails, the teacher arbitrates by deciding who is right and who is wrong. If that fails, the principal mediates the conflict. If that fails, the principal arbitrates.

Every student needs to learn how to manage conflicts constructively. Without training, many students may never learn how to do so. Teaching every student how to negotiate and mediate will ensure that future generations are prepared to manage conflicts constructively in career, family, community, national, and international settings. The process is neither easy nor quick. Reducing smoking in America took more than 30 years. Reducing drunk driving took more than 20 years. Ensuring that children and adolescents can manage conflicts constructively may take even longer. The more years students spend learning and practicing negotiation and mediation procedures, the more likely they will be to actually use the procedures skillfully both in the classroom and beyond the school door.

References

Deutsch, M. (1949). A theory of cooperation and competition. *Human Relations*, *2*, 129–152.

Deutsch, M. (1973). *The resolution of conflict*. New Haven, CT: Yale University Press.

Elam, S., Rose, L., & Gallup, A. (1994, September). The 26th annual Gallup poll of the public's attitudes toward the public schools. *Phi Delta Kappan*, *76*, 41–56.

Johnson, D. W. (1967). The use of role reversal in intergroup competition. *Journal of Personality & Social Psychology*, *7*, 135–141.

Johnson, D. W. (1970). *Social psychology of education*. Edina, MN: Interaction Book Co.

Johnson, D. W. (1971a). Role reversal: A summary and review of the research. *International Journal of Group Tensions*, *1*, 318–334.

Johnson, D. W. (1971b). Students against the school establishment: Crisis intervention in school conflicts and organizational change. *Journal of School Psychology*, *9*, 84–92.

Johnson, D. W. (1974). Communication and the inducement of cooperative behavior in conflicts: A critical review. *Speech Monographs*, *41*, 64–78.

Johnson, D. W. (1983). *Resolving marital conflicts constructively*. Edina, MN: Interaction Book Co.

Johnson, D. W. (1972/1993). *Reaching out: Interpersonal effectiveness and self-actualization* (5th ed.). Englewood Cliffs, NJ: Prentice-Hall.

Johnson D. W., & Johnson, F. (1975/1994a). *Joining together: Group theory and group skills* (5th ed.). Englewood Cliffs, NJ: Prentice-Hall.

Johnson, D. W., & Johnson, R. (1975/ 1994b). *Learning together and alone*. Englewood Cliffs, NJ: Prentice Hall.

Johnson, D. W., & Johnson, R. (1979). Conflict in the classroom: Controversy and learning. *Review of Educational Research*, *49*, 51–61.

Johnson, D. W., & Johnson, R. (1987). *Creative conflict*. Edina, MN: Interaction Book Co.

Johnson, D. W., & Johnson, R. (1989). *Cooperation and competition: Theory and research*. Edina, MN: Interaction Book Co.

Johnson, D. W., & Johnson, R. (1995a). *Creative controversy: Intellectual challenge in the classroom*. Edina, MN: Interaction Book Co.

Johnson, D. W., & Johnson, R. (1995b). *My mediation notebook* (3d ed.). Edina, MN: Interaction Book Co.

Johnson, D. W., & Johnson, R. (1995c). *Teaching students to be peacemakers*. Edina, MN: Interaction Book Co.

Johnson, D. W., & Johnson, R. (1995d). Teaching students to be peacemakers: Results of five years of research. *Peace and Conflict: Journal of Peace Psychology*.

Johnson, D. W., Johnson, R., & Holubec, E. (1993). *Circles of learning*. Edina, MN: Interaction Book Co.

Johnson, D. W., Johnson, R., & Johnson, F. (1976). Promoting constructive conflict in the classroom. *Notre Dame Journal of Education*, *7*, 163–168.

Johnson, D. W., Johnson, R., & Stevahn, L. (1995). *Three new studies on conflict resolution/peer mediation training*. Paper presented at annual meeting of National Association for Mediation Education (NAME), Seattle.

Lewin, K. (1951). *Field theory in social science*. New York: Harper.

Opotow, S. (1991). Adolescent peer conflicts. *Education and Urban Society*, *23*(4), 416–441.

Watson, G., & Johnson, D. W. (1972). *Social psychology: Issues and insights* (2nd ed.). Philadelphia: Lippincott.

Enhancing the Educational Attainment of Minority Youth

Elsie G. J. Moore

Inequalities exist in the life opportunities of young Americans from various social classes and ethnic groups. This is obviously not a new observation. The issue became the focus of considerable sociopolitical concern in the early 1960s as larger segments of our society were confronted with the reality that some groups were experiencing unmitigated intergenerational poverty and social and cultural isolation at a time when the majority was benefiting from prosperity and opportunities for upward mobility in an expanding economy.

Although the historical social forces of segregation and exclusion on the bases of race and national origin undoubtedly had contributed to the problems, legally banning these practices was clearly not sufficient to solve them. The fact remained that most individuals in the excluded groups were not developing the skills and credentials required by an increasingly technical society. That poor children and those from isolated ethnic groups consistently showed lower levels of educational attainment and scholastic achievement was recognized as a major contributor to socioeconomic disparities.

Also, public education clearly was not entirely succeeding as the great "equalizer" in providing—regardless of family background—the opportunity to learn, develop, and achieve. Black Americans, Hispanics, Puerto Ricans, and other ethnic minority children were not developing literacy and mathematic skills at a level necessary to compete with their more advantaged agemates in the majority culture.

Although general agreement existed that the socioeconomic immobility of these groups was strongly related to their lack of educational achievement, considerable disagreement emerged over what factors were contributing to their school failure and how these factors might be mediated by social class and ethnic group membership. Many experimental intervention programs were developed with the common goal of reducing or eliminating the school achievement deficiencies of minority status children. The focus and content of these programs varied depending upon the theoretical orientation of program developers to the nature and causal sequence of factors in minority children's educational difficulties.

In addition to numerous isolated experimental programs, Project Head Start was implemented at the national level in 1965 with federal funds allocated for the War on Poverty. The purpose of this national program for poor and minority status children ages 3 to 5 years was to ameliorate handicaps that prevent children from benefiting from public education, and thereby to increase their potential for upward social mobility.

After more than two decades of educational innovations, interventions, and research, considerable disparities remain in the scholastic achievement and educational attainment of minority status youth and their majority culture peers. Why this is the case and what can be done to facilitate school success of minority status young people are the issues addressed in this chapter. Suggestions as to how counselors may play a role in enhancing the educational attainment of minority youths are particularly focused upon in this discussion.

A Closer Look at the Problem

Young people from certain ethnic groups consistently show lower levels of educational attainment (i.e., number of years of schooling completed) than their majority culture peers. Blacks and Hispanics, for example, show significantly lower educational attainment than their Anglo counterparts.

Comparative Studies

Recent estimates indicate that, among American youth between ages 18 and 23 in the summer of 1980, the proportion of Blacks who had not obtained a high school diploma was twice that of the White population (32% vs. 16%) (U.S. Department of Defense, 1982). The proportion of Hispanic youths in this age range who had not completed high school was even higher than that of Blacks—42%. Differences in the proportions of these ethnic groups, ages 18 to 22 years, who had completed at least 1 year of postsecondary education (i.e., some college) were not as great as those seen for high school completion, but they were considerable.

Regardless of ethnicity, individuals with more education obtain higher status jobs and, generally, higher salaries. Therefore, educational variation between groups is an important factor in the persistent inequalities in life opportunities and ultimate occupational and income attainment observed between them (Jencks et al., 1979).

Increasingly, educators and social science researchers are focusing not only upon how much schooling young people from various groups complete but also on the level and types of skills they attain while in the educational system. Technological advances have reduced the demand for unskilled and semiskilled workers while increasing the demand for clerical, technical, and professional workers. What this means is that basic literacy *and* numeracy skills are absolute prerequisites for performance in occupations at even the lowest end of the skilled labor continuum. Individuals with basic science, electronics, and mechanical knowledge, as well as basic academic skills (in reading, writing, and mathematics) can be expected to create a competitive advantage in selection for jobs, higher educational placements, and job-training programs leading to higher status and more lucrative careers in today's labor market.

Studies of academic skill development among American school-age children have consistently shown that, on the average, minority youth are not developing basic academic skills, such as reading, writing, mathematics, and science, at the same rate as their White counterparts. The discrepancy in skill development among minority status youth quite clearly relates to social and educational processes that undermine their opportunities for quality education.

This point was substantiated by Coleman et al. (1966) in reporting the results of their national study of the skill development of American school children at various grade levels. The study demonstrated the unevenness with which public education serves individuals from various life circumstances. It alerted educators, social scientists, and policy makers to the fact that Black and other minority status children were not developing even basic academic skills at the same rate as their White agemates, even when they had the same amount of schooling. Subsequent studies such as the periodic National Assessment of Educational Progress, conducted by the Education Commission of the States, and analyses of results of the yearly administration of the Scholastic Aptitude Test (SAT) (see Jones, 1984, for a review of these studies) generally confirm the persistence of ethnic group differences in specific skill development over time.

Profile of American Youth

In 1980 a unique opportunity to examine the skill level of the contemporary American youth population, to assess their vocational potential (as indexed by aptitude test scores) and to compare the performance of persons of varying ethnic and educational backgrounds, resulted from a study sponsored by the Department of Defense in cooperation with the Department of Labor. This study, called *Profile of American Youth,* involved administration of the current version of the Armed Services Vocational Aptitude Battery (ASVAB) to nearly 12,000 young people ages 15 to 22 at the time of testing. The study sample was developed to yield data that could be projected to represent the entire U. S. population in this age range. Because the young people who were administered the ASVAB were participants in the Department of Labor's large-scale study, National Longitudinal Study (NLS) of Youth Labor Force Behavior, a considerable amount of background data were available for each person tested, including educational information, family background data, ethnicity, and so on.

What makes the results from the *Profile of American Youth* study so unique is that the data come from persons of all segments of our society who were sampled by direct home visits. Consequently, they give a much broader picture of the skill development of American young people than tests administered to school children (e.g., the National Assessment of Educational Progress) or to high school seniors who are college-bound [e.g., Scholastic Aptitude Test (SAT) and American College Testing (ACT) program results reported annually]. In addition, because the ASVAB is a broad-range aptitude test battery that assesses not only school-intensive skills such as reading, word knowledge, general science, and mathematics, but also technical skills such as electronics information, mechanical comprehension, and auto and shop information, the Profile study permits an analysis of vocationally relevant skills that usually are not covered in the routine testing of students.

Results of the Profile study revealed that for all American young people, poor and non-poor, Black, Hispanic, and White, the more schooling they complete, the higher are their skill levels in the school-intensive areas and the technical areas. But Black and Hispanic youth who had completed the same amount of schooling as their White peers, including those who had at least some college, generally scored considerably lower than Whites.

As a matter of fact, a clear pattern of increasing difference in level of skill development with education emerged when the performance of Black and White youths was compared. That is, the smallest difference in their scores was seen among those who had completed 8 or fewer years of education, and the greatest difference was seen among those who had completed at least some college. In the case of the Hispanic young people, the smallest differentiation of their skill level relative to White peers also was seen among those who had completed 8 or fewer years of schooling. Beyond this educational level, a larger, but essentially constant, difference was shown in favor of White youth. (See Bock & Moore, 1986, for a complete analysis and discussion of the Profile study results.)

Other Studies

Although researchers consistently have observed considerable differences in the level of skill development of ethnic minority youth as compared to that of their White peers, positive changes are beginning to appear. For example, Burton and Jones (1982), from their analysis of National Assessment of Educational Progress (NAEP) test results for children ages 9 and 13 years old between 1970 and 1980, reported a significant decline in performance differences between Black and White pupils in writing skills, science, mathematics, social studies, and reading. Similarly, Jones (1984) reported a decline in differences between Black and White students in SAT-Verbal and SAT-Mathematics performance between 1976 and 1983.

Even though considerable differences remain between the average scores of Black and White students, these trends of declining differences are encouraging. Why we now are beginning to see encouraging changes in the relative performance of White youth and their ethnic minority peers is difficult to specify. Most observers, however, conceptualize the declining differences as long awaited returns on societal investments in innovations, interventions, and general efforts to improve the quality of education available to ethnic minority youth.

Some Early False-Starts

In the 1960s and early 1970s the development of most experimental intervention programs aimed at facilitating school success of minority status children was predicated upon the belief that the children's academic difficulties were a consequence of cognitive deficiencies that characterized them at the onset of formal schooling (see Horowitz & Paden, 1973, for a review of these programs). That is, many psychologists, educators, and other authorities assumed that ethnic minority children did not develop prerequisite intellectual skills during the preschool years to allow them to optimally benefit from school instruction. Although theorists at the time differed in their ideas about why the children were deficient (whether the deficiencies were primarily the result of environmental factors or of biological factors), they did generally agree that children from certain ethnic minority groups were disproportionately deficient in the skills necessary for successful school performance and learning.

This notion of pervasive cognitive deficiency among ethnic minority children—particularly Black children—was attributable primarily to the consistent finding that the children on the average scored significantly lower on standardized intelligence tests than did their White peers. Indeed, ethnic group differences in IQ performance and performance on other standardized measures designed to assess learning potential were the empirical bases for assuming that cognitive deficits were the sources of the children's school achievement difficulties.

The logic of this assumption stems from the belief that IQ tests can inform us of the quality of cognitive functioning that characterizes all children and that differences in functioning indicated by variations in test scores play a significant causal role in differentiated school performance (Eckberg, 1979). Both facets of this assumption can be challenged on the basis of accumulated research findings on factors affecting minority children's IQ test performance (see Moore, 1986a, for a discussion of this issue).

In the belief that ethnic minority children suffered from cognitive deficiencies, most of the early programs were designed to provide experiences and instruction that were thought to promote cognitive competency in general and the development of prerequisite academic skills in particular. As might be expected, the effectiveness of those programs typically was evaluated by noting changes in children's IQ scores at the completion of the intervention.

Most of these early programs were successful in boosting the children's IQ scores, but follow-up data revealed that by the third grade the children's scholastic achievement was not significantly different from that of their ethnic peers who had not experienced special preparation for public school entry. Had the programs failed? The unqualified answer is *no,* they had not failed, but many of the guiding assumptions of the programs on which long-term projections for the children's school success were based were in error.

As our knowledge of human developmental processes evolves, we must adjust our assumptions and hypotheses. These early programs based their projections of future school success for the participating children on the assumption that experiences in early infancy and childhood have a lasting effect on the individual—an impact on development throughout the course of development.

Clarke and Clarke (1976) and Brim and Kagan (1980) have compiled evidence from a number of sources to indicate that the effects of early experience, both positive and negative, are not permanent over the life course. Human development is a dynamic process, and individuals change as a result of continual interaction between their person and their changing environments. From this perspective, Ramey and Haskins (1981) concluded that the failure of ethnic minority children to achieve in the public school system consistent with projections made on the basis of their IQ scores after program interventions was attributable to public school characteristics. That is, public schools do not generally provide continued support for these children's intellectual development at the level provided by high quality preschool programs.

The lesson to be learned from early attempts to enhance minority children's educational attainment is rather obvious. Attempts to boost the children's scholastic achievement and attainment cannot be a one-time effort in the preschool years. Efforts to facilitate their academic growth have to be reflected in all segments of the curriculum, in the process of classroom instruction, and in the planning and program development of administrators, teachers, and counselors.

Making the Schools Work for Minority Youths

Each school year a disproportionate number of ethnic minority children are relegated to inferior positions in the curriculum on the basis of test results such as IQ scores and reading readiness assessments (Scarr, 1981). These early school decisions later translate into lower track positions in high school (if the student does not drop out of school from boredom before that time) and generally lower skill development at the completion of their public school experience. The reason for this is that children who are placed in special education classes other than gifted classes often are stereotyped by the larger social system of the school as being not as capable as others.

Teachers, counselors, and other school personnel often use the lower standardized test performance of these children to set a similarly low ceiling on the type, amount, and level of exposure to curriculum materials and on acceptable levels of mastery. Instruction is limited to the level of the test score, with only modest attempts to provide intellectual growth experiences (Haskins, Walton, & Ramey,

1983). Consequently, the children get farther behind their peers who achieve higher curriculum placements early in the schooling process. The effects of this under-education are cumulative, resulting in greater disparities in skill development between groups at the higher educational levels than at lower levels.

Many unsophisticated users of test data interpret lower scores on standardized measures of the sort mentioned earlier as indicators of fixed deficits. Thus, they feel justified in setting lower educational standards and expectations for children who are thought to be less capable, especially if "hard" evidence, such as a test score, exists to verify that position. Therefore, test data users in the school setting must be aware of the importance of cultural relativity for determining educational potential. Schools and school personnel all too often have a monocultural view (i.e., that of the White middle-class) of what behaviors, skills, attitudes, and values on the part of a pupil and his or her family are indicative of a "high ability" child. This same view generally is reflected in the standardized test measures used to empirically support placement and classification decisions.

Children from different ethnic groups enter this system with learning experiences, skills, attitudes, and achievement orientations derived from their unique socialization experiences, which are quite often different from those expected or even desired by the school (Gilbert, 1985; Shade, 1982). But this does not mean that they have not developed the prerequisite cognitive skills to be successful learners of skills the schools are charged to provide. Schools must become more attuned to ethnic minority children's needs as learners and avoid relying on test scores to account for their failure to do so.

Certainly the standardized test scores of ethnic minority children can be useful—if used wisely and in conjunction with carefully collected observational data of the child in various contexts, not just the school classroom. These data can be used to identify the child's relative strengths and weaknesses in preparation for curriculum placements appropriate for her or his age. But these data must be used to capitalize on apparent strengths in the instructional process, and to plan and implement appropriate remediation, if necessary, to ensure the child's continual academic growth.

The Cultural Context of Educational Processes

School personnel have to recognize that the school context is not a culturally neutral environment. Gilbert (1985) noted that the culture of the school is one that encourages and expects competitive behavior among pupils, demonstrated competency in standard English in oral exchanges, willingness to follow pre-set rules for involvement in the instructional process (e.g., only one person speaks at a time), and that involvement is limited to cognitive participation, not affective and motorical participation.

Shade (1982) suggested that a particular style of information processing is required by the culture of the school for students to be remarkably successful in the educational process. Characteristics of this accepted style of information processing include the spontaneous tendency to focus on the task itself and to ignore the people in the situation, an attending preference for verbal rather than nonverbal cues, abstraction ability that separates ideas and concepts into parts and reconstitutes them into a unified whole, and an analytic thinking style. According to Shade, the schools expect and require cognitive strategies that are "sequential, analytic, and object-oriented" for school success, which means that children who are, as a result of their particular cultural socialization, "universalistic, intuitive, and . . . person oriented" are likely to experience achievement difficulties (p. 238).

More often than not, ethnic minority children enter the schools demonstrating information processing skills, attitudes, and understandings of involvement in the classroom that conflict with the instructional modes and expectations of the typical classroom teacher. Many believe that this mismatch between the skills and orientations to learning that ethnic minority children bring to the school and what the school system expects and values is a major source of the children's achievement difficulties (see Bock & Moore, 1986, for a review of this literature).

If this is the case, adjusting instructional modes to fit the styles of the children rather than attempting to force the children to be responsive to the preestablished style of the school could function to facilitate minority children's achievement. It also might function to facilitate their remaining in school through high school completion to the extent that the adjustment might encourage children's greater feelings of belonging to the system rather than feelings of "foreign-ness."

High Expectations of Pupils' Achievement

Much literature has accumulated on characteristics of so-called effective schools for poor and ethnic minority children—schools wherein these children show high academic achievement. Characteristics of effective schools generally include a strong leader who is knowledgeable about and involved in the instructional program, programs of instruction in reading and mathematics that are systematically implemented and for which goals of instruction are clearly articulated, and high expectations of children's achievement, particularly in basic verbal and numerical skills, by the teachers and administrative staff (Brookover et al., 1978; Edmonds, 1979).

The latter characteristic has been consistently found to affect the achievement of ethnic minority students. Those who experience school settings wherein high academic standards are set and school personnel, particularly teachers, expect them to be successful in achieving the standards show high achievement. Teachers in these situations tend to provide a considerable amount of encouragement, praise, and support for achievement efforts, and the children respond with continued persistence and efforts toward skill mastery.

Unfortunately, many ethnic minority children find themselves in educational settings wherein academic standards are low, as are expectations of their achievement. Why this is the case is not clear, but in these settings ethnic minority children appear to not only fail to achieve skill development at levels that would allow them to be competitive with peers from the majority culture but also develop lower personal standards of achievement and lower expectations of their own achievement potential.

Early Academic and Vocational Counseling

Ogbu (1978) theorized that the high dropout rate and lower scholastic achievement among Black students, in particular result from their lack of awareness of the relevance of the skills taught in school for future career options. If this is the case, teachers, counselors, and other school officials must make special efforts to continually demonstrate the relationship between the academic skills taught and their application to the larger world of work.

Moore (1986b) verified that Black youth have a significantly lower knowledge of the world of work—what people in various occupations actually do—than their White peers. This is perhaps the result of the rather limited representation of career roles available to ethnic minority young people in their home communities. The literature has consistently shown that Black youth, even those who attend college, show a limited range of vocational interests. They tend to gravitate toward the social sciences, education, and the health fields, while White college students favor biological and physical sciences, at least as freshmen (Astin, 1982).

Underrepresentation of ethnic minorities in scientific and technical careers has been the focus of considerable concern in recent years. This is because lucrative career opportunities in the contemporary economy are expanding in these areas, Ethnic minority youth, however, generally do not express an interest in these careers, nor are they prepared to be competitive for educational placements and job-training programs in these areas. Their lack of preparation is related to their lower average mathematics skills and science knowledge upon completion of their secondary education.

The literature clearly reveals that minority youths do not enroll in academic mathematics and science courses in high school in the same proportions as their White peers (Jones, 1984). Large numbers of ethnic minority students who aspire to careers in engineering or other mathematics-related careers, who are perceived as mathematically capable by their teachers and counselors, do not enroll in advanced level mathematics courses in high school. Obviously, better counseling would facilitate their preparation and achievement of career goals.

What Can Counselors Do?

Counselors' potential to facilitate the educational attainment of minority youth is enormous. Counselors can provide the leadership to develop systematic, comprehensive career exploration programs in elementary, junior high, and high schools that serve large numbers of ethnic minority students and can ensure that these programs are implemented and appropriately evaluated for effectiveness. Counselors can help classroom teachers develop strategies to demonstrate the relationship between skills taught in the classroom and effective, productive functioning in the larger world.

Further, counselors can monitor the use of standardized test results for purposes of classification and placement of ethnic minority students. They also can take the lead in dispelling the myth that any test score is fixed or is a stable index of what the child can achieve. Educating teachers and principals about the appropriate interpretation of standardized test scores would definitely facilitate the achievement efforts of these children.

Counselors can take the lead in developing opportunities for school personnel to explore their own cultural orientations and to consider how their ethnic minority pupils may differ from them on various dimensions. Along this line, teachers also might consider how cultural differences between them and their pupils may negatively impact the learning and achievement of pupils in their charge. Particular attention could be given to the possible mismatch between pupils' typical styles of perceiving and processing information and the style required to achieve under the teacher's preferred mode of instruction.

Finally, counselors can take the lead in educating school personnel on the importance of their expectations for children's achievement striving and attainment. Certainly, teachers and principals need to clarify their performance expectations for ethnic minority students. If they are low, educators should clarify how the expectations were formed and whether they can be verified in fact.

Obviously ethnic minority students' perception of the availability and openness of counselors to meeting with them and discussing their concerns and problems is important. From her study of successful rural Black adolescents, Courtland (1985) reported that many saw school counselors as important providers of academic and personal-social assistance. This component of what the researcher described as "positive school experiences" of these young people is particularly noteworthy in this context.

References

Astin, A. W. (1982). *Minorities in American higher education.* San Francisco: Jossey-Bass.

Bock, R. D., & Moore, E. G. J. (1986). *Advantage and disadvantage: A profile of American youth.* Hillsdale, NJ: Lawrence Erlbaum.

Brim, O. G., & Kagan, J. (1980). *Constancy and change in human development.* Cambridge: Harvard University Press.

Brookover, W. B., Schweitzer, J. H., Schneider, J. M., Beady, C, H., Flood, P. K., & Wisenbaker, J. M. (1978). Elementary school climate and school achievement. *American Educational Research Journal, 15,* 301–318.

Burton, N. W, & Jones, L. V. (1982). Recent trends in achievement levels of Black and White youth. *Educational Researcher, 11*(17), 10–14.

Clarke, A. B., & Clarke, A. D. B. (1976). *Early experience: Myth and evidence.* New York: Free Press.

Coleman, J. S., Campbell, E. Q., Hobson, C. J., McPartland, J., Mood, A. M., Weinfeld, F. D., & York, R. L. (1966). *Equality of educational opportunity.* Washington, DC: U.S. Government Printing Office.

Courtland, C. L. (1985). Successful rural Black adolescents: A psycho-social profile. *Adolescence, 20*(77), 129–142.

Eckberg, D. L. (1979). *Intelligence and race.* New York: Praeger.

Edmonds, R. (1979, March/April). Some schools work and more can. *Social Policy,* pp. 28–32.

Gilbert, S. E. II. (1985, October). Improving the success in school of poor Black children. *Phi Delta Kappan,* pp. 133–137.

Haskins, R., Walden, T., & Ramey, C. T. (1983). Teacher and student behavior in high and low ability groups. *Journal of Educational Psychology, 75,* 799–810.

Horowitz, F. D., & Paden, L. (1973). The effectiveness of environmental intervention programs. In B. Caldwell & H. Riccuiti (Eds.), *Review of Child Development Research* (Vol. 3) (pp. 331–402). Chicago: University of Chicago Press.

Jencks, C., Bartlett, S., Corcoran, M., Crouse, J., Eaglesfield, D., Jackson, G., McClelland, K., Mueser, P., Olneck, M., Schwartz, J., Ward, S., & Williams, J. (1979). *Who gets ahead?* New York: Basic Books.

Jones, L. V. (1984). White-Black achievement differences: The narrowing gap. *American Psychologist, 39*(11), 1207–1213.

Moore, E. G. J. (1986a). Family socialization and the IQ test performance of traditionally and transracially adopted black children. *Developmental Psychology, 22,* 317–326.

Moore, E. G. J. (1986b). *The influence of knowledge of the world of work on ethnic group differences in career aspirations.* Paper presented at the Annual Meeting of the American Educational Research Association, San Francisco, CA.

Ogbu, J. (1978). *Minority education and caste.* New York: Academic Press.

Ramey, C. T., & Haskins, R. (1981). Early education, intellectual development and school performance: A reply to Arthur Jensen and J. McVicker Hunt. *Intelligence, 5,* 41–48.

Scarr, S. (1981). Testing for children: Assessment and the many determinations of intellectual competence. *American Psychologist, 36*(10), 1159–1166.

Shade, B. (1982). Afro-American cognitive style: A variable in school success. *Review of Educational Research, 52,* 219–244.

U.S. Department of Defense. (1982). *Profile of American youth.* Washington, DC: Dept. of Defense, Office of Assistant Secretary of Defense, Manpower, Reserve Affairs, & Logistics.

Sexual Harassment in Schools: Crossing the Line

Walter H. Bera and Fran Sepler

In 1991 the Minnesota legislature passed a law requiring every secondary school to provide its students training and information about the prohibition of sexual harassment. Bills pending or soon to be introduced in other states aim for the same result. From our perspective, these developments have come as no surprise. In the 2 years we have grappled with the mysteries and ambiguities of sexual harassment between and among teens, we have found ourselves immersed in the various fictions of law, social rhetoric, and adolescent folklore and have been informed directly by the insights of hundreds of students and teachers. Sexual harassment between students clearly is prohibited, but a potential problem lies in the narrow scope and misguided approach of simplistic prohibitions—mere policies that lay out a lack of tolerance for sexual harassment. We hope to offer information and insights to school counselors, educators, and other concerned adults that will effectively prevent or reduce sexual harassment while avoiding approaches that may do little but rob students of the joys of growing up.

For the average person watching the Clarence Thomas–Anita Hill hearings in October, 1991, the previously peripheral issue of sexual harassment gained depth and a sense of importance. For some, it was an occasion for skepticism, for others an opportunity to connect their personal experience with the painful reality of sexuality turned weapon. Few, if any, media commentators or spokespeople went beyond the workplace to explore the site where the phenomenon originated: the halls and classrooms of schools. Ultimately this is the locale to which society must turn to examine the realities and foundations of sexual harassment .

North American culture has undergone a shift in perspective. Analysis and observation of human suffering within the context of "socially acceptable" behavior has led to laws and policies establishing the outer bounds of acceptable conduct. Behavior that might have been viewed as a typical and harmless right of teenage passage or mere bullying in years past now may fall under the rubric of Title VII or other federal laws that prohibit discriminatory behavior, including harassment based upon gender. In short, unwelcome behavior is more and more likely to be a matter of law. Yesterday's "have to put up with it" has become today's evidentiary concern. At the same time, in the sometimes murky worlds of childhood and adolescence, a prevailing caution and concomitant confusion cautions us to be wary of labeling developmentally driven behavior or social awkwardness as something insidious and problematic. The balance between protecting vulnerable people and interfering with the trial and error of child development is delicate.

In our work, we have seen 6-year-old children pushing one another labeled as "sexual harassment" by parents and teachers, and we have seen a single ignorant utterance or well meaning but awkwardly executed approach labeled as such by teenage students. Similarly, we have seen grossly insensitive and potentially damaging behavior overlooked as "natural." To pretend that the line between acceptable and unacceptable, or even lawful and unlawful, behavior is clear is a disservice to children, educators, and parents. In this chapter we attempt to help readers plumb the murky depths of the emerging issue of harassment without succumbing to divisive rhetoric or methodology.

Historical Background

Legal Prohibitions

The issue of unwanted or coercive sexual behavior in the workplace or schools was generally unaddressed before the rise of the civil rights and women's movements in the 1960s and 1970s (Sepler, 1990). The Civil Rights Act of 1964 and formation of the Equal Employment Opportunity Commission created a body of law prohibiting discrimination in the workplace and subsequently in public educational facilities. Title VII of the Federal Civil Rights Act defines sexual harassment as a form of sexual discrimination and protects individuals from discrimination and harassment in the workplace. In 1972 Congress approved the addition of Title IX, protecting individuals from sexual discrimination at school.

The Equal Employment Opportunity Commission (EEOC) defines sexual harassment as:

> ...unwelcomed sexual advances, requests for sexual favors, and other verbal or physical conduct of a sexual nature when (1) submission to such conduct is made either explicitly or implicitly as a term or condition of an individual's employment, (2) submission to or rejection of such conduct by an individual is used as the basis for employment decisions affecting such individual, or (3) such conduct has a purpose or effect of substantially interfering with an individual's work performance or creating an intimidating, hostile, or offensive working environment. [Federal Regulation 74,676 (1980) (codified 29 C.F.R.–160411 (1981)]

Colloquially, this language and most statutory language distinguishes two forms of sexual harassment. The first, *quid pro quo* (Latin meaning "this for that" or "something for something") prohibits the trading of sexual behavior or display for promotion or reward. It also prohibits punishing those who do not acquiesce to a demand or offer of sexual behavior as a condition of their employment. Easiest to understand of the two forms of sexual harassment, *quid pro quo* harassment is a relative rarity. According to EEOC data, it constitutes approximately 12% of harassment claims nationwide.

More difficult to conceptualize, *hostile environment harassment* means that sexual or gender-based language, conduct, or material have saturated the environment to a point that one or more individuals feel their ability to participate in the environment has been unreasonably affected. How does one differentiate sexual behavior that is merely uncomfortable or obnoxious and behavior that is illegal? The courts have provided some guidance by specifying the terms *unwelcome*, *pervasive,* and *offensive.*

1. *Unwelcome* refers to behavior that has not been requested, received willingly, or reciprocated.

2. *Pervasive* refers to behavior that is inescapable, repeated, and visible.

3. *Offensive* can be defined by behavior that is unreasonably unpleasant, producing fear, shame, disgust, or embarrassment.

The combination of these defined factors is what can lead to a hostile educational environment and constitutes behavior that is considered sexually harassing in the eyes of the law.

Legal Remedies

The EEOC is empowered to take legal action to enforce prohibition against discrimination in employment based upon race, color, religion, sex, or national origin. The EEOC may bring a civil suit in federal court for an injunction and other remedies against the offending party. Within a specified time period the aggrieved may seek a remedy [see Bureau of National Affairs, Equal Employment Opportunity Act of 1972, 1–28 (1973)].

State human rights laws also may provide avenues of legal relief to individuals. Most states now provide for a statutory prohibition of sexual harassment within schools. In some cases protected class status and relief offered by statute exceed that of the federal law and may offer more forgiving statutes of limitations for those who hesitate to bring a claim. Common-law claims for tortuous acts and damages resulting from those acts also are being made more frequently, often in concert with, or as an adjunct to, federal or state actions.

According to the EEOC, annual sexual harassment claims to the federal EEOC office have almost doubled in 5 years from 5,495 in 1988 to 10,513 in 1992. As a result of more complaints and heightened legal activity, businesses are taking the issue of workplace sexual harassment seriously. Sandroff (1992) reported that 81% of Fortune

500 companies have training programs on sexual harassment, compared with only 60% in 1987.

Sexual harassment in schools has been getting increasing attention. In February, 1992, the U. S. Supreme Court ruled that students who experience sexual harassment can seek damages from schools violating their civil rights (see later case studies for examples). Students in grade school, middle school, and high school who have made claims that they have been harassed by other students have brought EEOC, statutory, and common law claims against their school districts. Anxious to abate district liability, state legislatures are passing laws mandating that schools have sexual harassment policies and prevention education.

Sexual Harassment Versus Sexual Assault

We have found widespread confusion between the nature of sexual harassment and that of sexual assault or exploitation. From a theoretical and practical standpoint, the distinction between the two is important to clarify. Sexual harassment generally is considered a violation of an individual's human right to education or employment. In contrast to the harmful act of an individual, civil or human rights focus upon the behavior of the institutions and organizations in which behavior occurs. The school or organization is the entity mandated by law to prevent, investigate, and respond appropriately to such discrimination or harassment. The law requires not that students be provided with a "pristine environment," free from offensive behavior, but, rather, an expectation that if or when a school administrator or employer "knew or should have known" that an individual was being harassed based upon gender or sex, appropriate steps will be taken to halt the harassment and to assure that it will not recur.

Sexual assault, such as rape and child molestation, is a criminal offense. Law enforcement and social service agencies bear the burden for investigation, intervention, and prosecution of sexual assault. It involves behavior serious enough to result, upon conviction, in penalties including imprisonment. It is a crime against society. Whereas sexual harassment can create an atmosphere conducive to sexual abuse, these behaviors demand distinctly different responses from internal and external authorities.

Prevalence in Adult and College Populations

Even though prevalence numbers vary broadly because of differences in defining harassment, sexual harassment in its broadest context is a common experience of adult workers and college students. Many studies of workplace harassing behavior have been conducted from selected or random samples of female workers. For example, *Working Woman Magazine* conducted a survey of its readers and received 9,680 responses (Sandroff, 1992). The survey reported that 60% of its respondents (all female) had experienced sexual harassment. Contrary to the impressions gained from perusing the popular media, sexual harassment is a reality for men and women alike. The reality is that males also report sexual harassment and now bring 18% of sexual harassment complaints filed with the EEOC, as well as increasing numbers of common law complaints.

College student surveys report significant sexual harassment. For example, according to McKinney, Olsen, and Satterfield (1988), 35% of female and 9% of male university graduate students reported having been sexually harassed in school, predominantly by peers. This is consistent with results of a Roscoe, Goodwin, et al. (1987) finding of university undergraduates, in which harassment was reported by 28% of females and 12% of males in the institution.

Sexual Harassment in America's Schools

The landmark report, *Hostile Hallways: The AAUW Survey on Sexual Harassment in America's Schools* (American Association of University Women, 1993), was published in 1993. Commissioned by the AAUW and surveyed by the national firm of Louis Harris and Associates, 1,632 public high school students in grades 8 through 11 were surveyed in 79 schools across the continental United States. The survey has a 95% confidence level with a margin of error of plus or minus four percentage points. The survey encompassed representative samples of African-American, Hispanic, and Caucasian students. The results of this groundbreaking survey are reviewed here in an attempt to counter the many myths surrounding school-based sexual harassment.

Students were asked: "During your whole school life, how often, if at all, has anyone (this includes students, teachers, other employees, or anyone else) done the following things to you *when you did not want them to?*"[1] The following is the list of responses in descending order of reported frequency:

■ Made sexual comments, jokes, gestures, or looks.

■ Touched, grabbed, or pinched you in a sexual way.

■ Intentionally brushed against you in a sexual way.

■ Flashed or "mooned" you.

■ Spread sexual rumors about you.

■ Pulled at your clothes in a sexual way.

■ Showed, gave, or left you sexual pictures, photographs, illustrations, messages, or notes.

■ Blocked your way or cornered you in a sexual way.

■ Wrote sexual messages/graffiti about you on bathroom walls, in locker rooms, etc.

---

[1] The items listed were developed in consultation with experts in the field of sexual harassment.

- Forced you to kiss him/her.
- Said you were gay or lesbian.
- Pulled your clothing off or down.
- Forced you to do something sexual other than kissing.
- Spied on you as you dressed or showered at school.

Four of five students (81%) reported they had been the target of some form of harassment during their school lives. Consistent with the authors' experience, the gender gap is remarkably narrow: 85% of girls and 76% of boys experienced unwanted or unwelcome sexual behavior that interfered with their lives. The gender gap widens somewhat for the 58% of students who experienced harassment "often" or "occasionally," with 66% of the girls and 49% of the boys responding affirmatively.

When is the first sexual harassment experience most likely to occur? According to the AAUW report, the most vulnerable time for students is in the middle school years of sixth to ninth grade. The report indicates that 41% of the students who have been harassed fall within this age group. The most common forms of sexual harassment, reported by two thirds of all students surveyed, were sexual comments, jokes, gestures, or looks.

Who does the harassing? Of the students reporting harassment, one in four girls and one in 10 boys cited a school employee such as a teacher, a coach, or a bus driver as the harasser. As serious as these figures are, they do not account for the vast majority of harassment. Fully 79% of reported incidents are initiated by and directed against peers. Contrary to the assumption that primarily males sexually harass, 66% of all boys and 52% of all girls surveyed admitted they had sexually harassed someone in the school setting. Significantly, 94% of the admitted perpetrators claimed they themselves had been harassed, reflecting a harassed-harasser perpetration cycle.

Why do students sexually harass peers? The AAUW study indicates that ignorance, clumsiness, and peer influence drive sexual harassment. This is contrary to a frequent analysis that, regardless of the actors or situation, power is the primary motivator. When asked why they engaged in or experienced harassing behavior, students responded in the following order of frequency:

1. It's just a part of school life.
2. A lot of people do it.
3. It's no big deal.
4. I thought the person liked it.
5. I wanted a date with the person.
6. My friends encouraged me—"pushed me" into doing it.
7. I wanted something from that person.
8. I wanted that person to think I had some sort of power over them.

Where is sexual harassment most likely to occur? The AAUW survey indicated that the most common sites were:

1. School hallways.
2. Classrooms.
3. Outside of school.
4. Gym or sport area.
5. Cafeteria.
6. School bus or transportation.
7. Field trip.

Whom do students tell? The response of students in the AAUW survey confirms the critical role that peer-age friends can play in supporting targets of harassment. By far, students are most likely to tell a friend (63%). Significant gender differences reflect the gender socialization and stereotyping that boys should be the "strong, silent type" in response to adversity (Bolton, Morris, & MacEachron, 1989). Boys were more likely than girls to have told no one (27% and 15%, respectively). Only 7% of sexually harassed students said they told a teacher about the experience; again, girls were twice as likely as boys to have told a teacher. Of the students who experienced harassment, 23% remained silent or told no one.

What is the educational impact of sexual harassment? The academic impact of sexual harassment was profound. The impacts were:

1. Not wanting to attend school—nearly one in four students (23%).
2. Not wanting to talk in class.
3. Having a hard time paying attention in school.
4. Staying home from school or cutting class.
5. Getting a lower grade on a test paper.
6. Finding it hard to study.
7. Getting a lower grade in the class.
8. Thinking about changing schools.
9. Doubting whether he or she has what it takes to graduate from high school.

What are the emotional and behavioral consequences of sexual harassment? The responses were:

1. Feeling embarrassed.
2. Feeling self-conscious.
3. Being less sure of himself or herself or less confident.
4. Feeling afraid or scared.
5. Doubting whether he or she can have a happy romantic relationship.

6. Feeling confused about who he or she is.

7. Feeling less popular.

8. Interestingly, feeling more popular.

Nearly one in two students (49%) who were harassed said they avoid the person or persons who harassed them. More than twice as many girls as boys reported this response.

Despite the stereotype of males as harassers, a significant number of boys (76%) reported being targets of sexual harassment at school. This number was particularly high for African-American boys, most notably in the categories involving direct physical contact. Hispanic boys, on the other hand, were the least likely to experience non-physical forms of sexual harassment. In addition, boys most often were harassed by a girl acting alone.

Reflecting another form of prejudice, of the 14 types of sexual harassment outlined in the survey, 86% of all students reported they would be "very upset" if they were called gay or lesbian. The study noted that no other type of harassment, including actual physical abuse, provoked reaction this strong, especially in the boys. Of the boys who were called gay, nearly three in five said they had called someone else gay.

Sepler & Associates' Survey of Student Harassment

Sepler & Associates conducted gender-segregated focus groups with 420 students between ages 12 and 18 enrolled in the sixth through the 12th grades in urban, suburban, and rural school districts. The sample was not scientifically drawn, but the breadth and depth of the qualitative data gathered does provide another focal point on sexual harassment among students and enriches many of the insights of the AAUW survey.

Students were asked if they had experienced behavior from other students that made them "so ashamed, afraid, or embarrassed that they were distracted from their school work, avoided certain areas or classes, or skipped school altogether."[2] In response to this question, 302 students responded affirmatively. The comments below reflect the strong language used by the students in the focus groups. Because virtually every student described multiple acts, the frequency data mirror both the high incidence and the multiple responses to unwelcome behavior. Typically, the reaction of students who reported multiple incidents was at first to do nothing or to tell a friend. Students who reported ongoing incidents became more likely to tell parents or teachers or to file a complaint.

---

[2] This colloquial definition of sexual harassment was formulated in collaboration with teachers and attorneys attempting to create a "user friendly," yet legally accurate description of behavior that would rise to the level that legally constitutes sexual harassment.

Girls' Experiences

Of 240 subjects, 219 reported experiencing harassment. Girls described sexual harassment from boys as:

- Being called "cunt," "slut," "bitch," or "whore" while in groups (40%).
- Being "rated" or "ranked" based on gender (18%).
- Touching breast (16%).
- Publicly claiming, falsely or honestly, to have had sex with the girl (12%).
- Asking for or demanding sex (16%).
- Pulling shirt away from body and looking down (2%).
- Catcalls, jeers, sexist remarks (80%).
- Obscene notes, letters, phone calls (59%).
- Teasing regarding breast size (31%).
- Following, stalking, or sneaking up on repeatedly (19%).

Girls described sexual harassment from girls as:

- Being called "cunt," "slut," "bitch," or "whore" (38%).
- Spreading false rumors regarding the sexual activity of target (21%).
- Graffiti implying sexual promiscuity (14%).
- Sexual contact, including physical restraint and being forced to touch boys' genitals (11%).
- Betraying trust by sharing target's history of sexual activity (victimization and consensual) (9%).
- Making telephone advances at boys while claiming to be subject (7%).
- Being told that a boy wanted to see target and finding out it was a "set-up" (3%).

Boys' Experiences

Boys described sexual harassment from girls in the following ways (n = 83, total adds up to more than 100%):

- Receiving harassing or obscene phone calls (41%).
- Getting obscene notes (21%).
- Being subjected to repeated and unwelcome sexual advances (19%).
- Spreading false rumors regarding sexual activity of target (15%).
- Teasing or rumors regarding sexual orientation (11%).
- Touching genitals or "depantsing" (6%).
- "Ranking" or "rating" (4%).
- Following or stalking (2%).

Boys described sexual harassment by boys as:

■ Teasing or rumors regarding sexual orientation (22%).

■ Betraying trust regarding target's history of sexual activity, whether victimization or consensual (3%).

Students' responses to unwelcome behavior (within 3 months of incident):

■ Did nothing (98%).

■ Told friends (88%).

■ Confronted person or persons (44%).

■ Told parents (31%).

■ Told teacher (20%).

■ Filed complaint (16%).

■ Took legal action (3%).

Sexual Harassment Prevention Education

The rationale for sexual harassment prevention education rests on a number of realities:

1. Sexual harassment has affected the majority of students, female and male.

2. Sexual harassment has had significant impact on the targets—emotionally, behaviorally, and educationally.

3. Sexual harassment affects the school environment and affects the observers of harassment—teachers, students, and administrators.

4. The school may be mandated to provide information on its policies regarding sexual harassment.

5. The school can be held liable if it is found to be remiss in carrying out responsibilities regarding the prevention, investigation, and cessation of sexual harassment.

Sexual abuse prevention education programs developed in the 1980s are now used widely in school systems and can serve as a model for preventing harassment (Conte, Rosen, & Saperstein, 1986). Finkelhor (1986) reported that prevention education videos such as *TOUCH* and *No Easy Answers* (Anderson, 1983), which are directed primarily at children and adolescents, have some documented success in changing attitudes, indicated by a reduction in incidents. Finkelhor also emphasized the importance of prevention education aimed toward parents who need to educate themselves on the topic and improve their reactions when hearing about victimization. He recommended that efforts also focus on teachers and other adults who have contact with adolescents.

Finally he recommended further research in the prevention area, an area generally neglected in behavioral research.

Although readers may be aware of emerging literature and resources on sexual harassment and its prevention, harassment remains difficult to prevent. Selection and utilization of resources often is more a matter of happenstance than thoughtful consideration.

Crossing the Line Curriculum

One resource we recently developed is a sexual harassment prevention curriculum on the most commonly reported type of harassment: teen to teen. Entitled *Crossing the Line*, it consists of four 40-minute classroom sessions using a 30-minute interactive videotape of students in classrooms and hallways. The package features a teacher's guide, overhead transparencies, student handouts for each session, information for parents, and posters. Because *Crossing the Line* now is used in 48 states, we can bring a critical perspective to our own work and suggest a need for further resources.

Curriculum

In Session 1 we present a questionnaire to students, suggesting a variety of school scenarios and asking students to state their opinions about the appropriateness of each scenario. The first session, really a "pre-session," is designed to stimulate small-group discussion to examine attitudes toward sexual harassment. Session 2 aids students in exploring the legal and functional definitions of harassment, viewing a spectrum of behavior to help them understand where to draw the line. It features a videotaped scenario filmed five times with five different sets of dynamics, challenging students to understand the subtle ways in which a circumstance can range from delightful to grim to harmful. Session 3 uses two case examples that increase awareness and sensitivity by exploring the dynamics of common harassment situations and challenge students to come up with their own conclusions and solutions to these problem situations. The students discuss their insights and options. Session 4 features candid video statements by groups of male and female students presenting their personal views about various aspects of harassment. Class discussion follows each, to explore issues of personal responsibility and appropriate boundaries.

Evaluation

How do students respond to a sexual harassment prevention program? Can adolescents really relate to a topic that many adults find confusing or even incomprehensible? Can students learn respectful behavior and change their attitudes?

Crossing the Line was independently evaluated by Susan E. Akervik, an administrator and educator in Maplewood, Minnesota (Akervik, 1993). Evaluation results were obtained from a questionnaire filled out by 350 eighth-grade female and male students after they completed the four-session *Crossing the Line* sexual harassment prevention curriculum using a female/male presentation team. Her evaluation provided both quantitative and qualitative results, as seen in Tables 21.1 and 21.2. The results provide considerable hope for sexual harassment prevention education. An average of 69.4% of the students who participated in classroom presentations of *Crossing the Line* agreed the program was effective across the 10 major quantitative variables measured. An average of 9.1% disagreed. In addition, the qualitative responses indicate significant learning and attitudinal change as a result of the program.

Implementation Issues

After providing consultation and training in schools across the United States, we have made a number of observations of what is needed to effectively implement a school-based sexual harassment prevention program. The perspective has to be that there is a

Table 21.1 Crossing the Line Program: Quantitative Evaluation

[Instructions to students:

Please tell us what you think about *Crossing the Line*. For the following statements, put an X in the box that best explains how you feel about this program.] (Final percentages are rounded.)

	AGREE	DON'T KNOW	DISAGREE
1. The topics presented were clear and easy for me to understand.	95%	4%	1%
2. The program explained the school policy regarding sexual harassment.	83%	14%	3%
3. The program materials were at my level of understanding.	83%	13%	4%
4. The program helped me understand how to listen to others when my behavior is making someone else uncomfortable.	80%	16%	4%
5. The discussions helped me decide how I feel about sexual harassment.	72%	21%	7%
6. The program helped me understand how to tell others when I feel sexually harassed.	67%	25%	8%
7. The videotape helped me decide how I feel about sexual harassment.	64%	24%	12%
8. I will be able to apply what I learned in this program.	61%	35%	4%
9. Participating in the program was worth my time and effort.	58%	26%	16%
10. The program was interesting to me.	31%	37%	32%
AVERAGE	69.4%	21.5%	9.1%

Table 21.2 Crossing the Line Program: Quantitative Evaluation

What one thing did you like best about the sexual harassment curriculum?

    Very worthwhile in teaching the differences between harassment, flirting, and teasing
    Very well explained and in detail
    Like male/female presentation team
    Telling it straightforward; open and honest discussions
    You have choices
    How it affects other people
    It will help me for the rest of my life
    How to help someone
    It's okay to tell someone if you have been sexually harassed
    Videos and discussions, because they revealed other people's opinions and point of view
    How it can cut down on it recurring
    How to tell someone without offending them
    Videos looked real life because actors were the same age as us

What one thing did you like least about the sexual harassment curriculum? (This question had only four responses.)

    Made men out mainly to be the offenders and women to be the complainers
    Repetitiveness
    Explanation of difference between assault and harassment
    Want to know about the consequences

What would you like to change or add?

    More questions for situations where people give their perceptions
    More activities and group discussion
    Have skits or plays
    More emphasis on all kinds of harassment, not just sexual
    More of man's viewpoint of being harassed and how it feels
    How much it can alter one's life

What was the most important thing you learned about sexual harassment?

    Don't do it
    Nobody has to put up with it
    Now I know what to do
    It hurts feelings
    It's wrong and don't put up with it
    How easy it is to sexually harass someone
    Sexual harassment is not just touching, it's verbal too
    If you are a victim, tell someone
    Learn what it is and when to step forward
    To be more respectful of the opposite sex so as not to offend them
    Think before you speak and act
    Anyone can do the harassing or be harassed
    No means no

need for a multisystemic implementation. Bronfenbrenner (1979) was one of the first to note the importance of the "ecology" of human development. In a school system, the important parts of that school ecology are administrators, teachers, support staff, parents, and students.

1. *Administrators: Principals, Vice Principals, School Counselors, and Similar Personnel* should be the first ones exposed to the sexual harassment curriculum and policy, as well as provided consultation in how to manage sexual harassment reports rapidly and effectively.

2. *Teachers.* Teachers need to be familiar with the sexual harassment curriculum and policy. Presentation of a teacher-focused sexual harassment curriculum is similar in many ways to student presentations. The best dynamic occurs within an atmosphere of trust and frankness in which teachers can reflect on their own past experiences and those of their current students. This creates the personal and professional insights that lead to effective leadership and credibility when intervening in the student culture.

3. *Support Staff.* Often of low prestige or visibility, secretaries, teaching assistants, bus drivers, kitchen staff, assistant coaches, janitors, and others frequently are among the first to observe inappropriate behavior. They also are the least likely to be included in sexual harassment education. They must be a part of the solution.

4. *Parents.* When parents are involved in implementing a sexual harassment curriculum and are informed of policies that govern their children's behavior, many benefits can ensue. Feedback from parents often shows how much they have learned. With this awareness parents are more likely to offer open and vocal support to those implementing the curriculum and policy.

5. *Students.* Perhaps contrary to the most simple logic that focuses upon changing student behavior, we believe students should be the last ones in a school to be exposed to prevention and awareness materials. This helps put the adults who are critical as opinion leaders in the students' life in a position to provide real leadership and to avoid the divisiveness we often have observed when harassment incidents are investigated or students are disciplined in a school that has not spent adequate time with its employees and constituents. When all of the leaders in the school have a common understanding and agenda regarding student behavior, students can be exposed to a sexual harassment curriculum which goes beyond obligation and represents a substantive expectation in their educational environment.

Our experience tells us that sexual harassment prevention material is presented best by a male/female trainer team in groups small enough to foster student discussion. At the same time, we acknowledge that a single classroom teacher can be highly effective in presenting a concentrated and balanced program. If the student culture is fairly negative and insensitive, the material might best be presented first in same-gender groups that provide a safe atmosphere to discuss the issues and confront the attitudes. Attention should be paid to the socialization and psychological requirements of each gender. Issues of peer relations, male and female stereotypes, and verbal and relational skills should inform the presenter's approach (Gonsiorek, Bera, & LeTourneau, in press).

Conclusion

If sexual harassment is to be prevented, educators and students must deal with behaviors that, though not necessarily harassment from a legal standpoint, disrupt and harm the school environment. Exciting to us has been the experience of facilitating groups of students to build consensus and then receiving open letters about what *they* think the positive standards of behavior should be in their school. In some schools these self-generated standards of conduct have been so effective that they were hung in the school hallway for much of the academic year. Students generally want to be in a school environment that allows them to deal with problems as they arise and in which people will not be perfect but will respond when told they are behaving harmfully or insensitively.

Collective responsibility surpasses shame as a motivator for behavioral change. Repeatedly we visit educational institutions in which students have been briefed regarding the "thou shalt nots" of harassment and told that punishment will follow a violation of the rules. Too often this has been accompanied by harsh lectures regarding the abuse of power and occasionally male-blaming rhetoric. This approach is counter to our empirical knowledge—that in junior and senior high schools, half of the girls and two thirds of the boys admit sexually harassing others and that both genders have been harassed in similar numbers (American Association of University Women, 1993). It serves only to create resistance and hostility in those who may feel unfairly targeted or singled out.

Using the secondary school as a platform for unsupported political analysis may create a divisive dynamic that only exacerbates the sense that harassment is somebody else's problem. Far more effective is to engage students in a discussion of the myriad ways in which sexual harassment affects the school environment: gossip, fear, rumors, divisiveness, anxiety, uptight teachers. All of these make sense to students and assist the school community in contemplating an environment in which each and every student in any educational setting feels a personal stake in preventing harassment.

Problem solving, taking risks, being courageous, sticking up for others, stepping into situations that others may say are not anyone else's business, and tolerating others' honest and inadvertent mistakes empower and encourage students rather than posture them for adversarial finger-pointing. Our curriculum provides vignettes and structured discussion that many teachers supplement by having students share their own positive experiences in changing the behavior around them.

Finally, the missing link may be the cultural climate that teachers, staff, and parents create in schools. We frequently are disappointed when invitations to attend our school assemblies on sexual harassment prevention are issued to parents, urging them to attend and observe, and only the paltriest numbers attend. Parent information meetings are characterized by empty seats and embarrassed administrators. A school that can produce a hundred parents for an athletic event sometimes produces only a few on a subject that involves their students' capacity to receive a fair educational opportunity. Aggressive and creative marketing of a parents' night or even a more compulsory format for parental involvement in discussions of the school climate may be called for. When a student is disciplined for sexual harassment, the previously uninvolved parent often is the one who protests the loudest over too much or too little intervention.

Teachers, too, must be part of the solution. To credibly speak to students about interpersonal respect and sexual boundaries when a teacher's lounge is saturated with sexually demeaning humor and gender-bashing rhetoric is difficult. Likewise, when healthy sexuality and intimacy have been repressed to the point of stiff grimness in manner, students recognize and emulate the withholding of natural warmth and humor.

More than anything else, teachers must model the appropriate way to overcome discomfort or to challenge a peer; to hear criticisms or feedback on their behavior and respond without defensiveness and with a sense of personal investment. We have been deeply moved by the stories of educators struggling with this challenge, such as the male mathematics teacher who described his dawning recognition that he made a female student nervous when he stood behind her and the difficult decision he made, following one of our sessions, to acknowledge this to the student and ask her what manner of working together would be more comfortable. Educators must take the lead in creating an educational climate where understanding sexual harassment is a tool rather than a weapon.

Sexual harassment is a real problem in secondary schools, one that finally is getting the attention it so richly deserves. Yet the passion and politics of adult debate and passionate social analysis must be tempered by respect for the delicacy of the adolescent experience, the developmental tasks that teens face in forming intimate relationships, and the ultimate benefit to be gained by empowering rather than dictating to the next generation. This perhaps is said best in the thank-you note Fran Sepler received after working with a suburban school:

Today the boy came to my locker again, and I remembered what you said about [speaking and hearing each other]. I told him that I felt afraid. He got embarrassed and sort of sad, and said he was sorry. I'm not afraid of him anymore.

References

Akervik, S. (1993). *Crossing the Line—Program evaluation.* Unpublished study, Maplewood, MN.

American Association of University Women. (1993). *Hostile hallways: The AAUW survey on sexual harassment in America's schools.* Washington DC: AAUW Educational Foundation.

Anderson, C. (1983). *TOUCH* and *No Easy Answers.* Minneapolis: Illusion Theater. (videos)

Bolton, F., Morris, L., & MacEachron, A. (1989). *Males at risk: The other side of child sexual abuse.* Newbury Park, CA: Sage Publications.

Bronfenbrenner, U. (1979). *The ecology of human development.* Cambridge, MA: Harvard University Press.

Conte, J., Rosen, C., & Saperstein, L. (1986). An analysis of programs to prevent sexual victimization of children. *Journal of Primary Prevention, 6*(3), 141–155.

Finklehor, D. (1986). *A sourcebook on child sexual abuse.* Beverly Hills, CA: Sage Publications.

Gonsiorek, J., Bera, W., & LeTourneau, D. (in press) *Male adolescent sexual abuse: Clinical perspectives.* Beverly Hills, CA: Sage Publications.

McKinney, K., Olsen, C., & Satterfield, A. (1988). Graduate students' experiences with and responses to sexual harassment: A research note. *Journal of Interpersonal Violence, 3*(3), 319–325.

Roscoe, B., and Goodwin, M., et al. (1987). Sexual harassment of university students and student employees: Findings and implications. *College Student Journal, 21*(3), 254–273.

Sandroff, R. (1992). Sexual harassment: The inside story. *Working Woman,* June.

Sepler, F. (1990). Sexual harassment: From protective response to proactive prevention. *Hamline Journal of Public Law and Policy, 11*(1), 61–78.

CASE 1: KATY LYLE

It was 1987, and Katy, a cheerful 15-year-old, was making friends and enjoying her first weeks of high school. An attractive student, she was shy, friendly, popular and well liked.

Abruptly, in mid-October, everything changed.

"Guys' reaction to me kind of changed," she said. "They looked at me funny. They stayed away from me."

Only later did she learn from a senior male, "Do you know what they're writing about you on the bathroom walls? 'Katy Lyle is a slut.'"

She learned that the graffiti in the second-floor bathroom stall was growing daily in explicitness and vulgarity. Boys began referring to it as the "Katy Lyle stall" and they teased her about the messages. The teasing happened first thing in the morning when she boarded the bus and continued through the day, with peers questioning her about her proficiency at sex acts, asking her to "do" them or telling her they'd used "her" stall that morning.

Katy became more and more withdrawn. She was not going out with the friends she had made so recently. She studied a lot, babysat every weekend, practiced her saxophone, and just "felt blue" all the time.

She approached the guidance counselors and later the principal, asking them to please do something about the graffiti. "Each time I asked somebody, they said they'd take care of it. I thought they would, but no one did."

Katy continued to hear from others that the graffiti was still there. She heard excuses such as that custodians weren't allowed to paint and the district was supposed to hire painters, or that the custodians did wash off some of the words but that the writing would reappear.

Finally, before the summer that ended that first horrible year, she asked one of the male band members that she had met to sneak her into the bathroom so she could look for herself. She slipped in the bathroom door, walked to the center stall and stared. The whole inside of the stall was covered with writing about her in pencil, ballpoint, permanent marker, and scratched in razor blade.

"It was overwhelming," she said. "I was barraged. Things about farm animals and dogs and brothers....I actually took the time to read them all." Rejoining the band members on the bus, she eventually broke down and sobbed all the way to the concert but couldn't tell anyone why.

The next year was much the same. The principal and the guidance counselors made promises, and the graffiti and teasing continued. She took matters into her own hands. She brought forward a sexual harassment lawsuit, not really wanting the money but wanting the harassment to stop and for things to change.

"All I really wanted was an apology," she said. "Not even a public apology. Just a face-to-face apology."

She did not get the apology but did receive a settlement of $15,000 and an agreement from the district that all schools would post a sexual harassment policy and check bathroom stalls daily for graffiti. This came after more than a year of paperwork and negotiations.

(Excerpted and paraphrased with permission from a *Duluth News-Tribune* story dated January 12, 1993, by Laurie Hertzel)

CASE 2: JONATHAN HARMS

Ten-year-old Jonathan Harms has filed a complaint of sexual harassment against the Sauk Rapids-Rice School District. He reported that 12 students at Rice Elementary School repeatedly taunted him with profanity and obscenities, called him a girl, and told him he had sex with animals. The taunting occurred in class, in the school restroom and halls, on the playground, and on the bus. It started in first grade and continued until fourth grade, resulting in his leaving the school for a private school.

Sam Harms, Jonathan's father, said school officials failed to act despite repeated reports by both himself and his son until his son secretly tape-recorded the other students' harassing comments.

Jonathan said the harassment made him "upset, mad, and angry at the school and at home."

"I used to tell the playground supervisors [and teachers] when things like this happened," Jonathan said. "They never disciplined them. They would just say, 'Oh, that's not your business. Go play somewhere else.'"

Jonathan's father said Jonathan would "come home crying." He lost his concentration on simple tasks. His schoolwork declined rapidly. He didn't hand in reports."

School officials were provided with transcripts of the recording and decided to suspend five students for 5 days. The principal met with all parents involved.

The U. S. Education Department has decided to investigate the sexual harassment allegations. The Department of Civil Rights Office issues three types of findings: no violations; violations, but the school or district is complying with a plan to correct the problem and will be monitored for up to 2 years; or violation with refusal to comply. In the latter case, the school can lose its federal aid or be referred for civil prosecution.

(Excepted with permission from a *Minneapolis Star Tribune* article published May 20, 1993, and written by Maureen M. Smith)

CASE 3: AMBER AND TARA WOOLERY

Amber and Tara Woolery, sixth- and seventh-grade students, reported that for the past 3 years they have received sexually harassing letters and have been called "dirty bitch" and other names in the school hallways, on the bus, and in the classrooms. Another St. Cloud, Minnesota, student, Patti Langner Prom, who graduated in 1988, said she considered suicide during ninth grade because of ongoing harassment.

"If children are not emotionally safe [in the schools], that's going to hurt them just as much as guns and knives," said their father, Terry Woolery.

School principal John Clark said the school always calls the parents of students involved in discipline problems but how a school deals with students is not the business of parents of other students. Superintendent Jerry Hartley said, "It's better for adults to wait before stepping in before a student clearly can't cope with the problem."

"We don't condone harassment, but we also think people should solve their problems on their own," Hartley said.

(Excerpted with permission from a *St. Cloud Times* report dated May 28, 1993)

CASE 4: BOY'S EXPERIENCE IN EIGHTH GRADE

When in eighth grade, a boy described being "depantsed"—an adolescent "prank" in which a student's pants are yanked down below the buttocks. He described having several tenth-grade girls grab him and depants him and then mark his testicles with felt markers. He told only a friend, who told him to "forget the whole thing and avoid those girls." Now in eleventh grade, he shrugged while acknowledging it had been "quite a drag."

(Reported to authors)

CASE 5 : JUNIOR HIGH GIRL

A popular junior high girl who has startlingly brilliant red hair described a poll conducted by some students, male and female, who were wagering on the color of her pubic hair. She became extremely ashamed when the results were featured in a "gossip" column in the school newspaper. She felt compelled to laugh about it, insisting she didn't mind, even though she stated, "I thought seriously about killing myself for several weeks afterward."

(Reported to authors)

CASE 6: HIGH SCHOOL SENIORS

Throughout his school career a frail and introverted boy was teased incessantly by other boys as a "queer" and a "fag." As a senior in high school, he began dating another senior, who also saw herself as a social outcast. The two students were taunted verbally in the hallways and subjected to harassment on city streets by fellow students. On the senior retreat day, a picture of the couple was circulated, altered to show genitalia. Later that day, the two students attempted a mutual suicide, which was interrupted by a parent's unexpected arrival home.

When questioned later, both students attributed their suicide attempt to the harassing behavior they experienced from their fellow students.

(Reported to authors)

A Death at School: Issues and Interventions

Robert L. Wrenn

Jennifer Garcia, a third grader at Pratt Elementary, comes to school with a bandanna wrapped around her head. She has just finished her first trial run of chemotherapy with good success. Some of the other students kid her about how funny she looks, and Jennifer finally asks the teacher if she can go home.

Leroy Lincoln, a middle school student, is gunned down in the school's parking lot by a rival gang member. There is talk at school the next day about retribution for the young man who murdered Leroy.

Students at Centerview High come to their first class of the day having seen on TV the night before that two of their fellow students were in a car accident. Although students saw the accident reported on TV, they are not sure who the students were. All they know is that both students died immediately upon impact.

Bill McKerron, a student from your high school math class, had a party at his home on Sunday evening while his parents were away. He was showing off a handgun owned by his father to some of the kids at the party when it accidentally went off, hitting Jennifer Cook, another student from your class, in the head. Jennifer is at a local hospital in a coma. Students from your math class want to talk about the event.

A university class in media arts sits waiting for the instructor, only to find the department head and another person moving toward the front of the class. The department head introduces the "guest" as a University Mental Health Professional. The guest says to the class, "I'm sorry to have to tell you—your instructor died last night. It appears to have been suicide."

These are just a few of the kinds of death issues facing school personnel at all levels of education. You can add many more examples from your own experience. These also are examples of what I refer to as *teachable moments*. That is to say, students are eager to learn more about death, as well as to discuss and ask questions. They often are more ready to learn than we are to teach. We don't always know the right thing to say or do in death-related situations such as these. We wonder if someone else is more qualified or experienced to deal with such emotionally laden moments. Some deaths trigger anxiety or panic in us as they relate to worries and concerns we have in our personal lives for our own health and security or that of our loved ones.

Most schools do not have a plan of action for what to do in the event of death of a student, faculty member, or administrator. Of those that do, much of the plan has to do with issues of liability and imparting correct information about the death. The topic of support and education to the people involved often is not covered or even encouraged. In a sample of 423 public schools around the country, from pre-kindergarten through 12th grade, a national estimate was gathered as follows: 11% of the schools offer a course or unit on death education; 17% offer a grief support program; 25% have suicide prevention/intervention programs (Wass et al., 1990). At the university/college level a sample of 53 institutions across the country yielded the information that 38% had a written policy for dealing with the death of a student and 30% had training available for counseling survivors (Wrenn, 1991a).

Respondents to the latter survey were all members of the Association for Death Education and Counseling (ADEC), so these percentages from this university level survey are assumed to be larger than would be the case in a truly random sample of institutions of higher education. Death has yet to hit the "top 40" of our educational curriculum. As educators, we need to educate ourselves, then our peers, if we are to be seen as truly educated in this area of human and social affairs (Wrenn, 1992).

Death education, as is also true of sex education, is a topic about which our students should be informed and comfortable dealing with. Because many of us were protected from these topics as children, we have a tendency to pass along this attitude to our students. Teachers would do well to become better informed ourselves and to impart this information to our students in classes or during teachable moments. We can capitalize on those teaching moments, as they take place in our schools fairly often. We are not always aware when a death has occurred in the life of a student, faculty member, or administrator. When we are, we can use the moment to educate our young.

The remainder of this essay focuses on (a) basic developmental issues in children at different ages when dealing with a death in their lives, (b) factors that influence the process of grieving, (c) some interventions and resources that can be used to facilitate grieving and to educate our various constituencies about death, and (d) organizational issues.

Developmental Issues

Much current thinking is based on the belief that all higher forms of life within the animal kingdom grieve for their dead (Bowlby, 1977, 1980). Basic attachments, such as children to their parents, come from a need for *security* and *safety*. When these attachments are threatened or are taken from us at any age, we scramble to re-create a basis for security and safety and to establish meaning for what has happened.

From a developmental point of view, children up to approximately 5 years of age do not see death as final, irreversible, universal, or pertaining to them personally (Wass, 1991). Some exceptions can be observed in dying children. Nonetheless, most young children see everything as living (animistic), even the dead. They magically attribute power that brings the dead back to life or that relates death to taking place because someone (or God) wanted it to happen. We should not tell young children that people who are dead are "asleep" or are "on a trip," as the child's fantasy life will keep that person alive or make it difficult to sleep without worry.

Fox (1988) suggested that children have four tasks to deal with when they experience a death: They should be:

■ provided with *accurate* information about the death and a framework for interpreting the meaning of it all.

■ allowed to express their feelings and questions without censure.

■ given ways to commemorate the life of the deceased.

■ given permission to go on with living and loving.

This is not a bad lesson plan for any age group if you are called upon to develop a death education unit or to deal with a class in which one of its own members has died.

A number of theories and experiments have been advanced with an emphasis on child development as it relates to death (Erickson, 1963; Nagy, 1948; Piaget, 1960). As children progress in their understanding of the world their view of death also changes. Death comes to be seen more and more as pertaining to them ("I could die"), as final, irreversible, and universal. This is basically the mindset of a student of middle school years and beyond.

Factors That Influence the Process of Grieving

From the moment a student learns of a death, the grieving process begins. In the case of a slow, lingering death, the concept of anticipatory grieving (much debated in the literature) may elicit some amount of functional grieving even prior to a death. Doka (1989) referred to "disenfranchised grief," in which grieving is actively discouraged because we do not know how to deal with nonsanctioned relationships (e.g., abortion, death of a gay lover, stillbirth). In our culture, at home and school alike, we sometimes block and discourage the normal grieving process.

The literature presents many stage and task approaches, the most famous being that of Elisabeth Kubler-Ross (1969). Much of what I will discuss here, however, is from the clinical efforts of J. William Worden (1991). His book on *Grief Counseling* is a must for those who are interested in the basics of grief counseling and therapy. Worden (1991) proposed that everyone deals with four basic tasks in their grieving:

Task 1: To accept the reality of the loss. What helps the survivor in working on this task is whether (a) accurate information of the death is available, (b) the body can be viewed, (c) there will be a funeral or memorial service, (d) time is available to focus on the death (e.g., sitting shivah in the Jewish tradition), and (e) others acknowledge the death.

Task 2: To work through to the pain of grief. This is a difficult task for many because in our culture "life must go on," and we have a tendency to ask grieving people, "Are you okay now?" Institutions usually give us 3 days to grieve, and then it's back to work and things are supposed to be normal again. Primitive societies and some religions are much smarter about this, giving people at least a full year to work through the death of a person who was close to us.

We also have certain expectations as to how people should grieve. Anger, sadness, and guilt dominate the emotional menu of grief. These all have negative connotations, so we have to learn when we can display or discuss these feelings appropriately. A supportive environment goes a long way toward helping people work through this task. Peer support groups have been found to be the "therapy of choice" because peers who have experiences similar to the griever's are less threatening and more supportive. Not everyone cries, or needs to. Still, when someone with whom we have been close dies, most people are permanently changed in some ways.

Task 3: To adjust to an environment in which the deceased is missing. When a death takes a student, we have an empty seat in the classroom. This has to be acknowledged, at least tacitly, and, we would hope, openly. Everyone in the classroom must adjust to the change, and resentments and anger can arise when people are not sensitive to this change in the environment. Indications of our hesitation to impose on the grieving include difficulties in being at the site of the death, going to the home of the deceased, talking with those who were close to the deceased, and knowing how to acknowledge birthdays, holidays, anniversaries, and other events where the deceased normally would be. This pattern also points out our desire to detach from a perceived unpleasant situation. At just the times when a death should be acknowledged and mentioned, survivors of a death are ignored. Hospices are aware of this and often offer bereavement calls 3, 6, 9, and 12 months after a death, and even beyond. We should treat the survivor the same as before the death. If what you do or say comes from a base of honest empathy, it's hard to go wrong.

Task 4: To emotionally relocate the deceased and move on with life. One of the problems for people working on this task is the need to replace the kinds of things the deceased provided for us and the accompanying desire not to forget or abandon the deceased in some way. This means providing ways for survivors to remember the deceased while at the same time encouraging them to move on with life. Relocating the deceased means finding a suitable "place" psychologically for the deceased to be in the griever's mind so the deceased will not be forgotten or abandoned and normalcy of life can continue.

Grief can be manifested in four somewhat separate ways: (a) the expression of *feelings* such as sadness, anger, and guilt, (b) *body sensations* such as hollowness in the stomach, lack of energy, and shortness of breath, (c) *thought patterns* such as preoccupation, sense of the presence of the deceased, and dreams, and (d) *behaviors* such as treasuring objects of the deceased, withdrawing from people, and having disturbances in appetite and eating.

According to Worden (1991), seven factors seem to make the difference in how intensely people can be expected to grieve:

1. *Who the person was.* What was the nature of the relationship? Was it a close or a more distant relationship?

2. *The nature of the attachment.* Was the relationship functionally close? Was it a relationship on which the griever's survival or self-esteem depended? Was it an ambivalent relationship, one with a lot of unfinished business between the survivor and the deceased? All of these kinds of attachments increase the intensity of grieving. When a student commits suicide, this is the reason we look for anyone in an idealized or dependent relationship with the deceased who might want to join the deceased.

3. *Mode of death.* Each mode of death (natural, accidental, suicide, homicide) carries with it a different emphasis in the grieving process. Generally speaking, a suicide evokes more guilt, for example, and a homicide more anger.

4. *Historical antecedents.* What is the person's previous history of losses, and how did he or she cope? This is a particularly confusing area for educators who may know little about the personal lives of students in their classes. In opening up discussion, one good idea is to emphasize the importance of respect for people who are willing to relate personally about their own history of losses and *then*, if the class is willing to be respectful, encouraging students to respond to the question, "Have any of you had to go through this sort of thing before?" At the university level, if a student-run service is planned in memory of the deceased, inviting the parents or family members of a student who has died may be beneficial. This helps everyone work through the pain and evokes awareness of who cares and who can be counted on for later support.

5. *Personality variables.* How one will grieve relates to individual traits such as age, sex, shyness versus sociability, and threshold for anger.

6. *Social variables.* Ethnic and religious background determines in some ways what may be expected or unacceptable behavior from the griever, as does membership in certain organizations that have specific protocols.

7. *Concurrent stresses.* Other losses in the current or recent past may make grieving a cumulative matter. Multiple deaths within the family, as well as disasters that affect several people known to the survivor, complicate grieving. When we work clinically with bereaved people, we help them focus on each death separately rather than seeing the grieving process as a lump sum or aggregate.

Those who work with the survivors of a death must allow them time to grieve in their own way, help them interpret what is normal behavior, provide continuing support, and check out their defenses and coping styles so we can offer better personal guidance. Often, people in the community are willing to assist a school in time of need. Some of these resources are described later.

When having to notify someone of a death, we might want to ask ourselves these questions:

1. Do I have as much information as is possible to know?

2. Does one person in the organization serve as the "clearinghouse" for information?

3. Can I notify in person the people who need to hear about the death?

4. Can I get right to the point and not beat around the bush when saying, "I'm sorry to tell you, but we've just heard that Johnny Smith is dead."

5. Can you then wait for a response and not try to fill in the void in an effort to reduce your own anxiety?

6. Are others available who can offer more continued support?

7. Can I handle honestly the questions that will come forth? This means sometimes having to say, "I don't know, but I'll try to find out."

Examples of Interventions

Speaking as one educator to another, advanced degrees in psychology are not required to become a resource for your school or institution. What is needed is a desire to be helpful in situations where others fear to tread. Most organizations have enough of those situations to go around. This is not a place for "do-gooders." What is needed is someone who can see the educational value in offering a death education unit or facilitating a support group. The same wisdom required to become a good teacher, counselor, or administrator is what is needed to offer genuine help in a crisis situation or to plan a prevention program. Where there's a will—and honest empathy for those in need—there's a way.

Toward the end of this chapter, I will discuss some of the organizational issues at stake in deciding if you want to be involved in these situations. For many teachers and counselors, having a student (or a class) motivated to learn is what makes a teachable moment out of the opportunity for relating a death to anything you might want to say or do in class. Death, and how we as individuals, groups, societies, and countries relate to it, can become a unit in many different class content areas.

Schvaneveldt (1982) discussed ways of implementing death education in the high school setting. He suggested that curricular areas of focus for discussing death (a popular subject, especially for high school and university students) include, but are not limited to:

- being youthful in America.
- aging in America.
- cancer.
- suicide.
- how to deal with losses.
- death in literature and art.
- assassination and terrorism.
- childhood memories and how they are altered over time.
- media portrayal of death.
- death-related humor.
- euthanasia.
- dying for a cause you believe in.
- religious views on death.

Since the Schvaneveldt article, we have seen a dramatic rise in interest in the following topics, any of which can easily open up discussion among our students:

- gang violence murder (the highest rates of homicide in our country are found in the 15- to 24-year-old group).
- drive-by shootings.
- multiple suicides (suicide is the third leading cause of death of adolescents in the USA).
- right to life/right to death.
- hospice care.
- AIDS.

Some current topics in the media (films, TV, newspapers) also have a death theme. Field trips to a funeral home or a graveyard always produce questions of interest from students. The teachable moment will appear to you if you are ready to see it.

McLendon (1979) talked about developing materials for her eighth and ninth grade humanities classes, prompted by students' insistence that the topic be covered. Atkinson (1980) provided a wealth of ideas and references for classroom teachers to use in the elementary school setting. Glass (1990) concluded his research on death anxiety in public school children by suggesting that more than half of the students polled said they would go to their parents with questions about death. This being the case, he argued for the school to offer a program to the PTA or to parents interested in knowing more about what their children think. Someone in the community might be willing to facilitate the event. It could be a "Let's Talk" program in which students, school staff, and parents offer a panel presentation. *Death Studies* (1990) devoted an entire issue to suicide prevention in the schools. Other resources to get you started are listed at the end of this essay.

Some activities that have been particularly helpful at the preschool and elementary levels involve musical instruments, art techniques (e.g., clay, finger painting, drawing), body movement, reading stories, telling stories, puppetry, role playing, and guided imagery. Teachable moments in the nonschool environment include going to the airport to say goodbye to grandma or grandpa, the changing seasons of the year, asking questions about drawings that relate to death, and discussions about losing a toy, a pet, or a tooth.

Organizational Issues

In higher education, size and mission of the school determine much of what takes place when a student death occurs (Wrenn, 1991b). At the preschool, elementary, middle school, and high school levels a major variable is the lessening need of parents and school personnel to be protective as the child gets older. In spite of our intellectual understanding that even in death, children need and can benefit from careful exposure to the facts and feelings that come as part of a natural curiosity for learning, politics and policy often stand in our way.

Although many of you may not be working at the college or university level, I would like to relate a little of what we have learned and are doing at the University of Arizona. I believe that some of these ideas are transferable to any school organization, with appropriate modifications for age level, community awareness, experience of staff, and similar factors. I also recommend the excellent book on student death edited by Zinner (1985), especially for those at the college/university level.

We found at the University of Arizona that we were experiencing between 10 to 20 student deaths a year, and with an enrollment of 35,000 students, the national death rate estimate of 4 to 15 deaths per 10,000 student enrollment per year (*Chronicle*, 1989) placed us within the average range of deaths. More specifically, in my survey of colleges and universities in the United States and in Japan (Wrenn, 1991b), I found that the annual rate per 10,000 students was 4.5 deaths for the United States and 4.7 deaths for Japan. You might be interested in finding out if your school or school system has a record on this. Many don't. It will help you later in raising questions about how the school might intervene.

After connecting with the university police, dean of students, and mental health personnel, we developed an *Action Plan* for the campus. It simply lays out what we, as a community, need to do in the event of a death. It designates a point person (myself) to coordinate affairs and a point person (Public Information Officer) to triage information to the campus and the community as it becomes appropriate to do so. It indicates policies for "closing the records" and for Head Residents in campus residence halls. It includes sample letters and forms to family and others and discusses our policy on awarding posthumous degrees at commencement. It also indicates people to whom one can turn in time of need.

We sent copies of the *Action Plan* to all deans, department heads, and directors. We followed up with a one-page poster sheet for each department, with 10 easy-to-understand suggestions for encouraging appropriate and humane behavior at the time of a school death. These ideas can be found in Wrenn (1991a, 1991b), as well as in the boxed information.

What can happen when you make yourself available to assist when a member of the school community dies? A few examples from my experience are:

1. Being called to meet with a class whose instructor died the night before.

2. Being called to address a sorority experiencing the death of a sorority sister.

3. Being called to begin a memorial service in a small but closely knit academic department that just lost one of its favored graduate teaching assistants to death.

4. Being asked to see a student, faculty member, or administrator who was having "a tough time" coping with a death.

5. Teaching a course on Death and Dying in the curriculum.

6. Giving talks in the community.

HUMANE AND HELPFUL PROCEDURES IN THE EVENT OF A CAMPUS DEATH

■ Students, faculty, staff, and officials from the college/university attend the funeral or memorial service.

■ Letters of recognition of appreciation or achievement are given to the dying student or to the family posthumously.

■ One person is assigned to coordinate or handle information given to the press and to investigators.

■ The presence and support of the president, vice-president, dean, department head, and faculty members convey to the family and friends that the student was important and respected.

■ Police have good channels of communication with campus personnel.

■ Professionals are available to work with roommates, friends, and family of the deceased.

■ Some way, place, and time are provided for students and others associated with the deceased to ask questions and express their concern or anger.

■ Follow-up procedures are carried out with students or faculty members who are most affected.

■ Some public recognition of the death is issued, such as letters to those concerned.

■ Those closest to the deceased are encouraged to be involved in services and other events.

7. Writing articles on this topic.

8. Consulting with hospices (for me, this has become a new career).

I would not encourage you to drop what you are doing now and make this a new career. I would encourage you, however, to find people of vision and compassion within your school with whom you can share some of these ideas. Together, you might be able to try some things that will make your school a more humane place to be in times of crisis.

References

Atkinson, T. L. (1980). Teacher intervention with elementary school children in death-related situations. *Death Education, 4,* 149–163.

Bowlby, J. (1977). The making and breaking of affectionate bonds, I and II. *British Journal of Psychiatry, 130,* 201–210; 421–431.

Bowlby, J. (1980). *Attachment and loss: Loss, sadness, and depression* (Vol. 3). New York: Basic Books.

Chronicle of Higher Education, June 28, 1989, p. A24.

Corr, C. A., et al. (1994). *Death and dying: Life and living.* Pacific Grove, CA: Brooks/Cole.

Death Studies, 14(4), 1990.

Doka, K. J. (1989). *Disenfranchised grief.* Lexington, MA: Lexington Books.

Erickson, E. H. (1963). *Childhood and society* (2nd ed.). New York: Norton.

Fox, S. S. (1988). Helping the child deal with death teaches valuable skills. *Psychiatric Times* (August), pp. 10–11.

Glass, J. C., Jr. (1990). Changing death anxiety through death education in the public schools. *Death Studies, 14,* 31–52.

Kubler-Ross, E. (1969). *On death and dying.* New York: Macmillan.

McLendon, G. H. (1979). One teacher's experience with death education for adolescents. *Death Education, 3,* 57–65.

Nagy, M. A. (1948). The child's theories concerning death. *Journal of Genetic Psychology, 73,* 3–27.

Piaget, J. (1960). *The child's conception of the world.* Totowa, NJ: Littlefield, Adams.

Schvaneveldt, J. D. (1982, March). Developing and implementing death education in high schools. *High School Journal, 65*(6), 189–196.

Wass, H., et al. (1990). Death education and grief/suicide intervention in the public schools. *Death Studies, 14,* 253–268.

Wass, H. (1991). Helping children cope with death. In D. Papadatos & C. Papadatos (Eds.), *Children and death.* New York: Hemisphere Publishing.

Worden, J. W. (1991) *Grief counseling and grief therapy.* New York: Springer.

Wrenn, R. L. (1991a). College management of student death: A survey. *Death Studies, 15,* 395–402.

Wrenn, R. L. (1991b). College student death: Postvention issues for educators and counselors. Chapter 4 in D. Papadatos & C. Papadatos (Eds.), *Children and death.* New York: Hemisphere Publishing.

Wrenn, R. L. (1992). Educating the educators. *Thanatos* (Spring), pp. 33–35.

Zinner, E. S. (Ed.). (1985). *Coping with death on campus.* San Francisco: Jossey-Bass.

Intervention Procedures for Traumatic Crises in Schools

Beverley H. Johns
and John P. Keenan

The school community, like any other close-knit community, is seriously affected by the death of any of its members as well as by other major crises, such as an attempted suicide or a serious accident or illness. As stated by Watson, Poda, Miller, Rice, and West (1990), schools must have in place plans for the management of events that cannot be predicted. We believe that such guidelines must be developed not only for humanistic reasons but also to ensure that a rational, tempered atmosphere will prevail when traumatic crises occur.

In this chapter we provide general guidelines for dealing with traumatic crises in schools and specific guidelines to follow in the event of the death of a student or staff member or the potential death of a student.

Developing and Implementing a Basic Crisis Plan

Throughout this chapter, we have stressed the importance of being prepared for situations that may occur. Unpredictable crises are no exception: A crisis plan is a must. We are not suggesting that schools develop 300-page manuals that cover every possible type of disaster—no one would read them—but we do advocate the development of a basic disaster plan. The following is a step-by-step guideline for developing such a plan.

1. School officials should conduct periodic inventories of the potential for a disaster to occur in their school. For example, do any students or staff have serious illnesses? Is there a feeling of unrest among any group(s) of students?

2. Schools should review what other schools have done when crises have occurred. Educators can learn from both the mistakes and successes of other schools.

3. When developing policies and procedures for dealing with crises, school officials should seek assistance from the local police department. (All of the procedures provided in this paper were developed jointly by the police department and the school.) They should also seek input from all other agencies that would be impacted by the procedures.

4. All crisis policies and procedures should specify the following:

a. Who will serve as the school's spokesperson if this type of crisis occurs? According to St. John (1986), a single spokesperson should be designated to speak for the school. If more than one spokesperson is designated, there is the possibility that contradictory statements may be made.

    The spokesperson will also be the individual who talks to the press. As Jay (1989) discussed, responding to the media with "No comment" will encourage the media to get the story from other, far less reliable sources. The school spokesperson should stick to the facts and give the media as much information as has been verified. If a specific timeline exists for investigating the situation, he or she should let the media know that timeline.

b. Who will serve on a crisis intervention team?

c. What communication system will be used to alert students and staff of the crisis?

d. What special equipment will be needed for dealing with the crisis?

e. Who will tell the staff and who will tell the students (individual teachers, social workers, psychologists)?

f. Who will contact the students' parents?

g. Who will provide support and counseling to students and staff?

h. Who will determine whether any changes will need to be made in the school schedule?

i. Who will subsequently evaluate the process?

5. Once policies and procedures have been developed, they must be disseminated and explained to all personnel who would be impacted. Periodic reviews of the policies and procedures must be made.

6. Schools may wish, as St. John (1986) suggested, to index the crisis plan and place the plan and index in a loose-leaf binder. St. John recommended that the school administrator keep an outline of the crisis plan and all relevant phone numbers on a card in his or her wallet so they are always readily available.

7. Following any traumatic crisis, the school should, within a timely framework, assess the potential impact of the event on all parties involved and arrange appropriate follow-through to provide those parties with closure on the event. Jay (1989) noted the following three actions that the school should take after the immediate crisis is over:

a. Those who provided extra assistance, were courageous, and were patient throughout the crisis should be thanked.

b. Efforts should be made to help heal any wounds that remain after the crisis, to help allay any fears that may follow an accident, and to acknowledge the sadness that occurs after a loss.

c. The crisis team should consider what they could do better next time.

We cannot stress enough the importance of having a crisis plan in place. Few people will be level-headed enough to create such a plan "on the spot" when a crisis occurs. We are reminded of a sad event that occurred in the school at which one of us works. A dedicated and committed teacher was stricken with cancer. For five years, she continued to teach her class of students with severe behavioral disorders. When her illness became very serious, she was hospitalized and spent the last two weeks of her life in the hospital. Many of the staff and students had watched her brave effort to fight the illness and admired her courage. All of her students, some of whom had been in her class for three years, were devastated by her death, and the staff members were in a state of shock and sadness. All of the staff were grateful that the school had a plan in place for dealing with such sad events. No one was in any condition to create such a plan "on the spot."

In another incident that affected the staff and students in one of our schools this year, a young student was beaten, almost to death, by an older man on a weekend. On Monday, school personnel had to notify the staff and talk with the students. Many of the children were afraid that the same thing might happen to them. Counseling had to be made available to the students.

When dealing with any crisis, school personnel should always:

1. Stay calm.

2. Tell the truth.

3. Be as precise as possible.

4. Provide facts to the media. (We recommend that school personnel work with the press; remember, they will always have the last word.)

5. Follow the school's policies and procedures.

What to Do in the Event of the Death of a Student or Staff Member

The following outline details a sample action plan that a school may want to use in the event of the death of a student or staff member.

I. Foster Understanding

    A. The school administrator or designee notifies the crisis intervention team.

        1. When? The team should be called together whenever a student or staff member dies. The team should meet immediately, either during the school day or, if the crisis occurs outside of school hours, at 7:00 a.m. the following day, having been contacted at home by the principal. That meeting should be immediately followed by a full staff meeting to update staff, answer concerns, and outline the specific process to be followed.

2. Who/What? The members of the team and their roles follow:

a. School administrator or designee—chairs the team; formalizes or oversees its functioning; ensures that the team carries out its agenda.

b. School administrator or designee—directs staff on actions to be taken, contacts bereaved family for information about assistance needed, and funeral arrangements.

c. School administrator or designee—supervises and coordinates necessary activities that occur in school.

d. Psychologist and social worker—coordinate their roles and responsibilities.

e. School administrator or designee—contacts the press; contacts students' parents (e.g., sending a letter or memo or calling parents).

f. Teacher and alternate, selected by school administrator—serve as liaison with faculty.

g. Floating member, selected by school administrator—provides information to other team members on individual who has died, including his or her friends, enemies, etc.

B. The school administrator or other appropriate staff member contacts the family of the person who has died (this should be done before team meets, if possible) to:

1. Verify information and facts surrounding the crisis.

2. See how the family defines or understands the crisis (e.g., accident, illness, suicide).

3. See what the family's wishes are, if any, with regard to sharing information about funeral arrangements, etc., with students and staff.

4. Briefly outline the general process the school plans to follow.

C. School administrator or designee on crisis intervention team notifies faculty of the death. Also:

1. Identifies faculty who may be the most vulnerable to the crisis and provides support if necessary.

2. Prepares a paragraph to give to faculty members to *read to their classes* providing the true facts and briefly explaining what will happen next.

3. Leads a faculty meeting as soon as possible on the day of the death to explain events and procedures.

a. Two meetings may be needed so that teachers can cover one another's classes.

b. The faculty meeting may be held after school.

D. Students are notified.

1. Individual teachers announce the death to their classes rather than using written notification.
2. Teachers should offer a support system to students so that they may discuss their concerns.

E. School administrator or designee on crisis intervention team notifies parents of all students to explain the facts and any special arrangements to be made.

1. Notice can be hand-carried by each student.
2. Memo can be mailed to parents, though it will not arrive until the next day.
3. Parents of students close to the trauma or students having a hard time with it should be called.
4. If it is deemed necessary for a student to be dismissed from school, parents should be notified. The student should be picked up only by a parent or guardian.

F. School administrator or designee should be prepared to speak to the press, responding to press inquiries with a factual statement based on the immediate family's definition of the crisis and specifying what is being done in the school.

G. The crisis intervention team meets at the end of the day to review what has been done and what still needs to be done.

1. Reviews information dissemination.
   a. Was everyone notified, and how was news received?
   b. Is it necessary to update anyone? Parent letters can be written and mailed; an update memo can be provided to staff, who can read it to students the next day; a faculty meeting can be held after school to review progress.
   c. Were school administrator and all team members updated as described earlier?
   d. What was reported to the press, if anything, and how was the press handled?
2. Reviews adequacy of support services.
3. Reviews likely sequence of activity for those most affected by the crisis.
4. Reviews procedure for moving forward for students and faculty.

II. Assist in the Grieving Process

A. Grieving is appropriate for both students and staff, and everyone should be allowed to show their grief. (Note that it is appropriate to not grieve.)

1. Grief may come out as sadness, but anger must also be recognized as a part of the grieving process.

2. Close friends and enemies are most vulnerable when someone dies and should be seen in separate groups as determined by the crisis intervention team. (Worst enemies are at risk because of guilt and thinking, "I caused it.")

3. Teachers need to be sensitive to their students' need to grieve and should encourage students to participate in the programs noted in "B," below.

B. Grieving can be done in the following ways:

1. Group sessions in the classroom or elsewhere.

a. Groups may be open to anyone who needs and/or requests such sessions.

b. Specific groups may be brought together, such as close friends, enemies, and teachers who worked closely with the person who died.

2. Classroom discussions led by the teacher or a support team member, at the teacher's request.

3. Individual counseling:

a. By the social worker.

b. By the psychologist.

c. By the guidance counselor.

C. The student's belongings and school items, in the event of a student's death must be dealt with.

1. Personal belongings should be returned to the family in an appropriate manner.

2. What to do with school items, such as the student's desk, can be discussed with the class (e.g., remove it, leave it empty, etc.).

III. Explain School Policy for Commemorating the Death

A. Funerals:

1. School will not be closed for a student's funeral. However, the school will:

a. Provide support.

b. Help keep individuals from feeling isolated.

c. Clarify misinformation.

2. School may be closed for a faculty member's funeral.

3. Students who go to the funeral of another student or a staff member should be accompanied by an adult.

4. Experiences may be shared the next day, if needed, in class or with support services.

B. Suicides:

1. The school approach is to commemorate all lives that are cut short.

2. The school's emphasis should *not* be on glorifying the act but on discussing what can be done to prevent such acts in the future; a suicide should be viewed as a teachable moment.

3. The victim should not be eulogized.

4. The school schedule should be maintained as much as possible.

5. If the suicide occurs at school, the police should be called immediately and students should be kept away from the area of the building.

IV. Help Students and Staff to Move Forward

A. Students and faculty need to know that it is appropriate to go on with the business at hand even though they are still grieving and to know that laughter and fun are appropriate.

B. For adolescents, grieving may be a prolonged process, sometimes lasting throughout adolescence.

1. Students having a particularly hard time can be referred for counseling.

2. Students who are struggling at times but are able to function may require some understanding from time to time.

C. The crisis intervention team should meet to evaluate the situation and the effectiveness of the actions taken.

V. Points to Remember

A. Paradoxically, through a crisis such as death can come a closer, more caring, supportive school community.

1. Administrators and faculty can be seen in a more caring, supportive, human role.

2. Community relations can improve as a result of outreach to parents.

B. Numerous teaching points can be made during this period of time, for example:

1. How such a crisis may be prevented.

2. How to deal effectively, on a personal level, with a crisis.

3. How to handle crisis situations.

C. All staff, including teachers, administrators, and support team members should make note of students or staff who may require follow-up services and report their names to the school counselor or a member of the crisis intervention team.

What to do When a Student Makes a Suicide Threat

The July 22, 1996, issue of *Newsweek* featured an article entitled "Suicide's Shadow" (Gleck, 1996), which relayed the story of two young female students from

California who committed suicide just before graduating from ninth grade. Earlier in the school year, another student from the same school committed suicide. The events reminded the community of how dangerous the teenage years have become. The article included recent figures compiled by the Centers for Disease Control that show that teen suicide rates are rising steadily. Between 1980 and 1993, suicide rates rose 120% for 10- to 14-year-olds and 30% for 15- to 19-year-olds.

Some of the increase, as Liotta (1996) contended, is attributable to the fact that more students are depressed today than were in the past. Liotta listed a number of signs that may indicate the presence of depression in teenagers—and should be warning signs for parents and educators. These include lack of interest or pleasure, irritability, behavioral changes, loss of weight, change in eating habits, feelings of guilt, lack of energy, difficulty concentrating, low self-esteem, decline in school-work, sense of helplessness, sadness, sense of hopelessness, change in sleep patterns, restlessness, death-related thoughts, and suicidal thoughts.

With today's high rates of childhood depression, and increasing rates of teen suicide, one of the most common questions asked of us is what to do when a student makes a suicide threat at school. In our work with many students with serious emotional and behavioral problems, we have had to respond to such situations many times. We follow the guidelines set forth for educators by Guetzloe (1989), who made the following points about youth suicide and its prevention.

1. Never take a student's suicide threats or gestures casually. Do something, mobilize. A suicidal person may interpret any disregard of his or her suicidal signals as a covert wish that he or she should carry out the threat.

2. Do not be afraid to bring up the subject of suicide. The discussion will not encourage the student to go through with his or her plans; on the contrary, it will help the student to know that someone cares. By talking honestly with the student, you may save his or her life.

3. Question the student closely and carefully about a possible suicide plan. Ask: "Are you planning to hurt yourself?" "Do you have a gun (or pills)?" "When do you plan to do this?"

4. Do not debate the morality of suicide with the student. Do not preach. The suicidal person is not thinking about morality but about an unbearable emotional stress.

5. Through discussion with the student, identify the major stresses or events that precipitated the suicidal behavior. Do not pretend to understand when you are unsure about the student's feelings.

6. Do not respond to what the student says with such statements as, "You have so much to live for," or "Think of all the things you have that others don't." Such statements may make the student believe that his or her thoughts are ridiculous.

7. Encourage the student to make use of other supports, such as parents, friends, a minister, school personnel, neighbors, and the mental health clinic. Let the student know that you will help him or her make contacts with those supports.

8. If the problem was precipitated by the loss of a romantic relationship, do not make such comments as, "There are lots of fish in the sea," and do not pass judgment. The loss of love may feel like the end of the world to a teenager.

9. Never leave a suicidal student alone. Stay with the student.

10. Remove anything from the immediate environment that the student could use as a weapon, and remind the student's parents to do the same.

11. Mention school and community events that will occur later in the day, week, month, and so forth. Try to get a commitment from the student to attend or participate in those events.

12. Be aware of the student's responses to you. If the responses are accepting and the student's mood improves, continue with your present tactic. If, however, the student says, "Leave me alone!" respond with such statements as "I care about you," "I want to help you," and "I'll be here for you."

13. Be sure that the student has the telephone number of a crisis hotline or a counseling service.

14. Do not promise the student that you will keep his or her suicidal behavior secret. It must be reported to parents and a counseling center.

15. Try to get a commitment from the student to not hurt himself or herself and to call for help if he or she feels any kind of suicidal impulse again. You may want to write a contract with the student to get the student's commitment in writing.

16. Involve others in the school who may be able to provide support to the student. Other school personnel may assist in contacting the parents and the counseling service. Other staff may also be able to provide needed information about what is going on in the student's life.

17. Document all actions taken.

Specific Procedures for Suicide Threat Situations in Schools

We strongly recommend that all schools have in place specific procedures for dealing with suicide threats. Sample procedures that educators can adopt, or adapt, follow.

For all staff:

1. Take any suicide threat seriously.

2. Do not leave the student alone.

3. Remove anything from the immediate environment that could be harmful to the student.

4. Immediately inform the school social worker and administrator.

For the school social worker:

1. Talk to the student privately to assess the seriousness of the threat.

2. During all discussions, be supportive and encouraging; use active listening.

3. Do not hesitate to involve other significant staff members in developing an action plan for the student.

4. Keep the student's teacher(s) and the school administrator informed of what steps are being taken.

5. Call the local mental health center for consultation if needed. However, do not mention the student's name at this point.

6. If the student is under age 18, notify his or her parent or guardian and ask the parent to come in and sign a written release so that the local mental health agency can be contacted.

7. If the student is 18 years old or older and is her or his own guardian, discuss all plans with the student and obtain his or her permission to release information to others (by having the student sign a release of information form), including the student's parents and any other relatives with whom the student is living. If the threat of suicide is perceived to be imminent and the student is uncooperative, however, the student's signature is not needed: The parent should then be contacted immediately.

8. If the student's parent or guardian is willing to take the student to the local crisis evaluation site, offer to help in making the arrangements. Emphasize the need for immediate help if that is perceived to be the situation. Coordinate a plan of action with the local mental health center.

9. If the student's parent or guardian is unavailable and the threat of suicide is perceived to be imminent, seek the help of any significant other adult in the student's life, such as a relative, friend, minister, or doctor, and emphasize the need for immediate help. If any of these people are willing to help, offer to assist in making arrangements for transporting the student to the local crisis evaluation site. Coordinate this with the local mental health center.

10. If the student's parent or guardian or other significant adult is unwilling to help and the need for help is judged to be immediate, call the Children and Family Services hotline to report the neglect and to seek assistance. If necessary, call the local police for assistance in transporting the student to the local crisis evaluation site. Coordinate this with the local mental health center.

11. If the action specified in #9 or #10 is taken, a school staff member should accompany the student to the crisis evaluation site or meet the student there. If the student's parent or guardian does not arrive within a reasonable period of time, the staff member should contact the Children and Family Services hotline to report the neglect and to seek assistance.

12. Document the incident on a suicide threat record form.

School Security

In this section we provide practical tips for dealing with the following school security issues: weapons in the schools, bomb threats, visitors, procedures in place for dealing with crises in these areas, for they may occur in any school. To assist educators, we have included in this paper sample procedures that schools can adopt or adapt.

Weapons in Schools

J. Portner (1995) writes that a 1995 report issued by the U.S. Department of Justice stated that the number of teenagers arrested for weapons offenses—carrying or selling guns, explosives, or some types of knives—had more than doubled since 1985. According to the report, the increase in the number of juveniles arrested for gun possession reflected a larger trend of increased youth involvement in violent crimes.

Reports of student involvement in violent crime are all too common. Schools in cities and small towns, in rural and urban areas, have been affected. The following is just one of many such incidents. The Associated Press reported that on October 12, 1995, a suspended student walked through a back door at Blackville-Hilda High School in Blackville, South Carolina, armed with a revolver. He passed by two classrooms and entered a third, where he fired the gun at a math teacher. He then continued down the hall, where he confronted another math teacher, whom he shot to death.

With the increase in juvenile possession of weapons, schools must be prepared for incidents in which students confront school staff or other students with a weapon. Specific procedures must be in place. The following are our suggestions for what a teacher or other member of the school staff should do if he or she observes a student pointing a gun or other dangerous weapon at someone else in school.

1. Concentrate on staying calm. Instruct everyone not directly involved in the incident to leave the area. Another staff member should press an alarm button or immediately call the police from the nearest phone.

2. Stand a short distance from the student. Rather than directly facing the student, stand at an angle to the student's side. Use a nonconfrontational stance.

3. Focus on the student; avoid looking at the weapon.

4. Using a quiet and calm voice, attempt to negotiate with the student. Ask the student questions such as whether you can move back three steps. The more "yes"es you are able to get, the higher the chance that the student will not use the weapon. Further, the questioning will help you buy time until the police arrive. Again, the longer you can talk calmly to the student, the less likely it is that the student will use the weapon.

5. Do not attempt to disarm the student unless you believe that doing so is the *only* way to prevent the student from using the weapon.

6. When the police arrive, follow their directions.

It is illegal for a student to carry a gun, concealed or in the open, at school. If a teacher or other member of the school staff has reasonable cause to suspect that a student has a gun or other weapon in his or her possession at school, we recommend the following procedures.

1. Follow the school's search procedures. The search should be conducted by a team of school staff in an area that is away from other students but offers access to emergency exits, a phone, or both.

2. Should the staff conducting the search feel that the student is dangerous or threatening and in possible possession of a gun, the designated school officials should notify local police immediately.

3. Should a student suspected of having a concealed weapon refuse the search, the search team should explain to the student that, due to the perceived dangerousness of the situation, the police will be called if the student fails to comply with the staff search.

4. In the event that a weapon is confiscated during a search, school officials should notify the police and the student's parents. School officials should also call the police if a search reveals a questionable item (such as bullets) and request direction on how the school should proceed. Whenever a weapon is found, the law enforcement procedures for the illegal action should be invoked.

5. All searches should be documented by the individuals involved in the search. The student's behavior during the search, the reasonable cause for the search, the staff involvement, parent notification, and search results should be included in the documentation. In the case that a crime was committed, the documentation should be sent to the officer in charge of the case, to the local probation office, and to the assistant state's attorney.

6. In the case that a search reveals a student to be in possession of a knife, it is up to the school to determine whether the police should be involved. It is not a crime for a student to carry a pocketknife in school; a switchblade, however, is considered a weapon and its possession in school is illegal. We believe that it should be against school rules to carry *any* type of knife at school or at school events. We recommend that school staff confiscate any knife that is found and render consequences as specified in school policy.

Procedures for Handling Bomb Threats, Bombs Found, and Bomb Explosions in Schools

In any public institution, including schools, the possibility of a bomb threat always exists. In the author's small city (with a population of 20,000), the local police respond to several bomb threats every year. While it is true that the vast majority of bomb threats are false, they never should be ignored. A sound procedure for handling this type of threat is imperative.

In the Event of a Bomb Threat

In the event of a bomb threat at school, the following steps should be taken:

1. The school principal should immediately notify the local police and all necessary staff.

2. The police and the school principal should evaluate the seriousness of the threat based on the following:
   - Is there a sign of illegal entry into the school?
   - Has there been a report of missing chemicals from the Chemistry lab or elsewhere in the school?
   - Have other recent bomb threats proven to be hoaxes?
   - Is it a day that students may not want to be in school, such as the first day of spring?
   - Was there giggling in the background when the bomb threat call was made?
   - Has there been a recent pattern of student, parent, or staff unrest?
   - Which students have been reported absent on the day of the threat?

3. The police and school principal should conduct a search of the building.

In the Event That a Bomb Is Found

In the event that a bomb is found in the school, the following steps should be taken:

1. The area in which the bomb is found should be sealed off while the police remove the suspected device.

2. The school should be evacuated in stages starting with those rooms nearest the device.

3. School officials should instruct students and staff to reenter the building after being so advised by the police.

In the Event of a Bomb Explosion

In the event of a bomb explosion while staff or staff and students are in the school building, the following steps should be taken:

1. One of the alarm buttons to the police department should be pressed immediately, and the fire alarm should be activated.

2. If the phones in the school are still working, the fire department should be notified. If the phones are not working, the police should be asked to notify the fire department.

3. The building should be immediately evacuated and every effort should be taken to keep students calm. School officials should instruct students and staff to reenter the building only after being so advised by the police and the fire department.

4. School officials should develop a list of casualties.

5. School officials should notify the school attorney.

6. An information center, staffed by school officials, should be set up to handle all inquiries about injured persons and the status of the school.

7. If the decision is made to close the school for the rest of the day or longer, transportation should be arranged by school officials to get the students home.

8. School officials should fully document the incident.

Procedures for Handling School Visitors

Visitor control is perhaps one of the areas of school security that is most often overlooked. The authors have noticed that we are almost never challenged when we visit a school. Many schools simply ignore persons who are walking the hallways and have no procedure in place for visitor control. Schools are public-supported institutions and belong to the community. It is difficult to develop a mindset that the community should not necessarily be allowed free access to all school areas. The safety of children and staff must be balanced against the public expectation of free admittance to community schools. Visitor control is a means to accomplish this task.

The format we have used in the following sample is one that is common to many school handbooks.

Purpose: The school believes in maintaining a safe environment for students and staff at all times. To maintain safety and promote the orderly functioning of the educational environment, the school requires that all visitors adhere to the following procedures:

1. All visitors will use the administrative entrance to the building.
   1.1 Signs will be posted to indicate the appropriate entrance.

2. All visitors will check in with a secretary.
   2.1 Visitors will notify a secretary of their business with the school.
   2.2 Visitors will sign in and sign out on a visitor register.
   2.3 Visitors will wait in the designated visitor waiting area while the secretary notifies the staff of their arrival.

3. Visitors will be given a visitor badge for use on the day of their visit.
   3.1 The visitor is to wear the badge at all times while in the school.
   3.2 A visitor who is seen not wearing his or her badge will be asked to wear the badge or leave the school.

3.3 The visitor will return the badge to the secretary at the end of the visit.

4. Visitors will be escorted or directed to their destination by the secretary or school personnel.

5. All visits to the school, a classroom, or staff should be prearranged with school personnel.

    5.1 Visits during school hours should be for legitimate school business purposes.

    5.2 Classroom visits or observations should be prearranged with the classroom teacher, his or her supervisor, or another designated individual.

    5.3 Visitors who wish to monitor a classroom via an observation room must have permission from the teacher or his or her supervisor.

6. Students will be given an explanation of the school's expectations and procedures concerning visitors.

    6.1 At the beginning of the school year, teachers will explain the visitor procedures to their students.

    6.2 Students will be given directions (as specified herein) about what to do if they see a visitor in the school who is not wearing a visitor badge.

        a. Students will, calmly and quietly, immediately report the presence of the visitor to the nearest staff member.

        b. Students will not confront the visitor.

7. Staff will adhere to the following procedures with regard to school visitors.

    7.1 All staff will review the school's visitor procedures with their supervisors at the beginning of the school year.

    7.2 Staff will be aware of visitors and check to be sure that they are wearing their badges.

    7.3 In the event that a visitor is seen not wearing his or her visitor badge, the following procedures will be followed:

        a. Two to three staff members will, together, approach the visitor and ask him or her to walk with them to the visitor entrance, where they are to obtain a visitor badge and sign in.

        b. Should the visitor resist complying with the school procedures, one staff member should quietly leave the area to notify the school administrator and the police, if he or she feels that police involvement is needed. (That staff member will let the others know his or her intent by using a prearranged hand signal.)

        c. In the event that a visitor who resists complying with school rules is unruly or appears to be potentially dangerous, one staff member should immediately notify the police department for assistance. (Again, the staff member will use a prearranged hand signal to alert the other staff of his or her intent.) When talking to the police, the staff member will clearly state that the safety of the students may be at stake.

        d. The staff members who did not leave to notify the authorities should remain in the proximity of the visitor/intruder. The staff member who made the initial contact with the visitor/intruder should continue to talk to the intruder, if possible, to gain his or her compliance with the school procedures. The staff member who left to notify the authorities will, after doing so, alert all classroom teachers through a coded message over the intercom system to have everyone remain in the classrooms. (The code will be determined by staff at the beginning of the school year.) Teachers and staff in the classrooms will close and lock the classroom doors when this code is given.

e. Whenever a situation of visitor noncompliance arises, the staff members who intervened should, immediately after the incident, file a written summary of the incident with the school principal. A copy of the report should be placed in an appropriate file.

Procedures for Dealing With Hostage Situations in Schools

For the purposes of this discussion, we define a hostage situation as a situation in which one individual or a group of individuals prevents, through the use of verbal threats, intimidation, force, threats with weapons, or other means, another individual or group of individuals in a school from moving freely. In the event that an individual or group of individuals places students or staff in a hostage situation at school, we recommend that the following procedures be followed. The purpose of these procedures, as of all other procedures in this chapter, is to maintain the safety of all students and staff.

1. One entrance to the school will be designated as the official entrance into the building. A secretary will be stationed close to that entrance to check in visitors. All visitors shall check in with the secretary, who will explain the school procedures for visitors. All entrances other than the official entrance shall be locked, so that no one may enter through them during the school day.

2. An emergency alarm system shall be established whereby alarm buttons, directly connected to the local police station, will be strategically placed in the school. The alarms are to be used only in the following situations: a hostage situation, a situation in which an individual is brandishing a weapon with the intent to harm, and other situations that present clear and imminent danger to students, staff, or both, that cannot be managed without outside assistance. The alarm buttons shall be pressed only by school-designated officials.

3. A hand signal, which shall be determined by staff at the beginning of the school year, shall be used to indicate the need for someone to press an emergency alarm button. The signal shall also be used to indicate the need for further action, such as clearing the building.

4. In the event of a hostage situation in which a weapon is involved, all students and staff who are not hostages will be evacuated, to the preestablished location

including everyone in the administrative wing. The evacuation procedure will be the same as that established for fire drills with the exception that notification of the evacuation will be made by word of mouth rather than by audible alarm. The use of an alarm could escalate the hostage situation.

Students and staff who are evacuating will reassemble at a preestablished meeting area some distance from the school building. They will be directed to stay away from any window area or area visible to the hostage taker.

Teachers will be in charge of their students and will be responsible for keeping their classes occupied and calm.

Law enforcement officials will assist in transporting students to the preestablished location.

5. The staff member(s) (administrator or designee) directly dealing with the hostage situation should handle it in the following manner:

   a. Remain calm. (Bear in mind that as long as everyone is alive, your efforts are working.) Make every effort to keep everyone involved in the situation calm.

   b. Refrain from making any deals with the hostage taker. Law enforcement officials should be the only individuals to negotiate with a hostage taker.

   c. In the event that both students and staff are taken hostage, suggest that the hostage taker release the students.

   d. Cooperate with the hostage taker.

   e. Avoid trying to negotiate with the hostage taker other than to suggest the release of students.

   f. Avoid questioning any law enforcement tactics or actions while students or staff are being held hostage.

   g. Make every effort to keep the hostages from questioning law enforcement tactics.

   h. Remain patient. Expect that resolving the hostage situation will take time.

   i. Do not be alarmed if power is disconnected, food is not sent, or deadlines are missed. Such occurrences are not unusual in a hostage situation.

   j. Realize that experts are working hard to effect the hostage release. All of their tactics and actions, even those that may appear to be unrelated to the hostage release, do have that purpose.

   k. Know that law enforcement officials will act immediately if a violent act occurs. Should such an act occur, take cover, get away, and cooperate with any police command.

   l. In the aftermath of a hostage situation, avoid discussing the situation until law enforcement officials have completely finished their investigation.

   m. Be aware that bonding and sympathizing syndromes may occur in a hostage situation.

   n. Remember to respect the confidentiality of students and possible items of evidentiary value if you are interviewed by the media.

6. All staff should receive in-service training at the beginning of each school year on the procedures and precautions set forth herein. During that training, the

warning hand signal discussed previously shall be established. (We have used the following hand signal: The signaler puts one hand behind his or her back or out to the side and discretely extends one finger if the situation is manageable and no assistance is needed. If the situation is questionable and the signaler feels that he or she may need help, two fingers are extended to request assistance. If the signaler considers the situation dangerous, he or she extends three fingers to signal that another staff member should press the alarm button.)

References

Associated press. (1995, October 13). Teacher, student killed in high school shooting. *Jacksonville (Illinois) Journal-Courier,* p. 7.

Gleck, E. (1996, July 22). Suicide's shadow. *Newsweek,* pp. 40–42.

Guetzloe, E. (1989). *Youth suicide: What the educator should know.* Reston, VA: Council for Exceptional Children.

Jay, B. (1989). Managing a crisis in the school—tips for principals. *National Association of Secondary School Principals Bulletin, 73*(513), 14, 16–18.

Liotta, A. (1996). *When students grieve: A guide to bereavement in the schools.* Horsham, PA: LRP Publications.

Portner, J. (1995, November 22). Juvenile weapons offenses double in decade, report says. *Education Week,* p. 3.

St. John, W. (1986, October). How to develop an effective school communications crisis plan. *National Association of Secondary School Principals: Tips for Principals.* An occasional publication of the National Association of Secondary School Principals, 1904 Association Drive, Reston, Virginia 22091, 1–2.

Watson, R., Poda, J., Miller, C., Rice, E., & West, G. (1990). *Containing crisis: A guide to managing school emergencies.* Bloomington, IN: National Educational Service.

Courage for the Discouraged: A Psychoeducational Approach

Larry K. Brendtrow and Steven Van Bockern

The way one defines a problem will determine in substantial measure the strategies that can be used to solve it.

—Nicholas Hobbs

In the three decades since the Council for Children with Behavioral Disorders was formed, research about this population has exploded. Professionals working with these challenging children have encountered a cacophony of competing theories and methodology. Too often, proponents for purist viewpoints have been intolerant of other perspectives, berating alternative approaches as unscientific, dehumanizing, or obsolete. Most practitioners, however, have been skeptical of narrow approaches that offer a panacea. When facing a furious student, a single theory offers a slim shield indeed. Now, as our field matures, we finally are moving away from simplistic "one-size-fits-all" mindsets. The term *psychoeducational* has been used to describe approaches that blend multiple strategies of intervention.

Psychoeducational approaches planfully combine a variety of methods to meet the diverse needs of troubled children. These eclectic models can create a synergy wherein the whole is greater than the parts, but only if the diverse theoretical components are synthesized carefully (Macmillan & Kavale, 1986). We will review existing psychoeducational approaches and present a new model grounded in practice wisdom and modern developmental theory. At the onset, we must make a distinction between psychoeducation and unstructured eclecticism.

Pitfalls of Green Thumb Eclecticism

In an early study of services for emotionally handicapped children Morse, Cutler, and Fink (1964) found that in many settings no organized philosophy of treatment could be detected. Instead, staffs followed intuitive approaches that observers classified as naturalistic, primitive, or chaotic. Most seemed to use a "green thumb" eclecticism, trying out various procedures without apparent consistency or depth. Their style was neither organized nor proactive but, rather, consisted of spur-of-the-moment responses to individual academic or behavioral problems.

Without a guiding theory to influence selection of interventions, "try anything" eclecticism is like choosing a potluck meal while blindfolded. Among the pitfalls of green thumb eclecticism are:

1. *The flaws of folk psychology.* "Doing what comes naturally" with troubled and troublesome youth often entails attacking or avoiding them. These fight/flight responses are highly counterproductive. Harsh punishment easily escalates into hostility, and kindness often is exploited. If a whipping or a dose of love were all that were required, these kids would have been cured long ago.

2. *Contradictions in methodology.* If techniques drawn from different models are mixed together in potluck fashion, confusion sets in about what to do when theories suggest prescriptions that run counter to one another (Quay & Werry, 1988). For example, is planfully ignoring angry behavior better, or should one see this anger as a cry for help and communicate with the child?

3. *Incompatibility with teamwork.* When various team members invent idiosyncratic models of treatment, conflict and chaos reign. Russian youth work pioneer Makarenko (1956) observed that five weak educators inspired by the same principles is a better configuration than 10 good educators all working according to their own opinion.

4. *Inconsistency with children.* In programs in which adults are confused or inconsistent, anxious students become more agitated and antisocial students more manipulative. The most volatile possible combination is a dysfunctional staff team confronting a cunning and cohesive negative peer group.

Fortunately, we are not confined to naive "green thumb" eclecticism, as a number of thoughtful approaches merge multiple methods. Before presenting our own model, we briefly highlight four major approaches to the reeducation of troubled children.

Perspectives on Psychoeducation

In his book, *Caring for Troubled Children,* Whittaker (1980) identified four principal approaches that have shaped practice in North American programs of reeducation. These all represent different ways of defining emotional and behavioral problems, and they lead to different intervention strategies. Listed in historical sequence, the four models are:

1. *Psychodynamic:* Children are viewed as "disturbed" because of underlying emotional problems and unmet needs.

2. *Behavioral:* Children are viewed as "disordered" because of maladaptive patterns of learned behavior.

3. *Sociological:* Children are viewed as "maladjusted" because of association with peers who embrace negative values and behavior.

4. *Ecological:* Various ecosystems in the child's environment are seen as creating conflict and "dis-ease" in children.

Although each model has continued to develop with a separate tradition and literature, these approaches all have become more eclectic over time. Actually, as each model has become more comprehensive, it has been labeled as "psychoeducational" by at least some of its proponents:

1. *Psychodynamic psychoeducation places major emphasis on resolving inner conflicts of troubled children.* This blending of mental health concepts with education is tied to the early work of a number of outstanding European specialists who emigrated to North America around the time of World War II. Exemplary of this tradition is Fritz Redl (1902–1988), who was trained by August Aichorn and Anna Freud in Austria. Redl and Wineman (1957) worked with what they called highly aggressive youth in Detroit, and co-authored the classic book, *The Aggressive Child.* Collaborating with William Morse at the University of Michigan Fresh Air Camp for troubled youth, they trained an entire generation of professionals in this model of psychoeducation.

   Redl saw emotional disturbance as an exaggeration of feelings common to all individuals. What distinguishes the troubled child was the inability to manage those feelings. Redl also was concerned with behavior, but primarily as a way of understanding the "inner life" of children. His comprehensive approach includes some 20 techniques for "managing surface behavior," and a system for de-escalating crisis situations. He also designed the "life space interview," a counseling strategy used by front line staff (e.g., teachers, youth workers) to transform naturally occurring problems into opportunities for correcting distorted thoughts, feelings, and behaviors. Leading psychoeducational theorists include William Morse (1985) and Nicholas Long, who directs the Institute for Psychoeducational Training in Hagerstown, Maryland.

2. *Behavioral psychoeducation uses learning principles to modify the disordered behavior of children.* A prominent spokesperson for this version of psychoeducation is Arnold Goldstein of Syracruse University. His data-based belief is that disordered behavior has complex causes and thus is treated best with comprehensive interventions. He contends that powerful and lasting change requires methods that are both *multilevel* (directed both at the youth

and at the system) and *multimodal* (combining cognitive, affective, and behavioral interventions).

Goldstein (1988) has combined a variety of behavioral skill training methods into *The Prepare Curriculum* for teaching prosocial competence. Another widely used example of this merger of methods is *Aggression Replacement Training,* designed to address the deficits in social skills, anger control, and moral reasoning that characterize aggressive youth (Goldstein & Glick, 1987).

The eclectic behavioral approach known as the Boys Town Teaching Family Model (Coughlin & Shanahan, 1991) also qualifies for our definition of psychoeducational. This approach systematically integrates methods including social skills training, relationship building, nonaversive crisis intervention, and structured verbal interventions called "teaching interactions." The Boys Town model is used widely in both residential and public school settings. This model has been subjected to extensive research, and The Boys Town National Training Center in Boys Town, Nebraska, offers professional certification programs (Tierney, Dowd, & O'Kane, 1993).

3. *Sociological psychoeducation utilizes peer groups as a primary agent of change in values and behavior of troubled youth.* These programs grew from research showing that delinquent behavior develops through association with peers who support antisocial beliefs and behavior. The impact of peers is strong particularly among youth with weak parental attachments and controls. Unlike traditional group therapy, which treats individuals within a group, the aim of *guided group interaction* (GGI) is to win over the entire group to prosocial values and behavior, thereby encouraging change in individuals (Empey & Rabow, 1961).

Harry Vorrath extended the original GGI model into a comprehensive system for reeducation known as PPC, or *positive peer culture* (Vorrath & Brendtro, 1985). Peer group models are used most widely in residential treatment (Brendtro & Wasmund, 1989) and alternative schools and classes for troubled youth (Carducci & Carducci, 1984; Garner, 1982). PPC also has been proposed as an alternative approach to school discipline (Duke & Meckel, 1984). *Positive peer culture* groups identify problems and develop strategies to solve them. The goal is to create a prosocial ethos by making caring fashionable, demanding greatness instead of obedience, and challenging youth to assume responsibility for their lives. Brendtro and Ness (1983) described a "psychoeducational" approach using peer group strategies with other methods, which has been developed at the Starr Commonwealth Schools for troubled youth in Michigan and Ohio. The National Association of Peer Group Agencies provides research and training on this treatment model (Kern & Quigley, 1994).

4. *Ecological psychoeducation has been the most actively eclectic approach, borrowing freely from the more traditional models.* The leading author of this approach was Nicholas Hobbs (1918–1983) who created the Re-ED model at Vanderbilt University. (Re-ED is an acronym for Reeducation for Emotionally Disturbed Children.) The most recent model to develop, Re-ED borrows

generously from each of the foregoing models and is described as both *ecological* and *psychoeducational* (Lewis & Lewis, 1989). Hobbs was influenced strongly by European and French-Canadian psychoeducation, and he blended education, child care, and treatment into the role of "teacher-counselor."

A past president of the American Psychological Association, Hobbs was a powerful advocate for focusing on strength, health, and joy, rather than deviance and pathology. In *The Troubled and Troubling Child,* Hobbs (1982) argued that most emotional disturbance is not a symptom of individual pathology but, rather, a sign of malfunctioning human ecosystems. Re-ED professionals strive to develop competence in restorative relationships, working in close liaison with families and communities (Lewis & Lewis, 1989). The American Re-ED Association, a nationwide network of residential and school-based Re-ED programs, has grown from this ecological tradition. The Re-ED philosophy now is being applied to the challenging problems of urban schools in settings such as the Positive Education Program in Cleveland, Ohio (Cantrell, 1992).

Cross-fertilization has increased among all of these theories, albeit much of it random, as practitioners intuitively tinker with once pure models. Today, we find behaviorists advocating relationship building, psychodynamic programs using reinforcement concepts, and nearly universal recognition of the importance of group and ecological dynamics. In the face of this intermingling of theories, traditional concepts such as "behavioral" and "psychodynamic" no longer convey a clear meaning at the level of practice.

The Search for a Unifying Theme

A rich array of specialized methods now is available for treating troubled children and youth. What has been missing is a conceptual framework to bind together these separate components into a coherent system. As Yochanan Wozner (1985) of Israel observed, a "powerful reclaiming environment" for troubled youth requires a "unifying theme." This is a shared set of beliefs about program goals that gives consistency and cohesiveness to elements of the program. A unifying theme is essential to mold a common consensus among staff and youth about program mission.

We now propose a unifying theme for psychoeducation that grows from "empowerment" philosophy and psychology. This "new" paradigm challenges the deviance and deficit model that is common in many approaches to troubled children. Our model seeks to address the question, "What do all successful approaches have in common?"

In visiting an air show, one might see machines as diverse as biplanes and bombers, but each is able to fly only because it has been designed to the same fundamental principles of flight. Likewise, in spite of variations, all successful models of psychoeducation with troubled children must address the same fundamental needs of children. We have sought to identify these common principles that transcend successful work with children regardless of setting or theoretical model.

In our book *Reclaiming Youth at Risk* (Brendtro, Brokenleg, & Van Bockern, 1990), we proposed a unifying theme for the education and treatment of troubled children. Dr. Brokenleg, a Lakota Sioux psychologist, introduced us to sophisticated Native American child-rearing systems that created courageous, respectful children without the use of harsh punishments. We integrated this Native wisdom with the practice wisdom of great European pioneers in work with troubled youth. A note about each of these traditions will serve as an introduction to our model.

Psychologists Rogoff and Morelli (1989) contended that, to fully understand child development, one must break free of cultural biases and explore other cultural models. Centuries before European and American reformers would challenge Western patriarchal models of obedience, Native American tribes of North America had developed elaborate democratic institutions, governance systems, and models of education. These "primitive" peoples actually were far more advanced than the conquering Europeans in their understanding of child and youth development. When Europeans settled this new land, however, they imposed their obedience training system on Indian children, who were placed forcibly in militaristic boarding schools.

Martin Brokenleg's father was captured by the boarding school staff, who traveled the reservation each fall to harvest the next crop of first-graders. Now, several generations of Indian youth have been parented artificially in this environment, where they were beaten if they spoke their native language. Our research sought to reclaim traditional Native empowerment philosophies for use in developing contemporary approaches to youth at risk.

We also were intrigued to find great similarity between Native concepts of education and ideas expressed by Western educational reformers who challenged traditional European concepts of obedience training. These youth work pioneers worked at a time when democracy was replacing dictatorship in many nations. Attacking traditional authoritarian pedagogy, they included:

- *Maria Montessori*, Italy's first female physician, who created schools for disadvantaged youth and wrote passionately about the need to build inner discipline.

- *Janusz Korczak*, Polish social pedagogue, who proclaimed the child's right to respect and created a national children's newspaper so the voices of children might be heard.

- *John Dewey*, American pioneer of progressive education, who saw schools as miniature democratic communities of students and teachers working to pose and solve problems.

- *Anton Makarenko*, who after the Russian Revolution brought street delinquents into self-governing colonies where youth took turns as leaders of youth councils.

Now the wisdom of these early pioneers is being validated by modern psychological researchers.

The Circle of Courage

Early European anthropologists described Native American children as radiantly happy, courageous, and highly respectful, noting that their elders never subjected them to harsh punishment. The professional literature, however, shows little understanding of how tribal cultures could rear children with prosocial values and positive self-esteem. Long before the term "self-esteem" was coined, European youth work pioneers used a similar concept, which they called "discouragement." The obvious solution to discouragement is to help children develop courage. As we discovered, building courageous children was a central focus of Native American tribal cultures. Our modern "civilization," in contrast, produces millions of children of discouragement. How might we go about rearing courageous and respectful children?

In his definitive work, *The Antecedents of Self-Esteem,* Stanley Coopersmith (1967) concluded that childhood self-esteem is based on significance, competence, power, and virtue. Traditional Native child-care philosophy addresses each of these dimensions:

1. *Significance* is nurtured in an environment in which every child is treated as a "relative" and is surrounded by love and affection. This fosters a sense of *belonging.*

2. *Competence* is enhanced by nurturing each child's success and by celebrating the success of others. This provides all children abundant opportunities for *mastery.*

3. *Power* is fostered by practicing guidance without coercion. Even the youngest children learn to make wise decisions and thus demonstrate responsible *independence.*

4. The highest *virtue* is to be unselfish and courageously give of oneself to others. Children reared in altruistic environments learn to live in a spirit of *generosity.*

Lakota artist George Bluebird portrayed these concepts in a drawing of a medicine wheel called the "circle of courage," featured in Figure 24.1.

At first glance, the foregoing principles hardly seem debatable. They fit with humanistic values, psychology, and our own experience. After all, who would advocate the opposite of these concepts—alienation, failure, helplessness, and egotistic selfishness? Further, convincing youth themselves that these are important values is not difficult. Young people want to belong, succeed, have power over their lives, and be needed in the world. *Once these values are given primacy in our programs, their revolutionary quality becomes apparent.*

Whereas most of our traditional systems have been anchored in adult dominance, the Circle of Courage is a youth empowerment model. Table 24.1 shows how Native empowerment values mirror the foundations of self-esteem identified by Coopersmith (1967) and challenge the values of the dominant culture.

GENEROSITY

Patriarchal values and the developmental needs of children are strikingly disharmonious.

1. Instead of belonging, the hyperindividualism of Western society breeds an "ecology of alienation" (Bronfenbrenner, 1986).

2. In the place of mastery, traditional schools play a competitive zero-sum game in which enthroning "winners" ensures abundant losers.

3. When one's need for power is expressed by dominating others, all who are subjugated are disempowered.

Table 24.1 Empowerment Versus Patriarchal Values

FOUNDATIONS OF SELF-ESTEEM	NATIVE AMERICAN EMPOWERMENT VALUES	WESTERN PATRIARCHAL VALUES
Significance	Belonging	Individualism
Competence	Mastery	Winning
Power	Independence	Dominance
Virtue	Generosity	Affluence

4. A culture that equates worth with wealth provides its young a sanction for selfishness.

Successful programs for at-risk youth embody a unifying theme of values grounded in the holistic needs of children. Wozner (1985) defined the key difference among educational environments as whether they are "reclaiming" or "nonreclaiming." Reclaiming schools are organized to meet the needs both of the young person and of society. Nonreclaiming schools operate to perpetuate the system. The distinction is whether one is teaching students or tending school.

Blueprint for a Nonreclaiming School

These abstractions can be operationalized by examining some attitudes and practices of nonreclaiming schools. Next, with some hyperbole, we offer a compilation of comments we have heard in various schools.

Anti-Belonging

Greet newcomers with "report to the office" warning signs. Orient new students and their probably irresponsible parents by making them sign the discipline policy manual. Emphasize that the automatic response to "serious" behavior is exclusion in its many forms including in-school suspension (ISS), out-of-school suspension (OSS), or after school and Saturday (ASS) detention. If students quit, call them "dropouts" (pejorative). Be very businesslike lest you get entangled in "unprofessional" relationships. If kids don't respond, ship them to segregated "alternative" and special education programs to "get them out of our classrooms."

Teachers should not have to wet-nurse students, so get rid of that values clarification crap we are supposed to handle in homerooms. Put troublemaking special ed students, who can't be expelled, on homebound. [Authors' note: 40% of all students on homebound instruction are those with emotional and behavioral problems.] Make schools as large as possible to build better bands and ball teams. Ring bells every 50 minutes to mix 2,000 kids in narrow hallways. If they become hard to manage, hire more security guards so teachers are free to "teach."

Anti-Mastery

Organize instruction tightly around separate specialized subjects. Switch to a different group of students each period. You won't know them well, but at least one kid can't ruin your whole day. If students say they are having fun in a class, or if a teacher takes field trips, spread word in the lounge that no learning is going on. Make them work by themselves so they don't copy one another, follow a tight schedule, and have the shortest possible breaks between periods. Fill the policy manual with get-tough rules such as, "Students who skip school will be suspended" and "in-school suspension days will be counted as unexcused absences" and "students with 12 unexcused absences will fail the semester."

Emphasize competition with tough grading systems, tracking, and reduced expectations for difficult students. In all "real" classes make all students listen to professor-like lectures that are brain-antagonistic even in the university. Of course we don't mean those "popular" shop, art, and PE classes, because they are activity courses, not real education. If they don't hate it, they won't learn anything. What's all the fuss about outcome-based education? Let's stick to what has worked in the past. Use only the textbook and the "approved" curriculum. Maybe we need some more trophies for the top "winners" in sports and studies.

Anti-Independence

Impose systemwide discipline policies so we know who really runs this place. Give students a token student-government game to play so they won't challenge our control of really important issues. Make examples of troublemakers by announcing detention lists on the intercom. One thing we don't want is violence, so come down hard on bullies and let them know who's boss so they learn not to pick on others. Assume that if students engage in a spirited discussion about some current event, they are dodging real learning. Pace the room to keep on top of the class. Keep students anchored in their desks. Impose rules by fiat, put names on the board, and have surprise locker searches to keep them off-guard.

Use computers to schedule students because they probably just want to choose classes with their friends. Keep students in submissive roles so they learn to "respect" authority. (Years later the only teachers they will remember are the ones who don't take any crap.) Limit student choice of curriculum, because they aren't mature enough to make those decisions. I think it's time for another of those assertive discipline seminars. I felt so good after the last one, being reassured that this was my class and I was in charge.

Anti-Generosity

We have to do something to derail this foolish proposal that all students participate in volunteer service learning activities. This only steals time from real learning. Sure, maybe students need to feel needed, but if they want to be bleeding-heart social workers, let them do this on their own time. We have to do something about this cooperative learning movement. It's just a way of letting smart kids do the work for slow ones. Stop cross-age tutoring, because the older youth may take advantage of the younger ones.

And the notion of peer counselors really turns me off. Can you imagine what they would tell each other? Let them bring their problems to a trained guidance counselor. We shouldn't get into controversial social issues in school or teach values, except for the flag and patriotism. We have enough to do in the cognitive domain, so leave affective issues to parents. Also, put a stop to this multiculturalism in curriculum. Immigrant children should become American just as we had to. Today's kids will not produce unless you give them some reward or payoff, but, hey, that's the American system.

Although these comments may not be typical of most schools, a war undoubtedly is going on between tradition and reform in contemporary education. We believe, however, that conflict is the predictable reaction to the real changes sweeping education, and today's reform will be the mode of the future. The empowerment movement in schools must be seen as part of a broader cultural paradigm shift that is unsettling the established power relationships in Western culture.

Many traditionally powerless groups (e.g., women, people of color, ethnic minorities, and now children) are achieving fuller participation in an increasingly democratic world. A prominent example is the recent U. N. document on the rights of children, which has gained the status of international law. This shift to empowerment is a grassroots democracy movement that will impact all social institutions, including the school.

Mending Broken Circles

Only as we abandon our preoccupation with the control of deviance can we nurture the unmet developmental needs that drive most problem behavior. A growing research base shows that successful psychoeducational programs must nurture belonging, mastery, independence, and generosity in troubled children. Of course, other underlying physical and safety needs exist, but from the perspective of psychosocial development, these are four anchor points.

Belonging, mastery, independence, and generosity define social and mental health. As such, these are universal needs for all children and critical unmet needs for damaged children. Many students come to school already having experienced this "circle of courage" in their lives. Many others, however, come to us discouraged, with long histories of unmet needs.

- Instead of belonging, they are guarded, untrusting, hostile, withdrawn; or they seek attention through compensatory attachments.

- In place of mastery, they have encountered perpetual failure leading to frustration, fear of failure, and a sense of futility.

- Not having learned independence, they feel like helpless pawns, are easily misled, or seek pseudopower by bullying or defiance.

- Without a spirit of generosity, they are inconsiderate of others, self-indulgent, and devoid of real purpose for living.

Recently one of our graduate students surveyed high school students and asked them to "grade their schools" according to the criteria of belonging, mastery, independence, and generosity (Odney & Brendtro, 1992). Some of their comments will be used to introduce the following sections. After hearing their voices, we will identify a range of intervention techniques for mending broken circles of courage.

Fostering Belonging

Some of the teachers think they are too cool to talk to us. If you're walking down the hall, the teachers will put their heads down and look at the floor and keep walking.

—Helen

Pioneer Native American educator and anthropologist Ella Deloria described the central value of belonging in traditional Indian culture in these simple words: "Be related, somehow, to everyone you know." Treating others as kin forged powerful social bonds of community that drew all into the circle of relatives. From the earliest days of life, all children experienced a network of nurturance, wherein every older member in the tribe felt responsible for their well-being.

Theologian Martin Marty of the University of Chicago observed that throughout history the tribe, rather than the nuclear family, ultimately ensured survival of a culture. When parents faltered in their responsibility, the tribe always was there to nourish the new generation. The problem today is that we have lost our tribes. The school is the only institution beyond the family that provides ongoing relationships with all of our young. Schools could become the new tribes to support and nurture children at risk.

Early educational pioneers saw positive human attachments as the *sine qua non* of effective teaching. Johann Pestalozzi declared that love, not teaching, was the essence of education. In his classic book, *Wayward Youth*, Austrian August Aichorn (1935) argued that relationship was the heart of the reeducation process. His ethic was that affection rather than punishment must be dispensed to difficult youth because this is their primary unmet need. As educational literature became more "professional," however, relationship building was ignored temporarily. Now the importance of human attachment is the focus of a revival of interest.

Research shows that the quality of human relationships in schools and youth service programs may be more influential than the specific techniques or interventions employed (Brophy, 1986). Teachers with widely divergent instructional styles can be successful if they develop positive classroom climates. Building successful relationships, however, takes time and effort.

The late eminent psychiatrist Karl Menninger often noted that many of today's youth do not experience a sense of belonging at home. When they come to school and behave in unacceptable ways, they get another unbelonging message: "People who act like that don't belong here." Some youth quit trying to build human bonds and begin to protect themselves with a guarded, suspicious, withdrawn manner.

Others do not give up seeking attention, recognition, and significance. Instead they pursue "artificial belongings" in gangs, cults, or sexual promiscuity.

Hostile or withdrawn youth often are signaling to adults that they have learned by experience to expect rejection, and untrained people almost invariably give them what they are used to receiving. Many ways of reaching out to these unloved and sometimes unlovable children are possible if adults can overcome the fight or flight reactions that come so naturally. Following are strategies for meeting the needs for attachment and belonging, which have developed in various theoretical traditions.

1. *Psychodynamic* programs long have posited that strong, trusting relationships between troubled youth and adults were prerequisites to effective reeducation. Youth work pioneer August Aichorn concluded that love is the primary unmet need of many troubled children. Morse emphasized the importance of "differential acceptance," in which we accept the child but not the behavior. To accurately decode "testing" behaviors also is important. Many troubled children initially provoke well meaning adults to see if they will become hostile.

2. *Behavioral* research by Phillips and colleagues (1973) reported a failure to replicate their *achievement place model* when positive staff-student relationships were missing. Now called the *teaching family model*, relationship building components are central to this approach. The staff is trained to begin all corrective teaching interactions with a positive or empathy statement.

3. *Sociological* models use peer relationships as the foundation for treatment. This method is powerful particularly with youth who initially are inclined to trust peers more than adults. Peer concern rather than peer pressure is the basis for program success. Adults must model caring relationships and monitor confrontations carefully so students don't become targets of counteraggression (Brendtro & Ness, 1982).

4. *Ecological* models developed by Hobbs (1982) presume that the disturbed youth begins with a belief that most adults cannot be trusted. Only the people who can break down this barrier of trust can become predictable sources of support, affection, and learning. In Re-ED programs, "trust … is the glue that holds teaching and learning together, the beginning point of reeducation."

The emphasis on fostering attachments is also prominent in the middle school movement. Typically, schedules are designed so frequent and sustained contact between students and teachers is possible. Maeroff (1990) described one program in which a small team of four to five adults, including teachers, administrators, and counselors, serves 45 students. Each adult meets twice daily with a smaller advisory group of 8–10 students. In another middle school teachers greet their students as the buses arrive. Bells are eliminated, team- teaching is used, four award assemblies are held throughout the year, and F's have been changed to U's (Raebuck, 1990).

The celebration of belonging to a caring community is a central theme of effective schools. O'Gorman, a Catholic high school in Sioux Falls, South Dakota, invites new freshman students to a "unity weekend" retreat over the Labor Day holiday.

Some of the 90 trained senior volunteers welcome the new students, helping them carry sleeping bags and luggage into the school and providing leadership for the weekend activities. Students from outlying communities who have no preexisting peer relationships at this school receive a special invitation to a picnic and water-slide party hosted by a school counselor and the natural peer helper organization. Here, too, a strong advising system anchors each student in a close relationship with a small cadre of peers and a teacher-counselor.

Teachers in American schools traditionally have been attached to grade levels or subjects, not to cohorts of students. In contrast, Norwegian elementary school teachers often progress through the grades, remaining with one group of students for several years. In like manner, Holweide, a comprehensive secondary school in Cologne, West Germany, assigns teachers to teams of six or eight, which follow the same 120 students over the course of 6 years. In this structure the beginning and year-end rituals are eliminated, freeing more time for instruction. These teachers come to know their students in ways that tests never can approach (Shanker, 1990).

Positive attachments between adults and youth are the foundation of effective education. These individual bonds, however, must be part of a synergistic network of relationships that permeate the school culture. These include positive peer relationships among students, cooperative teamwork relationships among school staff, and genuine partnerships with parents. Administrators also must see their roles as co-workers in support of their staff, not as superiors trying to dominate. In the final analysis, only adults who are themselves empowered will be free to build empowering relationships with youth.

Fostering Mastery

> *I was walking down the hall and said "hi" to Mr. Nilson. He looked at me and said, "Oh, you're still here. You haven't dropped out yet, huh?" I know people have this in their head and think of me as being less than them. I would like to put Mr. Nilson in the situation I've had in my life, and I'll bet any amount of money he'd fold his cards.*
>
> —Lincoln

In traditional Native American culture, children were taught to celebrate the achievement of others, and a person who received honor accepted this without arrogance. Someone more skilled than oneself was seen as a model for learning, not as an adversary. The striving was for personal mastery, not to become superior to one's opponent. Recognizing that all must be nourished in competency, success became a possession of the many, not of the privileged few.

Maria Montessori, Italy's first female physician, decried the obedience tradition of schooling in which children sit silently in rows like "beautiful butterflies pinned to their desks." She tried to revolutionize learning with the belief that curiosity and the desire to learn come naturally to children.

The desire to master and achieve is seen in all cultures from childhood onward, a phenomenon that Harvard psychologist Robert White called "competence motivation." People explore, acquire language, construct things, and attempt to cope with their environments. It is a mark of humanness that children and adults alike desire to do things well and, in so doing, gain the joy of achievement.

Tragically, though, something often happens to the child's quest for learning in school, the very place where mastery is supposed to be nourished and expanded. Schooling in the traditional setting often fragments learning into subject areas, substitutes control for the natural desire to learn, co-opts naturally active children for hours in assembly line classes, ignores both individual and cultural differences, and is structured on competitive learning (Overly, 1979).

Children who lack skills in social or academic realms often appear resistant to learning. They withdraw from challenge and risk, avoiding most what they understand least. As Mary MacCracken (1981) said in her book *City Kid*, "When you have failed often and painfully enough, you will do almost anything to avoid having to try again" (p. 152).

Each of the treatment models has sophisticated strategies for breaking patterns of failure and futility. All address the crucial task of teaching social skills. Sometimes this is highly structured, as in direct instruction using formal curricula of social skills. In some models the demonstrated problem itself becomes the curriculum for teaching new ways of coping, as in life space interviews or peer counseling groups. Instead of communicating "I don't want to see any problems," educators and therapists are learning to use naturally occurring incidents as the basis for instruction. A sampling of promising methods for helping children achieve mastery and social competence follows.

1. *Psychodynamic* methods encourage creativity and self-expression in the curriculum to create a sense of mastery. Art, drama, music and poetry, literature— all can help youth connect with their feelings and surmount their problems. If problems cannot be eliminated immediately, they should be recast as learning opportunities. In the life space interview (LSI), real-world problems are grist for learning more adaptive ways of thinking, feeling, and acting. Instead of withdrawing from youth in times of crisis, the staff sees this as a unique window of opportunity for teaching coping skills.

2. *Behavioral* programs, of course, are grounded in learning theory. Among the most useful contributions are systematic social skills instruction to develop social competence and teach adaptive skills. These skills can be as diverse as asking for help and making friends. Students entering a *teaching family* program are taught up front how to accept criticism, using role playing and other realistic methods. Even before their first encounter with an adult, they are being given new coping strategies. Cognitive behavioral techniques are employed to replace irrational thinking or destructive self-talk with more accurate and adaptive thinking.

3. *Sociological* models train youth to assume problem-solving roles. The treatment group provides feedback about hurtful or inconsiderate behavior of members and encourages positive alternatives. For example, easily angered youth are

taught to understand and disengage from the put-down process, thereby inoculating themselves from the negative behavior of others. Of course, positive groups also foster positive attitudes toward school and teachers.

We recall a substitute teacher who most reluctantly accepted her first assignment to a class of delinquent youth in a peer treatment program. She was dumbfounded when the first discipline problem of the day was solved instantly by peers with a chorus of "leave the teacher alone so she can teach!"

4. *Ecological* Re-ED programs assume that competence and intelligence can be taught. Academic success itself is seen as a powerful therapy. By helping youth be good at something, especially schoolwork, one impacts a person's self-worth and motivation. Students also need opportunities for problem solving in interpersonal relationships in which they display "conspicuous ineptitude." This model also uses extensive adventure and outdoor education activities to reach students who don't respond to typical school structures.

Traditional educational approaches were developed centuries before any scientific understanding of the human brain. With increased knowledge of how the human brain functions, we now are able to restructure schooling so it is "brain friendly." Leslie Hart (1983), who has synthesized brain research related to education, suggests that the brain is designed to detect patterns and works best in nonthreatening, active, and social settings.

Writing in 1909 in *The Spirit of Youth and the City Streets*, Jane Addams observed that many of the difficulties of youth are related to the reality that they are highly spirited and adventurous. A distinctive feature of much youthful delinquency is the celebration of prowess. These youth are not motivated by the humdrum routine of most schools. Their search for fun and adventure often leads to excitement and kicks through risk-seeking behavior.

Wilderness education programs build on this spirit of adventure. When struggling against the elements of nature, even the most resistant youth has no need to defy the law of natural consequences (Bacon & Kimball, 1989). The Eckerd Wilderness Educational System operates a network of programs for youth at risk across the eastern United States. While totally abandoning the traditional classroom structure, its staff is able to make formidable academic and social gains with previously nonachieving youth.

Fostering Independence

This is probably the biggest part of school that I don't like. All through school, kids are herded around like sheep and are left with almost nothing to decide upon.

—Travis

Traditional Native culture placed a high value on individual freedom. In contrast to "obedience" models of discipline, Native education was designed to build "respect" by teaching inner discipline. Children were encouraged to make decisions, solve problems, and show personal responsibility. Adults modeled, taught values, and provided feedback and guidance, but children were given abundant opportunities to make choices without coercion.

Horace Mann once declared schooling in a democracy to be "an apprenticeship in responsibility." Early in the century Janusz Korczak of Poland founded a system of student self-governance in his orphanage for Warsaw street children. "Fifty years from now, every school in a democracy will have student self governance," he declared. But America continues to be uniquely out of step with many other nations that have implemented the principles of "democracy in education" for which American John Dewey is famous. We remain tethered to the obedience model, causing anthropologist Ruth Benedict to exclaim that our culture systematically deprives young people of the opportunity for responsibility and then complains about their irresponsibility.

A 6,000-year-old Egyptian stone bears the inscription: "Our earth is degenerate. Children no longer obey their parents." Similar calls are heard today, and those who think we have been too permissive could be expected to object to the notion of giving power to youth. The choice, however, is not between demanding obedience or total permissiveness. As Mary Wood says, adults need to continue to be in control—but of the learning environment rather than of the children. Put another way, we must make demands; however, we need to demand responsibility instead of obedience. Even when we intervene in behavior, the tone can be, "Why must adults handle this problem when you are mature enough to handle it yourselves?"

Youth deprived of power will get it somehow, often in a delinquent underground as they bully the weakest in their midst and sabotage our adult-dominated programs. Fortunately, all treatment models are recognizing the need to listen to the voices of youth, as seen in these strategies for teaching independence and self-control.

1. *Psychodynamic* approaches assume that many aggressive children lack sufficient self-management of emotions and behavior. The goal is to develop "controls from within." Redl and Wineman (1957) offered detailed behavior management strategies for providing external controls temporarily while at the same time using "clinical exploitation of life events" to teach the youth self-responsibility. Wood and Long (1991) outlined counseling methods to help children "master the existential crisis" of gaining responsible independence from adults.

2. *Behavioral* approaches to aggression also teach youth self-management skills for dealing with anger. These include recognizing "triggers" and "cues" for anger arousal, using self-administered "reminders" and "reducers" to lessen anger, and self-evaluation and reinforcement (Goldstein & Glick, 1987). Boys Town uses procedures whereby youth help decide the rules by which they will live in *teaching family* homes. Cognitive behavior theorist Meichenbaum (1993) now emphasizes that individuals construct their own personal realities, and the therapist's task is to help them take charge of reconstructing more positive personal outlooks to manage life stress.

3. *Sociological* models of group treatment reject the "patient" role and empower students to become agents of their own healing. Individuals are held accountable

for behavior, and excuses are turned back to the individual in a verbal technique called the "reversal of responsibility." For example, if a student rationalizes a fight, saying, "Well, he said things about my mother that were lies!" the group may respond, "Well, that's his problem, so why did you make his garbage yours?" By helping others with similar problems, youth develop a sense of control over their own destiny.

4. *Ecological* programs also use self-governing groups to implement behavioral programming (Lewis & Lewis, 1989). Any member can call together a problem-solving group. These groups often are led by youth. The group helps the member learn new strategies for avoiding the problem, thereby encouraging responsible behavior in all members. Rhodes (1992), a co-founder of the Re-ED model, has developed a life-impact curriculum that empowers children's thinking so they can "reconstruct their own reality."

The German youth work pioneer Otto Zirker once observed that when surrounded by walls, young people make wall climbing a sport. Faced with authoritarian structures, youth willingly enter into the counter-control game. Adults who struggle to manage behavior by power assertion believe they are engineering an orderly environment. The reality is more often a submerged negative subculture marked by chaos and disorganization (Wasmund, 1988).

In their study of effective alternative schools, *Expelled to a Friendlier Place*, Gold and Mann (1984) challenged the common practice of employing highly developed formal codes of conduct to manage behavior. Although these rule books make some adults feel secure, they are likely to be ignored or outmaneuvered if they are not owned by front-line staff and youth. Effective alternative schools are able to adapt flexibly to the needs of youth rather than make every decision "by the book." The emphasis shifts from pursuing rule violators to teaching values that foster inner control. Such is the case at the Thomas Harrington School in Harrisonburg, Virginia, where one rule applies equally to all students and staff: Respect people, respect property (Raebuck, 1990).

Independence for many youth is thwarted by inflexible and uncompromising structures. At the Jefferson County High School in Louisville, Kentucky, success with at-risk youth comes from flexible schedules (school is open from 8 A.M. to 9:30 P.M., 12 months a year), promise of success, treating students with respect, and awarding a regular high school diploma. The director of this alternative school, Buell Snyder, said, "I hire only teachers who agree to treat students with respect at all times, and I discard those who, despite their good intentions, infantilize or ridicule students" (Gross, 1990).

Fostering Generosity

I would have liked to tutor something or been a peer counselor. I could have helped someone and benefited from it myself if I had been given the chance to participate.

—Sondra

A central goal in Native American child rearing is to teach the importance of being generous and unselfish. Children were instructed that human relationships were more important than physical possessions. Describing practices a century ago, Indian writer Charles Eastman tells of his grandmother teaching him to give away what he cherished the most—his puppy—so he would become strong and courageous.

Pioneering German educator Kurt Hahn once observed that all young people desperately need some sense of purpose for their lives. Youth in modern society, however, do not have roles in which they can serve, and thus they suffer from the "misery of unimportance." Hahn advocated volunteer activities that tap the need of every youth to have some "grande passion." During the Hitler years he went to England, where he developed the basis of the Outward Bound movements.

Rousseau, Pestalozzi, Korczak, and many others also wrote of the importance of teaching youth the values of compassion and service to others. A century ago, William James noted that war always has fulfilled young men's need to be valuable to their community. He proposed a "moral equivalent to war" by involving youth in volunteer civic service. Although we seem to have lost sight of these basic truths for a time, there is now a healthy revival of the concept that we must offer opportunities to develop altruism, empathy, and generosity in modern youth (Kohn, 1990).

The following discussion highlights the increasing emphasis being placed on developing prosocial values and behavior as an antidote to hedonistic, antisocial lifestyles that characterize many modern youth.

1. Redl's *psychodynamic* model departs from traditional Freudian views that children experience too much guilt. Today, many youth seem not to have acquired the most basic sense of human concern. They suffer from too little guilt, and they can hurt or exploit others with impunity. Treatment for these children might involve "guilt-squeeze" life space interviews to foster empathy with victims, or "massaging numb values" to foster internalization of caring values.

2. *Behavioral* research suggests that teaching techniques to manage anger is not enough. Youth will choose prosocial alternatives only if they can move beyond egocentric moral reasoning. Thus, cognitive moral education is part of Goldstein's aggression replacement training. Everson (1994), from the Boys Town program, advocates teaching social skills as a way of fostering moral development. The goal is to create moral dilemmas in once self-centered youth. Now empowered with prosocial skills, youth have new options to act in caring ways.

3. *Sociological* group treatment models seek to "make caring fashionable" and to make youth uncomfortable with selfish, hurting behavior and thinking patterns. Positive peer culture programs teach youth to show concern by helping group members and then give them abundant opportunities to generalize helping behavior through service learning. For example, delinquent youth at Starr Commonwealth regularly "adopt" residents of nursing homes as grandparents, and they serve as basketball coaches to younger community children.

4. *Ecological* programs address the children and families who are alienated from community bonds. Re-ED involves students in community service in a variety

of ways including helping the elderly, operating a "roadblock" to solicit funds for a hospital, and distributing food and toys to needy families.

Every level of education has seen a revival of interest in volunteer service learning as an antidote to the narcissism and irresponsibility of modern lifestyles. All over the country in alternative and some traditional settings, examples of service learning can be found. At Chadwick School in Los Angeles, privileged students run a soup kitchen, help the mentally ill put on plays, work with disturbed children, and campaign for environmental protection. At Harlem's Rice High School in New York, students work with the sick and needy. In Connecticut students serve as the professional rescue squad for a semirural area. In all of these programs, young people's abilities to participate and help are valued (Lewis, 1990).

For 6 to 8 weeks in Shoreham-Wading River, students spend a double period, twice a week, in some community service activity. Students, for example, may work with elderly people or those with handicaps (Maeroff, 1990). Students in Petaluma, California, worked hard to clean up the endangered Adobe Creek. They hauled out 20 truckloads of junk, including washing machines, sofas, two beds, and 36 old tires. They planted willow trees. Now the group is trying to raise $200,000 for a fish hatchery. At least 25 ex-students are studying natural resources and wildlife at Humboldt State University in northern California. Three others are majoring in environmental law at other schools (Sims, 1990).

Service learning opens unusual programming possibilities with troubled children and youth who heretofore have seen themselves as "damaged goods." As they reach out to help others, they create their own proof of worthiness (Brendtro & Nicholau, 1985). Diane Hedin (1989) summarized various research studies supporting the positive results of volunteer service. These include increased responsibility, self-esteem, moral development, and commitment to democratic values.

Putting It All Together: The Michigan Study

Our thesis has been that reclaiming programs must address the critical variables of belonging, mastery, independence, and generosity. We close this essay by highlighting a recent study of more than 300 delinquent youth in Michigan correctional facilities (Gold & Osgood, 1992). The programs encompassed two state and two private treatment centers using positive peer culture (PPC) treatment methodology.

The Michigan researchers gathered exhaustive data from records, referral agencies, staff, students, and caregivers. They observed each youth from arrival until 6 months' follow-up after release. The population consisted of boys, generally 15 or 16 years old, who had been arrested from one to 20 times. The typical student was remarkably unsuccessful in school, with average academic achievement 4.2 grade levels below expectation. A third had not even attended in the period before placement. These youth are representative of those served currently by North American juvenile corrections programs.

The youth lived in 45 separate self-contained treatment/ classroom groups, each with its own interdisciplinary staff team. This enabled researchers to study the impact of these different treatment environments. Thus, though all programs used peer group treatment, they differed on variables such as the amount of autonomy given to youth and the closeness of staff and youth relationships. Variations in the group culture were related to success in the program and in the community after release.

Gold and Osgood reviewed prior research showing that homogeneous settings for aggressive youth typically spawn strongly negative youth countercultures. Instead of cooperating with treatment goals, students resist adult control, develop a code of silence against informing on one another, go underground to circumvent institutional rules, and use physical coercion to maintain a peer subculture committed to delinquent values and behavior. An ongoing debate in the research literature is considering why these negative subcultures form. Two competing explanations have been proposed:

1. Negative youth traits: Delinquent youth "import" into the reeducation setting their dysfunctional character traits. This is a collective example of the "bad apple" notion.

2. Negative institutional milieu: Depriving environments create aggressive countercultures. Harsh, coercive settings strip youth of autonomy and decision making, thus fostering rebellion.

Contrary to what might have been expected, Gold and Osgood found that delinquents in the Michigan settings regularly viewed their environments as safe and supportive. Although full consideration of their exhaustive study is beyond the scope of our current discussion, we highlight their findings related to the principles of belonging, mastery, independence, and generosity.

■ *Belonging:* The more troubled and beset youth are, the more they need close personal attachments to reconstruct their lives. Adults who do not form these bonds distance themselves from delinquent youth and thereby diminish their ability to influence them.

■ *Mastery:* Delinquent behavior often is provoked by scholastic failure. Teachers in successful school programs give students "uncommonly warm emotional support" and prevent them from failing. Youth who become interested in school and make achievement gains have better subsequent community adjustment.

■ *Independence:* Involving delinquent youth in decision making, even in highly secure settings, fosters the turnaround to prosocial behavior. Adult domination and authoritarian control feeds negative peer subcultures, which sabotage treatment goals.

■ *Generosity:* High value is placed on caring in peer-helping programs, and a key measure of progress is showing concern for other group members. Students who adopt prosocial norms have more positive experiences during treatment and gain access to more prosocial reference groups after leaving the program.

The Michigan research also shows that the "treatment versus custody" debate is bogus, as concern and control are both essential. Successful programs find ways to address developmental needs of youth as well as societal needs to stop destructive behavior. This requires adults who are authoritative but not authoritarian. These data contradict the currently popular boot-camp notion that the harsher the institutional experience, the greater is the deterrent effect. In reality, troubled youth need safe, positive environments where they can form corrective social bonds with caring adults and peers.

References

Addams, J. (1909). *The spirit of youth and the city streets.* New York: Macmillan.

Aichorn, A. (1935). *Wayward youth.* New York: Viking Press.

Bacon, S. B., & Kimball, R. (1989). The wilderness challenge model. In R. Lyman, S. Prentice-Dunn, & S. Gabel (Eds.), *Residential and inpatient treatment of children and adolescents.* New York: Plenum Press.

Brendtro, L., Brokenleg, M., & Van Bockern, S. (1990). *Reclaiming youth at risk: Our hope for the future.* Bloomington, IN: National Educational Services.

Brendtro, L., & Ness, A. (1982). Perspectives on peer group treatment: The use and abuse of guided group interaction/positive peer culture. *Children & Youth Services Review, 4*(4), 307–324.

Brendtro, L., & Ness, A. (1983). *Re-educating troubled youth: Environments for teaching and treatment.* New York: Aldine du Gruyter.

Brendtro, L., & Nicholau, A. (1985). Service learning with behaviorally disordered students. *[Monograph on severe behavior disorders of children and youth].* Council for Children with Behavior Disorders, Arizona State University, Tempe.

Brendtro, L., & Wasmund, W. (1989). The peer culture model. In R. Lyman, S. Prentice-Dunn, & S. Gabel (Eds.), *Residential and inpatient treatment of children and adolescents.* New York: Plenum Press.

Bronfenbrenner, U. (1986). Alienation and the four worlds of childhood. *Phi Delta Kappan, 67,* 430–436.

Brophy, J. (1986). Teacher influences on student achievement. *American Psychologist, 41,* 1069–1077.

Cantrell, M. (1992). Guns, gangs and kids. *Journal of Emotional & Behavioral Problems, 1*(1), Special issue.

Carducci, D., & Carducci, J. (1984). *The caring classroom.* Palo Alto, CA: Bull Publishing.

Coopersmith, S. (1967). *The antecedents of self-esteem.* San Francisco: W. H. Freeman.

Coughlin, D., & Shanahan, D. (1991). *Boys Town family home program training manual (3rd ed.).* Boys Town, NE: Father Flanagan's Boys' Home.

Duke, D., & Meckel, A. (1984). *Teacher's guide to classroom management.* New York: Random House.

Empey, L., & Rabow, J. (1961). The Provo experiment in delinquency rehabilitation. *American Sociological Review, 26,* 683.

Everson, T. (1994). The spiritual development of youth at risk. *Journal of Emotional & Behavioral Problems, 3*(10).

Garner, H. (1982). Positive peer culture programs in schools. In D. Safer (Ed.), *School programs for disruptive adolescents.* Baltimore: University Park Press.

Gold, M., & Mann, D. (1984). *Expelled to a friendlier place: A study of effective alternative education.* Ann Arbor: University of Michigan Press.

Gold, M., & Osgood, D. W. (1992). *Personality and peer influence in juvenile corrections.* Westport, CT: Greenwood Press.

Goldstein, A. (1988). *The prepare curriculum: Teaching pro-social competence.* Champaign, IL: Research Press.

Goldstein, A., & Glick, B. (1987). *Aggression replacement training: A comprehensive intervention for aggressive youth.* Champaign, IL: Research Press.

Gross, B. (1990). Here dropouts drop in—and stay! *Phi Delta Kappan, 71*(8), 625–627.

Hart, L. A. (1983). *Human brain and human learning.* New York: Longman.

Hedin, D. (1989). The power of community service. *Proceedings of Academy of Political Science, 31*(2), 201–213.

Hobbs, N. (1982). *The troubled and troubling child.* San Francisco: Jossey-Bass Publishers.

Kern, D., & Quigley, R. (1994). *Developing youth potential* [video]. National Association of Peer Group Agencies, Woodland Hills, 4321 Allendale Ave., Duluth, MN 55803.

Kohn, A. (1990). *The brighter side of human nature: Altruism and empathy in everyday life.* New York: Basic Books.

Lewis, A. (1990). On valuing young people. *Phi Delta Kappan, 71*(6), 420–421.

Lewis, W., & Lewis, B. (1989). The psycho-educational model: Cumberland House after 25 years. In R. Lyman, S. Prentice-Dunn, & S. Gabel (Eds.), *Residential and inpatient treatment of children and adolescents.* New York: Plenum Press.

MacCracken, M. (1981). *City kid.* New York: Signet Books.

Macmillan, D. L., & Kavale, K. A. (1986). Educational intervention. In H. Quay & J. S. Werry (Eds.), *Psychopathological disorders of childhood.* New York: John Wiley & Sons.

Maeroff, G. (1990). Getting to know a good middle school: Shoreham-Wading River. *Phi Delta Kappan, 71*(7), 505–511.

Makarenko, A. S. (1956). *Werke* [Works], (Vol. 5). Berlin: Volk & Wissen Volkseigener Verlag.

Meichenbaum, D. (1993). Changing conceptions of cognitive behavior modification: Retrospect and prospect. *Journal of Consulting & Clinical Psychology, 62*(2), 202–204.

Morse, W. C. (1985). *The education and treatment of emotionally impaired children and youth.* Syracuse, NY: Syracuse University Press.

Morse, W. C., Cutler, R., & Fink, A. (1964). *Public school classes for emotionally handicapped children.* Washington, DC: Council for Exceptional Children.

Odney, J., & Brendtro, L. (1992). Students grade their schools. *Journal of Emotional & Behavioral Problems, 1*(2), 2–9.

Overly, N. (Ed.). (1979). *Lifetime learning.* Alexandria, VA: Association of Supervision & Curriculum Development.

Phillips, E., et al. (1973). Achievement place: Behavior shaping works for delinquents. *Psychology Today 7*(1), 74–80.

Quay, H., & Werry, J. S. (Eds.). (1988). *Psychopathological disorders of childhood.* New York: John Wiley & Sons.

Raebuck, B. (1990). Transformation of a middle school. *Educational Leadership, 47*(7), 18–21.

Redl, F., & Wineman, D. (1957). *The aggressive child.* New York: Free Press. (combined version of two earlier books, *Children who hate* and *Controls from within*)

Rhodes, W. C. (1992). Empowering young minds. *Journal of Emotional & Behavioral Problems, 1*(2). (special issue on Life-Impact Curriculum)

Rogoff, B., & Morelli, G. (1989). Perspectives on children's development from cultural psychology. *American Psychologist, 44*(2), 343–348.

Shanker, A. (1990). The end of the traditional model of schooling and a proposal for using incentives to restructure our public schools. *Phi Delta Kappan, 71*(5), 345.

Sims, C. (1990). Teens mop up. *Outdoor, 5*(2), 23–24.

Tierney, J., Dowd, T., & O'Kane, S. (1993). Empowering aggressive youth to change. *Journal of Emotional & Behavioral Problems, 2*(1), 41–45.

Vorrath, H., & Brendtro, L. (1985). *Positive peer culture* (2nd ed.). New York: Aldine du Gruyter. (First edition published 1967)

Wasmund, W. (1988). The social climates of peer group and other residential programs. *Child & Youth Care Quarterly, 17,* 146–155.

Whittaker, J. (1980). *Caring for troubled children.* San Francisco: Jossey-Bass Publishers.

Wood, M., & Long, N. (1991). *Life space intervention: Talking with children and youth in crisis.* Austin, TX: PRO-ED.

Wozner, Y. (1985). Institution as community. *Child & Youth Services, 7,* 71–90.

School Violence and Disruption: Rhetoric, Reality, and Reasonable Balance

Peter E. Leone, Matthew J. Mayer,
Kimber Melmgren,
and Sheri M. Meisel

During the past few years the specter of school violence has caused many parents, teachers, and administrators to rethink their basic assumptions about the safety of schools. Tragic and senseless shootings of students by students in public schools in the United States have left us stunned and distraught. Images of school shootings and the demand that schools become safe for all children have shaped responses by politicians, parents, and school administrators (Sheley, 2000).

Recent and widely publicized school shootings raise a number of questions: Are public schools less safe than they were 10 years ago? Twenty years ago? Can teachers teach and children learn in an atmosphere where concerns about safety interfere with instruction and management? In addition to these questions, parents and others want to know who has been involved in these school shootings and whether schools have taken steps to ensure that these incidents don't happen in their schools.

Most parents and members of communities believe that schools should be places where children develop intellectually and socially. The idea that school violence, in whatever form, interferes with the orderly operation and safety of schools is anathema to the public. Beyond concerns about physical injury to children, disruption of the school environment interferes with others' learning and can create a climate of fear in which children avoid school or engage in behaviors to protect themselves (Chandler et al., 1998). There is also the concern that minor problems, if ignored, will escalate into major events.

The most current data on school violence and youth victimization in the United States indicate that violence has been declining since 1993. Data reported by the Federal Bureau of Investigation as part of the Uniform Crime Reports (Rand, 1998), as well as students' self-report of victimization that are part of the National Crime Victimization Surveys (Brener et al., 1999), indicate that violence perpetrated by and against youth continues to fall. In spite of this, many segments of the public believe that school violence is increasing (Brooks, Schiraldi, & Ziedenberg, 2000). Some of this misperception may be associated with the widely publicized school shootings at Columbine High School in Colorado and similar incidents in Kentucky, Oregon, and Michigan in the past few years.

Nevertheless, Uniform Crime Reports and data from other sources indicate that schools are the safest places for children to be. Fewer homicides and violent crimes are committed against children at school than in their homes or on the streets (Kaufman et al., 1998; Kaufman et al, 1999; Snyder & Sickmund, 1999). Students are greater than 100 times more likely to be the victim of a homicide away from school than at school (Kaufman et al., 1998).

Another issue that occasionally surfaces when the discussion turns to school violence is the role played by students with mental health problems or other disabling conditions. Some critics believe that special education rules and regulations have tied school principals' hands with regard to discipline and students with disabilities (Hymowitz, 2000). The reauthorization of IDEA (Individuals with Disabilities Education Act) in 1997, however, gave schools a great deal of latitude in responding to disciplinary problems exhibited by students with disabilities. Principals can unilaterally remove special education students involved in weapons or drug offenses and those at risk of harming themselves or others and place them in interim alternative programs (Bear, 1999).

In this chapter we examine issues related to school violence and disruption. We begin by examining the sociocultural context within which school violence occurs, using a nested ecological schema. The first section presents a review of major changes in the status of children and their families, a discussion of availability and consequences of easy access to firearms, and the increase in prevalence of violence in popular media. We also examine media coverage of recent, widely publicized school shootings and the effect that media coverage has on parents' and students' perceptions of school safety. In the second section of the chapter, we examine prevalence and trends in school violence, with particular attention to the use of firearms on school property. This discussion explores some of the difficulty associated with defining and measuring school violence.

We then discuss the challenge of balancing the right to education with the importance of maintaining safe and orderly schools. In particular, we look at available data on the role of students with disabilities in school suspensions and discuss possible interpretations of these data. Finally, we examine how local schools and school districts have addressed violence and disruption in their buildings and communities. We describe violence-prevention initiatives and present guidelines for parents, teachers, and administrators to assist in ensuring that their schools are safe places that promote academic achievement and healthy behavior among all children and adolescents.

The Contexts of School Violence

School violence is a multifaceted phenomenon. Preventing school violence and responding to violent acts that occur within schools require an understanding of the larger community and society. Human behavior is shaped by social-ecological contexts that include individuals with whom we interact daily as well as broad societal contexts that deliver messages about appropriate behavior and relationships among people (Bronfenbrenner, 1979). A widely accepted model (Tolan & Guerra, 1994) of youth and family violence depicts a nested ecological system (see Figure 25.1) of individual factors, close interpersonal relations (e.g., peers and family), proximal social contexts (e.g., school and neighborhood), and societal macrosystems (e.g., media and laws governing gun use). Schools have created prevention activities and

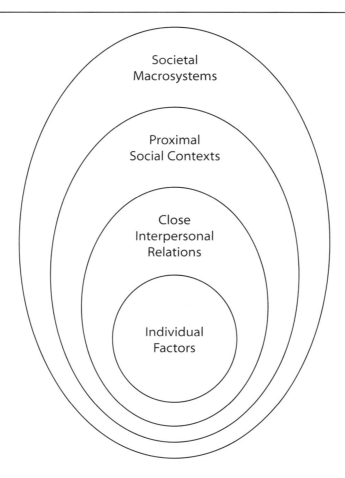

Source: Adapted from "Prevention of Delinquency: Current Status and Issues," (1994), by P. H. Tolan & N. G. Guerra, *Applied & Preventive Psychology, 3,* 254.

Figure 25.1   A Nested Ecological System of Influences on Youth Behavior developed school-wide management plans that have reduced disciplinary referrals and suspensions, addressing risk factors and needs at multiple levels (Taylor-Green et al., 1997; Sugai, Sprague, Horner, & Walker, 2000). These efforts and similar community-based initiatives have the potential to make schools more safe and orderly places for children. In this chapter, we will address aspects of the outer three levels of this nested system that surround the individual, looking at several school, family, and larger societal level factors.

The problem of school violence is linked to changes within our culture and society. Significant changes in family structure and changes in the status of children contribute to the problems that educators see in schools. Violence in the entertainment and news media has increased dramatically in recent years (Lichter, Lichter, & Amundson, 1999) and contributes to a sense that youth are being negatively influenced by the movies they see, the television they watch, the popular music they hear, and the video games they play.

Many youths have easy access to guns (Ward, 1999). At the same time, print and broadcast news media regularly report on a wide range of violent crime committed not just in our own communities but in any hamlet served by an affiliate or a subsidiary of a large media conglomerate (Goldstein, 1994). It is difficult to establish causal relationships between school violence and changes in family structure, violent themes in popular entertainment, the availability of guns, and the reporting of violence by the news media. In each of these areas, however, there have been significant changes in recent years.

Family Structure and Poverty

Changes in family structure and changes in the relative distribution of income within society in recent decades have affected children. In 1950, fewer than 20% of all children in the United States lived in households that were dual-earner nonfarm families and one-parent families. At present, nearly two thirds of all children live in dual-earner nonfarm and one-parent families (Hernandez, 1995). The effect of this drastic change in living arrangements is that fewer adults are at home and available to support students during the non-school hours. Although some of this change may have been offset by an increase in number of parents who work at home, evidence suggests that less time is available for parents to assist and monitor their children. Survey-based estimates suggest that from 4% to 23% of children regularly care for themselves, and several major surveys found that about 12% of children ages 5–12 were in self-care at least once a week (Kerrebrock & Lewit, 1999; U.S. Department of Education, 1999b).

Another major change since 1980 that affects children has been a shift in the distribution of family income. While the mean income of families in the United States has risen, there has been an increasing gap between children in families living at the lowest income levels and those at the highest levels. From 1968 to 1994, income inequality in the United States increased 22.4% (Weinberg, 1996). While the percentage of children living in luxury approaches 20%, an even larger percentage of children live in relative poverty or near-poor frugality (Hernandez, 1995; U. S. Bureau of the Census, 1998; Weinberg, 1996).

More recent data from the U.S. Bureau of the Census, based on the *Gini Index* and quintile shares of aggregate household income (widely used measures of income inequality), show for the most part, from 1993 to 1998, no significant change in income distribution (A. Jones, personal communication, July 17, 2000). Poverty and the availability of parents to supervise their children do not directly create or cause school violence and or disruption. Nevertheless, poverty is one of a number of factors that place youth at risk for school failure, dropout, and delinquent behavior (Walker & Sprague, 1999), and inadequate monitoring and supervision of children is associated with the development of antisocial behavior and delinquency (Patterson, 1982; Farrington, 1995; Hawkins et al, 2000).

Violence in the Entertainment Industry

A study by the Center for Media and Public Affairs documented the frequency with which violent images are featured in popular entertainment (Lichter et al., 1999). They examined made-for-television movies, television series, music videos, and movies, to determine the prevalence with which violent content was featured. They found that across all forms of entertainment, serious violent images or scenes were featured on the average of 14 times per hour of viewing. When just high violence shows were examined, they found an average of 54 violent acts per hour. Although causal effects between viewing violent images and engaging in violent or disruptive behavior in school are difficult to establish, evidence suggests that exposure to television violence does have an effect on violent behavior (American Psychological Association, 1993; Felson, 1996; Reiss & Roth, 1993).

Media Coverage of School Violence

During the past few years, news media have ratcheted up their coverage of violence in communities and across the country. The evening news and the daily paper chronicle violent acts, both local and across the country, involving juveniles and adults. In the wake of the tragic events and the massive media blitz at Columbine High School in April, 1999, a *USA Today* poll found that 68% of Americans surveyed thought that it was likely or very likely that a school shooting could occur in their town. Other polls of parents' perceptions of school safety taken in the past year revealed similar results (Brooks, Schiraldi, & Ziedenberg, 2000).

Consolidation within the media industry has placed control of radio, television, and newspapers in the hands of fewer and fewer companies (Howard, 1995). As corporate giants compete for audience share or circulation, reporting of violence has become a marketing tool to increase market share (Felson, 1996). Local events in one part of the country become national events as affiliate television and radio stations and newspapers carry reports throughout the country. Although juvenile crime rates fell in the 1990s, the public, informed by media coverage of violence, largely believed that juvenile crime was up and that schools were unsafe (Brooks et al., 2000).

Access to Guns

Handguns and other firearms are more widely available in the United States than in any other industrialized nation in the world, reflecting a permissive policy approach. A 1997 National Institute of Justice report estimated that approximately one third of all households in the United States have guns, with two thirds of gun owners possessing more than one gun (Cook & Ludwig, 1997). At the time of a recent survey 20% of gun owners reported having unlocked, loaded guns in their houses (Cook & Ludwig, 1997). In 1997, more than 4,200 children ages 0–19 were killed by firearms in the United States. More than 2,500 of these killings were homicides and another 1,200 were suicides (Ward, 1999).

Proportionately, young black males are more likely than white youths to be the victims of gun violence. Though federal law restricts sales of guns to minors by licensed gun dealers, in some states children as young as 12 can legally possess semi-automatic weapons and other firearms (Ward, 1999). Yet, unmistakably, the horrific killing of students by students in schools in recent years could not have happened without easy access to firearms by children.

Accountability, Achievement, and Zero Tolerance at the School Level

Our public schools also have changed dramatically during the past decade. Among other things, there has been an increased focus on accountability, information technology, and achievement. At the same time, there has been a decrease in tolerance of deviant behavior. Accountability and an emphasis on literacy for the Information Age have created a greater sense of urgency among educators. Teachers, principals, and superintendents are being asked to measure and demonstrate tangible academic gains in their students' performance. In this climate, disruptive students, particularly those who score poorly on tests that measure the performance of the classroom, school, or school district, are at-risk for being excluded from the education community.

Under the mantle of zero tolerance, schools and school boards have instituted policies that suspend students from school for a wide range of rule infractions that range from threats of violence to possession of weapons to use or possession of drugs on school property. Zero tolerance has created situations in which principals have no latitude or discretion in administering disciplinary sanctions. Thus, students have been suspended for sharing Midol tablets, for bringing a plastic knife to spread peanut butter at lunch, for sharing cough drops, for displaying a manicure kit with a 1-inch knife, and for sharing a prescription inhaler with a student experiencing anaphylactic shock (Tebo, 2000; Skiba & Peterson, 1999).

In sum, changes in the family and the status of children, increases in violent images in popular entertainment, changes in media coverage of violent events, increased availability of guns, and increased accountability at school all set the stage for understanding the current state of school violence and disruption. In the next section, we examine authoritative reports concerning school violence and discuss the difficulty of measuring school violence.

Understanding School Violence

Interest in school violence is a relatively recent phenomenon. How we conceptualize and define school violence shapes how schools think about and respond to the problem (Furlong & Morrison, 2000). Depending upon one's definition of the term, acts of school violence can range from threats of physical violence, to bullying, physical assaults, and homicide.

Data on School Violence

Schools are safer than individual homes and neighborhoods. Children are more likely to encounter serious violent crime away from school than at school. Multiple sources suggest that students are approximately three times safer in school than away from school (Elliott, Hamburg, and Williams, 1998; Kaufman et al., 1999; Snyder & Sickmund, 1999). There is less than a one in a million chance of a student experiencing a school-related violent death. Furthermore, the vast majority of school-related injuries are not violence-related and the majority of school crime is non-violent theft (U.S. Department of Education, 1999a).

The picture of school violence that has emerged over the past decade provides reason for concern, yet optimism for the future. The findings are mixed. In 1997, there were 202,000 serious violent crimes (rape, sexual assault, robbery, and aggravated assault) against students ages 12–18 in school and 2.7 million total school crimes (Kaufman et al., 1999). Centers for Disease Control (CDC) data collected in 1999 from the Youth Risk Behavior Surveillance (YRBS) (Kann et al., 2000) found:

- 6.9% carried weapons at school nationally during 30 days prior to the survey, with males (11.0%) reporting much higher rates of weapon-carrying than females (2.8%)

- 7.7% of students nationally reported having been threatened or injured with a weapon on school property during the past 12 months

- 14.2% of students had been in a physical fight at school during the prior 12 months.

Some longer-term data show that certain measures of violence in schools have remained fairly constant over the past 20 years while other measures of violence have shown a clear pattern of decrease during the 1990s. For example, YRBS data (Centers for Disease Control and Prevention, 2000) show a steady, dramatic decline in students reporting having carried a weapon on school property during the 30 days prior to the survey, from 11.8% in 1993 to 6.9% in 1999 (see Figure 25.2).

The same YRBS data show a similarly impressive decline in students reporting having carried a gun during the 30 days prior to the survey, from 7.9% in 1993 to 4.9% in 1999. Also, from 1993 to 1999, the percentage of students who reported having been in a physical fight at school during the 30 days prior to the survey dropped from 16.2% to 14.2%. The *Annual Report on School Safety* (U.S. Department of Education, 1999a) also reports a decline in several measures of school violence during the 1990s.

Several indicators of school violence have remained fairly constant over the past 20 years. For example, from 1976 to 1997, approximately 5% of high school seniors report having been injured with a weapon at school during the previous 12 months,

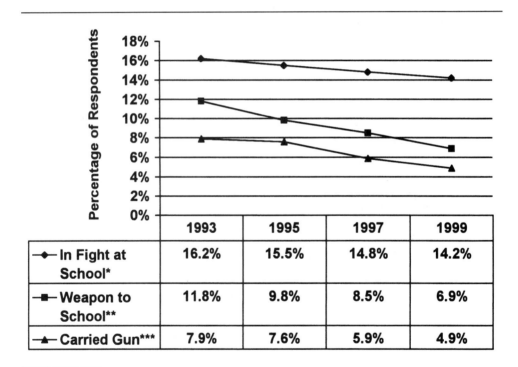

	1993	1995	1997	1999
◆ In Fight at School*	16.2%	15.5%	14.8%	14.2%
■ Weapon to School**	11.8%	9.8%	8.5%	6.9%
▲ Carried Gun***	7.9%	7.6%	5.9%	4.9%

Source: Centers for Disease Control and Prevention. (2000). *Fact Sheet: Youth Risk Behavior Trends*

*Involved in a fight *on school property* at least one time during the 12 months preceding the survey
** Carried a weapon *on school property* at least one time during the 30 days preceding the survey
*** Carried a gun at least one time during the 30 days preceding the survey

Figure 25.2 Self-Report of Risk Related Behaviors: 1993–1999 Trends according to data from the ongoing *Monitoring the Future* study (University of Michigan). During the same period, approximately 12% of seniors report having been injured without a weapon and about 12% report having been threatened with a weapon at school during the previous 12 months (U.S. Department of Education, 1999b; Institute for Social Research, 1997). Other data sources, such as the so-called Principals' and Disciplinarians' Report (U.S. Department of Education, 1998a), show relatively less crime in the schools. That report was based on incidents in which the school called the police. Understandably, administrators may be reluctant to call police or to submit reports suggesting that their school environment is out of control.

This discussion demonstrates that reported measures of school violence differ somewhat depending on the source. A reasonable question to ask is: Why do we see clear signs of decline in some measures, yet relative stability in other measures? Also, how do we decide whether, and to what extent, school violence and disruption is a serious problem? To begin to answer these questions, we need to consider a number of issues surrounding school violence, as well as community-based violence data collection and reporting.

Making Sense of the Numbers

National data on school violence come from several sources. Some sources focus on criminal acts per se, others focus on injury from a health agency perspective, and some privately commissioned surveys (e.g., Metropolitan Life Survey of the American Teacher) focus on various aspects of school violence. The FBI Uniform Crime Reporting (UCR) Program gathers reports from local law enforcement agencies directly or through respective state agencies (Cook & Laub, 1998). As illustrated by Cook and Laub, the UCR data can seriously underestimate true levels of violent crime and provide no information on age of victim or assailant.

Furthermore, some data on juvenile crime are presented in terms of arrests, whereas other data represent convictions. These two categories are quite different, as arrest figures can include innocent individuals (Loeber, Farrington, & Waschbusch, 1998, p. 21). Arrests records do not offer a viable sample of actual crime perpetrators (Cook & Laub, 1998). In addition, law enforcement agencies vary considerably in their reporting of data to the UCR system, thus making year-to-year and other comparisons risky.

A separate source of national level data on violence comes from the National Crime Victimization Survey (NCVS), using household interviews conducted every 6 months (since 1973), and from the School Crime Supplement (SCS) to the NCVS, which is conducted every 4 or 5 years. The NCVS provides information on victimization of youths age 12 and older. Like other forms of self-report, however, this one is subject to errors from a variety of sources, including sampling frame problems, instrument problems, and respondent errors such as inaccurate recall, comprehension problems, omissions, and telescoping effects (Biemer et al., 1991).

Data gathering methods to assess school violence vary considerably, and perceived violence is consistently reported at higher levels than self-reports of violent incidents (Furlong and Morrison, 1994). Methodologically, studies on school violence usually take a [confirmatory] hypothesis verification approach. That is, school violence is assumed to exist and survey questions elicit responses that confirm its existence. A Congressional Research Service report (U.S. Library of Congress, 1994) found problems in data collection efforts regarding school violence in terms of inconsistent definitions and wording of indicators, varying time frames among studies, and underreporting of criminal acts.

Reiss and Roth (1993) offer a detailed analysis of data collection issues pertaining to violence. They cite differences between UCR, NCVS, and National Center for Health Statistics (NCHS) data in terms of: "(a) domain of events, (b) unit of count, (c) timing of counting, and (d) sources of discretion and error in recording and counting events."

Furthermore, events that are measured are social constructs that depend on society's view of crime—something that changes over time. Reiss and Roth also note that crime incidents can be described differently as a function of the location and circumstance, whether they are defined in terms of the perpetrator (arrest) or victim (injury), and whether multiple offenders or offenses are involved. All of these issues can contribute to varying depictions of violent activity in the community as well as in schools.

Agencies responsible for data collection, analysis, and reporting have attempted to ameliorate the situation throughout the 1980s and 1990s. The CDC has supported many efforts to standardize definitions and reporting of injury-related data (CDC, 1997; Mercy, Ikeda, & Powell, 1998). The National Education Statistics Agenda Committee (U.S. Department of Education, 1996) assessed the current status of data collection and reporting among the states regarding criminal and violent behaviors in schools. The committee issued a report describing the existing state of affairs, providing model definitions for data collection and a description of a model data system that states could choose to implement.

Reconciling the differences between CDC data showing a clear decline in school violence and *Monitoring the Future* data that shows stability over two decades is a challenge. The participants, time frames, and wording of questions differ between these surveys. For example, several of the CDC-YRBS survey questions pertain to frequency of weapon-carrying and involvement in a fight. Several of the questions from the *Monitoring the Future* survey pertain to being threatened or injured with a weapon, and having property damaged or stolen.

Although we may choose to think of these questions as proxy variables for school violence and disruption, just because they fall under a common umbrella concept does not necessarily mean that they measure the same behaviors. They each need to be evaluated within the context of the specific survey effort. Unfortunately, no existing procedure allows clear reconciliation of these data differences. The best one can do is to conclude that some serious problems remain with school violence, but that there are several clear signals of an improving situation and that, generally speaking, schools are safe.

Balancing Educational Rights With an Orderly School Environment

Public schools are charged with providing all children with educational opportunities. School administrators and teachers have a vested interest in creating environments in which their students can best learn. Given the diversity and the numbers of children who walk through the public school doors, this is no small feat. School systems and personnel must constantly balance the need for orderliness and efficiency in schools with the rights and entitlements of individual students. Although the needs and desires of school systems often are aligned with the needs and desires of the students they serve, at times the two are at odds.

In the following sections we will discuss some of the entitlements due students in general, and how these entitlements have affected schools' abilities to provide appropriate educational environments. We also will discuss the impact of those additional entitlements afforded students with disabilities, including some of the pitfalls and misperceptions associated with these entitlements.

Educational Entitlements

Compulsory school-attendance laws give children the right, as well as the responsibility, to attend school. Schools must serve all the children in their communities—even children who prefer not to attend. The public schools cannot pick and choose whom they serve, even if picking and choosing would result in more efficiency, higher achievement scores for the school as a whole, or less disruption.

Over time, compulsory school-attendance laws have created problems for schools in jurisdictions where schools and school districts have not adapted to their changing school clientele. Problems have included truancy, disruptive or disrespectful behavior, drug use, threats of violence, and acts of violence. As problems have cropped up, individual schools, school districts, and governmental agencies have crafted ways for schools to deal with those problems. Responses have included (and continue to include) the use of behavioral modification strategies, timeouts, and corporal punishment. For serious violations of the school code, schools have expelled students and placed them into alternative education settings (Yell, 1990; Yell, Cline, and Bradley, 1995; Yell, 1998, ch. 15). Sometimes these responses have been effective in restoring order to the school environment. Other times these responses have gone too far and threatened the rights of the students to whom they are applied.

The U.S. Supreme Court has examined the issue of school discipline on several occasions. In 1977, the Court examined the constitutionality of corporal punishment (*Ingraham v. Wright,* 1977). Although the Court eventually decided that corporal punishment did not constitute "cruel and unusual punishment" and that students were not entitled to a hearing prior to the administration of corporal punishment (under the due process clause of the 14th Amendment), the justices did reiterate that individual teachers or administrators could be held liable or subject to criminal penalties if the corporal punishment administered was later found to be excessive. Even though the *Ingraham v. Wright* decision did not change the legal status of corporal punishment, the very fact that the Supreme Court heard this case influenced state legislatures to pass additional laws governing the use of corporal punishment (Yell, 1990; Yell, 1998, ch. 15). Corporal punishment remains an option for schools in some states, but its use is limited by requirements such as approval by the principal, presence of an adult witness, and prior parental approval. These limitations protect individual students from capricious and overzealous use of corporal punishment by frustrated school personnel.

Another disciplinary action that has been called into question is suspension from school. In 1975, the U.S. Supreme Court heard *Goss v. Lopez,* in which nine high school students alleged that their constitutional right to due process (under the 14th Amendment) had been violated when they were each suspended for up to 10 days without a formal hearing. In this case, the Court sided with the students, declaring that schools must provide evidence of a student's misconduct at a hearing prior to (or immediately following) the suspension. The Court ruled that students' rights to attend school supersede schools' rights to unilaterally exclude students for misconduct. Although school suspensions for disciplinary purposes are allowable, the process must include oral or written notice of the offense and the right to be heard (Yell, 1998, ch. 15).

In *Honig v. Doe* (1988), the Supreme Court set the stage for revised procedures in dealing with aggressive and violent students. This contributed to a change in attitudes among educators, politicians, and the public with regard to the behavior of students with disabilities. Bill Honig, Superintendent of Instruction for California schools, argued that a dangerousness exclusion to the "stay-put provision" of disability law existed, whereby schools could exclude students who threatened the safety of others. The Court denied his argument and made it clear that the stay-put provision held, and that schools could not unilaterally remove students considered dangerous while their change of placement was being appealed.

The Court's ruling also supported the position that a suspension of more than 10 days is a change of placement. The court affirmed that normal procedures, including temporary suspensions of up to 10 days, timeout, study carrels, and detention could be used with dangerous students (Sorenson, 1993; Tucker, Goldstein, and Sorenson, 1993; Yell, 1998).

In the last 5 to 10 years, particularly in the aftermath of the *Honig* decision, a number of state and local education agencies have revised school disciplinary codes to reflect the tenor of recent Safe and Drug-Free Schools legislation (Skiba & Peterson, 1999, 2000). This legislation was aimed at eliminating weapons and controlled substances on school grounds. This type of disciplinary approach—popularly referred to as zero tolerance—has serious flaws in its implementation. Some administrators have overlooked small infractions by otherwise well-behaved students (e.g., an honor student who forgets to remove a miniature Swiss army knife from his keychain), and others have enforced the letter of the law to such an unyielding extent that they attract national media attention (e.g., the second-grader who brought his grandfather's watch to show and tell; a 1-inch mini-pocketknife was attached; the student was suspended and sent to an alternative school for 1 month).

The real problem with a zero-tolerance posture is that serious punishments, such as suspensions from school, have been handed out in an arbitrary and inconsistent manner (Harvard University Civil Rights Project, 2000; Skiba & Peterson, 1999; Tebo, 2000). Students with disabilities who have behavioral problems and who typically have few advocates in the schools, as well as African-American students, are particularly vulnerable to harsh disciplinary tactics (Harvard University Civil Rights Project, 2000; Townsend, 2000).

Entitlements of Students With Disabilities

Although basic educational entitlements apply to all students, those with disabilities are afforded separate, additional protections under the IDEA, most recently amended and reauthorized in 1997. Provisions of IDEA pertaining to discipline are frequently a source of contention. For example, if a student engages in aggressive or disruptive behavior as a consequence of his or her disability, a school is not at liberty to unilaterally suspend that child from school for that very behavior. This is not to say, however, that schools have no recourse whatsoever when a student with a disability misbehaves.

A wide-range of commonly used discipline tactics are still available to use with students with disabilities. These include behavior management strategies, restrictions on privileges, and in-school suspension. Even suspension from school is still an option as long as that suspension does not last 10 days or become part of a pattern of suspensions that accumulate up to 10 days in length.

The stay-put provision of IDEA (IDEA Regulations, 34 C.F.R. § 300.514) is a common concern for teachers and administrators. When a student with a disability engages in serious acts of misconduct that could result in that student's removal from his or her current placement, school administrators and the student's parents often concur on a plan of action. When parents and school administrators disagree and parents request a due-process hearing, the stay-put provision comes into play. Under the stay-put clause, schools are not allowed to remove a student from his or her current placement while the disciplinary action is under review.

The stay-put provision often is misinterpreted to mean that children with disabilities can engage in dangerous conduct without fear of ever being removed to a more restrictive setting. To the contrary, if a student with a disability brings a weapon or controlled substance to school, that student is subject to the same disciplinary actions that apply to a student without a disability. The student then can be referred to an Interim Alternative Education Placement (IAEP).

Regardless of the disciplinary outcome, the school system must provide special education services to any student with a disability who ends up being suspended from school for more than 10 cumulative days in a school year. In addition, if a child with a disability engages in behavior that school administrators believe is likely to result in injury to self or others in the school community, the child with a disability can be removed to an IAEP for up to 45 days (Bear, 1999). The critical element is that the child with a disability not lose access to his or her educational services. The educational services provided to children with disabilities—including services designed to address their behavioral and social-skill deficits—are critical to their eventual success.

Occasionally schools use homebound instruction as an IAEP. These cases seem to violate both the spirit and intent of IDEA discipline provisions. Homebound instruction typically is limited to about 6 hours per week. In such circumstances, it is virtually impossible to provide appropriate academic instruction, and this level of service precludes meaningful implementation of a student's IEP.

Behaviors of Students With Disabilities

How often are students with disabilities involved in school violence and disruption? Apart from anecdotal accounts, it is difficult to find authoritative analyses, as data sources are limited. Several sources from recent years, however, present a partial picture and enable us to draw some tentative conclusions. We will examine two reports on implementation of the Gun-Free Schools Act, an analysis of suspensions and expulsions in Kansas, an analysis from Kentucky schools, a look at recent data from Maryland, and data regarding suspensions in Delaware and Minnesota. We also examine a national-level study of suspensions and expulsions by the Research Triangle Institute, a survey of state and local practices from state directors of special education services, and findings in the 21st Annual Report to Congress on IDEA.

Gun-Free Schools Reports

Subsequent to passage of the Gun-Free Schools Act of 1994, Congress mandated that annual reports be issued concerning implementation of the Act, including data on involvement of students with disabilities. The Act required each state receiving federal funds under the Elementary and Secondary Education Act (ESEA) to have a state law in effect mandating a minimum 1-year expulsion of students who brought a firearm to school, allowing chief administering officers the right to modify expulsion terms on a case-by-case basis.

During the 1996–97 school year, 6,093 students were expelled from school under the Act. Of the 43 states reporting on shortened expulsions, 39 states reported on the disability status of these students. Of the 699 students reported, 37% had disabilities under IDEA (U.S. Department of Education, 1998b). During the 1997–98 school year, 3,930 students were expelled from school under the Act. Of the 49 states reporting on shortened expulsions, 48 states reported on the disability status of these students. Of the 1,459 students reported, 38% had disabilities under IDEA (U.S. Department of Education, 1999c).

Suspensions and Expulsions in Kansas

Cooley (1995) examined suspension/expulsion data in Kansas, using survey data from 441 secondary school principals. This study found that students with disabilities had more than double the likelihood of suspension/expulsion than students without disabilities. Students with learning disabilities and behavior disorders were disproportionately represented among the students with disabilities who were suspended/expelled, compared to their proportions among students with disabilities in Kansas.

According to the researchers, however, students receiving special education services were no more likely than nondisabled students to engage in injury-causing behaviors. Furthermore, the acts committed by the suspended students with disabilities were found to be no different than those committed by nondisabled students. The report concluded that the students with disabilities were not receiving IEP-related services appropriate to their needs.

Analysis of Records in Kentucky

An analysis of records of 465 students in an Eastern Kentucky school district (Fasko, Grubb, and Osborne, 1995) found that about 20% of the suspended students were disabled, although students with disabilities composed about 14% of students included in the study. Approximately 83% of the suspensions were given to male students, and 17% to females. Males and females made up 53% and 47% of the student population, respectively.

Maryland Data

Data from Maryland (Maryland State Department of Education, 2000) showed that statewide, 64,103 students were suspended during the 1998–99 school year. Of those students, 15,669 (24.4%) were students with disabilities. Students with disabilities made up 13.1% of the statewide enrollment that year. Prior Maryland data for the 1997–98 school year (Maryland State Department of Education, 1999) provided an inconclusive picture of suspensions of students with disabilities because duplicated and unduplicated counts were mixed, using both incident- and person-specific data. This made comparisons to statewide percent of students with disabilities impossible, because, depending on relative rates of multiple offenses among disabled and nondisabled populations, different conclusions could be drawn.

Suspensions in Delaware

Along a similar vein, data from a study of suspensions in Delaware (cited in Sinclair and others, 1996) found that 23% of the incidents resulting in out-of-school suspensions during the 1994–95 school year involved special education students. These data were based on *incident* counts, not *person* counts. Therefore, we cannot conclude that 23% of the suspended students were special education students. Interestingly, the 1997–98 Maryland data (also not conclusive for similar reasons) found that 23.5% of short-term suspension incidents were associated with students with disabilities.

Suspensions in Minnesota

A University of Minnesota policy research brief (Sinclair et al., 1996) reported that in Minnesota, the overwhelming percentage of suspensions of students with disabilities involved students with learning disabilities and behavior disorders. The study found that, based on data from several other state studies, about 25% of suspension incidents were associated with students with disabilities.

Research Triangle Institute Report

Fiore and Reynolds (1996) conducted an exhaustive study gathering data on discipline issues in special education. The researchers found that for aggregated data from responding states and districts, approximately 20% of suspended students were students with disabilities, a percentage much larger than their proportion of the student population. Approximately 80% of the misconduct by students with disabilities was considered less serious, with about 20% of the misconduct falling into more serious categories. Also, the vast majority of students with disabilities who were suspended were males. Students with emotional disabilities were overrepresented among students with disabilities who were suspended.

The authors noted the paucity of available data on suspension/expulsion of students with disabilities. Only six states and 16 districts provided data on suspensions that included information on students with disabilities. The report demonstrated a tremendous variability among the states with regard to data systems on suspensions and on students with disabilities. The authors urged caution in interpreting the results, as many jurisdictions either had no such data-recording system or failed to provide the requested data. In turn, the available data cannot be construed as a nationally representative sample for students with disabilities.

21st Annual Report to Congress

The 21st Annual Report to Congress on IDEA (U.S. Department of Education, 2000) addressed school discipline and students with disabilities and reviewed some of the research cited above. Citing a 1994 Office of Civil Rights (OCR) report that found no overrepresentation of students with disabilities among suspended students, the Department of Education report discussed discrepant findings concerning discipline and students with disabilities.

Survey of State Departments of Education

A survey of state departments of special education (Morgan, Loosli, & Striefel, 1997) found improvements in maintaining and disseminating behavior standards compared to a similar survey done 5 years earlier. Of the 41 state respondents, 14 states reported that they had no such standards on behavioral procedures. The researchers found considerable variability among the states with regard to maintaining an information dissemination, monitoring, and training system for behavioral procedures for students with disabilities.

Conclusions Drawn from Studies

Although the data discussed above do not constitute a nationally representative sample of students with disabilities, we can still draw several tentative conclusions from these studies.

1. Mounting evidence suggests that a disproportionately high percentage (possibly close to 20%) of suspended students are students with disabilities, compared to a national proportion of about 11% of students ages 6–21 receiving services under IDEA. One OCR study (cited in the 21st Annual Report to Congress) contradicts this conclusion. Several studies demonstrate that students with learning disabilities and emotional disturbance are overrepresented among suspended students with disabilities.

2. Several studies have found that the majority of suspension-related behaviors seem to be nonviolent and generally do not result in injuries to others.

3. The nature of the suspension-related behaviors of students with disabilities may not be substantively different than the behaviors of the students' nondisabled peers.

4. Some evidence suggests that procedures to guarantee a system of consistent behavioral procedures for students with disabilities vary tremendously among the states and that students in some states may not be receiving appropriate services. Rather, suspension may be the procedure of choice in lieu of more proactive, supportive approaches.

Research by Mayer and Leone (1999), as well as publications by the Justice Policy Institute and the American Policy Forum (Brooks, Schiraldi, & Zeidenberg, 2000; Mendel, 2000) suggest that punitive, controlling approaches do little to solve continuing problems of school violence and disruption or juvenile crime in the community.

More data regarding specific school experiences with violence, individual school practices, and the role of students with disabilities will be gathered with the new School Survey on Crime and Safety (SSOCS), sponsored by the U.S. Department of Education, National Center for Education Statistics (NCES). NCES plans to conduct the SSOCS every 2 years, and the first SSOCS report is due in December 2000.

Gun-Free Schools Act suspension data revealed 37%– 38% representation by students with disabilities among cases shortened to less than one year for states reporting disability-related data. While it is logical that a relatively high percentage of cases meriting chief administering officer review would involve examination of disability-related factors, these data raise several concerns. *First,* the data (U.S. Department of Education, 1998b, 1999c), is a small and possibly unrepresentative subset of the complete dataset, precluding thorough analysis of the situation. The data must be interpreted with caution.

Second, there is reason to believe that often, students with disabilities get caught more often than nondisabled peers, because of problems with social communication, poor judgment, poor planning skills, and attributional biases that can lead to more confrontation with authority figures. These students may be more easily identified by the system for their infractions. That is not to lessen the egregiousness or unacceptability of such behaviors. Rather, it may simply point to a state of affairs in which students with disabilities are represented disproportionately in such cases, in part, because their nondisabled peers are more adept at eluding detection.

Third, the 37%–38% data could be fairly accurate, in which case schools need to develop new understandings and find more effective interventions to reduce weapon-carrying, particularly by students with disabilities. Additional research may shed more light on the exact nature of this phenomenon.

Schools clearly face many challenges in maintaining a safe and orderly environment. The next section presents several approaches to school- and community-based programming.

How Schools Have Responded to Problems of School Violence

Understanding and Shaping School Environments

School-based violence prevention initiatives are considered a best-practice approach to foster positive youth development (Dwyer & Osher, 2000; Mendel, 2000; Walker & Horner, 1996). Federal and state policy makers increasingly are viewing schools as excellent sites for prevention activities, although federal expenditures for these efforts are relatively modest (Gottfredson, 1997). Schools provide consistent access to youth in the early developmental years, and they employ staff members who are focused on ensuring successful academic and behavioral outcomes for students. Another critical advantage is that many risk factors (see Figure 25.3) associated with youth violence are school-related and therefore may be modified within school settings.

Schools should consider three fundamental principles when planning violence prevention initiatives. *First,* evidence strongly supports the effectiveness of *school-wide violence prevention* initiatives based conceptually on a public health model. This model organizes prevention efforts so that schools can systematically address the needs of all students, including those with severe academic, emotional, or behavioral problems.

Second, approaches that emphasize punishment, control, and containment have been demonstrated to be ineffective in preventing or intervening in disruption and violence; punitive orientations may actually exacerbate school disorder (Mayer & Leone, 1999).

INDIVIDUAL RISK FACTORS	PEER RISK FACTORS
• Poor academic skills • Impulsivity • Substance use • Poor social problem-solving skills • Inability to understand the perspective of others • Poor conflict-resolution skills • Difficulties in understanding the moral consequences of actions	• Low social status • Rejection by peers • Gang involvement • Shared deviant peer norms • Association with delinquent peer groups
FAMILY RISK FACTORS	SCHOOL/COMMUNITY RISK FACTORS
• Inconsistent discipline • Reliance on coercion • Harsh or abusive discipline • Poor monitoring of activities • Insecure attachments • Defensive communication • Deviant shared values • A high percentage of negative interactions • Low levels of emotional closeness • Inefficient use of family resources	• Lack of student/parent involvement • Low academic achievement • Lack of social organization and social support • Few opportunities for recreation • Unemployment and economic disparities • High levels of community crime • Availability of firearms

Source: *A Program Planning Guide for Youth Violence Prevention* (1996, p. 15), by N. G. Guerra and K. R. Williams (Boulder, CO: Center for the Study and prevention of Violence). Copyright © 1996 by the Institute of Behavioral Science, Regents of the University of Colorado. Reprinted by permission.

Figure 25.3   Risk Factors for Youth Violence

Third, effective school-wide prevention initiatives are comprehensive, have several components, and involve a broad range of services and supports provided over a sufficient period. Because the antecedents of youth violence are highly correlated (Dryfoos, 1990; Hawkins et al., 2000), prevention programs that address a range of interrelated risk and protective factors have greater potential than single-focus programs.

The public health approach underlying school-wide violence prevention initiatives was defined by the Institute of Medicine (1994) as a three-tiered ecological perspective incorporating a continuum of strategies at graduated levels of intensity. This

FOCUS ON SCHOOLS: CALVERTON MIDDLE SCHOOL

Calverton Middle School in Baltimore serves nearly 1,200 students in grades 6 through 8. The school has had a history of low achievement test scores, high rates of student and teacher absenteeism, and discipline problems. Seventy percent of the students at Calverton are eligible for free or reduced-price lunches. During the 1999–2000 school year, 56 of the 85 teachers at the school held provisional or probationary certification. Seven teachers were on long-term leave.

Performance at Calverton was among the lowest for middle schools in the state of Maryland. Daily attendance by students for the 1998–1999 school year averaged 69%, and during the Fall of 1999, more than 300 students were tardy to school each day. The school was chaotic and experienced frequent interruptions resulting from pulled fire alarms, fights, and classroom disruptions.

Scores on the statewide Maryland School Performance Assessment Program (MSPAP) from 1993–99 indicated that fewer than 6% of eighth grade students scored excellent or satisfactory in reading and fewer than 5% of eighth graders scored excellent or satisfactory in mathematics. On the Maryland State Department of Education's Middle School Performance Index (SPI), Calverton scored from 22.57 to 28.24 each year from 1993 to 1999. The SPI is the weighted average of a school's relative distance from the satisfactory standards, where a score of 100 is considered satisfactory. Several years ago, Calverton was placed on a list of schools eligible for reconstitution or takeover by the Maryland State Department of Education.

In February, 2000, a new principal, Karl Perry, assumed administrative responsibility for Calverton. To begin the process of turning Calverton into an effective and caring school, Perry, with the support of staff, instituted a series of measures designed to refocus the attention of staff and students on academic excellence. Following consultation with other administrative staff, the Five Ps—be Present, Punctual, Prepared, Polite, and Positive—were introduced. Perry's primary objectives in assuming the principalship were to gain control of the school and improve the school climate. Principal Perry also introduced the *Drop Everything And Read* (DEAR) program, a regular part of the school day at Calverton. He met with parents, local business owners, and members of the community to develop shared strategies to combat truancy and tardiness.

As a result of using an appropriately tailored combination of universal and selective level interventions, Calverton Middle School has showed early signs of improvement. For example, student attendance has risen from about 69% to over 76%. Tardy arrivals have dropped from about 300 per day during the Fall to about 150 during the Spring semester. Office referrals dropped from more than 2,600 during the Fall semester of 1999 to under 2,200 during the following semester.

model promotes the use of a comprehensive framework of *universal, selective,* and *indicated* prevention strategies (Tolan, Guerra, & Kendall, 1995).

- Universal strategies are the foundation of school-wide prevention efforts because they apply a primary prevention approach to the entire school population. Consistent use of these strategies provides sufficient support for a majority (80%–90%) of students in each school, thereby avoiding most instances of new problem behavior. Examples of universal prevention strategies include unambiguous behavioral expectations, proactive classroom management strategies, teacher expectations that support positive student outcomes, opportunities for positive attachment to school, consistent use of incentives and consequences, and school-wide literacy programs.

- Selective strategies provide increased support for a smaller number of students (10%–15%) in each school. Secondary prevention strategies such as small-group instruction, social-skills training, behavioral contracting, and mentoring are designed to avoid the escalation of emerging academic and behavioral problems.

- Indicated strategies support a relatively small number of students in each school (1%–5%) who demonstrate significant academic or behavioral problems requiring the most intensive level of support. Prevention strategies for these youth are individualized and often involve long-term involvement of education, mental health, social service, and juvenile justice agencies. Wraparound planning (Burns & Goldman, 1999) and school-based mental health services (Weist & Warner, 1997; Woodruff et al., 1999) are widely regarded as important advances in violence prevention for high-risk youth.

The variety of strategies incorporated in school-based violence prevention plans can be organized as individual or as environmental approaches. Prevention plans may focus on individual risk factors including alienation from school, truancy, poor academic performance, low levels of social competency, and antisocial behavior in the early grades. More broadly, prevention plans may focus on risk factors in the school and community, such as availability of drugs and weapons, negative peer experiences, and inadequate academic or behavioral support. Although examples of prevention strategies at the individual and environmental level are presented separately below, the interdependence of risk factors calls for integrated approaches that incorporate more than a single type of support.

Strategies frequently included in school-wide prevention plans that target individual risk factors include:

1. Instructional programs (identified as the most common prevention strategy used in schools) (Womer, 1997; Larson, 1994). These curriculum-based approaches focus on a range of social competency and academic skills with the goals of preventing or remediating academic failure, heightening awareness and knowledge of social influences on violent behavior, and teaching appropriate responses to these influences.

FOCUS ON SCHOOLS: RICHARD MONTGOMERY HIGH SCHOOL

Richard Montgomery High School (RMHS) in Rockville, Maryland, serves approximately 1,650 students in grades 9–12 in a suburban Washington, DC, school district. The school serves a diverse student body that is 12% African-American, 15% Asian, 16% Latino, and 55% non-Latino Caucasian students. Nearly 9% of students receive services because of limited English proficiency, 7% of the students receive special education services, and 10% of the students receive free and reduced-price meals. The mobility rate at RMHS is 6%. Students at RMHS perform well academically; approximately 500 students in the school are enrolled in the International Baccalaureate program—a rigorous college preparatory program—and 69% of students attend 2- or 4-year colleges after graduation.

In spite of average daily attendance above 90% and a strong academic program, the school has had an unacceptably high number of serious disciplinary incidents in recent years. In the 1997–98 school year, there were 35 serious disciplinary incidents at the school, including racial incidents, major vandalism, fights, and drug incidents. Mark Kelsch, a new principal appointed at the beginning of the 1998–99 school year, set out to reduce serious disciplinary incidents and improve academic performance of the school through greater participation and involvement of students and teachers in all aspects of the school. Kelsch's approach—a form of universal or primary prevention—combines a strong emphasis on relationships between adults and students and among students with rules that count and are fairly enforced.

The changes Kelsch has brought to RMHS include a daily 10-minute televised program produced by students and broadcast throughout the school. The program includes information from the principal, student groups, teaching staff, and others. Other changes include a focus on student achievement and recognition, reorganization of the school schedule so that all teachers in an academic area have common planning time, and consistent enforcement of attendance and tardy policies. These changes appear promising. During the 1999–2000 school year, 12 serious disciplinary incidents occurred—a reduction of nearly two thirds from just 2 years ago. The number of students losing course credit because of unexcused absences and being tardy to class dropped by 50% from the previous year. This past year Richard Montgomery High School received the Blue Ribbon Award for excellence from the U.S. Department of Education. For more information about the school, visit the web site: http://www.mcps.k12.md.us/schools/rmhs/

---

2. Behavior-management techniques designed to change antisocial behaviors and promote positive behavioral skills. These strategies will be most effective when based on systematic screening to identify students at risk for antisocial behavior (Sprague & Walker, 2000).

3. Peer strategies including peer coaching, mediation, and counseling.

4. Counseling and mentoring strategies.

Examples of environmental strategies are a strong academic mission, defining norms for appropriate behavior, promoting student attachment to school, and modifying organizational and structural conditions in the school by decreasing class size and providing a consistent climate of emotional support (Leone, 1997). In this context, prevention strategies should become a normative part of the school routine. For example, programs that teach nonviolent problem-solving strategies have a greater chance for success when the school climate regularly supports and models that approach to conflict (Gottfredson, 1997). School-wide prevention plans should be a high priority for the school and school system, a commitment reflected by strong administrative leadership at the school and district level and the provision of sufficient fiscal resources.

Efficacy of These Approaches

Although prevention science strongly supports the efficacy of school-wide approaches that incorporate multiple interventions and link schools and their environmental contexts, research on the impacts of these approaches is lacking (University of Vermont, 1999). As a result, numerous prevention initiatives have been implemented but reliable data of their effectiveness are not widely available. Despite the limited availability of rigorous evaluation studies in the 1990s, efforts to document the effectiveness of youth violence prevention programs are increasing. Schools using prevention plans report positive outcomes including improved academic performance and staff morale (Dwyer and Osher, 2000), as well as reduced behavior problems, reflected by fewer disciplinary referrals and suspensions (Sugai, Sprague, et al., 2000).

In an exhaustive study of school-based crime prevention efforts, Gottfredson (1997) found positive effects for programs that clarify behavioral norms, offer comprehensive instruction in a range of social-competency skills over a long period, provide behavior modification, and restructure schools to create smaller and more supportive units of instruction. Evidence also points to approaches that are *not* effective, including insight-oriented individual counseling and peer counseling (Gottfredson, 1997; Tolan & Guerra, 1998).

Our discussion of the advantages and strategies associated with school-wide prevention approaches is extended in the next section. We also present examples of research-based, school-wide prevention programs that show promise in reducing school disorder and promoting successful academic and social outcomes.

Promising Approaches

Numerous programs across the United States have shown positive results. Although it is beyond the scope of this chapter to review specific programs, we highlight three promising approaches to provide a perspective of the wider prevention and early intervention landscape. The listing of resources and websites (at the end of the chapter) leads to many other excellent program approaches and models.

Positive Behavioral Interventions and Supports: PBIS

Positive behavioral interventions and supports (PBIS) is a systems approach to creating and sustaining school environments that foster academic and behavioral competence for all students. As compared with traditional school-based approaches that target problem behavior demonstrated by individual students, PBIS focuses broadly on identifying policies and practices of the school itself that support or impede successful outcomes.

In this approach, classroom management and instructional practices are viewed as parallel processes; effective teaching of both academic and social skills involve strategies such as direct instruction, positive reinforcement, modeling, and precorrection (Sugai, Kameenui, et al., 2000). The PBIS framework emphasizes data-based assessment of the school climate and individual student progress through measures such as disciplinary referrals, attendance rates, and suspension rates. Functional behavior assessments are used in response to more intense problem behaviors.

Skill-Building: Violence Prevention Curricula

Violence prevention curricula based on social learning theory are used widely in school settings to improve students' problem-solving and anger-management skills, and to increase their knowledge of nonviolent responses to interpersonal conflict (Kenney & Watson, 1999). Conflict resolution and social skills are taught directly as a distinct curriculum or through integration in other coursework.

Numerous models for violence prevention through problem solving are available. For example, an interpersonal cognitive problem-solving approach with demonstrated effectiveness focuses on primary prevention in the elementary grades (Shure, 1999). In this approach, parents and teachers are trained to instruct children directly in using specific thinking and communication skills designed to prevent conflict in school and at home. *Second Step* is a violence prevention curriculum designed for use in preschool through ninth grade (Frey, et al., 2000). The curriculum emphasizes building protective social and emotional competencies and reducing aggressive and antisocial behaviors.

The Violence Prevention Curriculum for Adolescents (Prothrow-Stith, 1987) is designed to teach alternatives to aggressive behavior and to create supportive classroom environments in urban schools. Evidence suggests that the program is effective in reducing aggressive conflicts among students.

Mental Health and Social Services in Schools: Linkages to Learning

Linkages to Learning is a primary prevention model for the delivery of mental health, health, and social services for at-risk children and their families at 11 elementary and middle schools in Montgomery County, Maryland. The program was established in 1992 as a joint effort among public and private nonprofit agencies to respond to the increased needs of low- income children and their families. Parents are viewed as partners in this effort, taking an active role in developing solutions to individual, family, and community challenges. The overall goal of the program is to address social, emotional, and somatic health problems that undermine children's ability to succeed in school.

Participating children and families receive mental health assessment and counseling; assistance in obtaining shelter, food, housing, and employment; medical/dental care; assistance with immigration, translation, and transportation; and educational support including academic tutoring, mentoring, and adult education classes. Researchers at the University of Maryland completed a comprehensive longitudinal impact evaluation of children in a participating school and a control school (Fox et al., 1999). The evaluation found positive outcomes for children and parents, including improved academic achievement and behavioral functioning at home and school, increased consistency in parenting practices and overall family cohesion.

Developing a Plan to Prevent School Violence

In this section we present an overview of the major steps involved in establishing an effective school-wide violence prevention plan.

1. Assessing school needs.

Even though fundamental principles for organizing effective prevention plans can be identified and consistently applied, schools cannot follow "one size fits all" formulas or blueprints. The first step in developing a violence prevention plan that incorporates promising practices and responds to the local school context is to conduct a needs assessment.

A systematic needs assessment enables the staff to understand the structural, economic, cultural, linguistic, and developmental variations that influence the functioning of specific schools. The unique features of schools that would be addressed in needs assessment include differences in size and physical structure; personal and cultural attributes of students, staff, and the community; prior experiences with prevention strategies; and current perceptions of the level of order and disorder. Using information gathered in needs assessment helps to shape a school-wide prevention plan that incorporates specific performance goals tailored to the strengths and priorities of each school and community (Walker & Horner, 1996).

2. Developing parent and community support.

Because schools operate within environmental contexts, prevention initiatives that incorporate strong parent and community partnerships can mediate positive outcomes for youth. Kellam (2000) underscores the promise or perils associated with school/community partnerships when he emphasizes that "how prevention program leaders relate to community concerns will dictate the fate of their efforts (p. 2)."

Effective school-wide prevention plans operate best when they involve individual parents and parent organizations in meaningful ways. Parent/school collaboration enhances opportunities for schools to work successfully with troubled youth, extending prevention initiatives beyond schools and into local communities.

Links between the school and the larger community may take many forms, including collaboration among child-serving agencies, local business, law enforcement, and advocacy organizations. An important consideration in developing community support is to ensure that violence prevention initiatives are culturally competent. This is especially critical given the differential application of school disciplinary practices that result in the disproportionate suspension of African American youth (Townsend, 2000).

3. Developing a leadership team.

School-wide prevention plans that are actively supported by school- and district-level personnel, students, and families will likely produce the most effective and durable results. Team-based decision making can enhance ownership and acceptance of school violence prevention plans. Such a leadership team would be composed of staff members representing the various disciplines and roles within the school (e.g., general and special education teachers, counselors and school psychologists, administrators, paraprofessionals), and may include students, parents, and community members. Given the many risk factors associated with youth violence, the leadership team also could function as the organizational mechanism for systematic collaboration with mental health, social service, law enforcement, and other community agencies.

The leadership team conducts and analyzes the needs assessment, formulates short- and longer-term goals, identifies potential prevention strategies, monitors progress, and evaluates results (Dwyer & Osher, 2000). Teams can be formed specifically to address school-wide prevention efforts, or they can be built from and coordinated with other school-based management teams that exist in many schools.

4. Providing staff development.

As is the case in all school reform efforts, staff training is essential to ensure understanding, support, and consistent use of the school-wide violence prevention plan. Carefully designed and implemented training, available for *all* school staff, operationalizes the concept of a school-wide violence prevention agenda. This training involves teachers, counselors, bus drivers, cafeteria workers, clerical staff, and others working in the school. An important focus of training is skill development that supports achievement of instructional and behavioral competence for all students.

The content of training is also tailored for staff with specialized responsibilities, such as members of the leadership team. Further, given the complex nature of youth violence, staff development should reflect sustained rather than isolated training activities. Inservice training that follows this approach supports the reliable and consistent application of prevention strategies throughout the school.

5. Evaluating the plan.

Evaluation is the systematic collection and analysis of relevant data to inform decision making (Muraskin, 1993). Despite growing evidence supporting the use of school-wide violence prevention plans, specific prevention programs and practices have not typically been evaluated through rigorous research. Without benefit of evaluation, school staff and policy makers may respond to troubling behavior based more on political expediency than empirically validated practice.

Evaluation begins with needs assessment and can extend to process, outcome, and cost-benefit research (Flannery, 1998). When examining school-wide prevention programs one or more of the major types of evaluation may be appropriate to use.

■ *Process evaluations* address the qualities that make school-wide prevention programs work or not work.

■ *Outcome evaluations* focus on determining the impact of school-wide prevention programs on the school climate and for individual students.

■ *Cost-benefit evaluations* identify whether specific programs are cost-effective.

Evaluation design has been constrained by difficulties in identifying and measuring outcomes related to prevention of violence in schools (discussed in previous section). Further, the impact of violence prevention programs has not been measured reliably because most evaluations have focused on immediate results in a limited number of sites rather than on longer-term results and replication in different types of schools and communities.

Challenges Ahead: Next Steps

Many reports have shown that school and community-based adolescent violence has been declining in recent years and that schools are considerably safer than surrounding neighborhoods. At the same time, addressing school violence remains an appropriate concern for educators, parents, political leaders, and other members of the community. We've learned from program evaluations, as well as a vast body of research in the fields of education, mental health, social services, and juvenile justice, that school violence must be addressed on the individual, family, school, neighborhood, and larger societal levels. Multifaceted interventions must target specific risk factors, be developmentally appropriate, and be culturally sensitive. In addition, interventions should involve parents and members of the community, promote interagency collaboration, address multiple levels of the child's life (e.g., school, family, neighborhood), and involve an evaluation component.

Schools will continue to face challenges while working with students with disabilities. State and local school systems must develop, disseminate, and monitor the interventions used in addressing behaviors of students with disabilities, using research-based best practices. Schools need to explore alternatives to school suspension, keeping students engaged in their school responsibilities and promoting their academic success. Responsive and flexible approaches require, and real progress demands, long-term investment and commitment. There are no quick fixes. Schools should examine their climate and programming to ensure that they are addressing their students' needs. Successful school programs require a buy-in by <u>all</u> school staff—teachers, support staff, and school administration—not just by a particular program's leadership team.

Data collection and analysis of prevention efforts should be ongoing, using rigorous methodology, as exemplified by the PBIS approach (Sugai, Kameenui, et al., 2000). School- and community-based programs have to maintain ongoing data collection and record keeping and should evaluate student and family needs and progress. At present, the role of students with disabilities in school violence and disruption is not well understood. Meaningful prevention and intervention efforts require thorough understanding of the challenges facing school administrators in serving students with disabilities, particularly those with behavioral problems.

In the face of pressure to offer politically expedient responses to media accounts of school violence and disruption, all members of the community must cultivate a balanced approach to the problem. Parents, educators, administrators, local officials, and other community members should gather accurate information relevant to their community circumstances and needs. A wide range of resources and supports now available from federal agencies, public interest advocacy groups, and private foundations are listed below.

A Final Note

Professionals sometimes are affected by the pressures and circumstances of their daily working environment and may react to problems by seeking the most expedient solution. In addressing the complex needs of students with behavioral difficulties, we must force ourselves to take stock of the situation and proceed thoughtfully, in a reasonable and balanced manner. Teamwork and collaboration among all stakeholders, careful study and thorough planning, and a commitment to reflection and self-evaluation all hold the promise of ultimate success.

Resources

Reports Available On-Line

Many reports issued under the auspices of the U.S. Department of Education can be obtained (via mail) through the *ED Pubs* online ordering system at http://www.ed.gov/pubs/edpubs.html

Annual Report on School Safety 1999 available on-line at http://www.ed.gov/PDFDocs/InterimAR.pdf

*Early Warning Timely Response*available on-line at
http://www.ed.gov/offices/OSERS/OSEP/earlywrn.html

Indicators of School Crime and Safety 1999 available on-line at
http://nces.ed.gov/pubs99/1999057.pdf

Juvenile Offenders and Victims, 1999 National Report available on-line at
http://www.ncjrs.org/html/ojjdp/nationalreport99/toc.html

Less Hype, More Help (American Youth Policy Forum) available on-line at
http://www.aypf.org/whatsnew.htm

Metropolitan Life Survey of the American Teacher, 1999 available on-line at
http://www.metlife.com/Companyinfo/Community/Found/Docs/report9.pdf

Safeguarding Our Children: An Action Guide available on-line at
http://www.ed.gov/offices/OSERS/OSEP/ActionGuide/

School House Hype (Justice Policy Institute) available on-line at
http://www.cjcj.org/schoolhousehype/ *School House Hype II* (Justice Policy
Institute/Children's Law Center) available on-line at
http://www.cjcj.org/schoolhousehype/

*Violence and Youth, Psychology's Response (American Psychological Association,
1993)* included free as part of a kit: "Creating Safe Schools: A Resource
Collection for Planning and Action [Kit]" Can be obtained (via mail) under
"School Safety" category at ED PUBS at http://www.ed.gov/pubs/edpubs.html

Organizations With Websites and On-Line Resources

Center for Effective Collaboration and Practice (CECP)
Website at http://www.air-dc.org/cecp/

Center on Juvenile and Criminal Justice (CJCJ)
Website at http://www.cjcj.org

Center for the Prevention of School Violence
Website at http://www.ncsu.edu/cpsv/

Center for the Study and Prevention of Violence
Website at http://www.colorado.edu/cspv/

Kentucky Center for School Safety Website at http://www.kysafeschools.org/

National Center on Education, Disability, and Juvenile Justice (EDJJ)
Website at http://www.edjj.org/

National School Safety Center Website at http://www.nssc1.org/

National Youth Gang Center Website at http://www.iir.com/nygc/

Office of Juvenile Justice and Delinquency Prevention (U.S. Dept. of Justice)
Website at http://ojjdp.ncjrs.org/

Partnerships Against Violence Network (PAVNET)
Website at http://www.pavnet.org/

Positive Behavioral Interventions and Supports (PBIS)
Website at http://www.pbis.org/english/index.html

Safe and Drug-Free Schools Program (U.S. Dept. of Education)
Website at http://www.ed.gov/offices/OESE/SDFS/

Books

Elliott, D., Hamburg, B., & Williams, K. (Eds.) 1998. *Violence in American schools.* New York: Cambridge.

Gabarino, J. (1999). *Lost boys.* New York: Simon and Schuster.

Loeber, R., & Farrington, D. P. (Eds.) 1998. *Serious and violent juvenile offenders.* Thousand Oaks, CA: Sage.

Tonry, M., & Moore, M. H. (Eds.) 1998. *Youth violence.* Chicago: University of Chicago Press.

References

American Psychological Association. (1993). *Violence and youth: Psychology's response.* Washington, DC: Author.

Bear, G. G. (1999). *Interim alternative educational settings: Related research and program considerations.* Alexandria, VA: National Association of State Directors of Special Education, Project Forum.

Biemer, P. P., Groves, R. M., Lyberg, L. E., Mathiowetz, N. A., & Sudman, S. (1991). *Measurement Errors in Surveys.* New York: Wiley.

Brener, N. D., Simon, T. R., Krug, E. G., & Lowry, R. (1999). Recent trends in violence-related behaviors among high school students in the United States. *Journal of the American Medical Association, 282*(5), 440–446.

Bronfenbrenner, U. (1979). *The ecology of human development: Experiments by nature and design.* Cambridge, MA: Harvard University Press.

Brooks, K., Schiraldi, V., & Ziedenberg, J. (2000). *School house hype: Two years later.* Washington, DC: Justice Policy Institute.

Burns, B. J., & Goldman, S. K. (Eds.) (1999). Promising practices in wraparound for children with serious emotional disturbance and their families. *Systems of care: Promising practices in children's mental health, 1998 series, Vol. IV.* Washington, DC: Center for Effective Collaboration and Practice, American Institutes for Research.

Centers for Disease Control and Prevention. (1997). *Recommended framework for presenting injury mortality data.* Morbidity & Mortality Weekly Report, 1997; 46 (No. RR-14): 4–5.

Centers for Disease Control and Prevention. (2000). *Fact sheet: Youth risk behavior trends.* [online], http://www.cdc.gov/nccdphp/dash/yrbs/ trend.htm

Chandler, K. A., Chapman, C. D., Rand, M. R., & Taylor, B. M. (1998). *Students' reports of school crime: 1989 and 1995.* Washington, DC: U.S. Departments of Education and Justice. (NCES 98-241/NCJ-169607)

Cook, P. J., & Laub, J. H. (1998). The epidemic in youth violence. In M. Tonry, & M. H. Moore (Eds.), *Youth Violence* (pp. 27–64). Chicago: University of Chicago Press.

Cook, P. J. & Ludwig, J. (1997, May). Guns in America: National survey on private ownership and use of firearms. *Research Brief* (NIJ Rep. No. NCJ-165476). Washington, DC: U.S. Department of Justice, National Institute of Justice.

Cooley, S. (1995). *Suspension/expulsion of regular and special education students in Kansas: A report to the Kansas State Board of Education* (ERIC Document Reproduction Service No. ED 395 403). Topeka: Kansas State Board of Education.

Dryfoos, J. (1990). *Adolescents at risk.* New York: Oxford University Press.

Dwyer, K. & Osher, D. (2000). *Safeguarding our children: An action guide.* Washington, DC: U. S. Departments of Education and Justice, American Institutes for Research.

Elliott, D., Hamburg, B., & Williams, K. (Eds.). (1998). *Violence in American schools.* New York: Cambridge.

Farrington, D. P. (1995). The challenge of teenage antisocial behavior. In M. Rutter (Ed.), *Psychological disturbances in young people: Challenges for prevention* (pp. 83–130). New York: Oxford University Press.

Fasko, D., Grubb, D. J., & Osborne, J. S. (1995, November). *An analysis of disciplinary suspensions.* Paper presented at annual meeting of Mid-South Educational Research Association, Biloxi, MS. (ERIC Document Reproduction Service No. ED 393 169)

Felson, R. B. (1996). Mass media effects on violent behavior. *Annual Review of Sociology, 22,* 103–128.

Fiore, T. A., & Reynolds, K. S. (1996). *Analysis of discipline issues in special education.* Research Triangle Park, NC: Research Triangle Institute. (ERIC Document Reproduction Service No. ED 425 607)

Flannery, D. J. (1998). *Improving school violence prevention programs through meaningful evaluation.* New York: ERIC Clearinghouse on Urban Education. (ERIC Document Reproduction Service No. ED 417 244)

Fox, N., Leone, P., Rubin, K., Oppenheim, J., & Friedman, K. (1999). *Final report on the linkages to learning program and evaluation at broad acres elementary school.* Unpublished manuscript, University of Maryland at College Park.

Frey, K. S., Hirschstein, M. K., & Guzzo, B. A. (2000). Second step: Preventing aggression by promoting social competence. *Journal of Emotional & Behavioral Disorders, 8*(2), 102–112.

Furlong, M. & Morrison, G. (1994). Introduction to miniseries: School violence and safety in perspective. *School Psychology Review, 23*(2), 139–150.

Furlong, M., & Morrison, G. (2000). The *school* in school violence: Definitions and facts. *Journal of Emotional & Behavioral Disorders, 8*(2), 71–82.

Goldstein, S. Z. (1994). Corporate communication: A futurist vision. *Communication World, 11*(1), 26–28.

Goss v. Lopez, 419 U.S. 565 (1975).

Gottfredson, D. C. (1997). School-based crime prevention. In L. W. Sherman, D. C. Gottfredson, D. L. MacKenzie, J. Eck, P. Reuter, & S. D. Bushway. *Preventing crime: What works, what doesn't, what's promising: A report to the United States Congress.* [online] http://www.preventingcrime.com/report/index.htm

Gun-Free Schools Act, 20 U.S.C. § 1415 (e) (3).

Harvard University Civil Rights Project. (2000). *Opportunities suspended: The devastating consequences of zero tolerance and school discipline policies.* [online] http://www.law.harvard.edu/groups/civil-rights/conferences/zero/zt_report2.html

Hawkins, J. D., Herrenkohl, T. I., Farrington, D. P., Brewer, D., Catalano, R. F., Harachi, T. W., & Cothern, L. (2000, April). Predictors of youth violence. *Juvenile Justice Bulletin.* Washington, DC: U.S. Department of Justice, Office of Juvenile Justice and Delinquency Prevention.

Hernandez, D. J. (1995). Changing demographics: Past and future demands for early childhood programs. *The Future of Children, 5*(3), 145–160.

Honig v. Doe, 479 U.S. 1084 (1988).

Howard, H. H. (1995). TV station group and cross-media ownership: A 1995 update. *Journalism & Mass Communication Quarterly, 72*(2), 390–401.

Hymowitz, K. S. (2000). Who killed school discipline? *City Journal, 10*(2), 34–43.

Ingraham v. Wright, 430 U.S. 651 (1977).

Institute of Medicine (1994). *Reducing risks for mental disorders.* Washington, DC: National Academy Press.

Institute for Social Research. (1997). *Monitoring the future study.* Ann Arbor: University of Michigan.

Kann, L., Kinchen, S. A., Williams, B. I., Ross, J. G., Lowry, R., Grunbaum, J. A., & Kolbe, L. J. (2000). Youth risk behavior surveillance—United States, 1999. *Morbidity & Mortality Weekly Report, 49* (SS–5).

Kaufman, P., Chen, X., Choy, S. P., Chandler, K. A., Chapman, C. D., Rand, M. R., & Ringel, C. (1998). *Indicators of school crime and safety, 1998*. Washington, DC: U.S. Departments of Education and Justice. (NCES 1998-251/NCJ-172215).

Kaufman, P., Chen, X., Choy, S. P., Ruddy, S. A., Miller, A. K., Chandler, K. A., Chapman, C. D., Rand, M. R., & Klaus, P. (1999). *Indicators of school crime and safety, 1999*. Washington, DC: U.S. Departments of Education and Justice. (NCES 1999-057/NCJ-178906)

Kellam, S. G. (2000). Community and institutional partnerships for school violence prevention. In S. G. Kellam, R. Prinz, & J. F. Sheley, *Preventing school violence: Plenary papers of the 1999 Conference on Criminal Justice Research and Evaluation—Enhancing Policy and Practice Through Research* (Vol. 2, pp. 1–21). Washington, DC: U.S. Department of Justice, National Institute of Justice.

Kenney, D. J., & Watson, S. (1999, July). Crime in the schools: Reducing conflict with student problem solving *Research brief* (NIJ Rep. No. NCJ-177618). Washington, DC: U.S. Department of Justice, National Institute of Justice.

Kerrebrock, N., & Lewit, E. M. (1999). Children in self-care. *The Future of Children, 9*(2), 151–160.

Larson, J. (1994). Violence prevention in the schools: A review of selected programs and procedures. *School Psychology Review, 23*, 151–164.

Leone, P. E. (1997). The school as a caring community: Proactive discipline and exceptional children. In J. Paul, M. Churton, W. Morse, A. Duchnowski, B. Epanchin, P. Osnes, & L. Smith (Eds.), *Special education practice: Applying the knowledge, affirming the values, and creating the future.* (pp. 91–103). Pacific Grove, CA: Brooks-Cole.

Lichter, S. R., Lichter, L. S., & Amundson, D. (1999). *Merchandizing mayhem: Violence in popular culture.* Washington, DC: Center for Media and Public Affairs.

Loeber, R., Farrington, D. P., & Waschbusch, D. A. (1998). Serious and violent juvenile offenders. In R. Loeber & D. P. Farrington (Eds.), *Serious and violent juvenile offenders* (pp. 13–29). Thousand Oaks, CA: Sage.

Maryland State Department of Education (1999, January). *Suspensions from Maryland public schools (1997–98).* Baltimore: MSDE Results Branch.

Maryland State Department of Education (2000, January). *Suspensions from Maryland public schools (1998–99).* Baltimore: MSDE/PRIM-Information Management Branch.

Mayer, M. J., & Leone, P. E. (1999). A structural analysis of school violence and disruption: Implications for creating safer schools. *Education & Treatment of Children, 22*, 333–358.

Mendel, R. (2000). *Less hype, more help.* Washington, DC: American Youth Policy Forum.

Mercy, J. A., Ikeda, R., & Powell, K. E. (1998). Firearm-related injury surveillance: An overview of progress and challenges ahead. *American Journal of Preventive Medicine, 15*(38), 6–16.

Metropolitan Life Insurance Company. (1999). *Metropolitan Life survey of the American teacher, 1999: Violence in America's Public Schools.* New York: Author.

Morgan, R. L., Loosli, T. S., & Striefel, S. (1997). Regulating the use of behavioral procedures in schools: A five year follow-up survey of state department standards. *Journal of Special Education, 30*(4), 456–470.

Muraskin, L. D. (1993). *Understanding evaluation: The way to better prevention programs* [online], http://ed.gov.offices/OUS/eval/primer1.html

Patterson, G. R. (1982). *Coercive family process.* Eugene, OR: Castalia.

Prothrow-Stith, D. (1987). *Violence prevention curricula for adolescents.* Newton, MA: Education Development Center.

Rand, M. (1998). *Criminal victimizations 1997: Changes 1996–97 with trends 1993–97.* Washington, DC: US Department of Justice, Bureau of Justice Statistics.

Reiss, A. J. & Roth, J. A. (Eds.). (1993). *Understanding and preventing violence.* Washington, DC: National Academy Press.

Sheley, J. F. (2000). Controlling violence: What schools are doing. In S. G. Kellam, R. Prinz, & J. F. Sheley, *Preventing school violence: Plenary papers of the 1999 Conference on Criminal Justice Research and Evaluation—Enhancing Policy and Practice Through Research* Vol. 2, pp. 37–57). Washington, DC: US Department of Justice, National Institute of Justice.

Shure, M. B. (1999, April). Preventing violence the problem-solving way. *Juvenile Justice Bulletin.* Washington, DC: U.S. Department of Justice, Office of Juvenile Justice & Delinquency Prevention.

Sinclair, M. F., et al. (1996, December). On a collision course? Standards, discipline, and students with disabilities, *Policy Research Brief, 8*(4). Minneapolis: Institute on Community Integration, University of Minnesota. (ERIC Document Reproduction Service No. ED 404 793)

Skiba, R. J., & Peterson, R. L. (1999). The dark side of zero tolerance: Can punishment lead to safe schools? *Phi Delta Kappan, 80*(5), 372–378.

Skiba, R. J., & Peterson, R. L. (2000). School discipline at a crossroads: From zero tolerance to early response. *Exceptional Children, 66*(3), 335–347.

Snyder, H. N., & Sickmund, M. (1999). *Juvenile offenders and victims: 1999 national report.* Washington, DC: Office of Juvenile Justice and Delinquency Prevention.

Sorenson, G. (1993). Update on legal issues in special education discipline. *Education Law Reporter, 81,* 399–411.

Sprague, J. & Walker, H. (2000). Early identification and intervention for youth with violent behavior. *Exceptional Children, 66*(3), 367–379.

Sugai, G. M., Kameenui, E. J., Horner, R. H., & Simmons, D. C. (2000). *Effective instructional and behavioral support systems: A school-wide approach to discipline and early literacy.* [online], http://ericec.org/ osep/eff-syst.htm

Sugai, G. M., Sprague, J. R., Horner, R., & Walker, H. M. (2000). Preventing school violence: The use of office discipline referrals to assess and monitor school-wide discipline interventions. *Journal of Emotional & Behavioral Disorders, 8*(2), 94–102.

Taylor-Greene, S., Brown, D., Nelson, L., Longton, J., Gassman, T., Cohen, J., Swartz, J., Horner, R. H., Sugai, G., & Hall, S. (1997). School-wide behavioral support: Starting the year off right. *Journal of Behavioral Education, 7,* 99–112.

Tebo, M. G. (2000). Zero tolerance, zero sense. *ABA Journal, 86,* 40–45.

Tolan, P. H. & Guerra, N. G. (1994). Prevention of delinquency: Current status and issues. *Applied & Preventive Psychology, 3,* 251–273.

Tolan, P. H., & Guerra, N. G. (1998). *What works in reducing adolescent violence: An empirical review of the field.* Boulder, CO: Center for the Study and Prevention of Violence, University of Colorado.

Tolan, P. H., Guerra, N. G, & Kendall, P. C. (1995). Introduction to special section: Prediction and prevention of antisocial behavior in children and adolescents. *Journal of Consulting & Clinical Psychology, 63*(4), 515–517.

Townsend, B. L. (2000). The disproportionate discipline of African American learners: Reducing school suspensions and expulsions. *Exceptional Children, 66*(3), 381–391.

Tucker, B. P., Goldstein, B. A., & Sorenson, G. (1993). *The educational rights of children with disabilities: Analysis, decisions and commentary.* Horsham, PA: LRP.

U.S. Bureau of the Census, Current Population Reports (1998). *Measuring 50 years of economic change using the March current population survey* (Rep. No. P60-203). Washington, DC: U.S. Government Printing Office.

U.S. Department of Education, National Center for Education Statistics. *Recommendations of the crime, violence, and discipline reporting task force* (Rep. No. NCES 97-581). 1996. Washington, DC: National Education Statistics Agenda Committee.

U.S. Department of Education, National Center for Education Statistics (1998a). *Violence and discipline problems in U.S. public schools: 1996–1997* (Rep. No. NCES 98-030). Washington, DC: Author, 1998.

U.S. Department of Education, Office of Elementary and Secondary Education and Planning and Evaluation Service. (1998b). *Report on state implementation of the gun-free schools act—School Year 1996–97.* (Contract N0. EA94052001). Prepared by Westat, Rockville, MD.

U.S. Department of Education (1999a). *Annual report on school safety.* Washington, DC: Author.

U.S. Department of Education, (1999b). *The Condition of Education 1999.* Washington, DC: National Center for Education Statistics. (ERIC Document Reproduction Service No. ED 430 324)

U.S. Department of Education, Office of Elementary and Secondary Education and Planning and Evaluation Service. (1999c). *Report on state implementation of the Gun-Free Schools Act—school year 1997–98.* (Contract No. EA94052001). Prepared by Westat, Rockville, MD.

U.S. Department of Education (2000). *Twenty-first annual report to Congress on the implementation of the Individuals with Disabilities Education Act.* Washington, DC: Government Printing Office. Author.

U.S. Library of Congress, Congressional Research Service. *Violence in schools: An overview* (CRS Report for Congress No. 94-141 EPW). Washington, DC: Author.

University of Vermont. (1999). Prevention strategies that work: What administrators can do to promote positive student behavior. Burlington, VT: Department of Education, School Research Office.

Walker, H. M., & Horner, R. H. (1996). Integrated approaches to preventing antisocial behavior patterns among school-age children and youth. *Journal of Emotional or Behavioral Disorders, 4*(4), 194–220.

Walker, H. M. & Sprague, J. R. (1999). The path to school failure, delinquency, and violence: Causal factors and some potential solutions. *Intervention in School and Clinic, 35*(2), 67–73.

Ward, J. M. (1999). *Children and guns.* Washington, DC: Children's Defense Fund.

Weinberg, D. H. (1996). *A brief look at post-war U.S. income inequality* (Rep. No. P60-191). Washington, DC: U.S. Bureau of the Census.

Weist, M. D., & Warner, B. S. (1997). Intervening against violence in the schools. *Annals of Adolescent Psychiatry, 21,* 235–251.

Womer, S. C. (1997). *What kinds of school-based prevention programs are publicized?* Ellicott City, MD: Gottfredson Associates.

Woodruff, D. W., Osher, D., Hoffman, C. C., Gruner, A., King, M. A., Snow, S. T., & McIntire, J. C. (1999). The role of education in a system of care: Effectively serving children with emotional or behavioral disorders. *Systems of care: Promising practices in children's mental health, 1998 Series* (Vol. 3). Washington, DC: Center for Effective Collaboration and Practice, American Institutes for Research.

Yell, M. L. (1990). The use of corporal punishment, suspension, expulsion, and timeout with behaviorally disordered students in public schools: Legal considerations. *Behavior Disorders, 15,* 100–109.

Yell, M. L., Cline, D., & Bradley, R. (1995). Disciplining students with emotional and behavioral disorders: A legal update. *Education & Treatment of Children, 18,* 299–308.

Yell, M. L. (1998). *The law and special education.* Upper Saddle River, NJ: Prentice-Hall.

Disclaimer: The opinions stated in this chapter are those of the authors and do not represent U.S. Department of Education, Office of Special Education Programs or U.S. Department of Justice, Office of Juvenile Justice and Delinquency Prevention (OJJDP) policy. No endorsement of the Office of Special Education Programs, the U.S. Department of Education, or the OJJDP should be inferred.

Author Index

A

Abrahams, M.M., 139
Abramson, L.Y., 146
Achilles, C.M., 95
Adams, G.R., 64, 79, 268
Adelman, H.S., 25
Adelson, J., 329
Adler, Alfred, 239
Adler, J., 182
Ahrons, C.R., 304, 308
Aichorn, A., 522
Ainsworth, M., 201
Akervik, S., 473
Akiyama, K., 154
Albrecht, T.L., 109
Alexander, J.R., 269
Al-Khayyal, M., 343
Allen, F. H., 342
Al-Mabuk, R., 320, 324, 328, 332
Amara, I.A., 268
Ambert, A., 263, 265
Ambler, J., 308
Ambrosini, P.J., 136, 144
American Academy of Pediatrics, 55, 56
American Association for Marriage and Family Therapy (AAMFT), 22
American Association of Colleges, 70
American Association of University Women, 467
American Counseling Association, 22
American Psychiatric Association, 136

American Psychological Association (APA), 21, 30, 48, 199, 202, 539
American School Counselor Association, 22
Amundson, D., 538, 539
Anderson, C., 472
Anderson, J.C., 140, 148ñ149
Anderson, J.E., 66
Anderson, S., 20
Anderson-Johnson, C., 77
Andraski, F., 153
Angold, A., 140
Annuziata, J., 24, 26
Anthony, E.J., 271
Arday, S., 66
Armstrong, J.W., 320
Arnold, M.S., 6, 13
Arthur, G., 23
Arthur, J.L., 353
Askins, R.V., 72
Astin, A.W., 459
Atkinson, D.R., 14
Atkinson, T.L., 489
Attnaeve, C., 99, 106
Atwell, A.E., 268
Avery, A.W., 271
Axline, V., 19

B

Bachman, J.G., 55, 121, 124
Bacon, S.B., 526
Baer, P.E. 56
Baker, C.B., 253
Bakker, L., 135, 141
Baldwin, W., 61
Balow, I.H., 73

Bane, M.J., 261
Barbero, G.J., 136
Barnea, Z., 78
Barr, R.D., 90, 96
Barrett, K., 201
Bartlett, S., 452
Basile, S.K., 343, 344
Bates, J.E., 221
Bateson, G., 249, 374
Battjes, R.J., 78
Baumrind, D., 218, 219, 220, 221, 222, 327, 328, 333
Beady, C.H., 458
Beal, E.W., 271
Bear, G.G., 536, 547
Beavers, W.R., 376
Beavin, J., 373
Beck, A.T., 52, 135, 136, 144, 146
Beck, V., 99
Becker, G.S., 303
Bee, H., 319
Begley, S., 201
Behrens, J.T., 46, 140, 141, 145, 149
Belber, R., 232
Bell, C.S., 78
Bemak, F., 98
Benjamin, M.P., 346
Bentler, P.M., 55, 56, 78, 122
Bentovim, M., 20
Bera, W., 477
Berenson, B.G., 250
Bergen, A.E., 366
Berger, K., 319, 323, 324, 328, 329, 332
Berger, M., 110, 113
Berkan, W.A., 54, 77

Subject Index